PRACTICAL MATHEMATICS

for Home Study
Arithmetic, Geometry, Algebra & Trigonometry

C. I. PALMER

WARNING

Remember that the materials and methods described here are from another era. Workers were less safety conscious then, and some methods may be downright dangerous. Be careful! Use good solid judgement in your work, and think ahead. Lindsay Publications Inc. has not tested these methods and materials and does not endorse them. Our job is merely to pass along to you information from another era. Safety is your responsibility.

Write for a complete catalog of unusual books available from:

Lindsay Publications Inc
PO Box 12
Bradley IL 60915-0012

PRACTICAL MATHEMATICS

FOR

HOME STUDY

BEING THE ESSENTIALS OF

ARITHMETIC, GEOMETRY,
ALGEBRA AND TRIGONOMETRY

BY

CLAUDE IRWIN PALMER

ASSOCIATE PROFESSOR OF MATHEMATICS ARMOUR INSTITUTE OF TECHNOLOGY

FIRST EDITION

THIRD IMPRESSION

McGRAW-HILL BOOK COMPANY, Inc.
239 WEST 39TH STREET. NEW YORK

Practical
Mathematics
for Home Study
by Claude Irwin Palmer

ISBN 0-917914-77-5

5 6 7 8 9 0

PREFACE

During the past fifteen years the author has taught classes in practical mathematics in the evening school at the Armour Institute of Technology, Chicago. These classes have been composed of men engaged in practical pursuits of various kinds. The needs of these men have been carefully studied; and, so far as possible, those mathematical subjects of interest to them have been taken up. The matter presented to the classes has necessarily been of an intensely practical nature. This has been worked over and arranged in a form that was thought most suitable for class use; and was printed in Palmer's Practical Mathematics, four volumes, in 1912 and appeared in a revised edition in 1918.

The four volume edition has been used by thousands of men for home study. It is to meet the needs especially of such men that this one volume edition has been made. The subject matter includes all that is in the four volumes; and to this has been added a few new topics together with many solutions of exercises, and suggestions that makes the text more suitable for home study. It is hoped that it will find a place in the library of the man who applies elementary mathematics, and who wishes occasionally to brush up his mathematics.

Usually when the practical man appreciates the fact for himself that mathematics is a powerful tool that he must be able to use in performing his work, he finds that even the arithmetic that he learned at school has left him. A student of this kind is discouraged if required to pursue the study of mathematics in the ordinary text-books.

This work has been written for the adult. The endeavor has been to make the student feel that he is in actual touch with real things. The intention has been to lay as broad a foundation as is consistent with the scope of the work.

The nearly 3000 drill exercises and problems are, in most

v

cases, new. Many of them are adapted from engineering and trade journals, from handbooks of various kinds, and from treatises on the steel square and other mechanical devices; other problems are from the author's experience; and a large number of the specially practical problems were proposed by members of the classes pursuing the course during its growth.

Much information on various matters to which mathematics is applied, is incidentally given in the problems. Many devices and methods used by the practical man are given. Care has been taken to make these true to practice; but, in so wide a range of matter, there are undoubtedly errors. It is thought that the answers to the exercises are given to a reasonable degree of accuracy. It is hoped that the volume, as a whole, will not be found unmathematical.

The main features of Part I are the concise treatment of various subjects in arithmetic and their applications, checks of processes, degree of accuracy possible in solutions, and contracted processes.

In Part II, the endeavor has been to state definitions so as to give a clear idea of the term or object defined, and yet not to be too technical. Wherever possible, the attempt is made to discuss a fact or principle of geometry in such a way that its reasonableness will be apparent. While the subjects are treated in the mathematical order, many applications are given under separate headings. Such are brickwork, lumber, the steel square, screw threads, circular mils, belt pulleys, and gear wheels.

In Part III, the intention is to give sufficient drill in algebra for one who wishes to make direct applications to practical problems. Much attention is given to formulas and their transformations. The equation is applied to many practical problems. Graphical methods are considered, and many articles on special subjects are given.

In Part IV, the intention is to give sufficient work in logarithms to secure a fair degree of skill in computations. In trigonometry, those parts are emphasized that may be applied directly to practical problems; while the portions chiefly necessary as an aid in·the study of more advanced mathematical subjects, are either treated very slightly or omitted.   Many applications are given.   The tables are given to four decimal places.

The author wishes to acknowledge his great indebtedness to the more than 1000 men who made up his classes during the growth of this work, and to the hundreds of men from various parts of the country who have offered kindly criticisms and suggestions; for, without their help and sympathy, the present results would have been impossible.

Because of the remarkable success of the previous editions, it is with the greatest pleasure that this special edition is submitted to our practical men.

C. I. Palmer.

Chicago,
  June, 1919.

A WORD WITH THE STUDENT

One of the lessons of the Great War and the strenuous efforts necessary to carry it on, has been to bring forcibly to our minds the great usefulness of mathematics. The war activities have exhibited the extensive mathematical needs of those who aim to render the most efficient service under the most trying circumstances. The young men of the country realize the need for a working knowledge of mathematics, and see clearly that the need so emphasized by the war conditions is being carried over into the days of peace and into the period of great industrial activity that is sure to follow.

This volume being entitled Practical Mathematics does not mean that all exercises are such as would be called practical. It means that, in the main, the exercises, outside of those intended for pure drill, are such as may arise in some practical field of work. The endeavor has been to utilize the material afforded by the shops and the laboratories as well as in the trades and in engineering.

The practical man realizes that, for him, mathematics is a chest of tools together with many more or less complicated pieces of machinery that he may use to accomplish his purpose. To apply mathematics, then, he must be able to run its machinery not only accurately but speedily. To do this a great deal of work must be done in the arithmetical processes themselves. The student must drill himself on the fundamental operations—addition, subtraction, multiplication, and division—both in whole numbers and in fractions, until the processes become to a large degree mechanical. That is, he should be able to do these operations with but little expenditure of mental energy. This drill is best gained by doing many exercises especially set for this purpose. Each student who is studying alone, that is, without being in a class, must of necessity be his own judge as to how much drill he needs. For most people such drill is tedious and uninteresting, and it requires a strong will to force oneself to do the proper amount of such work.

That these ideas are not new is evident from the following quotation in quaint old English, taken from an arithmetic printed more than two hundred years ago: "Therefore, Courteous Reader, if thou intendest to be a Proficient in the Mathematicks, begin cheerfully, proceed gradually, and with Resolution, and the end will crown thy Endeavours with Success; and be not so slothfully Studious, as at every Difficulty thou meetest withal to cry, *Ne plus ultra*, for Pains and Diligence will overcome the greatest Difficulty: To conclude, That thou may'st so read as to understand, and so understand, as to become a Proficient, is the hearty desire of him who wisheth thy Welfare, and the Progress of Arts. From my School at *St. George's* Church in *Southwork, October 27, 1684.*"

CONTENTS

PART I

ARITHMETIC

CHAPTER I

PRELIMINARY WORK AND REVIEW

CHAPTER II

COMMON FRACTIONS

CHAPTER III

DECIMAL FRACTIONS

CHAPTER IV

SHORT METHODS AND CHECKS

CHAPTER V

WEIGHTS AND MEASURES

CHAPTER VI

PERCENTAGE AND APPLICATIONS

CHAPTER VII

RATIO AND PROPORTION

CHAPTER VIII

DENSITY AND SPECIFIC GRAVITY

CHAPTER IX

POWER AND ROOTS

PART II

GEOMETRY

CHAPTER X

PLANE SURFACES. LINES AND ANGLES

CHAPTER XI

TRIANGLES

CHAPTER XII

CIRCLES

CHAPTER XIII

GRAPHICAL METHODS

CHAPTER XIV

PRISMS

CHAPTER XV

CYLINDERS

CHAPTER XVI

PYRAMIDS, CONES, AND FRUSTUMS

CHAPTER XVII

THE SPHERE

CHAPTER XVIII

VARIOUS OTHER SOLIDS

PART III

ALGEBRA

CHAPTER XIX

NOTATION AND DEFINITIONS

CHAPTER XX

FORMULAS AND TRANSLATIONS

CHAPTER XXI

POSITIVE AND NEGATIVE NUMBERS

CHAPTER XXII

ADDITION AND SUBTRACTION

CHAPTER XXIII

EQUATIONS

CHAPTER XXIV

MULTIPLICATION

CHAPTER XXV

DIVISION, SPECIAL PRODUCTS, AND FACTORS

CHAPTER XXVI

EQUATIONS

CHAPTER XXVII

FRACTIONS

CHAPTER XXVIII

EQUATIONS AND FORMULAS

CHAPTER XXIX

EQUATIONS WITH MORE THAN ONE UNKNOWN

CHAPTER XXX

EXPONENTS, POWERS, AND ROOTS

CHAPTER XXXI

QUADRATIC EQUATIONS

CHAPTER XXXII

VARIATION

CHAPTER XXXIII

GRAPHICS

PART IV

CHAPTER XXXIV

LOGARITHMS

CHAPTER XXXV

INTRODUCTION, ANGLES

CHAPTER XXXVI

TRIGONOMETRIC FUNCTIONS

CHAPTER XL

TRIGONOMETRIC RATIOS OF MORE THAN ONE ANGLE

CHAPTER XLI

SOLUTION OF OBLIQUE TRIANGLES

TABLES

PRACTICAL MATHEMATICS

PART ONE
ARITHMETIC

CHAPTER I

PRELIMINARY WORK AND REVIEW

1. Language of mathematics.—Mathematics has a language of its own, with certain signs and symbols peculiar to it. It is as necessary to become familiar with these signs and symbols and their uses, in order to understand the language of mathematics, as it is for the shorthand writer to become familiar with the symbols used in his work. Failure to fix them in mind, and to learn the definitions and technical terms keeps many students from mastering the mathematical subjects they take up.

Some of the best known symbols of mathematics are the Arabic numerals, 1, 2, 3, 4, 5, 6, 7, 8, 9, 0, the signs of addition, +, subtraction, −, multiplication, ×, division, ÷, and equality, =, and the letters of the alphabet. Other symbols will be explained as used.

In the study of mathematics much time should be devoted: (1) to the expressing of verbally stated facts in mathematical language, that is, in the signs and symbols of mathematics; (2) to the translating of mathematical expressions into common language.

The signs and symbols of mathematics are used for convenience. They have gradually come into use by general agreement. In some cases the symbols are abbreviations of words, but often have no such relation to the thing they stand for. We cannot tell why they stand for what they do any more than we can tell why the words for cat and dog stand for the different animals they do. They mean what they do by *common agreement* or by *definition*.

1

2. How to attack a problem.—A problem in mathematics should not be attacked as a puzzle. No guesswork has any place in its consideration. The statement of the problem should be clear and so leave but one solution possible. This is the business of the author or the one who states the problem. The following points concern the student:

(1) *The problem should be read and analyzed so carefully that all conditions are well fixed in mind.* If the problem cannot be understood there is no use in trying to solve it. Of course, if the answer is given, a series of guess-operations may obtain it, but the work is worse than useless.

(2) *In the solution there should be no unnecessary work.* Shorten the processes whenever possible.

(3) *Always apply some proof or check to the work if possible.* A wrong answer is valueless. Accuracy is of the highest importance, and to no one more than to the practical man. If a check can be applied there is no need of an answer being given to the problem.

In this text the answers follow most of the exercises. They are given for the convenience of the student in checking his work, and great care must be taken not to misuse them. An answer should never assist in determining how to solve a problem. It is best, then, not to look at the answer till the problem is solved.

3. Definitions.—In order to be exact in ideas and statements, it is necessary to give certain definitions. It would seem, however, that for the practical man, technical terms should be omitted so far as possible. It is usually sufficient to make the term understood, though the definition may not be a good one technically. In mathematics more than in almost any other subject, each word used has a *definite* and *fixed meaning.*

The following definitions are inserted here to help to recall to mind some of the terms used:

(1) An **integer,** or an **integral number,** is a whole number.

(2) A **factor,** or a **divisor,** of a whole number is any whole number that will exactly divide it.

(3) An **even number** is a number that is exactly divisible by 2.

Thus, 4, 8, and 20 are even numbers.

(4) An **odd number** is an integer that is not exactly divisible by 2.

Thus, 5, 11, and 47 are odd numbers.

(5) A **prime number** is a number that has no factors except itself and 1.

Thus, 1, 2, 7, 11, and 17 are prime numbers.

(6) A **composite number** is a number that has other factors than itself and 1.

Thus, 6, 22, 49, and 100 are composite numbers.

(7) A **common factor,** or **divisor,** of two or more numbers is a factor that will exactly divide each of them. If this factor is the largest factor possible it is called the **greatest common divisor:** abbreviated to G. C. D.

Thus, 4 is a common divisor of 16 and 24 but 8 is the G. C. D. of 16 and 24.

(8) A **multiple** of a number is a number that is divisible by the given number. If the same number is exactly divisible by two or more numbers it is a **common multiple** of them. The least such number is called the **least common multiple:** abbreviated to L. C. M.

Thus, 36 and 72 are common multiples of 12, 9, and 4, but 36 is the L. C. M.

4. Rules for finding divisor of numbers.—It is often convenient to be able to tell without performing the division, whether or not a given number is divisible by another. The following rules will assist in this. Their proofs are simple but are not given here.

(1) A number is divisible by 2 if its right-hand figure is 0 or one divisible by 2.

(2) A number is divisible by 3 if the sum of its digits is divisible by 3.

Thus, 73245 is divisible by 3 since $7+3+2+4+5 = 21$ is divisible by 3.

(3) A number is divisible by 4 if the number represented by its two last digits on the right is divisible by 4, or if it ends in two zeros.

Thus, 87656 is divisible by 4 since 56 is divisible by 4.

(4) A number is divisible by 5 if the last figure on the right is 0 or 5.

(5) An even number the sum of whose digits is divisible by 3 is divisible by 6.

(6) No convenient rule can be given for 7; the best thing to do is to test by trial.

(7) A number is divisible by 8 if the number represented by the last three digits on the right is divisible by 8.

Thus, 987672 is divisible by 8 since 672 is divisible by 8.

(8) A number is divisible by 9 if the sum of its digits is divisible by 9.

(9) A number is divisible by 11 if the difference between the sum of the odd digits and the even digits, counting from the right, is divisible by 11.

Thus, 47679291 is divisible by 11 since $(9+9+6+4)-(1+2+7+7)=11$ is divisible by 11.

Note. This rule is of little value since the division can be tried about as easily as the rule can be applied.

The following facts are of some value:

(10) A factor of a number is a factor of any of its multiples.

(11) A common factor of any two numbers is a factor of the sum or the difference of any two multiples of the numbers.

5. Relative importance of signs of operation.—(1) In a series of operations denoted by the signs of addition, $+$, subtraction, $-$, multiplication, $\times$, and division, $\div$, the multiplications must be performed first, the divisions next, and lastly the additions and subtractions.

(2) If several additions, or several multiplications, occur together they may be performed in any order.

(3) If several subtractions, or several divisions, occur together they *must* be performed in the order in which they come from left to right.

The rules as stated here are in agreement with the best usage in algebra and in formulas used in practical work.

Examples. (1) $12+3-2+9+7-3=26$, by performing the operations in the order in which they occur.

(2) $120 \div 3 \times 5 \times 2 \div 2 = 2$, by first performing the multi-

plications and then the divisions in the order in which they occur.

(3) $12 \div 3 + 8 \times 2 - 6 \div 2 + 7 \times 2 \times 3 - 9$
$= 12 \div 3 + 16 - 6 \div 2 + 42 - 9$
$= 4 + 16 - 3 + 42 - 9 = 50$, by first performing the multiplications, then the divisions, and then the additions and subtractions.

EXERCISES 1

In the exercises 1 to 10, first perform the multiplications, then the divisions, and finally the additions and subtractions, each in the order in which they occur.

1. $14 + 16 - 3 + 10 - 4 - 6 = ?$ *Ans.* 27.
2. $16 \div 8 + 4 \times 2 \times 3 - 16 \times 2 \div 4 = ?$ *Ans.* 18.
3. $15 - 2 \times 3 - 15 \div 5 + 4 = ?$ *Ans.* 10.
4. $60 - 25 \div 5 + 15 - 100 \div 4 \times 5 = ?$ *Ans.* 65.
5. $17 \times 3 + 27 \div 3 - 40 \times 2 \div 5 = ?$ *Ans.* 44.
6. $56 - 7 + 525 \div 5 \times 7 \times 3 + 15 - 7 \times 8 = ?$ *Ans.* 13.
7. $864 \div 12 - 124 \div 31 + 54 \div 27 = ?$ *Ans.* 70.
8. $4 \times 27 \div 9 \times 4 + 9 \times 2 - 3 \times 6 \div 9 = ?$ *Ans.* 19.
9. $4963 \div 7 + 144 \div 72 - 14 \times 9 = ?$ *Ans.* 585.
10. $13 \times 9 \times 62 + 44 \div 4 - 17 \times 22 = ?$ *Ans.* 6891.
11. Time yourself in doing the following ten multiplications:
    (1) 347×371.   (6) 3249×987.
    (2) 547×682.   (7) 4444×888.
    (3) 433×925.   (8) 8764×2233.
    (4) 986×478.   (9) 9898×4257.
    (5) 3587×729.   (10) 9999×8888.
12. Check your work in the above ten multiplications by doing the multiplying, using the first number in each case as the multiplier.
13. Time yourself in doing the following divisions.   Check your work by finding the product of the divisor and quotient, and comparing it with the dividend.
    (1) $395,883 \div 9$.   (5) $4,518,976 \div 784$.
    (2) $64,362 \div 17$.   (6) $783,783 \div 4147$.
    (3) $306,192 \div 48$.   (7) $1,312,748 \div 437$.
    (4) $87,168 \div 384$.   (8) $4,495,491 \div 499$.
14. Do the following multiplications and check the work by dividing the product by the multiplier and comparing the result with the multiplicand:
    (1) 843×329.   (3) 4493×345.
    (2) 4327×987.   (4) 8397×9327.

15. Do the following divisions and check the work by finding the product of the divisor and quotient, then adding the remainder and comparing the result with the dividend:

(1) 43,962 ÷ 97.

(2) 842,637 ÷ 233.

(3) 467,234 ÷ 487.

(4) 9,372,468 ÷ 375.

(5) 4,343,764 ÷ 983.

(6) 3,784,328 ÷ 2345.

16. The cost of constructing 275 miles of railway was $4,195,400. What was the cost per mile? *Ans.* $15,256.

17. The circumference of a drive wheel of a locomotive is 22 ft. How many revolutions will it make in going 44 miles if there are 5280 ft. in one mile? *Ans.* 10,560.

18. If a power plant consumes 277 tons of coal at $3.10 per ton each day, what is the cost of the coal to run the plant one year of 365 days? Check the work.

19. A hog weighing 78 lb. requires 400 lb. of grain for each 100 lb. gain in weight. If the price of 56 lb. of grain increases in price from 42 cents to $1.54 what should be the increase in price of hogs per 100 lb.? *Ans.* $8.

20. When 56 lb. of corn cost 56 cents, hogs sold at $5.60 per 100 lb. live weight; and when corn cost $1.82 for 56 lb., they sold at $15.10 per 100 lb. How much more or less does the farmer make per hundred if it takes 400 lb. of corn for each 100 lb. increase in weight of hogs? *Ans.* In second case 50 cents more.

21. How many tons of silage, 2000 lb. per ton, should be stored for 20 cows, the intention being to feed each cow 40 lb. a day for 5 months, then 30 lb. a day for 2 months, then 20 lb. a day for 2 months? Consider 30 days to a month. *Ans.* 90.

22. Give three divisors of 192. Give three multiples of 72. Give a common divisor of 144 and 192. Give the greatest common divisor of these numbers. Give three common multiples of 15, 8 and 20. Give the least common multiple of these numbers. Is there a greatest common multiple?

23. Find the prime factors of each of the following: 1188; 148,225; 89,964; 36,992,000.

Solution.

The work is best carried out by selecting the smallest prime factors, leaving the larger till later. The prime factors of the number are all of the divisors used. The prime factors of 1188 are 2, 2, 3, 3, 3, 11.

$$2 \overline{)1188}$$
$$2 \overline{)594}$$
$$3 \overline{)297}$$
$$3 \overline{)99}$$
$$3 \overline{)33}$$
$$11 \overline{)11}$$
$$1$$

24. Tell which of the following numbers are exactly divisible by each of 2, 3, 4, 5, 6, 7, and 9: 324; 7644; 3,645,111; 4550; 3645; 49,875; 23,147,355.

6. Cancellation.—Often in solving problems, a fractional form like the following is obtained:

$$\frac{64\times25\times8\times12\times17}{48\times15\times32\times17\times24}.$$

If we do all the multiplications above the line and below the line, and then perform the division which the line indicates, we shall obtain the result. . It is often easy to avoid much of this work, however, by applying a principle of fractions. The process which is explained below is called **cancellation.**

$$\frac{\overset{2}{\cancel{64}}\times\overset{5}{\cancel{25}}\times\cancel{8}\times\cancel{12}\times\cancel{17}}{\underset{6}{\cancel{48}}\times\underset{3}{\cancel{15}}\times\cancel{32}\times\cancel{17}\times\underset{2}{\cancel{24}}}.$$

(1) It is seen that 17 is found both above and below the line; we draw a line through each of these. These numbers are then said to be cancelled.

(2) Now notice that the numbers 64 and 32 are divisible by 32. Cancel 64 and 32 and place 2 above 64 which is the number of times 32 is contained in 64.

(3) Next, divide 48 and 8 by 8 and cancel them, writing the quotient 6 below 48.

(4) Divide 25 and 15 by 5 and cancel them, writing the quotient 5 above 25 and 3 below 15.

(5) In a similar manner 12 and 24 are cancelled; also 2 and 2.

In this manner we have replaced the given form by the simpler one $\frac{5}{6\times3}=\frac{5}{18}$. This is the answer.

It should be noted that when no factor remains either above or below the line after the cancellation is finished, we retain one of the unit factors which we neglected to write when cancelling.

Thus, $\dfrac{\cancel{4}\times\cancel{8}\times\cancel{16}\times\cancel{10}}{\underset{3}{\cancel{12}}\times\underset{10}{\cancel{80}}\times\underset{3}{\cancel{48}}}=\dfrac{1}{9}.$ *Ans.*

Remark. It should be remembered that this method of simplifying cannot be used when there are additions or subtractions indicated in the problem.

In such a case the operations above the line must be performed first, then those below, and lastly the result above must be divided by the result below.

$$\text{Thus, } \frac{4+200-6\times2}{38+98-12\times6}=\frac{192}{64}=3. \; Ans.$$

These processes may be restated in the following:

RULE. (1) *Any factor above may be divided into any factor below the line.*

(2) *Any factor below may be divided into any factor above the line.*

(3) *Any factor common to factors one above and one below may be divided into each.*

(4) *The answer is obtained by dividing the product of the numbers remaining above the line by the product of the numbers remaining below the line. If no number remains above or below, use 1.*

EXERCISES 2

Use cancellation to find the results in the following:

1. $\dfrac{5\times8\times3\times16}{8\times15\times4}$.   *Ans.* 4.

2. $\dfrac{20\times56\times12}{21\times10\times18}$.   *Ans.* $3\frac{5}{9}$.

3. $\dfrac{57\times119\times16}{17\times12\times19}$.   *Ans.* 28.

4. $\dfrac{77\times100\times18\times14}{25\times11\times49\times16}$.   *Ans.* 9.

5. $\dfrac{18\times100\times13\times12}{26\times25\times9\times3}$.   *Ans.* 16.

6. $\dfrac{16\times12\times7\times11}{24\times22\times7\times18}$.   *Ans.* $\frac{2}{9}$.

7. $\dfrac{90\times89\times88\times87}{1\times2\times3\times4}$.   *Ans.* 2 555,190.

8. $\dfrac{1200\times515\times70\times100}{5\times35\times103}$.   *Ans.* 240,000.

9. $\dfrac{180\times132\times140\times75}{15\times70\times44\times36}$.   *Ans.* 150.

10. $\dfrac{750\times4500\times5760}{2400\times750\times50}$.   *Ans.* 216.

11. $\dfrac{144\times1728\times999}{96\times270\times33}$.   *Ans.* $290\frac{34}{55}$.

12. $\dfrac{1320\times432\times660}{4400\times297\times288}$.   *Ans.* 1.

13. $\dfrac{15\times2+45\times4}{60\times2}$.   *Ans.* $1\frac{3}{4}$.

14. $\dfrac{99-25+14\times7}{50+2\times18}$.   *Ans.* 2.

15. $\dfrac{16+3\times7-4\times2+167}{94-7\times9+3\times6}$.   *Ans.* 4.

16. $\dfrac{256\times6+125\times3-14\times76}{17\times27+32\times40-1618}$.   *Ans.* 7.

Analyze the following and shorten the computation as much as possible by cancellation.

17. If 18 men can do a piece of work in 14 days, how many men will do the work in 21 days?

Analysis. If 18 men can do a piece of work in 14 days, one man can do the work in 18×14 days. It will take as many men to do the work in 21 days as 21 is contained times in 18×14.

Operation.

$$\frac{\overset{6}{\cancel{18}}\times\overset{2}{\cancel{14}}}{\underset{3}{\cancel{21}}}=12$$

Hence it takes 12 men to do the work in 21 days.

18. A man worked 16 days for 30 bushels of potatoes worth 88 cents a bushel. What did he earn per day? *Ans.* $1.65.

19. How many days at $1.50 must 24 men work to pay for 360 bushels of wheat worth $1.20 a bushel? *Ans.* 12.

20. How many acres of potatoes yielding 150 bushels to the acre and worth 25 cents a bushel will amount to as much as 65 acres of wheat yielding 18 bushels to the acre and worth $1.05 per bushel? *Ans.* $32\frac{1}{2}\frac{6}{?}$.

21. If 8 men, in 15 days of 10 hours each, can throw 1000 cu. yd. of earth into wheelbarrows, how many men will be required to throw 2000 cu. yd. of earth into wheelbarrows in 20 days of 8 hours each? *Ans.* 15.

Suggestion. Analyze the problem and state in the following form for cancellation:

$$\frac{8\times15\times10\times2000}{20\times8\times1000}.$$

22. A gardener sells 75 crates of berries, 24 boxes in a crate, at 8 cents a box, and receives in return 12 rolls of matting, 40 yards in a roll. Find the price of the matting per yard. *Ans.* 30 cents.

23. A merchant bought 15 car-loads of apples of 212 barrels each, 3 bushels in each barrel, at 45 cents per bushel. He paid for them in cloth at 25 cents a yard. How many bales of 500 yd. each did he give? *Ans.* 34 and 172 yd. over.

24. How many bushels of potatoes at 55 cents a bushel must be given in exchange for 44 sacks of corn, each containing 2 bushels, at 30 cents a bushel? *Ans.* 48.

7. Applying rules.—The practical man often has to apply a rule in solving a problem. This rule may be given to him by a fellow workman, or it may be taken from a handbook. The rule may be one, the reasonableness of which is apparent, but often it is not. Many rules are the results of experience, others of experiment, and still others are mere "rules of thumb," that is, they merely state a combination of numbers which gives the result desired.

In the following problems, read the rule carefully before applying it.

RULE. To find the number of revolutions of a *driven* pulley in a *given* time, multiply the *diameter* of the *driving* pulley by its number of *revolutions* in the given time and divide by the *diameter* of the *driven* pulley.

25. A pulley 48 in. in diameter and making 65 revolutions per minute (R. P. M.) is driving a pulley 26 in. in diameter. Find its number of P. P. M. *Ans.* 120.

26. Find the R. P. M. of a pulley 8 in. in diameter driven by a 28-in. pulley, making 36 R. P. M. *Ans.* 126.

27. Find the R. P. M. of a pulley 44 in. in diameter driven by a 32-in. pulley, making 66 R. P. M.   *Ans.* 48.

RULE.   To determine the width of belt required to transmit a given *horse-power* at a given speed of the belt: For *single leather* or 4-*ply rubber belts*, multiply the number of horse-power to be transmitted by 33,000 and divide the product by the product of the speed of the belt, in feet per minute, multiplied by 60.   The quotient will be the width of the belt in inches.

28. What is the required width of belt to transmit 100 horse-power with a belt speed of 3500 ft. per minute?

Solution. $\dfrac{100 \times 33000}{3500 \times 60} = \dfrac{110}{7} = 15\frac{5}{7}$ in.

29. Find the width of a single leather belt to transmit 75 horse-power, with a belt speed of 3000 ft. per minute.   *Ans.* 13$\frac{3}{4}$ in.

30. For heavy double leather or 6-ply rubber belts, use 100 instead of 60 in the rule.   Find the width of such a belt to transmit 135 horse-power with a belt speed of 3600 ft. per minute.   *Ans.* 12$\frac{3}{8}$ in.

RULE.   To determine the horse-power a belt of given width will transmit when running at a given speed: For *single leather* or 4-*ply rubber belts*, multiply width of belt in inches by 60 and the product by speed of belt in feet per minute and divide the product by 33,000.   The quotient will be the number of horse-power that the belt will transmit with safety.

31. How many horse-power will a 10-in. single leather belt transmit, if running at 4000 ft. per minute?   *Ans.* 72$\frac{8}{11}$.

32. How many horse-power will a 36-in. heavy double leather belt transmit, running at 4500 ft. per minute?   (Use 100 instead of 60 in the rule.)   *Ans.* 491 nearly.

The first letter of a word is often used in mathematics instead of the word itself.   When two or more such letters are written together with no sign between them it is understood that multiplication is indicated.

If H stands for horse-power,

P for effective pressure in pounds of steam per square inch,

L for length of piston stroke in feet,

A for area of piston in square inches,

and N for number of strokes per minute,

then the *rule* for finding the horse-power of a steam engine may be stated in the following abbreviated form:

$$H = \frac{PLAN}{33000}.$$

33. Find H if $P = 55$ lb. per square inch, $L = 2$ ft., $A = 195$ sq. in., and $N = 80$.

Solution. $H = \dfrac{55 \times 2 \times 195 \times 80}{33000} = 52.$

34. Find H if $P = 70$, $L = 2$, $A = 165$, and $N = 90$. *Ans.* 63.

35. Find H if $P = 85$, $A = 95$, $L = 2$, and $N = 190$. *Ans.* 93 nearly.

36. A railroad uses 2,240,000 ties each year. If 350 trees grow on one acre and three ties are cut from a locust tree that is 30 years old, how many acres of locust trees must be planted each year to supply the ties?
Ans. 2133⅓.

37. If 9 men can cut 28 cords of wood in 4 days of 6 hours each, how many cords can 15 men cut in 16 days of 9 hours each? *Ans.* 280.

38. A marble slab 20 feet long, 5 feet wide, and 4 inches thick weighs 850 pounds. What is the weight of another slab of the same marble 16 feet long, 4 feet wide, and 2 inches thick? *Ans.* 272 pounds.

39. If 24 men in 18 days of 8 hours each can dig a ditch 95 rods long, 12 feet wide, and 9 feet deep, how many men in 24 days of 12 hours each will be required to dig a ditch 380 rods long, 9 feet wide, and 6 feet deep?
Ans. 24.

CHAPTER II

COMMON FRACTIONS

DEFINITIONS AND GENERAL PROPERTIES

8. The number 6 when divided by 3 gives a quotient of 2. This may be written $\frac{6}{3} = 2$. If now we attempt to divide 6 by 7, we are unable to find the quotient as above. The division may be written $\frac{6}{7}$. This is called a **fraction.**

$\frac{1}{7}$ means that a unit is divided into 7 equal parts. The fraction $\frac{6}{7}$ indicates that 6 of the 7 equal parts are taken.

9. Definitions.—A **fraction** is an indicated division, which in a simple form expresses one or more of the equal parts into which a unit is divided.

The divisor or the number below the line in the fraction is called the **denominator** of the fraction. The denominator tells into how many parts the unit is divided.

The dividend, or the number above the line in the fraction, is called the **numerator** of the fraction. The numerator tells how many of the parts, into which the unit is divided, are taken.

The numerator and the denominator are called **the terms** of the fraction.

The **value** of a fraction is the number that it represents.

10. Mixed number.—Just as we have whole numbers and fractional numbers, so we have numbers made up of whole numbers and fractions.

Thus, we may have $2\frac{2}{3}$ which is read 2 and $\frac{2}{3}$ and means $2 + \frac{2}{3}$.

Definition. A **mixed number** is one composed of a whole number and a fraction.

11. Proper and improper fractions.—If the fraction shows fewer parts taken than the unit is divided into, its value is evidently less than 1. If the fraction shows as many or more parts taken than the unit is divided into, the fraction is evidently equal to or greater than 1.

Thus, $\frac{3}{4}$ shows fewer parts taken than the unit is divided into, and is less than 1; $\frac{4}{4}$ shows as many parts taken as the unit is divided into and is equal to 1; and $\frac{7}{4}$ shows more parts taken than the unit is divided into, and is greater than 1. Then $\frac{3}{4}$ is a proper fraction, while $\frac{4}{4}$ and $\frac{7}{4}$ are improper fractions.

Definitions. A **proper fraction** is one in which the numerator is less than the denominator. An **improper fraction** is one in which the numerator is equal to or greater than the denominator.

It should be noted that an indicated division is often called a fraction, even though the division can be performed exactly, that is, without a remainder.

Thus, $\frac{12}{3}$, $\frac{24}{12}$, $\frac{44}{11}$ are fractions.

12. Comparison of fractions.—If two fractions have equal numerators and equal denominators they are evidently equal in value.

If two fractions have *equal denominators*, the one that has the *larger numerator* is the *greater* in value. Explain why.

Thus, of $\frac{5}{7}$ and $\frac{3}{7}$, $\frac{5}{7}$ is the larger.

If two fractions have *equal numerators*, the one that has the *larger denominator* is the *smaller* in value. Explain why.

Thus, of $\frac{7}{8}$ and $\frac{7}{9}$, $\frac{7}{9}$ is the smaller.

If two fractions have *both numerators* and *denominators unequal*, their values cannot be compared so easily.

Thus, the values of $\frac{3}{4}$ and $\frac{5}{6}$ can be more easily compared when the fractions are changed to fractions that have the same denominator. See **Art. 18**.

13. In order to get the right viewpoint, it is well for the student to note that before he took up fractions he had learned to add, subtract, multiply, and divide whole numbers; here he has new numbers, fractions, to deal with. It is now necessary to learn how to perform the fundamental operations on fractions. They must be combined not only with other fractions but with whole numbers. The main thing in this chapter is to do these fundamental operations. But to do these in all cases it is necessary to be able to change the fractional numbers in various ways, that is, to reduce to lower or higher terms, change fractions to common denominators, mixed numbers to improper fractions, and improper fractions to mixed numbers.

The student studying alone must determine for himself how many exercises he needs to do in order that he may secure the necessary accuracy and speed.

14. Principles.—Since a fraction is an indicated division the following principles may be stated for fractions:

(1) *Multiplying or dividing both numerator and denominator by the same number does not change the value of the fraction.*

(2) *Multiplying the numerator or dividing the denominator by a number multiplies the fraction by that number.*

(3) *Dividing the numerator or multiplying the denominator by a number divides the fraction by that number.*

15. Reduction of a whole or a mixed number to an improper fraction.—*Example.* Reduce 5 to 6ths.

Since $1 = \frac{6}{6}$, $5 = 5 \times \frac{6}{6} = \frac{30}{6}$. *Ans.* By principle (2).

Example 2. Reduce $7\frac{3}{5}$ to 5ths.

$$\text{Since } 1 = \frac{5}{5}, \ 7 = 7 \times \frac{5}{5} = \frac{35}{5}.$$
$$\therefore \ 7\frac{3}{5} = \frac{35}{5} + \frac{3}{5} = \frac{38}{5}. \ Ans.$$

The three dots, $\therefore$, as used above form a symbol meaning hence or therefore.

Rule. *To reduce a whole number to a fraction of a given denominator, first change 1 to a fraction of the given denominator and then multiply the numerator by the given whole number. With a mixed number, reduce the whole number to a fraction and then add to the numerator of this fraction the numerator of the fractional part of the mixed number.*

16. Reduction of an improper fraction to a whole or mixed number.—*Example 1.* Reduce $\frac{32}{4}$ to a whole number.

$$\frac{32}{4} = 32 \div 4 = 8. \ Ans.$$

Example 2. Reduce $\frac{47}{9}$ to a mixed number.

$$\frac{47}{9} = 47 \div 9 = 5\frac{2}{9}. \ Ans.$$

Rule. *To reduce an improper fraction to a whole or mixed number, perform the indicated division. The quotient is the number of units. If there is no remainder, it reduces to a whole number. If there is a remainder, it reduces to a mixed number of which the quotient is the whole number part and the remainder the numerator of the fractional part.*

EXERCISES 3

1. Reduce the following numbers to sixths: 7, 11, 40, 17, 19.   To thirds.
To tenths.

2. Reduce the following mixed numbers to improper fractions: $2\frac{1}{3}$, $7\frac{5}{8}$, $9\frac{4}{7}$, $12\frac{4}{5}$, $17\frac{2}{3}$, $18\frac{1}{8}$, $22\frac{11}{13}$, $46\frac{1}{9}$.

3. Reduce the following improper fractions to whole or mixed numbers:

$\frac{17}{2}$, $\frac{19}{3}$, $\frac{27}{4}$, $\frac{32}{8}$, $\frac{49}{7}$, $\frac{60}{8}$, $\frac{71}{3}$, $\frac{97}{16}$, $\frac{47}{13}$, $\frac{156}{21}$, $\frac{493}{17}$, $\frac{9296}{463}$, $\frac{7928}{97}$, $\frac{9999}{445}$, $\frac{37684}{841}$.

17. Reduction of fractions to lowest terms.—*Definition.*

A fraction is in its **lowest terms** when the numerator and denominator are *prime* to each other, that is, when there is no integer that will divide both of them.

Example. Reduce $\frac{75}{105}$ to its lowest terms.

$$\frac{75}{105} = \frac{15}{21} = \frac{5}{7}.$$

Since dividing both numerator and denominator by the same number does not change the value of the fraction, both terms may be divided by 5. Thus $\frac{15}{21}$ is obtained. Both terms of this fraction are divided by 3, and $\frac{5}{7}$ is obtained. Since 5 and 7 are prime to each other, the fraction is in its lowest terms. Both terms could have been divided by 15 and the reduction made in one step.

RULE. *To reduce a fraction to its lowest terms, divide both terms successively by their common factors, or divide by the greatest common divisor of the terms.*

EXERCISES 4

Reduce the following fractions to their lowest terms:

1. $\frac{5}{15}$, $\frac{9}{12}$, $\frac{14}{21}$, $\frac{9}{27}$.   **2.** $\frac{7}{35}$, $\frac{25}{35}$, $\frac{21}{28}$, $\frac{24}{32}$.

3. $\frac{16}{24}$, $\frac{17}{34}$, $\frac{19}{38}$, $\frac{21}{42}$.   **4.** $\frac{72}{100}$, $\frac{16}{124}$, $\frac{19}{57}$.

5. $\frac{336}{384}$.   *Ans.* $\frac{7}{8}$.   **6.** $\frac{720}{960}$.   *Ans.* $\frac{3}{4}$.

7. $\frac{888}{360}$.   *Ans.* $\frac{4}{5}$.   **8.** $\frac{216}{252}$.   *Ans.* $\frac{6}{7}$.

9. $\frac{960}{1536}$.   *Ans.* $\frac{5}{8}$.   **10.** $\frac{352}{384}$.   *Ans.* $\frac{11}{12}$.

11. $\frac{8172}{2196}$.   *Ans.* $1\frac{4}{9}$.   **12.** $\frac{8040}{9420}$.   *Ans.* $\frac{11}{17}$.

13. $\frac{5043}{6940}$.   *Ans.* $\frac{19}{20}$.   **14.** $\frac{777}{1111}$.   *Ans.* $\frac{7}{11}$.

15. $\frac{1430}{1320}$.   *Ans.* $1\frac{1}{12}$.   **16.** $\frac{1858}{7842}$.   *Ans.* $\frac{679}{3821}$.

17. $\frac{76200}{128600}$.   *Ans.* $\frac{381}{643}$.   **18.** $\frac{17895}{63720}$.   *Ans.* $\frac{1191}{6248}$.

19. Reduce the following per cents to fractions in their lowest terms: (The sign % takes the place of the denominator 100). 5%, 10%, 40%, 25%, 35%, 42%, 45%, 30%, 28%, 75%, 80%, 95%, 98%, 14%.

18. Reduction of several fractions to fractions having the same denominator.—*Definition.* Fractions that have the

same denominator are called **similar** fractions or fractions with a **common denominator.**

Example 1. Reduce $\frac{1}{2}$ and $\frac{1}{3}$ to fractions which have 6 for a denominator.

The fraction $\frac{1}{2}$ may be changed to 6ths by multiplying both its terms by a number which will make the denominator 6. This will not change the value of the fraction. This multiplier is obtained by dividing 6 by 2 which gives 3.

$$\therefore \; \tfrac{1}{2} = \frac{1\times3}{2\times3} = \tfrac{3}{6}.$$

$$\text{Likewise} \quad \tfrac{1}{3} = \frac{1\times2}{3\times2} = \tfrac{2}{6}.$$

Example 2. Reduce $\frac{7}{9}$, $\frac{3}{8}$, and $\frac{5}{6}$ to 72ds.

Both terms of $\frac{7}{9}$ are multiplied by $72 \div 9 = 8$,
both terms of $\frac{3}{8}$ are multiplied by $72 \div 8 = 9$,
both terms of $\frac{5}{6}$ are multiplied by $72 \div 6 = 12$.

$$\therefore \; \tfrac{7}{9} = \tfrac{56}{72}, \; \tfrac{3}{8} = \tfrac{27}{72}, \text{ and } \tfrac{5}{6} = \tfrac{60}{72}.$$

RULE. *To reduce several fractions to fractions having a common denominator, multiply both terms of each fraction by a number found by dividing the common denominator by the denominator of that fraction.*

19. Least common denominator.—In the preceding the common denominator, 72, was given. Usually the denominator is not given but we are asked to reduce the given fractions to fractions having a least common denominator. When this is the case we find the least common multiple of the denominators of the given fractions, and this is the **least common denominator** (L. C. D.) for all the fractions.

Example. Reduce $\frac{4}{9}$, $\frac{7}{12}$, and $\frac{13}{24}$ to fractions with a L. C. D.

The L. C. M. of 9, 12, and 24 is 72. If we divide 72 by each of the given denominators we get the numbers to be used as multipliers.

$$\therefore \; \tfrac{4}{9} = \tfrac{32}{72}, \; \tfrac{7}{12} = \tfrac{42}{72}, \text{ and } \tfrac{13}{24} = \tfrac{39}{72}.$$

Remark. Usually the fractions dealt with have such denominators that their L. C. D. can be seen by inspection. The student should endeavor to determine 'it in this way wherever possible. If it cannot be seen by inspection, a good way to find it is as follows:

Rule. *Divide the given denominators by a prime number that will divide two or more of them, then divide the remaining numbers and the quotients by a prime number that will divide two or more of them. Continue this as long as possible. The L. C. D. is the continued product of all the divisors and the quotients or numbers left.*

Example. Find the L. C. D. of $\frac{11}{30}$, $\frac{7}{45}$, $\frac{14}{135}$, and $\frac{18}{25}$.

Process.

$$
\begin{array}{r}
5)\overline{30,\ 45,\ 135,\ 25} \\
3)\overline{6,\quad 9,\quad 27,\quad 5} \\
3)\overline{2,\quad 3,\quad 9,\quad 5} \\
\overline{2,\quad 1,\quad 3,\quad 5}
\end{array}
$$

L. C. D. $= 5\times3\times3\times2\times3\times5 = 1350$. *Ans.*

EXERCISES 5

Change as indicated.

1. $\frac{1}{2}$, $\frac{1}{3}$, and $\frac{1}{4}$ to 12ths.
2. $\frac{5}{6}$ and $\frac{4}{7}$ to 42ds.
3. $\frac{2}{3}$, $\frac{3}{4}$, and $\frac{5}{8}$ to 24ths.
4. $\frac{7}{9}$, $\frac{8}{9}$, and $\frac{2}{3}$ to 63ds.
5. 2, $\frac{1}{7}$, and $\frac{5}{8}$ to 42ds.
6. 2, $\frac{2}{3}$, $\frac{4}{5}$, and 5 to 30ths.
7. $\frac{4}{5}$, $\frac{3}{4}$, $\frac{1}{2}$, and $\frac{7}{20}$ to 100ths.
8. $\frac{2}{3}$, $\frac{5}{8}$, $\frac{1}{5}$, and $\frac{5}{6}$ to 120ths.
9. $1\frac{5}{16}$, $\frac{9}{13}$, $\frac{7}{8}$, and $\frac{3}{4}$ to 208ths. *Ans.* $\frac{195}{208}$, $\frac{144}{208}$, $\frac{182}{208}$, $\frac{156}{208}$.
10. $\frac{4}{9}$, $\frac{5}{11}$, $1\frac{7}{22}$, and $\frac{3}{44}$ to 396ths. *Ans.* $\frac{176}{396}$, $\frac{180}{396}$, $\frac{306}{396}$, $\frac{27}{396}$.

Change the following to fractions having a L. C. D.

11. $\frac{1}{2}$ and $\frac{3}{5}$. *Ans.* $\frac{5}{10}$, $\frac{6}{10}$.
12. $\frac{4}{7}$ and $\frac{7}{11}$. *Ans.* $\frac{44}{77}$, $\frac{49}{77}$.
13. $\frac{3}{10}$ and $\frac{12}{25}$. *Ans.* $\frac{15}{50}$, $\frac{24}{50}$.
14. $\frac{9}{13}$ and $\frac{8}{17}$. *Ans.* $\frac{153}{221}$, $\frac{104}{221}$.
15. $\frac{4}{9}$ and $\frac{3}{37}$. *Ans.* $\frac{148}{333}$, $\frac{27}{333}$.
16. $1\frac{7}{15}$ and $1\frac{4}{9}$. *Ans.* $\frac{288}{45}$, $\frac{282}{45}$.
17. $\frac{4}{5}$, $\frac{11}{12}$, $1\frac{7}{12}$, and $\frac{9}{40}$. *Ans.* $\frac{96}{120}$, $\frac{440}{120}$, $\frac{10}{120}$, $\frac{27}{120}$.
18. $\frac{3}{20}$, $\frac{1}{4}$, $\frac{11}{32}$ and $\frac{5}{8}$. *Ans.* $\frac{24}{160}$, $\frac{40}{160}$, $\frac{55}{160}$, $\frac{100}{160}$.
19. $2\frac{3}{16}$, $4\frac{1}{20}$, $7\frac{5}{12}$. *Ans.* $2\frac{45}{240}$, $4\frac{12}{240}$, $7\frac{100}{240}$.

20. Change the following to 100ths and then write as per cents: $\frac{1}{2}$, $\frac{1}{4}$, $\frac{4}{5}$, $\frac{1}{5}$, $\frac{2}{5}$, $\frac{3}{5}$, $\frac{4}{5}$, $\frac{1}{10}$, $\frac{3}{10}$, $\frac{7}{10}$, $\frac{9}{10}$, $\frac{1}{20}$, $\frac{3}{20}$, $\frac{7}{20}$, $\frac{9}{20}$, $\frac{11}{20}$, $\frac{13}{20}$, $\frac{17}{20}$, $\frac{19}{20}$, $\frac{1}{25}$, $\frac{3}{25}$, $\frac{7}{25}$, $\frac{9}{25}$, $\frac{17}{25}$, $\frac{1}{50}$, $\frac{17}{50}$, $\frac{49}{50}$.

ADDITION OF FRACTIONS

20. *Example* 1. Add $\frac{7}{12}$, $\frac{5}{12}$, and $\frac{11}{12}$.

Just as 7 apples + 5 apples + 11 apples = 23 apples, so 7 twelfths + 5 twelfths + 11 twelfths = 23 twelfths.

The work may be arranged as follows:

$$\tfrac{7}{12}+\tfrac{5}{12}+\tfrac{11}{12}=\tfrac{23}{12}=1\tfrac{11}{12}.\quad \textit{Ans.}$$

Example 2. Find the sum of $\frac{7}{12}$, $\frac{8}{15}$, $\frac{17}{30}$.

Here the fractions must first be reduced to fractions having a L. C. D. The L. C. M. of 12, 15, and 30 is 60.

2

Then $\frac{7}{12}+\frac{8}{15}+\frac{17}{30}=\frac{35}{60}+\frac{32}{60}+\frac{34}{60}=\frac{101}{60}=1\frac{41}{60}$. *Ans.*

Example 3.　Find the sum of $3\frac{3}{4}$, $5\frac{4}{7}$, $2\frac{9}{14}$, $7\frac{1}{2}$.

The whole numbers and the fractions may be added separately, and then these sums united.　The work may be written as here.

$3\frac{3}{4}+5\frac{4}{7}+2\frac{9}{14}+7\frac{1}{2}=3\frac{21}{28}+5\frac{16}{28}+2\frac{18}{28}+7\frac{14}{28}=17\frac{69}{28}=19\frac{13}{28}$. *Ans.*

A more convenient way of writing the mixed numbers for adding, is to write them under each other, and add, similar to the method of adding whole numbers.

$$3\frac{3}{4}=3\frac{21}{28}$$
$$5\frac{4}{7}=5\frac{16}{28}$$
$$2\frac{9}{14}=2\frac{18}{28}$$
$$7\frac{1}{2}=7\frac{14}{28}$$
$$\text{\emph{Ans.} } 17\frac{69}{28}=19\frac{13}{28}$$

RULE.　*To add fractions that have a L. C. D., add the numerators of the fractions and place the sum over the L. C. D.　If this gives an improper fraction, it should be reduced to a whole or mixed number.　If the fractions do not have a L.C.D., first reduce them to fractions with a L. C. D.　To add mixed numbers, add the whole numbers and fractions separately and then unite the sums.*

EXERCISES 6

Add the following and express the sum in the simplest form.

1. $\frac{2}{8}+\frac{5}{8}+\frac{4}{8}+\frac{3}{8}$.

2. $\frac{4}{5}+\frac{3}{5}+\frac{7}{5}+\frac{6}{5}$.

3. $\frac{3}{16}+\frac{9}{16}+\frac{11}{16}+\frac{13}{16}$.

4. $\frac{4}{5}+\frac{3}{4}+\frac{7}{20}$.

5. $7+\frac{6}{9}+4\frac{3}{4}+7\frac{1}{4}$.

6. $9\frac{1}{7}+3\frac{4}{5}+6$.

7. $41\frac{1}{2}+40\frac{1}{4}+3$.

8. $9\frac{1}{2}+7\frac{1}{3}+8\frac{1}{4}$.

9. $\frac{3}{10}+\frac{8}{11}+\frac{5}{8}+\frac{3}{4}$.　　　*Ans.* $1\frac{183}{220}$.

10. $\frac{2}{8}+\frac{12}{5}+\frac{5}{3}+\frac{11}{4}$.　　　*Ans.* $8\frac{2}{5}$.

11. $1\frac{11}{4}+4\frac{2}{5}+1\frac{25}{6}$.　　　*Ans.* 60.

12. $1\frac{4}{9}+1\frac{7}{5}+\frac{8}{17}$.　　　*Ans.* $5\frac{61}{85}$.

13. $214\frac{1}{3}+517\frac{7}{45}+145\frac{5}{12}$.　　*Ans.* $876\frac{43}{8}$.

14. $3\frac{3}{4}+17\frac{3}{4}+28\frac{5}{12}+3\frac{7}{12}$.　*Ans.* $53\frac{5}{12}$.

15. $\frac{2}{8}+\frac{5}{6}+\frac{3}{4}+\frac{1}{2}+\frac{3}{8}+\frac{1}{12}+\frac{7}{12}$.　*Ans.* $3\frac{2}{8}$.

16. $2\frac{2}{3}+7\frac{5}{8}+11\frac{1}{12}+14\frac{3}{4}+17\frac{11}{12}$.　*Ans.* $54\frac{1}{4}$.

17. $371\frac{1}{16}+614\frac{18}{8}+81\frac{3}{4}$.　*Ans.* $1067\frac{47}{16}$.

18. $145\frac{7}{8}+36+\frac{11}{12}+194+\frac{87}{8}$.　*Ans.* $376\frac{11}{44}$.

19. $126\frac{2}{3}+35+15\frac{5}{8}+58\frac{1}{4}+9\frac{8}{10}$.　*Ans.* $245\frac{2}{8}$.

20. $16\frac{2}{3}+14\frac{1}{3}+17\frac{1}{2}+19\frac{3}{4}+27\frac{5}{12}$.　*Ans.* $95\frac{2}{3}$.

21. $16\frac{1}{2}+19\frac{2}{8}+24\frac{7}{10}+29\frac{7}{30}+14$.　*Ans.* $103\frac{2}{8}$.

22. A merchant sold to different customers $5\frac{2}{3}$ yards of cloth, $7\frac{3}{4}$ yards, $15\frac{1}{2}$ yards, $9\frac{1}{4}$ yards, and $3\frac{5}{8}$ yards.　Find the total number of yards sold.

Ans. $41\frac{19}{24}$.

23. A farmer has $10\frac{1}{2}$ acres in one field, $8\frac{3}{4}$ acres in another, and $30\frac{1}{4}$ acres in a third. How many acres in the three fields. *Ans.* $49\frac{1}{2}$.

24. In five days a steamer sails the following distances: $384\frac{3}{4}$ miles, $372\frac{7}{8}$ miles, $356\frac{1}{2}$ miles, $392\frac{3}{4}$ miles, and $345\frac{3}{8}$ miles. How far did it sail in the five days? *Ans.* $1852\frac{1}{4}$ miles.

SUBTRACTION OF FRACTIONS

21. *Example* 1. Subtract $\frac{4}{11}$ from $\frac{9}{11}$.

Since like numbers can be subtracted we can subtract 4 elevenths from 9 elevenths and have the remainder 5 elevenths. This may be written $\frac{9}{11} - \frac{4}{11} = \frac{5}{11}$. *Ans.*

Example 2. Subtract $\frac{7}{11}$ from $\frac{2}{3}$.

Here the fractions must first be reduced to fractions having the same denominator. It may be written

$$\frac{2}{3} - \frac{7}{11} = \frac{22}{33} - \frac{21}{33} = \frac{1}{33}.\ Ans.$$

Example 3. $7\frac{2}{3} - 3\frac{3}{5} =$ what?

In this case the fractional part of the subtrahend is less than that of the minuend. The fractional parts of mixed numbers are reduced to fractions having the L. C. D., the fractional parts subtracted, and then the whole numbers.

Solution.
$$7\frac{2}{3} = 7\frac{10}{15}$$
$$3\frac{3}{5} = 3\frac{9}{15}$$
$$Ans.\ 4\frac{1}{15}$$

Example 4. $7\frac{1}{2} - 3\frac{2}{3} =$ what?

In this case the fractional part of the subtrahend is greater than the fractional part of the minuend. The fractions are changed to fractions having the L. C. D. as before. It is then noticed that the fraction $\frac{4}{6}$ in the subtrahend is larger than $\frac{3}{6}$ in the minuend and so cannot be subtracted from it. To overcome this difficulty we take 1 from the 7 and change it to sixths. This gives $6\frac{9}{6}$ instead of $7\frac{3}{6}$. The subtraction is then made as before.

Solution.
$$7\frac{1}{2} = 7\frac{3}{6} = 6\frac{9}{6}$$
$$3\frac{2}{3} = 3\frac{4}{6} = 3\frac{4}{6}$$
$$Ans.\ 3\frac{5}{6}$$

RULE. *To find the difference between two fractions having a common denominator, find the difference of the numerators and write it over the common denominator. If the fractions do not have a L. C. D. reduce them to such before subtracting. If the numbers are mixed numbers, subtract the fractional parts and then the whole numbers.*

EXERCISES 7

Subtract the following and give the results in their simplest forms.

1. $\frac{3}{4}-\frac{1}{2}$.   2. $\frac{7}{8}-\frac{3}{4}$.   3. $\frac{9}{10}-\frac{2}{5}$.

4. $\frac{8}{17}-\frac{3}{34}$.   5. $\frac{7}{9}-\frac{5}{36}$.   6. $2\frac{1}{2}-\frac{3}{4}$.

7. $8\frac{1}{2}-\frac{6}{7}$.   8. $7-4\frac{4}{9}$.   9. $9\frac{4}{7}-1\frac{6}{7}$. ·

10. $\frac{13}{17}-\frac{8}{102}$.   *Ans.* $28\frac{8}{51}$.   11. $\frac{17}{111}-\frac{2}{17}$.   *Ans.* $\frac{167}{1887}$.

12. $\frac{79}{81}-\frac{4}{72}$.   *Ans.* $1\frac{49}{162}$.   13. $4\frac{2}{3}-1\frac{7}{10}$.   *Ans.* $2\frac{29}{30}$.

14. $8\frac{3}{4}-2\frac{5}{8}$.   *Ans.* $6\frac{3}{20}$.   15. $9\frac{7}{8}-3\frac{5}{6}$.   *Ans.* $5\frac{43}{45}$.

16. $463\frac{3}{8}$ / $146\frac{7}{14}$ 17. $346\frac{5}{8}$ / $146\frac{2}{3}$ 18. $461\frac{4}{5}$ / $145\frac{5}{8}$

19. $469\frac{8}{11}$ / $21\frac{3}{22}$ 20. $192\frac{3}{13}$ / $142\frac{3}{26}$ 21. $229\frac{1}{4}$ / $163\frac{2}{3}$

22. $230\frac{2}{3}$ / $103\frac{5}{8}$ 23. $117\frac{2}{3}$ / $96\frac{7}{8}$ 24. $403\frac{1}{12}$ / $231\frac{1}{6}$

Simplify the following, that is, do the operations indicated:

25. $12\frac{2}{3}+28\frac{5}{8}-15\frac{2}{3}$.   *Ans.* $25\frac{23}{30}$.   28. $4\frac{4}{5}-\frac{9}{7}-\frac{2}{3}+6\frac{2}{3}$.   *Ans.* $9\frac{85}{504}$.

26. $5\frac{3}{8}+2\frac{1}{2}-3\frac{1}{4}$.   *Ans.* $4\frac{1}{4}$.   29. $14+6\frac{1}{2}-9\frac{3}{4}$.   *Ans.* $10\frac{3}{4}$.

27. $4\frac{3}{4}-2\frac{1}{2}+1\frac{1}{3}$.   *Ans.* $3\frac{53}{60}$.   30. $\frac{4}{7}+13-(6\frac{7}{8}-\frac{3}{8})+\frac{4}{3}$.   *Ans.* $8\frac{1}{42}$.

The parentheses indicate that the enclosed operations must be performed first. Thus, in the above, $\frac{3}{8}$ must be subtracted from $6\frac{7}{8}$ before they are subtracted from 13.

31. $\frac{6}{7}+17+1\frac{3}{14}-(6+9\frac{1}{2})$.   *Ans.* $2\frac{4}{7}$.

32. $4\frac{3}{4}+3\frac{3}{8}+6\frac{1}{4}-(1\frac{3}{4}+1\frac{2}{3})$.   *Ans.* $10\frac{43}{8}$.

33. $7\frac{3}{8}+6\frac{1}{2}-2\frac{3}{8}+\frac{6}{7}+2\frac{5}{14}$.   *Ans.* $14\frac{11}{14}$.

34. $3\frac{1}{2}+4\frac{1}{3}+1\frac{5}{6}-(\frac{6}{7}+2\frac{8}{21})$.   *Ans.* $6\frac{8}{21}$.

35. $7\frac{5}{8}+2\frac{3}{4}-3\frac{5}{7}+(1\frac{3}{8}+1\frac{1}{9})$.   *Ans.* $9\frac{15}{56}$.

Do as many of the following as you can without a pencil.

36. A boy had $\$\frac{4}{5}$ and spent $\$\frac{1}{2}$; how much money did he have left?

37. A man bought $2\frac{1}{2}$ tons of coal and had $1\frac{1}{4}$ tons delivered; how much was left to be delivered?

38. A man had $5\frac{3}{4}$ acres of land and sold $3\frac{1}{2}$ acres; how many acres did he have left?

39. A man weighed $159\frac{3}{4}$ lb. on Monday and $154\frac{1}{2}$ lb. on the following Saturday; how many pounds did he lose?

40. A man had $\$7\frac{1}{2}$ and paid a debt of $\$3\frac{3}{4}$; how much did he have left?

41. A man sold $\frac{1}{2}$ of his farm at one time and $\frac{1}{3}$ of it at another; what part of his farm did he sell? What part did he have left?

42. A coal dealer had 10 tons of coal. He sold $3\frac{1}{2}$ tons to one customer, $2\frac{3}{4}$ tons to another and the remainder to a third customer. How much did he sell to the third customer?

43. A tank full of water has two pipes opening from it, one will empty $\frac{1}{2}$ of the water in the tank in one hour and the other $\frac{1}{3}$ of it; what part will both pipes empty in one hour? What part remains in the tank?

44. Find the distance around the figure with dimensions as given.

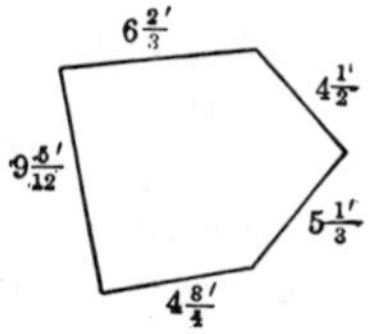

45. One coal wagon drew $6\frac{7}{10}$ and $8\frac{4}{5}$ tons of coal on two successive days; another wagon drew $7\frac{9}{20}$ and $9\frac{2}{3}$ tons on the same days. How much more did the latter draw than the former?

FIG. 1.

22. Resultants.—The combined effect of several forces is called the **resultant.** Thus, a pull of 100 lb. toward the east and at the same time a pull of 75 lb. toward the west gives a resultant pull 25 lb. toward the east.

The resultant of pulls of 150 lb. toward the east, 85 lb. toward the west, and 75 lb. toward the west is a pull of 10 lb. toward the west.

46. Using E for east, W for west, N for north, and S for south; find the resultants of the following:

(1) $48\frac{1}{2}$ lb. W, $92\frac{3}{4}$ lb. E, $76\frac{3}{8}$ lb. E, and $91\frac{1}{2}$ lb. W.   (2) $125\frac{3}{16}$ lb. N, $75\frac{5}{8}$ lb. N, $47\frac{3}{8}$ lb. S, and $156\frac{7}{16}$ lb. S.

$Ans.$ (1) $29\frac{1}{8}$ lb. $E;$ (2) 3 lb. $S.$

MULTIPLICATION OF FRACTIONS

23. Multiplication of fraction and integer.—*Example* 1. Multiply $\frac{3}{5}$ by 4.

To multiply $\frac{3}{5}$ by 4 is to find a fraction that is 4 times as large as $\frac{3}{5}$. By **Art. 14,** multiplying the numerator of a fraction multiplies the value of the fraction.

$$\therefore \tfrac{3}{5} \times 4 = \frac{3 \times 4}{5} = \frac{12}{5} = 2\tfrac{2}{5} \cdot \ Ans.$$

Example 2.   Multiply 8 by $\frac{2}{3}$.

Since in finding the product of two numbers either may be used for the multiplier without changing the product,

$$\therefore 8 \times \tfrac{2}{3} = \tfrac{2}{3} \times 8 = \tfrac{16}{3} = 5\tfrac{1}{3} \cdot \ Ans.$$

Example 3.   Multiply $\frac{3}{14}$ by 7.

Here we may use the principle that dividing the denominator multiplies the value of the fraction, or the operation may be thought of as one in cancellation.

$$\tfrac{3}{14}\times 7 = \frac{3}{14\div 7} = \tfrac{3}{2} = 1\tfrac{1}{2}.\ Ans.$$

$$Or\ \tfrac{3}{14}\times 7 = \frac{3\times 7}{14} = \tfrac{3}{2} = 1\tfrac{1}{2}.\ Ans.$$

Here the 7 and 14 are cancelled.

Rule. *To multiply a fraction by an integer or an integer by a fraction, multiply the numerator or divide the denominator of the fraction by the integer.*

Remark. When a whole number is multiplied by a whole number the product is larger than the multiplicand; but whenever the multiplier is a proper fraction the product is smaller than the multiplicand. Here we cannot think of multiplication as a shortened addition.

We often write $\tfrac{2}{3}$ of 6 for $\tfrac{2}{3}\times 6$.

The meaning is the same in each case

24. Multiplication of a fraction by a fraction.—

Example 1. Multiply $\tfrac{2}{3}$ by $\tfrac{5}{7}$.

$\tfrac{2}{3}$ by $\tfrac{5}{7}$ is the same as $\tfrac{5}{7}$ of $\tfrac{2}{3}$, but $\tfrac{5}{7}$ of $\tfrac{2}{3}$ is 5 times $\tfrac{1}{7}$ of $\tfrac{2}{3}$ and $\tfrac{1}{7}$ of $\tfrac{2}{3}$ has a value $\tfrac{1}{7}$ as large as $\tfrac{2}{3}$.

By **Art. 14,** the value of a fraction is divided when the denominator is multiplied.

$$\therefore\ \tfrac{1}{7}\ of\ \tfrac{2}{3} = \frac{2}{3\times 7} = \tfrac{2}{21}.$$

$$And\ \tfrac{5}{7}\ of\ \tfrac{2}{3} = 5\ times\ \tfrac{2}{21} = \frac{2\times 5}{21} = \tfrac{10}{21}.$$

These steps may be combined as follows:

$$\tfrac{2}{3}\times \tfrac{5}{7} = \frac{2\times 5}{3\times 7} = \tfrac{10}{21}.\quad Ans.$$

Example 2. Multiply $\tfrac{14}{18}$ by $\tfrac{3}{7}$.

$$\tfrac{14}{18}\times \tfrac{3}{7} = \frac{\overset{2}{\cancel{14}}\times \cancel{3}}{\underset{3}{\cancel{18}}\times \cancel{7}} = \tfrac{1}{3}.\quad Ans.$$

Cancellation should be used when it will shorten the work.

Example 3. Multiply $\tfrac{3}{5}$ by $\tfrac{9}{13}$ by $\tfrac{26}{27}$.

$$\tfrac{3}{5}\times \tfrac{9}{13}\times \tfrac{26}{27} = \frac{\cancel{3}\times \cancel{9}\times \cancel{26}^{2}}{5\times \cancel{13}\times \cancel{27}_{9}} = \tfrac{2}{5}.\quad Ans.$$

RULE. *To multiply a fraction by a fraction, multiply the numerators together for the numerator of the product, and the denominators together for the denominator of the product. Cancel when convenient.*

Remark. A form like $\frac{2}{3}$ of $\frac{3}{4}$ of $\frac{7}{8}$ is often called a compound fraction.

25. Multiplication of mixed numbers and integers.—

Example 1. Multiply $7\frac{3}{5}$ by 6.

$$7\tfrac{3}{5}\times 6=\frac{38}{5}\times 6=\frac{228}{5}=45\tfrac{3}{5}. \quad \textit{Ans.}$$

Example 2. Multiply $8\frac{1}{3}$ by $3\frac{2}{5}$.

$$8\tfrac{1}{3}\times 3\tfrac{2}{5}=\frac{\overset{5}{\cancel{25}}}{3}\times\frac{17}{\cancel{5}}=\frac{85}{3}=28\tfrac{1}{3}. \quad \textit{Ans.}$$

RULE. *To multiply two numbers, one or both of which are mixed numbers, reduce the mixed numbers to improper fractions and multiply as with fractions.*

Remark. The work may often be simplified by using the following methods:

Example 3. Multiply 47 by $16\frac{4}{5}$.

Process.

$$\begin{array}{r} 47 \\ \underline{16\frac{4}{5}} \\ 5)\underline{188} \\ 37\frac{3}{5} \\ 282 \\ \underline{47} \\ 789\frac{3}{5} \end{array}$$

Explanation. Multiply 47 by 4 and divide by 5, which is the same as multiplying 47 by $\frac{4}{5}$; this gives $37\frac{3}{5}$. Then multiply 47 by 16 in the ordinary way for multiplying whole numbers. Add these three partial products and the entire product is $789\frac{3}{5}$.

Example 4. Multiply $25\frac{2}{5}$ by $6\frac{1}{3}$.

Process.

$$\begin{array}{r} 25\frac{2}{5} \\ \underline{6\frac{1}{3}} \\ \frac{2}{15} \\ 8\frac{1}{3} \\ 2\frac{2}{5} \\ \underline{150\phantom{\frac{1}{1}}} \\ 160\frac{13}{15} \end{array}$$

Explanation. $\frac{2}{5}\times\frac{1}{3}=\frac{2}{15}$; $25\times\frac{1}{3}=8\frac{1}{3}$; $\frac{2}{5}\times 6=2\frac{2}{5}$; $25\times 6=150$.

The entire product equals the sum of these partial products.

If several fractions and mixed numbers are to be multiplied together it is usually best to reduce all to fractions for then the work may be shortened by cancellation.

Example 5.   Find the product of $\frac{7}{9}\times3\frac{2}{3}\times9\times4\frac{2}{11}\times\frac{3}{22}$.

$$\frac{7}{9}\times3\frac{2}{3}\times9\times4\frac{2}{11}\times\frac{3}{22}=\frac{7}{\cancel{9}}\times\frac{\cancel{11}}{\cancel{3}}\times\frac{\cancel{9}}{1}\times\frac{\cancel{46}}{\cancel{11}}\times\frac{\cancel{3}}{\cancel{22}}=\frac{161}{11}=14\frac{7}{11}. \quad Ans.$$

EXERCISES 8

Find the product of each of the following; without pencil when possible.

1. $\frac{2}{8}\times4$.
2. $\frac{7}{8}\times4$.
3. $\frac{4}{4}\times2$.
4. $\frac{4}{5}\times5$.
5. $\frac{9}{16}\times8$.
6. $\frac{9}{16}\times5$.
7. $7\times\frac{2}{3}$.
8. $8\times\frac{4}{5}$.
9. $9\times\frac{7}{3}$.

10. $25\times\frac{7}{10}$.
11. $5\times\frac{9}{13}$.
12. $15\times1\frac{2}{3}$.
13. $27\times1\frac{7}{9}$.
14. $45\times2\frac{1}{5}$.
15. $55\times2\frac{1}{5}$.
16. $\frac{1}{2}$ of $\frac{3}{4}$.
17. $\frac{4}{5}\times\frac{5}{4}$.
18. $\frac{7}{10}\times\frac{5}{14}$.

19. $\frac{8}{9}\times\frac{27}{32}$.
20. $\frac{3}{4}$ of 20.
21. $\frac{4}{5}$ of 30.
22. $\frac{5}{9}$ of 63.
23. $\frac{3}{10}$ of 120.
24. $\frac{2}{3}$ of 99.
25. $\frac{3}{11}$ of 22.
26. $6\frac{1}{4}\times8$.
27. $4\frac{5}{12}\times6$.

28. What is 3 times 4 bushels?   3 times 4-fifths?   3 times $\frac{4}{7}$? $3\times\frac{4}{11}$?

29. What is $\frac{1}{3}$ of 9 quarts? $\frac{1}{3}$ of 9-tenths? $\frac{1}{3}$ of $\frac{9}{11}$? $\frac{1}{3}\times\frac{9}{13}$?

30. A can is $\frac{4}{5}$ full of milk.   If $\frac{1}{3}$ of this is drawn off, what part of the whole can is drawn off?   What part remains in the can?

31. It took a boy living in the country 50 minutes to walk to school. He could drive with a horse in $\frac{3}{5}$ of this time. How long did it take him to drive?

32. On one field a farmer harvested 230 bushels of wheat and on a second $\frac{4}{5}$ as much. How many bushels were harvested on the second field?

33. One-third of the water in a tank will flow from a certain opening in 1 hour. If the tank holds 60 barrels how many barrels will flow out in 2 hours?

34. If two pipes open from a tank, one of which can empty $\frac{1}{4}$ of the tank in 1 hour, and the other $\frac{1}{5}$ of it in 1 hour, what part of the tank will both empty in 1 hour? If the tank holds 60 barrels, how many barrels will flow out in 2 hours if both pipes are open?   *Ans.* $\frac{9}{20}$, 54.

35. The circumference of a circle is about $3\frac{1}{7}$ times the diameter. Find the circumference of a circle if the diameter is 7 ft., 21 ft., 6 ft.

36. The diagonal of a square is very nearly $1\frac{5}{12}$ the length of one side. Find the diagonal when one side is 12 in., 6 in., 84 ft.

37. If you have a vacation of 100 days, and spend $\frac{2}{5}$ in the country, $\frac{3}{20}$ camping, and the remainder in the city, how many days do you spend in each place?

38. A boy has $2.50. He spends $\frac{2}{5}$ of it for a fishing rod, $\frac{3}{10}$ of it for a reel, and the remainder for a line. How much did he spend for each?

39. $\frac{27}{85}\times16$.　　*Ans.* $1\frac{1}{15}$.　　**40.** $\frac{49}{720}\times96$.　　*Ans.* $6\frac{8}{15}$.

41. $\frac{375}{878}\times96$.　　*Ans.* $62\frac{1}{2}$.　　**42.** $28\frac{5}{12}\times14$.　　*Ans.* $397\frac{5}{6}$.

43. $816\frac{3}{4}\times17$.　　*Ans.* $13883\frac{1}{4}$.　　**44.** $956\frac{4}{5}\times29$.　　*Ans.* $27747\frac{1}{5}$.

45. $12\frac{1}{2}\times62\frac{1}{2}$.　　*Ans.* $781\frac{1}{4}$.　　**46.** $12\frac{3}{8}\times3\frac{4}{5}$.　　*Ans.* $47\frac{23}{40}$.

47. $13\frac{1}{2}\times9\frac{3}{4}$.　　*Ans.* $131\frac{5}{8}$.　　**48.** $23\frac{1}{2}\times18\frac{4}{5}$.　　*Ans.* $441\frac{4}{5}$.

49. $14\frac{4}{5}\times10\frac{2}{5}$.　　*Ans.* $153\frac{23}{25}$.　　**50.** $212\frac{2}{3}\times7\frac{1}{2}$.　　*Ans.* 1595.

51. Multiply $1\frac{1}{2}$ by $1\frac{1}{2}$, $2\frac{1}{2}$ by $2\frac{1}{2}$, $3\frac{1}{2}$ by $3\frac{1}{2}$, $10\frac{1}{2}$ by $10\frac{1}{2}$.

52. Can you make a rule for finding the product of two factors that are the same and end in $\frac{1}{2}$? See **Art. 43** (5).

The product of two factors that are exactly alike is called the square of one of them. Thus, the square of $4\frac{1}{2}$ is $4\frac{1}{2}\times4\frac{1}{2}=20\frac{1}{4}$.

Find the square of each of the following by your rule: $7\frac{1}{2}$, $9\frac{1}{2}$, $11\frac{1}{2}$, $16\frac{1}{2}$, $12\frac{1}{2}$, $20\frac{1}{2}$, $100\frac{1}{2}$.

53. $\frac{2}{3}\times\frac{3}{4}\times\frac{3}{5}=$ what?　　　　　　　　*Ans.* $\frac{3}{10}$.

54. $\frac{2}{3}\times\frac{2}{3}\times1\frac{1}{2}\times\frac{7}{8}=$ what?　　　　　*Ans.* $\frac{7}{8}$.

55. $\frac{9}{23}\times2\frac{1}{4}\times7\frac{2}{3}\times\frac{9}{28}\times3\frac{1}{2}=$ what?　　　*Ans.* $7\frac{19}{32}$.

56. If hogs are worth $9\frac{3}{4}$ cents a pound, what is a hog weighing 325 lb. worth?　　　　　　　　　　　　　　　　　*Ans.* \$31.68$\frac{3}{4}$.

57. In Chicago in 1912, carpenters received 65 cents per hour. How much was this for an 8-hour day? For one week of $5\frac{1}{2}$ days?

Ans. \$5.20; \$28.60.

58. In the same city, a bricklayer received $72\frac{1}{2}$ cents an hour. How much could a man earn in a year if he worked 225 days of 8 hours each?

Ans. \$1305.

59. In 1908, a stonecutter in New York received $56\frac{3}{20}$ cents an hour. If a man worked 50 weeks a year and $5\frac{1}{2}$ days per week, $8\frac{1}{2}$ hours a day, how much would he earn a year?

Solution. $56\frac{3}{20}\times8\frac{1}{2}\times5\frac{1}{2}\times50=\frac{1123}{20}\times\frac{17}{2}\times\frac{11}{2}\times\frac{50}{1}=\$1312.50\frac{5}{8}$. *Ans.*

60. A man earns $62\frac{1}{2}$ cents an hour and his two sons each $22\frac{3}{4}$ cents an hour. How much do the three earn per week of $5\frac{1}{2}$ days of $8\frac{1}{2}$ hours each?

Ans. \$50.49.

61. A gang of men mix and place an average of $43\frac{15}{16}$ cu. yd. of concrete per hour. How many cubic yards do they place in a day of $8\frac{3}{4}$ hours?　　　　　　　　　　　　　　　　*Ans.* 381.

62. An alloy, used for bearings in machinery, is $\frac{5}{6}$ copper, $\frac{4}{29}$ tin, and $\frac{3}{29}$ zinc. How many pounds of each in 346 lb. of the alloy?

Ans. $286\frac{13}{18}$; $47\frac{23}{29}$; $11\frac{27}{29}$.

63. An alloy, called "anti-friction metal," is $\frac{37}{1000}$ copper, $\frac{111}{125}$ tin, and $\frac{3}{40}$ antimony. Find the weight of each metal in a mass of the alloy weighing 1250 lb.　　*Ans.* $46\frac{1}{4}$ lb.; 1110 lb.; $93\frac{3}{4}$ lb.

64. Find the cost of $27\frac{3}{5}$ sq. ft. of plate glass at $66\frac{2}{3}$ cents per square foot.　　　　　　　　　　　　　　　　　*Ans.* \$18.40.

65. A pumping engine in Chicago pumps on an average of $17,361\frac{1}{9}$ gallons per minute, how many gallons is this in 24 hours?

Ans. 25,000,000.

66. An ice-plant has an output of 45 tons daily. What is the value of this output for a year of 320 days at \$3$\frac{3}{5}$ per ton?　　*Ans.* \$51,840.

67. Nickel steel will stand a pull of 90,000 lb. per square inch of cross section. What pull will a bar of $1\frac{15}{16}$ sq. in. cross section stand?

Ans. 174,375 lb.

68. The average yearly fire loss in the United States from 1897 to 1906 was $2\frac{7}{10}$ per capita. If the population averaged 75,000,000, what was the average loss per year? *Ans.* \$202,500,000.

69. In the European countries for the same period as in the previous exercise, the average fire loss per capita was $\frac{1}{3}$. What would have been saved in the United States if the fire loss had been the same as in the European countries? *Ans.* \$177,500,000.

70. The circumference of a circle is very nearly $\frac{355}{113}$ times the diameter. What is the circumference of a circle that is $24\frac{7}{10}$ in. in diameter?

Ans. $77\frac{183}{226}$ in. nearly.

71. If the diagonal of a square is very nearly $1\frac{5}{12}$ the length of one side, find the diagonal in feet of a square $\frac{3}{4}$ miles on a side. A mile is 5280 ft. *Ans.* 5060 ft.

72. Remembering that 6 per cent means $\frac{6}{100}$, find the value of the following:

(a) 6% of \$7.25.

(b) 9% of \$820.

(c) 12% of \$75.20.

(d) 20% of 476 bushels

(e) 30% of 9227 bushels.

(f) 45% of 325 acres.

(g) 75% of \$3276.

(h) 95% of 396 miles.

(i) 82% of 7684 bushels.

(j) 65% of 4762.

Ans. (a) \$0.43$\frac{1}{2}$; (e) $2768\frac{1}{10}$ bu.; (g) \$2457; (j) $3095\frac{3}{10}$.

DIVISION OF FRACTIONS

26. Division of a fraction by an integer.—*Example* 1. Divide $\frac{3}{7}$ by 4.

(1) Since to divide by 4 is to find one of the 4 equal parts and to get $\frac{1}{4}$ of a number is to find one of the 4 equal parts, we have

$$\frac{3}{7} \div 4 = \frac{1}{4} \text{ of } \frac{3}{7} = \frac{3}{28}. \quad Ans.$$

(2) Or, using the principle that multiplying the denominator of a fraction divides the value of the fraction, we have

$$\frac{3}{7} \div 4 = \frac{3}{7 \times 4} = \frac{3}{28}. \quad Ans.$$

(3) In division of fractions, we can often divide the numerator and thus divide the fraction.

Example 2. Divide $\frac{925}{11}$ by 25.

$$\frac{925}{11} \div 25 = \frac{925 \div 25}{11} = \frac{37}{11} = 3\frac{4}{11}. \quad Ans.$$

This may be written $\frac{925}{11} \div 25 = \frac{925}{11} \times \frac{1}{25} = \frac{37}{11} = 3\frac{4}{11}. \quad Ans.$

RULE. *To divide a fraction by an integer, divide the numerator, or multiply the denominator, of the fraction by the integer; or multiply the fraction by 1 over the integer.*

27. Division by a fraction.—*Example* 1. Divide 6 by $\frac{2}{3}$.

(1) If we reduce 6 to thirds, we may divide the numerators, since then the numbers will both be thirds, and so be *like* numbers.

$$6 \div \frac{2}{3} = \frac{18}{3} \div \frac{2}{3} = 18 \text{ thirds} \div 2 \text{ thirds} = 9. \quad Ans.$$

(2) Since there are 3 times $\frac{1}{3}$ in 1, and $\frac{1}{2}$ as many times $\frac{2}{3}$, there are $\frac{1}{2}$ times 3, or $\frac{3}{2}$ times $\frac{2}{3}$ in 1. Now $\frac{3}{2}$ is $\frac{2}{3}$ inverted. Hence we can find how many times the fraction $\frac{2}{3}$ is contained in 1 by inverting the fraction. $\frac{2}{3}$ will be contained 6 times as many times in 6 as it is contained in 1.

$$\therefore 6 \div \frac{2}{3} = 6 \times \frac{3}{2} = 9. \quad Ans.$$

Definition. The **reciprocal** of a number is 1 divided by that number. Thus, $\frac{3}{2}$ is the reciprocal of $\frac{2}{3}$. $\frac{1}{4}$ is the reciprocal of $\frac{4}{1}$ or 4.

Example 2. Divide $\frac{48}{65}$ by $\frac{14}{39}$.

$$\frac{48}{65} \div \frac{14}{39} = \frac{48}{65} \times \frac{39}{14} = \frac{21}{10} = 2\frac{1}{10}. \quad Ans.$$

Example 3. Divide $4\frac{4}{5}$ by $3\frac{1}{3}$.

First reducing each to improper fractions, we have

$$4\frac{4}{5} \div 3\frac{1}{3} = \frac{24}{5} \div \frac{10}{3} = \frac{24}{5} \times \frac{3}{10} = \frac{36}{25} = 1\frac{11}{25}. \quad Ans.$$

RULE. *To divide a whole number or a fraction by a fraction, invert the divisor and multiply by the dividend. If either or both dividend and divisor are mixed numbers, first change to improper fractions.*

28. Special methods in division.—The work of division may often be simplified by one of the following methods:

Example 1. Divide $56\frac{2}{3}$ by 5.

Process.	*Explanation.*
$5)56\frac{2}{3}$	$56 \div 5 = 11$ with a remainder of 1.
$11\frac{1}{3}$ *Ans.*	$1\frac{2}{3} \div 5 = \frac{5}{3} \div 5 = \frac{1}{3}$.

Example 2. Divide 75 by $3\frac{2}{3}$.

Process.

$3\frac{2}{3}) \; 75$
$11)225$
$\qquad 20\frac{5}{11} \quad Ans.$

Explanation. Since multiplying both dividend and divisor by the same number does not change the quotient, we can multiply both by the denominator in the divisor, then divide as before.

Example 3.   Divide $125\frac{2}{3}$ by $2\frac{3}{4}$.

Process.

$2\frac{3}{4})125\frac{2}{3}$

$11)502\frac{2}{3}$

$45\frac{33}{33}$ *Ans.*

Explanation. The same as in the preceding, multiply both by the denominator in the divisor. Then divide as in example 6.

EXERCISES 9

Divide the following, using the pencil only when necessary:

1. $\frac{8}{9} \div 4$.
2. $\frac{12}{23} \div 3$.
3. $\frac{17}{4} \div 3$.
4. $\frac{9}{11} \div 4$.
5. $\frac{21}{13} \div 7$.

6. $\frac{121}{13} \div 11$.
7. $\frac{144}{25} \times 12$.
8. $5 \div \frac{1}{2}$.
9. $17 \div \frac{2}{3}$.
10. $16 \div \frac{4}{5}$.

11. $\frac{1}{2} \div \frac{3}{8}$.
12. $\frac{9}{7} \div \frac{5}{14}$.
13. $\frac{4}{5} \div \frac{8}{10}$.
14. $\frac{9}{16} \div \frac{3}{4}$.
15. $\frac{17}{3} \div \frac{15}{3}$.

16. $32\frac{1}{2} \div 4$.
17. $326\frac{2}{3} \div 2$.
18. $764\frac{3}{8} \div 4$.
19. $21\frac{3}{4} \div 2$.
20. $28\frac{2}{8} \div 3$.

21. $96\frac{3}{4} \div 8$.
22. $122\frac{2}{3} \div 3$.
23. $27\frac{2}{3} \div 5$.
24. $86\frac{3}{4} \div 3$.
25. $192\frac{4}{5} \div 5$.

26. If the denominator of a fraction is multiplied by 3, how is the unit of the fraction changed? How changed if multiplied by 6? By 5? Illustrate with the fraction $\frac{2}{3}$.

27. If $\frac{1}{4}$ in. on a map represents 1 mile, how many miles are represented by 6 in. on the map?

28. In the drawing of a house, $\frac{1}{8}$ in. in the picture represents 1 ft. in the actual house. Find the dimensions of the rooms that measure as follows: $2\frac{1}{4}$ in. by $2\frac{7}{8}$ in., $1\frac{1}{2}$ by $1\frac{3}{4}$, $1\frac{3}{16}$ by $1\frac{7}{16}$, $\frac{11}{16}$ by $\frac{15}{16}$.

In the following, x is used for the number that is to be found:

29. $\frac{2}{3} \div 6 = x$.

30. $3 \div x = 6$.

31. $\frac{2}{8} \div x = 5$.

32. $x \div \frac{1}{3} = 7$.

33. $\frac{75}{9} \div 15 = \frac{x}{9}$.

34. $\frac{48}{9} \div \frac{2}{3} = \frac{x}{9}$.

35. $\frac{8}{5} \div 4 = \frac{9}{x}$.

36. $\frac{17}{8} \div 9 = \frac{17}{x}$.

37. $\frac{2}{3} \div x = \frac{4}{7}$.

38. If a man can do a piece of work in 3 hours, what part of it can he do in 1 hour? In 2 hours?

39. If a man can do $\frac{1}{3}$ of a piece of work in 1 hour, in how many hours can he do all the work? $\frac{2}{3}$ of the work?

40. If a man can do $\frac{2}{5}$ of a piece of work in 2 hours, in how many hours can he do all the work? $\frac{4}{5}$ of the work? $\frac{1}{2}$ of the work? $\frac{7}{25}$ of the work?

41. If a boy can run $\frac{2}{3}$ of a mile in 6 minutes, how many minutes will it take him to run a mile? $\frac{1}{2}$ a mile? $\frac{1}{4}$ of a mile?

42 If John can do $\frac{1}{3}$ of a piece of work in 1 hour and Henry can do $\frac{1}{2}$ of it in 1 hour, what part of the work can they both do in 1 hour? How many hours will it take them to do the whole work if they work together?

$Ans.$ $\frac{5}{6}$; $1\frac{1}{5}$.

43. One boy can hoe a patch of potatoes in 3 hours and another boy can hoe the same patch in 4 hours. In how many hours can they hoe the potatoes if they work together?

Solution. The first boy can hoe $\frac{1}{3}$ of the patch in one hour, and the second boy $\frac{1}{4}$ of the patch in one hour. Together they can hoe $\frac{1}{3} \times \frac{1}{4} = \frac{7}{12}$ of the patch in one hour. They can hoe the entire patch in $1 \div \frac{7}{12} =$ $1 \times \frac{12}{7} = \frac{12}{7} = 1\frac{5}{7}$ or $1\frac{5}{7}$ hours.

44. A water tank that holds 60 barrels has two pipes opening from it. One of these can empty the tank in 4 hours when running alone, and the other pipe can empty the tank in 12 hours when running alone. If both of the pipes are running at the same time, how long will it take them to empty the tank? $Ans.$ 3 hours.

45. If one pipe can empty a tank in 4 hours, and another pipe can empty it in 12 hours, in how many hours will both pipes empty the tank when running together? $Ans.$ 3.

46. If a boy earns $\$\frac{3}{4}$ a day, in how many days will he earn \$9.

$Ans.$ 12.

47. If a man earns $\$\frac{3}{2}$ in 1 hour, in how many hours will he earn \$15?

$Ans.$ 10.

48. $\frac{275}{36} \div 175.$	$Ans.$ $\frac{11}{252}.$	**55.** $3\frac{11}{15} \div 7\frac{24}{25}.$	$Ans.$ $\frac{985}{597}.$
49. $\frac{161}{6} \div 42.$	$Ans.$ $\frac{23}{35}.$	**56.** $\frac{7}{257} \div 2\frac{7}{41}.$	$Ans.$ $2\frac{145}{71}.$
50. $\frac{87}{188} \div 1\frac{5}{6}.$	$Ans.$ $1\frac{7}{75}.$	**57.** $10\frac{18}{23} \div 1\frac{9}{115}.$	$Ans.$ 10.
51. $100 \div 4\frac{7}{8}.$	$Ans.$ $20\frac{16}{39}.$	**58.** $5\frac{2}{9} \div \frac{74}{343}.$	$Ans.$ $24\frac{1}{9}.$
52. $4\frac{10}{11} \div 10\frac{4}{11}.$	$Ans.$ $\frac{9}{19}.$	**59.** $7\frac{5}{29} \div 3\frac{11}{15}.$	$Ans.$ $1\frac{8}{9}.$
53. $31\frac{7}{9} \div 1\frac{62}{9}.$	$Ans.$ 18.	**60.** $104\frac{3}{11} \div 8\frac{9}{7}.$	$Ans.$ $11\frac{17}{37}.$
54. $3\frac{8}{17} \div 2\frac{16}{21}.$	$Ans.$ $1\frac{253}{336}.$	**61.** $115\frac{7}{8} \div 20\frac{3}{8}.$	$Ana.$ $5\frac{5}{8}.$

In the following five exercises, reduce all to fractions, take reciprocals of each divisor and cancel.

62. $2\frac{1}{3} \times 3\frac{1}{2} \times \frac{4}{17} \times 2\frac{7}{12} \div 20\frac{2}{3}.$

Process.

$$2\frac{1}{3} \times 3\frac{1}{2} \times \frac{4}{17} \times 2\frac{7}{12} \div 20\frac{2}{3} = \frac{7}{3} \times \frac{7}{2} \times \frac{\overset{2}{\cancel{4}}}{17} \times \frac{31}{12} \times \frac{3}{\underset{2}{\cancel{62}}} = \frac{49}{204}. \quad Ans.$$

63. $5\frac{1}{8} \times 9\frac{2}{8} \div 8\frac{4}{7} \div 9\frac{1}{7} \div 3\frac{6}{25} \div \frac{2}{145}.$ $Ans.$ $14\frac{7}{12}.$

64. $\frac{16}{17} \times 29\frac{3}{4} \times 13\frac{3}{8} \div 15\frac{3}{4} \div 2\frac{7}{8}.$ $Ans.$ $8\frac{88}{125}.$

65. $\frac{9}{16} \times 13\frac{1}{2} \times 2\frac{6}{8} \times 9\frac{1}{4} \div \frac{27}{43} \div (1\frac{1}{10} \times \frac{6}{8} \times 26\frac{1}{4}) \div \frac{8}{5}.$ $Ans.$ $2\frac{6}{85}.$

66. $8\frac{3}{4} \times 1\frac{8}{25} \times \frac{3}{14} \times 1\frac{1}{12} \times 1\frac{3}{5} \times 7\frac{1}{3} \times 1\frac{2}{8} \div 6\frac{3}{8} \div 1\frac{8}{9} \div 12\frac{5}{6} \div 2\frac{3}{25}.$ $Ans.$ $1\frac{1}{2}.$

67. Find the value of $\frac{7}{4} \div (\frac{2}{3} + \frac{5}{6}) - \frac{1}{4}.$ $Ans.$ $\frac{11}{12}.$

Parentheses indicate that the inclosed operations must be performed first. For example, in the above, $\frac{2}{3}$ is added to $\frac{5}{6}$ and then $\frac{7}{4}$ is divided by the sum.

68. Find the value of $2\frac{7}{8} - 7\frac{23}{27} + 5\frac{17}{18} - 56\frac{3}{4}.$ $Ans.$ $61\frac{49}{54}.$

69. Simplify (a) $\frac{4\frac{2}{3}}{2\frac{5}{6}}$, (b) $\frac{\frac{5}{6}}{\frac{9}{2}}$, (c) $\frac{\frac{1}{2}}{\frac{7}{16}}$, (d) $\frac{3\frac{3}{4}}{\frac{1}{3}}$. $Ans.$ $1\frac{11}{17}$, $\frac{5}{6}$, $1\frac{1}{7}$, $11\frac{1}{4}$.

70. From $75\frac{5}{42}$ take $12\frac{9}{14}$.   *Ans.* $62\frac{10}{21}$.

71. Multiply $2\frac{1}{2} \div \frac{7}{8}$ by $\frac{1}{2}$ of $(\frac{7}{8} + \frac{3}{4})$.   *Ans.* $2\frac{9}{28}$.

72. Find the value of $\dfrac{3\frac{2}{7} \times 8\frac{1}{6}}{4\frac{2}{3} \times 2\frac{1}{16}}$.   *Ans.* $2\frac{68}{93}$.

Suggestion. First, multiply $3\frac{2}{7}$ by $8\frac{1}{6}$, second, $4\frac{2}{3}$ by $2\frac{1}{16}$, then divide the first product by the second.

73. $13\frac{4}{9} - 2\frac{5}{18} - 6\frac{9}{16} + 3 - 1\frac{5}{12} + 8\frac{7}{8} - \frac{23}{72} - 10\frac{18}{48} = ?$ *Ans.* $4\frac{25}{72}$.

74. $(\frac{2}{3} \times \frac{5}{8} \times \frac{6}{25}) \div (\frac{2}{5} \times \frac{1}{2} \times \frac{5}{8}) = ?$ *Ans.* $\frac{4}{5}$.

75. Evaluate $\dfrac{\left(2\frac{5}{8} \div \frac{4}{1\frac{5}{10}}\right) \times 2}{2 - \frac{\frac{1}{4}}{2} \div 5}$.

Solution. The word evaluate means that the indicated operations should be performed and the value of the expression found. At first decide what operations must be performed first, what second, and so on. Then do these operations as simply as possible.

$$\frac{\left(2\frac{5}{8} \div \frac{4}{1\frac{5}{10}}\right) \times 2}{2 - \frac{\frac{1}{4}}{2} \div 5} = \frac{(\frac{21}{8} \div 8) \times 2}{2 - \frac{1}{8} \div 5} = \frac{2\frac{1}{8} \times \frac{1}{8} \times 2}{2 - \frac{1}{40}} = \frac{\frac{21}{32}}{\frac{79}{40}} = \frac{21}{32} \times \frac{40}{79} = \frac{105}{316}. \quad Ans.$$

76. Evaluate $\dfrac{(3\frac{1}{2} - 2\frac{1}{4}) \div 1\frac{2}{3}}{1\frac{2}{3} + 2\frac{1}{2}}$.   *Ans.* $\frac{9}{50}$.

77. Add $\frac{2}{3} \times \frac{5\frac{1}{3}}{\frac{5}{6}}$ to $\frac{6}{7} \times (4\frac{1}{2} - 2\frac{7}{9})$.   *Ans.* $14\frac{19}{630}$.

78. Subtract $\frac{2}{3}$ of $\frac{5}{9}$ from $\frac{7}{8}$ of $\frac{6}{8}$.   *Ans.* $\frac{5}{18}$.

79. $\frac{2}{5}$ of 20 is $\frac{7}{10}$ of what number?   *Ans.* $11\frac{3}{7}$.

80. Find the simplest expression for $\dfrac{1}{3\frac{1}{5}} - \dfrac{2\frac{1}{4}}{9} + \dfrac{3\frac{5}{8}}{2} - \dfrac{\frac{4}{9}}{4\frac{4}{7}}$.   *Ans.* $1\frac{3}{4}$.

Perform the operations indicated in the following five exercises:

81. $\dfrac{\frac{2}{5} + \frac{3}{8} + \frac{1}{4} - \frac{7}{12}}{3\frac{1}{3} - 2\frac{1}{2}}$. *Ans.* $\frac{13}{60}$.   **82.** $\dfrac{(4\frac{1}{2} + 7\frac{1}{2}) \div 3\frac{1}{3}}{\frac{1}{7} \times 2\frac{2}{7} \times 5\frac{1}{4}}$.   *Ans.* 2.

83. $2\frac{1}{4} \times \dfrac{10\frac{3}{4} - 4\frac{11}{12}}{6\frac{3}{16} + 7\frac{2}{3}} \times \dfrac{3\frac{5}{11}}{1\frac{2}{8} \times 9\frac{1}{11}}$.   *Ans.* $\frac{9}{55}$.

84. $\dfrac{1}{1\frac{1}{3} + 2\frac{1}{4}} \times 1\frac{2}{19} \div \dfrac{5\frac{1}{4} + 4\frac{1}{3}}{3\frac{2}{3} + 4\frac{1}{4}}$.   *Ans.* $\frac{100}{387}$.

85. $\left(\dfrac{3\frac{2}{3}}{\frac{5}{9} \times 1\frac{2}{3}} \times \frac{5}{9} \div \dfrac{7\frac{1}{3}}{31\frac{1}{9}}\right) \times \dfrac{7\frac{2}{3} - 4\frac{1}{2}}{\frac{1}{14} \times 3\frac{5}{8}}$.   *Ans.* $144\frac{188}{203}$.

In the following four exercises, the letters stand for values as follows: $a = 14\frac{2}{7}$, $b = 16\frac{2}{3}$, $c = 33\frac{1}{3}$, and $d = 27\frac{2}{3}$; find the values of the fractions expressed by the letters.

86. $\dfrac{a \times b + c}{c - b}$.   *Ans.* $16\frac{2}{3}$.   **88.** $\dfrac{c - d + b - a}{b \times c - d}$.   *Ans.* $\frac{507}{33257}$.

87. $\dfrac{d + c + b}{a \times c - d}$.   *Ans.* $\frac{1681}{9419}$.   **89.** $\dfrac{c \times d \div b}{(b \div c) \times d}$.   *Ans.* 4.

90. An alloy is composed of 92 lb. of copper, 17 lb. of zinc, and 7 lb. of tin. What part of the alloy is of each metal?

Ans. $\frac{23}{29}$ copper; $\frac{17}{116}$ zinc; $\frac{7}{116}$ tin.

91. Three men did a piece of work in $26\frac{1}{2}$ days for which they received $344\frac{1}{4}$. What was the average pay per day for each man?

Ans. $4\frac{1}{3}$.

29. Pitch and lead of screw threads.—The **pitch** of a screw thread is the distance from the center of the top of one thread to the center of the top of the next.

The **lead** of a screw thread is the distance the screw will move forward in a nut for each complete turn of the screw.

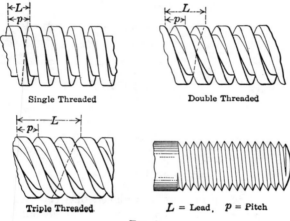

Single Threaded

Double Threaded

Triple Threaded L = Lead. P = Pitch

FIG. 2.

For a single-threaded screw the pitch and the lead are equal; but for a double-threaded screw, the lead is twice the pitch; and for a triple-threaded screw, the lead is three times the pitch.

In a single-threaded screw, there is only one thread running around the screw; in a double-threaded screw there are two threads running side by side around the screw; and a triple-threaded screw has three threads side by side running around the screw.

The above statements are made clearer by reference to the figure.

92. According to the Franklin Institute standards for the dimensions of bolts and nuts, a $\frac{5}{8}$-in. bolt has 11 threads per inch. What is the pitch? The lead if single-threaded? How many full turns of the nut will it take to advance the bolt $2\frac{1}{4}$ in.? *Ans.* $\frac{1}{11}$ in.; $\frac{1}{11}$ in.; $24\frac{3}{4}$.

93. A $4\frac{1}{4}$-in. bolt has $2\frac{7}{8}$ threads per inch. What is the pitch? What is the lead if triple-threaded? *Ans.* $\frac{8}{23}$ in.; $1\frac{5}{23}$ in.

94. In a special threaded screw for a screw-power stump puller, the screw is double-threaded with a pitch of $\frac{11}{16}$ in. How many turns of the nut are required to lift the stump $4\frac{1}{3}$ ft.? *Ans.* $37\frac{9}{11}$.

30. The micrometer.—The screw is used in very many mechanical devices. Many of these will be used in illustrative problems in later chapters. The use of the screw in measuring small distances where great accuracy is required, is illustrated in the ordinary **micrometer** shown in Fig. 3.

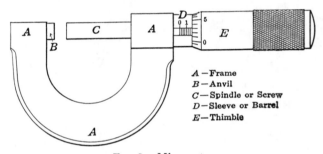

A —Frame
B —Anvil
C —Spindle or Screw
D —Sleeve or Barrel
E —Thimble

Fig. 3.—Micrometer.

The object to be measured is placed between the **anvil,** B, and the **spindle,** C. The spindle has a thread cut 40 to the inch on the part inside the **sleeve,** D. The thimble, E, is outside the sleeve and turns the spindle. The thimble has a beveled end that is divided into 25 equal divisions. The sleeve is graduated into divisions each $\frac{1}{40}$ of an inch, every fourth of which is marked 1, 2, 3, etc. The numbered marks then represent tenths of an inch.

If the thimble is turned through one of its graduations, the spindle is evidently advanced $\frac{1}{25}$ of $\frac{1}{40}$ in. $= \frac{1}{1000}$ in. The vernier, which will be described later (**Art. 157**) enables one to read to $\frac{1}{10}$ of one of the graduations on the thimble and hence makes it possible to measure $\frac{1}{10}$ of $\frac{1}{1000}$ in. $= \frac{1}{10000}$ in.

The readings of a micrometer are usually stated in decimals of an inch.

95. Find the distance the spindle advances when the thimble makes 7 full turns and 17 divisions.　　　　　*Ans.* $\frac{192}{1000}$ or 0.192 in.

96. What is the measurement when the reading on the sleeve is 5 graduations and on the thimble 14?　　　　*Ans.* $\frac{189}{1000}$ or 0.139 in.

31. Screw gearing.—Spiral or screw gearing is often used

where it is desired to reduce the speed greatly. The teeth are arranged in the same manner as the threads of a screw. A screw wheel may have one tooth or any number of teeth. A one-toothed wheel corresponds to a one-threaded screw, a many-toothed wheel to a many-threaded screw.

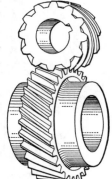

In Fig. 4, the upper wheel has 12 teeth, and corresponds to a 12-threaded screw; while the lower wheel has 36 teeth, and corresponds to a 36-threaded screw. Here the smaller wheel makes three revolutions while the larger is revolving once. If the smaller had but one tooth or was single threaded, it would make 36 turns to one of the larger wheel.

Fig. 4.—Righthand spiral gears.

When the number of threads or teeth on the smaller wheel is few, the smaller wheel is called a **worm,** and the larger the **worm wheel.**

97. If a worm is 2-pitch and single-threaded, how many inches will it cause the circumference of the worm wheel to advance for one revolution of the worm? How many inches if double-threaded? If triple-threaded? If 6-threaded? (2-pitch means 2 threads to the inch.)

98. If a single-threaded worm, making 20 revolutions per second, turns a worm wheel having 54 teeth, Fig. 5, how many revolutions per minute will the worm wheel make?　　　*Ans.* $22\frac{2}{9}$.

99. In turning a piece in a turning lathe the distance the cutting tool advances along the piece for each revolution is called the feed. The feed is usually given as a fraction of an inch. How long will it take to turn a piece $2\frac{1}{2}$ ft. long, if it makes 17 revolutions per minute, and the feed is $\frac{1}{16}$ in.?　　　*Ans.* $28\frac{4}{17}$ minutes.

100. How many turns per minute is a piece making if 4 ft. of length is turned in 75 minutes when the feed is $\frac{3}{32}$ in.?　　　*Ans.* $6\frac{62}{9}$.

101. What feed is necessary to run a cut of 45 in. in 10 minutes at 36 revolutions per minute?　　　*Ans.* $\frac{1}{8}$ in.

3

102. In planing an aluminum casting of width $10\frac{1}{2}$ in. and length $12\frac{3}{4}$ in., find the time required if cutting speed is 40 ft. per minute, return speed 80 ft. per minute, and feed $\frac{1}{64}$ in.   *Ans.* 27 minutes nearly.

Suggestion. The cutting tool cuts a strip $\frac{1}{64}$ in. wide each time across. Or it takes 64 times across to plane a strip one inch wide. If the cut is

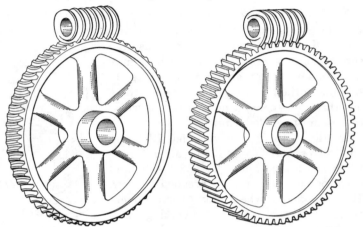

Lefthand single thread.   Righthand double thread
Fig. 5.—Worm and worm wheel.

made the long way of the casting it takes $64 \times 10\frac{1}{2} = 672$ cuts. The return strokes take one-half the time of the cutting strokes. No allowance is made for over run in the strokes.

103. A $\frac{7}{16}$-in. twist-drill has a speed of 130 revolutions per minute (R. P. M.) when cutting steel. How long will it take to drill through a $\frac{5}{8}$-in. plate if 120 revolutions are required to drill 1 in.?

Ans. $\frac{15}{26}$ minutes.

Fig. 6.—Twist drill.

104. A $1\frac{3}{16}$-in. drill makes 66 R. P. M. in iron and has a feed of $\frac{1}{80}$ in. How long will it take to drill 20 holes through a $\frac{3}{4}$-in. plate if $\frac{1}{2}$ minute is allowed for setting for each hole?   *Ans.* $28\frac{2}{11}$ minutes.

105. In drilling through mild steel $1\frac{5}{8}$ in. thick, a hole 1 in. in diameter is drilled in $1\frac{3}{4}$ minutes; find the distance drilled per minute.

Ans. $\frac{13}{14}$ in.

106. A $\frac{5}{16}$-in. drill can make 320 R. P. M. in brass. If 120 turns are made to drill 1 in., find how many holes can be drilled in a $\frac{5}{8}$-in. plate in 1 hour if $\frac{1}{4}$ the time is used in setting the drill.   *Ans.* 192.

107. The following rule is often used to find the weight of round steel and wrought iron: Square the diameter in inches and multiply by $\frac{8}{3}$, the product is the weight in pounds of 1 ft. of the bar. (The product of a number multiplied by itself is the square of the number.) Using this rule find the weights of round bars of steel of the following dimensions:

(1) Diameter $\frac{7}{8}$ in., length $12\frac{1}{2}$ ft.　　　　*Ans.* $25\frac{25}{48}$ lb.

(2) Diameter $2\frac{5}{8}$ in., length $2\frac{1}{4}$ ft.　　　　*Ans.* $41\frac{11}{32}$ lb.

(3) Diameter $8\frac{3}{4}$ in., length $1\frac{5}{8}$ ft.　　　　*Ans.* $326\frac{2}{3}$ lb.

108. Three pipes can empty a reservoir in 6, 5, and 4 hours respectively. How long will it take them to empty it if running together?

Ans. $1\frac{23}{37}$ hours.

Solution. Since the first pipe can empty the reservoir in 6 hours, it can empty $\frac{1}{6}$ of the reservoir in 1 hour. Reasoning in the same manner, the second pipe can empty $\frac{1}{5}$ of it in 1 hour, and the third pipe $\frac{1}{4}$ of it in 1 hour. Hence, the three pipes can empty $\frac{1}{6}+\frac{1}{5}+\frac{1}{4}=\frac{37}{60}$ of the reservoir in 1 hour. To empty the whole reservoir, it will take all the pipes together, $1 \div \frac{37}{60} = 1\frac{23}{37}$ hours.

109. In the preceding exercise, how long will it take to empty the reservoir if it is full to begin with, and the first two pipes are emptying out of and the third emptying into the reservoir?　　*Ans.* $8\frac{4}{7}$ hours.

110. Three pipes open from a tank. The first alone can empty it in 6 hours, the second in 4 hours, and the third in 3 hours. How many hours will it take to empty the tank if the pipes are all running together?

Ans. $1\frac{1}{3}$.

111. In the previous exercise the tank is full to begin with and the first and third pipes are emptying out of, and the second emptying into the tank. How long will it take to empty the tank?　*Ans.* 4 hours.

112. If A can do a piece of work in 9 hours and B can do the same work in 6 hours, how long will it take them if working together? What part can each do in 1 hour? What part of the work can both together do in 1 hour?　　　　　　*Ans.* $3\frac{3}{5}$ hours; $\frac{1}{9}$ and $\frac{1}{6}$; $\frac{5}{18}$.

113. If A can do a piece of work in $10\frac{1}{2}$ days and B can do the same work in $8\frac{2}{5}$ days, what part of the work can they both do in one day? In how many days can they do the work if working together?

Ans. $\frac{3}{14}$; $4\frac{2}{3}$.

114. If one gang of men can do a piece of work in 20 days, and another gang can do the same piece of work in 25 days, how long will it take both gangs working together to do the work?　　*Ans.* $11\frac{1}{9}$ days.

115. A contractor is to grade a street in 30 days. Fifteen men work on the grading for 20 days and do one-half of the work. How many men must work for the next 10 days to finish the grading?　*Ans.* 30.

116. In 10 days, 15 men do $\frac{3}{20}$ of a piece of work. How many men will it take to finish the work in 15 days?

117. How many turns must be made with a triple-threaded screw having $4\frac{3}{4}$ threads to the inch to have it advance a distance of 3 in.?

118. The lead screw on the table of a milling machine has a double thread with a pitch of $\frac{1}{4}$ in. How many inches per minute is the feed if the lead screw is making 4 R. P. M.?

119. A man who owns $\frac{5}{7}$ of a city block valued at \$140,000, sold $\frac{17}{20}$ of his share. What is the value of the part he has left?
Ans. \$15,000.

120. A merchant bought a stock of goods for \$7426.50 and sold $\frac{1}{2}$ of it at an advance of $\frac{1}{3}$ the cost, $\frac{1}{4}$ of it at an advance of $\frac{1}{4}$ the cost, and the remainder at a loss of $\frac{1}{10}$ the cost. Did he gain or lose and how much?
Ans. Gained \$1516.24.

121. A sum of money is divided among four persons. The first received $\frac{3}{10}$ of the amount, the second $\frac{1}{4}$, the third $\frac{1}{5}$, and the fourth the remainder which is \$5000. What is the amount each received?
Ans. \$6000; \$5000; \$4000; \$5000.

122. If it takes 4 tons of coal to heat as much as 6 cords of wood, which is the cheaper if coal is \$7$\frac{3}{4}$ a ton and wood \$5$\frac{1}{4}$ a cord? How much more will one cost than the other to heat a house that requires 11 tons of coal a year?
Ans. Coal, \$1$\frac{3}{4}$.

123. Which is the cheaper and how much, to have a 17$\frac{1}{2}$ cent an hour boy take 13$\frac{3}{4}$ hours to do a certain piece of work, or have a 42$\frac{1}{2}$ cent an hour man do it in 4$\frac{3}{4}$ hours?
Ans. The man 38$\frac{3}{4}$ cents cheaper.

124. A piece of work when forged weighed 214$\frac{1}{2}$ lb. After being turned down it weighed 156$\frac{3}{4}$ lb. The forging cost 16$\frac{1}{2}$ cents a pound and the metal turned off sold at 3$\frac{1}{4}$ cents a pound. Find the net cost of the metal in the finished piece.
Ans. \$33.51$\frac{9}{16}$.

125. A machinist drills 6 holes through a piece that is 2$\frac{3}{4}$ in. thick. The drill is 1$\frac{7}{8}$ in. in diameter and makes 154 R. P. M. with a feed of $\frac{1}{50}$ in. How many minutes does it take if 3 minutes are used in setting for each hole?
Ans. 23$\frac{5}{14}$.

126. A hole 6$\frac{3}{4}$ in. deep is drilled with a 1$\frac{1}{8}$-in. drill making 126 R. P. M. What feed is required to drill the hole in 3$\frac{3}{4}$ minutes?
Ans. $\frac{1}{70}$ in.

127. To change from Centigrade thermometer reading to Fahrenheit, the following formula is used: $F = \frac{9}{5}C + 32°$, where C is the Centigrade reading and F the Fahrenheit. (1) Find F when $C = 22\frac{1}{2}°$. (2) Find F when C is 720°.
Ans. (1) 72$\frac{1}{2}$°; (2) 1328°.

128. To change Fahrenheit thermometer reading to Centigrade, the following formula is used: $C = \frac{5}{9}(F - 32°)$, where C is the Centigrade reading and F the Fahrenheit. (1) Find C when $F = 81\frac{1}{2}°$. (2) Find C when $F = 1760°$.
Ans. (1) 27$\frac{1}{2}$°; (2) 960°

129. In inspecting steamboilers, the following formula is often used:

$$t = \frac{PRF}{T \times \%},$$

where t = thickness of plate in inches,
$\quad P$ = steam pressure in pounds per square inch,
$\quad R$ = radius of boiler in inches ($\frac{1}{2}$ of diameter),
$\quad F$ = factor of safety,
$\quad T$ = tensile strength of boiler plate in pounds,
$\quad \%$ = percentage of strength in joints.

Find the thickness of the boiler plate which should be used for a boiler 50 in. in diameter to carry 120 lb. of pressure if the tensile strength is 60,000 lb. Use 50% as the strength of·the joints and a factor of safety of 6. *Ans.* $\frac{3}{8}$ in.

Solution. $t = \dfrac{PRF}{T \times \%} = \dfrac{120 \times 25 \times 6}{60000 \times \frac{50}{100}} = \frac{3}{5}$

130. Find the thickness of the boiler plate for a 72-in. boiler to carry a pressure of 90 lb. with a tensile strength of 60,000 lb. Use 50% as the joint strength and a factor of safety of 6. *Ans.* $\frac{5}{8}$ in. nearly.

131. The following formula is used in finding the diameter of a steamoiler

$$D = \frac{2tT \times \%}{PF},$$

where D = diameter of boiler in inches,

t = thickness of plate in inches,

T = tensile strength of boiler plate in pounds,

P = steam pressure in pounds per square inch,

F = factor of safety,

$\%$ = percentage of strength in joints.

Find the diameter for a steamboiler having a $\frac{3}{8}$-in. plate, allowing 50% for strength of joints and a factor of safety of 6, with a tensile strength of 60,000 lb., and 125 lb. pressure per square inch. *Ans.* 50 in.

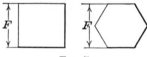

Fɪɢ. 7.

132. Find the number of lines in a paper of 38 pages, two columns to the page, each 10½ in. long, and 15 lines in 2 in. How many words if they average 11 words to the line? How long would it take to read such a paper at the rate of 170 words a minute?

133. The distance F across the flats in a bolt head or nut, either a square or a hexagon (Fig. 7), is equal to 1½ times the diameter of the bolt plus $\frac{1}{8}$ in. As a formula this is

$$F = 1\tfrac{1}{2}D + \tfrac{1}{8}.$$

Test the widths across the flats in the following table taken from a manufacturer's catalog:

Diameter of bolt D	$\frac{1}{4}$	$\frac{5}{16}$	$\frac{3}{8}$	$\frac{7}{16}$	$\frac{5}{8}$	$\frac{3}{4}$	$\frac{7}{8}$	$1\frac{1}{8}$	$1\frac{5}{8}$	$1\frac{3}{4}$	2
Width across flats F	$\frac{1}{2}$	$\frac{19}{32}$	$\frac{11}{16}$	$\frac{25}{32}$	$1\frac{1}{16}$	$1\frac{1}{4}$	$1\frac{7}{16}$	$1\frac{13}{16}$	$2\frac{9}{16}$	$2\frac{3}{4}$	$3\frac{1}{8}$

CHAPTER III

DECIMAL FRACTIONS

32. Definition.—Fractions that have 10, 100, 1000, etc. for denominators are **decimal fractions.**

Thus, $\frac{53}{100}$, $\frac{3756}{10000}$, $\frac{76}{1000}$, $\frac{4326}{1000}$ are decimal fractions.

In writing a decimal fraction it is convenient to omit the denominator, and indicate what it is by placing a point (.), called a **decimal point,** in the numerator so that there shall be as many figures to the right of this point as there are ciphers in the denominator.

Thus, $\frac{53}{100}$ is written 0.53; $\frac{3756}{10000}$ = 0.3756; $\frac{76}{1000}$ = 0.076; $\frac{4326}{1000}$ = 4.326.

In such numbers as 0.53 and 0.3765, the cipher is printed at the left of the decimal point for clearness; but it is not necessary and is often omitted.

It is to be noted that when there are fewer figures in the numerator than there are ciphers in the denominator, ciphers are added on the left of the figures to make the required number.

From the meaning of the decimal fraction, it is seen that the misplacing of the decimal point changes the meaning greatly. For each place it is moved to the right, the value of the decimal fraction is multipled by 10; and for each place it is moved to the left, the value is divided by 10.

Thus, 2.75 becomes 27.5 when the point is moved one place to the right, and 0.275 when the point is moved one place to the left. In the first case 2.75 is multiplied by 10, and in the second case it is divided by 10.

It is well to recall the fact that when we have a number such as 3333, where the same figure is used throughout, the values expressed by the threes vary greatly. For every place a three is moved toward the left, its value is increased ten times; and as we pass from left toward the right, each three has one-tenth the value of the one to the left of it. Since the above relations hold when we pass to the right of

38

the place representing units, we have the following relative values of the places:

Thousands | Hundreds | Tens | Units | Decimal point | Tenths | Hundredths | Thousandths | Ten-thousandths | Hundred-thousandths | Millionths | Ten-millionths | Hundred-millionths

0 0 0 0   0 0 0 0 0 0 0 0

33. Reading numbers.—The whole number 23,676 is read twenty-three thousand six hundred seventy-six. It should be noticed that no word *"and"* is used in reading a whole number.

A decimal is read like a whole number except that the name of the right-hand place is added.

For example, the number 0.7657 is read, seven thousand six hundred fifty-seven ten-thousandths.

When a whole number and a decimal fraction are written together the word *"and"* is used between the two parts in reading.

Thus, 73.2658 is read, seventy-three *and* two thousand six hundred fifty-eight ten-thousandths.

Where one person is reading numbers for another to write, it is not customary to proceed in the above manner.

Thus, the number 23.6785 may be read twenty-three, point, sixty-seven, eighty-five. Or we may read it, two, three, point, six, seven, eight, five.

EXERCISES 10

Write the following in figures:

1. Three hundred fifty-six ten-thousandths.
2. Two hundred fifty-six and twenty-three thousandths.
3. One hundred fifty-five millionths.
4. Four hundred fifty-six thousandths.
5. Four hundred and fifty-six thousandths.
6. Three hundred twenty-five and twenty-five ten-thousandths.

Read the following:

7. 23.462.   11. 1200.3604.
8. 2003.203.   12. 10,101.2301.
9. 0.4256.   13. 5867.0067.
10. 4200.0056.   14. 10,000.0001.

34. Reduction of a common fraction to a decimal fraction.—
A decimal fraction differs from a common fraction only in
having 1 with a certain number of ciphers annexed for the
denominator.   The common fraction can then be changed to
a decimal by reducing it to a fraction having 1 with ciphers
for a denominator.

It is evident from the method of reducing a common fraction
to one with a different denominator, that a common fraction
can be changed to a decimal only when its denominator is contained an exact number of times in 10,100,1000, or 10000, etc.

Thus, $\frac{2}{5} = \frac{4}{10}$ or 0.4, and, $\frac{9}{16} = \frac{5625}{10000}$ or 0.5625, but $\frac{2}{7}$ cannot be expressed
exactly as a decimal because 7 is not exactly contained in 10, 100, or
1000, etc.

To reduce a common fraction to a decimal proceed as
follows:

RULE. *Annex ciphers to the numerator and divide by the
denominator.   Place the decimal point so as to make as many
decimal places in the result as there were ciphers annexed.*

Thus, $\frac{7}{8} = 0.875$,   *Process.*   8)7.000
                                                   ‾‾0.875‾

and $\frac{2}{7} = 0.2857+$ *Process.*   7)2.0000
                                                   ‾0.2857+‾

The sign, +, placed after the number indicates that there
are still other figures if the division is carried further.

A common fraction in its lowest terms will· reduce to an
exact decimal only when its denominator contains no other
prime factors than 2 and 5.

Thus, $\frac{3}{64}$ reduces to an exact decimal for 64 is made up of $2\times2\times2\times$
$2\times2\times2$, while $\frac{7}{12}$ cannot be reduced to an exact decimal for its denominator contains the factor 3.

35. Decimal fraction to common fraction.—To change a
decimal fraction to a common fraction proceed as follows:

RULE. *Replace the decimal point by a denominator having 1 and as many ciphers as there are decimal places in the original fraction.* (See **Art. 32.**)

Thus, $2.375 = \frac{2375}{1000}$, which may be written as a mixed number, $2\frac{375}{1000} = 2\frac{3}{8}$.

EXERCISES 11

Reduce the following to decimals:

1. $\frac{25}{27}$. 2. $\frac{2}{3}$. 3. $\frac{19}{64}$.

4. $\frac{297}{425}$. 5. $21\frac{32}{625}$. 6. $62\frac{329}{1000}$.

Reduce the following to common fractions or mixed numbers in their lowest terms:

7. 0.440. 8. 0.98. 9. 0.03125.

10. 0.00096. 11. 14.06225. 12. 42.030125.

13. Reduce the following decimals of an inch to common fractions in their lowest terms: 0.375; 0.359375; 0.28125; 0.171875; 0.078125.

$Ans.$ $\frac{3}{8}$; $\frac{23}{64}$; $\frac{9}{32}$; $\frac{11}{64}$; $\frac{5}{64}$.

14. Express the following in their simplest common fractional form: $3.04\frac{8}{9}$; $0.00\frac{8}{9}$; $0.28\frac{4}{7}$; $0.714\frac{2}{7}$; $0.484\frac{3}{8}$; $0.87\frac{1}{2}$. $Ans.$ $3\frac{19}{450}$; $\frac{1}{250}$; $\frac{2}{7}$; $\frac{5}{7}$; $\frac{31}{64}$; $\frac{7}{8}$.

Suggestion. $3.04\frac{8}{9} = \dfrac{304\frac{8}{9}}{100} = \dfrac{\frac{2738}{9}}{100} = \frac{2738}{900} = 3\frac{19}{450}$.

15. Change the following per cents to their simplest common fractional forms: $87\frac{1}{2}\%$; $133\frac{1}{3}\%$; $\frac{5}{7}\%$; $185\frac{5}{7}\%$; $1.85\frac{5}{7}\%$; $2.21\frac{15}{18}\%$.

$Ans.$ $\frac{7}{8}$; $\frac{4}{3}$; $\frac{1}{140}$; $1\frac{9}{7}$; $\frac{13}{700}$; $\frac{3651}{180000}$.

16. Tell without trial which of the following common fractions will reduce to exact decimals: $\frac{4}{7}$; $\frac{5}{32}$; $\frac{7}{15}$; $\frac{16}{49}$; $\frac{4}{25}$; $\frac{7}{35}$; $\frac{14}{125}$; $\frac{37}{250}$; $\frac{41}{66}$; $\frac{3}{8}$; $\frac{127}{128}$.

17. Change the following decimals of an inch to the nearest 64ths of an inch: 0.394; 0.709; 1.416; 1.89.

$Ans.$ $\frac{25}{64}$; $\frac{45}{64}$; $1\frac{27}{64}$; $1\frac{57}{64}$.

36. Addition of decimals.—RULE. *Write the numbers so that the decimal points are under each other. Add as in whole numbers, and place the decimal point in the sum under the other decimal points.*

Example. Add 36.036, 7.004, 0.00236, 427, 723.0026.

$$\begin{array}{r} 36.036 \\ 7.004 \\ 0.00236 \\ 427. \\ 723.0026 \\ \hline 1193.04496 \end{array} \quad Ans.$$

37. Subtraction of decimals.—RULE. *Write the numbers so that the decimal points are under each other; subtract as in* *whole numbers, and place the decimal point of the remainder under the other decimal points.*

Example.   Subtract 46.8324 from 437.421:

437.421
46.8324
───────
390.5886   *Ans.*

38. Multiplication of decimals.—RULE. *Multi . ns in whole numbers, and point off as many decimal pla.. . .u the product as the sum of the numbers of the places in the factors.*

Example 1.	*Example 2.*
Multiply 7.32 by 0.032.	Multiply 0.00264 by 0.000314.

7.32	0.00264
0.032	0.000314
────	─────────
1464	1056
2196	264
────────	792
0.23424 *Ans.*	─────────────
	0.00000082896 *Ans.*

Multiplying a whole number or a decimal by 0.1 moves the decimal point one place to the left; by 0.01, two places; by 0.001, three places; etc.   If it is necessary, zeros are prefixed to the multiplicand.

Thus, 32.4 × 0.0001 = 0.00324.

Multiplying by 10, 100, 1000, etc., moves the decimal point 1, 2, 3, etc., places to the right.

39. Division of decimals.—RULE. *If the number of decimal places in the dividend is less than the number in the divisor, annex ciphers to the dividend till there are as many or more decimal places as in the divisor.   Divide as in whole numbers, and point off as many decimal places in the quotient as there are more decimal places in the dividend than in the divisor.*

Example 1.	*Example 2.*
Divide 0.4375 by 0.125.	Divide 4365 by 0.005.

0.4375|0.125   0.005)4365.000
 ─────┬─────   ──────────────
  375 │ 3.5   *Ans.*   873.000   *Ans.*
  625
  625

Dividing by 0.1, 0.01, 0.001, etc., moves the decimal point 1, 2, 3, etc., places to the right.   Dividing by 10, 100, 1000, etc., moves the decimal point 1, 2, 3, etc., places to the left.

40. Accuracy of results.—Often we are asked to give a result correct to a certain number of decimal places. Thus, if in working a problem we have a result as 47.264735, and wish to write it correct to three places, it is 47.265—. Correct to two places, it is 47.26+, correct to one place, 47.3—, correct to five places 47.26474—.

The last place taken is written one larger when the next figure to the right is 5 or more.

The part to the right of the last place taken is thrown away when the first figure of it is less than 5.

In this way we call a half or more of the last unit taken, a whole one of those units, and throw away anything less than a half.

The sign, +, is used to show that the accurate result is larger than the one given, that is, that something has been thrown away; and the sign, −, is used to show that the accurate result is smaller than the one given, that is, that something has been added.

EXERCISES 12

Add up and test by adding down:

1.	**2.**	**3.**
864.2	5.82	49.235
43.276	.486	86.426
.21.004	41.987	92.784
9824.246	987.	46.324
47.02	201.478	33.867
39.09	804.008	99.847
		34.396

4. $18\frac{1}{3}+17\frac{2}{3}+29\frac{5}{6}+14.672+34\frac{2}{7} = ?$ *Ans.* 114.791+.

5. $87.46\frac{1}{2}+93.27\frac{4}{7}+43.2906+0.0047+17\frac{1}{6} = ?$ *Ans.* 241.2027−.

6. $8.706+7.898+43\frac{2}{9}+89\frac{3}{20}+14\frac{6}{7} = ?$ *Ans.* 163.833+.

7. $1-0.640726 = ?$ *Ans.* 0.359274.

8. $2-1.798642 = ?$ *Ans.* 0.201358.

9. $4.8728-0.987 = ?$ *Ans.* 3.8858.

10. $75.0075-2.75903 = ?$ *Ans.* 72.24847.

11. $476.84-86.4396 = ?$ *Ans.* 390.4004.

12. From one thousand take five-thousandths.   *Ans.* 999.995.

13. From three million and one-millionth take one-tenth.

    Ans. 2999999.900001.

14. $78.896-53.5987 = ?$ *Ans.* 25.2973.

15. $81.35-11.678956 = ?$ *Ans.* 69.671044.

16. From nine hundred nine take nine hundred and nine thousandths.

    Ans. 8.991.

17. From 37.75¾ take 4.43⅝.   *Ans.* 33.32125.

18. One quart liquid measure has 57.75 cu. in., and 1 quart dry measure has 67.200625 cu. in.   How many cubic inches larger is the dry quart than the liquid quart?   *Ans.* 9.450625.

19. $3.62 \times 0.0037 = ?$ *Ans.* 0.013394.

20. $2.53 \times 0.00635 = ?$ *Ans.* 0.0160655.

21. $0.00076 \times 0.0015 = ?$ *Ans.* 0.00000114.

22. $7.789 \times 4.924 = ?$ *Ans.* 38.353+.

23. $2.236 \times 799 = ?$ *Ans.* 1786.564.

24. $2.967 \times 2.967 = ?$ *Ans.* 8.803+.

25. $8.943 \times 1\frac{2}{3} = ?$ *Ans.* 14.905.

Why would it be best not to reduce $1\frac{2}{3}$ to a decimal before multiplying? The multiplication can be carried out readily as shown here, the process is as if the multiplicand were a whole number.

Process.

$$
\begin{array}{ll}
8.943 & \\
\underline{1\frac{2}{3}} & \\
2\ 981 & = \frac{1}{3} \text{ of } 8943 \\
5\ 962 & = \frac{2}{3} \text{ of } 8943 \\
\underline{8\ 943} & = 1 \times 8943 \\
14.905 & = 1\frac{2}{3} \times 8.943
\end{array}
$$

26. $2.43\frac{3}{8} \times 9.5\frac{5}{8} = ?$ *Ans.* 23.218−.

27. $0.0439 \times 49\frac{1}{3} = ?$ *Ans.* 2.1657+.

28. $\frac{4}{5} \times 3.1416 \times 7.1 \times 7.1 \times 7.1 = ?$ *Ans.* 1499.2176−.

29. $9.3 \times 0.0042 \times 0.0027 = ?$ *Ans.* 0.000105+.

30. $49367 \times 0.0021 \times 0.0094 = ?$ *Ans.* 0.9745+.

31. $0.8\frac{2}{3} \times 9\frac{4}{5} \times 0.3375 = ?$ *Ans.* 2.7781+.

32. Multiply 3¾ thousandths by 3¾ hundredths.

                                                 Ans. 0.0001406+.

33. 1 kilogram equals 2.2046 pounds; how many pounds in 275.3 kilograms?   *Ans.* 606.926+.

34. Multiply each of the following numbers by 0.1, 0.01, 0.001, 0.0001, 10, 100, 1000, 10,000: 94, 47.368, 0.023, 3.42.

35. $67.56785 \div 0.035 = ?$ *Ans.* 1930.51.

36. $0.567891 \div 8.2 = ?$ *Ans.* 0.069255.

37. Divide 43.769 by 4.76 correct to four places.

Process.

$$
\begin{array}{r|l}
43.769000 & 4.76 \\
\cline{1-1}
4284 & 9.1951 \\
\cline{1-1}
929 & \\
476 & \\
\cline{1-1}
4530 & \\
4284 & \\
\cline{1-1}
2460 & \\
2380 & \\
\cline{1-1}
800 & \\
476 & \\
\cline{1-1}
324 &
\end{array}
$$

Ans. is 9.1952−.

Explanation. Since the quotient is to be correct to four places, the dividend must contain four more decimal places than the divisor. Three zeros are added to make this number. Since the fifth decimal figure in the quotient is not less than 5, the answer is 9.1952 −.

In the next 5 exercises, find the result correct to four decimal places.

38. $9.375 \div 4.76 = ?$ *Ans.* 1.9695+.
39. $89.7201 \div 3.276 = ?$ *Ans.* 27.3871 −.
40. $34.675 \div 4.375 = ?$ *Ans.* 7.9257+.
41. $43.45 \div 3.1416 = ?$ *Ans.* 13.8305+.
42. $3.1416 \div 6.67 = ?$ *Ans.* 0.4710+.
43. Divide 324.8 by 4000.

Explanation. Cancel the zeros in the divisor. Since this divides the divisor by 1000, the dividend must be divided by 1000, this is done by moving the decimal point three places to the left.

Process.
$4\cancel{000})0.3248$
0.0812

44. (*a*) $25 \div 500$ (*b*) $2 \div 2000$ (*c*) $9009 \div 11{,}000$
      (*d*) $1.44 \div 12{,}000$ (*e*) $3.075 \div 5000$ (*f*) $5684 \div 14{,}000$
45. (*a*) $1 \div 0.0001$ (*b*) $0.66 \div 0.011$ (*c*) $525 \div 0.025$
      (*d*) $0.00072 \div 8$ (*e*) $6600 \div 0.0022$ (*f*) $3.03 \div 0.03$
46. Divide $3.1416 \times 1.25 \times 50$ by $0.8 \times 2.75 \times 3$.

Explanation. The cancelling may be done as in whole numbers, paying no attention to the decimal point. When through, point off as many places in the result as the difference between the sum of those above and the sum of those below the line. Thus, in the example there are six

Process.

$$\frac{\overset{119}{\overset{1309}{\overset{3927}{3.1416}}} \times \overset{5}{1.25} \times 50}{0.8 \times 2.75 \times \underset{11}{3}} = 29.750.$$

places above and three below the line; hence, the result has three decimal places. If there are more places below than above, add ciphers until there are as many above as below.

Find the value of the following:

47. $\dfrac{2.75 \times 46.2 \times 100}{2.5 \times 2.8}$ to units.   *Ans.* 1815.

48. $\dfrac{0.7854 \times 5 \times 5 \times 8}{1.25}$ to three places.   *Ans.* 125.664.

49. $\dfrac{6.4 \times 0.84 \times 9.6 \times 1.44}{8 \times 9.2 \times 1.28}$ to three places.   *Ans.* 0.789 −.

50. $\dfrac{0.7854 \times 6 \times 6 \times 12.5 \times 1728}{231 \times 31.5}$ to two places.   *Ans.* 83.93+.

51. $\dfrac{8.5 \times 9.25 \times 3.66 \times 1728}{2150.42}$ to two places.   *Ans.* 231.24 −.

52. What is the inside diameter of a pipe which is 7.34 in. outside diameter and is made of iron 0.743 in. thick?   *Ans.* 5.854 in.

53. A hundred pounds of coke were found to contain 5.79 lb. of ash and 0.597 lb. of sulphur, the rest was carbon. How much carbon was there?   *Ans.* 93.613 lb.

54. A steam pump delivers 26.44 gallons per stroke. A gallon of water weighs 8.355 lb. What weight of water will it deliver in 117 strokes?   *Ans.* 25,846 lb.

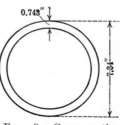

FIG. 8.—Cross section of pipe.

55. In 1 lb. of phosphor bronze 0.925 is copper, 0.07 is tin, and 0.005 is phosphorus. How much of each is there in 369.523 pounds of phosphor bronze? $Ans.$ 341.8088 $-$; 25.8666 $+$; 1.8476 $+$ lb.

56. A certain paper weighs 68 lb. per ream of 500 sheets. If the paper costs $5\frac{3}{4}$ cents per pound, how much will $2\frac{3}{20}$ reams cost?
                    $Ans.$ \$8.41.

57. Manganese bronze contains the following: copper 0.89, tin 0.1, manganese 0.01. How much of each metal is there in a propeller weighing $2378\frac{5}{8}$ lb.? $Ans.$ 2117.16 $+$; 237.88 $+$; 23.79 $-$ lb.

58. Add $\dfrac{4\frac{1}{5}}{6\frac{3}{10}}$ and $\dfrac{2\frac{1}{4}}{7\frac{4}{7}}$, divide the result by $7\frac{13}{21}$, and change the quotient to a decimal. $Ans.$ 0.125.

59. From $\frac{4}{21}\times 2\frac{4}{5}$ subtract the product of 0.075 and $1\frac{4}{5}$, divide the remainder by 12, and change the result to a decimal. $Ans.$ 0.0375.

60. Simplify $\dfrac{(3.2+0.004-1.111)\times 0.25}{(4\div 0.2)-17.907}$. $Ans.$ 0.25.

61. Simplify $(1\frac{3}{5}+1\frac{1}{2}-0.024)\div(15\frac{1}{2}-1.209)$. $Ans.$ 0.214 $+$.

62. Simplify $\dfrac{(\frac{1}{2}\div 3\frac{1}{4})\times 0.00025}{0.075}$. $Ans.$ 0.0005128 $+$.

63. Simplify $\dfrac{(3.71-1.908)\times 7.03}{2.2-\frac{74}{333}}$. $Ans.$ 6.405 $+$.

64. Simplify $\dfrac{(201+2.25\times 0.004)\div(1.0337-31.09\times 0.03)}{4.5\div 960}$.
                    $Ans.$ 424,573.5 $-$.

65. How many lengths each 0.0275 of a foot are contained in 27.2375 ft.? $Ans.$ 990.45 $+$.

66. The expenditures of the British Naval Service were as follows: for the year 1906–7, £31,472,087; for the year 1907–8, £31,251,156; express these sums to the nearest dollar if £1 = \$4.8665.
                    $Ans.$ \$153,158,911; \$152,083,751.

67. A wood dealer charged \$33.62 for a pile of wood containing $7\frac{3}{4}$ cords. What error did the dealer make if wood was worth \$4.25 a cord?
                    $Ans.$ \$0.68.

68. If a circle is 3.1416 times as far around as through it, find the number of feet around a cart wheel 3.75 ft. through. Find the distance around the earth if the diameter is 7918 miles.
                    $Ans.$ 11.781; 24,875 $+$ miles.

69. Find the value of:

27,750 shingles at \$4.25 per thousand. $Ans.$ \$117.94.
47,256 ft. of lumber at \$45 per thousand. $Ans.$ \$2126.52.
126,450 bricks at \$7.75 per thousand. $Ans.$ \$979.99.
45,350 ft. of gas at \$0.85 per thousand. $Ans.$ \$38.55.

70. What is the cost of carbon-steel rails to lay 6 miles of street car track, if the rails weigh 129 lb. per yard, and cost \$28 per ton. (1 mile = 1760 yd.) $Ans.$ \$38,142.72.

71. It has been determined by experiment that each square foot of steam radiation will give off to the surrounding air about 3 heat units per hour per degree difference between the air in the room and the steam radiator. If the temperature of the radiator is 212° and that of the room 70°, how many heat units will be given off per hour on 24,000 sq. ft. of radiating surface? How many pounds of coal will it take to make this steam if 1 lb. of coal contains 10,000 heat units?

Ans. 10,224,000; 1022.4.

72. Nickel steel will stand a pull of about 90,000 lb. per square inch in cross section. What pull will a bar 0.786 in. wide and 0.237 in. thick stand? *Ans.* 16,765+ lb.

Suggestion. The area of the cross section is found by multiplying 0.786 by 0.237.

73. The composition of white metal as used in the Navy Department is as follows: tin 7.6 parts, copper 2.3 parts, zinc 83.3 parts, antimony 3.8 parts, and lead 30 parts. Find the number of pounds of each in 635 lb. of the white metal.

Ans. tin 38; copper 11.5; zinc 416.5; antimony 19; lead 150.

Suggestion. Adding 7.6+2.3+83.3+3.8+30 = 127 =whole number of parts.

635 ÷ 127 = 5 = number of pounds for each part.

Multiply 5 lb. by number of parts of each.

74. In 1909 the number of horses in the United States was 20,640,000. They were valued at $1,974,052,000. Find the average price per head.

Ans. $95.64+.

75. A reamer that is 6 in. long is 1.2755 in. in diameter at the small end, and 1.4375 in. at the larger end. Find the taper per foot. (The taper per foot means the decrease in diameter per foot of length.)

Ans. 0.324 in.

76. A creditor receives $0.76 on each dollar due him. If he loses $326.40, how much was due him? What would he have received if $7642 had been due him? *Ans.* $1360; $5807.92.

77. It cost, for labor and materials, $38,692.38 to construct 7500 ft. of car track. What was the average cost per foot? What would be the cost for 100 miles at the same rate? (1 mile = 5280 ft.)

Ans. $5.159 − ; $2,723,943.55.

78. During 1908 the Daly-West mine marketed 12,760 tons of crude ore; containing 2,683,830 lb. of lead; 343,376 lb. of copper; 454,149 oz. of silver; and 441.86 oz. of gold. Find its value if lead is worth 3.925 cents per pound; copper 13.208 cents per pound; silver 52.864 cents per ounce; and gold $18.842 per ounce. *Ans.* $399,100.28.

79. One cubic foot of water weighs 62.5 lb.; find the volume of 1 lb. of water. Of 23 lb. *Ans.* 0.016 cu. ft.; 0.368 cu. ft.

80. One cubic foot of ice weighs 57.5 lb.; find the volume of 1 lb. of ice. Of 49.3 lb. *Ans.* 0.0174 − cu. ft.; 0.857 + cu. ft.

81. How many times as heavy as ice is water? How many times as heavy as water is ice? *Ans.* 1.087 − ; 0.92.

82. If the fire under a steam boiler requires 3 lb. of coal per horsepower per hour, find the cost of coal at $3.75 a ton to run a 160 horsepower boiler for 30 days of 10 hours each. *Ans.* $270.

83. A column of water 2.302 ft. high gives a pressure at the base of 1 lb. per square inch. Find the height of a column of water to give a pressure of 256.3 lb. per square inch. Find the pressure per square inch of a column of water 1 ft. high. A column 237.4 ft. high.
Ans. 590.0+ ft.; 0.4344+ lb.; 103.1+ lb.

84. The Auditorium Building in Chicago has a cubic content of 9,128,744 cu. ft., and cost 36 cents per cubic foot. Find the total cost.
Ans. $3,286,347.84.

85. Using U. S. standard, the gage and thickness for sheet steel is as follows: No. 00, 0.34375 in.; No. 2, 0.265625 in.; No. 4, 0.234375 in.; No. 7, 0.1875 in.; No. 13, 0.09375 in.; No. 28, 0.015625 in. Find the approximate thickness of each in a common fraction of an inch having 8, 16, 32, or 64 for a denominator. *Ans.* $\frac{11}{32}$, $\frac{17}{64}$, $\frac{15}{64}$, $\frac{3}{16}$, $\frac{3}{32}$, $\frac{1}{64}$.

86. If it costs $106.50 per day to run a gang of men and a rock crusher giving a daily output of 200 cu. yd. of crushed rock, find the cost per cubic yard. *Ans.* $0.5325.

87. In building a certain canal lock 2140 cu. yd. of concrete were used. It cost $1.77 a cubic yard for mixing and placing the concrete. The material for the concrete was as follows:

3010 barrels of cement, at $3.02,
1377 cu. yd. of broken stone at $1.37,
393 cu. yd. of screened pebbles at $0.90,
459 cu. yd. of gravel at $0.67,
500 cu. yd. of sand at $1.78.

Find the cost of the concrete work. *Ans.* $16,315.72.

88. In building a concrete viaduct containing 2111 cu. yd., the total cost was 1908 barrels of cement at $1.60; 1105 cu. yd. of sand at $1.95; 1468 cu. yd. of stone at $1.48; lumber for forms $1140; tools, hardware, etc., $527.75; water $63.00; labor $7262. Find the average cost per cubic yard of concrete. *Ans.* $7.756+

89. Number 8 (B. & S.) gage sheet steel is 0.1285 in. thick and weighs 5.22 lb. per square foot. (1) Find the thickness of a pile of 56 such sheets. (2) Find the nearest whole number of sheets to make a pile 1 ft. thick. (3) Find the weight of this number of sheets if each sheet has 4 sq. ft. *Ans.* 7.196 in.; 93; 1941.8+ lb.

90. Number 25 (B. & S.) gage sheet copper is 0.0179 in. thick and weighs 0.811 lb. per square foot. Answer the same questions as in exercise 91. *Ans.* 1.0024 in.; 670; 2173.5− lb.

91. An iron chain made of 1$\frac{3}{8}$-in. round iron has a breaking strain of 88,301 lb. If the chain weighs 17.5 lb. per foot, how long would the chain have to be to break of its own weight if suspended from one end?
Ans. 5046− ft.

92. Answer the same question as in exercise 93 for a chain made of $\frac{5}{16}$-in. round iron, the chain weighing 0.904 lb. per foot and breaking under a strain of 4794 lb. *Ans.* 5303+ ft.

93. How much must be paid for 1600 ft. of steel bar weighing 1.87 lb. per foot and costing $4.65 per hundred pounds? *Ans.* $139.13.

94. If a steel tape expands 0.00016 in. for every inch when heated, how much will a tape 100 ft. long expand?

95. A round piece of work being turned in a lathe is 1.4275 in. in diameter. What is the diameter after a cut $\frac{1}{64}$ in. deep is taken in the work?   *Ans.* 1.39625 in.

96. The inside diameter of a steam cylinder before boring was 26 in. The diameter after boring was 26.3125 in. How deep a cut was taken in boring? In boring, 20 turns were made in a minute. How long would it take to bore a distance of 28 in. if the feed was 0.0625 in.?

Ans. $\frac{5}{32}$ in.; 22.4 minutes.

97. Under a load of 325 lb. a wire 112 in. long and 0.09074 in. in diameter lengthened 0.265 in. What was the stretch per foot to four decimal places?   *Ans.* 0.0284 in.

98. In mixing a quantity of concrete using 1 part Portland cement, $2\frac{1}{2}$ parts of sand, 3 parts of gravel, and 5 parts of broken stone, it was found that 1 barrel of cement averaged 1.18 cu. yd. of concrete. If a barrel of cement contains $3\frac{3}{4}$ cu. ft., how many cubic feet of material were put into one cubic yard of concrete? Explain how this could be.

Ans. 36.55 cu. ft.

Fig. 9.

41. Proportions of machine screw heads. A. S. M. E. standard.—In the following four problems are given the four standard heads. The proportions are based on and include the diameter of the screw, diameter and thickness of the head, width and depth of the slot, radius for round and fillister heads, and included angle of flat-headed screw.

(1) *Oval fillister head machine screws.*
A =diameter of body.
$B = 1.64A - 0.009$ =diameter of head and radius of oval.
$C = 0.66A - 0.002$ =height of side.
$D = 0.173A + 0.015$ =width of slot.
$E = \frac{1}{2}F$ =depth of slot.
$F = 0.134B + C$ =height of head.

4

99. Given the values of A find those of B, C, D, E, and F.

A	B	C	D	E	F
0.216	0.3452	0.1406	0.052	0.093	0.1868
0.398	0.6437	0.2607	0.084	0.173	0.3469
0.450	0.729	0.295	0.093	0.196	0.3927

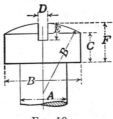

FIG. 10.

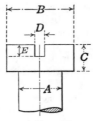

FIG. 11.

Suggestion. The values of B, C, D, E, and F are to be found from the given value of A.

$$B = 1.64 \times 0.216 - 0.009 = 0.3452.$$
$$C = 0.66 \times 0.216 - 0.002 = 0.1406.$$

(2) *Flat fillister head machine screws.*
A = diameter of body.
$B = 1.64A - 0.009 =$ diameter of head.
$C = 0.66A - 0.002 =$ height of head.
$D = 0.173A + 0.015 =$ width of slot.
$E = \frac{1}{2}C =$ depth of slot.

100. Given the values of A find those of B, C, D, and E.

A	B	C	D	E
0.112	0.1747	0.0719	0.034	0.036
0.177	0.2813	0.1148	0.046	0.057
0.320	0.5158	0.2092	0.070	0.105

(3) *Flat head machine screws.*
A = diameter of body.
$B = 2A - 0.008 =$ diameter of head.
$C = \dfrac{A - 0.008}{1.739} =$ depth of head.
$D = 0.173A + 0.015 =$ width of slot.
$E = \frac{1}{2}C =$ depth of slot.

101. Given the values of A find those of B, C, D, and E.

A	B	C	D	E
0.086	0.164	0.045	0.030	0.015
0.242	0.476	0.135	0.057	0.045
0.372	0.736	0.209	0.079	0.070

(4) *Round head machine screws.*
A = diameter of body.
$B = 1.85A - 0.005$ = diameter of head.
$C = 0.7A$ = height of head.
$D = 0.173A + 0.015$ = width of slot.
$E = \frac{1}{2}C + 0.01$ = depth of slot.

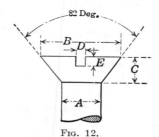

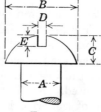

FIG. 12.　　　　　　　　　　FIG. 13.

102. Given the values of A find those of B, C, D, and E.

A	B	C	D	E
0.073	0.130	0.051	0.028	0.035
0.164	0.298	0.115	0.043	0.067
0.398	0.731	0.279	0.084	0.149

103. The formula for determining the number of threads per inch on machine screws is

$$N = \frac{6.5}{A + 0.02},$$

where N is the number of threads per inch, and A the diameter of the screw.

Compute the number of threads per inch for machine screws of the following diameters: 0.242, 0.398, 0.450, 0.563, 0.750. In each case give the answer to the nearest whole number.

Ans. 25; 16; 14; 11; 8.

CHAPTER IV

SHORT METHODS AND CHECKS

42. Contracted methods and approximate results.—As a rule the practical man does not need a large number of decimal places. The results of all measurements are at best only an approximation of the truth. The accuracy depends upon the instruments, the method used, and upon the thing measured. All that is necessary is to be sure that the magnitude of the error is small compared with the quantity measured. It is clear that in a dimension of several feet, a fraction of an inch would probably not make much difference; but if the dimension was small, such an error could not be allowed.

The man in practical work uses instruments which are of such accuracy as to secure results suitable to his purpose. If he requires measurements accurate to 0.001 in., it is not necessary for him in a computation to carry his work to 0.00001 in. A good rule to go by is not to calculate to more than one more decimal place than measurements are made.

Thus, if a measurement of 3.265 in. is made, and it is to be multiplied by 3.1416, it is not necessary to multiply in the usual way, as then there would be seven decimal places, while the measurement was accurate to only three places. If the multiplication is performed by multiplying first by the left-hand figure of the multiplier, and then passing toward the right, we have the following forms:

Form in full.	*Contracted form.*
3.265	3.265
3.1416	3.1416
9795	9795
3265	3265
13060	1306
3265	32
19590	19
10.2573240	10.2572

52

It will be noticed that one more decimal place is retained than the desired number.

In a similar manner, division can be contracted. Suppose it is required to divide 0.04267 by 3.278, and secure an answer correct to four significant figures.

The division in the full and contracted forms is as follows:

$$
\begin{array}{r|l}
0.042670000 & 3.278 \\
3278 & \overline{0.013017} \\
\hline
9890 & \\
9834 & \\
\hline
5600 & \\
3278 & \\
\hline
23220 & \\
22946 & \\
\hline
274 &
\end{array}
\qquad
\begin{array}{r|l}
0.042670 & 3.278 \\
3278 & \overline{0.013017} \\
\hline
9890 & \\
9834 & \\
\hline
56 & \\
32 & \\
\hline
24 & \\
22 & \\
\hline
2 &
\end{array}
$$

Hence the result correct to four significant figures is 0.01302 −.

It is easy to follow the method in obtaining the above, but it is hardly worth spending time upon unless one is to do much computing of this kind.

EXERCISES 13

Solve the following by contracted forms:

1. 3.14159×3.14159 correct to four decimal places.

Ans. 9.8696.

2. $9,376,245 \div 3724$ correct to the unit's place.   *Ans.* 2518.

3. $100 \div 3.14159$ correct to 0.01.   *Ans.* 31.83.

4. $87,659,734 \div 5467$ correct to five significant figures.

Ans. 16,034.

5. 45.8636×26.4356 correct to five significant figures.

Ans. 1212.4.

6. 6.234×0.05473 correct to four significant figures.

Ans. 0.3412.

7. 4.326×0.003457 correct to five significant figures.

Ans. 0.014955.

43. Other methods.—Numerous short methods in multiplication and division can be given. A few of the most useful ones are given here. If benefit is to be derived from them, they must be very carefully fixed in mind, and used whenever occasion arises.

(1) *To multiply a number by* 5, 50, 500, *etc., multiply by* 10, 100, 1000, *etc., and divide by* 2.

Why will this give the result?

Example. $7856 \times 50 = 785600 \div 2 = 392800.$ *Ans.*

Multiply the following without using the pencil:

76×50	432×50	5.5×5
96×5	768×500	4.35×50
88×500	47×50	79.2×5000

(2) *To multiply by* 25, 250, *etc., multiply by* 100, 1000, *etc., and divide by* 4.

Why will this give the result?

Example. $32 \times 250 = 32000 \div 4 = 8000.$ *Ans.*

Multiply the following without using the pencil:

256×25	8956×25	728×250
74.92×250	492×2500	942.3×2500

(3) *To multiply a number by* 125, *multiply by* 1000 *and divide by* 8.

Why will this give the result?

Example. $848 \times 125 = 848000 \div 8 = 106000.$ *Ans.*

Multiply the following:

920×125	4.76×125	72.88×125	55.5×125

(4) *To multiply a number by* $33\frac{1}{3}$, $16\frac{2}{3}$, $12\frac{1}{2}$, $8\frac{1}{3}$, *or* $6\frac{1}{4}$, *multiply by* 100 *and divide by* 3, 6, 8, 12, *or* 16.

Example. $84 \times 8\frac{1}{3} = 8400 \div 12 = 700.$ *Ans.*

Multiply the following:

$48 \times 33\frac{1}{3}$	$42.6 \times 16\frac{2}{3}$	$32\frac{1}{2} \times 16\frac{2}{3}$	$41\frac{2}{3} \times 8\frac{1}{4}$
$96 \times 12\frac{1}{2}$	$3.97 \times 8\frac{1}{3}$	$33\frac{1}{4} \times 33\frac{1}{3}$	$19\frac{4}{5} \times 6\frac{1}{4}$
$72 \times 6\frac{1}{4}$	$4.76 \times 33\frac{1}{3}$	$98.76 \times 16\frac{2}{3}$	$27\frac{2}{3} \times 12\frac{1}{2}$

This rule can be used easily in multiplying a number by $37\frac{1}{2}$, $62\frac{1}{2}$, $87\frac{1}{2}$, $83\frac{1}{3}$, and other fractional parts of 100 or 1000.

Multiply the following:

$24 \times 62\frac{1}{2}$	$35 \times 333\frac{1}{3}$	$42\frac{2}{3} \times 62\frac{1}{2}$
$32 \times 87\frac{1}{2}$	$476\frac{1}{2} \times 625$	$71\frac{3}{5} \times 37\frac{1}{2}$
$36 \times 83\frac{1}{3}$	$672 \times 62\frac{1}{2}$	$47\frac{3}{5} \times 333\frac{1}{3}$
$64 \times 37\frac{1}{2}$	$272 \times 87\frac{1}{2}$	$36\frac{2}{5} \times 83\frac{1}{3}$

(5) *To multiply a number ending in* $\frac{1}{2}$, *as* $2\frac{1}{2}$, $4\frac{1}{2}$, $11\frac{1}{2}$, *by itself, multiply the whole number by the whole number plus* 1 *and add* $\frac{1}{4}$ *to the product.*

Examples. $8\frac{1}{2} \times 8\frac{1}{2} = 8 \times 9 + \frac{1}{4} = 72\frac{1}{4}$. *Ans.*

$11\frac{1}{2} \times 11\frac{1}{2} = 11 \times 12 + \frac{1}{4} = 132\frac{1}{4}$. *Ans.*

The reason may be shown as follows:

$3\frac{1}{2} \times 3\frac{1}{2} = 3 \times 3 + 3 \times \frac{1}{2} + \frac{1}{2} \times 3 + \frac{1}{2} \times \frac{1}{2}$.

But $3 \times \frac{1}{2} + \frac{1}{2} \times 3 = 1 \times 3$ and $\frac{1}{2} \times \frac{1}{2} = \frac{1}{4}$.

Hence $3\frac{1}{2} \times 3\frac{1}{2} = 3 \times 4 + \frac{1}{4} = 12\frac{1}{4}$.

Multiply the following:

$5\frac{1}{2} \times 5\frac{1}{2}$	$12\frac{1}{2} \times 12\frac{1}{2}$	$20\frac{1}{2} \times 20\frac{1}{2}$	$18\frac{1}{2} \times 18\frac{1}{2}$
$7\frac{1}{2} \times 7\frac{1}{2}$	$14\frac{1}{2} \times 14\frac{1}{2}$	$25\frac{1}{2} \times 25\frac{1}{2}$	$150\frac{1}{2} \times 150\frac{1}{2}$
$9\frac{1}{2} \times 9\frac{1}{2}$	$16\frac{1}{2} \times 16\frac{1}{2}$	$40\frac{1}{2} \times 40\frac{1}{2}$	$59\frac{1}{2} \times 59\frac{1}{2}$

Putting in the decimal form, we have

$8\frac{1}{2} \times 8\frac{1}{2} = 8.5 \times 8.5 = 72.25$.

Now removing the decimal point, we have

$85 \times 85 = 7225$.

Multiply the following:

7.5×7.5	135×135	505×505
12.5×12.5	95×95	615×615
11.5×11.5	155×155	925×925

(6) *Divisions.* By using the inverse operations to those given in the preceding rules, we may divide by $33\frac{1}{3}$, $16\frac{2}{3}$, $12\frac{1}{2}$, 125, 250, $8\frac{1}{3}$, etc.

Make the rules for divisions.

$84 \div 12\frac{1}{2} = 84 \div 100 \times 8 = 6.72$.

$9 \div 16\frac{2}{3} = 9 \div 100 \times 6 = 0.54$

$32 \div 125 = 32 \div 1000 \times 8 = 0.256$.

$450 \div 61\frac{1}{4} = 450 \div 100 \times 16 = 72$.

$23 \div 250 = 23 \div 1000 \times 4 = 0.0092$.

The multiplications in such problems can usually be performed without using the pencil.

Divide the following:

$800 \div 12\frac{1}{2}$	$492 \div 16\frac{2}{3}$	$720 \div 8\frac{1}{3}$
$37.6 \div 250$	$923 \div 33\frac{1}{3}$	$783 \div 12\frac{1}{2}$
$7.62 \div 12\frac{1}{2}$	$436 \div 3\frac{1}{3}$	$7.29 \div 125$
$927 \div 333\frac{1}{3}$	$43.9 \div 250$	$8927 \div 166\frac{2}{3}$

44. Checking.—No check can be made that is absolutely certain to detect an error, but there are many very useful devices for checking the accuracy of the work.

(1) *Addition.* A simple way to check addition is to re-add, taking the figures in some other order. Add first up and then down, is very satisfactory.

(2) *Subtraction.* An error in a subtraction will generally be detected by adding the remainder to the subtrahend. If this gives the minuend the work is correct.

Example.

Minuend	37249
Subtrahend	18496
Remainder	18753

$$37249 = subtrahend + remainder.$$

(3) *Multiplication.* A good way to check multiplication is to interchange the multiplicand and multiplier and multiply again.

A very convenient and quick method is to proceed as follows:

(*a*) Add the digits in the multiplicand. If this sum has more than one digit, add these. Continue till a number of one digit is found.

(*b*) Add the digits of the multiplier as directed in (*a*).

(*c*) Multiply together the numbers obtained in (*a*) and (*b*), and add digits till a number of one digit is found.

(*d*) Add digits of product as directed in (*a*).

(*e*) Compare results of (*c*) and (*d*). If they are the same the work checks.

Check.	*Example.*
Summing digits as directed in (*a*), for multiplicand gives 1, for multiplier gives 6, $6 \times 1 = 6$. Sum of digits from product gives 6. Since this is the same as obtained before, the work is checked.	34768 *Multiplicand* 492 *Multiplier* —————— 69536 312912 139072 —————— 17105856 *Product*

(4) *Division.* Division can be checked by multiplying the divisor by the quotient and then adding the remainder. The result should be the dividend.

A quicker way to check is to add the digits as directed for checking multiplication: (*a*) the dividend; (*b*) the divisor; (*c*) the quotient; (*d*) the remainder. Multiply the results in (*b*) and (*c*), add the result in (*d*), and then add the digits in this result which should give the same as the result of (*a*) if the work is correct.

<table>
<tr><td>*Check.*</td><td>*Example.*</td></tr>
</table>

Dividend 4923567|476 *Divisor*

(a) Sum of digits, dividend 9,   476 |10343 *Quotient*

(b) sum of digits, divisor 8,   1635

(c) sum of digits, quotient 2,   1428

(d) sum of digits, remainder 2.   2076

    $8 \times 2 + 2 = 18.$ 1904

Sum of digits of $18 = 9$, which   1727

is the same as the sum in   1428

(a) and so checks the work.   299 *Remainder*

The preceding rules apply as well to decimals as to whole numbers, but do not check the position of the decimal point.

EXERCISES 14

First multiply then divide the following and check as directed in the preceding article.

1. 435678 by 4537.

2. 980765 by 789.

3. 60385 by 4327.

4. 342153 by 7651.

5. 45.654 by 345.

6. 456.78 by 45.32.

7. 1230.8 by 3.876.

8. 32418 by 8.098.

9. 4.6543 by 1.0876.

10. 32.654 by 7.547.

CHAPTER V

WEIGHTS AND MEASURES

45. English system.—The English system of weights and measures is the one in common use in the United States. The most used tables and equivalents of this system follow. The problems which are given later are inserted as material for review of work which it is supposed the student has done previously. Suggestions on solutions are given for some of the exercises that follow but no general methods are given as to how to solve such exercises.

(1) *Measures of time.*

60 seconds (sec.)	= 1 minute (min.)
60 minutes	= 1 hour (hr.)
24 hours	= 1 day (da.)
365 days	= 1 common year (yr.)
366 days	= 1 leap year.

(2) *Measures of length.*

12 inches (in. or ")	= 1 foot (ft. or ')
3 feet	= 1 yard (yd.)
5½ yards	= 1 rod (rd.)
320 rods	= 1 mile (mi.)
5280 feet	= 1 mile.
1760 yards	= 1 mile.

(3) *Measures of area.*

144 square inches (sq. in. or in.^{2})	= 1 square foot (sq. ft. or ft.^{2})
9 square feet	= 1 square yard (sq. yd. or yd.^{2})
30¼ square yards	= 1 square rod (sq. rd. or rd.^{2})
160 square rods	= 1 acre (A.)
640 acres	= 1 square mile (sq. mi.)

(4) *Measures of volume.*

1728 cubic inches (cu. in. or in.^{3})	= 1 cubic foot (cu. ft. or ft.^{3})
27 cubic feet	= 1 cubic yard (cu. yd. or yd.^{3})
128 cubic feet	= 1 cord (cd.)

(5) *Liquid measures.*

2 pints (pt.)	= 1 quart (qt.)
4 quarts	= 1 gallon (gal.)
31½ gallons	= 1 barrel (bbl.)
231 cubic inches	= 1 gallon.

(6) *Dry measures.*

2 pints (pt.)	= 1 quart (qt.)
8 quarts	= 1 peck (pk.)
4 pecks	= 1 bushel (bu.)
2150.42 cubic inches	= 1 bushel.

It should be carefully noted that dry and liquid measures are very different. For instance, 4 quarts in liquid measure contain 231 cu. in., while in dry measure they contain 268.8 cu. in. nearly.

(7) *Measures of weight (Avoirdupois).*

7000 grains (gr.)	= 1 pound (lb.)
16 ounces (oz.)	= 1 pound.
100 pounds	= 1 hundred weight (cwt.)
2000 pounds	= 1 ton (T.)
2240 pounds	= 1 long ton.

In practice it is customary to consider 1 cu. ft. of water as 62.5 lb. or 1000 oz. (See **Table II.**)

EXERCISES 15

1. Reduce 27 yd. 2 ft. 11 in. to inches.   *Ans.* 1007 in.

2. Reduce 18 hr. 20 min. 35 sec. to seconds.   *Ans.* 66,035 sec.

3. Reduce 4 T. 7 cwt. 35 lb. 9 oz. to ounces.   *Ans.* 139,769 oz.

4. Reduce 8 bu. 3 pk. 7 qt. 1 pt. to pints.   *Ans.* 575 pt.

5. Reduce 8 A. 25 sq. rd. 4 sq. yd. to square yards.

$\qquad\qquad$ *Ans.* 39,480¼ sq. yd.

6. Reduce 5937 sq. in. to higher denominations.

$\qquad\qquad$ *Ans.* 4 yd.² 5 ft.² 33 in.²

Suggestion. First divide 5937 by 144, the number of square inches in a square foot. The quotient is the number of square feet and the remainder is square inches.

Then divide by the number of square feet in one square yard.

7. Multiply 12 cu. yd. 15 cu. ft. 1115 cu. in. by 6.

$\qquad\qquad$ *Ans.* 75 yd.³ 12 ft.³ 1506 in.³

8. How many iron rails each 30 ft. long will be required to lay a railroad track 26 miles long?   *Ans.* 9152.

9. Find the value of a field 180 rods long and 94½ rods wide, at $18.00 per acre.   *Ans.* $1913.625.

10. Reduce 17 pints to the decimal of a gallon.   *Ans.* 2.125 gal.

11. How many steps does a man take in walking 2 mi. 76 rd. if he goes 2 ft. 8½ in. each step?   *Ans.* 4362.1 —

Suggestion. Divide the total number of inches by the number of inches in one step.

12. Find the weight of 1 gal. of water.

$\qquad\qquad$ *Ans.* 133.68+ oz. = 8 lb. 5.68 oz.

13. How many sacks each containing 2 bu. 1 pk. can be filled from a bin containing 245 bu ?   *Ans.* 109 sacks nearly.

14. A large steamship will hold 75 barge loads of wheat at 8500 bu. to the barge. A freight car 40 ft. long will carry 950 bu. Find the length of a train carrying enough wheat to load the steamship, allowing 2 ft. between cars

15. What decimal part of a foot is $\frac{1}{16}$ in.? $\frac{3}{8}$ in.? What decimal part of a yard is each?   *Ans.* 0.0052+; 0.03125; 0.00173+; 0.010417−.

16. Reduce the following to decimal parts of a foot: (a) 1 in., (b) 2 in., (c) 3½ in., (d) 7¾ in.

$\quad$ *Ans.* (a) 0.0833+, (b) 0.1667−, (c) 0.2917−, (d) 0.61458+.

17. Reduce each in exercise 16 to a decimal part of a yard.

$\quad$ *Ans.* (a) 0.02778−, (b) 0.0556−, (c) 0.0972+, (d) 0.20486+.

18. Reduce the following to decimal parts of a pound avoirdupois: (a) ¾ oz., (b) 1½ oz., (c) 3 oz., (d) 7½ oz., (e) 13 oz., (f) 4½ oz.

$\quad$ *Ans.* (a) 0.046875, (b) 0.09375, (c) 0.1875, (d) 0.46875,
$\quad\quad\quad\quad\quad\quad\quad\quad\quad\quad\quad$ (e) 0.8125, (f) 0.28125.

19. Reduce 3.36 in. to a decimal fraction of a rod.

$\quad$ *Ans.* 0.01697 − rd.

20. Reduce a pressure of 22.5 lb. per square foot to ounces per square inch.   *Ans.* 2.5 oz.

$\quad$ *Suggestion.* The cancellation is $\dfrac{22.5 \times 16}{144} = 2.5$.

21. What is the cost per hour for lighting a room with 68 burners each consuming 2¼ cu. in. per second, the price of gas being 85 cents per thousand cubic feet?   *Ans.* 27.1 − cents.

22. A clock that gains 1 min. in 10 hr. is correct at Monday noon. What is the correct time when the clock registers noon on the following Monday?   *Ans.* 43 min. 14 − sec. past 11 A. M.

23. How many feet per second are equivalent to 30 miles per hour?

$\quad$ *Ans.* 44 ft.

24. If sound travels at the rate of 1125 ft. per second, in what time would the report of a gun be heard when fired at a distance of 1.276 miles?   *Ans.* 5.989 − sec.

25. A train travels 316 miles in 10 hr. 34 min.; what distance will it travel in 27 hr. 17 min. at the same rate?   *Ans.* 815.9+ mi.

26. A tank holding 7 bbl. has 2 pipes opening from it; one empties out 2 qt. in 5 sec., and the other 17 gal. per minute. How long will it take to empty the tank if both pipes are open?   *Ans.* 9.587 − min.

27. If it takes 4 qt. of oats for one feeding for a horse; how many bushels of oats will it take to feed 5 horses one year, giving them 2 feedings per day?   *Ans.* 456¼ bu.

28. A carload of potatoes has a total weight of 55,600 lb. The car alone weighs 15,675 lb. How many bushels of potatoes in the carload if potatoes weigh 60 lb. per bushel?   *Ans.* 665.41 bu.

29. A tank that holds 25.6 bbl. will hold how many bushels?

$\quad$ *Ans.* 86.62+.

30. A bin that holds 13 bu. will hold how many gallons?

$\quad$ *Ans.* 121.02 − gal.

31. How long would it take a cannon ball going at the rate of 1950 ft. per second to reach the sun, if the sun is distant 93,000,000 miles?

Ans. 8 yr. nearly.

32. Supposing the distance travelled by the earth about the sun to be 596,440,000 miles per year, what is the average hourly distance travelled, taking the year to be 365¼ days? Find the average distance per second.

Ans. 19 miles per second, nearly.

33. Find the area in acres of a farm which is represented on paper as a rectangle 3¾ in. by 10½ in. on a scale of $\frac{1}{16}$ in. to the rod.

Ans. 63 acres.

34. If 4 oz. of the white of egg is used in cleansing 50 gal. of wine, how many eggs will it take for 17 bbl. of wine? One egg contains 1.1 oz. of white.

Ans. 39 eggs.

35. The total cost of making a cement walk 300 ft. long, 5 ft. wide, and 6 in. thick, where the cement was hand mixed, was as follows: Foreman, 8 hours; laborers, 120 hours at a cost of $53.20; cement, $86.00; gravel, $34.08. Find the total cost per square yard and per square foot.

36. A farmer drew a load of potatoes to market for which he received 76 cents a bushel. If the wagon and load weighed 3710 lb. and the empty wagon weighed 1150 lb., find what he received for the potatoes. 60 lb. of potatoes make 1 bu.

37. How many pounds of charcoal does it take to make 3 tons of gunpowder, if the powder is $\frac{1}{10}$ sulphur, ¾ saltpeter, and the rest charcoal?

Ans. 900.

38. How many barrels of flour, 196 lb. each, does it take to run a bakery one week of 7 days if the output is 6000 loaves a day, and there are 9½ oz. of flour in each loaf? *Ans.* 127 bbl. 45¼ lb.

39. (*a*) Find the number of cubic feet in a barrel to the nearest 0.001. (*b*) Find the number of cubic feet in a bushel to the nearest 0.00001.

Ans. 4.211 cu. ft.; 1.24446 cu. ft.

40. A new copper cent weighs 48 grains. How many pounds will $50 in these weigh? *Ans.* 34⅔ lb.

41. One of the largest diamonds in the world weighs 3025¾ carats. How many pounds avoirdupois is this, correct to the nearest 0.0001? A carat is 3.168 grains. *Ans.* 1.3694 lb.

42. If railroad ties are placed 18 in. apart from center to center, how many miles will 34,320 ties reach? *Ans.* 15$\frac{9}{44}$ mi.

43. How many rails, each 30 ft. in length, are used in laying two railroad tracks from New York to Chicago a distance of 870 mi.? Find the weight of these rails at 90 lb. per yard.

Ans. 612,480 rails; 275,616 tons.

44. Supposing the distance from the earth to the sun to be 91,713,000 miles, and that the sun's light reaches the earth in 8 min. 18 sec., what is the velocity of light per second? *Ans.* 184,163 miles nearly.

45. The pressure of the atmosphere is 14.7 lb. per square inch. Find the pressure in pounds per square foot. *Ans.* 2116.8 lb.

46. A column of water how high will give a pressure of 1 lb. per square inch?   *Ans.* 2.3 ft. nearly.

47. If the ends of an iron beam, bearing 5 tons at its middle, rest upon stone piers, required the necessary bearing surface of each pier if the stone will support 200 lb. per square inch of surface.   *Ans.* 25 in.[2]

By bearing surface is meant the area of the stone in contact with the beam.

48. One voussoir (or block) of an arch ring presses its neighbor with a force of 50 tons. If the joint has a surface of 5 sq. ft., find the pressure per square inch.   *Ans.* 138.9— lb. per square inch.

49. Work is done when resistance is overcome. It is measured by the product of the force times the distance over which the force acts. As a formula this is $w = f \times s$, where w is the work, f the force, and s the distance. If the force is in pounds and the distance in feet then the work is in foot-pounds.

A steam crane lifts a block of granite weighing 2 tons 80 ft. Find the work done in foot-pounds.   *Ans.* 320,000 ft. lb.

50. How many foot-pounds of work is necessary to pump 100 bbl. of water to a height of 120 ft.? Use 1 bbl. = 4.211 cu. ft.

Ans. 3,158,250 ft. lb.

51. How many foot-pounds of work is done in lifting an elevator weighing 3 tons to the top of a building 220 ft. high? If the elevator is raised through this height in 2 minutes, how many foot-pounds of work is done per second? If an engine of one horse-power can do 550 foot-pounds of work per second, an engine of what horse-power will be necessary to lift the elevator to the top in 2 minutes?

52. A man weighing 165 pounds ascends a stairs to a height of 60 ft. in 20 seconds. How many horse-power does he exert?

THE METRIC SYSTEM

46. From a study of weights and measures in the United States, it is seen that a legal standard, the troy pound, has been established for the use of the mint; but that beyond that, our weights and measures in ordinary use rest on custom only with indirect legislative recognition. It is seen that the metric weights and measures are made legal by direct legislative permission, and that standards of both systems have been equally furnished by the Government to the several states; that the customary system has been adopted by the Treasury Department for use in the custom-houses, but that the same department has by formal order adopted the metric standards as "fundamental standards" from which measures of the customary system shall be derived.

Commercial intercourse between nations makes it advisable, if not necessary, to have a uniform system of weights and measures. Such relations cause those countries not already using the metric system to make more and more use of that system. For instance, large orders for locomotives placed in the United States by foreign governments or by corporations in those countries, have made it a matter of good business to carry out the manufacturing in metric units of measure.

The European war, beginning in 1914, made it necessary for large manufacturing plants in this country to make considerable use of the metric system. It is stated on good authority that the first six months following the entrance of the United States into the great war advanced the use of the metric system in this country more than had the previous ten years.

A few manufacturing companies have for several years quoted sizes of reamers, drills, and other tools in the metric system as well as in the ordinary system. At present this custom is becoming increasingly more general.

47. Measure of length. The meter.—The length of the meter was at first determined as one ten-millionth part of the distance from the equator to the north-pole. It was afterward found that there had been a slight error in this determination. At present the meter is the length at 0°C. of a certain bar, made of 90 per cent platinum and 10 per cent iridium, called the International Meter, and kept at the International Bureau of Weights and Measures, near Paris.

The two copies of the meter which the United States has are made of the same material. One of these is used as the working standard, and the other is kept for comparison. To insure still greater accuracy, these are compared at regular intervals with the International Meter.

48. Legal units.—As has been stated the Treasury Department has determined that the meter shall be the "fundamental standard" of length. By the act of July, 1866, Congress fixed the relation, 1 meter = 39.37 in. This is the only legal relation between the two systems, and is used in the Office of Standards of Weights and Measures in this country in deriving the inch, foot, yard, etc., from the meter. Determined in this way the customary units are legal.

In the Philippine Islands, Porto Rico, and Guam the metric

system is in general use, and is the sole legalized system for these islands.[1]

49. Measure of surface.—There is no fundamental standard of surfaces or areas as there is of the measures of length. But as the measures of areas are based upon the units of length, and as these are standards, the measures of areas may be so considered.

50. Measures of volume. Cubic and capacity measures.— In the United States the fundamental standards of volume are: (1) the cubes of the linear units based on the International Meter; (2) the liter, which is the volume of the mass of one kilogram of pure water at its greatest density; (3) the gallon, which is 231 cu. in.; (4) the bushel, which is 2150.42 cu. in. The liter here used is almost exactly 1 cubic decimeter, and the inch is derived from the meter according to the relation, 1 meter = 39.37 in.

51. Measures of mass.—The fundamental standard of mass (weight) in the United States is the International Kilogram, a cylinder of 90 per cent platinum and 10 per cent iridium, preserved at the International Bureau of Weights and Measures, near Paris. As in the case of the meter, one of the two copies of the kilogram possessed by the United States is used as a working standard, and the other is kept under seal and used only to compare with the working standard from time to time. To insure still greater accuracy, these are compared at regular intervals with the International Kilogram.

By act of Congress of July 28, 1866, the pound is derived from the kilogram. The relation established at that time was 1 kilogram = 2.2046 avoirdupois pounds. This relation has since been made more nearly accurate and is 1 kilogram = 15,432.35639 grains, which would change the first relation to 1 kilogram = 2.20462234 lb. avoirdupois, or 1 lb. avoirdupois = 453.5924277 grams. This value is the one used by the National Bureau of Standards in Washington. It is thus seen that the avoirdupois pounds, ounces, etc., in common use

---

[1] See Introduction to "Laws Concerning Weights and Measures of the United States," compiled by Louis A. Fisher and Henry D. Hubbard of the Bureau of Standards, Washington, D. C.

are derived from the kilogram, and so are fixed and definite derived units.

The established relation between the troy pound and the avoirdupois pound is 1 troy pound $= \frac{5760}{7000}$ avoirdupois pounds.

When made, the standard kilogram was supposed to be the exact mass of one cubic decimeter or 1 liter of pure water at the temperature of its greatest density. It has been found that this is not exactly true, but the difference is very slight, the kilogram being about 25 parts in 1,000,000 too heavy. This difference is so very small that it could hardly affect any ordinary problem.

52. Tables and terms used.—In the customary system of weights and measures we have about 150 different terms and 50 different numbers, ranging all the way from 2 to 1728. These numbers bear no relation to one another. In the metric system we have only 14 different terms and but a single number, and that is the number 10.

In the metric system the different terms used are the following:

> **meter**—the unit of length,
> **liter**—the unit of volume,
> **are**—the unit of area,
> **gram**—the unit of weight,
> **myria**—which denotes 10,000,
> **kilo**—which denotes 1000,
> **hecto**—which denotes 100,
> **deka**—which denotes 10,
> **deci**—which denotes 0.1,
> **centi**—which denotes 0.01,
> **milli**—which denotes 0.001.

Terms which are sometimes used are:
> **millier**—which denotes 1,000,000,
> **quintal**—which denotes 100,000,
> **stere**—which is 1 cubic meter.

To these might be added **mikron** and **mikrogram**.

If the foregoing terms are carefully fixed in mind the tables are easily formed.

5

(1) Measures of length.

10 millimeters (mm.)	= 1 centimeter (cm.)	= 0.01 meter
10 centimeters	= 1 decimeter (dm.)	= 0.1 meter
10 decimeters	= 1 **meter** (m.)	
10 meters	= 1 dekameter (Dm.)	= 10 meters
10 dekameters	= 1 hectometer (Hm.)	= 100 meters
10 hectometers	= 1 kilometer (Km.)	= 1000 meters
10 kilometers	= 1 myriameter (Mm.)	= 10,000 meters

(2) Measures of surface.

100 square millimeters (mm.^{2})	= 1 sq. centimeter (cm.^{2})
100 square centimeters	= 1 sq. decimeter (dm.^{2})
100 square decimeters	= 1 sq. **meter** (m.^{2}) = 1 centare (ca.)
100 square meters	= 1 sq. dekameter (Dm.^{2}) = 1 are (a.)
100 square dekameters	= 1 sq. hectometer (Hm.^{2}) = 1
	hektare (Ha.)
100 square hectometers	= 1 sq. kilometer (Km.^{2})

(3) Measures for land.

| 100 centares (ca.) | = 1 **are** (a.) |
| 100 ares | = 1 hectare (Ha.) |

(4) Measures of volume.

1000 cubic millimeters (mm.^{3})	= 1 cu. centimeter (cm.^{3} or cc.)
1000 cubic centimeters	= 1 cu. decimeter (dm.^{3}) = 1 liter (l.)
1000 cubic decimeters	= 1 **cu. meter** (m.^{3}) = 1 kiloliter (Kl.)

(5) Measures of capacity.

10 milliliters (ml.)	= 1 centiliter (cl.)
10 centiliters	= 1 deciliter (dl.)
10 deciliters	= 1 **liter** (l.) = 1 dm.^{3}
10 liters	= 1 dekaliter (Dl.)
10 dekaliters	= 1 hectoliter (Hl.)
10 hectoliters	= 1 kiloliter (Kl.) = 1 m.^{3}

(6) Measures of weight.

10 milligrams (mg.)	= 1 centigram (cg.)
10 centigrams	= 1 decigram (dg.)
10 decigrams	= 1 **gram** (g.)
10 grams	= 1 dekagram (Dg.)
10 dekagrams	= 1 hectogram (Hg.)
10 hectograms	= 1 kilogram or kilo (Kg.)
10 kilograms	= 1 myriagram (Mg.)
10 myriagrams	= 1 quintal (Q.)
10 quintals	= 1 millier, tonneau, or metric ton (T.)

To these may be added the following used in scientific work:

| 1 mikron (μ) | = 0.000001 meter. |
| 1 mikrogram (γ) | = 0.000001 gram. |

Note. A chart showing very clearly the relations of the different measures can be secured by addressing the Bureau of Standards, Washington, D. C.

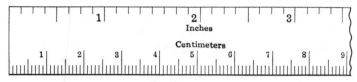

FIG. 14.

53. Equivalents.—To be remembered.

1 gallon	= 231 cubic inches (established by law).
1 bushel	= 2150.42 cubic inches (established by law).
1 meter	= 39.37 inches (established by law).
1 gram	= 15.432 grains.
1 pound avoirdupois	= 7000 grains.
1 inch	= 2.54 centimeters (approximately).
1 kilogram	= 2.2 pounds (approximately).

For Reference.

Lengths

1 inch	= 2.54001 cm.
1 foot	= 30.4801 cm.
1 kilometer	= 3280.83 ft. = 0.62137 mi.
1 mile	= 1.60935 Km.

Areas

1 sq. in.	= 6.45163 cm.^{2}
1 sq. ft.	= 0.0929034 m.^{2}
1 sq. yd.	= 0.836131 m.^{2}
1 cm.^{2}	= 0.155 sq. in.
1 m.^{2}	= 10.76387 − sq. ft. = 1.19599 − sq. yd.
1 are	= 119.5985 sq. yd.
1 acre	= 40.4687 ares.

Volumes, capacities

1 cu. in.	= 16.38716 cc.
1 cu. ft.	= 28.317 liters or dm.^{3}
1 pt. (liquid)	= 473.179 cc. = 0.473179 liters or dm.^{3}
1 pt. (dry)	= 550.614 cc. = 0.550614 liters or dm.^{3}
1 qt. (liquid)	= 946.358 cc. = 0.946358 liters or dm.^{3}
1 qt. (dry)	= 1101.228 cc. = 1.101228 liters or dm.^{3}
1 cm.^{3}	= 0.0610234 cu. in.
1 liter	= 61.0234 cu. in.
1 liter	= 2.11336 pt. (liquid) = 1.81616 pt. (dry).
1 liter	= 1.05668 qt. (liquid) = 0.90808 qt. (dry).

Weights (mass)

1 grain	= 0.0647989 gram.
1 ounce (avoirdupois)	= 28.3495 grams.
1 pound (avoirdupois)	= 453.5924277 grams = 0.45359+ Kg.
1 ton (short)	= 907.185 kilograms.
1 gram	= 15.43235639 grains.
1 kilogram	= 2.20462 pounds (avoirdupois).
1 metric ton	= 2204.62 pounds (avoirdupois).

54. Simplicity of the metric system.—The men who devised the metric system endeavored to invent a system of weights and measures that would be as simple as possible; and they undoubtedly succeeded in making a system that is simpler than any other in use.

Many look upon the system as difficult because they consider the difficulties of changing from the English to the metric system, or from the metric to the English, as difficulties of the metric system. In reality this is not the case, as all such difficulties would disappear if the metric system were in universal use.

The simplicity of the metric system lies in the two facts: first, it is decimal, and therefore fits our decimal notation; second, its units for lengths, surfaces, solids, and weights are all dependent on one unit, the meter.

Ability to handle the metric system easily, depends, in great part, on understanding thoroughly the terms used. It is of first importance then to learn well these terms and their meanings. For instance, the word decimeter should mean, at once, one-tenth of a meter.

Because of the decimal relations between the different terms used, the changing from one unit to another is a very simple matter. In reducing to higher denominations, we divide by 10, 100, 1000, etc., by removing the decimal point to the left.

Thus, to change 3768 cm. to meters, we divide by 100 by removing the decimal point two places to the left, and have 3768 cm. = 37.68 m.
In a similar manner, 72,468 g. = 72.468 Kg., and
$$8643 \text{ l} = 86.43 \text{ Hl.}$$

It should be noticed that we never write 4 Km. 7 Hm. 3 Dm. 5 m. but write it 4735 m. The former way of writing it would be similar to writing $7.265 in the form 7 dollars 2 dimes 6 cents 5 mills.

In reducing to lower denominations, the multiplication is performed by moving the decimal point to the right.

Thus, 25 m. = 250 dm. = 25,000 mm. and 16 Kg. = 16,000 g.

55. Relations of the units.—It cannot be impressed upon the mind of the student too strongly that he should understand clearly the relations between the units of different kinds of measure. He must know that a liter is a cubic decimeter, that a kilogram is the weight of a liter of pure water, that an are is a square dekameter, and so on. He should notice that in the surface measures, when using square meters, dekameters, etc., the scale is 100; while in using cubic meters, dekameters, etc., for volumes, the scale is 1000.

Thus, $2m.^2 = 200$ $dm.^2 = 20,000$ $cm.^2$
and $3m.^3 = 3000$ $dm.^3 = 3,000,000$ cc. $= 3,000,000,000$ $mm.^3$

56. Changing from English to metric or from metric to English systems.—The changing from one system to another is simply a matter of multiplication or division.

(1) Thus, to express 17 m. in inches,

1 m. = 39.37 in.

17 m. = 39.37 in. × 17 = 669.29 in.

(2) Also, to express 2468 lb. in kilograms,

2.2 lb. (approx.) = 1 Kg.

2468 lb. = 2468 ÷ 2.2 = 1121.8 Kg.

Or using the equivalent 1 lb. = 0.45359 Kg.,

2468 lb. = 0.45359 Kg. × 2468 = 1119.46 Kg.

The disagreement in the results is on account of 2.2 lb. being a rough approximation.

The United States Bureau of Standards has compiled numerous tables of equivalents for use in the custom houses. By the use of these tables, a conversion from one system to another, is made by simply referring to the proper table and reading the result.

For further information the following pamphlets can be obtained gratis from the Bureau of Standards, Washington, D. C.: History of Standard Weights and Measures of the

United States, Table of Equivalents, and the International Metric System of Weights and Measures.

EXERCISES 16

1. Express the following, first, in meters, and second, in millimeters: 456 cm., 1763 Dm., 27 Km.   *Ans.* 4.56 m., 17,630 m., 27,000 m., 4560 mm., 17,630,000 mm., 27,000,000 mm.

2. Express the following in m.^{2}: 75 cm.^{2}, 125 mm.^{2}, 0.025 Dm.^{2}, 0.0029 Km.^{2} *Ans.* 0.0075 m.^{2}, 0.000125 m.^{2}, 2.5 m.^{2}, 2900 m.^{2}

3. Expres the following in terms of m.^{3}: 1756 l., 467 Kl., 4937 dl., 0.1067 Dl., 735,432 dm.^{3}, 764 Dm.^{3} *Ans.* 1.756 m.^{3}, 467 m.^{3}, 0.4937 m.^{3}, 10.67 m.^{3}, 735.432 m.^{3}, 764,000 m.^{3}

4. Reduce 750 l. to liquid quarts; 326 l. to dry quarts; 75 m. to inches; 576 cm. to feet; 27 m.^{3} to bushels; 9276 mm.^{3} to gallons; 12 Dm.^{3} to barrels.   *Ans.* 792.51 qt., 296.03408 qt., 18.8976 ft., 766.19 bu., 0.00245 gal., 100,636.19 bbl.

Solution.   From **Art. 47** find 1 l. = 1.05668 qt. (liquid).
∴ 750 l. = 1.05668 qt. ×750 = 792.51 qt. *Ans.*

In the fifth part, 27 m.^{3} to bushels, the change is not so easy from the equivalents given.

27 m.^{3} = 27,000 dm.^{3} or liters.
1 l. = 0.90808 qt. (dry).
∴ 27,000 l. = 0.90808 qt. ×27,000 = 24,518.16 qt.

Divide this by 32 because 1 bu. = 32 qt.
∴ 27 m.^{3} = 766.19 bu. *Ans.*

5. Reduce 456 in. to meters; 43.5 ft. to centimeters; 327 gal. to liters; 92.87 qt. (dry) to liters; 756 bu. to cubic meters;
Ans. 11.58 m., 1325.88 cm., 1237.84 l., 102.27 l., 26.64 m.^{3}

6. No. 16 gage sheet steel is $\frac{1}{16}$ in. thick and weighs 40 oz. per square foot.   Find thickness in millimeters (four decimal places), and the weight per square meter in kilograms (two decimal places).
Ans. 1.5875 mm., 12.21 — Kg. per m.^{2}

Solution.   To find the weight in Kg. per m.^{2}, first find the weight of a square meter in ounces and then change to pounds and to kilograms.

1 m.^{2} = 10.76387 ft.^{2}
∴ 1 m.^{2} weighs 40 oz. × 10.76387 = 430.5548 oz. = 26.9097 lb.
1 lb. = 0.45359 Kg.
∴ 26.9097 lb. = 0.45359 Kg. × 26.9097 = 12.20597 Kg. *Ans.*

7. No. 24 gage sheet steel is 0.635 mm. thick and weighs 4.882 Kg. per m.^{2} Find thickness in decimal of inch (three decimal places), and weight per ft.^{2} in ounces.   *Ans.* 0.025 in., 16 oz. per ft.^{2}

8. Find the difference between $3\frac{15}{16}$ in. and 10 cm.
Ans. $3\frac{15}{16}$ in. larger by 0.0005 in.

9. Feb. 12, 1912, Oscar Mathieson, of Norway, set a new world's record in ice skating.   He made 1500 m. in 2 min. 20 sec.   This is a mile in what time?

Solution. 2 min. 20 sec. = 140 sec.

$$1500 \text{ m.} = \frac{1500 \times 39.37}{12} \text{ ft.}$$

$$\frac{1500 \times 39.37}{12 \times 140} = \text{ number of feet in 1 sec.}$$

$$\frac{5280 \times 12 \times 140}{1500 \times 39.37} = 150.2 = \text{ number of sec. to go 1 mi.}$$

150.2 sec. = 2 min. 30.2 sec. *Ans.*

10. The same day in Chicago, Harry Kaad won the mile race in 3 min. 23⅔ sec. This is 1500 m. in what time?   *Ans.* 3 min. 9.6 sec.

11. In describing the making of reenforced concrete the necessary pressure is given as 25 kilos per square centimeter. How many pounds is this per square inch?   *Ans.* 355.58+.

12. Find in kilograms the weight of air in a room 10.5 by 8.3 by 4 meters, air being 0.001276 times as heavy as water.

         Ans. 444.8136 Kg.

13. Find the weight in kilograms of the mercury in a tube of 1 cm.² cross section and 760 mm. long, mercury being 13.596 times as heavy as water.   *Ans.* 1.0333 − Kg.

14. If a map is made on a scale of 1 to 60,000, how many kilometers do 79 mm. on the map represent?   *Ans.* 4.74.

15. If a person in breathing uses 0.25 m.³ of air a minute, how long will it take 6 persons to use the air in a room 6 m. long, 3.5 m. high, and 5.3 m. wide?   *Ans.* 74.2 min.

16. A block of stone weighs 7643 Kg. A cubic decimeter of the stone weighs 2.7 Kg. Find the volume of the block in cubic meters.

         Ans. 2.83074 m.³

17. Find the area in hectares of a triangular field whose base is 70 m. and the altitude 60 m.   *Ans.* 0.21 Ha.

18. How many liters of water are contained in a reservoir 10 m.×6 m.×4 m.? What is the weight of the water in kilograms?

         Ans. 240,000 l., 240,000 Kg.

19. Find the capacity in liters of a rectangular tank 2 m.×9 dm.×8 dm.   *Ans.* 1440 l.

20. What is the length of a centigram of wire 255 mm. of which weighs 0.172 g.?   *Ans.* 14.83 − mm.

21. A liter of mercury weighs 13.596 Kg.; how many mm.³ of mercury weigh 1 g.?   *Ans.* 73.551.

22. A man's height is 174 cm. What is his height in feet and inches?   *Ans.* 5 ft. 8.5+ in.

23. Express the following readings in centimeters: 29.9 in., 30.0 in., 30.1 in., 30.2 in.

     Ans. 75.946 cm., 76.200 cm., 76.454 cm., 76.708 cm.

24. Express the following in inches to the nearest 0.01: 71.119 cm., 73.659 cm., 74.929 cm.   *Ans.* 28.00 in., 29.00 in., 29.50 in.

25. Cast copper being 8.8 times as heavy as an equal volume of water, what is the weight of 5 cm.³?   *Ans.* 44 g.

26. A velocity of 32.2 ft. per second is how many centimeters per second?   *Ans.* 981.5 −.

27. A rate of 1 mile in 2 min. 6 sec. is how many kilometers per minute? How many meters per second?   *Ans.* 0.7664 −, 12.77 +.

28. A rate of 30 miles per hour is at the rate of one kilometer in how many minutes?   *Ans.* 1.243 −.

29. A pressure of 14.7 lb. per square inch is how many grams per cm.²?

Solution. $\dfrac{14.7}{6.45163}$ = number of lb. per sq. cm.

$\dfrac{14.7 \times 453.5924}{6.45163}$ = 1033.5 + = number of g. per sq. cm.

CHAPTER VI

PERCENTAGE AND APPLICATIONS

57. Per cents as fractions.—To one who thoroughly understands fractions, percentage offers no new difficulties. The words per cent mean by the hundred. The symbol % means per cent. Thus, 10% means 10 per cent or $\frac{10}{100}$ or 0.10. In a similar way:

5%	=0.05	$=\frac{1}{20}$	50%	=0.50	$=\frac{1}{2}$
10%	=0.1	$=\frac{1}{10}$	60%	=0.60	$=\frac{3}{5}$
12½%	=0.12½	$=\frac{1}{8}$	62½%	=0.62½	$=\frac{5}{8}$
16⅔%	=0.16⅔	$=\frac{1}{6}$	75%	=0.75	$=\frac{3}{4}$
20%	=0.20	$=\frac{1}{5}$	80%	=0.80	$=\frac{4}{5}$
25%	=0.25	$=\frac{1}{4}$	83⅓%	=0.83⅓	$=\frac{5}{6}$
33⅓%	=0.33⅓	$=\frac{1}{3}$	87½%	=0.87½	$=\frac{7}{8}$
37½%	=0.37½	$=\frac{3}{8}$	90%	=0.90	$=\frac{9}{10}$
40%	=0.40	$=\frac{2}{5}$			

To change a fraction as $\frac{2}{5}$ to an equivalent form in per cent, reduce it to a fraction having 100 for a denominator.

Thus, $\frac{2}{5} = \frac{40}{100} = 40\%$;

or $\frac{2}{5} = \frac{2}{5}$ of 100% = 40%.

Similarly $\frac{7}{8} = \frac{7}{8}$ of 100% = 87½%.

A per cent expressed as $\frac{2}{5}\%$, does not mean $\frac{2}{5}$ but $\frac{2}{5}$ of 1%, which is the same as $\frac{2}{5}$ of $\frac{1}{100} = \frac{2}{500} = \frac{1}{250} = 0.004$. In the same way $\frac{3}{8}\% = \frac{3}{8}$ of $\frac{1}{100} = \frac{3}{800} = 0.00375 = 0.375\%$.

It should be carefully noticed that the sign % does the duty of two decimal places.

Thus, $0.05 = 5\%$, $0.0005 = 0.05\%$, $1.07 = 107\%$, and $4.33\frac{1}{3} = 433\frac{1}{3}\%$.

58. Cases.—The problems of percentage usually occurring are of the following forms:

(1) What is 37½% of 720?

(2) 45 is what per cent of 450?

(3) 85 is 62½% of what number?

These three forms can be stated in general terms if the following definitions are given:

The number of which the per cent is taken is the **base**.

The number of per cent taken is called the **rate**.

The part of the base determined by the rate is the **percentage**.

The sum of the base and percentage is the **amount**.

The base minus the percentage is the **difference**.

The three problems now become the cases:

Case I. *Base* and *rate* given to find *percentage*.

Case II. *Base* and *percentage* given to find *rate*.

Case III. *Percentage* and *rate* given to find *base*.

These three cases of percentage correspond to the three cases in multiplication; when any two of the numbers, multiplicand, multiplier, and product, are given, to find the third.

$$In\ multiplication, \left\{ \begin{array}{l} multiplicand\ \text{corresponds} \\ \quad \text{to base} \\ multiplier\ \text{corresponds to} \\ \quad rate \\ product\ \text{corresponds to} \\ \quad percentage \end{array} \right\} in\ percentage.$$

Case I corresponds to: *multiplicand* and *multiplier* given to find the *product*.

Product = multiplicand × multiplier.

Case II corresponds to: *multiplicand* and *product* given to find the *multiplier*.

Multiplier = product ÷ multiplicand.

Case III corresponds to: *multiplier* and *product* given to find the *multiplicand*.

Multiplicand = product ÷ multiplier.

59. Rules and formulas.—In the language of percentage these become:

Case I. *Percentage = base × rate.*

This may be written as a formula if *b* stands for base, *p* for percentage, and *r* for rate. The formula is

$$p = b \times r.$$

Case II. *Rate = percentage ÷ base.* The formula is

$$r = p \div b.$$

Case III. Base = *percentage ÷ rate.* The formula is

$$b = p \div r.$$

60. Solutions. *Problem* (1) is solved thus:

By fractions. $37\frac{1}{2}\%$ of $720 = \frac{3}{8}$ of $720 = 270$. *Ans.*

By formula. Using the formula $p = b \times r$, gives the same result, for then $p = 720 \times 0.37\frac{1}{2} = 270$. *Ans.*

Problem (2). *By fractions.* 45 is what per cent of 450 means 45 is how many hundredths of 450, that is, some number of hundredths of 450 is 45.

Then 45 is $\frac{45}{450} = \frac{1}{10} = \frac{10}{100} = 10\%$ of 450.

By formula. $r = p \div b$ gives $r = 45 \div 450 = 0.1 = 10\%$.

Problem (3). *By fractions.* 85 is $62\frac{1}{2}\%$ of what number is the same as 85 is $\frac{5}{8}$ of what number. It is now a simple problem in fractions and may be reasoned thus:

If 85 is $\frac{5}{8}$ of some number then 17 is $\frac{1}{8}$ of that number, and 136 is $\frac{8}{8}$ of that number.

Hence the number $= 136$. *Ans.*

By formula. $b = p \div r$ gives $p = 85 \div 0.62\frac{1}{2} = 136$. *Ans.*

EXERCISES 17

Solve the following exercises without a pencil if possible.

1. What is $\frac{1}{4}$ of 24?   0.25 of 24?   25% of 24?
2. What is $\frac{3}{4}$ of 36?   0.75 of 36?   75% of 36?
3. What is $\frac{1}{3}$ of 45? $0.33\frac{1}{3}$ of 45? $33\frac{1}{3}\%$ of 45?
4. What is $\frac{2}{3}$ of 48? $0.66\frac{2}{3}$ of 48? $66\frac{2}{3}\%$ of 48?
5. What is $\frac{1}{5}$ of 60?   0.20 of 60?   20% of 60?
6. What is $\frac{4}{5}$ of 70?   0.80 of 70?   80% of 70?
7. What is $\frac{1}{8}$ of 72? $0.12\frac{1}{2}$ of 72? $12\frac{1}{2}\%$ of 72?
8. What is $\frac{5}{8}$ of 48?   0.625 of 48?   62.5% of 48?
9. What is $\frac{1}{16}$ of 64? $0.06\frac{1}{4}$ of 64? $6\frac{1}{4}\%$ of 64?
10. What is 25% of 16?   of 48?   of 90?   of 240?
11. What is $33\frac{1}{3}\%$ of 75?   of 42?   of 96?   of 720?
12. What is 4% of 25?   of 75?   of 300?   of 1000?
13. What is 7% of 20?   of 14?   of 55?   of 300?
14. 5 is what per cent of 10?   of 20?   of 40?
15. 8 is what per cent of 16?   of 40?   of 80?
16. 30 is what per cent of 90?   of 240?   of 360?
17. What % is 8 of 150? $7\frac{1}{2}$ of 12?   *Ans.* $5\frac{1}{3}\%$; $62\frac{1}{2}\%$.
18. What % is $\frac{3}{8}$ of $12\frac{1}{2}$? $27\frac{3}{8}$ of 600?   *Ans.* $4\frac{4}{5}\%$; $4\frac{3}{8}\%$.
19. 20% of what number is 3?   7?   14?   17?
20. $33\frac{1}{3}\%$ of what number is 7?   8?   14?   90?
21. $62\frac{1}{2}\%$ of what number is 5?   20? $\frac{5}{8}$? $\frac{19}{4}$?
22. $37\frac{1}{2}\%$ of a number is 72; find the number.   *Ans.* 192.
23. 20% off of what number leaves 48?   *Ans.* 60.

Suggestion. 20% off a number leaves 80% of the number.

24. 30% off of what number leaves 50?   *Ans.* 71¾.
25. 33⅓% off of what number leaves 12?   *Ans.* 18.
26. 68 is 15% less than what number?   *Ans.* 80.
27. 49 is 30% less than what number?   *Ans.* 70.
28. 18 is 80% more than what number?   *Ans.* 10.
29. 80 is 33⅓% more than what number?   *Ans.* 60.
30. 98 is 40% more than what number?   *Ans.* 70.
31. 87½ is 37½% less than what number?   *Ans.* 140.

32. If oranges that cost 25 cents a dozen are sold at 3 for 10 cents what part of the cost is gained? What per cent?

33. Pencils are bought at 15 cents a dozen and sold for 2 cents each. What part of the cost is gained? What per cent?   *Ans.* 60%.

34. Bought a horse for $75 and sold it for $100; find the gain per cent.   *Ans.* 33⅓%.

35. Find the gain per cent in each case if a horse was bought at the following prices: $50, $40, $25, $10, $5, and $1; and sold for $100. Find the gain per cent if the horse was given to the seller.

36. I bought a bicycle for $100 and after using it one year sold it for $55. Find the per cent of discount.   *Ans.* 45%.

37. A gas bill was 25% higher last month than this. If it is $6.40 this month, what was it last month?

38. A horse was bought for $100 and sold for $90. What was the loss per cent?

39. A man sold a suit of clothes gaining ¼ the cost. What part of the cost was the selling price? What was the gain per cent? What per cent of the selling price was the cost?

40. A quantity of wool was bought for $360, and ¾ of it was then sold for the cost of the whole. What per cent would have been gained if the entire amount had been sold at the same rate?   *Ans.* 33⅓%.

41. A man spent 16⅔% of his salary for board and room. If he spent $6.50 a week for board and room, what was his yearly salary? (52 weeks per year.)   *Ans.* $2028.

61. Applications.—*Example* 1. The population of a certain city in 1900 was 52,600, and in 1905 was 61,805. Find the gain in population in the 5 years. What was the gain for each 100 of the population during the 5 years? State this increase as a per cent of the population in 1900. What was the average per cent of increase per year?

Discussion. 61,805 − 52,600 = 9205 = gain in 5 years. 9205 ÷ 526 = 17.5 = gain per 100 of the population. Since, asking for the per cent of gain is the same as asking for the number of increase for each 100 of the population, therefore, stated in per cent this is 17.5 % of the population.

17.5% ÷ 5 = 3.5% = average per cent of increase per year, based on the population in 1900.

Example 2. In a certain machine $\frac{2}{5}$ of the energy supplied to the machine is lost in friction and other resistances. What is the per cent of efficiency? If $\frac{1}{8}$ of the loss of energy is in a certain part of the machine, what per cent of the total loss is in this part?

Discussion. If in a machine it is known that $\frac{2}{5}$ of the energy expended is wasted in frictional and other resistances, we say that 40% is wasted, meaning that $\frac{40}{100}$ is useless for doing work. This does not state the actual numerical amount of energy wasted; all it tells is that for every 100 units of work expended on the machine, 40 units disappear. Such percentages enable comparisons of different machines to be made. If one machine has an efficiency of 60% and another of 70%, we know that the second is 10% more efficient than the first. If we know that $\frac{1}{8}$ or $12\frac{1}{2}$% of the 40% loss is in a certain part, this gives a percentage of a percentage. The solution of the problem is:

$\frac{2}{5} =$ part of the energy lost,

$\frac{3}{5} = 60\% =$ efficiency of the machine,

$\frac{1}{8}$ of $\frac{2}{5} = \frac{1}{20} = 5\% =$ loss in the particular part of the machine.

62. Averages and per cent of error.—The data for practical calculations are in many cases either the result of measuring quantities, or of experimental observations, and in each case are liable to error. To obtain a result which can be relied upon, a number of measurements or observations are taken and the average or mean result calculated.

The average, or mean result, is obtained by adding all the measured results together and dividing the sum by the number of them. This average is accepted as the best approximation to the truth. The error of any particular observation is obtained by finding the difference between it and the average. This error can often be most conveniently expressed as a per cent, and is spoken of as the per cent of error. We always take the correct value, or in this case the average value, as the base.

Example. In measuring the diameter of a steel rod with a micrometer, the separate measurements are: 0.3562 in., 0.3569 in., 0.3567 in., 0.3570 in., and 0.3565 in. Find the average measurement, and the per cent of error in the largest and the smallest measurements.

Solution and discussion.

0.3562 in. + 0.3569 in. + 0.3567 in. + 0.3570 in. + 0.3565 in. = 1.7833 in.

1.7833 in. ÷ 5 = 0.35666 in. = average.

0.3570 in. − 0.35666 in. = 0.00034 in. = error in largest measurement.

Using the formula $r = p \div b$ gives

$r = 0.00034$ in. ÷ 0.35666 in. = 0.00095 + = 0.095% = per cent of error in largest measurement.

0.35666 in. − 0.3562 in. = 0.00046 in. = error in smallest measurement.

$r = 0.00046$ in. ÷ 0.35666 in. = 0.0013 = 0.13% = per cent of error in the smallest measurement.

It should be emphasized that the per cent of error in any measurement is always found by using the correct measurement as the base and the error as the percentage.

63. List prices and discounts.—The prices of machines and materials, printed in catalogs and price lists, are usually subject to discounts. Often the discount is so large that the list price gives no idea of the actual cost. In preparing an estimate, it is necessary to know what discounts are given from a price list.

Discounts are usually given thus: 60% and 10% off or simply 60 and 10 or perhaps "sixty and ten." This does not mean a discount of 70%, but that a discount of 60% is first made and then a discount of 10% on the remainder. Thus, if the list price is $3.50 with 60% and 10% off, we find 60% of $3.50, which is $2.10. Then deduct this from $3.50 leaving $1.40. Now get 10% of $1.40, which is $0.14, and deduct it from $1.40, leaving $1.26 as the actual cost.

Similarly we may have discounts of 40%, 10%, and 4%, or 40, 10, and 4 off. These are deducted in turn as with the two discounts.

EXERCISES 18

1. 62% of 2000 = ?   *Ans.* 1240.
2. What is ⅜% of $28.80?   *Ans.* $0.108.
3. 37½% of 4000 = ?   *Ans.* 1500.
4. 300 is 7½% of what number?   *Ans.* 4000.
5. What per cent of $104 is $18.20?   *Ans.* 17½%.
6. What per cent of 300 is 272?   *Ans.* 90⅔%.

7. The indicated horse-power of an engine is 10.6, the actual effective horse-power is 8.96. What per cent of the indicated horse-power is the actual? *Ans.* 84$\frac{36}{53}$%.

8. A bankrupt has $5760, and with that sum can pay 40% of his debts; find his entire indebtedness. *Ans.* $14,400.

9. For collecting a bill an attorney received $2.52, which was 1$\frac{1}{8}$% of the bill; find the amount of bill. *Ans.* $224.

10. A milkman sold milk at 7 cents a quart, which was 233$\frac{1}{3}$% of the cost; find cost per quart. *Ans.* 3 cents.

Suggestion. 233$\frac{1}{3}$% = $\frac{7}{3}$. If 7 cents is $\frac{7}{3}$ of the cost, what is the cost?

11. What is the net price per barrel of oil, the list price of which is $18.00, subject to a discount of 12$\frac{1}{2}$% and 4% off for cash?
Ans. $15.12.

12. A tradesman marks his goods at 25% above cost and deducts 12% of the amount of a customer's bill for cash. What per cent does he make?
Ans. 10%.

Suggestion. Suppose the cost is $20. The marked price is 25% above $20 or $25. A deduction of 12% on $25 is $3. Hence the selling price is $25 − $3 = $22. The gain is $22 − $20 = $2. What per cent is $2 of $20? This gives the gain per cent.

13. If 1225 pounds of coal were fired to a boiler and 152 pounds were taken out of the ashpit as ash and waste, what per cent of the coal was taken from the ashpit. *Ans.* 12.4+%.

14. The weight resting on the drivers of a locomotive is 158,700 pounds. If this is 68.72% of the total weight; find the weight of the locomotive.

15. A man who receives 42$\frac{1}{2}$ cents an hour works a day of 8 hours, and 4 hours overtime at pay for time and a half. What does he receive in all? What per cent is the overtime pay of the total?
Ans. $5.95; 42$\frac{6}{7}$%.

16. A firm increases the wages of its employees 12$\frac{1}{2}$%. Find the wages of a man who was getting $3.40. Of a boy who was getting $1.60 a day. A man now receives $6.30 a day. What did he receive before the increase? *Ans.* 3.82\frac{1}{2}$; $1.80; $5.60.

17. A tank whose capacity is 168 gallons, discharges 72 gallons per hour, which equals 25% less than it receives. In what time will it be filled? *Ans.* 7 hours.

Suggestion. If 72 gal. is 25% or $\frac{1}{4}$ less than it receives per hour, 72 gal. = $\frac{3}{4}$ of what it receives per hour. Hence it receives 96 gal. per hour. Then the tank receives 24 gal. per hour more than it discharges.

18. One mill is gaged at 767 barrels of flour a day, which equals 18% more than the amount for another. What is the value of the daily output of the latter at $5 a barrel? *Ans.* $3250.

19. The usual allowance made for shrinkage when casting iron pipes is $\frac{1}{8}$ in. per foot. What per cent is this? *Ans.* 1.04 + %.

20. Find the cost of an article that is listed at 80 cents, 40 and 6 off.
Ans. 45.12 cents.

21. Find the cost of a machine quoted at $25.50, 40% and 10% off with a further discount of 4% for cash.   *Ans.* $13.22.

22. When rock is crushed or broken into fragments of nearly uniform size it increases in bulk and has voids, or inter-spaces, of from 30 to 55 per cent of the whole volume. Find the number of cubic yards when crushed occupied by 1 cu. yd. of solid rock, if voids are (*a*) 30%; (*b*) 35%; (*c*) 40%; (*d*) 45%; (*e*) 55%.

Ans. (*a*) 1.43; (*b*) 1.54; (*c*) 1.67; (*d*) 1.82; (*e*) 2.22.

Suggestion. The volume of the rock, 1 cu. yd., is 30% less than or 70% of bulk of crushed rock. Using formula

$$b = p \div r \text{ gives } b = 1 \div 0.70 = 1.43 - . \ Ans.$$

23. A team of horses and a wagon cost, say $400. If money is worth 6%, depreciation in value of team and wagon is 25% per year, teamster's wages are $2.00 per day while working, and cost per month for keeping team is $18.50; find the amount that should be charged per day for man and team, counting 250 days actually worked per year.   *Ans.* $3.384.

24. In the preceding problem what would be the gain per year from the team if $5.00 a day was charged for services, deduction being made for depreciation in value?   *Ans.* $404.

25. In estimating the amount to charge per day for the use of a steam-roller, a contractor has the following data: first cost of steam-roller $3000; money worth 6%; days actually worked per year, 100; depreciation in value of the machine, $200 per year. Find price to be charged per day for use of roller.   *Ans.* $3.80.

26. The actual cost of removing a cubic yard of rock in excavating a certain canal is $1.10. What price should be put in the estimate, if 12% is to be allowed for superintending, and 10% on the cost, including superintending, is allowed for profit?   *Ans.* $1.3552.

27. A house depreciates in value each year at the rate of 4% of its value at the beginning of each year, and its value at the end of two years is $6451.20. Find the original value.   *Ans.* $7000.

Suggestion. $6451.20 ÷ 96 = $6720. This is the value at beginning of second year.

28. A house valued at $4000 rents for $27.50 per month. The repairs on house each year amount to $40, and the taxes are $17.50. What interest does the property pay on the investment, no allowance being made for change in value of house?   *Ans.* $6\frac{13}{16}$%.

29. In making a certain machine, 750 lb. of iron are used at an average cost of 8 cents per pound. There are used in the work on the machine, 20 hr. of time at 30 cents per hour, 7 hr. at 60 cents and 4 hr. at 16 cents. If 20% is allowed on cost as profit, what is the selling price of the machine? What will it be listed at if sold at 30 and 5 off?

Ans. $85 nearly, $127.82.

30. An article is listed at $225, and sells at 40 and 10 off. How will the 40% discount be changed to offset an increase of 15% in cost of production?   *Ans.* 31%, or better, 30%.

Solution. It is desired to find a first discount so that the net price, that is, the price after the discounts are made from the list price will be 15% more than the net price when discounts of 40% and 10% are used.

A discount of 40% and 10% off from $225 leaves $121.50. This is the old net price.

$121.50 + 15% of $121.50 = $139.725 = new net price.

$139.725 ÷ 0.90 = $155.25 = price after new first discount is deducted from list price.

$225 − $155.25 = $69.75 = amount of first discount.

$69.75 ÷ $225 = 0.31 = 31% = the first discount.

31. The composition of white metal is to be 4 parts by weight of copper, 9 antimony, and 97 tin. Express these as per cents, and find the weight of each material required to make 2376 lb. of the alloy.

Ans. Copper $3\frac{7}{11}$%, 86.4 lb.; antimony $8\frac{2}{11}$%, 194.4 lb.; tin $88\frac{2}{11}$%, 2095.2 lb.

32. For the two months ending Feb. 28, 1908, there were exported from the United States $27,531,617 worth of iron and steel, including machinery. During the same time in 1909 it was $21,276,547. Find the decrease per cent. *Ans.* 22.7 + %.

33. The output of Canadian pig iron for 1908 was 563.672 tons, a decrease of 3% from 1907. What was the output in 1907?
Ans. 581,105 tons.

34. Steel billets that were selling at $26 per ton dropped to $23 per ton. What is the per cent of reduction? *Ans.* $11\frac{7}{13}$%.

35. The water-power in use in the United States is 5,300,000 horse-power. The undeveloped is 8,100,000 horse-power. What per cent of the total water-power is developed? *Ans.* 39.55 + %.

36. A ton of coal from the Rock Island field has 11.57% moisture, and 6.27% of the dry coal is ash. How many pounds of ash in a ton of the coal? *Ans.* 110.89 +.

37. If 2.346 g. of an ore give 0.362 g. of copper, what per cent of copper does the ore contain? *Ans.* 15.43 + %.

38. 2.3656 Kg. of ore give 0.7 g. of gold and 2.5 g. of silver. Find the per cent of each. *Ans.* 0.0296 − %; 0.1057 − %.

39. A merchant buys rubber door mats at $48.00 a dozen less discounts of 40%, 15%, and 5%. What should he sell them apiece in order that he may make 35%? *Ans.* $2.62 −.

40. $1\frac{1}{4}$-in. basin plugs are listed by the jobber at $1.20 a dozen. The retailer gets discounts of 50 and 10 off, and sells them at 15 cents each. Find his gain per cent. *Ans.* $233\frac{1}{3}$%.

41. If the author gets 10% of the selling price of a book, how many books, selling at 75 cents each, must be sold to pay the author $117.30? *Ans.* 1564.

42. In a compound of two substances *A* and *B*, their weights are in the ratio of 1.3498 to 1. What is the per cent of each in the compound? *Ans.* 57.44 + %; 42.56 − %.

43. Two substances A and B form a compound and have a total weight of 3.267 g. If the compound has 24.725% of A and 75.275% of B, find the weight of each substance in the compound.

Ans. 0.8078 − g.; 2.4592 +g.

44. Find the cost of a steam boiler listed at $500 subject to discounts of 40%, 10%, and $7\frac{1}{2}$%.   *Ans.* $249.75.

45. Marshall Field and Co. quotes an article of silverware at $25 with discounts of 40, 10, 5, and 6% off in 10 days. Find net cost if paid in 10 days.   *Ans.* $12.06 −.

46. The recorded measurement of a city block is 528 ft. By chaining carefully the length is 527.75 ft. Find the per cent of error in the recorded length. How wide is a man's lot recorded as 30 ft.?

Ans. 0.047 + %; 29.986 − ft.

47. A sample of nickel-steel contained 24.51% of nickel and 0.16% of carbon. How much of each nickel and carbon in 2240 lb. of nickel-steel?

Ans. 549.024 lb.; 3.584 lb.

48. If a $3\frac{1}{2}$% nickel-steel rail is used to maintain a curve in a street-car track, it lasts three times as long as carbon-steel. How much will be saved per ton when one nickel-steel rail is worn out, if nickel-steel costs $56 per long ton and carbon-steel $28? It costs $2.00 a ton for laying, and the old rails are worth $16.00 per ton, besides 20 cents a pound is realized on the nickel.   *Ans.* $15.68.

49. In an experiment to show the loss of pressure for different kinds of valves in water pipes, a globe valve in a 3-in. pipe caused the pressure to fall from 80 lb. to 41 lb. per square inch; while a gate valve caused a loss of pressure of 4 lb. per square inch. Find (a) the per cent of loss for globe valve, (b) for gate valve, (c) what per cent loss through gate valve is of loss through globe valve.   *Ans.* $48\frac{3}{4}$%; 5%; 10.26 − %.

50. In an analysis of the best quality of crucible cast steel, the following was found: carbon 1.2%, silicon 0.112%, phosphorus 0.018%, manganese 0.36%, sulphur 0.02%, iron 98.29%. Find the number of pounds of each substance if the total weight is 176.5 lb.

Ans. 2.118; 0.1977 − ; 0.0318 − ; 0.6354; 0.0353; 173.4818 +.

51. Find the cost of the following at 83% discount:

350 ft., 8-in. sewer pipe	at $0.50
4 elbows	at $2.00
3 T branches	at $2.25
4 traps	at $6.60

Ans. $36.75.

52. The mean effective pressure on the piston of a steam engine, found from the indicator diagram, was 59.75 lb. per square inch. The boiler pressure was 87 lb. per square inch. What per cent of the boiler pressure was the mean effective pressure?   *Ans.* 68.7 − %.

53. The grade of a railroad track is given in per cent. A grade of 1% is a rise of 1 ft. in 100 ft. If a railroad has a constant grade of $1\frac{1}{4}$%, what is the rise in $3\frac{1}{2}$ miles?   *Ans.* 231 ft.

54. The total rise in a $1\frac{3}{4}\%$ grade is 43.6 ft. Find the length of the track having this grade. *Ans.* $2491\frac{3}{7}$ ft.

55. A railroad rises 112.7 ft. in $3\frac{1}{2}$ miles. Find the average grade. *Ans.* $0.61 - \%$.

56. The mechanical efficiency of a machine is the relation between the work put into the machine and the work gotten out of it. Mechanical efficiency is usually stated as a per cent. Thus, if 100 units of work are put into a machine and only 80 units gotten out the mechanical efficiency, or simply the efficiency, is 80%. What is the efficiency of the engine of exercise 7?

57. At what advance must a shopkeeper mark goods costing 90 cents that he may allow a 20% discount and yet gain 25%? *Ans.* $50\frac{5}{8}$ cents.

58. A man purchases ice at 50 cents per 100 lb. At what rate must he sell it after it has lost 10% of its weight by melting to gain 20%?

64. Interest.—Interest is money that is paid for the use of money. It is usually reckoned at a certain rate per cent per year. The base on which the interest is reckoned is called the **principal.**

In percentage, the time did not enter, but in reckoning interest the time has to be taken into account. The interest on a sum of money for *one year* at a certain rate is the principal multiplied by the rate; for *two years* it is twice as much; and for any period of time it is the interest for one year multiplied by the time in years.

If p stands for principal, I for interest, r for rate per cent, and t for time in years, the interest is found by the formula

$$I = p \times r \times t.$$

The **amount,** A, is the principal plus the interest.

Many short methods for reckoning interest can be given, but here it is not the intention to enter into them.

Example 1. Find the interest and amount of $350 for 5 years at 6%.

$$I = p \times r \times t = \$350 \times 0.06 \times 5 = \$105.00. \ Ans.$$
$$A = p + I = \$350 + \$105.00 = \$455.00. \ Ans.$$

Example 2. Find the interest on $750 for 2 yr. 7 mo. at 8%.

Here the time is $2\frac{7}{12}$ years, since in getting the time in years we use 12 months for a year, 30 days for a month, and 360 days for a year.

$$\therefore I = \$750 \times 0.08 \times 2\frac{7}{12} = \$155.00. \ Ans.$$

It is usually best to use cancellation.

$$\text{Thus,} \frac{750 \times 8 \times 31}{100 \times 12} = 155.$$

Example 3. Find the interest on $375 for 2 yr. 5 mo. 15 da. at 5%.

Here the time is $\frac{885}{360}$ years.

$$\therefore I = \$375 \times 0.05 \times \tfrac{885}{360} = \$46.09. \ Ans.$$

EXERCISES 19

Find the interest and amount of each of the following:

1. $700 for 3 yr. at 8%.   *Ans.* $168.00; $868.00.
2. $14.30 for 2 yr. 9 mo. at 8%.   *Ans.* $3.15; $17.45.
3. $245.60 for 2 yr. 7 mo. 21 da. at 8%.   *Ans.* $51.90; $297.50.
4. $436.75 for 1 yr. 2 mo. 15 da. at 5%.   *Ans.* $26.39; $463.14.
5. $325.25 for 2 yr. 9 mo. 12 da. at 6½%.   *Ans.* $58.84; $384.09.
6. $87.50 for 3 yr. 3 mo. at 7%.   *Ans.* $19.91; $107.41.
7. $480 for 6 yr. 3 mo. at 15%.   *Ans.* $450; $930.
8. $18.20 for 9 yr. 9 mo. 9 da. at 5¾%.   *Ans.* $10.23; $28.43.
9. A note for $225 at 6% runs for 9 mo. What is the amount of the note when due?   *Ans.* $235.13.
10. A note for $390.00 at 7% runs for 3 yr. 6 mo. What is the amount due?   *Ans.* $485.55.

CHAPTER VII

RATIO AND PROPORTION

65. Ratio.—There are several ways of stating the relation of one quantity to another. If the size or magnitude of the quantities are thought of, a very convenient way of comparing them is to state the ratio of one to the other.

The **ratio** of one number to another is the quotient of the first number divided by the second.

Thus, the ratio of $6 to $2 is 3, and may be stated in the form $\frac{\$6}{\$2}$ or $6 : $2. In either case it is read "the ratio of $6 to $2."

From the idea of a ratio it is evident that we can state a ratio between two magnitudes only when the magnitudes are alike. That is, a ratio cannot be stated between such quantities as dollars and bushels.

The two numbers used in a ratio are called the **terms** of the ratio. The first one is named the **antecedent** and is the dividend; the second is named the **consequent** and is the divisor.

The ratio $2 : 3$ is the **inverse** of the ratio $3 : 2$.

Since a ratio in the form $4 : 3$ is an indicated division or a fraction, the principles applying in division or to a fraction likewise apply to a ratio.

The expressions *"in the same ratio as," "in the same proportion," "proportionally,"* and *"pro rata"* all have practically the same meaning.

When it is said that $20 is divided between two men in the ratio of 2 to 3, it is meant that one gets $2 as often as the other gets $3. That is, of each $5, one gets $2 and the other $3. Hence one gets $\frac{2}{5}$ of $20 or $8, and the other gets $\frac{3}{5}$ of $20 or $12.

EXERCISES 20

1. Find the value of the following ratios: $8:2$; $9:4$; $17:2\frac{1}{2}$; 44 hours: 3 hours; 7 bu.:2 bu.; $4\frac{1}{2}:3\frac{1}{2}$; $9\frac{1}{3}:16$.

2. A room is 16 ft. by 12 ft. What is the ratio of its length to its width?

3. Two gear wheels have 80 teeth and 30 teeth respectively. What is the ratio of the numbers of teeth?

4. One city has a population of 8000 and a second a population of 20,000. What is the ratio of their populations? What part is the first of the second? What per cent? How many times as large as the first is the second? What difference is there in the ideas involved in the questions?

5. Write the inverse ratios to the following: 7:2; 9:2⅓; 10 ft.:90 ft.; 23½:2⅘.

6. Divide $50 between A and B in the ratio of 3:7.

7. A man rode 250 miles partly by rail and partly by boat. What distance did he travel by each if their ratio is as 3 to 2?

Ans. 150 mi.; 100 mi.

8. Fifty-one students entered a class and 33 of them finished the work. What per cent finished? What is the ratio of the number that finished to the whole number?

9. A worm wheel makes 6 turns per minute and the worm 180 turns per minute. What is the ratio of the reduction of speed? *Ans.* 30 to 1.

66. Proportion.—A proportion is a statement of equality between two ratios.

Thus, 2:3 =4:6 and 4 men:8 men =$6:$12, are proportions.

The first and last terms of a proportion are called the **extremes.** The second and third terms are called the **means.**

In the first proportion above, 2 and 6 are the extremes and 3 and 4 the means.

By inspecting several proportions the following principles will be evident:

(1) *The product of the means of any proportion is equal to the product of the extremes.*

(2) *The product of the two means divided by either extreme gives the other extreme.*

(3) *The product of the two extremes divided by either mean gives the other mean.*

Example 1. Find the value of h from the proportion 25 : 100 = 7 : h.

Solution. Applying principle (2), $h = \dfrac{100 \times 7}{25} = 28$. *Ans.*

Example 2. If 15 tons of coal cost $63 what will 27 tons cost at the same rate per ton?

Solution. Since the same relation holds between the cost

prices as between the amounts of coal, the ratio of 15 tons to 27 tons must equal the ratio $63 to the cost of 27 tons. Let x stand for the number of dollars 27 tons cost, and we can state the proportion,

$$15 : 27 = 63 : x.$$
$$\therefore x = \frac{27 \times 63}{15} = 113.40.$$
$$\therefore 27 \text{ tons cost } \$113.40. \ Ans.$$

Example 3. If 25 men can do a piece of work in 30 days, in how many days can 35 men do the same work?

Solution. It is evident that 35 men can do the work in less time than 25 men, hence the ratio of the number of days is equal to the inverse ratio of the number of men. Using x for the number of days required,

$$35 : 25 = 30 : x.$$
$$\therefore x = \frac{25 \times 30}{35} = 21\tfrac{3}{7}.$$

$\therefore$ 35 men can do the work in $21\tfrac{3}{7}$ days. *Ans.*

Example 4. An inclined plane as shown in the figure rises 38 ft. in 100 ft., find the height h it will rise in 28 ft.

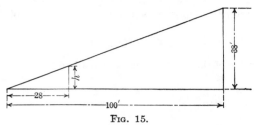

FIG. 15.

Solution. Here the proportion is

$$100 : 28 = 38 : h.$$
$$\therefore h = \frac{28 \times 38}{100} = 10.64.$$

$\therefore$ the rise in 28 ft. is 10.64 ft. *Ans.*

The proportion could as well be stated $100 : 38 = 28 : h$.

Definition. If the rise of a road bed is h ft. in 100 ft., the **grade** of the road is $\dfrac{h}{100}$, or the ratio of the rise to the horizontal distance.   Thus, if a road rises 3 ft. in 100 ft. the grade is $\dfrac{3}{100} = 3\%$.

Example 5.   What is the grade of a road bed that rises 1.2 ft. in a horizontal distance of 40 ft.?

Solution.   Let h stand for the number of feet rise in 100 ft. It is evident that the ratio $\dfrac{h}{100}$ = the ratio $\dfrac{1.2}{40}$. But $\dfrac{1.2}{40}$ = 0.03.   ∴ the grade is 0.03 or 3%, *Ans.*

Example 6.   If a bell metal is 25 parts copper to 12 parts tin, what is the weight of each in a bell weighing 1850 lb.?

Solution.   The ratio of the number of parts of each metal to the whole number of parts equals the ratio of the weight of each metal to the whole weight.   Use c to stand for the number of pounds of copper, and t for the tin.   Then we have

$$25 : 37 = c : 1850,$$
$$\text{and } 12 : 37 = t : 1850.$$
$$\therefore c = \frac{25 \times 1850}{37} = 1250,$$
$$\text{and } t = \frac{12 \times 1850}{37} = 600.$$

∴ weight of copper is 1250 lb. and tin is 600 lb. *Ans.*

EXERCISES 21

Find the value of the letter in the exercises 1 to 6.

1. $17:45 = 14:x$.   *Ans.* $x = 37\frac{1}{17}$.

2. $3\frac{3}{4}:9\frac{1}{5} = 6:x$.   *Ans.* $x = 15\frac{7}{15}$.

3. $16\frac{1}{5}:29\frac{1}{2} = 50\frac{2}{5}:x$.   *Ans.* $x = 88\frac{1}{2}$.

4. $3:x = 5:25$.   *Ans.* $x = 15$.

5. $75:85 = x:170$.   *Ans.* $x = 150$.

6. $r:11 = 17:121$.   *Ans.* $r = 1\frac{6}{11}$.

7. If a train travels 378 miles in 11 hours, how far will it travel in 17 hours?   *Ans.* $584\frac{2}{11}$ miles.

8. If 10 men can do a piece of work in 20 days, how long will it take 25 men to do it?   *Ans.* 8 days.

9. If a ship sails 256 miles in $11\frac{1}{2}$ hours, how far will it sail a the same rate in 179 hours?   *Ans.* $3984\frac{16}{23}$ miles.

10. The roof of a house rises 2 ft. in a run of 3 ft., how far will it rise in a run of 20 ft.?   *Ans.* 13 ft. 4 in.

11. A road bed rises $2\frac{1}{2}$ ft. in 200 ft., what is the grade?   In how many feet will it rise 1 ft.?   *Ans.* $1\frac{1}{4}\%$; 80.

12. If 16½ tons of hay cost $61.875, find the cost of 28 tons at the same rate.   *Ans.* $105.

13. The mixture for a casting has 4 parts of copper, 3 parts lead, and 2 parts tin. How many pounds of each in a casting weighing 96 lb.?   *Ans.* 42⅔; 32; 21⅓.

Work the following 4 exercises by proportion.

14. What per cent is 59.1 of 51.3?

Solution. 100% stands for the base, then, using x for the number of per cent required, the proportion is

$$51.3 : 51.9 = 100 : x.$$

$$\therefore x = \frac{59.1 \times 100}{51.3} = 115.2.$$

$$\therefore 59.1 \text{ is } 115.2\% \text{ of } 51.3.$$

15. 46 is what per cent of 79?   *Ans.* 58.23 − %.

16. 146 is 17% of what number?   *Ans.* 858.82 +.

17. 3% of a number is 426, what is the number?   *Ans.* 14,200.

67. Measuring heights.—There are several methods for determining the height of a standing tree. One of the simplest is to measure the shadow of the tree and the shadow of a straight pole of known length set upright in the ground. Then if H stands for the height of the tree, h for the height of the pole, S for the length of the shadow of the tree, s for that of the pole, we have the proportion

$$s : S = h : H.$$

EXERCISES 22

1. Find the height of a tree that casts a shadow 115 ft. long when a pole 8 ft. high casts a shadow of 5 ft.

Solution. 5 : 8 = 115 : H.

$$\therefore H = \frac{115 \times 8}{5} = 184.$$

$\therefore$ height of tree is 184 ft. *Ans.*

2. Find the height of a church steeple that casts a shadow 84 ft. long when a pole 11 ft. long casts a shadow of 7 ft. 9 in. *Ans.* 119 ft. nearly.

The two following methods with the figures are given in Bulletin 36 of the Bureau of Forestry, U. S. Department of Agriculture.

(1) A method used when the sun is not shining is to set two poles in a line with the tree as shown in Fig. 16. From a point S on one pole sight across the second pole to the base and to the top of the tree. Let an assistant note the points a and b where the lines of vision cross the second pole and measure the distance between these points, ab, also measure the distance from the sighting point on the first pole to the base

of the tree, SB, and to the lowest point on the second pole, Sb.   Then the following proportion is true:

$$Sb:SB = ab:AB.$$

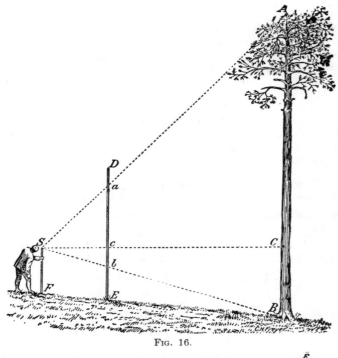

FIG. 16.

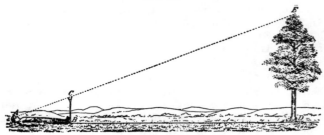

FIG. 17.

3. Find the height of a tree when $Sb = 6$ ft., $SB = 40$ ft., and $ab = 9$ ft.
Ans. 60 ft.

(2) Another method sometimes used is as follows: The observer walks on level ground to a point A at a convenient distance AD from the foot of the tree.   He then lies on his back as shown in Fig. 17.   An assistant

notes on an upright staff erected at his feet the exact point C where his line of vision to the top of the tree E crosses the staff. The height of the staff BC is measured, and his own height AB from his feet to his eyes, then the following proportion is true:

$$AB:BC = AD:DE.$$

4. Find the height of the tree DE if $AB = 5\frac{1}{2}$ ft., $BC = 8$ ft., and $AD = 90$ ft.   *Ans.* 131 ft. nearly.

68. The lever.—A stiff bar or rod supported at some pivotal point, about which it can move freely, is called a **lever**. The pivotal point is called the **fulcrum**. The lever enters in one form or another into many mechanical devices.

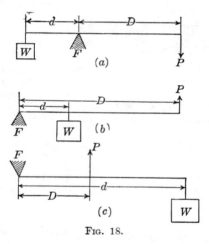

Fig. 18.

In Fig. 18, F stands for fulcrum, W for the weight lifted, P for the force that does the lifting, D for the distance from the fulcrum to the point of application of the force, and d for the distance from the fulcrum to the point where the weight is attached. In all possible relations of the fulcrum, weight, and force the following proportion holds:

$$P:W = d:D.$$

That is, the applied force is to the weight inversely as their distances from the fulcrum. This means that a small force will balance a larger weight only if the weight is nearer the fulcrum than the force.

EXERCISES 23

1. Given $P = 150$ lb., $D = 12\frac{1}{2}$ ft., $d = 1\frac{1}{2}$ ft., find W.   *Ans.* 1250 lb.

2. Given $P = 200$ lb., $D = 9\frac{3}{4}$ ft., $W = 775$ lb., find d.

Ans. 2 ft. 6.2 − in.

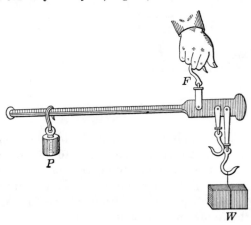

3. Given $P = 160$ lb., $W = 900$ lb., $d = 1\frac{1}{4}$ ft., find D.

Ans. 7 ft. $\frac{3}{8}$ in.

4. Given $W = 160$ lb., $D = 3\frac{1}{2}$ ft., $d = 8\frac{1}{3}$ ft., find P.

Ans. 381 lb. nearly.

5. In a wire cutter the wire is placed $\frac{1}{2}$ in. from the fulcrum and the pressure of the hand is 7 in. from the fulcrum. Find the resistance of the wire if the hand exerts a force of 40 lb.

Ans. 560 lb.

Fig. 19.

6. In pulling a nail from a board with a hammer as shown in Fig. 19, find the resistance of the nail at the start if $P = 50$ lb., $D = 10$ in., and $d = 1\frac{1}{2}$ in.   *Ans.* $333\frac{1}{3}$ lb.

7. In the ordinary steel-yard, Fig. 20, what must be the weight P to

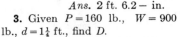

Fig. 20.

balance a weight W of $17\frac{1}{2}$ lb. if it is $1\frac{1}{4}$ in. from fulcrum to application of W and $8\frac{1}{2}$ in. from application of P to fulcrum?   *Ans.* 2 lb. 9.2 − oz.

8. If the steel-yard is turned over so that the distance from the fulcrum to W is $\frac{1}{2}$ in., what weight W will $1\frac{1}{2}$ lb. at P balance when P is $20\frac{3}{4}$ in. from the fulcrum?   *Ans.* $62\frac{1}{4}$ lb.

69. Hydraulic machines.—A principle known as *Pascal's Law* states that pressure exerted on a liquid in a closed vessel is transmitted equally and undiminished in all directions.

In Fig. 21, if the area of a is 1 sq. in. then a pressure of 1 lb. at a gives a pressure of 1 lb. on each square inch of the surface of C. If the area of the top of C is 100 sq. in. then a pressure of 1 lb. at a will lift a weight of 100 lb. at A.

If a, A, p, and P are the areas and pressures respectively then we have the proportion

$$a : A = p : P.$$

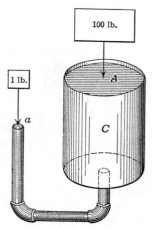

FIG. 21.

EXERCISES 24

1. A pressure of 5 lb. on the cork of a jug filled with water gives how many pounds pressure tending to force out the bottom of the jug? The area of the cork is $1\frac{1}{2}$ sq. in. and the area of the bottom is 245.6 sq. in.

Ans. $818\frac{2}{3}$ lb.

2. A hydraulic lifter used to raise heavy weights has the pressure applied to a piston having an area of $\frac{1}{2}$ sq. in. by a lever. From the fulcrum to the point attached to the small piston is 4 in., and to the point where a force of 100 lb. is applied is 22 in. Find the weight that can be raised on a piston having an area of 75.6 sq. in.

Solution. Let x = pressure in pounds applied on small piston.
Then $100:x=4:22$. From which $x=550$.
And $0.5:75.6=550:P$.

$$\therefore P = \frac{550 \times 75.6}{0.5} = 82,160.$$

Hence a weight of 82,160 lb. can be raised.

3. A supply pipe for a 14-in. plunger hydraulic elevator piston is $1\frac{1}{4}$ sq. in. in area, and the pressure in the supply pipe is pumped up to 150 lb. per square inch. What is the total pressure on the 14-in. plunger if it has an area of 153.94 sq. in.? *Ans.* 23,091 lb.

CHAPTER VIII

DENSITY AND SPECIFIC GRAVITY

70. Density.—Experience tells us that some bodies are heavier than others; that is, of two bodies of the same size, one weighs more than the other. Take a cubic foot of metal and one of wood; suppose the metal weighs 500 lb. and the wood 50 lb., then the metal is ten times as heavy as the wood, or the ratio of their densities is as 10 to 1. We also say that the density of the metal is 500 lb. per cubic foot.

Water has a density of about 62.5 lb. per cubic foot. In the metric system the density of water under standard conditions is one gram per cubic centimeter.

The **density** of a body is its mass per unit volume. For our purpose the mass is the same as the weight. Strictly speaking, the weight of a body near the earth is the force with which the earth attracts the mass of the body.

71. Specific gravity.—The term specific gravity is used for the ratio of the densities of two bodies. Thus, the specific gravity of the metal with reference to the wood is 10, which means that the metal is ten times as heavy as the wood. It should be carefully noticed that the specific gravity of a substance is an abstract number, that is, a number with no name attached.

72. Standards.—For convenience the standard to which other substances are referred, in stating specific gravities, is water for solids and liquids.

RULE. *The specific gravity of a substance is obtained by finding the weight of a certain volume of it and dividing this weight by the weight of the same volume of the standard.*

Thus, to find the specific gravity of a stone it is necessary to find its weight, and the weight of an equal volume of water. The weight of the stone divided by the weight of the water gives the specific gravity of the stone.

The specific gravity of any other body could be found in the same manner. Some difficulty might be found in doing

94

the weighing, but a little ingenuity will devise a plan. Various methods for doing the weighing are discussed in physics. Water is taken as the standard because of its abundance. All substances can be referred to it, but gases are usually compared with air or hydrogen gas.

If w stands for the weight of the body whose specific gravity is to be found, s the weight of the same volume of the standard, and g for the specific gravity, the rule may be stated as a formula:

$$w \div s = g.$$

73. Use.—Tables of the specific gravities of the various substances are given for use in making computations. In **Table VIII** are given the specific gravities of a few of the more common substances.

If it is required to find the weight of a block of iron 2 ft. by 3 ft. by 1 ft. we could find the number of cubic feet in the block which is 6. This times the weight of a cubic foot of water gives the weight of an equal volume of water, or $62.5 \times 6 = 375$ lb. The weight of the water multiplied by the specific gravity of iron gives the weight of the iron, or 375 lb. $\times 7.2 = 2700$ lb.

In terms of the letters already used, since $w \div s = g$,

$$w = s \times g.$$

Example 1. Find the specific gravity of a rock if 1 cu. ft. of it weighs 182 lb.

Solution. Since water weighs 62.5 lb. per cubic foot the specific gravity of the rock is found thus:

$$182 \text{ lb.} \div 62.5 \text{ lb.} = 2.912.$$

$\therefore$ specific gravity of the rock is 2.912.

Example 2. How many cubic inches are there in 1 lb. of cork, if its specific gravity is 0.24?

Solution. Since 1728 cu in, of water weigh 62.5 lb. 1728 cu. in. of cork weigh 0.24×62.5 lb.

$\therefore$ 1 cu. in. of cork weighs $\dfrac{0.24 \times 62.5}{1728}$ lb.

And $1 \div \dfrac{0.24 \times 62.5}{1728} = \dfrac{1728}{0.24 \times 62.5} = 115.2.$

$\therefore$ there are 115.2 cu. in. in 1 lb. of cork.

EXERCISES 25

1. Find the weight of 176 cu. in. of copper.   *Ans.* 56+ lb.
2. Find the weight of 37 cu. ft. of cast iron.   *Ans.* 16,650 lb.
3. A stone weighs 3 lb. in air and 1.75 lb. in water. Find its specific gravity.   *Ans.* 2.4.
4. What is the specific gravity of a substance 40 cu. in. of which weighs 6 lb.?   *Ans.* 4.147+.
5. Two cubic feet of cast iron immersed in water weigh how much?
Solution. From **Table VIII**, 2 cu. ft. of cast iron weigh in air 2×450 lb. $= 900$ lb.
2 cu. ft. of water weigh 2×62.5 lb. $= 125$ lb.
Weight of iron in water $= 900$ lb. $- 125$ lb. $= 775$ lb.
6. A piece of metal weighing 243 lb. floats in mercury (s. g. 13.6) with $\frac{9}{17}$ of its volume immersed. Determine the volume and the specific gravity of the metal.   *Ans.* s. g. $= 7.2$; Vol. $= 933.1$ in.^{3}
7. The specific gravity of ice is 0.92, of sea water 1.025. What part of an iceberg is below the surface of the water when floating?
          Ans. 0.8975.
8. A balloon containing 10,200 cu. ft. will lift how great a weight if filled with hydrogen gas?   *Ans.* Less than 756.5 lb.
9. An irregular shaped mass of iron (s. g. 7.22) weighed in air 126 lb. Find its volume. What would be its weight if immersed in water?
          Ans. 482.5 − in.^{3}; 108.55 − lb.
10. A pond $\frac{3}{4}$ acre in area is frozen over. Find the weight in tons of the ice if it is $3\frac{1}{2}$ in. thick and the specific gravity of ice is 0.92.
          Ans. 273.95 tons.
11. Find the weight of a cubic meter of iron (s. g. 7.22) in kilograms. What is the weight in pounds?   *Ans.* 7220 Kg.; 15935.6 lb.
12. Find the number of liters in a vat 2 m. $\times 75$ cm. $\times 50$ cm. Also find the weight in Kg. of the sulphuric acid (s.g. 1.84) required to fill it.
          Ans. 750 l.; 1380 Kg.
13. Find the value of 17 l. of sulphuric acid at 5 cents per Kg.
          Ans. $1.56.
14. Mercury weighs 13.596 times as much as water at its greatest density. What is the pressure per square centimeter of a column of mercury 76 cm. high?   *Ans.* 1033.296 g.
15. A column of mercury how high would cause a pressure per square inch equal to 14.7 lb.?   *Ans.* 29.89+ in.
16. A tank 1.85 m. long, 1.35 m. wide, and 85 cm. deep is filled with sea water (s. g. 1.025). What is the weight of the water?
          Ans. 2175.95 − Kg.
17. Sandstone of specific gravity 2.5 is crushed. Find the weight of 1 cu. yd. of the crushed stone if the voids are 35%. (See Ex. 22, p. 80).
Solution. If 35% are voids, 65% is rock.
Weight $= 0.65 \times 27 \times 62.5 \times 2.5 = 2742 +$ lb.

18. Granite of specific gravity 2.8 is crushed. Find the weight of 1 cu. yd. of the crushed rock if voids are 40%. *Ans.* 2835 lb.

19. A casting of iron when immersed in water displaces 2 quarts; find the weight of the casting. *Ans.* 30 lb.

20. An irregular shaped steel forging was found to displace 6.75 quarts of water; find the weight of the forging. (Use s. g. of steel = 7.85).

Ans. 111 lb. nearly.

21. A wooden pattern for a casting weighs 2¾ pounds. An aluminum casting is to be made. Find the weight of the casting if the specific gravity of the wood is 0.52 and that of the aluminum is 2.6.

Ans. 13¾ lb.

CHAPTER IX

POWERS AND ROOTS

74. Powers.—When we have several numbers multiplied together, as $3 \times 4 \times 6 = 72$, we call the numbers 3, 4, and 6, **factors** and 72 the **product.** If now we make all the factors alike, as $3 \times 3 \times 3 \times 3 = 81$, we call the product by the special name **power.** We say 81 is a power of 3, and 3 is the **base** of the power.

A **power** is a product obtained by using a base a certain number of times as a factor.

If the base is used twice as a factor the power is called the second power; three times as a factor, the third power; and so on for any number of times.

75. Exponent of a power.—Instead of $3 \times 3 \times 3 \times 3$, we may write 3^4. The small figure, placed at the right and above the base, shows how many times the base is to be used as a factor, and is called an **exponent.**

The **exponent** of a **power** is a number placed to the right and above a base to show how many times the base is used as a factor.

It should be noted that the use of the exponent gives us a short concise way of writing a continued product where the factors are all alike.

76. Squares, cubes, involution.—The second power of a number is called the **square** of the number, as 3^2.

The third power of a number is called the **cube** of the number, as 5^3.

The higher powers have no special names. 3^4 is called the **fourth power** of 3, 5^7 the **seventh power** of 5, etc.

Involution is the process of finding the powers of numbers.

EXERCISES 26

1. Find the square of 7, of 27, of 92, of 736. Find the square of the square of 3, of 7, of 10.

2. Find the cube of 7, of 8. Find the square of the cube of 3.

Ans. 343; 512; 729.

3. Find the fourth power of 5. What is the difference between the fourth power of a number and the square of the square of the same number?

4. Find values of the following: (a) 792^2, (b) 35^3, (c) 3^4, (d) 2^{16}.

Ans. (a) 627,264, (b) 42,875, (c) 81, (d) 65,536.

77. Roots.—If we take 9 and separate it into the two equal factors 3 and 3, that is, $9 = 3 \times 3$, then one of these factors, 3, is called the **square root** of 9. The process is just the inverse of that by which the power is found. Similarly $64 = 4 \times 4 \times 4$, and we say 4 is the **cube root** of 64.

The **square root** of a number is one of the two equal factors into which a number is divided.

The **cube root** is one of the three equal factors into which a number is divided; the **fourth root** is one of the four equal factors; and so on for the higher roots.

78. Radical sign and index of root.—To indicate a root, we use the sign $\sqrt{}$, which is called the **radical sign**. A small figure, called the **index** of the root, is placed in the opening of the radical sign to show what root is to be taken. Thus, $\sqrt[3]{64}$ indicates the cube root of 64. The small 3 is the index of the root.

Since the square root is the most frequently written root, the index 2 is omitted. Thus, the square root of 625 is written $\sqrt{625}$ and not $\sqrt[2]{625}$. Higher roots are indicated as $\sqrt[4]{243}$, $\sqrt[7]{128}$.

Evolution is the process of finding a root of a given number.

79. Square root.—The numbers 1, 4, 9, 16, 25, 36, 49, 64, 81, which are the squares of the numbers 1, 2, 3, 4, 5, 6, 7, 8, 9, respectively, should be carefully remembered. It will be noticed that these are the only whole numbers less than 100 of which we can find the square roots. Such numbers as these are called **perfect squares.** As we pass to numbers above 100, the perfect squares become still more scarce.

The square root of 49 is 7, but the square root of 56 cannot be expressed as a whole number, nor can it be expressed as a decimal exactly. We can find it to any desired number of decimal places, and so as accurately as we wish. It remains to devise a method by which this may be done.

The practical man who wishes to find the square root of a number does not care greatly why he goes through a certain process; but it is very important to him that he shall be able to find the root quickly and accurately. In what follows then the attempt is made to tell in as simple a manner as possible how to find the root.

80. Process for the square root of a perfect square.— *Example 1.* Find $\sqrt{522729}$.

Explanation.	*Process.*

First, separate the number into **periods** of two figures each, beginning at the right, and placing a mark between them. The number of periods thus formed is equal to the number of figures in the root.

$$52'27'29\ (723\ \textit{Ans.}$$
$$\underline{49}$$
$$142\ \overline{\smash{|}\ 327}$$
$$\underline{|\ 284}$$
$$1443\ \overline{\smash{|}\ 4329}$$
$$\underline{|\ 4329}$$

Find the largest perfect square which is equal to, or less than, the left-hand period, 52. This perfect square is 49. Write it under 52; and put its square root, 7, to the right as the first figure of the root. Now subtract 49 from 52 and bring down the next period, 27, and unite with the remainder 3, thus obtaining 327.

Take twice 7, the first figure of the root, and write it to the left of 327. Find how many times this, 14, is contained in 32, which is 2, for the second figure of the root. Place this figure 2 in the root, and also to the right of 14, making 142. Now multiply 142 by 2, and write the product, 284, under 327. Subtract 284 from 327 and bring down and unite the next period, 29, with the remainder, 43, thus obtaining 4329.

In the above work 327 is called the **first remainder;** 14, the **trial divisor;** 142, the **true divisor;** and 4329, the **second remainder.**

Next multiply 72 by 2, and write it at the left of 4329 as the second trial divisor. Find how many times 144 is contained in 432, which is 3, for the third figure of the root. Place this figure, 3, in the root and also at the right of 144, making 1443, the second true divisor. Multiply 1443 by 3 and write the product under 4329. This gives no remainder. Therefore, 723 is the exact square root of 522,729, that is, $723 \times 723 = 522,729$.

Example 2. Find $\sqrt{6780816}$.

Explanation.

First, separate the number into periods of two figures each as in example 1. As before, we find the greatest square, 4, in the left-hand period, write it

Process.

$$6'78'08'16\,(2604\ \ Ans.$$
$$\underline{4}$$
$$46\ \ |\overline{278}$$
$$\ \ \ \ |276$$
$$5204\ |\ \overline{20816}$$
$$\ \ \ \ \ \ |\ 20816$$

under 6 and put the square root, 2, of this square for the first figure of the root. Subtract the square, 4, from 6, and bring down the next period, 78, and unite it with the 2, making the first remainder, 278.

Take twice 2 for a trial divisor. Find how many times it is contained in the first remainder, excepting the right-hand figure; that is, find how many times 4 is contained in 27. The number is 6, which write as the second figure of the root, and also at the right of the trial divisor. This makes 46 the true divisor. Multiply the true divisor by 6, and subtract the product, 276, from the first remainder. Bring down and unite the next period to the difference, making the second remainder, 208.

Multiply the root already found by 2, and get the second trial divisor, 52. Find how many times this is contained in 20, which gives 0 for the next figure of the root. Place this 0 in the root and also to the right of 52, making 520, the second true divisor. Now, since the 0 written in the root is the multiplier, nothing is gained by multiplying the true divisor by it, and subtracting from 208. This part of the process is omitted, and the next period, 16, is united with 208, making 20,816, the third remainder.

The third trial divisor is twice the root, 260, which gives

520. This is contained in 2081, 4 times. Place the 4 as the next figure of the root, and also to the right of 520, making 5204, the third true divisor. Multiply this by 4 and subtract from the third remainder. As the remainder is zero, 2604 is the exact square root of 6,780,816.

81. Square root of a number containing a decimal.–

Example. Find $\sqrt{665.1241}$.

Here the division into periods is made by beginning at the decimal point and going in both directions. The rest of the work is the same as in examples 1 and 2, **Art. 80.**

Process.

$$6'65.'12'41\,(\underline{25.79}\ Ans.$$
$$\underline{4}$$
$$45\,\overline{\big|265}$$
$$225$$
$$507\,\overline{\big|4012}$$
$$3549$$
$$5149\,\overline{\big|46341}$$
$$46341$$

The student should note that the second trial divisor, 50, is contained 8 times in the first three figures of the second remainder, 4012. However, if 8 were used as the root, it would give a number larger than 4012 when the true divisor was multiplied by it. The relations noted here should help to make clear why we give to the trial divisor its name.

The decimal point in the root is so placed that there are as many whole number *figures* in the root as there are whole number *periods* in the number of which the root is extracted. The position of the decimal point can also be determined so that there will be as many decimal places in the root as there are decimal periods in the number of which the root is being extracted.

If the decimal part of the number consists of an odd number of figures a cipher is annexed to make a full period at the right.

Thus, in pointing off 53.76542 into periods it is 53'.76'54'20.

82. Roots not exact.—Most numbers are not perfect squares, but the roots may be found to any desired number of decimal places. When extracting the root of a number not a perfect square, one must determine how many decimal places he wishes in the answer, and then annex ciphers to the right of the number till there are as many decimal **periods** as there are to be decimal **places** in the root. The root is then extracted in the usual manner. We stop when the desired number of figures is found in the root.

Example. Find $\sqrt{27}$ to three decimal places in the root.

Explanation.

Since three decimal places are required in the root, annex three periods of ciphers to the right of 27. These are the decimal periods. Extract the root as before. Place the decimal point in the root as in example of **Art. 81.** It will be noticed

Process.

$$
\begin{array}{r}
27.'00'00'00(5.196 \ Ans. \\
25 \\
\hline
101 \quad \overline{200} \\
101 \\
\hline
1029 \quad \overline{9900} \\
9261 \\
\hline
10386 \quad \overline{63900} \\
62316 \\
\hline
1584
\end{array}
$$

that there is a remainder; this is disregarded as it affects the next figures only, that is, the fourth and following figures in the decimal part of the root.

83. Root of a common fraction.—If the numerator and the denominator of the fraction are each a perfect square, find the square root of each separately.

Example 1. Find $\sqrt{\frac{144}{625}}$.

The $\sqrt{144} = 12$, and $\sqrt{625} = 25$.

Hence $\sqrt{\frac{144}{625}} = \frac{12}{25}$. *Ans.*

If the numerator and denominator are not each a perfect square, reduce the fraction to a decimal and then extract the square root as in **Art. 81.**

Example 2. Find $\sqrt{\frac{2}{7}}$.

Reducing to a decimal, $\frac{2}{7} = 0.28571428 \cdots$.

$$\sqrt{0.28571428} = 0.5345.$$

Hence, $\sqrt{\frac{2}{7}} = 0.5345$ to four decimal places.

It is worth noting here that the square root of $\frac{2}{7}$ may be found by extracting the square root of both numerator and denominator, and then dividing the square root of the numerator by the square root of he denominator. This process would require two extractions of roots and one long division, and so make the work about three times what it is if the fraction is first reduced to a decimal and then the root extracted.

84. Short methods.—*Partly division.* If it is required to extract the square root of a number to, say, five decimal places, making, say, seven figures in the root, the work may be shortened by extracting the root in the usual way till four figures are obtained, and then dividing the last remainder found by the corresponding trial divisor to obtain the last three figures of the root. In general, extract root till more than *half* the required number of figures are found, and then for the other figures of the root divide the remainder by the corresponding trial divisor.

Process.

Example 1. Find $\sqrt{178}$ to five decimal places.

$$1'78.'00'00'00'00(13.34166 \quad \textit{Ans.}$$
$$\underline{1}$$

23	78
	69

263	900
	789

2664	11100
	10656

$$2668) \quad 444000(166$$
$$\underline{2668}$$
$$17720$$
$$\underline{16008}$$
$$17120$$
$$\underline{16008}$$
$$1112$$

The process may be contracted still further by using contracted division when dividing.

Method by factoring. When the number of which the square root is to be extracted can be factored into two factors, one of which is a perfect square and the other the number 2, 3, 5, 6, or 7, a very useful short method may be obtained. For this purpose it is necessary first to have found the following square roots:

$$\sqrt{2} = 1.4142, \qquad \sqrt{3} = 1.73205, \qquad \sqrt{5} = 2.23607,$$
$$\sqrt{6} = 2.4494, \qquad \sqrt{7} = 2.6457.$$

Of these the most useful are the roots of 2 and 3.

Example 2. Find the $\sqrt{32}$.

$32 = 16 \times 2$, so we may write

$$\sqrt{32} = \sqrt{16} \times \sqrt{2} = 4 \times 1.4142 = 5.6568. \quad \textit{Ans.}$$

Example 3. Find $\sqrt{125}$.

$$\sqrt{125} = \sqrt{25} \times \sqrt{5} = 5 \times 2.236 = 11.180. \quad \textit{Ans.}$$

85. Rule for square root.—After carefully following through the solutions of the preceding examples, the following rule should be understood:

RULE. (1) *Begin at the decimal point and point off the whole number part and the decimal part into periods of two figures each. If there is an odd number of figures in the whole number part, the left-hand period will have only one figure. If there is an odd number of figures in the decimal part, annex a cipher so that the right-hand period shall contain two figures.*

(2) *Find the greatest square in the left-hand period and place it under that period. The square root of this greatest square is the first figure of the required root. Subtract the greatest square from the left-hand period and bring down and unite with the remainder the next period of the number. This is the first remainder.*

(3) *Take twice the root already found for a trial divisor, which write at the left of the remainder. Find how many times this trial divisor is contained in the remainder omitting the right-hand figure. This gives the next figure of the root, which place in the root and also at the right of the trial divisor, forming the true divisor. Multiply the true divisor by the figure last placed in the root and write the product under the remainder. Subtract and bring down and unite the next period in the number. This process is repeated for each figure of the root.*

(4) *If at any time the trial divisor will not be contained in the corresponding remainder, place a cipher in the root and at the right of the trial divisor, bring down another period, and continue as before.*

(5) *Point off in the root as many decimal figures as there are decimal periods in the number of which the root is extracted.*

86. Cube root.—The extraction of cube root is so seldom used that it is thought best to omit the usual consideration of it. It is found in a very simple manner by the use of logarithms, by which means any one root is as easily found as another. (See **Art. 313**.)

EXERCISES 27

Find the square root of the following:

1. 516,961. *Ans.* 719.
2. 23,804,641. *Ans.* 4879.

3. 0.3364.   *Ans.* 0.58.
4. 0.120409.   *Ans.* 0.347.
5. 1159.4025.   *Ans.* 34.05.
6. 2 to four decimals.   *Ans.* 1.4142.
7. 786,432 to two decimals.   *Ans.* 886.81.
8. 7,326,456 to two decimals.   *Ans.* 2706.74.
9. 3 to five decimal places.   *Ans.* 1.73205.
10. 5 to three decimal places.   *Ans.* 2.236.
11. 6 to four decimal places.   *Ans.* 2.4495.
12. 7 to five decimal places.   *Ans.* 2.64575.
13. $\frac{49}{189}$.   *Ans.* $\frac{7}{13}$.
14. $27 \div 156.25$ to four decimals.   *Ans.* 0.4157.

Suggestion. First perform the division, and then extract the root of the quotient.

15. $\frac{7}{9}$ to four decimal places.   *Ans.* 0.8819.

In each of the exercises from 16 to 23, carry the root to five decimal places:

16. 143.	*Ans.* 11.95826	**20.** 287.	*Ans.* 16.94107.
17. 164.	*Ans.* 12.80624.	**21.** 396.	*Ans.* 19.89975.
18. 92.	*Ans.* 9.59166.	**22.** 416.	*Ans.* 20.39608.
19. 278.	*Ans.* 16.67333.	**23.** 539.	*Ans.* 23.21637.

24. Find the square roots of the following by short methods: (a) 28, (b) 72, (c) 288, (d) 75, (e) 147, (f) 192, (g) 432.

     Ans. (a) 5.2915, (b) 8.4852, (c) 16.971, (d) 8.6603, (e) 12.1244, (f) 13.8564, (g) 20.7846.

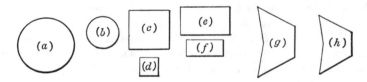

Fig. 22.—Similar figures.

87. Similar figures.—The following principles are useful in solving many problems:

(1) *The areas of similar figures are in the same ratio as the squares of their like dimensions.*

(2) *The volumes of similar solids are in the same ratio as the cubes of their like dimensions.*

Similar figures are such as have the same shape.

In Fig. 22 the following pairs are similar: (a) and (b); (c) and (d); (e) and (f); (g) and (h).

EXERCISES 28

1. If the diameter of (*a*) is 6 in. and of (*b*) is 4 in., how many times as large as (*b*) is (*a*)?

Solution. Area of (*a*): area of (*b*) = $6^2:4^2$ = 36: 16 = $2\frac{1}{4}$. *Ans.*

2. Find the ratio of areas of (*e*) to (*f*), if the shorter side of (*e*) is 9 ft. and of (*f*) 5 ft. *Ans.* 3.24.

3. If a round steel rod $\frac{1}{2}$ in. in diameter, hanging vertically, will support 12,000 lb., what will a rod $\frac{7}{8}$ in. in diameter support?

Ans. 36,750 lb.

4. Given that the electrical resistance is inversely in the same ratio as the areas of the cross sections of the conductors of the same material; find the ratio of the resistances of two copper wires of diameters $\frac{1}{8}$ in. and $\frac{1}{3}$ in. respectively. *Ans.* 64:9.

5. Two steam boilers of the same shape are respectively 12 ft. and 18 ft. long. Find the ratio of their surfaces. *Ans.* 4:9.

6. How many times as much gold leaf will it take to cover a ball 10 in. in diameter than to cover a ball 6 in. in diameter? *Ans.* $2\frac{7}{9}$.

7. Two balls of steel are respectively 7 in. and 15 in. in diameter. The second is how many times as heavy as the first? *Ans.* 9.84 −.

8. Which is the cheaper, oranges $2\frac{1}{2}$ in. in diameter at 30 cents a dozen or 3-in. oranges at 40 cents a dozen? What should the larger ones sell at to give the same value for the money as the smaller at 30 cents a dozen? *Ans.* The 3-in. oranges; 52 cents a dozen nearly.

Suggestion. The price the 3-in. oranges should sell at is given by the proportion: $(2\frac{1}{2})^3:3^3 = 30:x$.

9. Two balls of the same material are 10 in. and 3 in. in diameter respectively. If the smaller ball weighs 9 lb. what is the weight of the larger? *Ans.* $333\frac{1}{3}$ lb.

10. The formula $V = \sqrt{2gh}$ gives the velocity V in feet per second a body will have after falling from a height h. Find the value of V for a stone that has fallen 400 ft. In the formula $g = 32.2$.

Ans. 160.5 ft. nearly.

Suggestion. As in this exercise, the evaluation of a formula often requires the extraction of a square root. The numbers that the letters stand for are put in place of the letters and we have

$$V = \sqrt{2 \times 32.2 \times 400} = \sqrt{25760} = 160.5 -.$$

11. The effective area of a chimney is given by the formula

$$E = A - 0.06\sqrt{A},$$

where E = the effective area, and A = the actual area of the flue. Find the effective area if $A = 86$ sq. in. If $A = 3.14$ sq. ft.

Ans. 85.44 sq. in.; 3.03 sq. ft.

12. When the pressure of water at the place of discharge is known, the rate of flow is given by the formula

$$V = 12.16\sqrt{P},$$

where V = velocity of discharge in feet per second, and P = pressure in pounds per square inch at the place of discharge. Find the rate of discharge if the pressure as given by a pressure gage is 50 lb. per square inch.   *Ans.* 85.98 ft. per second.

13. As in the last, find the velocity of discharge if the pressure is 200 lb. per square inch. Compare the result with that of the preceding.

                     Ans. 171.97 ft. per second.

PART TWO
GEOMETRY

CHAPTER X

PLANE SURFACES. LINES AND ANGLES

88. In this and the following chapters are discussed some of the facts established in geometry, and some of their applications to practical problems. The endeavor is to illustrate and make clear the principles and thus lay a broad foundation, rather than to follow narrow special lines. Many special problems, however, are given. From these the individual student can select those that are suited to his needs.

There are many terms which, although quite familiar to the student, are used in geometry with such exactness as to require a careful definition or explanation. Point, line, angle, surface, and solid are such terms. Like all simple terms, such as number, space, and time, they are difficult to define; but it is hoped the explanations given will lead to a reasonable understanding of them.

89. Definitions.—A **material body,** as, for example, a block of wood or an apple, occupies a definite portion of space.

In geometry no attention is given to the *substance* of which the body is composed. It may be *iron, stone, wood,* or *air,* or it may be a *vacuum.* Geometry only considers the *space* occupied by the substance. This space is called a **geometric solid** or simply a **solid.**

If one thinks of a brick, and then considers the brick removed and thinks of the space that the brick occupied, he has an illustration of a geometric solid.

A solid has *length, breadth,* and *thickness.*

A boundary face of a solid is called a **surface.**

A surface has *length* and *breadth* but no *thickness.*

109

The boundary of a surface, or that which separates one part of a surface from an adjoining part, is called a **line**.

A line has *length* only.

That which separates one part of a line from an adjoining part is called a **point**.

A point has neither *length, breadth,* nor *thickness.* It has *position* only.

A point is read by naming the letter placed upon it. A line is read by naming the letters placed at its ends, or by naming

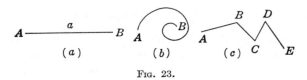

(a) (b) (c)

FIG. 23.

the single letter placed upon it. Capital letters are usually used at the ends of a line, while a small letter is placed upon a line. In Fig. 23(a), the line is read "the line AB" or simply "the line a."

A **straight line** is a line having the same direction throughout its whole extent. See Fig. 23(a).

A **curved line** is a line that is continually changing in direction. See Fig. 23(b).

A **broken line** is a line made up of connected straight lines. See Fig. 23(c).

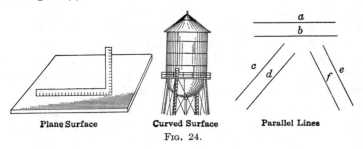

Plane Surface   Curved Surface   Parallel Lines

FIG. 24.

If a surface is such that any two points in it can be connected by a straight line lying wholly in the surface, it is called a **plane surface** or simply a **plane**.

A carpenter determines whether or not the surface of a

board is a plane by laying the edge of his square or other straightedge on the surface in different positions, and observing if the straightedge touches the surface at all points.

A **curved surface** is a surface no part of which is a plane surface. Thus, the surface of a circular pipe and the surface of a ball are curved surfaces.

Parallel lines are lines in the same plane and everywhere the same distance apart.

In Fig. 24 are shown pairs of parallel lines.

90. Angles.—Two straight lines which meet at a point form an **angle.** The idea of what an angle is, being a simple one, is hard to define. One should guard against thinking of the point where the two lines meet as the angle. This point is called the **vertex** of the angle.

FIG. 25.

The two lines are called the **sides** of the angle. The difference in the directions of the two lines forming the angle is the **magnitude** of the angle. For a further discussion of an angle see **Art. 317.**

An angle is read by naming the letter at the vertex, or by naming the letters at the vertex and at the ends of the sides.

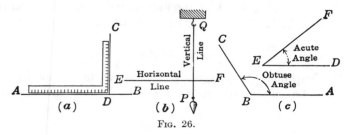

FIG. 26.

When read in the latter way, the letter at the vertex must always come between the other two.

Thus, the angle in Fig. 25 is read "the angle *b*," "the angle *ABC*," or "the angle at *B*."

If one straight line meets another so as to form equal angles, the angles are **right angles,** and the lines are **perpendicular** to each other.

In Fig. 26 (*a*), lines *AB* and *CD* are perpendicular to each other.

A **vertical line** or a **plumb line** is the line along which a string hangs when suspended at one end and weighted at the other.

A **horizontal line** is a line that is perpendicular to a vertical line. Fig. 26(*b*).

If a right angle is divided into 90 equal parts, each part is called a **degree**. It is usually written 1°.

An **acute angle** is an angle that is less than a right angle. An **obtuse angle** is an angle that is greater than a right angle and less than two right angles. See Fig. 26(*c*).

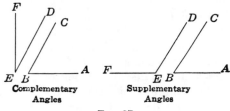

Complementary Angles   Supplementary Angles

Fig. 27.

Two angles whose sum is one right angle, or 90°, are called **complementary angles,** and either one is said to be the **complement** of the other. Two angles whose sum is two right angles, or 180°, are called **supplementary angles,** and either one is said to be the **supplement** of the other.

SURFACES

91. Polygons.—A **polygon** is a plane surface bounded by any number of straight lines. Any one of these lines is called

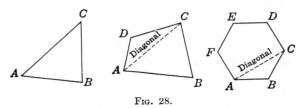

Fig. 28.

a **side.** The point where two sides meet is called a **vertex.** The distance measured around the polygon, or the sum of the lengths of the sides, is called the **perimeter** of the polygon.

A **triangle** is a polygon having three sides.

A **quadrilateral** is a polygon having four sides.

A **pentagon** is a polygon having five sides.

A **hexagon** is a polygon having six sides.

An **octagon** is a polygon having eight sides.

A **regular polygon** is one whose sides are all equal and whose angles are all equal.

A **diagonal** is a line joining any two vertices not adjacent in a polygon.

92. Concerning triangles.—A line drawn from any vertex of a triangle perpendicular to the opposite side and ending in it is called an **altitude** of the triangle. Since a triangle has three vertices, each triangle has three altitudes. The altitude

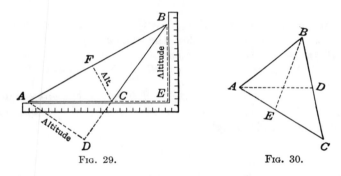

FIG. 29.   FIG. 30.

may meet the opposite side, as *CF* in triangle *ABC*, Fig. 29; or the opposite side may have to be extended to meet it, as *AD* and *BE*, Fig. 29.

A line drawn from any vertex of a triangle to the center of the opposite side is called a **median.** It is evident that in any triangle there are three medians.

In Fig. 30, *AD* is a median.

A line drawn through the vertex of an angle and dividing the angle into two equal parts is called the **bisector** of the angle. The bisector of an angle of a triangle is often taken as the length of the bisector of an angle of the triangle from the vertex to the opposite side.

BE in Fig. 30 is the bisector of the angle *ABC* of the triangle.

8

It is evident that there are three bisectors of the angles in any triangle.

93. Concerning quadrilaterals.—A **parallelogram** is a quadrilateral whose opposite sides are parallel. See Fig. 31(a).

A **rectangle** is a parallelogram whose angles are right angles. See Fig. 31(b).

A **square** is a rectangle whose sides are all equal. See Fig. 31(c).

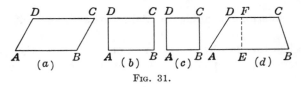

Fig. 31.

A **trapezoid** is a quadrilateral with only two sides parallel. The parallel sides are called the **bases**. The **altitude** is the distance between the two bases.

Fig. 31(d) is a trapezoid; AB and DC are the bases, and EF is the altitude.

The forms just discussed are very important, as any figure bounded by straight lines may be thought of as composed of rectangles and triangles.

EXERCISES 29

In the following exercises use a ruler and a hard lead pencil. Letter all figures.

1. Draw two curved lines. Two broken lines.

2. Draw several parallel lines.

3. Draw a right angle. An acute angle. An obtuse angle.

4. Draw perpendicular lines. If two lines are perpendicular to each other is one of them vertical? Illustrate by a drawing.

5. Draw vertical and horizontal lines. Is a vertical line always perpendicular to a horizontal line?

6. Estimate the size as nearly as you can and draw an angle of 45°. Of 30°. Of 60°. Of 120°. Of 135°. Of 180°. Which are acute angles? Which obtuse angles?

7. Draw two complementary angles. Two supplementary angles.

8. Draw a triangle. A quadrilateral. A pentagon. A hexagon. An octagon. A regular hexagon.

9. How many diagonals have each of the polygons of exercise 8?

10. What are the vertices of each polygon of exercise 8? What are the perimeters?

11. Draw a triangle having all its angles acute, and draw its three altitudes.

12. Draw a triangle having all its angles acute, and draw its three medians. Draw the three bisectors of its angles.

13. Draw triangles each having one obtuse angle, and follow the directions of exercises 11 and 12.

14. Draw a rectangle. A square. A parallelogram. A trapezoid. A quadrilateral that is not any of these. Draw their altitudes.

15. Name objects in nature, or objects made by man that are of the forms asked for in the preceding exercises.

AREAS OF POLYGONS

94. The rectangle.—How to find the area of a rectangle is illustrated in Fig. 32. Suppose that this represents a rectangle whose length AD is 5 ft., and width AB is 4 ft. The rectangle is divided into small squares 1 ft. on a side, and so each represents 1 sq. ft. Since there are 4 rows of squares each containing 5 sq. ft., there are 4×5 sq. ft. $= 20$ sq. ft. in the rectangle. What is said will also be true if the lengths of the sides are fractional. This leads to the following:

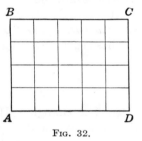

Fig. 32.

RULE. *The area of a rectangle is equal to the product of its length and its width.*

Remark. The length and the width of the rectangle must be in the same unit before taking their product. The product is then square units of the same kind as the linear units. Thus, if the unit of length is the foot, the product will be square feet.

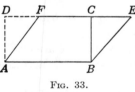

Fig. 33.

95. The parallelogram.—A parallelogram and a rectangle, each having the same base and altitude, are equal in area. This is illustrated in Fig. 33. $ABCD$ is the rectangle and $ABEF$ is the parallelogram. The altitude BC is the same for each, and they have the same base, AB. Since the part BCE of the parallelogram may be cut off and fitted on ADF, it is evident that the parallelogram is just equal to the rectangle. Therefore, we have the following:

Rule.   *The area of a parallelogram is equal to the product of its base and its altitude.*

96. Formulas.—A rule stated in letters and signs is called a **formula.** It is a shorthand way of stating a rule.

If A is used as an abbreviation for area, b for base, and a for altitude, the rule for the area of a rectangle or a parallelogram is given in the following formula:

$$[1] \quad A = ab.$$

The form ab means altitude times base.

Since the altitude times the base equals the area, by using well-known principles of division we have for the rectangle or parallelogram the following:

Rule.   (1) *The altitude equals the area divided by the base.* (2) *The base equals the area divided by the altitude.*

These rules written as formulas are:

$$[2] \quad a = A \div b,$$
$$[3] \quad b = A \div a.$$

97. The triangle.—If a triangle and a parallelogram have the same base and have their altitudes equal, the triangle has half the area of the parallelogram.

This is illustrated in Fig. 34. ABCD is the parallelogram.

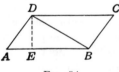

The diagonal BD divides it into two triangles ABD and BCD, which are equal.

From this and the rule for the area of a parallelogram, it is clear that the following is true:

Fig. 34.

Rule.   *The area of any triangle is equal to one-half of its base times its altitude.*

If the area and either base or altitude of a triangle are given, the other dimension (altitude or base) is found by dividing twice the area by the given dimension.

If A stands for the area, a for the altitude, and b for the base, we have these formulas for the triangle:

$$[4] \quad A = \tfrac{1}{2}ab,$$
$$[5] \quad a = 2A \div b,$$
$$[6] \quad b = 2A \div a.$$

EXERCISES 30

1. Compute the areas of the following figures using the dimensions as given.

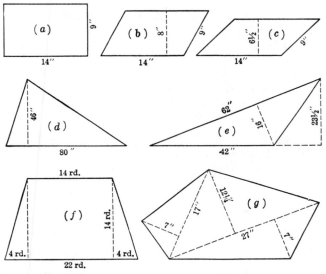

Fɪɢ. 35.

2. If the sides only of a parallelogram are given can its area be found?

3. Draw two triangles and find their areas by drawing the three altitudes of each and measuring the sides and altitudes.

98. Area of a triangle when the three sides only are given.— If a, b, and c stand for the three sides of a triangle; and if s stands for one-half the sum of a, b, and c, then the area A of the triangle is given by the formula:

$$[7]\ \ A = \sqrt{s(s-a)\ (s-b)\ (s-c)}.$$

This formula cannot well be derived here, but it is found in geometry. The area of the triangle can also be found by constructing it to scale, as explained later. The altitude can then be measured and the area be found by taking one-half the product of the base and the altitude.

Since a formula is a rule stated in symbols, the above formula may be stated as the following rule for the area of a triangle when the three sides only are given:

Rule. *Find half the sum of the three sides. Subtract each side from this half sum. Take the continued product of the half sum and the three differences. The square root of this product is the area of the triangle.*

This rule can be illustrated best by an example.

Example. Find the area of a triangle with sides 40 rd., 28 rd., and 36 rd.

Solution. $a = 40,\ b = 28,\ c = 36.$
$$s = \tfrac{1}{2}(40+28+36) = 52.$$
$$s - a = 52 - 40 = 12.$$
$$s - b = 52 - 28 = 24.$$
$$s - c = 52 - 36 = 16.$$
$$A = \sqrt{52 \times 12 \times 24 \times 16} = \sqrt{239,616} = 489.506.$$
$$\therefore \text{area} = 489.506 - \text{rd.}^2 \quad Ans.$$

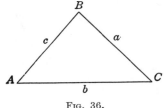

Fig. 36.

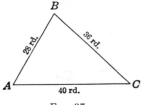

Fig. 37.

With very ordinary instruments this triangle can be constructed to scale and measured, and the area found to within half a square rod of the computed area.

99. Area of trapezoid.—A diagonal of a trapezoid divides it into two triangles which have the same altitude, and have

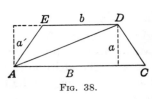

Fig. 38.

as bases the two bases of the trapezoid. Thus, in the trapezoid of Fig. 38, the diagonal AD divides the trapezoid into 'two triangles ACD and ADE. The area of $ACD = \tfrac{1}{2}$ of $AC \times a$ and area of $ADE = \tfrac{1}{2}$ of $ED \times a'$. But $a = a'$, hence the sum of the areas of the two triangles $= \tfrac{1}{2}(AC + ED) \times a$.

Now the area of the trapezoid can evidently be found by finding the sum of the areas of the two triangles into which it is divided; or what amounts to the same thing, by the following:

RULE. *The area of a trapezoid equals one-half the sum of the two bases times the altitude.*

If *B* and *b* stand for the two bases and *a* for the altitude of the trapezoid, the formula is

$$[8] \quad A = \tfrac{1}{2}(B+b) \times a.$$

Example. Find the area of a trapezoid whose lower base is 20 rd., upper base 14 rd., and altitude 9 rd.

Solution. By formula [8], $A = \tfrac{1}{2}(B+b)a$. Putting the numbers of the example in place of the letters of the formula,

$$A = \tfrac{1}{2}(20+14) \times 9 = 153.$$

$\therefore$ area = 153 sq. rd. *Ans.*

EXERCISES 31

1. Find the parts not given in the following exercises which refer to parallelograms:

    (1) Base 22½ in. altitude 19 in. area ————.

    (2) Base ———— altitude 47 rd. area 426 rd.²

    (3) Base 33⅓ ft. altitude ———— area 433⅔ ft.²

    (4) Base ———— altitude 102⅔ in. area 9367 in.²

        Ans. (1) 427½ in.²; (2) $9\frac{3}{47}$ rd.; (3) $13\frac{1}{700}$ ft.; (4) $91\frac{64}{307}$ in.

2. Find the number of acres in a farm 160 rd. long and 80 rd. wide.
    Ans. 80.

3. Find the number of square feet in a floor 16 ft. 8 in. by 13 ft. 6 in.
    Ans. 225.

4. Find the number of square meters in a rectangle 77 m. long and 5 Dm. wide.
    Ans. 3850.

5. A box 6 in. long, 4 in. wide, and 3 in. deep has six rectangular faces. Find the area of the surface of the box.
    Ans. 108 in.²

6. Find the area of a triangle whose base is 25 ft. and whose altitude is 12 ft. 4 in.
    Ans. 154⅙ ft.²

7. How many acres are there in a triangular lot whose base is 432 ft. and altitude 320 ft.?
    Ans. 1.59 —.

8. Find the number of hectares in a triangular field whose base is 196.8 m. and altitude 85 m.
    Ans. 0.8364.

9. Find the base of a triangle whose area is 20 acres and altitude 80 rd.
    Ans. 80 rd.

10. A rectangular field 48 rd. long contains 9 acres. Find the width.
    Ans. 30 rd.

11. If the perimeter of a rectangle is 96 ft. and the length is three times the breadth, find the area.
    Ans. 432 ft.²

12. A rectangular garden 56 ft. long and 40 ft. wide· has a path 6 ft. wide around it. Find the area of the path.   *Ans.* 1296 ft.²

13. A box of tin sheets for roofing, containing 112 sheets 14 in. by 20 in., will cover 170 ft.² What per cent of surface covered is allowed for joints and waste?

Solution. Without allowing for joints and waste each box would cover $\dfrac{14 \times 20 \times 112}{144} = 217\frac{7}{9}$ sq. ft.

$217\frac{7}{9}$ sq. ft. -170 sq. ft. $= 47\frac{7}{9}$ sq. ft. $=$ allowance for joints and waste.

$47\frac{7}{9}$ sq. ft. $\div 170$ sq. ft. $= 0.28+ = 28+\%$.

14. How many bricks each 9 in. by 4½ in. by 1¾ in. will it take to pave a court 16 ft. by 18 ft., if bricks are laid flat? If laid on edge?

Ans. flat 1024; edge 2634.

15. How many paving blocks each 4 in. by 4 in. by 10 in., placed on their sides, will it take to pave an alley 600 ft. long and 12 ft. 6 in. wide?

Ans. 27,000.

16. What will be the expense of painting the walls and ceiling of a room 12 ft. 6 in. by 16 ft. and 10 ft. 4 in. high at 15 cents per square yard?   *Ans.* $13.15.

17. Find the cost of sodding a lawn 31 ft. wide and 52 ft. long at 18 cents per square yard.

Ans. $32.24.

18. Find the number of square feet in the floor of the room shown in Fig. 39.

Ans. 277½ ft.²

Suggestion. Divide into rectangles and trapezoids.

FIG. 39.

19. At 15 cents per square foot, find the cost of building a cement walk 6 ft. wide, on two sides of a corner lot 33 ft. by 100 ft.

Ans. $125.10.

20. Find the area of a trapezoid whose bases are 17 in. and 11 in. respectively and whose altitude is 13 in.   *Ans.* 182 in.²

21. Find the area of a triangle whose sides are 13 in., 15 in., and 21 in.

Ans. 96.79— in.²

22. Find the area of a triangle whose sides are 54 in., 32 in., and 22 in.

Ans. 0 in.²

23. Find the area of a triangle whose base is 27 in. and altitude 14 in.

Ans. 189 in.²

24. Find the area of a board 14 ft. long and 18 in. wide at one end and 12 in. at the other.   *Ans.* 17.5 ft.²

25. Find the cost of painting both sides of a solid board fence 260 ft. long and 6 ft. high at 60 cents a square. How many gallons of paint will it take for two coats if 1 gallon will cover 250 sq. ft. two coats? (1 square = 100 sq. ft.)   *Ans.* $18.72; 12½ gal. nearly.

26. How much did it cost to harvest a field of wheat 156 rd. by 76 rd., if cutting and binding cost $1.50 per acre, setting up 25 cents an acre, and hauling $1.25 an acre? *Ans.* $222.30.

27. Find the area in acres of a farm which is represented on paper as a rectangle $3\frac{3}{4}$ in. by $10\frac{1}{2}$ in. on a scale of $\frac{1}{16}$ in. to the rod.

Ans. 63 A.

28. Find the area of Fig. 40(*a*). *Ans.* 23.592 in.[2]
29. Find the area of Fig. 40(*b*). *Ans.* 6.02 in.[2]
30. Find the area of Fig. 40(*c*). *Ans.* 8.625 in.[2]

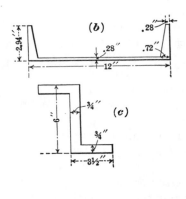

Fɪɢ. 40.

31. Find the area of the footing for a column with a load of 168,000 lb. if the safe bearing load of the soil is 4000 lb. per square foot.

Ans. 42 sq. ft.

32. How many square yards of plastering will be required for the four side walls of a hall 90 ft. long, 50 ft. wide, and 20 ft. high, with 4 doors $5\frac{1}{2}$ ft. by 10 ft., 14 windows 5 ft. by 11 ft., and a baseboard 9 in. high around the room? Find the cost at 40 cents per square yard. Find the contractor's profit at 20%.

LUMBER

100. Measuring lumber.—Lumber is measured in board measure. Timber used in framework is counted as lumber. Lumber and timber are sold by the 1000 ft. board measure. This is sometimes written 1000 ft. B.M., but more often it is indicated by the single letter M.

One **board foot** is 12 in. square and 1 in. thick, and so contains one-twelfth of a cubic foot. The number of board feet in a stick of timber is the number of cubic feet times 12. The following rule may be used to find the number of board feet in a stick of timber:

RULE. *Take the product of the end dimensions in inches, divide by 12, and multiply the quotient by the length in feet.*

The student should make clear to himself the correctness of this rule.

Example. Find the number of board feet in a stick of timber 6 in. by 8 in. and 14 ft. long.

Solution. $\dfrac{6\times8}{12}\times14 = 56$ ft. B.M. *Ans.*

Lumber less than 1 in. is counted as if 1 in. thick in buying and selling. In widths a fraction of $\frac{1}{2}$ in. or more is counted as 1 in.

Usually lumber is cut in lengths containing an even number of feet, as 12, 14, and 16 ft. Longer lengths than these are usually special, but classifications vary greatly. There are sixteen or more associations in America with specifications governing the classification of lumber, and these specifications differ more or less.

Timber work is usually paid for at an agreed price per M, the timber to be measured in the work.

101. Estimations.—There are various rules regarding the estimating of the amount of lumber required in a structure. In general, all that is necessary is to find the number of board feet in the lumber required and add a certain per cent for waste in cutting, matching, etc. Regardng this, the student can consult a handbook specially prepared for those in this line of work.

102. Shingles.—Shingles are 16 in. or 18 in. in length, are counted as 4 in. wide, and put up in bunches of 250. The part of the shingle that is exposed when laid is said to be "laid to the weather." The part so exposed varies from 4 in. to 6 in. So a single shingle covers a space 4 in. wide and from 4 in. to 6 in. long.

In laying shingles, the estimating is often made by the *square,* an area 10 ft. by 10 ft. or containing 100 sq. ft.

In stating the number of shingles, give the number so that only whole bunches will be required. Thus, do not give a number as 5650 but as 5750.

The following table allows for waste and gives the number of square feet covered by a thousand shingles, and also the number of shingles required to cover a square, when laid at various distances to the weather.

Inches to the weather	Area covered by 1000 shingles	No. to cover a square
4	100 sq. ft	1000
4¼	110 sq. ft	910
4½	120 sq. ft	833
5	133 sq. ft	752
5½	145 sq. ft	690
6	157 sq. ft	637

EXERCISES 32

1. Find the number of feet of lumber it will take to build a tight board fence 5½ ft. high and 70 ft. long, boards 1 in. thick and nailed at top and bottom to pieces of 2 in. by 4 in. stuff. (No waste allowed.)
Ans. 478.

2. Find cost of lumber at $32.00 per M to build a walk 30 ft. long and 8 ft. wide; plank to be 2 in. thick and laid crosswise on 4 pieces of 4 in. by 4 in., running lengthwise. *Ans. $20.48.*

3. Find the amount of lumber to floor a room 30 ft. by 40 ft. with strips 3 in. wide, allowing ⅛ for matching and 15% for waste.

4. Find how many shingles it will take to shingle a roof 36 ft. by 40 ft. if shingles are laid 4½ in. to the weather. (Use the table of **Art. 102.**)

Solution. $\dfrac{36 \times 40}{100} = 14.4 =$ number of squares.

$833 \times 14.4 = 11,995 =$ number of shingles required.

∴ 12,000 shingles must be bought.

5. How many board feet in 26 pieces of 2 in. by 4 in. by 14 ft. long, 20 pieces of 3 in. by 10 in. by 16 ft. long? *Ans. 1043.*

6. What will it cost at $28 per M to cover the floor of a barn 32 ft. by 42 ft. with 2-in. plank? *Ans. $75.26.*

7. How many board feet are there in 3 sticks of timber 12 in. by 14 in. and 22 ft. long? *Ans. 924.*

8. Find the total cost of shingling the two sides of a roof each 18 ft. by 40 ft. Redwood shingles at $4.75 a thousand are used, and the laying, nails, etc., cost $1.90 per square. Shingles are to be laid 5 in. to the weather. (Use the table of **Art. 102.**) *Ans. $79.61.*

9. What does the following cost at 25 cents a foot:

1 piece ⅞ in. by 6 in. by 10 ft.
1 piece ⅝ in. by 8 in. by 12 ft.
1 piece ⅞ in. by 18 in. by 4 ft.
2 pieces ¼ in. by 6 in. by 8 ft.?

Ans. $6.75.

10. Find the cost of the following bill of lumber if the quarter sawed is $90 per M and the common sawed is $65 per M:

2 pieces 1½ in. ×2½ in. ×12 ft. quarter sawed
2 pieces ⅜ in. × 8 in. ×12 ft. quarter sawed
1 piece ¾ in. ×2½ in. ×12 ft. quarter sawed
1 piece ¾ in. × 2 in. ×12 ft. quarter sawed
5 pieces ¾ in. × 3 in. ×12 ft. quarter sawed
1 piece ⅞ in. ×10 in. ×12 ft. quarter sawed
1 piece ½ in. ×10 in. × 6 ft. common sawed
6 pieces ½ in. × 6 in. ×12 ft. common sawed
4 pieces ¼ in. × 6 in. ×12 ft. common sawed.

Ans. $9.18.

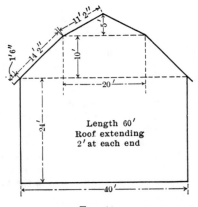

Length 60'
Roof extending
2' at each end

Fɪɢ. 41.

11. Fig. 41 is the end of a barn. Find the area of one end. Find the area of the roof. The rafters are placed 16 in. from center to center. Find the number of board feet in the rafters if made of 2 in. × 6 in. (Use 12-ft. stuff for short rafters.) Find number of feet of lumber to cover ends, sides and roof. Find how many shingles it will take for the roof if laid 4½ in. to the weather.

Ans. 1310 ft.²; 3434⅔ ft.²; 2744; 8935; 28,750.

12. A ship builder gave $300 for a standing oak tree to make a long ship timber. The cost of felling, hewing, and hauling was $275. If the timber was 18 in. square and 98 ft. long, find the number of board feet in it and the cost per thousand feet. *Ans.* 2646; $217.31.

13. Find the number of board feet in the following list of framing timber for a house:

Girders......................	5 pieces 6 in. × 8 in. ×20 ft.
Sills.........................	16 pieces 6 in. × 6 in. ×16 ft.
First floor beams...............	45 pieces 3 in. ×10 in. ×28 ft.
Second floor beams.............	45 pieces 3 in. × 8 in. ×28 ft.
Ribbons......................	16 pieces 1 in. × 8 in. ×20 ft.
Plates........................	32 pieces 2 in. × 4 in. ×16 ft.
Outside wall studs..............	156 pieces 2 in. × 4 in. ×20 ft.
Inside wall studs...............	200 pieces 2 in. × 4 in. ×12 ft.
Rafter studs..................	90 pieces 2 in. × 8 in. ×24 ft.
Collar beams.................	45 pieces 2 in. × 6 in. ×16 ft.

Ans. 14,673.

CHAPTER XI

TRIANGLES

THE RIGHT TRIANGLE

103. A right triangle is a triangle having one right angle. The side opposite the right angle is called the **hypotenuse,** and the sides about the right angle are called **base** and **altitude,** the base being the side the triangle is supposed to rest upon.

The right triangle is of great importance as it is of very common occurrence in practice. The solution of the right triangle depends upon the following relation established in geometry.

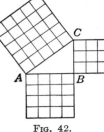

FIG. 42.

The square formed on the hypotenuse is equal to the sum of the squares formed on the other two sides.

This may be illustrated as in Fig. 42. AC is the hypotenuse and is 5 units in length. AB is the base, 4 units long. BC is the altitude, 3 units long. Here it is easily seen that the square on AC is equal to the sum of the squares on AB and BC. Hence $\overline{AC}^2 = \overline{AB}^2 + \overline{BC}^2$, or in general, if c stands for the hypotenuse, b for base, and a for altitude, then $c^2 = a^2 + b^2$. From this are derived the three following formulas, by which any side can be found if the other two are known.

[9] $c = \sqrt{a^2 + b^2}.$
[10] $a = \sqrt{c^2 - b^2}.$
[11] $b = \sqrt{c^2 - a^2}.$

Example. Find the hypotenuse of a right triangle whose base is 14 ft. and altitude 16 ft.

Solution. Using formula [9], $c = \sqrt{a^2 + b^2}.$

$$\therefore c = \sqrt{16^2 + 14^2} = \sqrt{452} = 21.26+ \text{ ft. } Ans.$$

EXERCISES 33

In the following right triangles, solve for the parts named in the exercise:

1. $a = 25$, $b = 16$, find c and area.

Ans. $c = 29.68$; area $= 200$ square units.

2. $c = 46$, $b = 30$, find a and area.

Ans. $a = 34.87 +$; area $= 523.05 +$ square units.

3. Area $= 2$ acres, $a = 15$ rd.; find b and c.

Ans. $b = 42.667 -$ rd.; $c = 45.23 -$ rd.

4. $a = 16$, $c = 20$, find b and area.

Ans. $b = 12$; area $= 96$ square units.

5. Find length of the diagonal of a rectangle 16 ft. by 14 ft.

Ans. 21.26 ft.

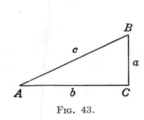

FIG. 43.

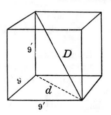

FIG. 44.

6. Find the diagonal of a cube 9 ft. on an edge. *Ans.* $15.588 +$ ft.

Suggestion. In Fig. 44, the line marked D is called the diagonal of the cube. First find d and then D.

$$d = \sqrt{9^2 + 9^2} = \sqrt{162}.$$
$$D = \sqrt{162 + 9^2} = \sqrt{243}$$
$$= \sqrt{81 \times 3} = 9\sqrt{3}.$$

7. A man swims at right angles to the bank of a stream at the rate of 3.5 miles per hour. If the current is 7.5 miles per hour, find the rate the man is moving. *Ans.* $8.28 -$ miles per hour.

Suggestion. The rate the man is moving is the length of the hypotenuse of a right triangle having a base $= 3.5$ mi. and an altitude $= 7.5$ mi.

8. The diagonal of a rectangle is 130 and the altitude is 32. Find the area. *Ans.* 4032 square units.

9. What is the length of the longest line that can be drawn within a rectangular box 12 ft. by 4 ft. by 3 ft.? *Ans.* 13 ft.

10. The hypotenuse of a right triangle, with base and altitude equal, is 12 ft. Find the length of the base and altitude. *Ans.* $8.485 +$ ft.

11. The base of a triangle is 20 ft. and the altitude is 18 ft. What is the side of a square having the same area? *Ans.* $13.416 +$ ft.

12. The area of a rectangular lawn is 5525 m.², and the length of one of its sides is 8.5 Dm. Find the length of its diagonal in meters to three decimal places. *Ans.* $107.005 -$ m.

13. A steamer goes due north at the rate of 15 miles per hour, and another due west at 18 miles per hour. If both start from the same place, how far apart will they be in 6 hours?　　*Ans.* 140.58+ miles.

14. What is the length of the diagonal of a room 20 ft. by 16 ft. by 12 ft.?　　*Ans.* 28.284+ ft.

15. Find cost at $20 per M of roof boards on a third-pitch roof of a barn 45 ft. by 65 ft., if projections at ends and eaves are 2 ft. (In a third-pitch roof the distance of the ridge above the plate is one-third the width of the building.)　　*Ans.* $80.15.

Suggestion. Distance of ridge above plate = ⅓ of 45 ft. = 15 ft.
Length of rafters without projection = $\sqrt{22.5^2 + 15^2} = 27.04$ ft.
Total length of rafters = 2 ft. +27.04 ft. = 29.04 ft.
Area of one side of roof = 29.04 ×69 = 2003.76 sq. ft.

16. How many thousand shingles will it take to cover the above roof, if shingles are laid 4½ in. to the weather and a double row is put at the beginning on each side? (No allowance for waste.)
　　Ans. 32,500 nearly.

17. In fitting a steam pipe to the form *ABCD*, Fig. 45, making a bend of 45°, the fitter takes $BC = CE + \tfrac{5}{12}CE$. What is the error if $CE = 18$ in.? What is the correct length of *CB*, and what is the per cent of error by the fitter's method?

Ans. Error, 0.0442−; correct, $CB = 25.4558+$ in.; % of error, 0.17+.

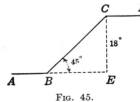

FIG. 45.

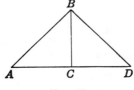

FIG. 46.

18. In cutting a rafter for a half-pitch roof a carpenter makes the length of the rafter $AB = 1$ ft. 5 in. for every foot there is in *AC*, Fig. 46. If $AC = 8$ ft., find *AB* by this rule. What is the per cent of error by this method?　　*Ans.* Carpenter's method, 11 ft. 4 in.; correct, 11 ft. 3.76+ in.; error, 0.17+ %.

19. To find the diagonal of a square, multiply the side by 10, take away 1% of this product, and divide the remainder by 7. Test the accuracy of this rule.　　*Ans.* 0.006 − % too large.

Solution. Take a square with a side of, say, 25 in.
$$10 \times 25 = 250$$
$$1\% \text{ of } 250 = \underline{2.5}$$
Remainder = 247.5
$$247.5 \div 7 = 35.357\,+ \text{ in.} = \text{diagonal, by rule.}$$
By formula for hypotenuse, diagonal = $\sqrt{25^2 + 25^2} = 35.355+$ in.
Hence error = 35.357 in. − 35.355 in. = 0.002 in.
$$0.002 \div 35.355 = 0.006 - \% = \text{per cent of error.}$$

It is evident that this rule is very accurate and is also easy of application.

20. Show that the following rules are correct   They are very useful in many problems connected with a square.

(1) *The diagonal of a square equals a side of the square multiplied by* $\sqrt{2}$.

(2) *The side of a square equals one-half the diagonal multiplied by* $\sqrt{2}$.

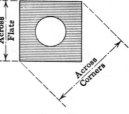

The number of decimal places used in $\sqrt{2}$ will depend upon the degree of accuracy desired.   Pipe fitters usually use $\sqrt{2} = 1.41$. It is often necessary to take three or more decimal places. $\sqrt{2} = 1.4142136$ to seven decimal places.

Fig. 47.

21. Use rule (1) in obtaining the correct values in exercises 17, 18, and 19.

22. What is the distance across the corners of a square nut that is $3\frac{3}{8}$ in. on a side?   Use rule (1).

Fig. 48.

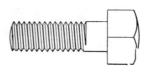

Fig. 49.—Cap screw.

23. What must be the diameter of round stock so that a square bolt head $1\frac{3}{4}$ in. on a side may be milled from it?

24. Find the distance across the flats of the square head of a cap screw that may be milled from round stock $1\frac{1}{8}$ in. in diameter.   Use rule (2) of exercise 20.

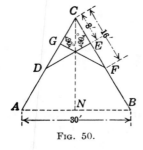

Fig. 50.

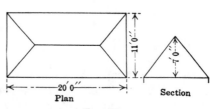

Fig. 51.

25. Fig. 50 shows a "scissors" roof truss with the lengths $AB = BC = AC = 30$ ft., $CD = CF = 16$ ft., and $CG = CE = 8$ ft.   Find the lengths of NC and FG.   *Ans.* $NC = 25$ ft. $11\frac{3}{4}$ in.; $FG = 13$ ft. $10\frac{1}{4}$ in.

9

26. A smokestack is held in position by three guy wires that reach the ground 49 ft. from the foot of the stack.   Find the length of a guy wire if they are fastened to the stack 70 ft. from the ground.

Ans. 85.4+ ft.

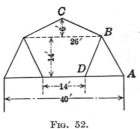

Fig. 52.

27. An engine shaft is centered 9 ft. below and 3 ft. to the left of the center of a line shaft.   Find the distance between the centers of the two shafts.   *Ans.* 9 ft. $5\frac{7}{8}$ in.

28. The dimensional sketch, Fig. 51, shows plan and section of a roof.   It has to be boarded.   What will be the number of feet of boards required?   *Ans.* 356.

29. In the gambrel roof shown in section in Fig. 52, find the lengths of rafters and parts not given.

Ans. $AB = 15$ ft. $7\frac{3}{4}$ in.; $DB = 15$ ft. $2\frac{3}{4}$ in.; $BC = 14$ ft. $3\frac{3}{4}$ in.   All to the nearest $\frac{1}{4}$ in.

SIMILAR TRIANGLES

104. Triangles that have the same shape are said to be similar.

In Fig. 53(*a*), *ABC* and *ADE* are similar.   In (*b*) *ABC* and *A'B'C'* are similar.

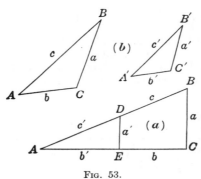

Fig. 53.

Draw two triangles as in (*a*) and measure the sides *a*, *b*, *c* and *a'*, *b'*, *c'*.   Then determine the ratios *a* : *b*, *a* : *c*, *b* : *c*, *a'* : *b'*, *a'* : *c'* and *b'* : *c'*.   Follow the same directions for the triangles in (*b*).   Now compare the values of the ratios and notice whether or not they are equal.

The results of the above should lead to the following: *a* : *b* = *a'* : *b'*; *a* : *c* = *a'* : *c'*; and *b* : *c* = *b'* : *c'*.

Two triangles that have the angles of one equal respectively to the angles of the other are smilar.

The sides about the equal angles in the similar triangles are called **corresponding sides.**

Thus, c and c' are corresponding sides. Other corresponding sides are a and a', and b and b'.

From the proportions given above, we arrive at the following principle:

Corresponding sides of similar triangles form a proportion.

Example. To find the distance between the points P and Q on opposite banks of a stream, Fig. 54, where P is inaccessible.

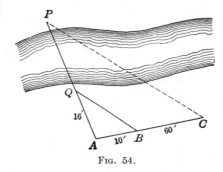

Fig. 54.

Solution. As shown in the figure, measure distances $AQ = $ 16 ft., $AB = 10$ ft., and $BC = 60$ ft. Because triangles AQB and APC are made similar we have the proportion

$AB : AQ = AC : AP$

$\therefore 10$ ft. : 16 ft. $= 70$ ft. : AP

$\therefore AP = \dfrac{16 \times 70}{10} = 112$ ft.

$\therefore PQ = 112$ ft. $- 16$ ft. $= 96$ ft. *Ans.*

105. Tapers.—The man in the machine shop often finds it necessary to determine the **taper per foot** of a piece that is to be turned, in order that he may set his lathe properly. By the **taper per foot** is meant the **decrease** in **diameter** if the piece is 1 ft. long.

In Fig. 55(a), the taper is evidently $4\frac{1}{2}$ in. $- 3$ in. $= 1\frac{1}{2}$ in. per foot. In (b) the taper is $2\frac{1}{2}$ in. $- 2$ in. $= \frac{1}{2}$ in. in 4 in. Hence the taper per foot is 3 times as much or $1\frac{1}{2}$ in.

If l stands for the length of tapered part in feet, t for the taper in inches in this part, and T for the taper in inches per foot, then the following proportion is true by similar triangles:

$$[12]\ 1 : \mathbf{I} = t : T.$$

The taper for the total length of the piece is evidently the taper per foot times the length in feet.

Example. In Fig. 55(c), what is the taper per foot? What would be the taper for total length of piece?

Solution. Substituting in [12], $\frac{5}{12} : 1 = \frac{1}{2} : T$.

$$\therefore T = 1 \times \tfrac{1}{2} \div \tfrac{5}{12} = 1\tfrac{1}{5} \text{ in.}\quad Ans.$$

$1\tfrac{1}{5}$ in. $\times \tfrac{23}{12} = 2.3$ in. $=$ taper if it were tapered the full length.

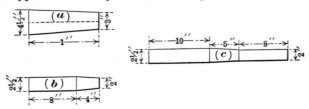

Fig. 55.

106. Turning.—In turning a piece in a lathe the taper is sometimes made by shifting the tailstock of the lathe. Since, when the piece is revolved, the same cut is made on all sides, it is necessary to set the tailstock over one-half of what the taper would be if the piece were tapered the full length. Thus, a piece 1 ft. long with a taper $1\tfrac{1}{4}$ in. per foot requires the tailstock to be set over $\tfrac{1}{2}$ of $1\tfrac{1}{4}$ in. $= \tfrac{5}{8}$ in.

If $D =$ the large diameter and d the small diameter of the tapered portion, L the total length of the piece, and l the length of the tapered portion, then the offset x of the tailstock is determined by the following formula:

$$[13]\ \mathbf{x} = \frac{\mathbf{D} - \mathbf{d}}{\mathbf{2}} \times \frac{\mathbf{L}}{\mathbf{l}}.$$

Example. A shaft 3 ft. long is to have a taper turned on one end 10 in. long, the large end of the taper being 4 in. in diameter and the small end $3\tfrac{1}{2}$ in. Find the distance to set over the tailstock.

Solution. $x = \dfrac{4 - 3\tfrac{1}{2}}{2} \times \dfrac{36}{10} = 0.9$ in. $Ans.$

EXERCISES 34

1. The following tapers per inch are what tapers per foot: 0.0026 in.; 0.0473 in.; 0.0379 in.?

2. How much will the tailstock need to be set over to give a taper of $1\frac{1}{8}$ in. per foot if the work is 1 ft. in length? If 8 in. in length?
Ans. $\frac{9}{16}$ in.; $\frac{3}{8}$ in.

3. The standard pipe thread taper is $\frac{3}{4}$ in. per foot. How much is this per inch? *Ans.* $\frac{1}{16}$ in.

4. Find the taper per foot to be used in turning a pulley with a 14-in. face crowned $\frac{3}{16}$ in. *Ans.* $0.32+$ in.

5. If the crowning of a pulley is $\frac{1}{24}$ of the width of the face, find the taper per foot to be used in turning a pulley with a 10-in. face.
Ans. 1 in.

Taper pin.   Taper $\frac{1}{4}$ in. per foot.

Taper-pin reamer.   Taper $\frac{1}{4}$ in. per foot.

Fig. 56.

6. A taper-pin reamer has a taper of $\frac{1}{4}$ in. per foot. If the diameter of the small end is 0.398 in. and the length of the flutes is $5\frac{1}{4}$ in., find the diameter of the large end of the flutes.

7. A taper reamer has a taper of $\frac{5}{8}$ in. per foot and the flutes are $3\frac{1}{2}$ in. long. If it is $\frac{3}{4}$ in. in diameter at the large end, find the diameter at the small end. *Ans.* 0.5677 in.

8. Find the taper per foot of a taper reamer that has a diameter of $\frac{11}{16}$ in. at the large end of the flutes, and $\frac{33}{64}$ in. at the small end if the flutes are $2\frac{3}{4}$ in. long. *Ans.* $\frac{3}{4}$ in.

9. A taper reamer has a taper of $\frac{3}{4}$ in. per foot. If the diameter of the large end is $1\frac{3}{16}$, find the diameter of the small end, the flutes being $3\frac{3}{4}$ in. long. *Ans.* $\frac{61}{64}$ in.

10. In Fig. 57, the timbers CB, DF, and EG are perpendicular to CA. From the given dimensions find the lengths of DF, EG, CF, DG, and AB. *Ans.* $EG = 4$ ft.; $DG = 10.770$ ft.; $AB = 32.311$ ft.

Suggestion. $CA : CB = DA : DF$.
Or $30 : 12 = 20 : DF$.
$$\therefore DF = \frac{12 \times 20}{30} = 8.$$
$$CF = \sqrt{10^2 \times 8^2} = \sqrt{164} = 12.806+$$

11. How much should the tailstock be offset to turn a taper on a piece of work 10 in. long, if the tapered portion is 4⅛ in. long and measures 1.275 in. in diameter at the large end and 0.845 in. at the small end?

Ans. 0.5212 in.

12. What is the offset of the tail center for turning a taper 18 in. long on a bar 26 in. long, if the diameters at the ends of the taper are 3⅛ in. and 2¾ in.? Ans. 0.27 +in.

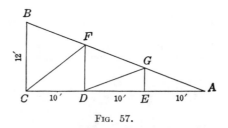

Fig. 57.

13. To find the distance across the lake in Fig. 58, measure $AB = 80$ rd.; $AD = 30$ rd.; $DE = 25$ rd., and find BC. Is it necessary to make right-angled triangles? Ans. 66⅔ rd.; no.

14. Show how to find the height of a smokestack CD of Fig. 59, when the foot of the stack cannot be reached.

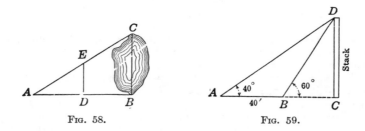

Fig. 58.   Fig. 59.

Suggestion. On a level place measure from A to B in a line with C, and measure angles BAD and CBD. Suppose the line AB is 40 ft. and the angles are 40° and 60° respectively. Construct a figure to scale on paper and measure the line that corresponds to the smokestack.

THE STEEL SQUARE

107. One of the most useful instruments known to man is the ordinary **steel square** or **carpenter's square** shown in Fig. 60. It is made in various sizes but the most common size is with the longer arm, called the **body, blade,** or **stock,**

24 in. in length and 2 in. in breadth, and the shorter arm, called the **tongue,** 16 in. or 18 in. in length and 1½ in. in breadth.

Many books, having in some cases five or six hundred pages, have been written on the uses of the steel square. Here we wish only to call attention to the fact that the principles involved in using the steel square are mainly those involved in the solution of the right triangle and in similar triangles. One who understands the right triangle can devise many uses

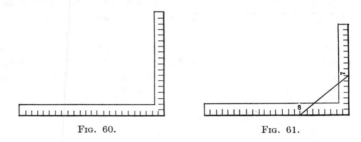

FIG. 60.   FIG. 61.

for the steel square, and can readily see the principles underlying the various uses of this instrument given in the treatises on the steel square.

Upon the ordinary steel square are found many figures, telling lengths of braces, board measures, etc. No attempt will be made here to explain these.

Example. By use of a steel square, find the length of the hypotenuse of a right triangle that has a base of 8 in. and an altitude of 7 in.

Solution. Measure the line drawn from the 8-in. mark on the blade to the 7-in. mark on the tongue. This measures about 10⅝ in. which is near enough for most practical purposes. By the right triangle method the hypotenuse $= \sqrt{8_2 + 7_2} = 10.63 +$ in. (See Fig. 61.)

This method can readily be applied to find the lengths of braces supporting two pieces that are perpendicular to each other; to find rafter lengths, lengths of the parts of a trestle, etc.

108. Rafters and roofs.—The **run** of a rafter is the distance measured on the horizontal from its lower end to a point under its upper end. The **rise** is the distance of the upper end above the lower end. In Fig. 62, AC is the run and CB the rise.

The slant of a roof is usually told by stating the relation of the *rise* to the *run*. It is often given by stating the **rise per foot of run;** as 6 in. to 1 ft.

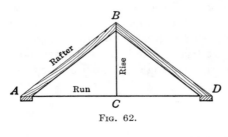

FIG. 62.

Another way is to state what is known as the **pitch** of the roof. A roof is said to be **half pitch, quarter pitch, full pitch,** etc., when the rise is $\frac{1}{2}$, $\frac{1}{4}$, 1, etc., times the full width of the building as represented in Fig. 62, where AD is the width of the building.

The relation between rise and pitch is shown by the following table:

12 ft. run to 4 ft. rise is $\frac{1}{6}$ pitch.
12 ft. run to 6 ft. rise is $\frac{1}{4}$ pitch.
12 ft. run to 8 ft. rise is $\frac{1}{3}$ pitch.
12 ft. run to 10 ft. rise is $\frac{5}{12}$ pitch.
12 ft. run to 12 ft. rise is $\frac{1}{2}$ pitch.
12 ft. run to 15 ft. rise is $\frac{5}{8}$ pitch.
12 ft. run to 18 ft. rise is $\frac{3}{4}$ pitch.
12 ft. run to 24 ft. rise is full pitch.

109. Uses of the square.
—The **bevel** or **slant** on the end of a brace or rafter, necessary to make it fit the part it rests against, can easily be marked by the square.

Example 1. Required to cut the lower end of a rafter that is to rest on the plate if the rise of the rafter is 8 ft. and the run 12 ft.

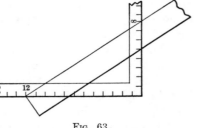

FIG. 63.

Discussion. Place the square as shown in Fig. 63 and mark along the lower edge. This gives the proper slant. Marking along the tongue gives the slant for the upper end of the rafter.

In placing the square on the stick it is only necessary to take the distances on the blade and tongue in the same ratio as the ratio of the run to the rise. In this case we could as well have taken 24 in. and 16 in. or 9 in. and 6 in.

Example 2. Required to cut a rafter for a V-shaped roof on a building 12 ft. wide if the rise of the rafter is to be 4 ft. The rafter is to be made of a piece of 2 in. by 4 in. and half its width is to project 18 in. beyond the plate.

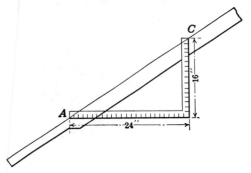

Fig. 64.

Discussion. Determine the slant for the plate end as described in example 1. Then place the square as shown in Fig. 64 so as to give a run of 24 in. to a rise of 16 in. The square is replaced with point A on C and this repeated as often as necessary to give a run of half the width of the building. In this case, it is necessary to place the square three times. In the last position, a mark along the tongue gives the slant of the upper end of the rafter and determines the length of the rafter. Any rafter can be cut in this way.

EXERCISES 35

1. Show with a carpenter's square how to determine the length of a brace for a run of 4 ft. 6 in., and a rise of 3 ft. 6 in. Show how to cut bevels on ends.

2. Show how to mark the slants for the legs of the sawhorse shown in Fig. 65. Compute the length of legs. *Ans.* 29¾ in. nearly.

3. In Fig. 66 is a plan of one end of a roof on a house 18 ft. in width and 28 ft. long. CB, DE, etc., are *common* rafters; AB and NB are *hip* rafters; and FG, HI, etc., are *jack* rafters. Find the lengths to cut the several rafters if the roof is ⅓ pitch. Show how to determine the slants at both ends of each.　The rafters do not extend beyond the plates and are placed 1 ft. 6 in. from center to center.

4. Find lengths of the common, hip, and jack rafters for the roof of which Fig. 67 is the plan.　It is $\frac{1}{2}$ pitch, rafters 1 ft. 6 in. from center to center, and extend 2 ft. beyond the plates.

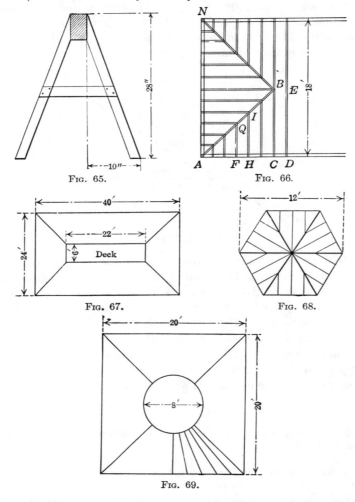

Fɪɢ. 65.　　　　　　　　　　　Fɪɢ. 66.

Fɪɢ. 67.　　　　　　　　　　　Fɪɢ. 68.

Fɪɢ. 69.

5. Fig. 68 is a plan of the roof of a hexagonal tower.　Find lengths of the rafters that end at the plates.　Full pitch and rafters 1 ft. 6 in. between centers.　Width of tower is 12 ft.

6. Fig. 69 represents the plan of a roof of a house 20 ft. square, with a flat circular portion 8 ft. in diameter. If the circle is one-third the width of the building above the plates and the rafters 2 ft. between centers on the plates, find the length of each rafter and show how to cut slants.

ISOSCELES AND EQUILATERAL TRIANGLES

110. Two other forms of triangles of common occurrence are *isosceles* and *equilateral triangles.*

A triangle which has two equal sides is called an **isosceles triangle.**

A triangle which has all of its sides equal is called an **equilateral triangle.**

The following facts are proved in geometry. The student should satisfy himself that they are true by constructing the figures and measuring the parts.

111. The isosceles triangle.—In Fig. 70 the isosceles triangle ABC has equal sides AC and BC.

The angles A and B opposite the equal sides are equal.

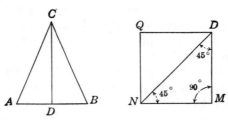

Fig. 70.

The line CD drawn bisecting the vertex angle, C, is perpendicular to and bisects the base, AB. That is, $AD = DB$. It also divides the isosceles triangle into two equal right triangles, BDC and ADC.

The line CD is then the *bisector* of the angle C, and also a *median* and an *altitude* of the triangle.

The diagonal of a square divides the square into two equal right isosceles triangles. In these isosceles triangles each of the equal angles is 45°

112. The equilateral triangle.—In Fig. 71, triangle ABC has its three sides equal and is an equilateral triangle.

The angles opposite the equal sides are equal, and therefore each angle equals 60°.

The line drawn from the vertex A and bisecting the angle is perpendicular to and bisects the opposite side BC. It also divides the equilateral triangle into two equal right triangles, ABD and ADC.

Furthermore, each of the lines BE and CF divides the triangle in the same manner that it is divided by AD.

Each of these lines then is a *bisector* of an angle, and also a *median* and an *altitude* of the equilateral triangle.

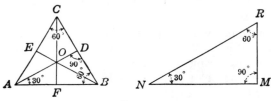

Fig. 71.

The point O where these three lines meet is called the **center** of the equilateral triangle. It is one-third the distance from one side to the opposite vertex. That is, $DO = \frac{1}{3}DA$, $FO = \frac{1}{3}FC$, and $EO = \frac{1}{3}EB$.

It follows then that $AO = 2DO$, $BO = 2EO$, and $CO = 2FO$.

Either of the triangles formed when an equilateral triangle is divided into two triangles by an altitude is a right triangle having acute angles of 30° and 60°. This triangle is very important in practical work. It is readily seen that, in such a right triangle, the hypotenuse is twice the shortest side. That is, $NR = 2MR$.

An altitude of an equilateral triangle equals one-half of a side times $\sqrt{3}$. As a formula, $a = \frac{1}{2}s\sqrt{3} = \frac{1}{2}s \times 1.732$, where $a =$ an altitude and $s =$ a side.

This is obtained by solving the right triangle AFC for FC. The student can easily carry through the work for any particular value of a side. The following is the derivation in general and involves some algebra.

Let s stand for one side of the equilateral triangle.

Then $FC = \sqrt{\overline{AC}^2 - \overline{AF}^2} = \sqrt{s^2 - (\frac{1}{2}s)^2} = \sqrt{\frac{3}{4}s^2} = \frac{1}{2}s\sqrt{3}$.

From this it follows that:

A side of an equilateral triangle equals twice the altitude divided by $\sqrt{3}$. As a formula, $s = 2a \div \sqrt{3}$.

Since the area of any triangle is one-half its base times its altitude, it follows that:

The area of an equilateral triangle equals the square of one-half a side times $\sqrt{3}$. As a formula, $A = (\frac{1}{2}s)^2\sqrt{3} = (\frac{1}{2}s)^2 \times 1.732$, where A is the area.

113. The regular hexagon.—Another form often used in practice is the *regular hexagon.* From geometry we learn the following facts which will appear true from a careful considera- tion of Fig. 72. The diagonals, drawn as shown, divide the hexa- gon into six equal equilateral triangles. The distance from the center O to any vertex is the same as the length of a side. The *area* of the regular hexagon is equal to six times the area of an equilateral triangle with sides equal to the sides of the hexagon. The altitude NO may be found by solving the right triangle ANO; or may be found by taking AN times $\sqrt{3}$.

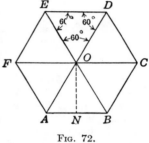

Fig. 72.

EXERCISES 36

1. Find the altitude of an isosceles triangle whose equal sides are 16 ft. and base 14 ft. *Ans.* 14.387+ ft.

2. Find the base of an isosceles triangle if equal sides are 18 in. and altitude 16.5 in. *Ans.* 14.387+ in.

3. Find the altitude of an equilateral triangle the sides of which are 12 ft. *Ans.* 10.392+ ft.

4. In Fig. 72, find ON if AB is 10 ft. *Ans.* 8.660+ ft.

5. Find the area of an equilateral triangle 18 in. on a side. *Ans.* 140.3− in.²

6. Find the area of an isosceles triangle whose base is 6 in. and equal sides 9 in. *Ans.* 25.456− in.²

7. Compute the area of a regular hexagon one of whose sides is 5 ft. *Ans.* 64.95+ ft.²

8. An equilateral triangle has an area of 21.217 in.² What is the length of one side? *Ans.* 7 in.

Solution. On page 141 it is stated that the area of an equilateral triangle equals the square of one-half a side times $\sqrt{3}$.

Or $\qquad A = (\tfrac{1}{2}s)^2 \times 1.732.$

Then $\qquad \tfrac{1}{2}s = \sqrt{A \div 1.732}.$

But A is given equal to 21.217.

$\qquad \therefore \ \tfrac{1}{2}s = \sqrt{21.217 \div 1.732} = \sqrt{12.25} = 3.5.$

Or $\qquad s = 2 \times 3.5 = 7.$

9. An isosceles triangle has a base 16 in. long and the equal sides 18 in. What is the area? *Ans.* 128.996+ in.²

10. Find the length of the steam pipe $ABCD$, Fig. 73, if $AD = 6$ ft., $CE = 16$ in., and angle $EBC = 30°$. *Ans.* 76.29− in.

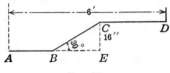

Fig. 73.

Suggestion. $\qquad BC = 2EC = 2 \times 16$ in. $= 32$ in.

$\qquad BE = \sqrt{3} \times EC = 1.732 \times 16 = 27.71+$ in.

Increase along $BC = 32$ in. $-27.71+$ in. $= 4.29-$ in.

Length of $ABCD = 72$ in. $+4.29-$ in. $= 76.29-$ in.

11. The hypotenuse of a right triangle is 5 ft. and one side is 4 ft. Show that the equilateral triangle made on the hypotenuse is equal to the sum of the equilateral triangles made on the other two sides.

Suggestion. Find the areas of the three triangles and show that the sum of the areas of the two smaller triangles equals the largest triangle. Use the formula $A = (\tfrac{1}{2}s)^2 \times 1.732$.

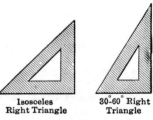

Isosceles
Right Triangle

30°-60° Right
Triangle

Fig. 74.

12. Two very convenient forms of triangles used by draftsmen are right triangles made of celluloid or rubber; one a right isosceles triangle having the acute angles each 45°, and one having acute angles of 30° and 60°. If one of the equal sides of the isosceles right triangle is 6 in., find the hypotenuse. *Ans.* 8.485 in.

13. If the shortest side of the 30°-60°-right triangle is 4 in. find the other sides. *Ans.* 6.928 in. and 8 in.

14. Using the draftsman's triangles, show how to construct the following angles: 15°, 75°, 105°, 120°, 135°, 150°.

15. A hexagonal nut for a $\frac{11}{16}$-in. screw is $1\frac{1}{4}$ in. across the flats. Find the diagonal, or the distance across the corners, of such a nut.

Ans. 1.443 in.

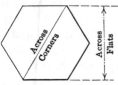

FIG. 75.

16. What is the distance across the corners of a hexagonal nut that is $\frac{3}{4}$ in. on a side? What is the distance across the flats of the same nut?

Ans. 1.5 in.; 1.299 in.

17. Show that the distance across the corners of a hexagonal nut is approximately 1.15 times the distance across the flats.

Suggestion. It is readily seen that the distance across the corners is twice the side of an equilateral triangle whose altitude is one-half the distance across the flats.

By **Art. 112,** $s = 2a \div \sqrt{3}$.

$\therefore 2s = 4a \div \sqrt{3} = 2a \times 1.15$.

But $2s =$ distance across corners,

and $2a =$ distance across flats.

18. In a standard hexagonal bolt nut the distance across the flats is given by the formula $F = 1.5D + \frac{1}{8}$, where F is the distance across the flats and D the diameter of the body of the bolt.

Find the distance across the flats and across the corners on a hexagonal nut for a bolt $1\frac{3}{4}$ in. in diameter. *Ans.* 2.75 in.; 3.1754 in.

19. To what diameter should a piece of stock be turned so that it may be milled to a hexagon and be $1\frac{3}{4}$ in. across the flats?

Ans. 2.0207 in.

20. Find the size of round stock to make bolts with hexagonal heads and having bodies of the following diameters: $\frac{1}{2}$ in., $1\frac{1}{2}$ in., $1\frac{1}{8}$ in., $1\frac{5}{16}$ in.

Ans. 1.0104 in.; 2.7424 in.; 2.0929 in.; 2.4177 in.

Suggestion. Distance ocross flats, $F = 1.5D + \frac{1}{8}$.

When $D = \frac{1}{2}$ in., $F = 1.5 \times 0.5 + 0.125 = 0.875$ in.

Diameter of stock = distance across corners = $\dfrac{0.875 \times 2}{\sqrt{3}} = 1.0104$ in.

By the rule of exercise 17, distance across corners = $0.875 \times 1.15 = 1.006$ in.

SCREW THREADS

114. In the United States there are in use several different kinds of screw threads. Here we will consider: *first,* the *sharp V-thread,* or *common V-thread;* and second, the *United States standard screw thread.* Other kinds will be considered on page 437.

115. Sharp V-thread.—The **sharp V-thread,** or **common V-thread,** is a thread having its sides at an angle of 60° to each other and perfectly sharp at the top and bottom.

The objections urged against this thread are, first, that the top, being so sharp, is injured by the slightest accident; and second, that in the use of taps and dies the fine sharp edge is quickly lost, thus causing constant variation in fitting.

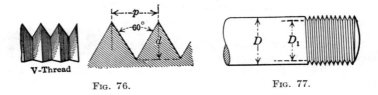

V-Thread

Fig. 76.   Fig. 77.

The common V-thread with a pitch of 1 in. has a depth equal to the altitude of an equilateral triangle 1 in. on a side. Hence its depth $= \frac{1}{2}\sqrt{3} = 0.866$ in. The root diameter equals the diameter of the bolt less twice the depth of the thread. We have then the following formulas:

$$p = \frac{1}{N},$$

$$d = 0.866p = \frac{0.866}{N},$$

$$[14] \quad D_1 = D - 2d = D - \frac{1.732}{N},$$

where $p =$ pitch, $d =$ depth of thread, $N =$ number of threads to the inch, $D =$ diameter of bolt, and $D_1 =$ root diameter.

116. United States standard thread.—The **United States standard screw thread** (U. S. S.) has its sides also at an angle of 60° to each other but has its top cut off to the extent of $\frac{1}{8}$ its depth and the same amount filled in at its bottom, thus making the depth $\frac{3}{4}$ that of the common V-thread of the same pitch. The distance f on the flat is $\frac{1}{8}$ its pitch.

This thread is not so easily injured, the taps and dies retain their size longer, and bolts and screws having this thread are stronger and have a better appearance.

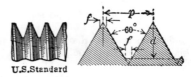

U.S.Standard

Fig. 78.

For the U. S. S. screw thread we have the following formulas:

$$p = \frac{1}{N},$$
$$d = 0.6495p = \frac{0.6495}{N},$$
$$[15] \ D_1 = D - 2d = D - \frac{1.299}{N}.$$

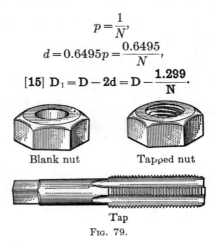

Blank nut   Tapped nut

Tap

Fig. 79.

The blank nut for a bolt is drilled with a tap drill the same size as the root diameter of the screw or bolt, or very nearly that size.

Table V can be used in computations connected with screw threads.

EXERCISES 37

1. Find the depths of common V-threads of the following number of threads to an inch: 10, 20, 5, 8, 40, 13.

Ans. 0.0866 in.; 0.0433 in.; 0.1732 in.; 0.1083 in.; 0.0217 in.; 0.0666 in.

2. Find the depths of U. S. S. threads of same pitches as in exercise 1.

Ans. 0.0649 in.; 0.0325 in.; 0.1299 in.; 0.0812 in.; 0.0162 in.; 0.0500 in.

10

3. Find the root diameter of a screw of outer diameter $\frac{1}{2}$ in. and 14 sharp V-threads to the inch.   *Ans.* 0.3763 in.

4. Show that the depth of any sharp V-thread in inches is $\frac{1}{2}\sqrt{3}$ divided by the number of threads per inch, or, what is the same thing, 0.866 divided by the number of threads per inch.

5. Check the depth of the sharp V-thread for five of the sizes given in **Table V**.

6. Using the formula, find the root diameter of the following common V-threads: $\frac{1}{4}$ in. diameter and 20-pitch, $\frac{3}{8}$ in.-16, $\frac{1}{2}$ in.-13, $1\frac{1}{2}$ in.-6, $2\frac{5}{16}$ in.-$4\frac{1}{2}$, $3\frac{1}{2}$ in.-$3\frac{1}{4}$.

Ans. 0.1634 in.; 0.2668 in.; 0.3668 in.; 1.2113 in.; 1.9276 in.; 2.9671 in.

7. Find the size of tap drill for a $\frac{9}{16}$-in. 12-pitch sharp V-thread nut.

Ans. 0.4182 in.

8. What is the tap drill size for the nut of a $\frac{9}{16}$-in. 20-pitch common double-threaded nut?   *Ans.* 0.4759 in.

9. Find the depth of the U. S. S. screw thread when there are 15 threads to the inch.   16 threads.   *Ans.* 0.0433 in.; 0.0406 in.

10. Show that the depth in inches of any U. S. S. is $\frac{3}{8}\sqrt{3} = 0.6495$ divided by the number of threads per inch.

11. Using the diameter of the screw, check the depth of the U. S. S. thread for five of the sizes given in **Table V**.

12. Using the formula, find the root diameter of the following U. S. S. threads: $\frac{5}{8}$ in.-11, 1 in.-8, $1\frac{3}{4}$ in.-5.

Ans. 0.507 in.; 0.838 in.; 1.490 in.

13. Check the root diameters for five sizes of screws found in **Table V**.

CHAPTER XII

CIRCLES

117. The importance of a geometrical form in the study of practical mathematics is determined, to a great extent, by the frequency of its occurrence in the applications. The circle occurs often, perhaps more frequently than any other geometric form in applied mathematics. Wires, tanks, pipes, steam boilers, pillars, etc., involve the circle. In the present chapter will be considered the more useful facts about the circle, and some of their applications. Again, the student is recommended to select those parts that are most closely connected with his work or interests.

118. Definitions.—A **circle** is a plane figure bounded by a curved line every point of which is the same distance from another point, called the center.

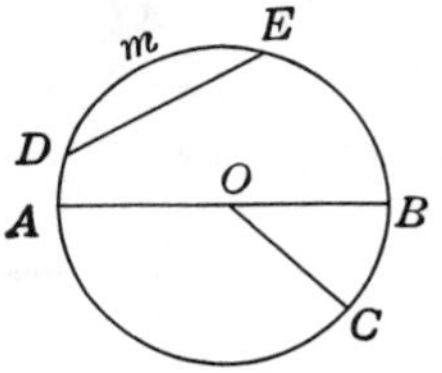

The curved line is called the **circumference.**

A line drawn through the center and terminating in the circumference is called a **diameter.**

A line drawn from the center to the circumference is called a **radius.**

Fig. 80.

Any part of the circumference is called an **arc.**

In Fig. 80, BC is an arc.

If the arc equals $\frac{1}{360}$ of the circumference it is 1° of arc. There are then 360° of arc in one circumference.

The straight line joining the ends of an arc is called a **chord.**

In Fig. 80, DE is a chord.

The chord is said to **subtend** its arc.

The chord DE subtends the arc DmE.

The area bounded by an arc and a chord is called a **segment.**

In Fig. 80, the area DmE is a segment.

147

The area bounded by two radii and an arc is called a **sector.**

In Fig. 80, the area *BOC* is a sector.

Circles are said to be **concentric** when they have a common center as in Fig. 81.

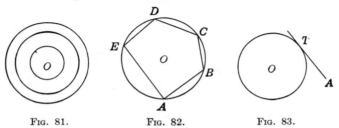

FIG. 81.   FIG. 82.   FIG. 83.

A polygon is **inscribed in** a circle when it is inside the circle and has its vertices on the circumference.   The circle is then **circumscribed about** the polygon.

The polygon *ABCDE* in Fig. 82 is inscribed in the circle *O*.

A line is **tangent** to a circumference when it touches but does not cut through the circumference.

In Fig. 83, *AT* is tangent to the circle *O* at the point *T*.

The point *T* where it touches the circle is called the **point of tangency.**

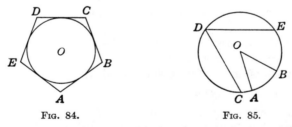

FIG. 84.   FIG. 85.

A polygon is **circumscribed about** a circle, or the circle is **inscribed in** a polygon, when the sides of the polygon are all tangent to the circle.

In Fig. 84, the polygon *ABCDE* is circumscribed about the circle *O*.

A **central angle** is an angle with its vertex at the center of the circle.

In Fig. 85, angle *AOB* is a central angle.

An **inscribed angle** is an angle with its vertex on the circumference of the circle.

In Fig. 85, angle *CDE* is an inscribed angle.

An inscribed or a central angle is said to **intercept** the arc between its sides.

The sides of the angle *AOB* intercept the arc *AB*, and the sides of the angle *CDE* intercept the arc *CE*.

119. Properties of the circle.—The student should become familiar with the following properties, and satisfy himself that they are true by actual drawings and measurements.

(1) *In the same circle or in equal circles, chords that are the same distance from the center are equal.*

(2) *A radius, drawn to the center of a chord, is perpendicular to the chord and bisects the arc which the chord subtends.*

In Fig. 86, the radius *OC* is drawn through the center of the chord *AB*. It is perpendicular to *AB*, and makes arc *AC* = arc *CB*. This appears true by measuring the parts in the drawing.

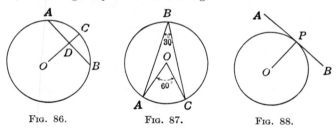

Fig. 86. Fig. 87. Fig. 88.

(3) *The angle at the center, that intercepts an arc, is double the inscribed angle that intercepts the same arc.*

In Fig. 87, the central angle *AOC* = 60°, and the inscribed angle *ABC* is measured and found to equal 30°.

The student should draw several such figures and measure the angles. (See **Art. 137** for measuring angles.)

(4) *The central angle has as many degrees in it as there are in the arc its sides intercept; and it is said that the central angle is measured by the arc its sides intercept.*

This is so because there are 4 right angles or 360° in the angles at the center, and the circumference also contains 360°.

(5) *The inscribed angle has one-half as many degrees as the arc its sides intercept, and hence the inscribed angle is measured by one-half the arc its sides intercept.*

(6) *A radius drawn to the point of contact of a tangent is perpendicular to the tangent.*

In Fig. 88, *OP* is drawn to the point of contact of the tangent *AB*. The angles can be measured and found to be right angles. Hence the radius is perpendicular to the tangent.

120. The segment.—In practical work it is often necessary to find the radius of the circle when we know the chord *AB* and the height of the segment *DC* of Fig. 89. If *r* stands for the radius of the circle, *h* for the height of the segment, and *w* for the length of the chord, we have the following formulas for finding *r*, *h*, and *w*:

$$[16] \ r = \frac{(\tfrac{1}{2}w)^2 + h^2}{2h},$$

$$[17] \ h = r - \sqrt{r^2 - (\tfrac{1}{2}w)^2},$$

$$[18] \ w = 2\sqrt{h(2r - h)}.$$

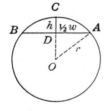 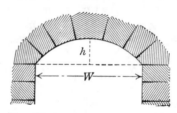

Fig. 89.

For the derivation of formula [16] the student is referred to exercise 35, page 306.

It should be noticed that these formulas are found by applying the principles of the right triangle.

Example. If the chord of the segment of a circle is 5 ft. 6 in. and the height of the segment is 10 in., find the radius of the circle.

Solution. From formula [16], $r = \dfrac{33^2 + 10^2}{2 \times 10} = 59.45$

∴ radius = 59.45 in.

The method given in this article for finding the radius of the circle when the length of the chord and the height of the segment are known is used by street car trackmen as follows: A straightedge 10 ft. long is laid against the rail on the inside of the curve. The distance from the center of the straightedge to the rail is measured. This is the height of the segment, or, as it is usually called, the "middle ordinate." The radius can now be found by the formula given.

For the use of the practical man, tables are arranged which give the radius corresponding to any "middle ordinate" for the 10-ft. chord.

121. Relations between the diameter, radius, and circumference.—If the diameter and the circumference of a circle be measured, and the length of the circumference be divided by the length of the diameter the result will be nearly $3\frac{1}{7}$. This value is the ratio of the circumference to the diameter of a circle, and cannot be expressed exactly in figures. In mathematics the ratio is represented by the Greek letter π (pi). The exact numerical value of π cannot be expressed. The value to four decimal places is 3.1416. (See **Table II.**)

Because of this relation, if the diameter, the radius, or the circumference is known, the other two can be found.

RULE. *The* **radius** *equals one-half the diameter, or the diameter equals twice the radius.*

The **circumference** *equals the diameter times* 3.1416.

The **diameter** *equals the circumference divided by* 3.1416.

If r stands for the radius, d for the diameter, and C for the circumference, the rules are stated in the following formulas:

[19] $C = \pi d$.
[20] $d = C \div \pi$.
[21] $C = 2\pi r$.
[22] $2r = C \div \pi$.

122. Area of the circle —The method of finding the area of a circle when the radius, diameter, or circumference is given is established in geometry. The following will show the reasonableness of the rules.

In Fig. 90, suppose the half of the circle AnB is cut as indicated from the center nearly to the circumference, and then spread out as in (*b*). The length AnB of (*b*) is the half circumference. Let the other half of the circle be cut in the same manner and fitted into the first half. It is evident that, if we make the number of the cuts large, the figure formed will be approximately a rectangle whose length is equal to one-half the circumference, and whose width is equal to the radius. We then have the following:

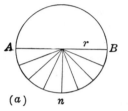 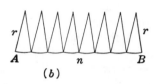

(a)　　n

(b)

Fig. 90.

RULE. *To find the area of a circle, multiply one-half the circumference by the radius.*

This may be put in either of the following forms which are usually more convenient to use.

RULE. *The area of a circle equals π times the square of the radius; or the area of a circle equals one-fourth of π times the square of the diameter.*

If A stands for the area, C for the circumference, d for the diameter, and r for the radius, these rules are stated in the following formulas:

[23] $A = \frac{1}{2}Cr.$

[24] $A = \pi r^2 = 3.1416 \times r^2.$

[25] $A = \frac{1}{4}\pi d^2 = 0.7854 \times d^2.$

From formula [24], if the area of the circle is given, the radius equals the square root of the quotient when the area is divided by π. Or, in a formula,

[26] $r = \sqrt{A \div \pi}.$

From formula [25], we get

[27] $d = \sqrt{A \div \frac{1}{4}\pi} = \sqrt{A \div 0.7854}.$

Example. Find the radius of a circle whose area is 28 ft.^{2}

Solution. Using formula [26] and putting in the numbers,

$$r = \sqrt{28 \div 3.1416} = \sqrt{8.9126} = 2.985.$$
$$\therefore \text{ radius} = 2.985 \text{ ft.}$$

123. Area of a ring.—In the ring, which is the area between the circumferences of two concentric circles, the area can be found by subtracting the area of the small circle from the area of the large circle.

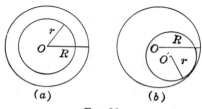

(a)   (b)

FIG. 91.

If A and a, R and r stand for the areas and the radii respectively of the two circles, and A_r for the area of the ring, then

[28] $A_r = A - a = \pi R^2 - \pi r^2 = \pi(R^2 - r^2) = \pi(R+r)(R-r).$

This last is a very convenient formula to use. It may be stated in words as follows:

RULE. *To find the area of a ring, multiply the product of the sum and the difference of the two radii by π.*

Example. Find the area of a ring of inner diameter 8 in. and outer diameter 12 in.

Solution. Using formula [28] and putting in the numbers,

$$A_r = 3.1416(6+4)(6-4)$$
$$= 3.1416 \times 10 \times 2 = 62.832.$$
$$\therefore \text{area} = 62.832 \text{ in.}^2$$

It should be noted that the rule holds even though the circles are not concentric, that is, the circles may be as in Fig. 91(*b*).

124. Area of a sector.—The area of a sector of a circle is equal to that fractional part of the area of the whole circle that the angle of the sector is of 360°. Thus, if the angle of the sector is 90°, the area of the sector is $\frac{90}{360}$ of the area of the circle.

Example. Find the area of a sector of 60° in a circle of radius 10 in.

Solution. In Fig. 92, the sector *AOB* has an angle of 60°. Its area equals $\frac{60}{360} \times \pi r^2$. If the radius is 10 in., the area of the sector is

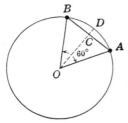

$$A = \tfrac{1}{6} \times 3.1416 \times 10^2 = 52.36 \text{ in.}^2 \ Ans.$$

If θ (the Greek letter theta) stands for the number of degrees in the angle of the sector, and the other letters the same as before, the area of the sector is given by the formula,

$$[29] \ A = \frac{\theta}{360} \times \pi r^2.$$

Fig. 92.

125. Area of a segment.—In Fig. 92, it is evident that the area of the segment *ABD* equals the area of the sector *AOB* minus the area of the triangle *AOB*. Since it requires a knowledge of trigonometry to find the area of a triangle when we have only two sides and an angle, or to find the area of a sector when the angle is unknown, we cannot usually find the area of a segment by geometry. (See page 434.)

If the angle and the lines in the segment are measured, the area of, first, the sector, and second, the triangle, can be found. The difference between these areas is the area of the segment.

Example 1. Find the area of a segment in a circle of radius $11\frac{1}{4}$ in. and subtending an angle at the center of 105°.

Solution. The dimensions are as shown in Fig. 93, where the parts are constructed accurately to scale and measured.

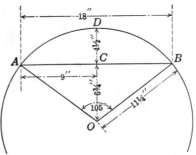

Fig. 93.

The area of sector $OADB = \frac{105}{360}$ of the area of the circle.

∴ area of sector $= \frac{105}{360} \times 3.1416 \times (11\frac{1}{4})^2 = 115.97 \text{ in.}^2$

Area of triangle $OAB = \frac{1}{2} \times 18 \times 6\frac{3}{4} = 60.75 \text{ in.}^2$

Area of segment = area of sector − area of triangle

$= 115.97 \text{ in.}^2 - 60.75 \text{ in.}^2 = 55.22 \text{ in.}^2 \ Ans.$

Many approximate rules are given to find the area of a segment. Perhaps the following are as good as any.

$$[30(a)] \quad A = \tfrac{2}{3}hw + \frac{h^3}{2w},$$

$$[30(b)] \quad A = \tfrac{4}{3}h^2\sqrt{\frac{2r}{h} - 0.608}.$$

In these rules A is the area of the segment, h the height, and w the width, while r is the radius of the circle to which the segment belongs.

If the height of the segment is less than one-tenth the radius of the circle, formula [30(a)] may be shortened to $A = \tfrac{2}{3}hw$.

Steam engineers often wish to find the area of a segment when the height is large compared with the radius, say, two-thirds of the radius. They then proceed as follows: In Fig. 94, let it be required to find the area of the segment CnD. Find the area of the half circle AnB, and then the area of the part $ACDB$ considered as a rectangle. The area of the segment is roughly the difference between these.

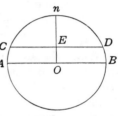

Fig. 94.

Example 2. Find the area of the segment whose chord is 10 ft. and height 1.5 ft.

Solution. By formula [30(a)].

$$A = \tfrac{2}{3} \times 1.5 \times 10 + \frac{1.5^3}{2 \times 10} = 10.17 - \text{ ft.}^2$$

By formula [30(b)], first finding r by formula [16],

$$r = \frac{5^2 + 1.5^2}{2 \times 1.5} = 9.083.$$

$$A = \tfrac{4}{3} \times 1.5^2 \sqrt{\frac{2 \times 9.083}{1.5} - 0.608} = 10.175 \text{ ft.}^2$$

126. The ellipse.—The **ellipse** is a figure bounded by a curved line such that the sum of the distances of any point in the boundary from two fixed points is constant, that is, always the same.

Thus, in Fig. 95, any point P has the distances $PF + PF'$ equal to the distances $P'F + P'F'$, drawn from any other point P'.

F and F' are the two fixed points and are called the **foci** (singular **focus**). The point O is the **center** of the ellipse. NA is the **major axis**, and MB is the **minor axis**. OA and OB are the **semi-axes**.

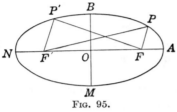

FIG. 95.

If a stands for OA and b for OB, it has been proved that the area of the ellipse is given by the formula,

[31] A=πab.

Example 1.   Find the area of an ellipse whose two axes are 30 ft. and 26 ft. respectively.

Solution.   Using formula **[31]** and putting in the values,

$$A = 3.1416 \times 15 \times 13 = 612.612 \text{ ft.}^2$$

While the area of an ellipse is easily found when the major and minor axes are given, the circumference, or perimeter, of the ellipse is determined with difficulty.   Various approximate formulas are given for finding the circumference of an ellipse. If the ellipse is very nearly the shape of a circle, that is, if the major and minor axes are nearly equal, then

[32(a)] P=π(a+b),

where P is the perimeter or circumference, a the semi-major axis, and b the semi-minor axis.

When the ellipse differs considerably from a circle, that is, when there is considerable difference between the major and minor axes, either of the following rules may be used to good advantage:

[32(b)] P=π[³⁄₂(a+b)−√ab],

[32(c)] P=π√2(a²+b²).

The exact formula derived by the methods of higher mathematics may be stated in the following form:

$$P = 2\pi a \left(1 - \tfrac{1}{4}e^2 - \tfrac{3}{64}e^4 - \tfrac{5}{256}e^6 - \tfrac{175}{16384}e^8 - \cdots \right),$$

where $e = \dfrac{\sqrt{a^2 - b^2}}{a}$.   This formula is not given with the intention that it should be used, as the computation required is considerable.

Example 2.   Find the circumference of an ellipse whose major axis is 18 in. and whose minor axis is 6 in.

Solution. Here $a = 9$ and $b = 3$.

By [**32(a)**], $P = 3.1416(9 + 3) = 37.699$ in.

By [**32(b)**], $P = 3.1416[\frac{3}{2}(9 + 3) - \sqrt{9 \times 3}] = 40.225$ in.

By [**32(c)**], $P = 3.1416\sqrt{2(9^2 + 3^2)} = 42.149$ in.

Formula [**32(b)**] is the best to use when the two axes are not very nearly equal.

EXERCISES 38

1. Using d for diameter, C for circumference, r for radius, and A for area of a circle, given the values in the first column to find those in the last two.

(a) $d = 75$ ft.	$C = 235.62$ ft.;	$A = 4417.86$ ft.^{2}
(b) $r = 23$ ft.	$C = 144.51$ ft.;	$A = 1661.90$ ft.^{2}
(c) $d = 34.6$ in.	$C = 108.70$ in.;	$A = 940.25$ in.^{2}
(d) $d = 24.5$ in.	$C = 76.97$ in.;	$A = 471.44$ in.^{2}
(e) $C = 86.08$ in.	$d = 27.4$ in.;	$A = 589.65$ in.^{2}
(f) $C = 158.02$ in.	$d = 50.3$ in.;	$A = 1987.13$ in.^{2}
(g) $A = 1452.20$ ft.^{2}	$d = 43$ ft.;	$C = 135.09$ ft.
(h) $A = 27171.6$ ft.^{2}	$r = 93$ ft.;	$C = 584.34$ ft.

2. Find the area of the cross section of a half-inch rod.

Ans. $0.196+$ in.^{2}

By the **cross section** is meant the area of the end of the rod when cut square off.

3. Find the area of the ring enclosed between two circles, the outer 9 in. and the inner 8 in. in diameter. *Ans.* 13.352 in.^{2}

4. The inner and outer diameters of a ring are $9\frac{1}{2}$ and 10 in. respectively. Find the area of the ring? *Ans.* 7.658 in.^{2}

5. Find the area of the ring in the cross section of a water main 40 in. in external diameter, if the iron is 1 in. thick in the shell.

Ans. $122.52+$ in.^{2}

6. In an elliptical garden the longest diameter is 36 ft. and the shortest 22 ft. Find the area of the garden. *Ans.* $622.04-$ ft.^{2}

7. In a steel plate 3 ft. by $2\frac{1}{2}$ ft. are 26 round holes, each $1\frac{3}{4}$ in. in diameter. Find the area of steel remaining. *Ans.* $1017.46+$ in.^{2}

8. At the center of one side of a barn 40 ft. on a side a horse is tied by a rope 70 ft. in length. Find the area he can graze over in square rods. *Ans.* $43.27+$ rd.^{2}

Suggestion. When the figure is drawn it is seen that the horse can graze over a half-circle having a radius of 70 ft., two quarter-circles having a radius of 50 ft., and two quarter-circles having a radius of 10 ft.

9. A 6-in. water pipe can carry how many times as much as an inch pipe?

Solution. Area of 6-in. pipe $= 0.7854 \times 6^2$ in.^{2}

Area of 1-in. pipe $= 0.7854 \times 1^2$ in.^{2}

$$\frac{\text{Area of 6-in. pipe}}{\text{Area of 1-in. pipe}} = \frac{0.7854 \times 6^2}{0.7854 \times 1^2} = \frac{6^2}{1^2} = 36. \ Ans.$$

The quotient or the ratio of the areas of two circles can always be found by dividing the square of one diameter by the square of the other. The radii may be used instead of the diameters.

The above is simply the principle that similar areas are in the same ratio as the squares of their like dimensions, applied to circles.

10. In putting up blower pipes, two circular pipes 11 in. and 14 in. in diameter respectively join and continue as a rectangular pipe 14 in. in width. Find the length of the cross-section of the rectangular pipe.   *Ans.* 17.78 + in.

11. How many times the area of the cross section of a $\frac{1}{16}$-in. wire is a half-inch wire?   *Ans.* 64.

12. If an inch pipe will empty 2 barrels in 15 minutes, how many barrels will an 8-in. pipe empty in 24 hours? (Make no allowance for friction.)   *Ans.* 12,288.

13. How many 3-in. steam pipes could open off from an 18-in. steam pipe?   *Ans.* 36.

14. The diameter of the safety valve in a boiler is 3 in. Find the total pressure tending to raise the valve when the pressure of the steam is 120 lb. per square inch.   *Ans.* 848.23 lb.

15. If the diameter of a piston is 30 in., find the total pressure on the piston when the pressure of steam is 100 lb. per square inch.   *Ans.* 70,686 lb.

16. A circular sheet of steel 2 ft. in diameter increases in diameter by $\frac{1}{200}$ when the temperature is increased by a certain amount. (a) Find the increase in the area of the sheet. (b) Find the per cent of increase in area.   *Ans.* (a) 0.03149 ft.²; (b) 1%.

17. How many No. 20 B. and S. copper wires will have the same cross section area as one No. 00? (See **Table VII.**)   *Ans.* 130.3 −

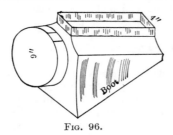

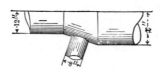

FIG. 96.   FIG. 97.

18. A hot-air pipe 9 in. in diameter passes into a boot as shown in Fig. 96, and a rectangular pipe of same capacity passes upward from the boot. If the rectangular pipe is 4 in. wide, find its length in cross section.   *Ans.* 15.9 + in.

19. Given two joining pipes 12 in. and 8 in. in diameter respectively, to find the diameter x of the continuation which has the same area. (See Fig. 97.)   *Ans.* 14.4 + in.

20. Given an elliptical pipe of longest and shortest axes 16 in. and 10 in. respectively, to find the diameter of the circular pipe having the same area of cross section.   *Ans.* 12.65— in.

21. Show by means of the carpenter's square how to find the diameter of a circle having the same area as the sum of the areas of two given circles.

Discussion. Suppose we take two circles 6 in. and 8 in. in diameter respectively. Lay off on one arm of the carpenter's square, as shown in

Fig. 98, the diameter of the 6-in. circle and on the other arm the diameter of the 8-in. circle. The line joining the ends of these, or the hypotenuse of the right triangle, is the diameter of the circle having the same area as the sum of the areas of the two given circles.

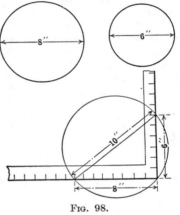

This is seen to be true in this particular case as follows:

Area of 6-in. circle $=6^2 \times 0.7854$ in.^{2}

Area of 8-in. circle $=8^2 \times 0.7854$ in.^{2}

Sum of areas $=(6^2+8^2) \times 0.7854$ in.^{2}

But $6^2+8^2=10^2$, and if 6 in. and 8 in. are respectively the altitude and base of a right triangle then 10 in. is the hypotenuse.

Fig. 98.

Hence the area of the circle equal to the sum is $10^2 \times 0.7854$ in.^{2} The diameter of this circle is evidently 10 in., which is the hypotenuse of the right triangle as drawn in the figure.

A similar discussion would apply to any two circles.

22. Show by means of the carpenter's square how to find the diameter of a circle having the same area as the sum of the areas of any number of given circles.

23. If the drive wheels of a locomotive are 66 in. in diameter, find the number of revolutions per minute to go 40 miles per hour.

Ans. 203.7+.

$$\frac{40 \times 5280 \times 12}{60 \times 66 \times 3.1416} = 203.7.$$

Solution. It is usual to work such problems as this by cancellation. Above the line are the numbers which give the inches in 40 miles. Below the line is 60, which we divide by to get the number of inches the train goes in 1 minute; and 66×3.1416, which is the number of inches in the circumference of the wheel.

24. Supposing that the driving wheels of a locomotive are 16 ft. in circumference, what number of revolutions must they make per minute so that the locomotive may attain a speed of 60 miles per hour?

Ans. 330.

25. A locomotive wheel 5 ft. in diameter made 10,000 revolutions in a distance of 24 miles. What distance was lost due to the slipping of the wheels?   *Ans.* 5¾ miles.

26. If an arc of a circle is equal in length to the radius, what is the value of the central angle which it measures?   *Ans.* 57.2958° −.

Solution. Since 2π times the radius equals the circumference, and the entire circumference measures an angle of 360° at the center of the circle, the number of degrees $= 360 \div 2\pi = 57.2958 -$.

27. The radii of two circles are 2 ft. and 4 ft. The area of the second is how many times the first?   *Ans.* 4.

28. The length of the circumference of a circle is 132 ft. Calculate the length of the diameter, the length of an arc of 40°, and the area of a sector of 80°. *Ans.* Arc 14.67 − ft.; dia. 42.017 − ft.; area 308.1+ ft.² ·

29. Find the weight of the iron hoops on a tank 15 ft. in diameter, there being 16 hoops weighing 3 lb. per linear foot. *Ans.* 2261.9+ lb.

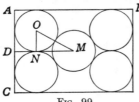

FIG. 99.

30. A regular hexagon, the perimeter of which is 42 ft., is inscribed in a circle. Find the area of the circle.   *Ans.* 153.9+ ft.²

31. What is the waste in cutting the largest possible circular plate from a piece of sheet steel 17 in. by 20 in.?
          Ans. 113.02 in.²

32. Four of the largest possible equal sized pipes are enclosed in a box of square cross section 18 in. on an edge. What part of the space do the pipes occupy?   *Ans.* 0.7854.

33. Find size of the box to enclose five 6-in. pipes, placed as in Fig. 99, and find the part the area of the pipes is of the area of the box.

          Ans. Box 12 in. by 16.392 in.; part occupied 0.7187+.

Solution. $AC = 12$ in., $AB = 2DM$.

$DM = DN + NM$, but $DN = 3$ in. and

$NM = \sqrt{OM^2 - ON^2} = \sqrt{6^2 - 3^2} = \sqrt{27} = 5.196$ in.

$\therefore DM = 3$ in. $+5.196$ in. $= 8.196$ in.

$\therefore AB = 2 \times 8.196$ in. $= 16.392$ in.

$\therefore$ area $= 12 \times 16.392 = 196.704$ in.²

Area of 5 circles $= 5 \times 0.7854 \times 6^2 = 141.372$ in.²

Part occupied by pipes $= 141.372 \div 196.704 = 0.7187+$.

34. If the diameter of a circle is 3 in., what is the length of an arc of 80°?   *Ans.* 2.0944 in.

35. The minute hand of a tower clock is 6 ft. long. What distance will the extremity move over in 36 minutes?   *Ans.* 22 ft. 7.4+ in.

36. The maximum circumferential velocity of cast-iron flywheels is 80 ft. per second. Find the maximum number of revolutions per minute for a cast-iron flywheel 8 ft. in diameter.   *Ans.* 191 nearly.

37. An emery wheel may have a circumferential velocity of 5500 ft. per minute. Find the number of revolutions per second an emery wheel 9 in. in diameter may make.   *Ans.* 39 nearly.

38. The peripheral speed of a grindstone of strong grain should not exceed 47 ft. per second. Find the number of revolutions per minute a grindstone 3 ft. in diameter may turn. *Ans.* 299 nearly.

39. The area of a square is 49 sq. ft. Find the length of the circumference and the area of the circle inscribed in this square.

Ans. 21.99+ ft.; 38.48+ ft.^{2}

40. Find the size of the largest square timber which can be cut from a log 24 in. in diameter. *Ans.* 16.97+ in.

41. A roller used in rolling a lawn is 6.5 ft. in circumference and 2.5 ft. wide. If the roller makes 10 revolutions in crossing the lawn once and must go up and back 12 times, what is the area of the lawn?

Ans. 3900 ft.^{2}

42. Three circles are enclosed in an equilateral triangle. If the circles are 10 in. in radius, find the sides of the triangle. *Ans.* 54.64 in.

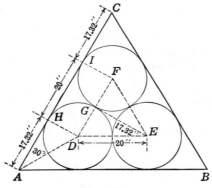

Fɪɢ. 100.

Suggestion. The circles are as shown in Fig. 100. The triangle DEG = triangle DAH. Hence $AH = GE = 10 \times \sqrt{3} = 17.32$ in., HI = the diameter of one of the circles = 20 in., and $IC = AH = 17.32$ in.

43. Using 4000 miles as radius of earth, find length in feet of one second of arc on the equator. *Ans.* 102.4− ft.

Note. 1° = 60 minutes and 1 minute = 60 seconds of arc.

44. Using 4000 miles as radius of earth, find the length in miles of arc of 1′ (*a*) on the parallel of 45° north; (*b*) on the parallel of 60° north.

Ans. (*a*) 0.823− miles; (*b*) 0.582− miles.

Suggestion. For the parallel of 45° north, CB is the radius. But $CB = OC$ since the triangle OCB is a right triangle with two equal angles. The relations are as shown in Fig. 101.

45. A bicycle is so geared that one revolution of the feet makes two revolutions of the wheels which are 28 in. in diameter How many revolutions per minute of the feet are necessary to go at the rate of 25 miles per hour? Suppose that the pneumatic tires are not well inflated,

11

what is the per cent of loss in distance made if the compression in the tire is ½ in.?   *Ans.* 150+; 3.6 − %.

Suggestion. If the compression of the pneumatic tire is ½ in., the wheel acts as if it were ½ in. less in radius.

46. What is the per cent of error in taking 4 times *CA* in Fig. 102 as the circumference of circle *O*?   *Ans.* 0.66+% too large.

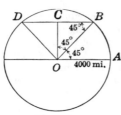

Fig. 101.

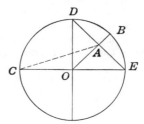

Fig. 102.

47. In the same circle, what is the per cent of error in taking 4(*DE*+½*AB*) as the circumference?   *Ans.* 0.65 − % too small.

48. If statements in numbers 46 and 47 gave the exact length of the circumference, what would be the value of π in each case?

Ans. In No. 46, $\pi = \sqrt{10} = 3.16228 -$; in No. 47, $\pi = 3.1213+$.

49. Make a construction as shown in Fig. 103, and *AB* is approximately the quadrant of the circle. Find the per cent it differs from the correct value.   *Ans.* 0.4+% too large.

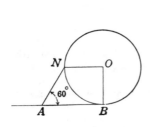

Fig. 103.

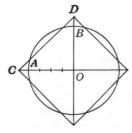

Fig. 104.

Suggestion. By the quadrant of the circle is meant the length of the arc *BN*.

50. Justify the following rule used by sheet-metal workers, or show the per cent of error if it is not correct: Divide the radius *AO*, Fig. 104, into four equal parts; place one of these parts from *A* to *C* and another from *B* to *D*, the ends of two perpendicular diameters. Connect *C* and *D*, which gives the side of the square of the same area as the circle.

Ans. 0.5+% too small.

51. The stem of a 4-in. safety valve, Fig. 105, is $2\frac{3}{4}$ in. from the fulcrum. Supposing the valve will blow when the gage reads 7 lb. without any weight on the lever (*i.e.,* that 7 lb. per square inch on the valve overcomes weight of valve and lever), at what pressure would it blow with a weight of 75 lb. 32 in. from the fulcrum?

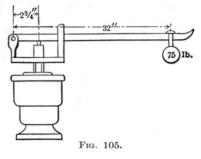

Fig. 105.

Ans. 76.4+ lb. per square inch.

Solution. If *P* represents the total number of pounds pressure on the valve necessary to lift the weight, then

2.75 : 32 = 75 : *P*. From which *P* = 872.73.

Area of valve = 0.7854 × 4² = 12.5664 sq. in.

Pressure to raise weight = 872.73 ÷ 12.5664 = 69.4 lb. per sq. in.

Total pressure = 69.4 lb. + 7 lb. = 76.4 lb. per sq. in.

52. What weight of ball would be required to allow the valve in exercise 51 to blow off at 80 lb.? *Ans.* 78.8+ lb.

53. If the original weight of 75 lb. is used, at what distance from the fulcrum should it be placed to allow the valve to blow off at 80 lb.? *Ans.* 33.6+ in.

54. The following is an approximate formula for determining the number of inscribed tangent circles in a larger circle:

$$N = 0.907\left(\frac{D}{d} - 0.94\right)^2 + 3.7,$$

where *N* is the number, *D* the diameter of the enclosing circle, and *d* the diameter of the inscribed circles. This formula can be used to find the number of wires that can be put in a casing of given size.

Apply the above formula and find how many wires $\frac{1}{2}$ in. in diameter can be placed inside a 5-in. pipe. *Ans.* 78.

55. How many steel balls 0.4 in. in diameter can rest at the bottom of a closed pipe $2\frac{1}{2}$ in. in diameter? *Ans.* 29.

56. In a circle of radius 5 ft. there is a chord 6 ft. 6 in. in length. Find the height of the segment. *Ans.* 1.200+ ft.

57. A segment of a circle cut off by a chord 4 ft. 6 in. in length has a height of 1 ft. 10 in. Find the radius of the circle. *Ans.* 27.57 − in.

58. Find the area of a sector in a circle whose radius is 28 cm., if the sector contains an angle of 50° 36'. *Ans.* 346.19 − cm.²

59. Find the area of a sector whose arc is 99.58 m. long and radius 86.34 m. *Ans.* 4298.87 − m.²

60. Test formula [**30(a)**] by taking the segment as half the circle 60 in. in diameter.

Ans. By [**30(a)**] *A* = 1425 in.² As $\frac{1}{2}$ a circle *A* = 1414 − in.²

61. Find the radius of a circle in which a chord of 10 ft. has a middle ordinate of 3 in. *Ans.* 50 ft. 1.5 in.

62. The Gothic Arch is formed by two arcs each $\frac{1}{8}$ of a circle. The center of each circle is at the extremity of the width of the arch, that is, the radius equals the width. Find the area of such an arch of radius 6 ft. (See Fig. 106.)   *Ans.* 22.11 ft.[2]

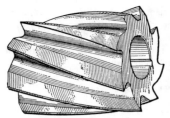

FIG. 106.

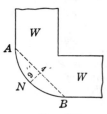

FIG. 107.

63. In Fig. 107, W, W is a wall with a round corner, of dimensions as given from A to B, on which a molding, gutter, or cornice is to be placed; find the radius of the circle of which arc ANB is a part. *Ans.* 3 ft. $\frac{1}{2}$ in.

64. Each of four steam engines is supplied by a 6-in. steam pipe. These open off from a single steam pipe. Find the diameter of the larger pipe that it may have the same capacity as the four 6-in. pipes.

Ans. 12 in.

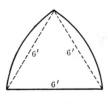

FIG. 108.—Milling cutter.

65. A milling cutter $4\frac{1}{2}$ in. in diameter is cutting soft steel at the rate of 45 ft. per minute. Find the number of revolutions per minute.

Ans. 38.2 −.

66. How many turns per second must a drill $\frac{1}{2}$ in. in diameter make so that the outer edge of the lip will have a cutting speed of 35 ft. per minute? *Ans.* 4.46 −.

67. The distance between the center of the crank pin C, Fig. 109, and the center of the flywheel at D is 20 in. What is the length of the stroke

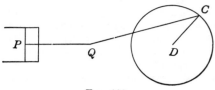

FIG. 109.

of the piston? If the flywheel makes 144 R. P. M., find the average speed of the piston in feet per minute. *Ans.* 40 in.; 960 ft. per min.

68. The "piston speed" in a Corliss engine should be 600 ft. per minute.

How many revolutions per minute should be made by an engine having a 20-in. stroke? By an engine having a 36-in. stroke?

Ans. 180; 100.

69. Which would occupy the greater portion of the square shown in Fig. 110, the four small circles or the large circle? *Ans.* Both the same.

70. The drivers on a locomotive are making 210 R. P. M., and are 76 in. in diameter. Find the speed of the loco-motive in miles per hour if 2% is allowed for slipping. *Ans.* 46.53 mi. per hr.

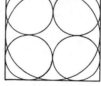

Fig. 110.

71. In a Corliss engine the high-pressure cylin-der is 22 in. in diameter. What must be the diameter of the low-pressure cylinder in order that it may have double the area of the high-pressure cylinder? *Ans.* 31.1+ in.

72. If the total pressure on the piston of a brake cylinder is 8100 lb., what is the diameter of the cylinder if the pressure is 60 lb. per square inch? *Ans.* 13.1+ in.

73. A 10-in pipe is to be branched off into two equal pipes. What must be the diameter of each of these pipes if the two pipes shall equal the area of the 10-in. pipe? *Ans.* 7.07+ in.

74. A machine screw ⅝ in. in diameter has 12 sharp V-threads to the inch. Find the root diameter. Find the tensile strength at 50,000 lb. per square inch. Give answer to the nearest 100 lb. *Ans.* 9100 lb.

75. What should be the area of the opening of a cold-air box for a hot-air furnace in order to supply 7 hot-air pipes 9 in. in diameter and one pipe 14 in. in diameter, if the area of the cold-air opening is ¾ the area of the hot-air pipes? *Ans.* 449.4+ sq. in.

76. A cylinder of a double-acting engine is 26 in. in diameter and the length of the stroke is 30 in. Compute the pressure on each side of the piston if the piston rod is 3½ in. in diameter and the steam pressure in the cylinder is 150 lb. per square inch. (Use formula [**28**].)

Fig. 111.

77. In practice piston rings for a steam engine are turned so that they are 1½% larger in diameter than the diameter of the cylinder barrel. They then have a piece cut out and are sprung into place. Find the diameter of the ring for a cylinder 24 in. in diameter. Find the length of the piece to be cut out if when sprung into place it has a clearance of 1/16 in. between ends. Give dimensions to the nearest 32nd of an inch.

Ans. 24⅜ in.; 1³⁄₁₆ in.

78. Find the speed of a belt running over a pulley having a diameter of 22 in. and making 320 R. P. M., if ½% is allowed for slipping.

Ans. 1834— ft. per minute.

79. If the greatest and least diameters of an elliptical manhole are 2 ft. 7 in. and 2 ft. 3 in. respectively, find its area. Find its perimeter, using formulas [**32**(b)] and [**32**(c)].

Ans. 4.565 ft.²; 91.2+ in. and 91.3 in.

80. Find the length in feet of the arc of contact of a belt with a pulley, if the pulley is 3 ft. 6 in. in diameter and the arc of contact is 210°.

Ans. 6 ft. 5— in.

81. As in the preceding, find the length of the arc of contact if it is 120° and the diameter of the pulley is 16 in. *Ans.* 16¾ in.

REGULAR POLYGONS AND CIRCLES

127. It is often necessary to determine the dimensions of a regular polygon inscribed in or circumscribed about a given circle, or to determine the size of a circle that can be inscribed in or circumscribed about a given polygon.

Such problems are readily solved by trigonometry, and some of them may be solved by geometry. In either case, though, the computation may be long and tedious. For this reason handbooks give rules by which the computations can be readily made. In the table on page 167 are classified certain facts about the **regular polygons** named. These facts can readily be applied to polygons of any size.

(1) **To find the area of a polygon when the length of one side is given.**—*Multiply the square of the side by a number given in column* (3).

This rule is an application of the principle that similar areas are in the same ratio as the squares of their like dimensions. Show that this is the case.

Example. Find the area of a regular pentagon having sides of 7 in.

Area = 7² × 1.7204774 in.² = 84.30339 in.²

(2) **To find the side of a polygon when its area is given.**— *Divide the area of the polygon by a number from column* (3). *The square root of the quotient is the required side of the polygon.*

Example. The area of an octagon is 4376 ft.²; find a side of the polygon.

Side = √(4376 ÷ 4.828) = 30.106 ft.

(1) No. of sides	(2) Name of polygon	(3) Area when side = 1	(4) Radius of circumscribed circle	(5)	(6) Radius of inscribed circle when side = 1	(7) Length of sides when radius of circumscribed circle = 1	(8) Angle at center	(9) Angle between adjacent sides
			When perpendicular from center = 1	When side = 1				
3	Triangle	0.4330127	2.	0.5773	0.2887	1.732	120°	60°
4	Square	1.	1.414	0.7071	0.5	1.4142	90°	90°
5	Pentagon	1.7204774	1.238	0.8506	0.6882	1.1756	72°	100°
6	Hexagon	2.5980762	1.156	1.	0.866	1.	60°	120°
7	Heptagon	3.6339124	1.11	1.1524	1.0383	0.8677	51° 26′	128° 34$\frac{2}{7}$′
8	Octagon	4.8284271	1.083	1.3066	1.2071	0.7653	45°	135°
9	Nonagon	6.1818242	1.064	1.4619	1.3737	0.684	40°	140°
10	Decagon	7.6942088	1.051	1.618	1.5388	0.618	36°	144°
12	Dodecagon	11.1961524	1.037	1.9319	1.866	0.5176	30°	150°

(3) **To find the radius of the circumscribing circle when a side of the polygon is given.**—*Multiply the length of a side by a number chosen from column* (5).

This can be used to good advantage in drawing a regular polygon of a given side.

Example. Construct a regular decagon having sides of $2\frac{1}{2}$ in.

Radius of circumscribing circle $=2\frac{1}{2}\times1.618$ in. $=4.045$ in. With the compasses construct a circle of this radius. Then with the dividers open $2\frac{1}{2}$ in. step around the circle, which should be divided into 10 parts. Connect these points successively and the construction is complete.

(4) **To find the radius of the inscribed circle when a side of the polygon is given.**—*Multiply the length of a side by a number chosen from column* (6).

(5) **To find the length of the side of a polygon that can be inscribed in a circle of given radius.**—*Multiply the given radius by a number chosen from column* (7).

Example. Construct a regular heptagon in a circle of 3-in. radius.

A side of the polygon $=3\times0.8677$ in. $=2.6$ in. With the dividers open 2.6 in. step around the circle, which should be divided into 7 equal parts. Connect these points successively and the construction is complete.

EXERCISES 39

1. A round shaft is $3\frac{1}{4}$ in. in diameter. Find the length of the side of a triangular end that can be made on the shaft. Find the length of the side of a square end. Of a hexagonal end. Of an octagonal end.

Ans. $2.81+$ in.; $2.30-$ in.; $1\frac{5}{8}$ in.; $1.24+$ in.

Triangular

Pentagonal

Hexagonal

FIG. 112.

2. Find the diameter of a circular shaft so that it may have a triangular end $2\frac{1}{2}$ in. on a side. A pentagonal end $1\frac{1}{2}$ in. on a side. An octagonal end $1\frac{1}{8}$ in. on a side. *Ans.* $2.887-$ in.; $2.552-$ in.; $2.940-$ in.

Suggestion. Use rule (3).

3. A square taper reamer is to be made which must ream $1\frac{1}{8}$ in. at the small end and $1\frac{5}{8}$ in. at the back end. What must be the distance on the flat face at each end? *Ans.* 0.795+ in.; 1.149+ in.

4. What is the diameter of the bearing that can be turned on a triangular shaft of side 2 in.? On a hexagonal shaft of side $1\frac{5}{8}$ in.? *Suggestion.* Use rule (4). *Ans.* 1.155− in.; 2.815− in.

5. Find the difference between the area of a circle of radius 5 in. and the area of the inscribed regular triangle. The inscribed regular pentagon. Hexagon. Octagon. Decagon.
Ans. 46.065+ in.²; 19.10− in.²; 13.59− in.²; 7.94+ in.²; 5.08− in.²
Suggestion. Find the side of the inscribed polygon by rule (5) and its area by rule (1).

6. Find the radius and area of the largest circle that can be cut from a triangle every side of which is 4 ft. *Ans.* 1.155− ft.; 4.19− ft.²

7. The triangular end on a round shaft is 1.7 in. on a side. Find the diameter of the shaft. *Ans.* 1.96+ in.

8. The area of a regular hexagon inscribed in a circle is $24\sqrt{3}$. Find the area of the circle and the length of the circumference.
Ans. 50.266− ; 25.133−.

9. A square end 0.875 in. on a side must be milled on a shaft. What is the diameter to which the shaft should be turned? *Ans.* 1.237+ in.

10. A pipe 10 in. in diameter is connected to a hexagonal pipe of the same area in cross section. Find the edge of the hexagon of the cross section of the hexagonal pipe. *Ans.* 5.50− in.

TURNING AND DRILLING

128. Rules.—The **cutting speed** of a tool is the rate at which it passes over the surface being cut. This applies to a lathe tool in turning a piece of work, such as a car axle; or to a drill used in making holes in a metal of any kind.

The rate at which the tool can cut the metal without injuring the tool depends upon the material in the tool, as well as upon the kind of work being turned.

Since cutting speeds are usually given in feet per minute, the rate at which a tool is cutting can be found by the following:

RULE. *Multiply the circumference of the piece, or of the drill, in feet by the number of revolutions per minute. This gives the cutting speed in feet per minute.*

This applies to work turned in a lathe or to the drill in a drill press.

It follows from the above that the number of revolutions, allowable per minute, is found by the following:

RULE. *Divide the cutting speed in feet per minute by the circumference of the work in feet. This gives the number of revolutions per minute.*

129. Feed.—The **feed** of a tool is the sideways motion given to the cutting tool. It is expressed in one of the following ways:

(1) The feed is the part of an inch that the tool advances along the work for each revolution or stroke, as a feed of $\frac{1}{16}$ inch.

(2) The feed is the number of revolutions or strokes necessary to advance the tool 1 inch, as a feed of 20 turns to the inch.

(3) The feed is the number of inches the tool advances in 1 minute, as the feed is $\frac{3}{4}$ inch per minute.

Thus, in turning a car axle, the shaving may be $\frac{1}{4}$ in. wide, which means that the tool must advance that distance along the axle for every revolution of the axle. That is, it will take 4 turns of the axle to cover 1 in. of its length with the turning tool.

130. Cutting Speeds.—Cutting speeds for carbon steel tools should be about 30 ft. per minute in steel, 35 ft. per minute in cast iron, and 60 to 100 ft. per minute in brass.

The general rule is to run high-speed steel tools, in steel, about double, and in iron about three times the speed of the carbon-steel tool.

The maximum speed given to any tool must be governed by the density and toughness of the material being cut, and by the way the tool "holds up."

The feed of a drill should be from 0.004 in. to 0.01 in. per revolution.

EXERCISES 40

1. In turning a brass rod 2 in. in diameter, what is the proper number of revolutions per minute if the cutting speed for brass is 100 ft. per minute? *Ans.* 191.

2. In turning a locomotive wheel 78 in. in diameter, what is the proper number of revolutions per minute, in order that the cutting speed may be 10 ft. per minute? *Ans.* 0.49 nearly.

3. In turning a tool-steel arbor, a carbon-steel turning tool is used. The cutting speed is 18 ft. per minute. How many revolutions per minute should the work make if the arbor is 3 in. in diameter?

Ans. 22.9.

4. A $\frac{3}{4}$-in. drill, cutting cast iron, may cut at the rate of 40 ft. per minute. How many revolutions per minute can it make? *Ans.* 203.7.

5. In turning a car wheel 27 in. in diameter, it makes $1\frac{3}{4}$ revolutions per minute. What is the speed of the cutting tool?

Ans. 12.37 ft. per minute.

6. How long will it take to turn off one layer from the surface of a car wheel 4 in. thick and 30 in. in diameter, if the cutting is 15 ft. per minute and the feed $\frac{1}{8}$ in.? *Ans.* $16\frac{3}{4}$ minutes nearly.

7. How long would it require to make one cut over the surface of a tool-steel arbor 2 in. in diameter and 10 in. in length, if the cutting speed is 18 ft. per minute and the feed of the cutting tool $\frac{1}{16}$ in. per revolution of the work? *Ans.* 4.65+ minutes.

8. In Kent's Mechanical Engineer's Pocket-book are given the following formulas for finding results in cutting speed problems:

Let $d =$ the diameter of the rotating piece in inches,
$n =$ the number of revolutions per minute, and
$S =$ the cutting speed in feet per minute, then

$$S = \frac{\pi dn}{12} = 0.2618dn; \quad n = \frac{S}{0.2618d} = \frac{3.82S}{d}; \quad d = \frac{3.82S}{n}.$$

Show that these are true and apply them to the preceding exercises.

9. The diameter of a piece of cast iron to be turned is 7 in. If the lathe makes 22 revolutions per minute, what is the cutting speed?

Ans. 40.3+ ft. per minute.

10. A piece of brass 4 in. in diameter is making 80 R. P. M. in a lathe. What is the cutting speed? *Ans.* 83.8− ft. per minute.

11. A wrought-iron shaft 2 in. in diameter and 30 in. long is turned at a cutting speed of 25 ft. per minute and a feed of $\frac{1}{40}$ in. Find the time for turning the shaft. *Ans.* 25.1+ minutes.

Solution. $30 \div \frac{1}{40} = 1200 =$ number of revolutions.
$$\frac{2 \times 3.1416 \times 1200}{12 \times 25} = 25.1328 = \text{number of min.}$$

12. The cutting speed in a certain case must not exceed 40 ft. per minute. The piece to be turned is $1\frac{3}{4}$ in. in diameter. How many revolutions per minute can it make? *Ans.* 87.3.

13. Give to the nearest sixteenth of an inch the length of a $\frac{3}{4}$-in. steel rod that is turned per minute, if the cutting speed is 36 ft. per minute and the feed $\frac{1}{25}$ in. *Ans.* $7\frac{5}{16}$ in.

14. In turning a car wheel 3 ft. in diameter, the highest rate of speed allowable for the cutter is 40 ft. per minute. How many revolutions per hour can the wheel make? *Ans.* 254.6.

15. A car axle may be turned with the cutter moving 9 ft. per minute. If the axle is $4\frac{1}{2}$ in. in diameter, how many revolutions can it make per minute? *Ans.* 7.64.

BELT PULLEYS AND GEAR WHEELS

131. The relation of size and speed of driving and driven gear wheels are the same as those of belt pulleys. In calculating for gears we use the diameter of the pitch circle, or the number of teeth as may be necessary.

A mechanic should be able to determine quickly and accurately the speed of any shaft or machine, and to find the size of a pulley in order that a shaft or machine may run at a desired speed. He should master the principles underlying the rules and formulas used as well as know how to use them. It is well then for the student to work many problems on pulley speeds before special formulas are taken up. This will help him to master the principles, and will make him independent of the formulas. It will also put him into position to derive the formulas.

For a complete discussion of questions connected with belts and belting see any mechanical engineer's handbook.

EXERCISES 41

1. A shaft having a pulley 6 in. in diameter makes 840 R. P. M. If this speed is to be reduced to 320 revolutions, what size of pulley should be used?

Solution. If the 6-in. pulley makes 840 R. P. M., a point on the belt moves $6 \times 3.1416 \times 840$ in. per minute. Then in order to make 320 R. P. M., the pulley must be $\dfrac{6 \times 3.1416 \times 840}{320}$ in. in circumference, and hence $\dfrac{6 \times 3.1416 \times 840}{320 \times 3.1416} = 15\frac{3}{4}$ in. in diameter.

2. The pulley on the armature shaft of a dynamo is 4 in. in diameter. This is to be belted to a driving shaft which makes 500 revolutions per minute. The speed of the dynamo must be 1700 revolutions per minute. What must be the size of the pulley placed on the shaft?

Ans. $13\frac{3}{5}$ in. in diameter.

3. A shaft has upon it two pulleys, each 8 in. in diameter. The speed of the shaft is 400 revolutions per minute. What must be the size of the pulleys of two machines if, when belted to the shaft, one of them has a speed of 300 revolutions per minute and the other 900?

Ans. $10\frac{2}{3}$ in. and $3\frac{5}{9}$ in. in diameter.

4. The pulley on the headstock of a lathe is 3 in. in diameter. This is belted to an 8-in. pulley on a shaft that makes 420 revolutions per minute. At what rate will a block of wood placed in the chuck revolve?

Ans. 1120 R. P. M.

5. If the wheels of an electric car are 2 ft., the axle cogwheel 8 in., and the cogwheel attached to the motor 12 in. in diameter, what must be the speed of the motor to carry the car a mile in 5 minutes?

Ans. 112.04+ R. P. M.

6. In two connected belt pulleys, or gear wheels, if D is the diameter of the driving wheel, d the diameter of the driven wheel, R the number of revolutions per minute of driver, and r the number of revolutions per minute of driven, find r in terms of D, d, and R.

$$Ans. \quad r = \frac{RD}{d}.$$

Discussion. In Fig. 113, A is the driving pulley and B is the driven pulley. It is evident that, since the belt does not slip, a point on the circumference of B must move as far in a minute as a point on the circumference of A.

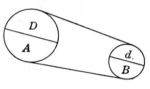

Since A makes R revolutions per minute, a point on its circumference will move $R\pi D$ units per minute. Similarly a point on the circumference of B will move $r\pi d$ units per minute.

FIG. 113.

$$\therefore R\pi D = r\pi d$$

$$\text{or } RD = rd \text{ and } r = \frac{RD}{d}.$$

7. In any system of pulleys or gears, the general rule holds: that the product of the diameters, or numbers of teeth, of the driving wheels and the number of revolutions per minute of the first driver must be equal to the product of the diameters, or the numbers of teeth, of the driven wheels and the number of revolutions per minute of the last driven wheel. As a formula this may be stated

$$r = \frac{R \times D \times D' \times D'' \times D''' \times \text{etc.}}{d \times d' \times d'' \times d''' \times \text{etc.}},$$

where D, D', D'', etc., are the diameters of the driving pulleys, d, d' d'', etc., are the diameters of the driven pulleys, R is the R. P. M. of the first driver, and r is the R. P. M. of the last driven pulley. Show why this is true.

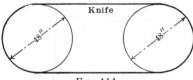

FIG. 114.

8. The number of revolutions the governor of a steam engine is intended to run is given by the builder. If the speed of the governor is 120 R. P. M., size of governor pulley 8 in., and the desired speed of the engine 90 R. P. M., find the diameter of the pulley to be put on the engine shaft to run the governor pulley.

$$Ans. \quad 10\tfrac{2}{3} \text{ in.}$$

9. An endless knife runs on pulleys 48 in. in diameter as shown in Fig. 114, at a rate of 180 R. P. M. If the pulleys are decreased 18 in. in diameter, how many R. P. M. will they have to make to keep the knife traveling at the original speed?

Solution.   180×3.1416×48 in. = rate per minute.

3.1416×30 in. = circumference of reduced pulleys.

$$\frac{180 \times 3.1416 \times 48}{3.1416 \times 30} = 288 = \text{number of R.P.M. of reduced pulleys.}$$

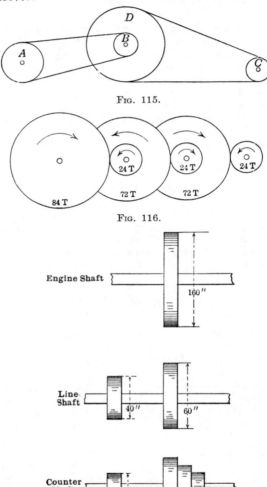

FIG. 115.

FIG. 116.

FIG. 117.

10. Adapt the formula of exercise 7 to the following: A train of wheels consists of four wheels each 12 in. in diameter of pitch circle, and three pinions 4 in., 4 in., and 3 in. in diameter respectively. The first three large wheels are the drivers and the first makes 36 revolutions per minute. Required the speed of the last wheel. *Ans.* 1296 R. P. M.

11. In the train of the preceding exercise, what is the speed of the first large wheel if the pinions are the drivers, the 3-in. pinion being the first driver and making 36 revolutions per minute? *Ans.* 1 R. P. M.

12. Pulleys are arranged as in Fig. 115. Pulley *A* makes 192 R. P. M., is the driver, and is 14 in. in diameter. Pulley *B* is 8 in. in diameter. Pulley *C* is 6 in. in diameter and is to make a required 1400 R. P. M. Find the diameter to make the pulley *D*, fastened to the same shaft as *B*, in order that *C* may have the desired number of revolutions per minute. *Ans.* 25 in.

13. Find the number of R. P. M. of the last gear shown in Fig. 116, if the gear having 84 teeth makes 36 R. P. M.

14. In Fig. 117, if a 160-in. pulley on the engine shaft drives a 60-in. pulley on the line shaft, and a 40-in. pulley on the line shaft drives an 18-in. pulley on the counter shaft, find the number of revolutions per minute of the counter shaft if the engine shaft runs at 80 R. P. M. *Ans.* 474 nearly.

THE MIL

132. The circular mil.—In most cases, electrical conductors have a circular cross section. We know that the area of a circle is found by the formula $A = \frac{1}{4}\pi d^2$, which brings in the inconvenient factor $\frac{1}{4}\pi$, or 0.7854. In order to avoid this factor, a new unit has been adopted for commercial work. This unit is the **circular mil** (abbreviation C. M.) which is the area of a circle one **mil**, or 0.001 inch, in diameter.

If *A* is the area in circular mils of any circle and *d* the diameter in mils, then, since a circle 1 mil in diameter has an area of 1 C. M., we have the proportion

$$\frac{1}{A} = \frac{1^2}{d^2}$$

for the areas of the circles are in the same ratio as the squares of the diameters. This proportion gives

$$A = d^2.$$

This stated in words is the following:

RULE. *The area of a circle in circular mils is the square of the diameter in mils, or thousandths of an inch.*

Thus, a 0000 gage B. and S. wire is 0.46 in. = 460 mils in diameter, and hence has an area of $460^2 = 211,600$ C. M.

If the area in circular mils is given, the diameter in mils can evidently be found by taking the square root of the area, or

$$d = \sqrt{A}.$$

133. The square mil.—The **square mil** is sometimes used, and is the area of a square 1 mil on a side. Since the area of a circle is $0.7854d^2$, it is seen that 0.7854 square mil $= 1$ C. M.

EXERCISES 42

1. Find the number of circular mils in the area of B. and S. gage wires Nos. 40, 20 and 10. (See **Table VII.**)

$Ans.$ $9.88+$; $1021.5+$; $10,383-$.

2. How many square mils in a bar $\frac{1}{2}$ in. by $\frac{3}{4}$ in. in cross section?

$Ans.$ 187,500.

3. How many circular mils are equal to 20,000 square mils?

$Ans.$ $25,464.8-$.

4. Find the diameter in mils and in inches of a circular rod having a cross section of 237,600 C. M. $Ans.$ $487.4+$ mils; $0.4874+$ in.

5. In ordinary practice, trolley wire is 0 or 00 B. and S. hard-drawn copper wire. What is the area of the cross section of each in circular mils? $Ans.$ $105,535-$ C. M. or $133,076+$ C. M.

CHAPTER XIII

GRAPHICAL METHODS

ANGLES

134. Units.—In measuring any magnitude, a unit of measure is necessary. In measuring length, there are various units, as the inch, foot, meter, and mile. Likewise in the measurement of angles, there are in use, as units, the **right angle,** the **degree,** and the **radian.**

Right angle as unit. When using the right angle as a unit, we speak of an angle as such a part of, or as so many times, a right angle.

The degree as a unit. The degree as a unit for measuring angles may be defined as the value of the angle formed by dividing a right angle into 90 equal parts. The degree is also used as a unit for measuring arcs. It is then defined as $\frac{1}{360}$ part of a circumference. In either case the degree is divided into 60 parts called minutes, and the minute into 60 parts called seconds. Degrees, minutes, and seconds of angle or arc are indicated by the signs °, ′, and ″.

For example, a measurement of 27 degrees, 47 minutes, 35 seconds is written thus: 27° 47′ 35″.

As already defined, if an angle has its vertex at the center of a circle and its sides formed by the radii of the circle, it is spoken of as an angle at the center of a circle. The number of degrees in the angle so placed is equal to the number of degrees in the arc of the circle intercepted between the sides of the angle.

Thus, in Fig. 118, AOB is an angle at the center. The number of degrees in this angle equals the number of degrees in the arc AB.

The angle AOB is said to be measured by the arc AB.

135. Circular measure, radian.—The unit of circular measure of angles is the **radian.** The **radian** is defined as the

12   177

angle which at the center of a circle is measured by an arc equal in length to the radius of the circle.

In Fig. 118, arc AB = radius OA, hence angle AOB is one radian.

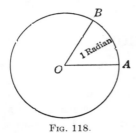

FIG. 118.

Since a circumference is 2π times the radius, there are 2π arc lengths equal to the radius in a circumference; and hence 2π radians are measured by the circumference of a circle, or 2π radians = 360°.

From this, π radians = 360° ÷ 2 = 180°, and

1 radian = 180° ÷ π = 57.29578° − .

Reduced to degrees, minutes, and seconds:

1 radian = 57° 17′ 44.8″.

In a similar manner, if 180° = π radians, then

1° = π radians ÷ 180 = 0.01745+ radians.

136. The protractor.—The protractor consists of a circular or semicircular scale of convenient diameter. The circumference of this scale is divided into degrees, half degrees, and sometimes into quarter degrees, as shown in Fig. 119. The

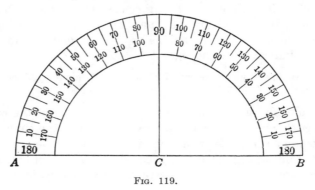

FIG. 119.

divisions of the scale are numbered from 0° to 180°, beginning at each end. The sum of the two readings at any point is 180°. This method of numbering enables one to measure an angle from either end of the protractor, or it enables one to set off angles in either a right- or a left-hand direction.

137. To measure an angle with protractor.—Place the protractor over the angle to be measured, so that the point C is on the vertex of the angle, and either half of the side AB will fall upon one side of the angle. The other side of the angle should pass through some mark on the scale of the protractor. The reading on the scale where this side of the angle crosses it is the measure of the angle in degrees. In work with the protractor, a hard pencil with sharp point should be used.

138. To lay off an angle with a protractor.—Draw one side of the angle and locate the vertex. Place side AB of protractor on side drawn and point C on the vertex. Locate reading of value of angle required on scale of protractor, and connect this with the vertex. The degree of accuracy with which an angle can be laid off depends upon the instruments and the one who uses them, but largely upon the size of the protractor. It is well then to use a fairly large protractor, one 5 or 6 in. in diameter.

EXERCISES 43

1. Draw three triangles and measure their angles. Find the sum of the angles of each triangle. Are their sums equal?

2. Draw a right triangle and measure the two acute angles. What is their sum?

3. Draw an equilateral triangle and measure the angles. What is their sum?

4. Draw an isosceles triangle and measure its angles. Are there two equal angles?

5. Construct angles of 26°, 75° 30′, 106° 45′, and 146° 15′.

6. Describe how an angle of $1\frac{1}{2}$ radians may be constructed.

7. How many radians in each of the angles: 27° 45′, 47° 26′, 109° 30′?
$Ans.$ $0.484+$; $0.8279-$; $1.911+$.

8. What is the value in degrees and decimals of degrees of each of the angles: 2 radians, $\frac{3}{4}$ radian, 1.75 radians?
$Ans.$ $114.5916°-$; $42.9718°+$; $100.2676°+$.

9. Draw a line AB $2\frac{1}{2}$ in. long; at A lay off an angle of 115° 30′ and draw line AC $\frac{3}{4}$ in. long; at B lay off an angle of 97° and draw line BD $1\frac{3}{8}$ in. long. Find length of CD by measuring.

10. Draw a parallelogram and measure its angles. What is their sum? How do the angles compare?

11. Draw a quadrilateral and measure its angles. What is their sum?

ANGLES BY CHORDS

139. An angle can usually be laid off more accurately by means of a table of chords than by the protractor, and the method is often more convenient. While with the protractor it is not easy to measure more accurately than to half degrees, with the table of chords the angle may be laid off to tenths of a degree.

In **Table VI** are given the lengths of the chords in a circle of radius 1, for central angles from 0° to 89.9°.

140. To find a chord length from the table.—To find the length of the chord for an angle of, say, 27.6°, find 20° in the left-hand column of the table; go to the right to column headed 7° and there find 0.467, the length of the chord for 27°. Now add to 0.467 the number 0.010, found still further to the right in the column headed 0.6°. This gives 0.477 as the length of the chord for 27.6°. This means that, if the vertex of the angle is at the center of a circle of radius 1 in., the chord has a length of 0.477 in.

For the length of the chord in a circle of any other radius, multiply this chord by the length of the radius of the given circle. Thus, for a circle of 6-in. radius, the chord for a central angle of 27.6° is 6×0.477 in. = 2.862 in.

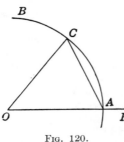

Fig. 120.

141. To lay off an angle.—How this can be done is best shown by an actual construction.

Example. Lay off an angle of 48.3°.

From **Table VI**, the chord for 48.3° is 0.818. Draw a line *OP*, Fig. 120. With *O* as a center and radius 1 in., draw the arc *AB*. With *A* as a center and with radius 0.818 in., strike the arc cutting *AB* at *C*. Connect *O* with *C*, and *AOC* is the angle 48.3° required.

For this construction there are required a pair of compasses, a ruler divided into 0.01 in., and a sharp pencil.

An angle larger than a right angle may be laid off by first constructing a right angle, and then laying off the remainder adjacent to this.

The table can be conveniently used if a radius is taken 10 units in length.

142. To measure an angle.—With the vertex of the angle as center and radius 1, draw an arc cutting both sides of the angle. Measure the chord drawn between these two points, and refer to the table of chords to find the angle.

An angle larger than 90° may be measured by first laying off an angle of 90°, and then measuring the remaining angle.

EXERCISES 44

1. In a circle of radius 1 in., find the lengths of the chords for the following angles:

(a) 43.8°.	*Ans.* 0.746 in.	(e) 63° 48′.		*Ans.* 1.057 in.
(b) 29.1°.	*Ans.* 0.503 in.	(f) 10° 40′.		*Ans.* 0.186 in.
(c) 13.3°.	*Ans.* 0.231 in.	(g) 43° 30′.		*Ans.* 0.741 in.
(d) 79.2°.	*Ans.* 1.275 in.	(h) 78° 15′.		*Ans.* 1.263 in.

2. Construct the following angles: (a) 60°, (b) 10° 45′, (c) 72.8°, (d) 115° 30′, (e) 145.3°, (f) 39.9°.

3. Draw the chords in a circle of 1 in. radius to form a regular polygon of 5 sides. (Each angle at the center is 72°.)

4. Inscribe regular polygons of 6, 7, 8, 9, 10, and 15 sides in a circle of radius 3 in.

Suggestion. Divide 360° by the number of sides to find the angle at the center of the circle determined by the side. From **Table VI** determine the length of the side, and space off the circumference using this length.

If the number of sides is 9, the angle at center is $360° \div 9 = 40°$. When the radius of the circle is 3, the side of the polygon is 2.052.

AREAS, GRAPHICAL METHODS

143. Drawing to scale.—If we wish to draw to scale the floor of a room 10 ft. by 20 ft., we may conveniently represent 1 ft. in the dimensions of the room by $\frac{1}{8}$ in. in the drawing. Whatever dimension is measured in the drawing and given in eighths of an inch can be interpreted as feet when applied to the floor. The map of a country may be drawn on a scale of 50 miles to an inch, or any other convenient scale.

144. To construct a triangle having given two sides and the angle between these sides.—Let the side $AB = 10$ ft., and $AC = 8$ ft., and the angle A between these sides be 47° 45′.

Choose a convenient scale, say, ⅛ in. for 1 ft. Draw line
AB, Fig. 121, in length $1\frac{0}{8}$ in.; lay off angle $BAC=47°\ 45'$;
make AC ⅜ in.; and draw CB. Then the triangle ACB is
the required representation of the triangle.

   If it is required to find the area of the triangle, the measured

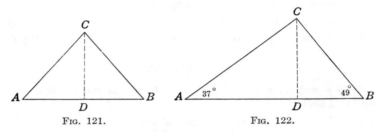

FIG. 121.   FIG. 122.

length of the altitude DC in eighths of an inch times one-half
of the base AB in the same unit, would give the area of the
triangle in square feet.

   **145. To construct a triangle when given two angles and
the side between these angles.**—Let the side $AB=30$ ft., the
angle $A=37°$, and the angle $B=49°$. Choose a scale, say,
$\frac{1}{16}$ in. for 1 ft. Draw line AB, Fig. 122, in length $\frac{30}{16}$ in.; lay
off angle $A=37°$, and $B=49°$; and extend the sides of these

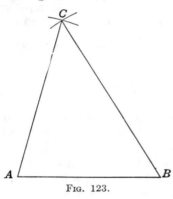

FIG. 123.

angles till they meet. Then
the triangle ACB is the required
triangle represented on a scale
of $\frac{1}{16}$ in. to 1 ft. The area of
this triangle can easily be found
by measuring the altitude DC
and applying the rule for the
area of a triangle.

   **146. To construct a triangle
when the three sides are
given.**—Let $AB=60$ rods,
$AC=70$ rods, and $BC=80$
rods. Choose a scale of, say,

40 rods to the inch. Then 60 rods is represented by $1\frac{1}{2}$ in.,
70 rods by $1\frac{3}{4}$ in., and 80 rods by 2 in. Draw AB, Fig. 123,
in length $1\frac{1}{2}$ in. With the compasses and a radius of $1\frac{1}{4}$ in.
draw an arc with A as center. With B as center, and radius

2 in., draw an arc to intersect this at *C*. Draw the lines *AC* and *BC*. Then triangle *ABC* is the required triangle.

In a similar manner other shaped figures may be constructed to scale. In many cases these drawings may be divided into triangles, squares, and rectangles, which may be measured, and so the entire area of the figure be found.

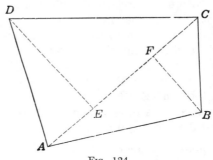

Fig. 124.

Example. A piece of ground in the form of a quadrilateral is represented by Fig. 124 to a scale of 40 rods to an inch. The area can be found by drawing the diagonal *AC* and the altitudes of the triangles *ACD* and *ABC*. The sum of the areas of these triangles equals the area of the quadrilateral *ABCD*.

147. Areas found by the use of squared paper.—It is often convenient to find the area of an irregular figure by drawing it on squared paper (paper accurately ruled into small squares). The figure will usually be drawn to some scale that uses the side of one of the small squares as a unit.

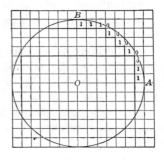

Fig. 125.

The method is most nearly accurate on irregular figures, and is liable to considerable error when the boundary has long straight lines, nearly parallel to the lines forming the squares.

As an illustration of the method, find the area of the circle in Fig. 125, if the circle is drawn on a scale of 1 in. to a side of the squares.

First, determine how many squares are wholly within the circle.

Second, count as whole squares the squares that are half or more than half within the circle, and neglect those squares that are less than half within the circle.

Here it is most convenient to count the squares in one quarter of the circle, and then multiply by 4 to get the area of the whole circle.

From the figure, it is seen that there are 30 whole squares in the quarter of the circle *AOB*. Counting the squares marked 1, gives 8 partial squares to be taken as whole squares. The squares marked 0 are not counted.

$30 + 8 = 38$ squares for the quarter circle.

$38 \times 4 = 152$ squares for the circle.

$\therefore$ area of the circle is 152 in.^{2}

By formula [**24**], area $= 3.1416 \times 7^2 = 154 -$ in.^{2}

148. Other methods for approximating areas.—(*a*) The planimeter is an instrument for estimating areas. There are several forms of this device; but, as instructions for its use are given with each instrument, it will not be described here.

(*b*) The area, when very irregular, can often be estimated quite accurately by cutting full size or to scale out of cardboard or sheet tin. Weigh on accurate scales the piece of tin or cardboard; also weigh a square unit of the same material. Divide the weight of the piece by the weight of the square unit. The quotient is the number of square units in the figure.

(*c*) Other methods will be found in **Chapt. XXXIII.**

EXERCISES 45

1. The two sides of a triangle are 18 ft. and 24 ft., respectively, and include an angle of 98°. Find the length of the other side, and find the area of the triangle by two separate sets of measurements, that is, draw two altitudes and use two sides as bases.

2. The base of a triangle is 10 ft., and the other two sides are 7 ft. and 5 ft. respectively. Find graphically the length of the altitude to the base. What is the area of the triangle?

3. Find the area of the triangle in exercise 2 by rule for the area of a triangle when the three sides are given.   *Ans.* 16.25 − ft.^{2}

4. In a triangle, one side is 28 ft. and the adjacent angles are 39° 45′ and 49° 30′. Find the lengths of the other sides and the area of the triangle.

5. The angles of a triangle are 48°, 78°, and 54°. Find the length of the side opposite the angle 78°, if the side opposite 48° is 32 ft.

6. The two sides AB and BC of a triangle are 44.7 ft. and 96.8 ft., respectively, the angle ABC being 32°. Find (a) the length of the perpendicular drawn from A to BC; (b) the area of the triangle ABC; (c) the angles at A and C.

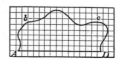

Ans. (a) 23.69 ft.; (b) 1147 ft.^{2}; (c) 22°; 126°.

FIG. 126.

7. Find the area of $AbcD$, Fig. 126, which is on a scale of 1 in. to the side of a square, by counting the squares.

8. Find the area of the ellipse in Fig. 127, which is on a scale of 4 rods to the side of a square, by counting squares. Find the area by formula [31], and compare results.

9. The quadrilateral in Fig. 128 is on a scale of 16 rods to the inch. Find its area by dividing into triangles.

10. Draw a triangle on a scale of ⅛ in. to the foot, having sides of 17 ft., 19 ft., and 23 ft. respectively. Draw any altitude of the triangle, measure it, and compute the area of the triangle. Check by drawing the other altitudes and computing the area again.

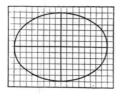

FIG. 127.

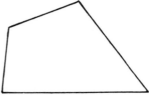

FIG. 128.

11. Draw the following to scale, using ¹⁄₁₆ in. to the rod, then find the area in acres. Start at a point A, go east 20 rd. to B, north 10 rd. to C, east 10 rd. to D, north 40 rd. to E, west 40 rd. to F, south 20 rd. to G, east 20 rd. to H, and then to A.   *Ans.* 9¹⁄₁₆ A.

12. Find the area of the following plot of ground: Start at A, go east 10 ft. to B, north 20 ft. to C, northeast 14.14 ft. to D, north 10 ft. to E, west 20 ft. to F, and south to A *Ans.* 550 ft.^{2}

VARIOUS USEFUL CONSTRUCTIONS

149. To divide a line of any length into a given number of equal parts.—In Fig. 129, let AB be the line which it is required to divide into seven equal parts. Draw a line AC, making any convenient angle with AB.   Take some convenient length, as a half inch, and beginning at A mark seven of these lengths on AC.   This determines the points a, b, c,

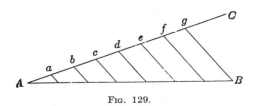

FIG. 129.

d, e, f, and g.   Draw a line from g to B, and draw lines parallel to gB through f, d, c, b, and a.   These lines divide AB into seven equal parts.

It is readily seen that this method can be used to divide any line into any number of equal parts.

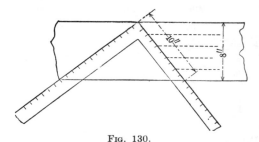

FIG. 130.

Example.   The carpenter makes use of this construction when he uses his steel square, as shown in Fig. 130, to divide a board of any width into any number of equal strips.   Here an 8-in. board is to be divided into five equal strips.   A number of inches divisible by 5, as 10 in., is taken on the square, and the square is placed as shown.   A mark is made on the board at the 2-in. divisions on the square. This divides the board as desired.

150. To cut off the corners of a square so as to form a regular octagon.—Draw the diagonals of the square, Fig. 131. With the compasses open a distance AO, one-half a diagonal, and with each vertex of the square as a center, strike the arcs at a and a', b and b', c and c', d and d'. Connect these points as shown in the figure, and get the regular octagon $bac'b'dca'd'$.

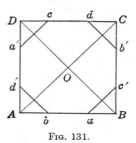

Fig. 131.

151. To divide a given circle into any number of equal parts by concentric circles.—Let the largest circle of Fig. 132 be the given circle, and let it be desired to divide it into four equal parts. Draw the radius OA and divide it into the same number of equal parts. Draw a semicircle on this radius as a diameter.

Erect perpendiculars to OA at each division point a, b,

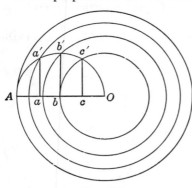

Fig. 132.

and c, and let them intersect the circumference of the semicircle at a', b', and c' respectively. Using Oc', Ob', and Oa' as radii and O as a center, draw the three concentric circles. These circles divide the original circle as desired.

152. To inscribe regular polygons.—(See **Arts. 127** and **140.**) (1) *To lay out a square in a circle.* Draw two perpendicular diameters as shown in Fig. 133, and connect their successive extremities. This gives the inscribed square $ACBD$.

(2) *To lay out a pentagon in a circle.* Draw two perpendicular diameters AB and CD, Fig. 134, bisect AO at F. With E as a center and ED as a radius, draw the arc DF. The length DF is equal to the side of the inscribed pentagon.

(3) *To lay out a hexagon in a circle.* The radius of the circle is equal to a side of the inscribed hexagon.

(4) *To lay out an equilateral triangle in a circle.* Connect the alternate vertices of the hexagon as shown in Fig. 135.

(5) *To lay out a regular heptagon in a circle.* Make a con-

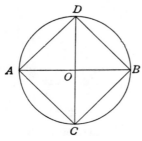

Fig. 133.

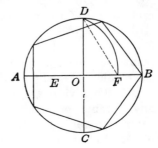

Fig. 134.

struction as shown in Fig. 136, and *AB* is very nearly the side of the inscribed regular heptagon.

(6) *To lay out a regular octagon in a circle.* Bisect the arcs of the inscribed square.

(7) *To lay out a regular decagon in a circle.* Bisect the

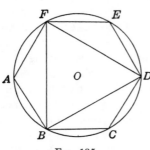

Fig. 135.

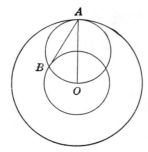

Fig. 136.

arcs of the inscribed regular pentagon.

153. To draw the arc of a segment when the chord and the height of the segment are given.—This method is to be used when it is not convenient to find the radius and use it. In Fig. 137, *AB* is the chord and *FC* is the height. Draw

AC; AD perpendicular to AC; CD parallel to FA; AE perpendicular to AF; and divide AF, DC, and AE into the same number of equal parts. Letter them as in the figure. Draw da, eb, fc, $C1$, $C2$, and $C3$. The points of intersection of these are points on the arc. The more equal parts the lines are divided into, the more points of the arc will be determined.

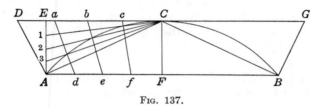

FIG. 137.

154. To find the radius of a circle when only a part of the circumference is known.—It often happens that one has a part only of a wheel or pulley from which he must determine the size of a new wheel or pulley. The method by bisecting the arcs is shown in Fig. 138. Let ABC be the arc given. Draw two chords AB and BC of any convenient lengths. Draw perpendicular bisectors of these. They will intersect

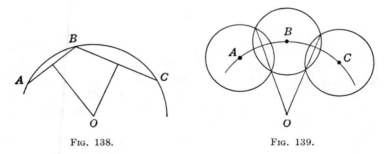

FIG. 138.   FIG. 139.

at a point O which is the center of the circle of which the given arc is a part.

What amounts to the same thing and is more quickly done is shown in Fig. 139. Draw three equal intersecting circles with their centers on the arc, then the lines drawn through the intersecting points as shown meet at the center of the circle of which the given arc is a part.

155. How to cut a strikeboard to a circular arc.—The
standard specifications of the American Concrete Institute
recommend that the surface of concrete highways be finished
to a crown corresponding to the arc of a circle. The height
of the crown at the center of the highway above the margin
of the pavement is recommended to be not more than $\frac{1}{50}$
and not less than $\frac{1}{100}$ of the width of the pavement. A carpenter or mechanic can readily lay out a curve of this kind
on a strikeboard. The method shown in Fig. 140 is based
upon a simple geometric fact and if properly followed will
give a true curve.

If the lower edge of the piece from which the strikeboard
is to be cut is not straight, the lay-out can be made to a chalk

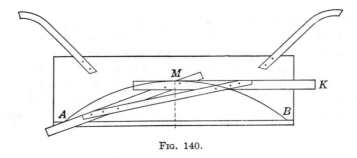

Fig. 140.

line, AB of the figure. Drive a stiff nail at each of the points
A and B, which mark the width of the pavement. Find the
mid-point between these nails and mark on the board a line
perpendicular to the line AB. Drive a nail at M as far above
the mid-point of the line AB as required by the cross section
for the crown height at center.

Take two light pieces of lumber which have straight edges,
and fasten them rigidly together so that they form the angle-
frame AMK. The line MK must be parallel to AB. Then if
one side of this angle-frame is held against the frame at M
and one at A, the intersection of the sides of the angle will be
a point of the curve desired. By shifting the angle-frame, the
intersection may be moved from M to A and points on the
curve marked as often as desired. By turning the angle-frame
over, the curve on the other half may be similarly marked.

156. The vernier.—The **vernier** is a device, invented by Pierre Vernier, by which measurements can be read with a much greater degree of accuracy than is possible by mere mechanical division and subdivision. There are two kinds of verniers, known as the *direct* and *reverse*. Only the *direct* will be described here.

The principle is shown in its essentials in Fig. 141, which is a portion of a graduated scale, having below it a sliding

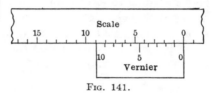

FIG. 141.

scale, which is the vernier. The vernier is so divided that 10 divisions of its scale just equal 9 divisions of the graduated scale. If the 0 mark on the vernier coincides with a division, say, the 0 division as in Fig. 141, of the graduated scale, then the division 1 on the vernier stands at 0.9 on the scale; 2 on the vernier at 1.8 on the scale; and so on for the other divisions.

If the vernier be moved along so that one of its divisions, as 4 in Fig. 142, coincides with a division of the scale, then the

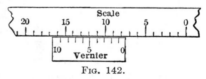

FIG. 142.

division on the vernier just to the right or left of the coinciding division lacks 0.1 of a scale division of coinciding with a scale division. The next division of the vernier to the right or left lacks 0.2 of a scale division of coinciding with a scale division, and so on. In this case, the 0 point on the vernier is removed 0.4 of a division to the left of a scale division.

The reading then in Fig. 142, that is, the distance from the 0 division on the scale to the 0 division on the vernier, is 7.4. If the scale division is tenths of an inch, then the reading is 0.74 in.

If the vernier is moved to the left so that 6 on the vernier coincides with a division on the scale, then 0 on the vernier is 0.6 of a scale division to the left of a scale division.

It is evident that any number of divisions on a scale could be equal to one greater number of divisions on a vernier, and the readings could be made in a similar way. For instance, in instruments for measuring angles, if the scale divisions are to $\frac{1}{2}°$, then a vernier with 30 divisions equaling 29 divisions of the scale will give a reading to $\frac{1}{30}$ of $\frac{1}{2}°$ or 1' of angle.

157. Micrometer with vernier.—A micrometer that reads to thousandths of an inch may be made to read to ten-thousandths of an inch by putting a vernier on the barrel, so that 10 divisions on the vernier correspond to 9 divisions on the

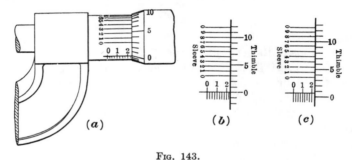

FIG. 143.

thimble. There are eleven parallel lines on the sleeve occupying the same space as ten lines on the thimble. These lines are numbered 0, 1, 2, 3, 4, 5, 6, 7, 8, 9, 0. The difference between one of the ten spaces on the sleeve and one of the nine spaces on the thimble is $\frac{1}{10}$ of a space on the thimble or $\frac{1}{10000}$ inch in the micrometer reading.

In Fig. 143(b), the third line from 0 on the thimble coincides with the first line on the sleeve. The next two lines do not coincide by $\frac{1}{10}$ of a space on the thimble, the next two marked 5 and 2 are $\frac{2}{10}$ of a space apart, and so on. When the micrometer is opened the thimble is turned to the left and each space on the thimble represents $\frac{1}{1000}$ inch. Therefore, when the thimble is turned so that the lines 5 and 2 coincide the micrometer is opened $\frac{1}{10}$ of $\frac{1}{1000}$ inch or $\frac{2}{10000}$ inch. If the thimble be turned further, so that the line 10 coincides with the line 7 on the sleeve as in (c), the micrometer has been opened $\frac{7}{10000}$ inch.

To read a micrometer graduated to ten-thousandths, note the thousandths as usual, then observe the number of divisions on the vernier until a line is reached which coincides with a line on the thimble. If it is the second line marked 1, add $\frac{1}{10000}$; if the third marked 2, add $\frac{2}{10000}$, etc.

As an exercise give the different readings shown in the figure.

CHAPTER XIV

PRISMS

158. Definitions.—Two planes are said to be parallel when they will not meet however far they be extended. That is, they are everywhere the same distance apart.

A line is parallel to a plane when it will not meet the plane however far it may be extended.

A line is perpendicular to a plane when it is perpendicular to every line of the plane that passes through its foot.

A **prism** is a solid whose ends, or **bases,** are parallel polygons, and whose sides, or **faces,** are parallelograms.

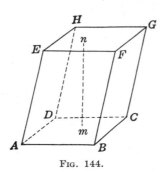

Fig. 144 is a prism. The bases $ABCD$ and $EFGH$ are parallel polygons. The faces $AEFB$, $BFGC$, etc., are parallelograms. The lines AB, BC, etc., and EF, FG, etc., are **base edges.** The lines AE, BF, etc., are **lateral edges.**

If the lateral edges are perpendicular to the bases of the prism, the prism is a **right prism.**

If the lateral edges are not perpendicular to the bases, the prism is an **oblique prism.**

FIG. 144.

In an oblique prism, the faces are parallelograms; but, in a right prism, they are rectangles.

A prism is called triangular, square, rectangular, hexagonal, etc.; according as its bases are triangles, squares, rectangles, hexagons, etc. Fig. 145 is a right triangular prism.

A **cross section** of a prism is a section that is perpendicular to the edges of the prism.

In Fig. 145, MNO or either base is a cross section.

The sum of the edges of the base is the **perimeter** of the base.

194

The **altitude** of a prism is the perpendicular line between the two bases, as *mn*, Fig. 144. In a right prism, the altitude is the same length as an edge. In an oblique prism, this is not true.

A right prism that has rectangles for bases is called a **rectangular solid.** The **cube** is a rectangular solid all of whose six faces are squares.

159. Surfaces.—The right prisms are the forms of prisms that are met with usually in practical work. They are the ones considered here.

The **lateral area** of a right prism is the area of its faces, not including the two bases. Since the faces are rectangles their areas can be easily found. As the area of each face is the product of its base by its altitude, the sum of the areas of the faces, or the lateral area of the prism is given by the following:

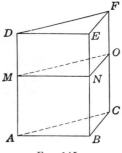

FIG. 145.

RULE. *The lateral area of a right prism equals the perimeter of the base times the altitude.*

The total area of the prism equals the lateral area plus the area of the two bases.

Since the cube has six equal square faces, the total area is six times the square of an edge.

If *S* stands for lateral area, *T* for total area, *A* for area of each base, *p* for perimeter of the base, *h* for altitude, and *a* for an edge, the rules are stated in the following formulas:

[33] $S = ph.$

[34] $T = ph + 2A.$

[35] $T = 6a^2,$ for the cube.

[36] $p = S \div h.$

[37] $h = S \div p.$

Example. Find the total area of a right triangular prism, of altitude 20 ft., if the edges of the base are 2 ft., 3 ft., and 4 ft.

Solution. $p=2+3+4=9.$

By [7], $A = \sqrt{s(s-a)\ (s-b)\ (s-c)}.$

But $s=\frac{1}{2}(2+3+4)=4\frac{1}{2},$

$$s-a=4\frac{1}{2}-2=2\frac{1}{2},$$
$$s-b=4\frac{1}{2}-3=1\frac{1}{2},$$
$$s-c=4\frac{1}{2}-4=\frac{1}{2}.$$

$\therefore A = \sqrt{4.5\times2.5\times1.5\times0.5} = \sqrt{8.4375} = 2.9047.$

By [34], $T=ph+2A.$

$\therefore T=9\times20+2\times2.9047=185.81-\text{ft.}^2\ Ans.$

160. Volumes.—In Fig. 146, there are as many cubic inches on the base $ABCD$ as there are square inches in its area, and since there are as many layers of cubic inches in the rectangular

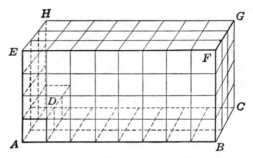

Fig. 146.

solid as there are inches in the altitude AE, the total number of cubic inches in the solid is found by multiplying the number of square inches in the base by the number of linear inches in the altitude.   Any right prism can be taken in the same manner as the rectangular solid; hence the following:

Rule.   *The volume of a right prism equals the area of the base times the altitude.*

If the prism is a rectangular solid this rule becomes:

Rule.   *The volume of a rectangular solid equals the continued product of the length, breadth, and height.*

If V stands for volume, and the other letters as before, we have these formulas:

[38] $V = Ah,$ for any prism.

[39] $V = a^3,$ for the cube.

[40] $h = V \div A.$

[41] $A = V \div h.$

Example 1. One of the concrete pillars to hold up a floor in a concrete building has a cross section that is a regular hexagon. The dimensions are as shown in Fig. 147. Find its weight if concrete weighs 138 lb. per cubic foot.

Solution. The volume is found by formula [38] $V = Ah$, where h is 12 ft. and A the area of a hexagon with one side 8 in.

$$A = 6 \times 4^2 \times 1.732 \text{ in.}^2 = \frac{6 \times 4^2 \times 1.732}{144} \text{ ft.}^2$$

$$\therefore V = \frac{12 \times 6 \times 4^2 \times 1.732}{144} \text{ ft.}^3$$

$$\text{Weight} = \frac{12 \times 6 \times 4^2 \times 1.732 \times 138}{144} = 1912 \text{ lb.}$$

Example 2. How deep is a cistern in the form of a hexagonal prism to hold 100 bbl. if the base is 4 ft. on an edge?

Fig. 147.

Solution. By formula [40], $h = V \div A$.

$V = 100$ bbl. $= 100 \times 31\frac{1}{2} \times 231$ cu. in.

$A =$ area of hexagon with edge of 4 ft.

Alt. of one triangle of hexagon $= 2 \times 1.732$
$= 3.464$ ft.

Area of hexagon $= 6 \times \frac{1}{2}(4 \times 3.464) = 41.568$ sq. ft.

41.568 sq. ft. $= 41.568 \times 144$ sq. in.

$$\therefore h = \frac{100 \times 31\frac{1}{2} \times 231}{41.568 \times 144} = 121.563 \text{ in.} = 10.13 \text{ ft. } Ans.$$

EXERCISES 46

1. Find the volume of the following rectangular solids:
(a) 8 ft. by 11 ft. by 32 ft.   *Ans.* 2816 ft.³
(b) 3 ft. by 4½ ft. by 7¾ ft.   *Ans.* 104⅝ ft.³
(c) 30 ft. 6 in. by 41 ft. 6 in. by 12 ft.   *Ans.* 15,189 ft.³
(d) 17 ft. 2 in. by 19 ft. 3 in. by 3 ft. 7 in. to nearest 0.001 ft.³
                                                  Ans. 1184.142+ ft.³
(e) 3 ft. 4 in. by 14 ft. 7 in. by 11 ft. 11 in. to nearest 0.001 ft.³
                                                  Ans. 579.282+ ft.³

2. If the inside dimension of a cubical tank is 4 ft., find the number of barrels it will hold when full.   *Ans.* 15.2− bbl.

3. Find the number of cubic yards of earth to be excavated in digging a cellar 40 ft. by 26 ft. by 7 ft.   *Ans.* 269.63−.

4. A rectangular solid has the three dimensions: 5.25 ft., 17.23 ft., and 4.062 ft. Find its capacity in bushels. *Ans.* 295.3 – bu.

5. Find the weight of a block of granite (specific gravity 2.9) 6 ft. by 7 ft. by $1\frac{1}{2}$ ft. *Ans.* $11,418\frac{3}{4}$ lb.

6. Find the weight of a solid cast-iron pillar in the form of a hexagonal prism 12 ft. high and 3 in. on edge of base.

Ans. 875 lb. nearly.

7. A common brick is 2 in. by 4 in. by 8 in. Find the number of bricks in a pile $8\frac{1}{2}$ ft. by 4 ft. by 10 ft. (Use cancellation.) *Ans.* 9180.

8. How many rectangular solids 3 in. $\times$4 in. $\times$9 in. will fill a box 4 ft. $\times$ 6 ft. $\times$8 ft.? *Ans.* 3072.

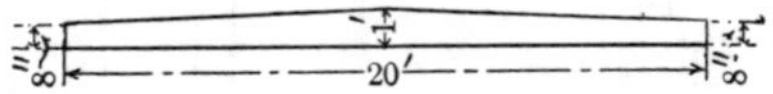

Fig. 148.

9. One hundred eighty square feet of zinc are required for lining the bottom and sides of a cubical vessel. How many cubic feet of water will it hold? *Ans.* 216.

10. A box car that is $36\frac{2}{3}$ ft. long and $8\frac{1}{6}$ ft. wide, inside measurements, can be filled with wheat to a height of $5\frac{1}{2}$ ft. Find how many bushels of wheat it will hold if $\frac{5}{4}$ cu. ft. are 1 bushel. *Ans.* $1317\frac{5}{9}$.

11. How many cubic yards of soil will it take to fill in a lot 50 ft. by 100 ft., if it is to be raised 3 ft. in the rear end and gradually sloped to the front where it is to be $1\frac{1}{2}$ ft. deep? *Ans.* $416\frac{2}{3}$.

Suggestion. The vertical cross section the long way of the lot is a trapezoid having parallel sides of lengths 3 ft. and $1\frac{1}{2}$ ft. respectively, and an altitude of 100 ft.

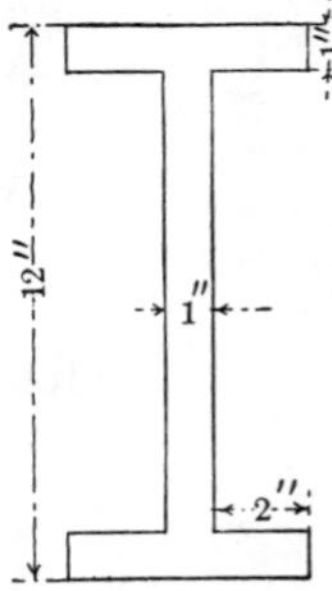

Fig. 149.

12. Find the number of cubic yards of crushed rock to make a road one mile in length and of cross section as shown in Fig. 148.

Solution. The area of the vertical cross section can be found by considering it as two trapezoids each having parallel sides of 8 in. and 1 ft. respectively, and altitudes of 10 ft.

Area of cross section $= (\frac{2}{3}+1)10 = 16\frac{2}{3}$ sq. ft.

No. of cu. ft. of rock $= 5280 \times 16\frac{2}{3} = 88,000$.

No. of cu. yd. of rock $= 88,000 \div 27 = 3259\frac{7}{27}$. *Ans.*

13. One cubic inch of steel weighs 0.29 lb. An I-beam has a cross section as shown in Fig. 149, and a length of 22 ft. Find its weight.

Ans. 1531+ lb.

14. Find the weight of steel beams 10 ft. in length and of the cross sections given in Fig. 40, page 121.

Ans. 821 lb.; 209.5 lb.; 300.2 lb.

15. Find what weight of lead will be required to cover a surface 48 ft. long and 32 ft. wide, with lead $\frac{1}{12}$ in. thick, allowing 5% of weight for joints. *Ans.* 4 tons nearly.

16. A rectangular box is made with $\frac{1}{8}$-in. sheet steel. Find weight of box (no allowance for corners) if it is 4 ft. by 3.4 ft. by 2.6 ft. (1 cu. in. = 0.29 lb.). *Ans.* 342.8 lb.

17. What length must be cut from a bar of steel $\frac{1}{2}$ in. by $1\frac{1}{4}$ in. in cross section in order to make 1 cu. ft.? *Ans.* 230.4 ft.

18. The base of a right prism is a triangle whose sides are 12 ft., 15 ft., and 17 ft., and its altitude is $8\frac{1}{2}$ ft. Find the lateral area.

Ans. 374 ft.²

19. Find the volume of the above prism. *Ans.* 745.872− ft.³

Suggestion. Use formula [7] to find the area of the base.

20. Find the volume of a cube whose diagonal is 8 in.

Ans. 98.534+ in.³

21. The cost of digging a ditch, including all expenses and profits, is estimated at 27 cents per cubic yard. Find the cost of digging a ditch 15 miles long, 10 ft. wide at the bottom, 20 ft. at the top, and 6 ft. deep. *Ans.* \$71,280.

22. A river is 76 ft. wide and 12 ft. deep and flows at the rate of $3\frac{1}{2}$ miles per hour. How many cubic feet of water per minute passes a given point on the river? *Ans.* 280,896.

Suggestion. The flow per minute is the volume of a prism of water of the cross section of the river and in length equal to the distance the water flows per minute.

23. A cistern 7 ft. long and 4 ft. broad holds 35 bbl. when three-fifths full; find the depth of the cistern. Find the cost of lining the bottom and sides with zinc at 5 cents per square foot.

Ans. 8 ft. 9.27+ in.; \$11.05.

24. An iron casting shrinks about $\frac{1}{8}$ in. per linear foot in cooling down to 70° Fahrenheit. What is the shrinkage per cubic foot?

Ans. 53.44− in.³

Suggestion. The shrinkage per cubic foot is the difference between a cubic foot and the volume of a cube $11\frac{7}{8}$ in. on an edge.

25. A fall of $\frac{7}{8}$ in. of rain is how many barrels per square rod?

Ans. $4\frac{5}{7}$.

26. A flow of 300 gallons per second will supply water for how deep a stream, if the stream is 4 ft. broad and flows 5 miles per hour?

Ans. $16\frac{13}{32}$ in.

Suggestion. The computation in the form of cancellation is

$$\frac{300 \times 231 \times 60 \times 60}{4 \times 5 \times 5280 \times 12 \times 12} = 16\tfrac{13}{32}.$$

27. Find cost at 40 cents a pound for sheet copper to line bottom and sides of a cubical vessel 7 ft. on an edge, if the sheet copper weighs 12 oz. per square foot. How many barrels will the vessel hold?

Ans. \$73.50; 81.45+.

28. A stream, flowing 5 miles per hour, must be of how large cross section to supply $1\frac{1}{2}$ in. in depth of water per week for 160 acres of land? *Ans.* $28\frac{2}{7}$ in.²

29. If a glass rod 1 in. long at 0° centigrade is increased to 1.000008 in. at 1° centigrade, find the increase in volume of. a cubic inch of glass when heated from 0° to 1° centigrade.   *Ans.* 0.000024 + in.³

STONEWORK

161. Terms.—A full description cannot be given here. For such the student is referred to a trade handbook.

Stonework where the stones are broken with the hammer only is called **rubble-work.** If the stones are laid in courses it is called **coursed rubble.** When the stones showing in the outside face of the wall are squared, the work is designated as **ashlar.** If all the stones of a course are of the same height, the work is called **coursed ashlar.** When the stones are of different heights it is called **broken ashlar.** Ashlar work is both hammer-dressed and chisel-dressed. Any stonework where any other tool than the hammer is used for dressing is called **cut-work.**

162. Estimating cost of stonework.—In estimating the cost of stonework, the custom varies greatly; we find it varying even among the contractors of the same city. Cut-work is often measured by the number of square feet in the face of the wall.

Rubble-work is almost universally measured by the perch, but the perch used varies greatly. The legal perch of 24¾ cu. ft. is seldom used by stone masons. The perch of 16½ cu. ft. is the one most used. That of 25 cu. ft. or of 22 cu. ft. is sometimes used.

Stonework on railroads is usually measured by the cubic yard.

Openings, as a rule, are not deducted if containing less than 70 sq. ft.

EXERCISES 47

1. Find the cost of laying a hammer-dressed ashlar wall, 45 ft. long, 6 ft. high and 2 ft. thick, at $2.75 a perch, using the 22-cu. ft. perch.
Ans. $67.50.

2. Find the cost of making a rubble-work wall at $3.25 a perch, including all the material, under a building 25 ft. by 60 ft., the wall to be 30 in. thick and 8 ft. high. Use the 16½-cu.ft. perch.   *Ans.* $630.30.

3. Find the cost of laying the stonework in two abutments for a bridge, each abutment to be 8 ft. high, 3½ ft. thick, 20 ft. long at the bottom and

15 ft. at the top. (The shape is a trapezoid.) The price for laying is $1.75 per cubic yard. *Ans.* $63.52.

4. Find the cost of building a sandstone rubble-work wall for a basement 36 ft. by 47 ft., 8 ft. high, and the wall 18 in. thick. (Use outside measurements and make no allowances for openings.) The stone costs $1.40 a perch (25 cu. ft.), and the labor of laying, including lime and sand, is $1.25 a perch. *Ans.* $211.15.

BRICKWORK

163. Brick.—The size of brick varies. In the United States, there is no legal standard. The common brick is approximately given as 8 in. by 4 in. by 2 in. In the New England States, they average about $7\frac{3}{4}$ in. by $3\frac{3}{4}$ in. by $2\frac{1}{4}$ in. In most of the western states, the common brick averages about $8\frac{1}{2}$ in. by $4\frac{1}{8}$ in. by $2\frac{1}{2}$ in. The brick from the same lot may vary as much as $\frac{3}{16}$ in., depending upon the degree to which they are burnt. The hard-burned bricks are the smaller.

Walls made from these bricks are about 9, 13, 18, and 22 inches in thickness, that is, 1, $1\frac{1}{2}$, 2, and $2\frac{1}{2}$ bricks.

Pressed bricks are usually larger than common bricks; the prevailing size is $8\frac{3}{8}$ in. by $4\frac{1}{8}$ in. by $2\frac{3}{8}$ in.

164. Estimating number, and cost of brickwork.—This cannot be discussed in full here. The student is referred to an architect's and builder's handbook for the details. Plain walls are quite universally figured at 15 bricks to the square foot, *outside measure*, of 8- or 9-in. wall; $22\frac{1}{2}$ bricks per square foot of 12- or .13-in. wall; 30 bricks per square foot of 16-, 17-, or 18-in. wall; and $7\frac{1}{2}$ bricks for each additional 4 or $4\frac{1}{2}$ in. in thickness of wall. These figures are used without regard to the size of the bricks, the effect of the latter being taken into account in fixing the price per thousand. No deduction is made for openings of less than 80 sq. ft., and when deductions are made for larger openings the width is measured 2 ft. less than the actual width. Hollow walls are measured as if solid. For chimney-breasts, pilasters, detached chimneys, and other forms the student is referred to a builder's handbook.

Example. Find the cost of brickwork in the walls of a house 26 ft. by 34 ft., no cross walls, the basement walls to be 13 in. thick; the first story walls, 13 in. thick; second story walls, 9 in. thick; height of basement walls to top of first floor joists, 9 ft.; from first floor joists to top of second floor joists, 10 ft. 6 in.; from second floor joists to plate, 9 ft. (The chimneys, openings, and pressed brickwork are not considered as the method of estimating has not been given.) The cost of brick and laying, including lime, sand, scaffolding, etc., is $10 per thousand.

Solution.   Basement and first story walls:

Girth of house $= 2 \times 26$ ft. $+ 2 \times 34$ ft. $= 120$ ft.

Height of wall $= 9$ ft. $+ 10$ ft. 6 in. $= 19\frac{1}{2}$ ft.

Thickness of wall is 13 in. and hence $22\frac{1}{2}$ brick are counted per square foot.   Hence the number of bricks required is

$$120 \times 19\frac{1}{2} \times 22\frac{1}{2} = 52,650.$$

Similarly for the second story,

$$120 \times 9 \times 15 = 16,200.$$

$\therefore$ total number of bricks $= 52,650 + 16,200 = 68,850.$

$\therefore$ cost $= \$10 \times 68.850 = \$688.50.$ *Ans.*

EXERCISES 48

1. Find the cost at $9.50 per thousand to cover brick, material, and labor to build a brick wall on the front and one side of a corner lot 50 ft. by 100 ft.; the wall to be $6\frac{1}{2}$ ft. high and a brick and a half thick, allowance being made for one opening 12 ft. in length (count it 2 ft. less).
Ans. $194.51.

2. The following is about the cost of furnishing and laying 1500 bricks, or one day's work:

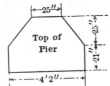

Fig. 150.

1500 bricks at $6.00 per M,
$\frac{3}{4}$ barrel of lime at $1.00,
9 bushels of sand at 5 cents,
1 day's work for mason at $5.76,
1 day's work for helper at $3.32.

Using this as a basis for estimating, find the cost of building the walls of an apartment house 25 ft. by 54 ft., 41 ft. high in front and 36 ft. in the rear.   The walls are to be 13 in. thick and no allowances for openings.
Ans. $1759.20.

3. Find the cost of common brick in the pier with a cross section as shown in Fig. 150, and a height of 12 ft. 6 in., at $7.00 per thousand. Count 20 brick to 1 cu. ft.
Ans. $24.15.

4. How many enamel brick 4 in. by 8 in. are required to face a wall 30 ft. long and 12 ft. high, deducting for two windows 4 ft. by 8 ft. and one door 3 ft. 4 in. by 10 ft.?
Ans. 1182.

CHAPTER XV

CYLINDERS

165. Definitions.—A **right circular cylinder,** or a **cylinder of revolution,** is a solid formed by revolving a rectangle about one of its sides as an axis.

Thus, in Fig. 151, the rectangle $OABO'$ is revolved about OO' as an axis. This forms the cylinder as drawn.

From this definition, the two bases are circles, and the lateral surface is a curved surface. The **axis** of the cylinder is the line OO' joining the centers of the bases. It is per-

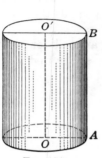

Fig. 151.

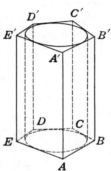

Fig. 152.

pendicular to the bases, and hence it is equal to the altitude of the cylinder. The **cross section** of a cylinder is a section perpendicular to the axis.

A cylinder is **inscribed in** a prism when its bases are inscribed in the bases of the prism (see Fig. 152). The prism is then **circumscribed about** the cylinder. A cylinder is **circumscribed about** a prism, or the prism is **inscribed in** the cylinder, when the bases of the prism are inscribed in the bases of the cylinder.

166. Area and volume.—If the lateral surface of a right cylinder could be peeled off and spread out, it would form a rectangle of width equal to the altitude of the cylinder,

203

and of length equal to the circumference of the base of the cylinder. From this we get the following:

RULE. *The area of the lateral surface of a right cylinder equals the circumference of the base times the altitude.*

The total area equals the lateral area plus the area of the two bases.

From a consideration similar to that for the prism, **Art. 160,** the volume of the cylinder is obtained by the following:

RULE. *The volume of a cylinder equals the area of the base times the altitude.*

The similarity of the cylinder and the prism is seen if the cylinder is thought of as a prism having a very great number of sides to the base.

The above rules hold when the cylinder is not circular.

Since the altitude times the cross section gives the volume, the altitude equals the volume divided by the area of the base or cross section. Also the area of the base equals the volume divided by the altitude.

If S stands for lateral area, T for total area, A for area of base, and h for altitude, the rules given are stated in the following formulas:

$$[42] \quad S = Ch = \pi dh = 2\pi rh.$$
$$[43] \quad V = Ah = \pi r^2 h = \tfrac{1}{4}\pi d^2 h.$$
$$[44] \quad h = V \div A = V \div \pi r^2.$$
$$[45] \quad A = V \div h.$$

167. The hollow cylinder.—The volume of a hollow cylinder may be found by subtracting the volume of the cylindrical hollow from the volume of the whole cylinder. If R is the radius of the cylinder, and r the radius of the hollow, then the volume of the hollow cylinder is as follows:

$$[46] \quad V = \pi R^2 h - \pi r^2 h = \pi h(R^2 - r^2) = \pi h(R+r)(R-r).$$

Example 1. Find the number of cubic inches of copper in a hollow cylinder 7 in. long, inner diameter 6 in. and outer diameter 8 in.

Solution. By [46], $V = \pi h(R+r)(R-r)$.

$\therefore V = 3.1416 \times 7(4+3)(4-3) = 153.938$ in.³

Example 2. Find the effective heating surface of a boiler of diameter 5 ft. and length 16 ft.; with 54 tubes $3\frac{1}{2}$ in. in diameter, assuming that the effective heating surface of the shell is one-half the total surface.

Solution. By [**42**], effective heating surface of the shell =
$\frac{1}{2}(\pi dh + 2 \times \frac{1}{4}\pi d^2) = \frac{1}{2}(3.1416 \times 5 \times 16 + 2 \times 0.7854 \times 5^2) =$

$$145.299 \text{ ft.}^2$$

Effective heating surface of 54 tubes

$$= \frac{3\frac{1}{2} \times 3.1416 \times 54 \times 16}{12} = 791.683 \text{ ft.}^2$$

∴ total heating surface = 145.299 + 791.683 = 937 ft.² nearly.

Example 3. What is the weight of a cylindrical shaft of marble 3 ft. in circumference and 9 ft. high?

Solution. $r = \frac{1}{2}(3 \div 3.1416) = 0.47746.$

By [**43**], $V = \pi r^2 h = 3.1416 \times 0.47746^2 \times 9 = 6.4457 \text{ ft.}^3$

Weight $= 2.7 \times 62.5 \times 6.4457 = 1087$ lb.

Since 62.5 lb. = weight of 1 cu. ft. of water, and 2.7 = specific gravity of marble.

EXERCISES 49

1. If the radius of the base of a right circular cylinder is 5 in. and the altitude is 8 in., find the lateral area, the total area, and the volume.
Ans. 251.33 in.²; 408.4 in.²; 628.3 in.³

2. If r, d, h, A, S, and V have the meanings given in the preceding articles:
(a) Given $A = 48$ sq. in. and $h = 16$ in.; find r, S, and V.
(b) Given $V = 4800$ cu. ft. and $A = 160$ sq. ft.; find d and S.
Ans. (a) $r = 3.909 -$ in.; $S = 393.0 -$ sq.in.; $V = 768$ cu. in.

3. Find the area of the rubbing surface in a steam cylinder $91\frac{1}{2}$ in. in diameter, the stroke of the piston being 6 ft. 8 in.
Ans. 159.7 − ft.²

4. Find the total area and the volume of a cylinder whose radius is 7 ft. and whose altitude is 12 ft.
Ans. 835.66 ft.²; 1847+ ft.³

5. Find the number of barrels each of the following cylindrical tanks will hold:
(a) Diameter 5 ft., depth 5 ft.   *Ans.* 23.3.
(b) Diameter 8 ft., depth 9 ft.   *Ans.* 107.4.
(c) Diameter 20 ft., depth 19 ft.   *Ans.* 1417.5.
(d) Diameter 30 ft., depth 20 ft.   *Ans.* 3357.3.
Suggestion. Use 1 bbl. = 4.211 cu. ft.

6. Find the number of cubic yards of earth removed in digging a tunnel 175 yd. long, if the cross section is a semicircle with a radius of 14 ft.   *Ans.* 5986.5.

7. A peck measure is to be made 8 in. in diameter. How deep should it be? (See Fig. 153.)   *Ans.* 10.695 in.

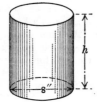

FIG. 153.

Suggestion. 1 pk. = ¼ of 2150.42 cu. in. = 537.605 cu. in.

Area of base = 8² × 0.7854 = 50.2656 sq. in.

Altitude = volume ÷ area of base.

8. A cylindrical oil tank 3 ft. in diameter and 10 ft. long will contain how many gallons of oil? *Ans.* 528.8 −.

9. The external diameter of a hollow cast-iron shaft is 18 in., and its internal diameter is 10 in. Calculate its weight if the length is 20 ft., and cast iron weighs 0.26 lb. per cubic inch.

Ans. 10,980 lb. nearly.

10. Water is flowing at the rate of 10 miles per hour through a pipe 16 in. in diameter into a rectangular reservoir 197 yd. long and 87 yd. wide. Calculate the time in which the surface will be raised 3 in.

Ans. 31.38 minutes.

Suggestion. Ten miles per hour is $\dfrac{10 \times 5280}{60} = 880$ ft. per minute.

Now find the number of cubic feet of water that will flow through the 16-in. pipe in 1 minute. Then find the number of cubic feet required to fill the reservoir 3 in. The quotient found by dividing the required number of cubic feet by the flow per minute is the time in minutes.

11. In a table giving weights and sizes of square nuts for bolts, a nut 2 in. square and 1¼ in. thick, with a hole 1 1/16 in. in diameter, has a given weight of 1.042 lb. Use wrought iron and find this weight.

12. Find the length of steel wire in a coil, if its diameter is 0.025 in. and its weight is 50 lb. (Use 1 cu. in. weighs 0.29 lb.)

Ans. 29,270 ft. nearly.

13. A cylindrical cistern is 6 ft. in diameter. Find the depth of the water when containing 10 barrels. *Ans.* 17.87 in.

14. A nugget of gold is dropped into a cylinder of water and raises the surface of the water 1¼ in. If the cylinder is 2 in. in diameter and 25 grains of gold are worth $1, find the value of the nugget.

Ans. $767.

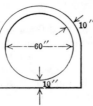

Fig. 1·54.

15. In a table giving size, etc., of wrought-iron washers, a washer 3½ in. in diameter with a hole 1½ in. in diameter is 5/32 in. thick. Find the number of these in a keg of 200 lb. *Ans.* 582.

16. Find the per cent of error in the following rule which applies to round bars, (a) for wrought iron, (b) for cast iron. Multiply the square of the diameter in inches by the length in feet, and that product by 2.6. The product will be the weight in pounds nearly.

Ans. (a) 1.5 − % too small; (b) 6.1 + % too large.

17. A conduit made of concrete has a cross section as shown in Fig. 154. How many cubic yards of concrete are used in making 500 yd. of this conduit? *Ans.* 1113.4 yd.³

18. In a table giving weights and areas in cross section of steel bars, a round steel bar $\frac{3}{8}$ in. in diameter has its area given as 0.1104 in.^{2} and weight 0.376 lb. per linear foot. Verify these results if steel weighs 489.6 lb. per cubic foot.

19. A water tank in a Pullman car has a vertical cross section as shown in Fig. 155, and a length of 52 in. Find its capacity in gallons. The arc is a part of a circle. *Ans.* 68.3 gal.

20. A rod of copper 8 in. long and 1 in. in diameter is drawn into wire of uniform thickness and 200 ft. long. Find the diameter of the wire. *Ans.* 0.0577 in.

21. The rain which falls on a house 22 ft. by 36 ft. is conducted to a cylindrical cistern 8 ft. in diameter. How great a fall of rain would it take to fill the cistern to a depth of $7\frac{1}{2}$ ft.? *Ans.* 5.712 in.

22. Find the weight of 7 miles of $\frac{1}{8}$-in. copper wire, if copper weighs 0.319 lb. per cubic inch. *Ans.* 1736.26 lb.

23. Find the greatest tensile force a copper wire 0.25 in. in diameter can stand without breaking. (See **Table VII.**)
Ans. Less than 1472.6 lb.

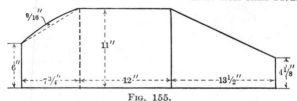

Fig. 155.

By tensile force is meant a pulling force. The problem asks how great a weight the wire will hold when hanging vertically.

24. Calculate the size of a square wrought-iron bar to stand a pull of 43,000 lb. (See **Table VII.**) *Ans.* 0.927 in. square.

25. What should be the diameter of a round cast-iron bar which is subjected to a tension of 30,000 lb., if the pull on each square inch of cross section is 2400 lb.? *Ans.* 3.991 in.

26. Find the pull per square inch necessary to break a rod $2\frac{1}{2}$ in. diameter, which breaks with a load of 270,000 lb.
Ans. 55,000 lb. nearly.

27. If a wrought-iron bar 2 in. by $1\frac{1}{4}$ in. in cross section breaks under a load of 125,000 lb., what load will break a wrought-iron rod $2\frac{1}{2}$ in. in diameter? *Ans.* 245,400 lb. nearly.

28. A cast-iron bar has an elliptical cross section with axes 6 in. and 4 in. Find the pull per square inch of cross section under a total tensile load of 125,000 lb. *Ans.* 6631 lb.

29. A wrought-iron cylindrical rod 2000 ft. long and $1\frac{1}{2}$ in. in diameter is suspended vertically from its upper end. What is the total pull at this end, and the pull per square inch of cross section?
Ans. 11,875 lb.; 6720 lb.

30. Find the length of a wrought-iron bar, supported vertically at its upper end, that will just break under its own weight. *Ans.* 15,000 ft.

31. About what is the strength of an 18 gage B. and S. wrought-iron wire? (See **Table VII.**) *Ans.* 63.8 lb.

32. A trolley wire is copper and 00 gage B. and S. Find the pull it will take to break the wire. *Ans.* 3130 lb.

33. A cylinder to cool lard is 4 ft. in diameter and 9 ft. long and makes 4 R. P. M. As the cylinder revolves, the hot lard covers the surface ⅛ in. deep. How many pounds of lard will it cool in 1 hour if the specific gravity of lard is 0.9? *Ans.* 15,900 nearly.

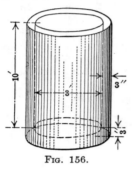

Fig. 156.

34. If a tank 5 ft. in diameter and 10 ft. deep holds 10,000 lb. of lard, what will be the depth of a tank of 2000 lb. capacity if its diameter is ⅔ ft.? If this tank has a jacket around it on the bottom and sides 3 in. from the surface of the tank, how many gallons of water will the space between the jacket and tank hold? *Ans.* 5⅝ ft.; 124 nearly.

35. Find the volume of a wash boiler if the bottom is in the form of a rectangle with a semicircle at each end. The rectangle is 10 in. by 14 in., and the semicircles are on the smaller dimensions. The depth of the boiler is 16 in. *Ans.* 15.14− gal.

36. Find the height of a 10-gallon wash boiler whose base is 10 in. wide with· semicircular ends, the length of the straight part of the sides being 9¼ in. *Ans.* 13.5− in.

37. A certain handbook gives the following "rules of thumb" for finding the volume in gallons of a cylindrical tank:

(1) V (in gal.) = (diameter in feet)$^2 \times 5\frac{7}{8} \times$ (height in feet).

(2) V (in gal.) = (diameter in feet)$^2 \times \frac{1}{2}$ of height in inches less 2% of same.

Find per cent of error for each rule.

Ans. (1) 0.003 + % too small; (2) 0.08 + % too large.

Remark. Rule (2) is a quick rule to apply if the 2% is disregarded. This rule is in common use by many estimators.

38. In making the pattern for a teakettle with an elliptical bottom to hold 6 quarts, it is decided to have the bottom an ellipse with axes 10 in. and 7 in. Find the height. *Ans.* 6.30+ in.

39. How long a piece of copper will it take to make the body of the above teakettle? $\left(\text{Use Cir.} = 2\pi \times \dfrac{a+b}{2}.\right)$ *Ans.* 26.70 in.

40. In drilling in soft steel, a $1\frac{9}{16}$-in. twist-drill makes 37 R. P. M. with a feed of $\frac{1}{30}$ in. Find the number of cubic inches cut away in 3¼ minutes. *Ans.* 3.1+.

41. A $\frac{3}{16}$-in. twist-drill makes 310 R. P. M. with a feed of $\frac{1}{125}$ in. Find the volume cut away in 3½ minutes. *Ans.* 0.24 − in.³

42. In turning a steel shaft 6 in. in diameter and 4 ft. long, the cutting speed was 36 ft. per minute and the feed 0.125 in. Find the time required for turning the shaft. If the depth of the cut was 0.05 in., find the amount of metal removed. *Ans.* 16¾ min. nearly; 45.2 in.³

43. Find the number of pounds of cast iron turned off per hour in the following: (Consider the cutting as if on a plane.)

Speed per min.	Depth of cut	Breadth of cut	
(a) 37.90 ft.	0.125 in.	0.015 in.	*Ans.* 13.3.
(b) 25.82 ft.	0.015 in.	0.125 in.	*Ans.* 9.06.
(c) 25.27 ft.	0.048 in.	0.048 in.	*Ans.* 10.9.

44. A steam chest cover is 42 in. by 24 in. How many steel studs 1¼ in. in diameter should be used to hold the cover, if the steam pressure is 160 lb. per square inch? The diameter of the bolts at the bottom of the thread is 1.065 in. Allow a stress of 11,000 lb. per square inch.

Ans. 16.5 bolts or 18 to make the number even.

Solution. 42×24×160 lb. = 161,280 lb. total pressure.

161,280÷11,000 = 14.662 in.² = area in cross section of all bolts.

0.7854×1.065² = 0.89082+ in.² = area of one bolt.

14.662÷0.89082 = 16.5 −.

∴ number of bolts is 18 to be even.

45. The flanges at the joining of two ends of flanged steam pipes 9 in. in inside diameter are bolted together by 12 bolts ¾ in. in diameter. If the pressure in the pipes is 200 lb per square inch, find what each bolt must hold. How much is this per square inch cross section of the bolts? Suppose that bolts have 10 pitch U. S. S. thread. This makes the root diameter 0.620 in. (See Fig. 157.)

Ans. 1060.3 lb.; 3512+ lb.

FIG. 157.

46. As in the last exercise, if the steam pipe is 18 in. in diameter, and allowing the same pull per square inch of cross section of each bolt, find the number of bolts 1⅛ in. in diameter at a joint of the pipe. (A 1⅛-in. bolt with 7 pitch U. S. S. thread is 0.940 in. in diameter at root of thread.) *Ans.* 22.

47. The following rule is often used to find the heating surface of any number of tubes in a steam boiler: Multiply the number of tubes by the diameter of one tube in inches, this product by its length in feet, and then by 0.2618. The final product is the number of sq. ft. of heating surface. Using this rule, what is the heating surface of 66 3-in. tubes each 18 ft. long? Does the rule give the correct result? *Ans.* 933 ft.²; yes.

48. To find the water capacity of a horizontal tubular boiler, find ⅔ the volume of the shell and subtract from this the volume of all the tubes. Find the water capacity of a horizontal tubular boiler 18½ ft. long, 66 in. in diameter, with 72 3-in. tubes. *Ans.* 227.6+ ft.³

49. The steam capacity of a horizontal boiler is often reckoned as

14

one-third the volume of the shell. Find the steam capacity of a horizontal boiler 18 ft. long and 78 in. in diameter. *Ans.* 199+ ft.³

50. Use the following rule and find the heating surface of a boiler 12 ft. long, 5 ft. in diameter, and having 52 2½-in. tubes.
Ans. 518.7 ft.² to 556.7 ft.²

Rule. In finding the heating surface in a horizontal boiler, it is customary to take one-half to two-thirds of the lateral area of the shell, the lateral area of the tubes, one-half to two-thirds the area of the ends of the boiler, and subtract the areas of both ends of the tubes.

51. A steam boiler is 72 in. in diameter, 18 ft. long, and contains 70 tubes 4 in. in diameter. Find the heating surface, using one-half in the rule. *Ans.* 1505+ ft.²

52. Find the steam capacity of a boiler 4 ft. in diameter and 16 ft. long, if the height of the segment occupied by the steam is 18 in.? Is this more or less and how much than one-third the total capacity of the boiler shell? *Ans.* 68.9 ft.³; 1.9 ft.³ more.

Suggestion. Using [30(b)] as the most convenient,

$$A = \frac{4}{3} \times 1.5^2 \times \sqrt{\frac{4}{1.5}} - 0.608 = 4.305 \, \text{ft.}^2$$

Volume = 16×4.305 ft.³ = 68.9 ft.³

53. The cylinder of a pump is 6 in. in diameter, the length of stroke 8 in., and the number of strokes per minute 160. Find the flow in gallons per minute if the pump is double acting, that is, pumps the cylinder full each stroke. *Ans.* 156.7− gal.

54. When the piston of a hand pump is 3 in. in diameter, and the supply of water is drawn from a depth of 25 ft., what pressure is required on the handle 24 in. from the fulcrum when the piston rod is attached 3¼ in. from the fulcrum? *Ans.* 10.39− lb.

55. The Cleveland Twist Drill Company records a test in which a 1¼-in. "Paragon" high-speed drill removed 70.56 cu. in. of cast iron per minute. The penetration per minute was 57½ in., the feed $\frac{1}{10}$ in., and the drill made 575 R. P. M. Do these numbers agree?

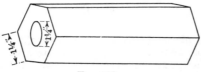

Fig. 158.

56. What will be the weight of a cast-iron pipe 10 ft. long, 2 ft. in outer diameter, and 1 in. thick? (Use 0.26 lb. per cubic inch.) *Ans.* 2254 lb.

57. A tank car with a cylindrical tank 8 ft. in diameter and 34 ft. long will hold how many gallons? What weight of oil will it hold if the specific gravity of oil is 0.94? *Ans.* 12,784 gal.; 100,400 lb.

58. Find the height of a cylindrical tank having a diameter of 30 in. in order that it may hold 4 barrels. *Ans.* 41$\frac{3}{16}$ in.

59. If a bar 1½ in. in diameter weighs 6.01 lb. per foot of length, what is the weight per foot of a bar 1½ in. square and of the same material? *Ans.* 7.65+ lb.

60. Find the weight of a hollow hexagonal bar 16 ft. long and weighing 0.28 lb. per cubic inch. The cross section is a regular hexagon $1\frac{1}{4}$ in. on a side, with a circle $1\frac{1}{4}$ in. in diameter, at the center. (See Fig. 158.)

Ans. $152\frac{1}{4}$ lb.

61. A cylindrical tank 22 ft. long and 6 ft. in diameter rests on its side in a horizontal position. Find the number of gallons of oil it will hold when the depth of the oil is 8 in. When 1 ft. 6 in. When 2 ft. 6 in. Use formula [**30(b)**] for finding the area of the segment.

Ans. 282.5 gal.; 909.3 gal.

62. The segment in Fig. 159 is a counter-balance $5\frac{1}{2}$ in. thick. Find its weight if made of cast iron weighing 0.26 lb. per cubic inch.

Solution. Area of segment AnB = area of sector $AOBn$ − area of triangle AOB.

Area of sector $AOBn = \frac{1}{6} \times 84^2 \times 0.7854 = 923.63$ in.²
Area of triangle $AOB = \frac{1}{2} \times 42 \times 21 \times \sqrt{3} = 763.81$ in.²
Area of segment $AnB = 923.63$ in.² $- 763.81$ in.² $= 159.82$ in.²
Volume of counter-balance $= 5\frac{1}{2} \times 159.82$ in.³ $= 879.0$ in.³
Weight of counter-balance $= 879.0 \times 0.26$ lb. $= 228.5$ lb. *Ans.*

63. What is the diameter of a single round rod in order that it may be as strong as three rods having diameters of $\frac{1}{2}$ in., 1 in., and $1\frac{1}{2}$ in. respectively? *Ans.* $1.87+$ in.

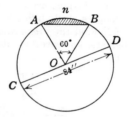

64. Because the body of a bolt is greater in diameter than the threaded part, when the bolt is under strain the two parts will not stretch uniformly. For this reason the bolt is most liable to break where the threaded part joins the other part. To overcome this a hole is sometimes drilled from the center of the head to the beginning of the threaded part. This hole is made of such size that the cross-sectional area of the body is the same as that at the root of the thread.

Fig. 159.

Find the diameter of the hole to be drilled in the following bolts in accordance with the preceding:

(a) Diameter of bolt $\frac{3}{4}$ in. with 10 U. S. S. threads to 1 in.
(b) Diameter of bolt $1\frac{3}{8}$ in. with 5 U. S. S. threads to 1 in.

Ans. (a) $0.422-$ in.; (b) 0.952 in.

65. In computing the safe working pressure for a steam boiler, a factor of safety of 5 is used. That is, the safe working pressure is $\frac{1}{5}$ of the bursting pressure. The bursting pressure in pounds per square inch is given by the formula

$$P = \frac{Ttk}{r},$$

where P = bursting pressure in pounds per square inch,
　　　　T = tensile strength of boiler plate per square inch,
　　　　t = thickness of boiler plate in inches,
　　　　r = radius of boiler in inches,
and 　　k = a constant depending upon the riveting and is 0.56 for single

riveted boilers, 0.70 for double riveted boilers, and 0.88 for triple riveted boilers. Derive the formula. (See Fig. 160.)

66. Find the bursting and the safe working pressure for a double riveted boiler 66 in. in diameter, made of plate $\frac{5}{16}$ in. thick, if tensile strength is 50,000 lb. per square inch. *Ans.* 331.4 lb.; 66.3 lb.

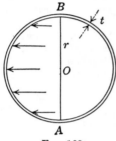

Fig. 160.

67. What would be the bursting pressure in pounds per square inch of a wrought iron pipe having an inside diameter of 3 in. and a shell $\frac{1}{8}$ in. thick? Use a tensile strength of 40,000 lb. per square inch. *Ans.* $3333\frac{1}{3}$ lb.

68. Holes are punched in sheets of metal by means of great pressure applied by a punch press. The pressure is usually reckoned at 60,000 lb. per square inch of surface cut over. For example, a hole 2 in. in circumference punched in a $\frac{1}{2}$-in. plate would require a pressure of $2 \times \frac{1}{2} \times 60,000$ lb., that is, the area of the cylindrical surface sheared off times 60,000 lb. Find the pressure necessary to punch a hole, having a diameter of $\frac{1}{2}$ in., through a steel plate $\frac{1}{8}$ in. thick. *Ans.* 11,781 lb.

69. Find the pressure necessary to punch at one blow a hole $\frac{3}{4}$ in. in diameter and a rectangular hole $\frac{3}{4}$ in. by $\frac{1}{4}$ in. through a steel plate $\frac{1}{2}$ in. thick. *Ans.* 130,686 lb.

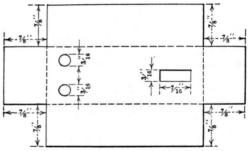

Fig. 161.

70. Find the blow necessary to cut out the corner squares and the holes in the box shown in Fig. 161. The dimensions are as given and the thickness of the sheet steel is $\frac{1}{32}$ in. *Ans.* 17,678 lb.

71. Many small metal articles in common use are punched out of sheet metal and pressed into shape. The blank is usually cut so as to have the same area as the area of the finished article (Fig. 162). For example, the blank for a cylindrical box, having a diameter of 1 in. and a depth of 2 in., would have an area equal to the combined area of the sides and bottom of the box. Find the area and diameter of the blank for this box.

Solution. Area $= 3.1416 \times (\frac{1}{2})^2 + 3.1416 \times 1 \times 2 = 7.06$ sq. in. 89

Diameter of blank $= \sqrt{7.0686 \div 0.7854} = 3$ in.

Note. In shallow articles, as pail covers, the diameter of the blank is often found by adding twice the depth to the diameter of the top.

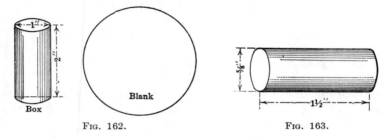

Fɪɢ. 162.   Fɪɢ. 163.

72. Find the diameter of the blank for a pail cover whose diameter is 8 in. and depth $\frac{3}{4}$ in. Work by both methods suggested above and compare results.

73. An aluminum cap for a paste bottle has the dimensions given in Fig. 163. Find the diameter of the blank from which it was pressed.

Ans. 2.035 in.

74. A shoe-blacking box has a diameter of 3 in. and a depth of 1 in. Find the diameter of the blank from which it was pressed.

Ans. 4.58 in.

CHAPTER XVI

PYRAMIDS, CONES, AND FRUSTUMS

168. Pyramid.—A **pyramid** is a solid whose base is a polygon, and whose sides are triangles with their vertices at a common point, called the **vertex** or **apex** of the pyramid. A pyramid is triangular, square, hexagonal, etc., according as its base is a triangle, square, hexagon, etc.

A **right pyramid,** or a **regular pyramid,** is a pyramid whose base is a regular polygon, and the sides or faces equal isosceles triangles.

Fig. 164 is a regular pyramid with a square base.

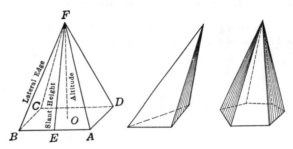

Fig. 164.

In a regular pyramid the **axis,** or the line drawn from the vertex to the center of the base, is perpendicular to the base. This line is the **altitude** of the pyramid.

In Fig. 164, *OF* is the altitude.

The **slant height** of a right pyramid is the line drawn from the vertex to the center of one edge of the base.

EF of Fig. 164 is the slant height.

A **lateral edge** is the line in which two faces meet.

BF of Fig. 164 is a lateral edge.

169. Cone.—A **circular cone** is a solid whose base is a circle, and whose lateral surface tapers uniformly to a point, called the **vertex** or **apex**. The axis of the cone is a straight line drawn from the vertex to the center of the base.

A **right circular cone** is a cone whose base is a circle and whose axis is perpendicular to the base.

In Fig. 165, *F-ABC* is a right circular cone.

This might also be defined as a solid formed by a right triangle revolved about one of its legs as an axis. It may be called a **cone of revolution**.

The **altitude** of a cone is the perpendicular line from the vertex to the base. The **slant height** is a straight line drawn from the vertex to the circumference of the base.

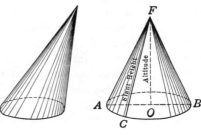

FIG. 165.

In Fig. 165, *OF* is the altitude, and *CF* the slant height.

170. Frustum.—If the top of a pyramid or a cone is cut off by a plane parallel to the base, the remaining part is called a **frustum** of a pyramid or a cone.

In Fig. 166, (*a*) and (*b*) are frustums.

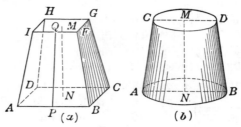

FIG. 166.

The **altitude** of a frustum is the perpendicular between the bases, as *NM* of Fig. 166. The **slant height** of the frustum of a right pyramid or cone is the shortest line between the perimeters of the two bases. It is perpendicular to the edge of each base in the frustum of a right pyramid; and is, therefore, the altitude of the trapezoids that form the faces of the frustum.

In Fig. 166(*a*), *PQ* is the slant height.

171. Areas.—The **lateral area** of a right pyramid is found by taking the sum of the areas of the triangles forming the faces of the pyramid.   Since the altitudes of these triangles are each the slant height of the pyramid, they are equal.   Because the base of a right pyramid is a regular polygon, the bases of the triangles are equal.   We then have the following:

RULE.   *The lateral area of a right pyramid or cone equals the perimeter of the base times one-half the slant height.*

The total area equals the lateral area plus the area of the base.

Since the faces of the frustum of a pyramid are trapezoids, we have, by use of formula [8], the following:

RULE.   *The lateral area of the frustum of a right pyramid or cone equals one-half the sum of the perimeters of the two bases times the slant height.*

The total area equals the lateral area plus the areas of the two bases.

That these rules apply to the cone as well as to the pyramid may be seen by thinking of the cone as a pyramid with a very great number of sides to the base.

Using S for lateral area, T for total area, h for altitude, s for slant height, p for perimeter (P and p for frustum), A for area of base (B and b for frustum), the rules may be written as the formulas:

[47] $S = \frac{1}{2}ps$, for pyramid or cone.

[48] $T = \frac{1}{2}ps + A$, for pyramid or cone.

[49] $S = \frac{1}{2}(P+p)s$, for frustum.

[50] $T = \frac{1}{2}(P+p)s + B + b$, for frustum.

172. Volumes.—A particular case of the volume of a

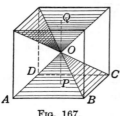

FIG. 167.

pyramid is seen as follows: The cube of Fig. 167 is divided into six equal pyramids with their vertices at the center of the cube.   The volume of the cube equals the area $ABCD$ times the altitude PQ.   Now the volume of one of the six pyramids, as $O\text{-}ABCD$, equals $\frac{1}{6}$ of the volume of the cube, and hence equals the area of the base $ABCD$ times $\frac{1}{3}$ of PO.

RULE.   *The volume of a pyramid or a cone equals the area of the base times one-third the altitude.*

Which may be written as the formula:

$$[51] \quad V = \tfrac{1}{3}Ah.$$

The volume of the frustum of a pyramid or cone is best stated in the following formula:

$$[52] \quad V = \tfrac{1}{3}h(B + b + \sqrt{B \times b}).$$

The volume of a frustum of a cone is usually more easily found by

$$[53] \quad V = \tfrac{1}{3}\pi h(R^2 + r^2 + Rr),$$

or $$[54] \quad V = \tfrac{1}{12}\pi h(D^2 + d^2 + Dd),$$

where R and D are radius and diameter respectively of lower base, and r and d of upper base.

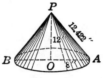

FIG. 168.

It should be noted that the volume of a pyramid is one-third the volume of a prism of the same base and altitude, and that the cone bears a like relation to the cylinder.

Example. Find the volume and the lateral area of a right cone of diameter 16 in. and altitude 12 in.

Solution. $A = \pi r^2 = 3.1416 \times 8^2 = 201.0624.$

$V = \tfrac{1}{3}Ah = \tfrac{1}{3} \times 201.0624 \times 12 = 804.25$ in.^{3}

$s = \sqrt{12^2 + 8^2} = 14.422$, since the altitude, radius, and slant height form a right triangle AOP of Fig. 168.

$S = \tfrac{1}{2}ps = \pi rs = 3.1416 \times 8 \times 14.422 = 362.465$ in.^{2}

EXERCISES 50

1. Find the volume of a right cone whose altitude is 8 in. and radius of base is 4.887 in. *Ans.* 200 in.^{3} nearly.

2. Find the volume and total area of a cone whose radius of base is 6 in. and altitude 5.3 in. *Ans.* 199.8+ in.^{3}; 263.9 in.^{2}

3. Find the volume and lateral area of a cone whose altitude is 8 in. and radius 6 in. *Ans.* 301.6− in.^{3}; 188.5− in.^{2}

4. The circumference of the base of a conical church steeple is 35 ft. and the altitude is 73 ft. Find the lateral area. *Ans.* 1281− ft.^{2}

Suggestion. Radius of base $= \tfrac{1}{2}(35 \div 3.1416)$. The altitude and radius are the altitude and base of a right triangle of which the hypotenuse is the slant height of the steeple.

5. Find the weight of a conical casting of iron 8 in. in diameter and slant height 14 in. *Ans.* 58.4 lb.

6. A pail is 10 in. in diameter on the bottom and 12 in. on top.   If the slant height is 11 in., what is the number of square inches of tin in the pail?   *Ans.* 458.67.

7. Find the total area and volume of a cone of revolution whose altitude is 12 ft., and the diameter of whose base is 10 ft.

Ans. 282.74 ft.²; 314.16 ft.³

8. The diameter of the top of a water pail is 12 in., the bottom is 10 in., and the altitude is 10½ in.   How many quarts will the pail hold?

Solution. By [**54**], $V = \frac{1}{12} \times 3.1416 \times 10.5(12^2 + 10^2 + 12 \times 10) = 1000.6$ in.³

$$1000.6 \text{ in.}^3 \div 57.75 \text{ in.}^3 = 17.33 - = \text{number of quarts.}$$

9. Find the lateral edge, lateral area, and volume of a regular pyramid, each side of whose triangular base is 10 ft., and whose altitude is 18 ft.

Ans. 18.90+ ft.; 273.45 − ft.²; 259.8+ ft.³

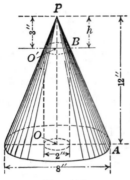

Fig. 169.

10. A cone 12 in. in altitude and with circular base 8 in. in diameter has a hole 2 in. in diameter bored through the center from apex to base.   Find the volume of the part remaining.   *Ans.* 169.646 in.³

Suggestion. The part cut away, as shown in Fig. 169, consists of a cylinder 9 in. in altitude and a cone 3 in. in altitude.   The height of the small cone can be found from the similar triangles *AOP* and *BO'P* in which we have the proportion

$$AO : BO' = OP : O'P,$$
$$\text{or } 4 : 1 = 12 : O'P. \quad \therefore O'P = 3.$$

11. Find the weight of a green fir log 215 ft. long, 4 ft. 6 in. in diameter at one end, and 20 in. in diameter at the other end, the specific gravity of fir being 0.78.   *Ans.* 42 tons nearly.

12. Hard coal dumped in a pile lies at an angle of 30° with the horizontal.   Estimate the number of tons in a pile of conical shape and 10 ft. high.   Large egg size weighs 38 lb. per cubic foot.   (See Fig. 170.)

Ans. 60 tons nearly.

Suggestion. Radius of base of pile $= 10 \times \sqrt{3}$ by **Art. 112.**

13. Find the number of tons of large egg coal in a pile 20 ft. broad and 100 ft. long with circular ends.   *Ans.* 99 tons nearly.

14. A tank of reenforced concrete is 160 ft. long, 100 ft. wide, and 10 ft. 6 in. deep outside dimensions.   The side walls are 8 in. thick at the top and 18 in. at the bottom, with the slope on the inside.   The bottom is 6 in. thick.

Fig. 170.

Find the number of cubic yards of cement in the tank and the capacity of the tank in barrels.   *Ans.* 503+; 36,670 bbl. nearly.

15. Find the weight of a tapered brick stack of 10 ft. inside diameter, with a wall 4 ft. thick at the base, 1 ft. 6 in. at the top, and 175 ft. high. A cubic foot of brick weighs 112 lb. *Ans.* 1095.5 tons.

Suggestion. Find the volume of a frustum of a cone with lower base 18 ft. in diameter and upper base 13 ft. in diameter. Subtract from this the volume of the cylinder 10 ft. in diameter.

16. A cast-iron driver in the form of a frustum of a square pyramid is used on a pile-driving machine. Find the weight of the driver if it is 16 in. high, 10 in. square at the bottom, and 7 in. square at the top.

Ans. 303.7 lb.

17. A cast-iron cone pulley is 34 in. long. The diameter of one end is 12 in. and of the other end is 5 in. A circular hole 2 in. in diameter extends the length of the pulley. Find the weight of the pulley.

Ans. 502.2 lb.

CHAPTER XVII

THE SPHERE

173. Definitions.—A **sphere** is a solid bounded by a curved surface, every point of which is equally distant from a point within, called the **center**. A straight line passing through the center and ending in the surface is called a **diameter**. A line extending from the center to the surface is a **radius**.

If the sphere is cut by a plane, the section is a circle. If the section is through the center of the sphere, it is called a **great circle**; if not through the center, it is called a **small circle**. The **circumference of a sphere** is the same as the circumference of a great circle.

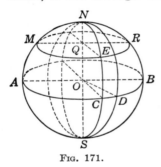

Fig. 171.

In Fig. 171, circles *ACB* and *NCS* are great circles, and *MER* is a small circle.

The parallels of latitude on the surface of the earth are small circles. The meridians of the earth all run through both the north and the south poles and, therefore, are great circles.

174. Area.—The following is proved in geometry:

RULE. *The area of the surface of a sphere equals four times the area of a circle of the same radius.*

Or stated as a formula:

$$[55] \quad S = 4\pi r^2 = \pi d^2,$$

where S is the area of the surface of the sphere, r the radius, and d the diameter.

The student may satisfy himself that this is true by winding evenly the surface of a ball with heavy cord, and then coiling the same cord into four circles of the same radius as the radius of the sphere.

The rule can be derived from the fact that a sphere has the

same area as the lateral area of a cylinder having the same radius as the sphere, and an altitude equal to the diameter of the sphere. Area of lateral surface of cylinder $= 2\pi r \times 2r = 4\pi r^2$.

175. Volume.—Geometry gives the following:

RULE. *The volume of a sphere equals the area of the surface times one-third of the radius.*

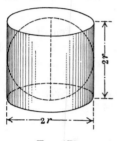

FIG. 172.

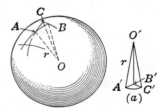

FIG. 173.

Or stated as a formula:

$$[56] \quad V = \tfrac{1}{3}Sr = \tfrac{4}{3}\pi r^3 = \tfrac{1}{6}\pi d^3 = 0.5236d.^3$$

The reasonableness of this may be seen by thinking of the surface of the sphere as divided into a large number of small polygons. Let these be so small that they may be considered as planes. Now if we think of the sphere cut into pyramids having these polygons as bases, and having their vertices at the center of the sphere, as shown in Fig. 173, the volume of one of these small pyramids, represented in (a) of the figure, is found by [51] to be $\tfrac{1}{3}r$ times the area of the small polygon. And the volume of all the small pyramids is equal to the whole surface of the sphere times $\tfrac{1}{3}r$. Hence $V = \tfrac{1}{3}Sr$.

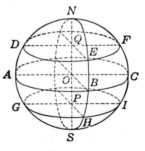

FIG. 174.

176. Zone and segment of sphere.—A portion of the volume of a sphere included between two parallel planes is a **segment of the sphere.** If both the planes cut the surface of the sphere, the segment is a **segment of two bases.** In Fig. 174, the segment between the planes *ABC* and *DEF* is a segment of

two bases.   The part of the sphere above *DEF* is a **segment
of one base.**

That portion of the surface of the sphere between two
parallel planes is a **zone.**   The **altitude** of the segment or
zone is the perpendicular between the parallel planes.

Thus, *OQ* is the altitude of the segment between the planes *ABC*
and *DEF*.

Here we can neither derive the rules for the area of a zone
and the volume of a segment nor make them seem reasonable
by any discussion.   They are of some importance practically,
especially the volume of the segment.

RULE.   *The area of a zone is equal to the circumference
of a great circle of the sphere times the altitude of the zone.*

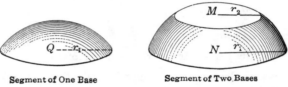

Segment of One Base   Segment of Two Bases

FIG. 175.

This rule is stated in the formula:

$$[57]\ Z = 2\pi rh,$$

where Z is the area of the zone, h the altitude, and r the
radius of the sphere.

It is readily seen from formula [57] that the area of any
two zones on the same or equal spheres are to each other as
their altitudes.   It also follows that any zone is to the surface of the sphere as the altitude of the zone is to the diameter of the sphere.

If a sphere is cut by parallel planes that are equal distances
apart, as the planes cutting the sphere in Fig. 174, then the
zones are all equal.

Since the parallels of 30° north and south latitude are in
planes that bisect the radii drawn to the north and south
poles, then one-half of the surface of the earth is within 30°
of the equator.

The volume of a spherical segment is given by the formula:

$$[58] \quad V = \tfrac{1}{2}h\pi(r_1{}^2 + r_2{}^2) + \tfrac{1}{6}\pi h^3,$$

where V is the volume, h the altitude, and r_1 and r_2 the radii of the bases of the segment. If the segment has only one base, one of the radii is zero.

Example 1. Find the surface, volume, and weight of a cast-iron ball of radius $12\frac{1}{2}$ in.

Solution. By [55], $S = 4\pi r^2 = 4 \times 3.1416 \times 12.5^2 = 1963.5$ in.^{2}

By [56], $V = \tfrac{1}{3}Sr = \tfrac{1}{3} \times 1963.5 \times 12.5 = 8181.25$ in.^{3}

Since 1 in.^{3} of cast iron weighs 0.26 lb.,

the weight $= 0.26$ lb. $\times 8181.25 = 2127.125$ lb.

Example 2. A sphere 8 in. in radius is cut by two parallel planes, one passing 2 in. from the center, and the other 6 in. from the center. Find the area of the zone, and the volume of the segment between the two planes, if both planes are on the same side of the center.

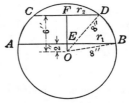

Fig. 176.

Solution. By [57], $Z = 2\pi rh = 2 \times 3.1416 \times 8 \times 4 = 201.06$ in.^{2}

$$r_1 = \sqrt{(OB)^2 - (OE)^2} = \sqrt{8^2 - 2^2} = \sqrt{60}.$$
$$r_2 = \sqrt{(OD)^2 - (OF)^2} = \sqrt{8^2 - 6^2} = \sqrt{28}.$$

By [58], $V = \tfrac{1}{2}h\pi(r_1{}^2 + r_2{}^2) + \tfrac{1}{6}\pi h^3$

$$= \tfrac{1}{2} \times 4 \times 3.1416(60 + 28) + \tfrac{1}{6} \times 3.1416 \times 4^3 = 586.43 \text{ in.}^3$$

EXERCISES 51

1. Find the volume and the area of the surface of a sphere 6 ft. in diameter. *Ans.* $113.1-$ ft.^{3}; $113.1-$ ft.^{2}

2. A sphere 4 in. in radius is cut from a cylinder 8 in. high and 8 in. in diameter. Find the volume cut away. *Ans.* $134.04+$ in.^{3}

3. The radius of a sphere is 2 ft. Find the area of the surface and the volume. *Ans.* $50.266-$ ft.^{2}; $33.51+$ ft.^{3}

4. How much will a sphere of cast iron weigh if it is 3 in. in diameter, and if cast iron weighs 0.26 lb. per cubic inch? *Ans.* 3.675 lb.

5. A cubic foot of lead weighs 712 lb. Find the weight of a ball 3 in. in diameter. *Ans.* 5.825 lb.

6. How many square feet of tin will it take to roof a hemispherical dome 40 ft. in diameter? *Ans.* $2513+$ ft.^{2}

7. Find how many acres of land on the surface of the earth, if one-fourth of the surface is land and the radius is 4000 miles.

Ans. 32,170,000,000 nearly.

8. Find the volume of a cylinder 2 ft. in diameter and 2 ft. in altitude; of a sphere 2 ft. in diameter; and of a cone 2 ft. in diameter and 2 ft. in altitude. Compare the three volumes. (See Fig. 177.)

9. Find the volume of the segment between two parallel planes 6 in. apart that cut a sphere 12 in. in radius, if one plane passes 2 in. from the center. There are two cases: (a) when the center of the sphere lies outside of the segment, and (b) when the center lies in the segment.

Ans. (a) 2186.6 − in.³; (b) 2638.9+ in.³

10. An iron ball 3 in. in diameter has a coating of lead 1 in. thick. Find the volume of the iron, of the lead, and the weight of each.

Ans. 14.137 in.³; 51.313 in.³; 3.676 − lb.; 21.141 − lb.

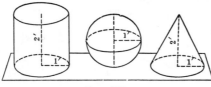

Fig. 177.

11. A ball of lead 2 in. in diameter is pounded into a circular sheet 0.01 in. thick. How large in diameter is the sheet?

Ans. 23 in. nearly.

12. A water tank, 6 ft. in total length and 18 in. in diameter, is in the form of a circular cylinder with two hemispherical ends. Find its capacity in gallons.

Ans. 72.7+ gal.

13. A hollow copper sphere used as a float weighs 10 oz. and is 5 in. in diameter. How heavy a weight will it support in water?

Ans. Less than 27.9 oz.

Suggestion. It will support a weight less than the weight of water displaced by the sphere minus the weight of the sphere.

14. A circular flower bed in a park is 25 ft. in diameter and is raised 2 ft. 6 in. in the center making a spherical segment. How many loads of dirt did it take to build it up if one load is 1½ cu. yd.? *Ans.* 15¼ nearly.

15. In a practical handbook the following rule is given as *nearly correct.* In fact, it is *correct.* The area of a flanged spherical segment, a vertical section of which is shown in Fig. 178, is equal to the area of a

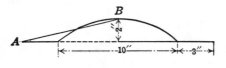

Fig. 178.

circle of radius equal in length to the line drawn from the top of the segment to the edge of the flange, that is, equal to a circle of radius *AB*.

Find the area of a flanged segment having dimensions as given in Fig. 178. Work both by the rule and by using the formulas for area of a ring and of a zone.

Solution. By [16], radius, *r*, of sphere of which zone is a part

$$=\frac{5^2+2^2}{2\times2}=7.25.$$

By [57], $Z = 2 \times 3.1416 \times 7.25 \times 2 = 91.1064$ in.²
By [28], area, A, of ring $= 3.1416(8+5)(8-5) = 122.5224$ in.²
91.1064 in.² $+ 122.5224$ in.² $= 213.63 -$ in.²
$AB = \sqrt{8^2 + 2^2} = \sqrt{68}$.

Area of circle having a radius $= \sqrt{68}$ is $3.1416 \times (\sqrt{68})^2 = 213.63 -$ in.², which is the same as the result by the first method.

16. Find the per cent of error in using the following rule: To find the weight of a cast-iron ball multiply the cube of the diameter in inches by 0.1377, and the product is the weight in pounds.

Ans. Rule is correct if 1 cu. in. of cast iron weighs 0.263 lb.

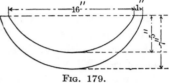

Fɪɢ. 179.

17. Fig. 179 is the vertical cross section of a casting, the inner and outer "skins" being spherical zones. Find the weight of metal at 0.35 lb. per cubic inch necessary to make the casting.

Ans. 176 lb. nearly.

Suggestion. Find the difference of the volumes of the two segments.

18. A hemispherical cap of aluminum is $3\frac{1}{2}$ in. in diameter. Find the diameter of the blank from which it is pressed. *Ans.* 4.95 − in.

19. Find the diameter of the blank if the cap in the preceding exercise has a flat ring $\frac{1}{2}$ in. wide around it. *Ans.* 5.70 + in.

20. Show that the volume of a round or button head of a machine screw is given by the formula

$$V = \pi h \left(\frac{D^2}{8} + \frac{h^2}{6} \right),$$

where D is the diameter of the head and h the height of the head.

Suggestion. In formula [58],

$$V = \tfrac{1}{2} h \pi (r_1^2 + r_2^2) + \tfrac{1}{6} \pi h^3.$$

But $r_1 = \dfrac{D^2}{2}$ and $r_2 = 0$.

$$\therefore V = \tfrac{1}{2} h \pi \frac{D^2}{4} + \tfrac{1}{6} \pi h^3 = \pi h \left(\frac{D^2}{8} + \frac{h^2}{6} \right).$$

Fɪɢ. 180.

21. Find the volume of the head of a round head machine screw if the diameter of the head is 0.731 in. and the height is 0.279 in.

Ans. 0.070 cu. in.

22. The water tank shown in Fig. 180 consists of a cylinder with a hemisphere below. The diameter is 20 ft. and the height of the cylindrical part is 22 ft. Find the capacity of the tank in gallons. *Ans.* 67,369 gal.

CHAPTER XVIII

VARIOUS OTHER SOLIDS

177. Anchor ring.—A ring formed of a cylinder bent into a circular form, as in Fig. 181, is called an **anchor ring.** The mean length of the rod in such a ring is the circumference of a circle of radius ON.

Any cross section of such a ring will be a circle. Since the ring may be considered as a cylinder bent into circular form, the area of the surface is $2\pi \times ON \times$ circumference of a cross section. If $ON = R$, and the radius of the cross section NM is r, we have for the area the formula:

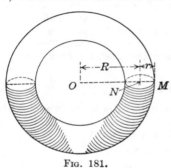

[59] $\mathbf{A = 2\pi R \times 2\pi r = 4\pi^2 Rr.}$

The volume is the same as the volume of a cylinder with an altitude that is equal to the mean circumference of the ring, hence the following:

[60] $\mathbf{V = 2\pi R \times \pi r^2 = 2\pi^2 Rr^2.}$

These rules may be generalized so as to apply to *any circular ring.* In general, the area of the sur-

FIG. 181.

face equals the perimeter of the cross section times the circumference drawn through the center of gravity of the cross section. The volume equals the area of the cross section times the circumference drawn through the center of gravity of the cross section.

EXERCISES 52

1. The cross section of a solid wrought-iron ring is a circle of 4 in. radius. The inner radius of the ring is 3 ft. Find the area of the surface and the volume of the ring.   *Ans.* 6316.6 in.²; 12,633.2 in.³

2. The cross section of the rim of a flywheel is a rectangle 6 in. by 8 in., the shorter dimension being in the diameter of the wheel. The wheel is 22 ft. in outer diameter. Find the volume of the rim and its weight if of cast iron. *Ans.* 22.515 ft.³; 10,132 lb.

3. Find the weight of a cast-iron water main 12 ft. in length, 2 ft. in outer diameter, and 1 in. thick. Solve both by considering it as a ring and as a hollow cylinder. *Ans.* 2709.6 lb.

4. Find the area of the surface and volume of a ring of outer diameter 10 in., made of round iron 1 in. in diameter. What is its weight at 0.28 lb. per cubic inch? *Ans.* 88.83 in.²; 22.207 in.³; 6.218 lb.

5. An anchor ring, 13 in. in outer diameter, of 1¼ in. round iron, has the same volume as what length of a bar 1¼ in. by 1½ in. in cross section? *Ans.* 24.16 in.

6. Find the weight of an anchor ring of cast iron, outer diameter 3 ft., the iron being circular in cross section and 6 in. in diameter. (Use 450 lb. per cubic foot.) *Ans.* 693.9 lb·

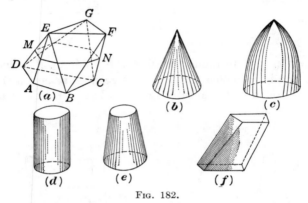

Fɪɢ. 182.

178. Prismatoids.—A **prismatoid** is a solid whose bases are parallel polygons and whose faces are quadrilaterals or triangles. One base may be a point, in which case the prismatoid is a pyramid; or one base may be a line, in which case it is wedge-shaped. The rule for finding the volumes of prismatoids holds in very many cases when the faces become curved surfaces and the prismatoid has become a cone, frustum of a cone, a cylinder, a sphere, a spindle of some kind, or one of various other forms that cannot well be described here. The rule is as follows:

RULE. *To find the volume of a prismatoid, add together the areas of the two bases and four times the area of a section midway between them and parallel to them, then multiply the sum by one-sixth the perpendicular between the bases.*

The rule may be stated in the formula:

$$[61] \quad V = \tfrac{1}{6}h(B_1 + 4M + B_2),$$

where B_1 and B_2 are the two bases and M the mid-section.

In Fig. 182 are given some forms to which the rule for the volume of a prismatoid will apply. The dimensions of the mid-section may be found by actually measuring the lines or by computing them.

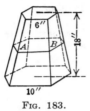

Fig. 183.

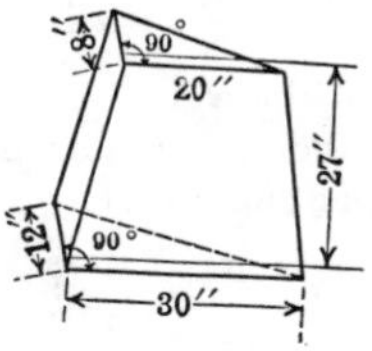

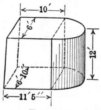

Fig. 184.

Example. By formula [61], find the volume of a frustum of a pyramid in which the bases are regular hexagons 10 in. and 6 in. on a side respectively and whose altitude is 18 in. (See Fig. 183.)

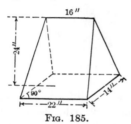

Fig. 185.

Fig. 186.

Solution. $AB = \tfrac{1}{2}(10 \text{ in.} + 6 \text{ in.}) = 8$ in.
Area of lower base $= 5^2 \times 1.732 \times 6 = B_1$.
Area of upper base $= 3^2 \times 1.732 \times 6 = B_2$.
$4 \times$ area of mid-section $= 4 \times 4^2 \times 1.732 \times 6 = 4M$.
$\therefore B_1 + 4M + B_2 = 1018.416$ in.^{2}
And $V = \tfrac{1}{6} \times 18 \times 1018.416 = 3055.248$ in.^{3}

EXERCISES 53

1. Use the rule for volume of prismatoids, and find the volumes called for in exercises 3, page 217; exercises 8 and 9, page 218.

2. Use formula [61] to find the volume of a hemisphere and check by the ordinary rule.

3. Use formula [61] to find the volume of the solid shown in Fig. 184.

Ans. 3420 in.[3]

4. Use formula [61] to find the volume of the solid shown in Fig. 185.

Ans. 3360 in.[3]

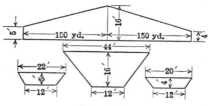

Fig. 187.

5. A concrete pier for a railway bridge has the dimensions shown in Fig. 186, the bases being rectangles with semicircles.   Find the number of cubic yards of concrete in 21 such piers.   *Ans.* 793.3+.

6. A railroad cut has the dimensions shown in Fig. 187, which shows the vertical section and three cross sections.   Find the volume of the earth removed in cubic yards.   *Ans.* 7972⅔ yd.[3]

PART THREE

ALGEBRA

CHAPTER XIX

NOTATION AND DEFINITIONS

179. General remarks.—In mathematics, the attempt is made to do certain things more easily and in less time than they can otherwise be done. In arithmetic, many processes were learned that saved time and labor. In performing these processes, certain signs and symbols were used to express the ideas. New signs and symbols were introduced as they were needed to express the new ideas that were involved.

Thus, there were used the numerals 0, 1, 2, 3, 4, 5, 6, 7, 8, and 9; the letters of the alphabet; and various signs among which are $+$, $-$, $\times$, $\div$, ( ), and $\sqrt{}$.

Algebra is a name applied to the continuation of arithmetic. The same signs and symbols are used in algebra as in arithmetic, and they have exactly the same meanings.

From time to time as we proceed, we shall find it convenient to add to the symbols and signs, in order that we may express new ideas or perform new processes. We shall also expect that many new, simpler, and more powerful methods of procedure will be developed; in fact, this is the chief aim in continuing the study of mathematics.

180. Definite numbers.—The numerals 0, 1, 2, 3, etc., have definite meanings. For instance, the symbol 4 represents the idea we call four. It may be 4 yards, 4 dollars, 4 pounds, or 4 of any other units; but, in any case, is a **definite number.** We have learned that the letter π represents a definite number, the ratio of the circumference to the diameter of a circle. This cannot be expressed exactly by the numerals 1, 2, 3, etc.; but has, none the less, a fixed value.

181. General numbers.—We have used the letter b to represent the number of units in the base of a triangle. Its value changed for different triangles, that is, it represented in a general way the length of the base of a triangle. Its value might be given as 10 ft., 6 in., or as any number of any sized units of length. Likewise, r represents the radius of a circle; but when it occurs in the formula $A = \pi r^2$, we do not think of a particular value for it. Such an idea as we represent by b or by r cannot be represented by the numerals. The idea is a **general number-idea.** It is usually represented by a letter of the alphabet.

In a particular discussion, the letter or letters used stand for the same value throughout the discussion. For example, when we are considering a particular circle the letter r represents a definite length as 10 ft.

182. Signs.—The signs $+$, $-$, $\times$, and $\div$ are **signs of operation.** They continue to have the same meaning as in arithmetic. As we have already seen, the sign $\times$ is not often expressed where a multiplication is indicated between numbers expressed by letters. The symbol $(\cdot)$ may be used instead; but usually no sign is expressed. Thus, $a \times b$ is written $a \cdot b$ or simply ab. Similarly, $2axy$ means 2 time a times x times y.

The **signs of grouping** are the **parentheses** ( ), the **brackets** [ ], the **braces** { }, and the **vinculum** ——. The first three are placed around the parts grouped, and the vinculum is usually placed over what is grouped. They all indicate the same thing; namely, that the parts enclosed are to be taken as a single quantity.

Thus, $12 - (10 - 4)$ indicates that 4 is to be subtracted from 10 and then the remainder is to be taken from 12. Hence $12 - (10 - 4) = 6$. Exactly the same thing is indicated by $12 - [10 - 4]$, $12 - \{10 - 4\}$, and $12 - \overline{10 - 4}$.

The vinculum is most frequently used with the radical sign. Thus, $\sqrt{6425}$.

It is to be noted that in the form $\dfrac{7-4}{3+4}$ the horizontal line serves as a vinculum and as a sign of division. It thus performs three duties: first, indicates a division; second, binds together the numbers in the numerator; and third, binds together the numbers in the denominator.

In performing the operations in a problem containing the

signs of grouping, the operations within the grouping signs must be considered first.

183. Algebraic expression.—An **algebraic expression** is any expression that represents a number by means of the signs and symbols of algebra.

A **numerical algebraic expression** is one made up wholly of numerals and signs. A **literal algebraic expression** is one that contains letters.

Thus, $14+13-(4+3)$ and $3ab-4cd$ are algebraic expressions; the first is numerical and the second is literal.

The value of an algebraic expression is the number it represents.

184. Coefficient.—If we have such an expression as $8abx$, 8, a, b, and x are factors of the expression. Any one of these factors or the product of any two or more of them is called the **coefficient** of the remaining part.

Thus, $8ab$ may be considered the coefficient of x, or $8a$ the coefficient of bx; but usually, by the coefficient, we mean the numerical part only. It is then called the **numerical coefficient.** If no numerical part is expressed, 1 is understood. Thus, $1axy$ is the same as axy.

185. Power, exponent.—If all the factors in a product are equal as $a \cdot a \cdot a \cdot a$, the product of the factors is called a **power** of one of them. The form $a \cdot a \cdot a \cdot a$ is usually written a^4. The small number to the right and above indicates how many times a is taken as a factor. (See **Arts. 74** and **75.**)

In the above power a is called the **base** and 4 the **exponent.**

The **exponent** of a **power** is a *number* written at the right and a little above the base. When it is a positive whole number it shows how many times the base is to be taken as a factor.

Thus, c^2 is read c square or c second power, and indicates that c is taken twice as a factor; c^3 is read c cube or c third power, and indicates that c is taken three times as a factor; c^4 is read c fourth power, and indicates that c is taken four times as a factor; c^n is read c nth power or c exponent n, and indicates that c is taken n times as a factor.

When no exponent is written the exponent is understood to be 1.

Thus, a is the same as a^1.

186. A **term** in an algebraic expression is a part of the expression not separated by a plus or a minus sign.

Thus, in $4ax+3c-d$, $4ax$, $3c$, and d are terms.

It is convenient to have names for algebraic expressions having different numbers of terms. A **monomial** is an algebraic expression consisting of one term. A **binomial** consists of two terms; and a **trinomial** consists of three terms. Any algebraic expression of two or more terms is called a **polynomial** or a **multinomial**.

Terms that are exactly the same or differ only in their coefficients, are called like **terms** or **similar terms**. Terms that differ otherwise than in their coefficients, are **unlike**, or **dissimilar terms**.

Thus, $6a^3x^2$, $-7a^3x^2$, and $16a^3x^2$ are like terms; while $6ax^2$, $-7a^3x^2$, and $16ayz$ are unlike terms.

187. Remarks.—The object of the exercises of this chapter is to recall the meanings and uses of signs and symbols, and to fix in mind the new ideas that have been given here. The doing of these exercises must not be slighted by the student, for he must become familiar with the mathematical way of stating ideas in order that he may be prepared for the work that comes later.

EXERCISES 54

Find the value of each of the following:
1. $3+6-2+4-1+7+2$.
2. $7+2\times6-3+8\times2-2$.
3. $8+16\div2-4+14\div7+21$.
4. $75+10+25\times6-3\times3-15$.
5. $150\div6+4\times25-75$.
6. $150\div5\times6+10\times9+17$.

Name the monomials in the following list, the binomials, the trinomials. Which of them are polynomials?

7. m^2+2v.	8. $7a^2b^2c$.	9. $4+9c+d$.
10. $ab+ac+ad$.	11. a^5+4c+d.	12. $17a^6b^2n$.
13. $a^2+b^2-c^2$.	14. $\frac{1}{2}gt^2$.	15. $\frac{4}{3}\pi r^3$.
16. $\frac{1}{3}h\pi r^2$.	17. $5x^2+3y$.	18. $7yz-4z^2-2y$.
19. $19xy-3z-2$.	20. $\frac{1}{4}x-\frac{2}{3}y-\frac{4}{5}z$.	21. $9x^2y^2+3xyz^3+3x^3y^2$.

22. What is the coefficient of v in Ex. 7? Of a^2b^2c in Ex. 8? Of c in Ex. 8? Of a^6 in Ex. 12? Of r in Ex. 16?

23. Name the numerical coefficients in Exs. 9, 13, and 20.

24. Name the exponents in Exs. 8, 11, and 18.

25. How many factors are there in Ex. 8? In Ex. 12?

Write the following in algebraic symbols:

26. The result of adding 7 times a to 9 times b.

27. The result of subtracting 10 times a from 6 times n.

28. The product of 3 times a^3 times b square.

29. The product of 7 times a fourth power times n cube times d.

30. The product of the sum of a and b, times the difference found by subtracting b from a.   *Ans.* $(a+b)(a-b)$.

31. The square of the sum of a, b, and c.   *Ans.* $(a+b+c)^2$.

32. The quotient of the sum of x and y divided by the difference when y is subtracted from x.

33. Express the product of m^3 and the sum of the two fractions, 2 divided by a and 3 divided by b.   *Ans.* $m^3\left\{\dfrac{2}{a}+\dfrac{3}{b}\right\}$.

34. Express the product of the sum of a, $2b$, and $3c$, and the sum of $3a$, $4b$, and $7c$.   *Ans.* $(a+2b+3c)(3a+4b+7c)$.

35. Express the square of the sum of a and b, plus the cube of the sum of m, n, and p.   *Ans.* $(a+b)^2+(m+n+p)^3$.

Translate the following algebraic expressions into English:

36. $12n+5m$.   **37.** $7n-14m$.   **38.** $x(m-n)$.

39. p^2x^2z.   **40.** $(3c+4d)(a+b)$.   **41.** $4+(14-3)$.

42. $\dfrac{m+n}{m-n}$.   **43.** $\dfrac{(x+y)^3}{(x-y)^2}$.   **44.** $\left\{\dfrac{1}{b}+\dfrac{1}{a}\right\}^2$.

45. $9a-(16-b)$.   **46.** $(x+y)^2+b^3$.   **47.** $\left\{\dfrac{2}{a+b}-\dfrac{1}{a-b}\right\}x^2$.

48. Write the following in a more compact form by using exponents:

(1) $4aaabbbb$.   (2) $27xxyyyzzz$.

(3) $17abbcccdddd$.   (4) $14aa+16bb+17ccc$.

49. Write in a more compact form by using exponents:

(1) $2\cdot2\cdot2\cdot3\cdot3$.   (2) $5\cdot5\cdot5\cdot3\cdot3\cdot2$.

(3) $7\cdot4\cdot4\cdot5\cdot5\cdot5$.   (4) $3\cdot3\cdot3\cdot3\cdot4\cdot4\cdot5\cdot5$.

50. Express each of the following as a single number without an exponent:

(1) 10^5.   (2) 4×10^7.   (3) 2.3×10^8.

(4) 8.62×10^7.   (5) 4.326×10^{11}.   (6) 2.763×10^{11}.

51. Express the following large numbers as a small number times a power of 10:

(1) 7000000000.   (2) 23460000000.   (3) 2456000000000.

(4) 427600000000.   (5) 5678000000000.   (6) 54237600000000.

52. Find the value of (1) $2^3\cdot4^2$, (2) $7^3\cdot2^2\cdot5$, (3) $2^4\cdot5^3\cdot7^2$.

53. Separate the following into prime factors and express compactly by using exponents:

(1) 864. (2) 1296. (3) 78400. (4) 94500. (5) 152100.

54. If $a=4$, what is the value of $3a$? Of $7a$? Of a^2? Of a^3? Of $4a^2$?

55. What is the value of $15a$ if a is 4, 7, $2\frac{3}{5}$, 0, $3\frac{1}{5}$, $8\frac{3}{5}$, $5\frac{1}{3}$?

56. If l is the number of feet in the length of a room and the length is
3 times the width, what is the width? $Ans.\ \dfrac{l}{3}.$

57. If there are 17 books on a shelf and 7 more are added to these,
how many are there? If n books are on the shelf and p books are added,
how many are there? If there are q books and t books are taken away,
how many are there left?

58. If s is the number of feet in the length of a line, how many feet
are there in twice this length? In half the length? In ¾ the length?

59. A boy can run a yards in 1 second. How far can he run in 10
seconds? In c seconds? In 1 minute? In d minutes?

60. If a train runs a miles in c hours, how far does it run in 1 hour? In

q hours? $Ans.\ \dfrac{a}{c}$ miles; $\dfrac{aq}{c}$ miles.

61. A grocer receives c cents for one pound of tea. How much does
he receive for 10 pounds? For p pounds?

62. A boy can walk m miles an hour. How many miles can he walk
in c hours? In d minutes? How many feet can he walk in e minutes?

$$Ans.\ mc;\ \dfrac{md}{60};\ 88me.$$

63. What number does $10t+u$ represent if $t=5$ and $u=6$? $Ans.$ 56.

64. What number does $100h+10t+u$ represent if $h=3$, $t=7$, and $u=9$?
If $h=9$, $t=8$, and $u=7$? $Ans.$ 379; 987.

65. What number does $1000a+100b+10c+d$ represent if $a=7$, $b=8$,
$c=2$, and $d=3$? $Ans.$ 7823.

66. If a, b, c, and d have the same values as in exercise 65, what number does $abcd$ represent? What does 7823 mean? $Ans.$ 336.

67. Is twice any whole number always an even number? If n is any
whole number, represent any even number. $Ans.\ 2n.$

68. If n is any whole number, does $2n-1$ represent an even number or
an odd number? Does $2n+1$ represent an even number or an odd
number?

CHAPTER XX

FORMULAS AND TRANSLATIONS

188. Subject matter.—In the present chapter, drill will be given in evaluating algebraic expressions and formulas, in translating verbally stated rules and principles into algebraic expressions and formulas, and in translating certain algebraic expressions and formulas into words.

In previous chapters many formulas have been used. To some extent the derivation of these was made clear. But one cannot thoroughly understand the derivation of formulas and the changes that can be made in them without a considerable knowledge of algebra. It is only through a thorough understanding of the *equation* that one gains the ability to change a formula to other forms that are more convenient for certain computations. The equation, in its turn, requires an understanding of the fundamental operations, factoring, and fractions in algebra for its manipulation. For these reasons we shall expect a more complete treatment of formulas later.

189. The slide rule.—The slide rule is a device consisting of sliding scales. It is used to make certain arithmetical calculations in a very simple manner. It gives the results in *multiplications, divisions, squares* and *square roots*, and *cubes* and *cube roots* at sight, and so saves time. However, the results are correct to only three or four figures when the common ten-inch slide rule is used. For this reason, the slide rule is to be relied upon for results only when it is sufficiently accurate. In other cases, it may be used to test the results obtained by ordinary computation. In all cases, however, one should be able to make the computations without using the slide rule.

The student is urged to acquaint himself with the slide rule and its uses. The computations in some of the exercises of this chapter may be made by means of this device. It is an invaluable instrument in making estimates.

It is not thought necessary to give a detailed description of the slide rule here nor to describe its uses, since with each instrument the buyer receives a booklet giving a full description of the device and its uses. At this point in his work, however, the student cannot expect to fully understand the uses of the slide rule as it is based in principle upon logarithms.

190. Evaluation of algebraic expressions.—A *numerical algebraic expression* has a definite value which may be found by performing the indicated operations.

Thus, $21 - (10+3) + 14 - 10 = 21 - 13 - 14 - 10 = 12.$

A *literal algebraic expression* has a definite value depending upon the values given the letters.

Thus, the expression abc, which means $a \times b \times c$, has a definite value if $a = 3$, $b = 4$, and $c = 10$. Putting these values in place of the letters we have $3 \times 4 \times 10 = 120$.

If any other set of values are assigned to a, b, and c, a definite value will be obtained for the product.

Example 1. Find the value of $\pi r^2 h$ if $\pi = 3.1416$, $r = 6$, and $h = 10$.

Substituting these values for the letters, the expression becomes $3.1416 \times 6^2 \times 10 = 1130.976$, the definite value.

Definition. When an algebraic expression is the statement of some rule or principle it is called a **formula.**

Example 2. Find the value of $a^3 + 3a^2b + 3ab^2 + b^3$, when $a = 2$ and $b = 3$.

Substituting the values in place of the letters,

$$a^3 + 3a^2b + 3ab^2 + b^3 = 2^3 + 3 \times 2^2 \times 3 + 3 \times 2 \times 3^2 + 3^3 = 125,$$

the definite value.

Example 3. Find the value of $\sqrt{s(s-a)(s-b)(s-c)}$, if $s = \dfrac{a+b+c}{2}$, and $a = 36$, $b = 22$, and $c = 20$.

Substituting in $s = \dfrac{a+b+c}{2}$, $s = \dfrac{36+22+20}{2} = 39.$

Substituting in $\sqrt{s(s-a)(s-b)(s-c)}$, we have

$\sqrt{39(39-36)(39-22)(39-20)} = \sqrt{37791} = 194.4 -.$ *Ans.*

EXERCISES 55

1. Express without exponents and find the value of the following:

(1) $2^3 \cdot 4^2$. (2) $7^2 \cdot 2^2 \cdot 5$.

(3) $2^4 \cdot 5^3 \cdot 7^2$. *Ans.* 98,000. (4) $3^3 \cdot 5^4 \cdot 7^2$.

(5) $7 \cdot 11^2 \cdot 5^3$. *Ans.* 105,875. (6) $3^4 \cdot 2^5 \cdot 13^2$. *Ans.* 438,048.

If $a = 2$, $b = 3$, and $c = 5$, find the values of the following:

2. $3a^2b^3$. *Ans.* 324.

3. $2ab^2 - c^2$. *Ans.* 11.

4. $3(a^2+b^2)$. *Ans.* 39.

5. $(a+b)^3$. *Ans.* 125.

6. $(a+c-b)^3$. *Ans.* 64.

7. $(c-a)^4$. *Ans.* 81.

8. $a(a^2+c^2-b^2)$. *Ans.* 40.

9. $ab^2(c^2-b^2)$. *Ans.* 288.

10. $(a+b)(c-b)$. *Ans.* 10.

11. $(c+b+a)(c-b+a)$. *Ans.* 40.

12. $a^2+2ab+b^2$. *Ans.* 25.

13. $(a^2+b^2)^2-c^2$. *Ans.* 144.

14. $c^3-(a^2+b^2)$. *Ans.* 112.

15. $(a^2+b^2)^2-(c^2-b^2)$. *Ans.* 153.

16. Find the value of the following when $r = 18$:

(1) $S = 4\pi r^2$. *Ans.* 4071.5+.

(2) $V = \frac{4}{3}\pi r^3$. *Ans.* 24,429+.

17. Find the value of the following when $r = 7$ and $h = 9$:

(1) $S = 2\pi rh$. *Ans.* 395.84+.

(2) $V = \pi r^2 h$. *Ans.* 1385.4+.

If $a = 1$, $b = 3$, $c = 5$, and $d = 0$, find the numerical values of the following:

18. $a^2+2b^2+3c^2+4d^2$. *Ans.* 94.

19. $a^4+4a^3b+6a^2b^2-4ab^3+b^4$. *Ans.* 40.

20. $\dfrac{12a^3-b^2}{3a^2}+\dfrac{2c^2}{a+b^2}-\dfrac{a+b^2+c^3}{5b^3}$. *Ans.* 5.

Suggestion. Remember that the lines in the fractions are vinculums and bind the terms in the numerators or denominators together, as well as indicate division. The multiplications, additions, and subtractions indicated in the numerators and denominators must be performed first. Thus, after substituting the values,

$$\frac{12 \times 1^3 - 3^2}{3 \times 1} + \frac{2 \times 5^2}{1+3^2} - \frac{1+3^2+5^3}{5 \times 3^3} = \frac{3}{3} + \frac{50}{10} - \frac{135}{135}.$$

If $a = 1$, $b = 2$, $c = 3$, $d = 5$, and $e = 8$, evaluate the following:

21. $b^2(a^2+e^2-c^2)$. *Ans.* 224.

22. $(a^2+b^2+c^2)(e^2-d^2-c^2)$. *Ans.* 420.

23. $e-[\sqrt{e+1}+2]+(e-\sqrt[3]{e})\sqrt{e-4}$. *Ans.* 15.

Evaluate the following when $a = 1$, $b = 2$, $c = 3$, $d = 4$, and $e = 5$:

24. $abc^2+bcd^2-dea^2$. *Ans.* 94.

25. $e^4+6e^2b^2+b^4-4e^3b-4eb^3$. *Ans.* 81.

26. $\dfrac{a^4+4a^3b+6a^2b^2+4ab^3+b^4}{a^3+3a^2b+3ab^2+b^3}$. *Ans.* 3.

27. $(a+b)(b+c)-(b+c)(c+d)+(c+d)(d+e)$. *Ans.* 43.

28. $(a-2b+3c)^2-(b-2c+3d)^2+(c-2d+3e)^2$.   *Ans.* 72.

29. $\sqrt{4c^2+5d^2+e}$.   *Ans.* 11.

30. $\sqrt{e^2+d^2+c^2-a^2}$.   *Ans.* 7.

31. Evaluate $(ac-bd)\sqrt{a^2bc+b^2cd+c^2ad-2}$, if $a=1$, $b=2$, $c=3$, and $d=0$.   *Ans.* 6.

32. If A stands for the number of square units in the area of a circle, and r stands for the number of linear units in the radius, state in words the following formula: $A=\pi r^2$.

33. In the above formula, can r be any number we please to make it? Can A? If we make $r=5$ in., can we then make A anything we please? Can π be any number we wish to make it? Is π a general number? Is A? Is r?

34. Using A, a, and b, state the following as a formula: The area of any triangle equals one-half of the base times the altitude.

35. Write a formula for finding the area of the cross section of a channel iron, using the letters given in Fig. 188.   *Ans.* $A=td+b(s+n)$.

36. Using the formula derived in the above exercise, find the areas of the cross sections of channel irons of the following dimensions:

Fig. 188.   Fig. 189.

No.	d	t	b	n	s	*Ans.* A
(1)	3 in.	0.17 in.	1.24 in.	0.38 in.	0.17 in.	1.19 in.²
(2)	5 in.	0.19 in.	1.56 in.	0.45 in.	0.19 in.	1.95 in.²
(3)	8 in.	0.22 in.	2.04 in.	0.56 in.	0.22 in.	3.35 in.²
(4)	10 in.	0.24 in.	2.36 in.	0.63 in.	0.24 in.	4.45 in.²
(5)	15 in.	0.40 in.	3.00 in.	0.90 in.	0.40 in.	9.90 in.²
(6)	6 in.	0.41 in.	3.15 in.	0.53 in.	0.46 in.	5.58 in.²
(7)	7 in.	0.45 in.	3.00 in.	0.525 in.	0.475 in.	6.15 in.²
(8)	10 in.	0.375 in.	3.00 in.	0.469 in.	0.406 in.	6.38 in.²

37. Write a formula for finding the area of the cross section of an I-beam, using the letters as given in Fig. 189.   *Ans.* $A=dt+2b(n+s)$.

38. Using the same letters for dimensions as in the last exercise, find the areas of the cross sections in the following I-beams:

No.	d	t	b	s	n	*Ans.* A
(1)	5 in.	0.21 in.	1.395 in.	0.21 in.	0.44 in.	2.86 in.²
(2)	9 in.	0.29 in.	2.02 in.	0.29 in.	0.627 in.	6.31 in.²
(3)	15 in.	0.80 in.	2.80 in.	0.80 in.	1.27 in.	23.59 in.²

39. Using B for base, P for percentage, R for rate, and A for amount, write the formulas for determining the different things called for in percentage.

40. If p stands for principal, i for interest, t for time in years, r for rate per cent, and a for amount, translate the following formulas into English:

(1) $i = prt$. (2) $a = prt + p$. (3) $a = i + p$. (4) $r = \dfrac{i}{pt}$.

(5) $p = \dfrac{i}{rt}$. (6) $t = \dfrac{i}{pr}$. (7) $r = \dfrac{a - p}{pt}$.

41. State in words the process of adding two fractions having a common denominator.   State the same as a formula, using a and b for the numerators and d for the common denominator.   *Ans.* $\dfrac{a}{d} + \dfrac{b}{d} = \dfrac{a+b}{d}$.

42. Do the same as in exercise 41, for subtracting fractions having a common denominator.

43. Translate the following into English:

(1) $\dfrac{a}{b} \div \dfrac{c}{d} = \dfrac{a}{b} \times \dfrac{d}{c}$.

(2) $\dfrac{n \times m}{d \times m} = \dfrac{n}{d}$.

(3) $\dfrac{n \div m}{d \div m} = \dfrac{n}{d}$.

(4) $\dfrac{n}{d} \times m = \dfrac{n \times m}{d}$.

44. Write the formula that states that a times the sum of b, c, and d equals s.   *Ans.* $s = a(b+c+d)$.

45. In exercise 44, find s: (1) if $a = 7$, $b = 6$, $c = 8$ and $d = 10$; (2) if $a = \frac{2}{3}$, $b = \frac{7}{8}$, $c = \frac{3}{4}$, and $d = \frac{7}{24}$.   *Ans.* 168; $1\frac{5}{18}$.

46. Write in algebraic symbols that if c, the cost, in dollars, of a harness, be increased by 5, the sum multiplied by 4 equals v, the cost, in dollars, of a horse.   If c is 45, find the value of v in the formula.
Ans. $v = 4(c+5)$; 200.

47. Using b_1 and b_2 for the bases and h for the altitude, state the following as a formula: The area of a trapezoid equals one-half the sum of the two bases times the altitude.   *Ans.* $A = \frac{1}{2}(b_1 + b_2)h$.

48. Using the formula of the preceding exercise, find the areas of the following trapezoids:

(1) $b_1 = 22.33$ in., $b_2 = 46.39$ in., $h = 26.43$ in.   *Ans.* $908.13+$ in.²
(2) $b_1 = 7.203$ in., $b_2 = 5.826$ in., $h = 3.243$ in.   *Ans.* $21.127-$ in.²

49. Write the formula stating that the area S of the surface of a sphere equals 4 times π times the square of the radius r.   Use the formula and find the area of the surface of a sphere 15 in. in radius.
Ans. $2827.4+$ in.²

50. Write a formula stating that the volume V of a sphere equals $\frac{4}{3}$ of π times the cube of the radius r.   Use this formula and find the volume of a sphere 12 in. in radius.   *Ans.* $7328.2+$ in.³

51. Write a formula stating that the volume V of a rectangular solid equals the length l times the breadth b times the height h.   Use this formula and find the number of cubic feet in a room 40 ft. by 30 ft. by 12 ft.   *Ans.* 14,400.

52. Find the perimeter of each form in Fig. 190.   *Ans.* (1) $4x$; (2) $2(a+b)$; (3) $2(x+y)+4b$; (4) $2(b+c+d+y)+4x$; (5) $2(a+b+d)$.

16

53. Find the area of each form in Fig. 190.　　　*Ans.* (1) x^2-y^2;
(2) $ab-2xy$; (3) $xy-2ab$; (4) $bc-y(2x+d)-d^2$; (5) $ab-cd$.

54. If a man is 35 years old, what was his age a years ago?　What will
it be b years from now?　　　　　　*Ans.* $35-a$ years; $35+b$ years.

55. If x years was the age of a man a years ago, what is his age now?
What will it be in c years from now? *Ans.* $x+a$ years; $x+a+c$ years.

56. Write in algebraic language: x diminished by a; y increased by b;
x divided by n; the nth part of x; one mth of a.

57. The sum of two numbers is a and one of the numbers is x, what is
the other number?　Express one mth of the first plus one nth of the

second number.　　　　　　　　　　*Ans.* $a-x$; $\dfrac{x}{m}+\dfrac{a-x}{n}$.

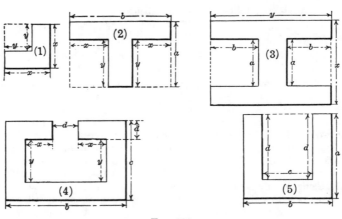

FIG. 190.

58. If x is the first of two consecutive numbers, what is the second?
What will represent each of three consecutive numbers, if x stands for
the middle one?　　　　　　　　*Ans.* $x+1$; $x-1$, x, and $x+1$.

59. Represent three consecutive even numbers if x is the middle one.

60. If the length of a stick is a feet, how many inches is it in length?

How many rods?　How many miles?　　　*Ans.* $12a$; $\dfrac{a}{16\frac{1}{2}}$; $\dfrac{a}{5280}$.

61. If d is the number of dollars an article costs, what is the number
of cents?　　　　　　　　　　　　　*Ans.* $100d$.

62. If a room is a yards, b feet, and c inches long, how many inches in
length is it?　　　　　　　　　　　*Ans.* $36a+12b+c$.

63. Given the product p and the multiplier m, find the multiplicand n.

　　　　　　　　　　　　　　　Ans. $n=\dfrac{p}{m}$.

64. Given the dividend d and the quotient q, find the divisor b.

$$Ans. \quad b = \frac{d}{q}.$$

65. Given the divisor d, the quotient q, and the remainder r, find the dividend D. $Ans. \quad D = dq + r.$

66. The difference between two numbers is n and the smaller one is a, what is the larger?

67. A number exceeds a by c, what is the number? $Ans. \quad a + c.$

68. Write in symbols that a exceeds b as much as c is less than d.

$$Ans. \quad a - b = d - c.$$

69. Express in symbols that one-half of m equals the nth part of the sum of a, b, and c. $Ans. \quad \tfrac{1}{2}m = \dfrac{a + b + c}{n}.$

70. If a cents is the price **per** quart for beans, what is the price per bushel? $Ans. \quad 32a$ cents.

71. The provisions that will keep a family of 9 persons 30 days will keep a family of 5 persons how many days? The provisions that will keep a family of a persons l days will keep b persons how many days?

$$Ans. \quad 54; \; \frac{al}{b}.$$

72. If it takes m men d days to dig a ditch, how many days will it take c men to dig it? $Ans. \quad \dfrac{md}{c}.$

73. How many pounds of sugar at c cents a pound will d dozen eggs at e cents a dozen buy? $Ans. \quad \dfrac{de}{c}.$

74. A cubical tank e ft. on an edge will hold how many barrels, if one barrel equals 4.211 cu. ft.? $Ans. \quad \dfrac{e^3}{4.211}.$

75. A box a ft. long, b ft. wide, and c ft. deep will hold how many bushels, if 1 bushel equals 2150.42 cu. in.? $Ans. \quad \dfrac{1728abc}{2150.42}.$

76. A man earned \$$a$ per day and his son \$$b$. How many dollars did they both earn in a month, if the man worked 26 days and the son 21 days? $Ans. \quad 26a + 21b.$

CHAPTER XXI

POSITIVE AND NEGATIVE NUMBERS

191. Meaning of negative numbers.—The degrees of temperature, indicated by the thermometer scale, are counted in two opposite directions from the zero point. We usually speak of a temperature as so many degrees above or below zero. In arithmetic we speak of temperature in this manner, but in algebra we seek some abbreviated form for stating the same thing. We might agree to use any convenient signs whatever. The signs + and − have been generally adopted. The + sign, placed before the number of degrees, indicates a temperature above zero; and the − sign indicates a temperature below zero. This use of these signs is different from the ordinary use in which they indicate addition and subtraction. Here they indicate the *sense* or *direction* in which the temperature is measured or counted.

Thus, +25° means 25° above zero, and −25° means 25° below zero.

The number preceded by the + sign is called a **positive number,** and the one preceded by the − sign, a **negative number.** Two numbers so related, one positive and one negative, may be called **relative numbers.** The following are further examples of relative numbers. They will help to fix the negative number-idea in mind.

Time is commonly measured forward and backward from a certain date. This might be shown by using the + and − signs.

Thus, 1918 A. D. might be written +1918, while 325 B. C. might be written −325.

A force acting in one direction and another in an opposite direction are designated as a + and a − force respectively. Money gained and resources are +, and money lost and liabilities are −.

192. Need of negative number.—The necessity for extending the number system so as to include negative numbers may be seen from the following subtractions, where the min-

244

uend remains the same, but the subtrahend increases by steps of 1 as we pass from left to right. This causes the difference to diminish by steps of 1 from left to right. When the difference becomes less than zero we indicate it by the sign − placed before the number.

6	6	6	6	6	6	6	6
3	4	5	6	7	8	9	10
3	2	1	0	−1	−2	−3	−4 etc.

193. Representation of negative and positive numbers.— For convenience, the positive and negative numbers may be represented on a horizontal line; the +, or positive, numbers to the right of a certain point, called zero, and the −, or negative, numbers to the left of the zero point. This method of representing them is found very convenient in explaining addition and subtraction.

It should be carefully noted that toward the right is the

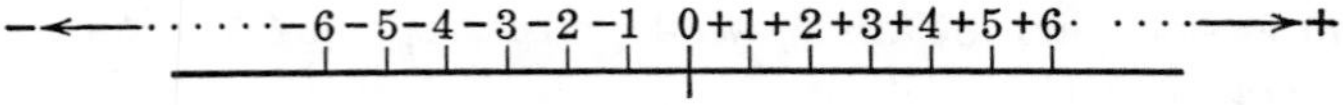

$$-\longleftarrow\cdots\cdots-6-5-4-3-2-1\ \ 0+1+2+3+4+5+6\cdots\cdots\longrightarrow+$$

Fig. 191.

positive direction and toward the left is the **negative direction,** no matter from what point we start.

The idea of negative number is opposite to that of positive number. For example, if a man walks five miles east, or in the positive direction, and then five miles west, or in the negative direction, he is at the starting-point. The negative distance has destroyed the opposite or positive.

194. Definitions.—Positive and negative numbers, together with zero, form the system called **algebraic numbers.**

The **absolute** or **numerical value** of a number is the value which it has without reference to its sign.

Thus, +5 and −5 have the same absolute value 5.

The signs + and − when used to show direction or sense are called **signs of quality** to distinguish them from the **signs of operation** used to indicate an addition or a subtraction.

The sign +, used as a sign of quality, is usually omitted; but the sign −, when a sign of quality, is expressed.

To show that the sign is one of quality it is sometimes

written with the number and enclosed in parentheses, as (-3), $(+4)$. $(-5)+(+2)$ indicates that a -5 is to be added to a $+2$.

195. Remarks on numbers.—What is the negative number and why do we need to trouble ourselves about it? The illustrations given above should help one to get the idea of negative number, and to see how it is forced upon us when we try to subtract a larger number from a smaller one.

In mathematics when a new number-idea appears, the first thing to do is to represent it by a symbol; and, second, find a way of operating with it. That is, we must determine how to add, subtract, multiply, and divide such numbers.

One of the first things we did in arithmetic was to determine methods of operating with positive whole numbers; then a little later, we did the same thing for the fractional numbers. In fact, much of the time spent in studying mathematics is spent in finding how to add, subtract, multiply, and divide numbers of different kinds, whole, positive, negative, fractional and combinations of these.

It now remains to devise methods and rules for operating with algebraic numbers. This must be done in such a way that no old rules or principles shall be violated. The student is asked to consider carefully each step taken and *to make every part seem reasonable.*

EXERCISES 56

1. A place is at $10°\ 25'$ east longitude. What sign may be used instead of the word east to show this?

2. New York is $74°$ west longitude. Designate this by means of a sign.

3. Chicago is $41°\ 45'$ north latitude, and 'Melbourne $37°$ south latitude. Designate these algebraically, that is, with signs.

4. A man overdraws his bank account. How may the banker indicate this on his books?

5. If the weight of a stone, weighing 100 lb., is written $+100$ lb., how may the upward lift of 500 lb. of a balloon be written?

6. What is meant by saying that a man is worth $+\$3000$? By $-\$2000$?

7. If a man has a $-\$200$, a $+\$300$, and a $-\$100$, what is he worth?

8. A man was born in the year -35 and died in the year $+48$. How old was he when he died? *Ans.* 83 years.

9. If a man has assets of $3000, and we represent it by a line 3 in. long drawn to the right of 0, how could we represent a liability of $1500?

10. A man walks 10 miles east and then 6 miles west. Write this in symbols.

11. If a body is heated 37° and then cooled down 42°, indicate the facts in symbols.

12. If 7 men came into a room and 8 men left the room, we could represent the fact by saying that $+7$ and -8 men came into the room. A man received $25 and spent $21. Write this as money received.

13. Remembering the positive and negative directions, draw a line; locate a zero point; and, with a unit of 1 in., locate positive and negative numbers to the right and left of zero. Start at $+5$ and go $+3$, -7, -4, $+6$, -10, $+2$, $+1$, and $+4$. Where do you stop?

Ans. At the zero point.

CHAPTER XXII

ADDITION AND SUBTRACTION

196. Definitions.—The aggregate value of two or more algebraic numbers is called their **algebraic sum.** The process of finding this sum is called **addition.**

197. Addition of algebraic numbers.—If we wish to add 3 to 4, we start with 4 and count 3 more, arriving at 7 which is the sum. If we consider the system of algebraic numbers arranged on a horizontal line, Fig. 192, we add a positive number by starting with the number we wish to add to, and count-

$$-10-9-8-7-6-5-4-3-2-1 \quad 0+1+2+3+4+5+6+7+8+9+10$$

ing toward the right as many units as there are in the number added.

Thus, in the above, we start at 4 and count toward the right to 7.

To add $+5$ to -3, we start at -3 and proceed 5 units toward the right, arriving at $+2$.

To add $+3$ to -7, we start at -7 and proceed 3 units toward the right, arriving at -4.

Since adding -3 to $+7$ is the same as adding $+7$ to -3, the result of adding -3 to $+7$ is $+4$. In order to start with $+7$ and arrive at $+4$, we must move in the negative direction, or toward the left. Therefore, we conclude that to add a negative number, we go toward the left.

.Thus, to add -4 to $+9$, we start at $+9$ and go 4 units toward the left, arriving at $+5$. To add -7 to $+2$, we start at $+2$ and go 7 units toward the left, arriving at -5. To add -4 to -5, we start with -5 and proceed 4 units toward the left, arriving at -9.

The above results are given here:

$+4$	-3	-7	$+7$	$+9$	$+2$	-5
$+3$	$+5$	$+3$	-3	-4	-7	-4
$+7$	$+2$	-4	$+4$	$+5$	-5	-9

248

198. Principles.—A careful consideration of the above will disclose the following principles:

(1) *The algebraic sum of two numbers with like signs is the sum of their absolute values, with the common sign prefixed.*

(2) *The algebraic sum of two numbers with unlike signs is the difference between their absolute values, with the sign of the one greater in absolute value prefixed.*

In adding three or more algebraic numbers, differing in signs, find the sum of the positive numbers, and then the sum of the negative numbers by principle (1), and then add these sums by principle (2).

Thus, in finding the sum of
+2, +10, −6, −3, −7, +9, we take
+2+10+9 = +21 and
(−6)+(−3)+(−7) = −16, then
+21+(−16) = +5, the sum.

199. Subtraction of algebraic numbers.—**Subtraction** is the *inverse* of addition. If we are given *one* of two numbers and their *sum*, subtraction is the process of finding the other number.

In arithmetic it is assumed that the minuend is always greater than the subtrahend. In the subtraction of algebraic numbers we not only may have the subtrahend larger than the minuend when the numbers are positive, but either or both subtrahend and minuend may be negative numbers.

Since subtraction is the inverse of addition, if we consider the system of algebraic numbers arranged along the horizontal line as in **Art. 197,** we have the following principles:

(1) *Subtracting a positive number is equivalent to adding a numerically equal negative number.*

(2) *Subtracting a negative number is equivalent to adding a numerically equal positive number.*

These may be combined in the following:

RULE. *Subtraction of algebraic numbers is performed by considering the sign of the subtrahend changed and proceeding as in addition of algebraic numbers.*

Applying the rule, we find the following algebraic differences:

$$
\begin{array}{cccccc}
+7 & +4 & -6 & -3 & -8 & +7 \\
+3 & +6 & -2 & -7 & +3 & -2 \\
\hline
+4 & -2 & -4 & +4 & -11 & +9
\end{array}
$$

It should be carefully noted that $4-3$ may be considered as a $+4$ minus a $+3$, or as a $+4$ plus a -3. It is this choice that causes more or less trouble to the beginner.

If the number with its sign of quality is inclosed in parentheses, we have, for example, $(+4)+(-6)-(+7)-(-11)+(+7)$. This may also be written $(+4)-(+6)-(+7)+(+11)+(+7)$, which is the same as $4-6-7+11+7$ where the signs indicate operations and all the numbers are positive.

EXERCISES 57

Find the sum in exercises 1 to 7.

1. $7,\ -10,\ -13,\ 16,\ 25,\ -3$.	*Ans.* 22.
2. $27,\ 46,\ -100,\ -16,\ 17$.	*Ans.* -26.
3. $3,\ 16,\ -21,\ -1,\ 2,\ 1$.	*Ans.* 0.
4. $\frac{2}{3},\ -\frac{3}{4},\ \frac{7}{8},\ -\frac{9}{16}$.	*Ans.* $\frac{1}{4}\frac{1}{8}$.
5. $-3\frac{3}{4},\ -7\frac{6}{10},\ 3\frac{3}{8},\ -\frac{7}{10}$.	*Ans.* $-8\frac{27}{40}$.
6. $3.25,\ -7.16,\ -10.3,\ 14.1$.	*Ans.* -0.11.
7. $14.17,\ -16.19,\ -26.3$.	*Ans.* -28.32.
8. From 17.6 take -14.3.	*Ans.* 31.9.
9. From -111 take -12.	*Ans.* -99.
10. From -46 take 75.	*Ans.* -121.

11. Is the absolute value of an algebraic number ever increased by subtraction? Illustrate.

12. Is the absolute value of an algebraic number ever decreased by addition? Illustrate.

13. How many degrees of latitude between places at $+37°\ 45'\ 17''$ and at $-16°\ 14'\ 53''$.   *Ans.* $54°\ 0'\ 10''$.

14. If a steamer is moving through still water at the rate of 20 miles per hour, and a man walks forward on the deck at the rate of 4 miles per hour, express the rate the man is moving with reference to the water. Suppose the man walks toward the stern of the boat at the same rate, how may the rate of the boat, and the rate of the man with reference to the boat, be expressed?

200. Addition and subtraction of literal algebraic expressions.—We add 5 bushels, 8 bushels, 10 bushels and get 23 bushels. So we have 5 bu.$+8$ bu.$+10$ bu.$=23$ bu.

Similarly, $6d+4d+7d=17d$,

$$4xy+7xy+8xy=19xy,\ \text{and}$$
$$16x^2y+\ 23x^2y+3x^2y=42x^2y.$$

In subtraction, we have $17a-5a=12a$ and

$$46x^3y^2-6x^3y^2=40x^3y^2.$$

We know that in arithmetic we cannot add or subtract

unlike things; neither can we do so here. If we wish to add $3a$ to $2b$, we indicate the addition, thus, $3a+2b$.

From these considerations, we have the following principle:

Monomials which are alike, or similar, can be added or subtracted by adding or subtracting the coefficients. If the monomials are unlike, the operations can only be indicated.

Examples of addition.

(1)	(2)	(3)
$+\ 3abc$	$-16xy^3$	$17ab$
$-\ 6abc$	$+\ 3xy^3$	$-3xy$
$+10abc$	$-\ 4xy^3$	$-4c^2$
$-16abc$	$-\ 7xy^3$	$+3a^2$
$-\ 3abc$	$+28xy^3$	
$-12abc$	$+\ 4xy^3$	$17ab-3xy-4c^2+3a^2$

Examples of subtraction.

(1)	(2)	(3)
$4ax^2$	$-21x^2y$	$14ab$
$-6ax^2$	$3x^2y$	$-6c$
$10ax^2$	$-24x^2y$	$14ab+6c$

201. Polynomials.—The addition and subtraction of polynomials is similar to that of monomials. *Write them so that like terms are in the same column, and combine the terms in each column as with monomials.*

Example of addition.

$+\ 3ax^2+14y^2-\ 3z$
$-\ 7ax^2-16y^2+\ 7z$
$+10ax^2-\ 4y^2+\ 9z$
$-\ 7ax^2+10y^2-11z$
$-\ \ \ ax^2+\ 4y^2+\ 2z$

Example of subtraction.

$17xy^2-14c^2+4a$
$10xy^2-\ 5c^2-8a$
$7xy^2-9c^2+12a$

202. Test or proof of results.—It is very important that one should be able to *test* the results. The problems in addition or subtraction of literal algebraic expressions may be tested by substituting some definite values for the general numbers.

Thus, if $a=1$, $b=1$, and $x=1$ in the following example, the test is as given.

Example.

$-\ 7ab+\ 4x^2-3bx$
$-\ 8ab-10x^2-4bx$
$-\ 9ab+11x^2+6bx$

$-24ab+\ 5x^2-\ bx$

Test.

$-\ 7+\ 4-3=-\ 6$
$-\ 8-10-4=-22$
$-\ 9+11+6=\ \ \ 8$

$-24+\ 5-1=-20$

The test depends upon the fact that the letters used may have any values whatever. We could just as well take $a = 1$, $b = 2$, $x = 3$. Of course, we usually choose values that make the computations as simple as possible.

EXERCISES 58

Write the sums in exercises from 1 to 11.

1. $3a$, $5a$, $7a$, $9a$.   *Ans.* $24a$.

2. $6ab$, $-4ab$, $3ab$, $-2ab$.   *Ans.* $3ab$.

3. $9x^2$, $10x^2$, $-14x^2$, $-13x^2$.   *Ans.* $-8x^2$.

4. $14x^2y^2$, $-11x^2y^2$, $-16x^2y^2$.   *Ans.* $-13x^2y^2$.

5. $2m + n$, $6m - 4n$, $7m - 2n$.   *Ans.* $15m - 5n$.

6. $p + 2q - r$, $2p - 3q$.   *Ans.* $3p - q - r$.

7. $a + 4b - 6c$, $-2b + 5c$.   *Ans.* $a + 2b - c$.

8. $-2x + 3y - 4z$, $x + y - z$.   *Ans.* $-x + 4y - 5z$.

9. $2x + 3a + m$, $2y - 3a - m$.   *Ans.* $2x + 2y$.

10. $a + 3c - 17$, $5a - 6c + 14$, $2a - 5c - 2$.   *Ans.* $8a - 8c - 5$.

11. $2a^2 - 4cd$, $-8a^2 - 7cd$, $-25a^2 + 16cd$.   *Ans.* $-31a^2 + 5cd$.

12. Subtract exercises 6 to 9 above.

13. From $3ax - 4cd$ take $10ax - 2cd$.   *Ans.* $-7ax - 2cd$.

14. From $17ab - 2c$ take $3ab - 4d$.   *Ans.* $14ab - 2c + 4d$.

15. From $m^2 - 2mn + n^2$ take $m^2 + 2mn + n^2$.   *Ans.* $-4mn$.

16. From $16x^2y^2z + 4a$ take $16a - 14cd$.   *Ans.* $16x^2y^2z - 12a + 14cd$.

17. Add and test by putting $x = 1$, $y = 2$, $z = 3$: $14x - 16y + 3z$, $7x + 2y - 7z$, $-16x - 2y + 4z$.

18. Add and test by putting $x = 1$ and $y = 2$: $3x + 2y - 4xy$, $7x - 4y + 2xy$.

19. Subtract and test by putting $x = 2$, $y = 1$, and $z = 3$: $3xy - 4xz - 3x^2$ from $-6xy + 5xz - 2y^2$.

20. From $17x^2y^3 - 16xz^3 + 14c^2d$ take $-16x^2y^3 + 43c^2d - 14xz^3$.
Ans. $33x^2y^3 - 2xz^3 - 29c^2d$.

21. Add $3ab - 2ac + 4df$, $7ac - 6df$, $4ab + 9ac - 3df$.
Ans. $7ab + 14ac - 5df$.

22. Add $7x^2 - 9y^2 - 11xy$, $10x^2 - 4xy - 11y^2 + 7x^2$.
Ans. $24x^2 - 20y^2 - 15xy$.

23. Add $11x^2y^3 - 16xy + 14ax^2 - 17x$, $16x^2y^3 + 14xy$, $17x^2y^3 - 43x + 27ax^2$.
Ans. $44x^2y^3 - 2xy + 41ax^2 - 60x$.

24. Add $x^2 + 2xy + y^2$, $x^2 - 2xy + y^2$, $-2x^2 + 2y^2$, $7x^2 - 12y^2$.
Ans. $7x^2 - 8y^2$.

25. Add $34ax - 75by + 60cz$, $16ax + 25by - 10cz$, $-41ax + 41by - 20cz$.
Ans. $9ax - 9by + 30cz$.

26. Add $142x^4 + 31x^3y + 9x^2y^2 + 10xy^3 - 15y^4$, $-130x^4 - 30x^3y + 2x^2y^2 - 8xy^3 + 20y^4$, $-11x^4 - 10x^2y^2$.   *Ans.* $x^4 + x^3y + x^2y^2 + 2xy^3 + 5y^4$.

27. Add and test by letting $x = 1$, $y = 2$, and $z = 3$: $17x - 9y$, $3z + 14x$, $y - 3x$, $x - 17z$, $x - 3y + 4z$.

28. Add and test by letting $x = 1$, and $y = 2$: $3x^2 + 2xy + 4y^2$, $4x^2 - 3xy - 2y^2$, $3x^2 + xy$.

29. Add and test by letting $m = 1$, $n = 1$, $p = 2$, and $q = 4$: $16m + 3n - p$, $p + 4q$, $-q + 7m - 3n$, $n - q$, $3n + 2p$.

30. Add $3ax - 4ab - xy + z - 3xy + 6ab + 7xy - 3z - 4ax - 6xy + ax$.
$$Ans.\ 2ab - 3xy - 2z.$$

31. Add $17ax^2 - 9axy + 6z - 24 + 6 + 2axy - 2z + ax^2 - 13 - 14ax^2 + 6axy - 4z$.
$$Ans.\ 4ax^2 - axy - 31.$$

32. Subtract $4m^2 - 6n^3 + 73x$ from $-m^2 - 8n^3 + 83x$.
$$Ans.\ -5m^2 - 2n^3 + 10x.$$

33. Subtract $10x^2y - 4xy + 16y^2$ from $3xy - 18y^2$.
$$Ans.\ -10x^2y + 7xy - 34y^2.$$

34. From $ax^2 + 3ay^2 - 4z^2$ subtract $2ax^2 + 3ay^2 - 4z^2$.　　$Ans.\ -ax^2$.

35. From $5abc + 3bcd + 7cde$ take $4abc - 10bcd - 8cde$.
$$Ans.\ abc + 13bcd + 15cde.$$

36. Take $2x^3 - y^2$ from the sum of $x^3 - 2xy + 3y^2$ and $xy + 4y^2$.
$$Ans.\ -x^3 - xy + 8y^2.$$

Given $A = a^3 + 3a^2b + 3ab^2 + b^3$, $B = -3a^2b + 3ab^2 - 3b^3$, and $C = a^3 - b^3$, find results in exercises 37 to 44. Test results by substituting values for a and b.

37. $A - B$.　　　**38.** $B - C$.　　　**39.** $C - A$.
40. $B - A$.　　　**41.** $C - B$.　　　**42.** $A - C$.
43. $A + B + C$.　　**44.** $A + B - C$.

45. From the sum of $0.4x^2 - 7.5a + 5m^2$ and $1 - 0.125a + 3m^3$ take $1.5a - 7.2x^2 - 3.25m^3$.　　$Ans.\ 7.6x^2 - 9.125a + 5m^2 + 6.25m^3 + 1$.

46. Find the sum of $\frac{1}{2}ab^2 - \frac{2}{3}cd^3 + \frac{2}{3}x^3$, $\frac{2}{3}ab^2 - \frac{1}{4}cd^3 - \frac{1}{3}x^3$, $\frac{1}{4}ab^2 + \frac{5}{12}cd^3 - \frac{3}{4}x^3$, and $\frac{3}{4}ab^2 + \frac{2}{3}cd^3 + 2x^3$.　　$Ans.\ 2\frac{1}{6}ab^2 + \frac{1}{6}cd^3 + 1\frac{7}{12}x^3$.

203. Terms with unlike coefficients.—It often happens that we wish to add or subtract terms where the coefficients that are to be united are not all numerical. For example, add d^2x, e^2x, and cx by uniting the coefficients of x. Here the coefficients of x are d^2, e^2, and c. Since these are unlike terms the addition can only be indicated; thus, $d^2 + e^2 + c$. We may write the sum then of d^2x, e^2x, and cx as $(d^2 + e^2 + c)x$. Similarly the sum of $6x$, $5x$, and $2x$ may be written $(6 + 5 + 2)x$; but here the coefficients can actually be united and expressed as one symbol, thus $13x$.

EXERCISES 59

Add the following by uniting the coefficients of the letter that is common in the terms.

1. $5ay$, $-6dy$, $4cy$, and $17y$.　　$Ans.\ (5a - 6d + 4c + 17)y$.
2. $3x^2y$, $-14xy$, $6x^3y$, and $7y$.　　$Ans.\ (3x^2 - 14x + 6x^3 + 7)y$.
3. bxy, $-bn$, $-14b$, and $3bx^2y$.　　$Ans.\ (xy - n - 14 + 3x^2y)b$.

4. $(a+b)d$, cd, $-dfg$, and $2d$.   *Ans.* $(a+b+c-fg+2)d$.
5. $(3x-y)n^4$, x^2n^4, and $(2x+3y)n^4$.   *Ans.* $(x^2+5x+2y)n^4$.
6. $(a+b-c)x$, $(a-b+c)x$, and $(2a-3b+4c)x$.
    Ans. $(4a-3b+4c)x$.
7. $(ac-cd+b)y$, $(2ac-3cd-b)y$, and $(4ac-6cd-4b)y$.
    Ans. $(7ac-10cd-4b)y$.

Subtract the second expression from the first in the following, uniting the coefficients of the common letters.
8. ay and by.   *Ans.* $(a-b)y$.
9. $3ab$ and $7bc$.   *Ans.* $(3a-7c)b$.
10. $4a^2x$ and $9b^2x$.   *Ans.* $(4a^2-9b^2)x$.
11. $(a+b)z$ and $(a-2b)z$.   *Ans.* $3bz$.
12. $(2a-3b+c)de$ and $(a+b-2c)de$.   *Ans.* $(a-4b+3c)de$.
13. $(4x+2y-3z)ab$ and $(3x-4y+2z)ab$.   *Ans.* $(x+6y-5z)ab$.
14. $(ab+cd-ef)x$ and $(ab-2cd-3ef)x$.   *Ans.* $(3cd+2ef)x$.
15. Find the perimeter of an irregular hexagon having sides of the following lengths: $2a+b$, $3a-2b$, $4a+b$, $2a-3b$, $2a+2b$, and $7a-5b$.
    Ans. $20a-6b$.

204. Signs of grouping.—When a sign of grouping is preceded by a $+$ or $-$ sign, it indicates that the expression enclosed by the sign of grouping is to be added to or subtracted from what precedes.

When a plus sign precedes a sign of grouping, we may remove the sign of grouping without making any change in signs.

Thus, $a+(b-c)=a+b-c$.

When preceded by a minus sign, the sign of grouping may be removed if the signs within it are changed.

Thus, $a-(b-c+d)=a-b+c-d$.

The reason for this change is the same as for the changing of the signs in the subtrahend when subtracting.

When there are several signs of grouping, one within another, they may be removed by first removing the innermost one, and then the next outer one, continuing till all are removed.

Example 1. Simplify $4x^2-5y^2+x-[6x^2-3x-(y^2-x)]$.
Beginning with the inner sign of grouping,
$$4x^2-5y^2+x-[6x^2-3x-(y^2-x)]$$
$$=4x^2-5y^2+x-[6x^2-3x-y^2+x]$$
$$=4x^2-5y^2+x-6x^2+3x+y^2-x$$
$$=-2x^2-4y^2+3x. \quad Ans.$$
Example 2. Simplify $8-\{7-[4+(2-x)]\}$.

Solution.
$$8-\{7-[4+(2-x)]\} = 8-\{7-[4+2-x]\}$$
$$=8-\{7-4-2+x\}$$
$$=8-7+4+2-x$$
$$=7-x. \ \ Ans.$$

The terms may be united as soon as like terms appear within a sign of grouping.

Thus, in the first step in example 2, the $4+2$ within the signs [ ] may be united; it then would be:
$$8-\{7-[6-x]\}$$
$$=8-\{7-6+x\}$$
$$=8-\{1+x\}$$
$$=8-1-x$$
$$=7-x. \ \ Ans.$$

EXERCISES 60

Simplify by removing the signs of grouping and uniting the like terms in the following:

1. $4a+7b-(3a+2b)$.   *Ans.* $a+5b$.
2. $5-3x+(-18+2x)$.   *Ans.* $-13-x$.
3. $11x+1-(-x+3)$.   *Ans.* $12x-2$.
4. $a-3a^2+7-(2a^2+5-3a)$.   *Ans.* $4a-5a^2+2$.
5. $x^3-z^3-(x^3+y^3-z^3)$.   *Ans.* $-y^3$.
6. $a-c+d-(a+c-d)-(d-c-a)$.   *Ans.* $a-c+d$.
7. $3x-(y-2x)+(z+y-5x)$.   *Ans.* z.
8. $z-[y-(z-x)]$.   *Ans.* $2z-x-y$.
9. $74-26-(15-8)$.   *Ans.* 41.
10. $63-[23-(14-8)]$.   *Ans.* 46.
11. $4a+[2a-(a+b)+b]$.   *Ans.* $5a$.
12. $3x-[2y+5z-(3x+y)]$.   *Ans.* $6x-y-5z$.
13. $a-[a-\{a-(2a-a)\}]$.   *Ans.* 0.
14. Let $a=7$, $x=10$, $y=-5$, and $z=-2$, and verify results in exercises 3, 4, 8, and 12.
15. $a+b-[a-b+\{a+b-(a-b)\}]$.   *Ans.* 0.
16. $a-2b-[3a-(b-c)-5c]$.   *Ans.* $4c-b-2a$.
17. $2a-\{b-[3a+(2b-a)]\}$.   *Ans.* $4a+b$.
18. $5x-(4x-[-3x-\{2x-x-1\}])$.   *Ans.* $1-3x$.
19. $24x^2+3xy-[2xy+6x^2-(x^2-4xy)+x^2]$.   *Ans.* $18x^2-3xy$.

205. Insertion of signs of grouping.—For the same reasons as given in the preceding articles, any terms of a polynomial may be enclosed in a sign of grouping preceded by a plus sign *without change of signs.* They may be enclosed in a sign of grouping preceded by a minus sign, *provided the sign of each term within is changed from* $-$ *to* $+$, *or from* $+$ *to* $-$.

Example. Enclose the last three terms in the following expression within parentheses: (1) preceded by a $+$ sign, and (2) preceded by a $-$ sign.

$$ax + by + cd - e.$$

(1) $ax + by + cd - e = ax + (by + cd - e).$

(2) $ax + by + cd - e = ax - (-by - cd + e).$

EXERCISES 61

Insert parentheses around all the terms that follow the first $-$ sign in each of the following:

1. $a - b + c.$

2. $2a + 3b - c - 2d.$

3. $4x - x^2 + y^2 - xy.$

4. $17x^2 - x^3y - xy + yz.$

5. $6 + 3x - 4x^2 + 5x^3 - 6x^4.$

6. $-a - b + c - d + e.$

Write the following with the last three terms of each enclosed in parentheses: (1) preceded by a $-$ sign, and (2) preceded by a $+$ sign.

7. $3x - 2y + 4 - 7z.$

8. $9x^2 + 4y^2 - 7xy - 4yz.$

9. $a + b + c - 3f + 4c^2.$

10. $8x + 4xy - 7z + 4.$

11. $4d^2 + 3c^3 - 4x + 3y.$

12. $2c - 4dx^2 + 3y - 7.$

Collect all the coefficients of x in the following within parentheses preceded by a $-$ sign.

13. $ax - bx + cx.$ *Ans.* $-(-a + b - c)x.$

14. $2cx - 4dx + 6ex - 2x.$ |s *Ans.* $-(-2c + 4d - 6e + 2)x.$

15. $x + 3ax - 4cx + dx.$ *Ans.* $-(-1 - 3a + 4c - d)x.$

16. $-x + 6cx - 4a^2x - ac^2x.$ *Ans.* $-(1 - 6c + 4a^2 + ac^2)x.$

In the following, group within parentheses the terms that have the same letter to the same power: (1) preceded by a $+$ sign, (2) preceded by a $-$ sign.

17. $3 - ab - xy + ac - xz + ad.$ *Ans.* (1) $3 + (-ab + ac + ad) + (-xy - xz),$ (2) $3 - (ab - ac - ad) - (xy + xz).$

18. $az - xy + ad - ac + px.$

19. $ab^2 - ac^2 + ad^2 - nm^2 + np^2 - nq^2.$

20. $acx^2 - bcy + 4ncd - 6 + 4x - 3y^2.$

21. $7 + y^2 - ay^2 + cz^2 - z^2 + 3dy^2 - 4bz^2.$

CHAPTER XXIII

EQUATIONS

206. Definitions.—An **equation** is a statement that two expressions are equal in value.

Thus, $A = \frac{1}{2}ab$ is an equation. So are $A = \pi r^2$; $V = \frac{4}{3}\pi r^3$; and $3x + 4 = 10$.

The part to the left of the equality sign is called the **first member** of the equation, and the part to the right, the **second member**.

If the area of a rectangle is 36 sq. ft. and the altitude is 4 ft., we have $36 = 4b$, where b stands for the base. Now it is easy to see that the statement, or equation, is true if, and only if, $b = 9$. Such an equation as this, where the letter whose value we wish to find has a certain value, is called a **conditional equation.** That is, this equation is true on the condition that $b = 9$, and for no other value of b.

Not all statements of equality are conditional. For instance, $\frac{x^2 - 4}{x + 2} = x - 2$ is an equation; but x may have any value whatever, and still make the equation true.

Thus, if $x = 3$, the equation becomes $\frac{9 - 4}{3 + 2} = 3 - 2$ or $1 = 1$. If $x = 4$ we get $2 = 2$. Similarly for any value we give x.

This kind of an equation is called an **identical equation** or an **identity.**

The number asked for in an equation or the letter standing for it is called the **unknown number,** the **unknown quantity,** or, briefly, the **unknown.**

The following definitions are stated for equations involving one unknown, but may easily be extended.

An equation that is true only on condition that the unknown has particular values is called a **conditional equation** or, briefly, an **equation.**

17
257

An equation that either involves no unknown, or that is true for any value whatever that may be given to the unknown, is called an **identical equation** or, briefly, an **identity.**

To **solve** an equation is to find the value or values of the unknown that will make the equation true.

207. The equation.—A large number of problems, that are solved by means of algebra, involve the equation in one form or another. This makes the equation the most important tool of algebra; in fact, it may be looked upon as a more or less complicated piece of machinery, with which the student should become very familiar.

To become familiar with the mechanism of the equation and its applications requires a great deal of time and much drill in solving equations. Much of the work in solving equations is mechanical, in that it does not require much thought in its performance. However, there is a reason for doing each step that is taken, and one should be able to give this reason.

208. Solution of equations.—As already stated, to solve an equation is to determine the value or values of the unknown number or numbers in the equation. This may be an easy matter, but it is often difficult. Here we shall start with very simple equations and endeavor to discover certain general methods of procedure in the solution.

Example 1. Find the value of x, if $x - 5 = 3$.

Here one readily sees by inspection that $x = 8$, but this does not help us in solving a more complicated equation. If, however, we notice that in order to determine $x = 8$, 5 is added to each member of the given equation, we have a method of procedure that we can apply to another like problem. We have then the *solution:*

Given equation, $\qquad\qquad x - 5 = 3.$
Adding 5 to each member, $\qquad x = 3 + 5.$
Collecting the terms, $\qquad\qquad x = 8.$

Example 2. Solve for x, if $x + 3 = 10$.

Solution. Given equation, $x + 3 = 10.$
Subtracting 3 from each member, $x = 10 - 3.$
Collecting the terms, $\qquad\qquad x = 7.$

Example 3. Solve for b, if $\quad 4b = 36.$

Solution. Given equation, $4b = 36$.

Dividing each member by 4, $b = 9$.

Example 4. Solve for x, if $4x + 5 - 7 = 2x + 6$.

Solution. Given equation, $4x + 5 - 7 = 2x + 6$.

Adding 7 to both members, $4x + 5 = 2x + 6 + 7$.

Subtracting 5 from both members, $4x = 2x + 6 + 7 - 5$.

Subtracting $2x$ from both members, $4x - 2x = 6 + 7 - 5$.

Collecting the terms, $2x = 8$.

Dividing both members by 2, $x = 4$.

Notice that when a term is added to or subtracted from both members of an equation, it is *transposed* from one member to the other and its sign is changed. Now by this transposing we can bring all the terms that contain the unknown into the *first member* and all the others into the *second member*. This gives a convenient form, for we wish finally to have an equation in which the form is:

$$unknown = some\ number.$$

Steps in solution. The solution of an equation that is in a simple form may then be carried out in the following three steps:

(1) *Transpose all terms containing the unknown to the first member, and all other terms to the second member. In each case change the sign of the term transposed.*

(2) *Collect the terms in each member.*

(3) *Divide each member by the coefficient of the unknown.*

It will be found later that there are other changes to be made in an equation that is not in a simple form, before these three steps are to be performed.

209. Axioms.—An **axiom** is a truth that we accept without proof.

The solutions of the equations and the changes mentioned in the preceding article suggest the following axioms:

(1) *If equal numbers are added to equal numbers, the sums are equal.*

(2) *If equal numbers are subtracted from equal numbers, the remainders are equal.*

(3) *If equal numbers are multiplied by equal numbers, the products are equal.*

(4) *If equal numbers are divided by equal numbers, the quotients are equal.*

(5) *Numbers that are equal to the same number or equal numbers are equal to each other.*

(6) *Like powers of equal numbers are equal.*

(7) *Like roots of equal numbers are equal.*

(8) *The whole of anything equals the sum of all its parts.*

210. Testing the equation.—The equation puts the question: What number, if any, must the unknown represent in order that the two members of the equation shall be equal? The solution of the equation answers this question, but it is always well to test or check the work. This may be done by substituting the number obtained for the unknown in place of the unknown letter. If the two members of the equation then become identical, the number substituted is the answer to the equation.

Example. Solve and test: $47r - 17 = 235 - 37r.$

Solution. Given equation, $47r - 17 = 235 - 37r.$

Transposing, $47r + 37r = 235 + 17.$

Collecting terms, $84r = 252.$

Dividing by the coefficient of r, $r = 3.$

Testing by substituting 3 for r in the equation,
$$141 - 17 = 235 - 111.$$

Collecting gives the identical equation, $124 = 124.$

EXERCISES 62

Solve and test the following equations:

1. $3x + 4 = 2x + 5.$ *Ans.* 1.
2. $3x - 4 = x + 12.$ *Ans.* 8.
3. $3x - 25 + 2x = 39 - 3x.$ *Ans.* 8.
4. $250x - 20 = 20x + 440.$ *Ans.* 2.
5. $5x + 7 = 2x + 9.$ *Ans.* $\frac{2}{3}$.
6. $4x - 4 = x + 7.$ *Ans.* $3\frac{2}{3}$.
7. $17x + 10 = 14x + 16.$ *Ans.* 2.
8. $3x + 14 + 2x = x + 26.$ *Ans.* 3.
9. $40x - 10 = 15x + 90.$ *Ans.* 4.
10. $8x + 25 = 2x + 28.$ *Ans.* $\frac{1}{2}$.
11. $16x - 3 = 6x + 8 - 23x.$ *Ans.* $\frac{1}{3}$.
12. $y - 2 + 7y = 14y + 7 - 8y.$ *Ans.* $4\frac{1}{2}$.
13. $2x + (5x - 5) = 7.$ *Ans.* $1\frac{5}{7}$.

Suggestion. First clear of parentheses and then proceed as before.

14. $12y - (2y + 1) = 38 + 7y.$ *Ans.* 13.

15. $(y + 3) - 27 = 10 - y - (y - 2).$ *Ans.* 12.

16. $18y - (2y + 6) - 17 = 14y - (14 - y).$ *Ans.* 9.

17. $35a - 64 + (13 - a) = 16a - (47 - 14a).$ *Ans.* 1.

211. The equation in solving problems.—As has been stated before, one of the things to be gained in the study of mathematics is to be able to express ideas in mathematical symbols. The student has already had some practice in this. We have stated various principles and rules as formulas, and have done much translating from English to mathematical language and from the language of mathematics to English in **Chapter XX.**

For this translating we cannot give rules as we can for the operations to be performed in the solutions of exercises. The student must first thoroughly understand the thing to be expressed; and, secondly, he must know the signs and symbols, that is, the language of mathematics. The following suggestions will help the student to state a problem in the form of an equation.

(1) *Read carefully* the statement of the problem, as it is given in words.

(2) Select the unknown number and represent it by some letter. If there are more unknown numbers than one, try to express the others in terms of the one first selected.

(3) Find *two expressions* which, according to the problem, represent the same number, and set them equal to each other. This forms the equation to be solved.

EXERCISES 63

1. A man is m years old. Give in algebraic symbols his age 10 years ago. Give his age n years age. Give his age s years from now.

2. A man is m years old. When will he be 50 years old? When was he 15 years old? When a years old?

3. A train runs n miles in 1 hour. How many miles will it run in 8 hours? In t hours? In m minutes?   *Ans.* $8n$; nt; $\dfrac{mn}{60}$.

4. A train runs x miles in 10 hours. How far does it run in 1 hour? In n hours? How long will it take to run 100 miles?

Ans. $\dfrac{x}{10}$; $\dfrac{nx}{10}$; $\dfrac{1000}{x}$.

5. How many cents in a dollars?   In b dimes?   In c dollars and d dimes?   *Ans.* $100a$; $10b$; $100c+10d$.

6. If x represents the number of bushels of apples bought, what was the price per bushel if $10 was the cost of all?

7. Find the cost per bushel of apples if 25 bushels at x dollars per bushel cost $10.   State as an equation and solve.

8. A room is three times as long as it is wide and its perimeter is 96 ft. Find the length and width.

Solution.

(1) Let x = number of feet in width.

(2) Then $3x$ = number of feet in length,

(3) and $x+x+3x+3x$ = perimeter.

(4) Also 96 = perimeter.

(5) $\therefore$ $x+x+3x+3x=96$, by axiom (5).

(6) Collecting terms, $8x=96$.

(7) Dividing by 8, $x=12$ = number of feet in width,
   and $3x=36$ = number of feet in the length.

Note that in statements (3) and (4) are two expressions for the same thing, the perimeter.   These two expressions put equal to each other in statement (5) give the equation to be solved.

9. In a company there are 64 persons, and the number of children is three times the number of adults.   How many are there of each?

Solution.

(1) Let x = the number of adults.

(2) Then $3x$ = the number of children,

(3) and $x+3x$ = number in the company.

(4) Also 64 = number in the company.

(5) $\therefore$ $x+3x=64$.

(6) $4x=64$.

(7) $x=16$ = the number of the adults.

(8) $3x=48$ = the number of the children.

10. If twice a number is added to six times the number the sum is 96. What is the number?   *Ans.* 12.

11. A horse and wagon cost together $214.   If the horse cost $76 more than the wagon, find cost of each.   *Ans.* horse $145; wagon $69.

12. The second of three numbers is 4 times the first and the third is 3 times the first.   If the first and second are added and the third subtracted from the sum, the remainder is 60.   Find the three numbers.
                                                      Ans. 30; 120; 90.

13. The number of copies of a book sold doubled each year for three years, and in that time 36,750 copies were sold.   How many were sold each year?   *Ans.* 5250; 10,500; 21,000.

14. A rectangular lot is 30 rods longer than it is wide.   Use w rods for the width and state in an equation that the perimeter is 260 rods.   Solve this equation and find the width and length of the field.
                                                   Ans. 50 rd.; 80 rd.

15. The sum of two numbers is 300 and their difference is 200. What are the numbers?

Solution.

(1) Let $x =$ the greater number.

(2) Then $300 - x =$ the lesser number,

(3) and $x - (300 - x) =$ the difference.

(4) Also $200 =$ the difference.

(5) $\therefore x - (300 - x) = 200$, by axiom (5).

(6) Simplifying, $x - 300 + x = 200$.

(7) Transposing, $x + x = 300 + 200$.

(8) Collecting terms, $2x = 500$.

(9) Dividing by coefficient of x, $x = 250$, the greater number.

(10) $300 - x = 50$, the lesser number.

Test. The sum of 250 and 50 is 300, and the difference is 200. Hence the conditions of the problem are satisfied.

16. A man has $77 in $1 bills and $10 bills. How many bills has he if he has the same number of each? *Ans.* 14.

Suggestion.

Let $x =$ number of each kind of bills.

Then $x =$ number of dollars represented in $1 bills,

and $10x =$ number of dollars represented in $10 bills.

$\therefore x + 10x = 77$.

17. If I have three times as many $5 bills as $2 bills and the amount of money in these bills is $85, how many of each kind of bills have I? *Ans.* 15; 5.

18. In my pocketbook are a certain number of silver dollars, twice as many quarters as dollars, and five times as many dimes as dollars. If the total amount of money is $4.00, find the number of coins of each kind. *Ans.* 2; 4; 10.

19. A shopper bought three articles. The second cost three times as much as the first and the third $3 more than the second. Find the cost of each if the total cost was $9. *Ans.* $\$\frac{6}{7}$; $\$2\frac{4}{7}$; $\$5\frac{4}{7}$.

20. Three tanks hold a total of 24,500 gallons. The first holds 4500 gallons more than the second, and the second 2500 gallons more than the third. How many gallons does each hold? *Ans.* 12,000; 7500; 5000.

21. Of two candidates for the same office, the successful one received a majority of 265. How many votes did each receive, if the total number of votes cast was 6793? *Ans.* 3529; 3264.

22. Find the three consecutive even numbers whose sum is 216. *Ans.* 70; 72; 74.

Suggestion.

Let $x =$ first number.

Then $x + 2 =$ second number, and $x + 4 =$ third number.

23. Find the four consecutive odd numbers whose sum is 88. *Ans.* 19; 21; 23; 25.

24. Find the three consecutive numbers whose sum is 66.

Ans. 21; 22; 23.

25. Divide $210 between A, B, and C so that B shall have $35 less than A and $20 more than C. *Ans.* $100; $65; $45.

26. One angle is the complement of another. If 14° is subtracted from the second and 14° added to the first, the first will be 44° larger than the second. Find the two angles. *Ans.* 53° and 37°.

Two angles are said to be complements of each other if their sum is 90°. (See **Art. 90.**)

27. The difference between two angles is 14°. Find the angles if they are complements of each other. *Ans.* 52° and 38°.

28. A father and son earn $188 a month. If the son's wages were doubled, he would receive $62 less than his father. How much does the son receive? *Ans.* $42.

29. Three men, A, B, C, raised 4080 bushels of wheat. A raised three times as many bushels as B and 330 bushels more than C. How many bushels did each raise? *Ans.* A, 1890 bu.; B, 630 bu.; C, 1560 bu.

30. The sum of four angles about a point is 360°. The second is twice the first, the third three times the second, and the fourth is 10° greater than the first. Find the angles. *Ans.* 35°, 70°, 210°, 45°.

CHAPTER XXIV

MULTIPLICATION

212. Fundamental ideas.—Multiplication of whole numbers in arithmetic may be thought of as a *shortened process of addition*. For instance,

$$5 \times 3 = 5 + 5 + 5 = 15. \tag{1}$$

We say that the multiplicand is used as an addend[1] as many times as there are units in the multiplier.

This idea of multiplication must be enlarged in order to include the multiplying by a fraction. Thus, $8 \times \frac{3}{4} = \frac{8 \times 3}{4}$; that is, we multiply by the numerator and divide by the denominator of the multiplier.

For multiplication in algebra we shall retain its arithmetical meaning when the multiplier is a positive whole number or fraction, but shall have to extend the meaning to include negative numbers.

From the arithmetical meaning, since the multiplier is positive, we have,

$$(-5) \times (+3) = (-5) + (-5) + (-5) = -15. \tag{2}$$

Now we know that when we multiply two positive abstract numbers together, it does not matter which is used as the multiplier. If we assume that this principle holds when one of the numbers is negative, we have,

$$(-5) \times (+3) = (+3) \times (-5) = -15.$$

This gives us the following meaning for multiplication by a negative number:

To multiply by a negative number is to multiply by its absolute value and then change the sign of the product.

Thus, to multiply $+5$ by -3 we multiply $+5$ by $+3$ getting $+15$, and then change the sign of the result. That is,

$$(+5) \times (-3) = -15. \tag{3}$$

[1] An addend is one of the numbers to be added in an addition problem.

265

Likewise, to multiply -5 by -3 we multiply -5 by $+3$ getting -15, and then change the sign of the result. That is,

$$(-5)\times(-3) = +15. \qquad (4)$$

In (**1**), (**2**), (**3**), and (**4**) we have examples of all the combinations possible of two algebraic numbers.

213. From the above considerations we see that in finding the product of two algebraic numbers:

(1) *The numerical part of the product is the product of the absolute values of the multiplicand and multiplier.*

(2) *The sign of the product is plus when the signs of the multiplicand and multiplier are alike, and minus when their signs are unlike.*

This is called the law of signs in multiplication. It may be stated as follows:

$$+\times+ = +,$$
$$-\times- = +,$$
$$+\times- = -,$$
$$-\times+ = -.$$

214. Concrete illustration.—For those who find the foregoing difficult to understand, the following may clear up matters.

There is a machine shop employing laborers and apprentices. The laborers are paid $15 per week, and the apprentices are charged $3 per week.

Suppose that an increase in the number of men or dollars is positive, and a decrease in either is negative. Thus, a number of laborers or apprentices taken in will be called positive, and a number let go will be called negative; while the number of dollars received from an apprentice is positive and the number of dollars paid a laborer is negative.

On these suppositions we have:

(1) If apprentices are increased by 5, the amount of money is increased $15 per week. That is,

$$(+3)\times(+5) = +15.$$

(2) If apprentices are decreased by 5, the amount of money is decreased $15 per week. That is,

$$(+3)\times(-5) = -15.$$

(3) If laborers are increased by 5, the amount of money is decreased by \$75 per week. That is,

$$(-15) \times (+5) = -75.$$

(4) If laborers are decreased by 5, the amount of money is increased by \$75 per week. That is,

$$(-15) \times (-5) = +75.$$

From these considerations, we may deduce the same rules as already given.

215. Continued products.—To find the product of three or more numbers, we find the product of the first two, and then multiply this product by the third, and so on till all the numbers have been used.

By applying principles (1) and (2) of **Art. 213,** we obtain the following:

(1) *The product of an odd number of negative factors is negative.*

(2) *The product of an even number of negative factors is positive.*

(3) *The product of any number of positive factors is positive.*

Thus, $(-2)(-2)(-2)(-2)(-2) = -32$, while
$(-2)(-2)(-2)(-2)(-2)(-2) = +64$.

The first one of these equals $(-2)^5$, and is then read "*the fifth power of* -2." The second is $(-2)^6$.

It should be noted that such a form as $(-2)^5$ does not mean the same as -2^5, though they may be equal. The form -2^5 is read "*minus 2 to the fifth power.*"

Thus, $(-2)^2 = (-2)(-2) = 4 = 2^2$,
$(-2)^3 = (-2)(-2)(-2) = -8 = -2^3$,
$(-2)^4 = (-2)(-2)(-2)(-2) = 16 = 2^4$,
$(-2)^5 = (-2)(-2)(-2)(-2)(-2) = -32 = -2^5$,
$-2^5 = -(2)(2)(2)(2)(2) = -32$,
$(-3)^2(-2)^3 = (-3)(-3)(-2)(-2)(-2) = -72$,
$(4^2)(3^2) = 4 \cdot 4 \cdot 3 \cdot 3 = 144$.

EXERCISES 64

1. Find the product of -7, -8, and $+10$.   *Ans.* 560.
2. Find the product of -2, -40, $+75$, and -60.
3. Find cube of -7, of $+8$, of -21.

Find values of the following:

4. $(-4)^5$.   *Ans.* -1024.   **5.** $(-8)^4$.   *Ans.* 4096.

6. $(-1)^{10}$.   *Ans.* $+1$.   **7.** $(-4)^3(-3)^2$.   *Ans.* -576.

8. $2(+6)^2(-6)^2$.   *Ans.* 2592.

If $x=2$, $y=-3$, $z=-4$, find value of:

9. x^3y^2.   *Ans.* 72.   **10.** xyz.   *Ans.* 24.

11. y^3z.   *Ans.* 108.   **12.** $x^2y^2z^2$.   *Ans.* 576.

13. $(6)(-5)(-2)y^3$.   *Ans.* -1620.

14. $15\cdot(-2)\cdot(-3)+4\cdot(-5)\cdot6$.   *Ans.* -30.

15. $1\cdot2\cdot3+3\cdot4\cdot5+(-5)\cdot(-6)\cdot(-7)$.   *Ans.* -144.

16. $4\cdot(-3)\cdot5+2\cdot(-3)\cdot4+3\cdot(-3)\cdot4$.   *Ans.* -120.

17. $(-2)^5\cdot(-3)^4-(-4)\cdot6\cdot(-7)$.   *Ans.* -2760.

18. $(-3)^3-3^3+(-2)^5-2^5$.   *Ans.* -118.

19. $(-2)\cdot(-3)+(-4)\cdot(-5)+(-5)\cdot(-6)$.   *Ans.* 56.

20. $1\cdot2\cdot3\cdot4\cdot5-(-1)(-2)(-3)(-4)(-5)$.   *Ans.* 240.

21. $4\cdot5\cdot6\;7-(-4)(-5)(-6)(-7)$.   *Ans.* 0.

216. Law of exponents.—The law which applies to exponents that are positive integers is derived from the definition given in **Art. 185.**

Since $a^5 = a\cdot a\cdot a\cdot a\cdot a$,

and $\quad a^3 = a\cdot a\cdot a$,

then $\quad a^5\cdot a^3 = a\cdot a\cdot a\cdot a\cdot a\cdot a\cdot a\cdot a = a^8$,

and $\quad a^5\cdot a^3 = a^{5+3} = a^8$.

In general $a^n = a\cdot a\cdot a\cdot a\cdots$ to n factors[1]

and $\quad a^m = a\cdot a\cdot a\cdot a\cdots$ to m factors,

then $\quad a^n\cdot a^m = a\cdot a\cdot a\cdot a\cdot a\cdots$ to $(n+m)$ factors,

and $\quad a^n\cdot a^m = a^{n+m}$.

Similarly, when there are any number of factors we have $a^n\cdot a^m\cdot a^p\cdot a^r\cdots = a^{n+m+p+r\cdots}$.

LAW. *The product of two or more powers of the same base is equal to that base affected with an exponent equal to the sum of the exponents of the powers.*

217. To multiply a monomial by a monomial.—

Example. Multiply $14a^3b^2$ by $-3a^4b^3$.

Process.

$$14a^3b^2$$
$$-\ 3a^4b^3$$
$$\overline{-42a^7b^5}$$

Discussion. Since the multiplier is composed of the factors -3, a^4, and b^3, the multiplicand may be multiplied by each successively. In each case the product for any one of these factors is obtained by multi-

---

[1] A repetition of dots, as a, b, c,···, is the sign of continuation. It is read "and so on."

plying a single factor in the multiplicand by it. We multiply by -3, by multiplying 14 by -3, which gives $-42a^3b^2$. This is multiplied by a^4, by multiplying the a^3 by a^4, which gives $-42a^7b^2$. This is multiplied by b^3, by multiplying the b^2 by b^3, which gives $-42a^7b^5$, the answer.

The multiplication is carried out by determining in the following order:

(1) *the sign of the product,*
(2) *the coefficient of the product,*
(3) *the letters of the product,*
(4) *the exponents of these letters.*

Thus, in the above example the sign is $+ \times - = -$; the coefficient is $14 \times 3 = 42$; the letters are a and b; and the exponents are, for a, $3+4=7$, and for b, $2+3=5$.

This plan should be carefully followed by the beginner.

218. To multiply a polynomial by a monomial.—

RULE. *The product is found by multiplying each term of the multiplicand by the multiplier, and taking the algebraic sum of these partial products.*

Example. Multiply $7ax^3 - 21ab^4 - 3x^2$ by $2a^2b^3x^4$.

Process. $\dfrac{\begin{array}{l} 7ax^3 - 21ab^4 - 3x^2 \\ 2a^2b^3x^4 \end{array}}{14a^3b^3x^7 - 42a^3b^7x^4 - 6a^2b^3x^6}$

Explanation. The first term at the left of the product is obtained by multiplying the first term at the left of the multiplicand by the multiplier. The second and third terms in the product are obtained in a similar manner. In each of the multiplications we have a monomial by a monomial, which has been discussed in the previous article.

219. To multiply a polynomial by a polynomial.—

RULE. *Multiply every term of the multiplicand by each term of the multiplier, write the like terms of the partial products under each other, and find the algebraic sum of the partial products.*

Example 1. Multiply $x^2 + 3xy - 2y^2$ by $2xy - 2y^2$.

Process.

$2xy$ times $(x^2 + 3xy - 2y^2) =$
$-2y^2$ times $(x^2 + 3xy - 2y^2) =$
Adding these we get,

$$\begin{array}{l} x^2 + 3xy - 2y^2 \\ 2xy - 2y^2 \\ \hline 2x^3y + 6x^2y^2 - 4xy^3 \\ \quad\quad - 2x^2y^2 - 6xy^3 + 4y^4 \\ \hline 2x^3y + 4x^2y^2 - 10xy^3 + 4y^4 \end{array}$$

Example 2.　Multiply $3a^2+3b^2+ab$ by $b^3-2a^2b+ab^2$.

Process.

$$3a^2+3b^2\ \ \ +ab$$
$$b^3-2a^2b\ \ +ab^2$$
$$\overline{3a^2b^3+3b^5+ab^4}$$
$$-6a^2b^3\qquad\qquad-6a^4b-2a^3b^2$$
$$a^2b^3\qquad+3ab^4\qquad\qquad+3a^3b^2$$
$$\overline{-2a^2b^3+3b^5+4ab^4-6a^4b+\ a^3b^2}$$

220. Test.—Problems in multiplication can be tested by substituting convenient numerical values for the letters. It is best to use values larger than 1, since with 1 the exponents are not tested, as any power of 1 is 1.

Test of example 1, by letting $x=2$ and $y=2$.

$$x^2\ +3xy-2y^2\qquad\qquad=4+12-8=8$$
$$2xy-2y^2\qquad\qquad\qquad=8-8\qquad=0$$
$$\overline{2x^3y+6x^2y^2-4xy^3}$$
$$-2x^2y^2-6xy^3+4y^4$$
$$\overline{2x^3y+4x^2y^2-10xy^3+4y^4}=32+64-160+64=0.$$

The work is probably correct if the product of the values of the two factors equals the value of the product.

EXERCISES 65

Find the product of the following:

1. $10ab^2$ and $3a^3b$.　　　　　　　　　　　*Ans.* $30a^4b^3$.
2. $16n^4x^5$ and $-2n^6x^2$.
3. $4a^2x^3y^4$ and $-5x^6y$.　　　　　　　　　*Ans.* $-20a^2x^9y^5$.
4. $-17x^2y^7$ and $-3a^3x^2$.
5. $-5m^3n^2d^2y^3$ and $-2m^{10}n^6c^2y^2$.　　　*Ans.* $10m^{13}n^8c^2d^2y^5$.
6. $-x^2y^3$ and $-x^4y^2z^3$.
7. $-3x^2y^3$, x^2, y^3, and $4xy$.　　　　　　*Ans.* $-12x^5y^7$.
8. $3PQ$, Q^2, and $4P^2Q^3$.　　　　　　　　*Ans.* $12P^3Q^6$.
9. $-\tfrac{2}{3}ax^2$, $\tfrac{3}{4}a^2x^3$, and $-\tfrac{1}{2}ax$.　　　*Ans.* $\tfrac{1}{4}a^4x^6$.
10. a^n, a^{2n+1}, a^{3n+2}, and a^{n+1}.　　　　*Ans.* a^{7n+4}.
11. $(a^3)^2$ or a^3 times a^3.　　　　　　　*Ans.* a^6.
12. $(m^2n^3)^4=?$　　　　　　　　　　　*Ans.* m^8n^{12}.
13. $(4a^2b^4)^3=?$　　　　　　　　　　*Ans.* $64a^6b^{12}$.
14. $(a^nb^m)^c=?$　　　　　　　　　　*Ans.* $a^{cn}b^{cm}$.
15. $a^5b^2c\cdot a^2b^5c\cdot ab^5c^2\cdot ab^2c^5$.　　　*Ans.* $a^9b^{14}c^9$.
16. $x^4y^2z\cdot x^2y^4z^3\cdot x^6y^7z$.　　　　　　*Ans.* $x^{12}y^{13}z^5$.
17. $3a^4c^2\cdot-4a^5c\cdot-2a^6c^4$.　　　　　　*Ans.* $24a^{15}c^7$.
18. $pqr^2\cdot-p^2qr\cdot-pq^2r$.　　　　　　　*Ans.* $p^4q^4r^4$.
19. $(6xyz)\cdot(-7axy^2)\cdot(-2a^3x^2y^6z^2)$.　　*Ans.* $84a^4x^4y^9z^3$.
20. $5b^2\cdot(5+6b^2-7b^4)$.　　　　　*Ans.* $25b^2+30b^4-35b^6$.

21. $-7x^2y \cdot (-3x^2y^2 + 2xy)$. $\qquad$ *Ans.* $21x^4y^3 - 14x^3y^2$.

22. $25ab^2 \cdot (2x^4b^3 + 2c^2d)$. $\qquad$ *Ans.* $50ab^5x^4 + 50ab^2c^2d$.

23. $-5x \cdot (-3a + 2a^2 + 4)$. $\qquad$ *Ans.* $15ax - 10a^2x - 20x$.

24. $-15x^7y^8 \cdot (m^7n^8x^2y^2 - 13p^9q^{10})$. $\quad$ *Ans.* $-15m^7n^8x^9y^{10} + 195p^9q^{10}x^7y^8$.

25. $-3x^3y^5z^7 \cdot (x^8y^6z^4 - 13x^4y^2)$. $\qquad$ *Ans.* $-3x^{11}y^{11}z^{11} + 39x^7y^7z^7$.

26. $3c^2de \cdot (3cd^2e + 6cde^2 - 5cde)$. $\qquad$ *Ans.* $9c^3d^3e^2 + 18c^3d^2e^3 - 15c^3d^2e^2$.

27. $4x^2y^3 - 7xy^4 + 14a^2$ by $-4x^3$. $\qquad$ *Ans.* $-16x^5y^3 + 28x^4y^4 - 56a^2x^3$.

28. $2x - 3y$ by $4x + y$. $\qquad$ *Ans.* $8x^2 - 10xy - 3y^2$.

29. $x^2 - 2y$ by $4x + y^2$. $\qquad$ *Ans.* $4x^3 - 8xy + x^2y^2 - 2y^3$.

30. $-3x + 7$ by $2x - 1$. $\qquad$ *Ans.* $-6x^2 + 17x - 7$.

31. $5x + 4y$ by $3x - 2y$. $\qquad$ *Ans.* $15x^2 + 2xy - 8y^2$.

32. $ax - by$ by $ax + by$. $\qquad$ *Ans.* $a^2x^2 - b^2y^2$.

33. $a^2x^2 - 2y^2$ by $a^2x^2 + 2y^2$. $\qquad$ *Ans.* $a^4x^4 - 4y^4$.

34. $a^2 + ab + b^2$ by $a - b$. $\qquad$ *Ans.* $a^3 - b^3$.

35. $a^2 - ab + b^2$ by $a + b$. $\qquad$ *Ans.* $a^3 + b^3$.

36. $a^2 - ab + b^2$ by $2a - 4b$. $\qquad$ *Ans.* $2a^3 - 6a^2b + 6ab^2 - 4b^3$.

37. $2x + 3y - z$ by $2x - 3y + z$. $\qquad$ *Ans.* $4x^2 - 9y^2 + 6yz - z^2$.

38. $a^2 + ab + b^2$ by $a^2 - ab + b^2$. $\qquad$ *Ans.* $a^4 + a^2b^2 + b^4$.

39. $x^2 - 2xy + y^2$ by $x^2 + 2xy + y^2$. $\qquad$ *Ans.* $x^4 - 2x^2y^2 + y^4$.

40. $6x^2 + 2x + 1$ by $x^2 - x - 1$. $\qquad$ *Ans.* $6x^4 - 4x^3 - 7x^2 - 3x - 1$.

41. $c^2 + 3cd + 4d^2$ by $c^2 - 3cd - 4d^2$. $\qquad$ *Ans.* $c^4 - 9c^2d^2 - 24cd^3 - 16d^4$.

42. $x^2 - 4x + 16$ by $x + 5$. $\qquad$ *Ans.* $x^3 + x^2 - 4x + 80$.

43. $n^2 - 50n - 100$ by $n + 2$. $\qquad$ *Ans.* $n^3 - 48n^2 - 200n - 200$.

44. $a^3 - 3a^2b + 3ab^2 - b^3$ by $a^2 - ab$.

$\qquad$ *Ans.* $a^5 - 4a^4b + 6a^3b^2 - 4a^2b^3 + ab^4$.

45. $4x^3 - 3x^2y + 5xy^2 - 6y^3$ by $5x + 6y$.

$\qquad$ *Ans.* $20x^4 + 9x^3y + 7x^2y^2 - 36y^4$.

46. $4y^2 - 10 + 2y$ by $2y^2 - 3y + 5$. $\qquad$ *Ans.* $8y^4 - 6y^2 - 8y^3 + 40y - 50$.

47. $a^4 - a^3b + a^2b^2 - ab^3 + b^4$ by $a + b$. $\qquad$ *Ans.* $a^5 + b^5$.

48. $2ac^2 - 3by$ by $2c^3 - 3y^2$. $\qquad$ *Ans.* $4ac^5 - 6bc^3y - 6ac^2y^2 + 9by^3$.

49. $a^3 + 3a^2x + 3ax^2 + x^3$ by $a^3 - 3a^2x + 3ax^2 - x^3$.

$\qquad$ *Ans.* $a^6 - 3a^4x^2 + 3a^2x^4 - x^6$.

50. $x^4 + x^2y^2 + y^4$ by $x^2 - y^2$. $\qquad$ *Ans.* $x^6 - y^6$.

Signs of grouping are often used to enclose factors of a product. Thus, $(a + b)(a - b)$ means the same as $(a + b)$ times $(a - b)$. To free the expression of these signs of grouping, the indicated multiplications are performed.

Free the following of signs of grouping and simplify:

51. $(a + b)(a - b)$. $\qquad$ *Ans.* $a^2 - b^2$.

52. $(2x + 7)(3x^2 - 8)$. $\qquad$ *Ans.* $6x^3 + 21x^2 - 16x - 56$.

53. $(3x^2 + ab)(3x^2 - ab)$. $\qquad$ *Ans.* $9x^4 - a^2b^2$.

54. $5(x^2 - ab) + 6(x^2 + ab)$. $\qquad$ *Ans.* $11x^2 + ab$.

55. $-3ab(ab - a^2) + 2ab(a^2 - b^2)$. $\qquad$ *Ans.* $-3a^2b^2 + 5a^3b - 2ab^3$.

56. $-2(-2a^4 + 3a^3b - b^4) + 3(a^4 + 2a^3b - 2b^4)$. $\qquad$ *Ans.* $7a^4 - 4b^4$.

57. $2(x^2 - 3x + 1) - (x + 4)(x - 1)$. $\qquad$ *Ans.* $x^2 - 9x + 6$.

58. $2(n + 1)(n - 1)(n + 2) - 4n(1 - n)(n + 3)$.

$\qquad$ *Ans.* $6n^3 + 12n^2 - 14n - 4$.

Solution. $2(n+1)(n-1)(n+2) = \quad 2n^3 + 4n^2 - 2n - 4$

Subtracting, $4n(1-n)(n+3) \quad = -4n^3 - 8n^2 + 12n$

$$\overline{\qquad 6n^3 + 12n^2 - 14n - 4.}$$

59. $2x^2[x^2 - 3x(x-y)] + (x^2 + xy - y^2)(x^2 - y^2 + xy^2).$

$\quad\quad\quad$ *Ans.* $-3x^4 + 7x^3y - 2x^2y^2 - xy^3 + y^4 + x^3y^2 + x^2y^3 - xy^4.$

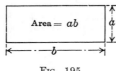

Fig. 193.

Fig. 194.

60. Find the area of a rectangle $2x+5$ ft. in length and $x-6$ ft. wide.

$\quad\quad\quad$ *Ans.* $2x^2 - 7x - 30$ sq. ft.

61. Find the volume of a rectangular solid $2x-3$ ft. wide, $7x-2$ ft. long, and $x+4$ ft. deep. $\quad\quad$ *Ans.* $14x^3 + 31x^2 - 94x + 24$ cu. ft.

62. Find the volume of a right circular cylinder if the altitude is h ft. and the radius $2h-4$ ft. $\quad\quad$ *Ans.* $\pi(4h^3 - 16h^2 + 16h)$ cu. ft.

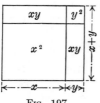

Fig. 195.

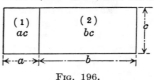

Fig. 196.

63. A hollow square has dimensions as shown in Fig. 193. Find its area. $\quad\quad\quad\quad\quad\quad\quad\quad$ *Ans.* $3s^2 + 28s + 32.$

64. A ring has dimensions as shown in Fig. 194. Find its area.

$\quad\quad\quad\quad\quad\quad\quad\quad$ *Ans.* $\frac{1}{4}\pi(27a^2 + 150a + 32).$

221. Representation of products.—If a is the number of units in the altitude in Fig. 195 and b is the number of units in

Fig. 197.

the base, then the product ab is the number of square units in the area of the rectangle in the figure.

Similarly, the two rectangles in Fig. 196 represent the product of $(a+b)$ by c. The part marked (1) represents the partial product ac, and the part marked (2) represents the partial product bc.

Fig. 197 shows that $(x+y)(x+y) = x^2 + 2xy + y^2$. The whole figure is a square $x+y$ on a side. This is made up of a square x units on a side, having x^2 square units; a square y

units on a side, having y^2 square units; and two rectangles each x units by y units, having xy square units each. Hence the whole figure contains $x^2+2xy+y^2$ square units.

EXERCISES 66

Find the product in each of the following, and show the product and the partial products by drawings.

1. $(a+b+c)d$.
2. $(a+b+c)(d+e)$.
3. $(a+b+c)^2$.
4. $(x+y)(x-y)$.
5. $(x-y)^2$.
6. $(a+b+c)(d+e+f)$.

222. Approximate products.—By multiplication we get the formula $(1+a)(1+b) = 1+a+b+ab$.

If in this formula a and b are small fractions, the product ab will be very small compared with a and b. The value of $(1+a)(1+b)$ will then be approximately $1+a+b$.

Thus, if $a=0.05$ and $b=0.02$, the approximate value of $(1+a)(1+b) = 1+0.05+0.02 = 1.07$, while the exact value is $1.05 \times 1.02 = 1.071$. $1.071 - 1.07 = 0.001 = $ difference.

Example. If $a=0.01$ and $b=0.02$ find the per cent of error in the product $(1+a)(1+b)$ if the term ab is disregarded.

Solution. The approximate value of $(1+0.01)(1+0.02) = 1+0.01+0.02 = 1.03$.

The exact value $= 1+0.01+0.02+0.0002 = 1.0302$.

The error $= 1.0302 - 1.03 = 0.0002$.

The per cent of error is obtained by finding what per cent 0.0002 is of 1.0302.

$\therefore 0.0002 \div 1.0302 = 0.0002- = 0.02-\%$. *Ans.*

EXERCISES 67

1. Find per cent of error if term ab is disregarded when $a=0.001$ and $b=0.002$. *Ans.* $0.0002-\%$.

2. Calculate the value of 1.002×1.05 to three decimal places by using the approximate method. *Ans.* 1.052.

3. To how many places can the product of 1.02×1.0024 be found by the approximate method? *Ans.* 4.

4. How much error per cent is there in assuming $(1+a)(1+b) = 1+a+b$ when $a=0.003$ and $b=0.005$? *Ans.* $0.0015-\%$.

5. In assuming $(1+a)^3 = 1+3a$, what is the per cent of error when $a=0.0002$? When $a=0.002$? When $a=0.02$? When $a=0.2$?
Ans. $0.000012-\%$; $0.0012-\%$; $0.114-\%$; $7.41-\%$.

18

6. In measuring the radius of a circle of correct length 1 ft., there is an error of 1%. Find the per cent of error in the area of the circle determined from the measured radius.   *Ans.* 2% nearly.

7. If in determining the area of a triangle by drawing to scale and measuring the base and altitude, the base is measured $1\frac{1}{2}$% and the altitude 2% too large respectively, find per cent of error in area, disregarding the product term.   *Ans.* $3\frac{1}{2}$%.

8. Find the approximate products of the following:

(1) 1.003×1.012.   (4) 0.97×0.98,
(2) 1.02×0.97.   (5) 0.996×0.997.
(3) 1.004×0.998.   (6) 0.985×0.996.

9. In measuring a rectangle the length is measured 2% too large and the width 3% too small. If the area is computed from these measurements, find the per cent of error in the area.

Ans. 1% nearly, too small.

10. If, in measuring a triangle, the base is measured 1% too large and the altitude $1\frac{1}{2}$% too small, find the per cent of error in the area computed from these measurements.   *Ans.* $\frac{1}{2}$% nearly, too large.

11. If the error in a number is 1%, what is the per cent of error in the square of the number? In the cube of the number?

Ans. 2%; 3% nearly.

CHAPTER XXV

DIVISION, SPECIAL PRODUCTS, AND FACTORS

223. Division.—Division is the *inverse* of multiplication. That is, the quotient must be an expression that multiplied by the divisor will give the dividend.

From the law of signs and the law of exponents in multiplication we have the following:

(1) *In dividing, like signs give a positive, and unlike signs give a negative sign for the quotient.*

(2) *In dividing powers of the same base, the exponent of the quotient equals the exponent of the dividend minus the exponent of the divisor.*

This applies, by definition of the positive integral exponent, only when the exponent of the dividend is larger than the exponent of the divisor.

Thus, $a^5 \div a^3 = a^2$; but when the exponents are equal and we subtract we obtain the exponent 0, which is meaningless.

In dividing the same powers of the same base, the quotient is 1.

Thus, $a^3 \div a^3 = 1$ and, in general, $a^n \div a^n = 1$.

224. Division of one monomial by another.—It is well for the beginner to carry out the work of a division in a regular order as in multiplication. (See **Art. 217.**) The steps in division are:

(1) *Determine the sign of the quotient.*

(2) *Determine the coefficient.*

(3) *Determine letters and exponents.*

Remember that in the process of division we divide where we multiply in multiplication, and we subtract exponents where we add exponents in multiplication.

Example. Divide $25a^4x^5$ by $-5a^2x^3$.

Process, carried out in steps.

275

$$25 \div -5 = -5,$$
$$a^4 \div a^2 = a^2,$$
$$x^5 \div x^3 = x^2,$$
$$\therefore 25a^4x^5 \div -5a^2x^3 = -5a^2x^2. \quad Ans.$$

The last only should be written down in performing the work. The first three steps are mental operations and are placed here for guidance.

The division of one monomial by another may also be performed as a cancellation. If we recall that an expression like $4a^2b^3$ means $4 \cdot a \cdot a \cdot b \cdot b \cdot b$, we may write $16a^3b^5c^3 \div 4a^2b^3$ in the form.

$$\frac{\cancel{4} \cdot 4 \cdot \cancel{a} \cdot \cancel{a} \cdot a \cdot \cancel{b} \cdot \cancel{b} \cdot \cancel{b} \cdot b \cdot b \cdot c \cdot c \cdot c_,}{\cancel{4} \cdot \cancel{a} \cdot \cancel{a} \cdot \cancel{b} \cdot \cancel{b} \cdot \cancel{b}}.$$

Now cancel the factors common to the dividend and divisor. The product of the factors remaining in the dividend is the quotient.

This process is too long for rapid work, but it may clear up points in division that trouble the student.

225. Test.—The work in division can be tested the same as in multiplication by substituting convenient values for the letters. It may also be tested by multiplying the divisor by the quotient, when the product will be the dividend.

EXERCISES 68

Divide the following and test:

1. $16x^2y$ by $2xy$.
2. $14x^3z^4$ by $-7xz$.
3. $10x^4yz^3$ by $3x^2z^2$.
4. $-22a^2b$ by $-2ab$.   *Ans.* $-6ab$.
5. $100a^4x^3$ by $-5a^4x$.
6. $18a^3b^2x$ by $-3a^2bx$.   *Ans.* $4xy^2$.
7. $-20x^3y^4$ by $-5x^2y^2$.   *Ans.* $4xy^2$.
8. $-42a^3m^2y^3$ by $7a^2m^2$.   *Ans.* $-6ay^3$.
9. $-13a^2y^2$ by $-13ay^2$.   *Ans.* a.
10. $8a^2y^3$ by $-8a^2y^3$.   *Ans.* -1.
11. $18a^6b^5$ by $-6a^3b$.   *Ans.* $-3a^3b^4$.
12. $3ax^3$ by $7ax$.   *Ans.* $\frac{3}{7}x^2$.
13. $5a^4x^3c$ by $-2a^2$.   *Ans.* $-\frac{5}{2}a^2x^3c$.
14. $3^3 \cdot 2^4 a^2$ by $3^2 \cdot 2^2 a^2$.   *Ans.* $3 \cdot 2^2$.
15. $-5^4a^3c^5$ by -5^2ac^4.   *Ans.* 5^2a^2c.
16. $7^5ac^4xy^2$ by -7^4ac^4y.   *Ans.* $-7xy$.

226. Division of a polynomial by a monomial.—

Example. Divide $24a^5y^3 - 96a^5y^6$ by $8a^4y^3$.

Process. $$8a^4y^3) \frac{24a^5y^3 - 96a^5y^6}{3a \quad -12ay^3}.$$

RULE. *The division is performed by dividing each term of the dividend by the divisor, beginning at the left.*

EXERCISES 69

Divide the following and test by multiplication:

1. $14ax + 28ay + 84az$ by $14a$.   *Ans.* $x + 2y + 6z$.
2. $12a^3 + 3a^4 + 18a^5$ by $3a^3$.   *Ans.* $4 + a + 6a^2$.
3. $3x^5 - 16x^3 + 14x^2$ by x^2.   *Ans.* $3x^3 - 16x + 14$.
4. $2 \cdot 3^3 + 4 \cdot 3^2 + 3^4$ by 3^2.   *Ans.* $2 \cdot 3 + 4 + 3^2$.
5. $2 \cdot 3^2 \cdot 5 - 3 \cdot 3^3 \cdot 7 \cdot 5$ by 3^2.   *Ans.* $2 \cdot 5 - 3 \cdot 3 \cdot 7 \cdot 5$.
6. $25ax^2y^3 - 10x^3y^4 - 5x^2y^3$ by $5x^2y^3$.   *Ans.* $5a - 2xy - 1$.
7. $21a^3x^3 - 7a^2x^2 + 14ax$ by $7ax$.   *Ans.* $3a^2x^2 - ax + 2$.
8. $42a^3 - 11a^2 + 28a$ by $7a$.   *Ans.* $6a^2 - 1\frac{4}{7}a + 4$.
9. $24x^4y^2 - 8x^4y^5 - 24xy^2$ by $8x$.   *Ans.* $3xy^2 - x^3y^5 - 3y^2$.
10. $4x^4y^6 + 8x^7y^3 - 12x^6y^4$ by $2x^2y^2$.   *Ans.* $2x^2y^4 + 4x^5y - 6x^4y^2$.
11. $\frac{1}{4}a^5b^2 + 5a^3b^4 - 7a^4b^3$ by $-1\frac{1}{2}a^2b^2$.   *Ans.* $-\frac{1}{6}a^3 - 3\frac{1}{3}ab^2 + 4\frac{2}{3}a^2b$.
12. $3.25a^7 - 5.2a^6 + 9.75a^3$ by $0.25a^3$.   *Ans.* $13a^4 - 20.8a^3 + 39$.
13. $a^2(a+b) + a^3(a+b)$ by a^2.   *Ans.* $a + b + a(a+b)$.
14. $3(a-b) + 6a(a-b)$ by $(a-b,$.   *Ans.* $3 + 6a$.
15. $(a-b)(c+d) + (a-b)(x+y)$ by $(a-b)$.   *Ans.* $c + d + x + y$.

227. Factors of a polynomial when one factor is a monomial.

—In exercise 1 of the preceding list, each term of $14ax + 28ay + 84az$ can be divided by $14a$. The quotient is $x + 2y + 6z$. Now the product of $x + 2y + 6z$ and $14a$ is $14ax + 28ay + 84az$. We say that $14a$ and $x + 2y + 6z$ are the factors of $14ax + 28ay + 84az$.

The factors of a polynomial similar to the above are a monomial, containing all that is common to each term of the polynomial, and the quotient found by dividing the polynomial by the monomial.

Example. Factor $4a^2x - 2ax^2 + 6a^2x^2$.

The monomial factor is $2ax$. This is seen by inspection. Dividing the polynomial by $2ax$ we find $2a - x + 3ax$ which is the other factor. The factors are written in the form $2ax(2a - x + 3ax)$.

The work may be tested by finding the product of the factors, which gives the expression that was to be factored.

EXERCISES 70

Find factors of the following and test the work by multiplication:

1. $ay+ax+ac$.   **5.** $x^2-x^3+x^4$.

2. $14+21a$.   **6.** $54a^4+63a^7$.

3. $20a+30b+40$.   **7.** $a^4b^2-a^3b^4-a^2b^6$.

4. $2^2 \cdot 3+2^3 \cdot 5$.   **8.** $16+32a-24a^3$.

9. $(x-2)a+(x-2)b$.   *Ans.* $(x-2)(a+b)$.

Suggestion. Consider $(x-2)a$ and $(x-2)b$ as the terms of the polynomial. Then $(x-2)$ is common to the two terms, and is the factor to use as a divisor in finding the other factor.

10. $(c-d)b^4-(c-d)c^2x$.   *Ans.* $(c-d)(b^4-c^2x)$.

11. $(3a-5)n+(3a-5)p$.   *Ans.* $(3a-5)(n+p)$.

12. $3(2a+4b)+3(3a-6b)$.   *Ans.* $3(5a-2b)$.

13. $16a^2(a+b)+16a^2(c-d)$.   *Ans.* $16a^2(a+b+c-d)$.

14. $(a-b)^3+2a(a-b)^2$.   *Ans.* $(a-b)^2(3a-b)$.

228. Squares and square roots of monomials.—By the principles of multiplication already given, the *square of a monomial may be found as follows:*

(1) *The sign is always plus.*

(2) *The numerical coefficient is the square of the numerical coefficient of the monomial.*

(3) *The exponent of any letter is twice the exponent of the same letter in the monomial.*

Thus, $(5a^2b^3)^2=25a^4b^6$, $(-4a^3b^2d)^2=16a^6b^4d^2$, and $(\frac{1}{3}x^3y)^2=\frac{1}{9}x^6y^2$.

The *square root* of a monomial can be found by doing the inverse processes to those for finding the *square* of a monomial.

(1) *The square root can be found of a positive number only.*

(2) *The numerical coefficient is the square root of the numerical coefficient of the monomial.*

(3) *The exponent of any letter is one-half the exponent of the same letter in the monomial.*

It follows that the monomial of which the square root is to be taken must have a numerical coefficient that is a perfect square and all the exponents must be even numbers. Otherwise the square root cannot be found exactly.

Thus, $\sqrt{16a^4b^2}=4a^2b$ and $\sqrt{225x^4y^6z^2}=15x^2y^3z$; but $\sqrt{10a^4b^6}$ can only be expressed as $\sqrt{10}a^2b^3$; and $\sqrt{35a^3b}$ cannot be found.

EXERCISES 71

Find the indicated square or square root of the following when possible. When not possible, tell what change in the expression would make it possible.

1. $(3ab^3)^2$.

2. $(-2x^2y^2)^2$.

3. $(-9ac^2d)^2$.

4. $(\frac{1}{2}am^3r)^2$.

5. $(-\frac{1}{3}x^3y^4z)^2$.

6. $(11m^4n^5x)^2$.

7. $(x^3y^4z^5)^2$.

8. $(-20x^5y^4)^2$.

9. $\sqrt{16x^4y^6}$.

10. $\sqrt{25m^4n^6}$.

11. $\sqrt{13a^6z^4}$.

12. $\sqrt{256x^8y^{10}}$.

13. $\sqrt{9a^7b^2}$.

14. $\sqrt{49a^6b^4z^6}$.

15. $\sqrt{576x^4y^2}$.

16. $\sqrt{-16x^6z^4}$.

17. $\sqrt{x^6y^8z^4}$.

18. $\sqrt{3s^2y^6}$.

19. $\sqrt{\pi^2R^2r^2}$.

20. $\sqrt{\left(\frac{\pi}{2}\right)^2 D^2d^2}$.

21. $\sqrt{\left(\frac{W}{2}\right)^2 h^6z^2}$.

229. The square of a binomial.—By multiplication

$$(a+b)^2 = a^2 + 2ab + b^2,$$
$$(a-b)^2 = a^2 - 2ab + b^2.$$

Here a and b are general numbers, so we may use the statements as formulas to find the square of the sum or the difference of any two numbers. These formulas may be translated into words as follows:

(1) *The square of the sum of two numbers equals the square of the first plus twice the product of the first by the second plus the square of the second.*

(2) *The square of the difference of two numbers equals the square of the first minus twice the product of the first by the second plus the square of the second.*

The use of these principles will save much work in multiplication.

Example 1. Find the value of $(cd+e)^2$.

The square of the first term $= (cd)^2 = c^2d^2$.

Twice the product of the first by the second $= 2(cd)e = 2cde$.

The square of the second term $= e^2$.

$$\therefore (cd+e)^2 = c^2d^2 + 2cde + e^2.$$

Example 2. $(2a+b^2)^2 = 4a^2 + 4ab^2 + b^4$.

Example 3. $(2x^2-3y^3)^2 = 4x^4 - 12x^2y^3 + 9y^6$.

EXERCISES 72

Write the products of the following without actual multiplication, and then test by actual multiplication.

1. $(m+2)^2$.

2. $(a+2b)^2$.

3. $(x+2y)^2$.

4. $(3x+y)^2$.

5. $(x^2+4)^2$.

6. $(2x^2-3)^2$.

7. $(2x-7)^2$.

8. $(ax^2-4y)^2$.

9. $(3ax-4y)^2$.   *Ans.* $9a^2x^2-24axy+16y^2$.
10. $(2a^2y^3-3y)^2$.   *Ans.* $4a^4y^6-12a^2y^4+9y^2$.

230. Factors of a trinomial square.—A *trinomial square* is a trinomial that is the square of a binomial.

Thus, $a^2+2ab+b^2$ is a trinomial square because it is the square of the binomial $a+b$. Its factors then are evidently $(a+b)(a+b)$. Likewise, the factors of $a^2-2ab+b^2$ are $(a-b)(a-b)$. The factors of $4x^2-12x+9$ are $(2x-3)$ $(2x-3)$.

It should be carefully noticed that a trinomial square has two positive terms, each of which is the square of a monomial; and one term, either positive or negative, that is twice the product of the square roots of the other two terms. If this term is positive the factors are sums, and if negative the factors are differences.

Thus, $9a^4-24a^2y^2+16y^4$ is a trinomial square, for $9a^4$ and $16y^4$ are each positive and squares of the monomials $3a^2$ and $4y^2$ respectively; and $24a^2y^2$ is twice the product of these square roots. The factors are $(3a^2-4y^2)(3a^2-4y^2)$.

Since by definition the **square root** of a number is one of its two equal factors, the square root of a trinomial square is one of its two equal factors.

EXERCISES 73

Determine which of the following are trinomial squares. Factor and find the square root when possible.

1. $x^2+2xy+y^2$.
2. $4x^2-4xy+y^2$.
3. $9x^4+18x^2y^2+9y^2$.
4. $16x^4-8x^2y+y^2$.
5. x^2-2x-1.
6. x^4+4x^2+4.
7. x^2+3x+9.
8. $25x^{10}+10x^5+1$.
9. $14x^2+6x+8$.

10. $25b^2+16x^2-50bx$.
11. $4x^4+y^4+4x^2y^2$.
12. $225a^2-270a+81$.
13. $\frac{1}{4}x^2+\frac{1}{3}xy+\frac{1}{9}y^2$.
14. $81a^4-108a^2y^2+36y^4$.
15. $4x^2y^2+4xy+1$.
16. $25z^4-70yz^2+49y^2$.
17. $100+a^2+20a$.
18. $16x^2+25y^2-50xy$.

231. The product of the sum of two numbers by the difference of the same two numbers.—By multiplication

$$(a+b)(a-b)=a^2-b^2.$$

Since a and b are general numbers, we may use this statement as a formula and so write at once, without actual multiplication, the product of the sum and the difference of any two numbers. The formula may be translated into words as follows:

The product of the sum and the difference of two numbers equals the difference of their squares.

Example 1. $(2c+3b)(2c-3b) = 4c^2-9b^2$.

Example 2. $(16+2)(16-2) = 16^2-2^2 = 256-4 = 252$.

Example 3. $102 \times 98 = (100+2)(100-2) = 10{,}000-4 = 9996$.

EXERCISES 74

Find the product of the following without actual multiplication and test by actual multiplication·

1. $(2+2y)(2-2y)$.

2. $(3x-y)(3x+y)$.

3. $(12x-13)(12x+13)$.

4. $(16x^2y-2)(16x^2y+2)$.

5. $(x^3+y^3)(x^3-y^3)$.

6. $(3t^2-4t)(3t^2+4t)$.

7. $(4x^2y^3+1)(4x^2y^3-1)$.

8. $(2 \cdot 3^3-5)(2 \cdot 3^3+5)$.

9. $[a+(b+1)][a-(b+1)]$.

10. $[(x+y)+z][(x+y)-z]$.

11. $(2c+d+e)(2c+d-e)$.

Suggestion. This may be written

$$[(2c+d)+e][(2c+d)-e] = (2c+d)^2-e^2 = 4c^2+4cd+d^2-e^2. \quad Ans.$$

12. $(a+b-2c)(a+b+2c)$.

13. $(x^2-y^2-xy)(x^2+y^2+xy)$.

Suggestion. This may be written

$$[x^2-(y^2+xy)][x^2+(y^2+xy)] = x^4-(y^2+xy)^2 = \text{etc.}$$

14. $(x^2-y^2-xy)(x^2-y^2+xy)$.

15. $(7+x+y)(7-x-y)$.

16. $(3-x+y)(3+x+y)$.

Suggestion. This may be written

$$[(3+y)-x][(3+y)+x] = (3+y)^2-x^2 = \text{etc.}$$

17. $(a-y-z)(a-y+z)$.

18. $[4a-(x-2b)][4a+(x-2b)]$.

19. $(11x^3y-z^4)(11x^3y+z^4)$.

20. $(30x^2y^3+3xy)(30x^2y^3-3xy)$.

21. 95×105.

22. 995×1005.

23. $64+56$.

24. 75×85.

25. 505×495.

26. 706×694.

232. Factors of the difference of two squares.—From a consideration of the preceding it is easily seen that the difference of two squares can be factored into two binomial factors that are, respectively, the sum and the difference of the square roots of these squares.

Example 1. $4-a^2 = (2+a)(2-a)$.

Example 2. $16a^4-9y^2 = (4a^2+3y)(4a^2-3y)$.

Example 3. $(a+b)^2-2^2 = (a+b+2)(a+b-2)$.

Example 4. $a^2-b^2+2bc-c^2 = a^2-(b^2-2bc+c^2) = a^2-(b-c)^2 = (a+b-c)(a-b+c)$.

EXERCISES 75

Factor the following and test by multiplication:

1. $4-x^2$.	**2.** $16-4y^2$.	**3.** a^2-1.
4. $1-9x^4$.	**5.** $81a^2-16b^2$.	**6.** 7^2-5^2.
7. $225-64a^2$.	**8.** $36a^4-49b^2$.	**9.** $4a^2b^2-25a^2c^2$.
10. $64a^4b^6-100c^2d^2$.	**11.** $3^2a^4-2^2b^4$.	**12.** $2^2 \cdot 3^4 d^2-5^2c^2$.

13. $(x+y)^2-z^2$.   Ans. $(x+y+z)(x+y-z)$.
14. $(a+b)^2-64$.   Ans. $(a+b+8)(a+b-8)$.
15. $x^2+y^2-2xy-z^2$.   Ans. $(x-y+z)(x-y-z)$.
16. $25-(a+b)^2$.   Ans. $(5+a+b)(5-a-b)$.
17. $25-(a-b)^2$.   Ans. $(5+a-b)(5-a+b)$.
18. $P^2-4PC+4C^2-C^2$.   Ans. $(P-C)(P-3C)$.
19. $(3a-b)^2-(2a+2b)^2$.   Ans. $(5a+b)(a-3b)$.
20. $(2x-7)^2-(3x-1)^2$.   Ans. $(5x-8)(-x-6)$.

233. The product of two binomials having one common term.—By multiplication, we find the following products:

(1) $(a+2)(a+3) = a^2+5a+6$.
(2) $(a-2)(a-3) = a^2-5a+6$.
(3) $(a+2)(a-3) = a^2-a\ -6$.
(4) $(a-2)(a+3) = a^2+a\ -6$.
(5) $(a+b)(a+c) = a^2+(b+c)a+bc$.

From an inspection of these, the truth of the following statement can be seen:

The product of two binomials, having one common term and the other terms unlike, is a trinomial consisting of the square of the common term, the algebraic sum of the unlike terms times the common term, and the product of the unlike terms.

Thus, in (1) above, the common term is a and the unlike terms are 2 and 3. The square of the common term is a^2. The algebraic sum of the unlike terms is $2+3=5$, and this times the common term is 5 times $a=5a$. The product of the unlike terms is $2\times3=6$. Hence the result $(a+2)(a+3)=a^2+5a+6$.

Likewise in (3), the square of the common term is a^2. The algebraic sum of the unlike terms is the sum of $+2$ and -3, or -1. This times the common term, a, is $-a$. The product of the unlike terms is $2\times-3=-6$. Hence the result $(a+2)(a-3)=a^2-a-6$.

EXERCISES 76

Find the products of the following without actual multiplication and test by actual multiplication:

1. $(x+3)(x+4)$.	**2.** $(x-4)(x+3)$.	**3.** $(x-3)(x+4)$.
4. $(x-3)(x-4)$.	**5.** $(x+7)(x+8)$.	**6.** $(x-7)(x-8)$.
7. $(x+7)(x-8)$.	**8.** $(x-7)(x+8)$.	**9.** $(2n-4)(2n+5)$.

10. $(2n+4)(2n+5)$. **11.** $(x+1)(x-11)$.
12. $(r-16)(r+17)$. **13.** $(x^2+6)(x^2-5)$.
14. $(2x+7)(2x-18)$. **15.** $(5a+3)(5a-6)$.
16. $(6+8)(6-5)$. **17.** $(xy+2)(xy-3)$.
18. $(3+xy)(4+xy)$. **19.** $(2x+3)(4x+3)$.
20. $(3x-4)(3x+9)$.

234. To factor a trinomial into two binomials with one common term.—By a careful study of the preceding exercises, we may determine how to proceed in factoring such trinomials as the products in those exercises. The method of factoring those forms will best be seen by considering examples.

Example 1. Factor $a^2+9a+20$.

This has one term, a^2, that is a perfect square; a, the square root of this, is to be the common term of the factors, if there are any. The unlike terms of the factors must have a product of $+20$ and a sum of $+9$. By inspection we see that $+5$ and $+4$ have such a product and sum. Hence the factors of $a^2+9a+20$ are $(a+5)(a+4)$.

Example 2. Factor a^2-a-20.

As before, the common term is a. The unlike terms have a product of -20 and a sum of -1. The product being $-$, one of the terms is $-$ and one $+$. The sum being $-$, shows that the larger in absolute value is $-$. This gives -5 and $+4$ as the numbers.

Hence $a^2-a-20=(a-5)(a+4)$.

235. Other forms.—Many trinomials that appear to be of the kind here considered cannot be factored in this way.

For instance, x^2+7x+5 cannot be factored as here, for we can find no integral numbers which have a sum of 7 and a product of 5.

There is still another class of trinomials, those where the binomial factors have no common term, and many other expressions which can be factored. These will not be taken up here, either because they are too difficult or because they are of less use than the ones considered.

EXERCISES 77

Factor the following if possible; if not, change a term so that they may be factored. Test your work by multiplication.

1. $b^2-7b+12$. **2.** $b^2+11b+30$. **3.** c^2-c-30.
4. x^2+2x-8. **5.** $a^2-3x-10$. **6.** $x^2+15x+56$.

7. $y^2 - y - 56$.

8. $a^2 + 3a + 14$.

9. $x^2 - 15x + 56$.

10. $r^2 + 20r + 64$.

11. $x^2 y^2 + 3xy + 2$.

12. $x^2 - 3x + 16$.

13. $a^2 + 9a - 10$.

14. $a^2 - a - 132$.

15. $a^2 - a - 72$.

16. $x^2 + 6a - 72$.

17. $x^2 - x - 90$.

18. $x^2 + 15x - 34$.

19. $x^2 - 12x - 45$.

20. $a^2 + 4a - 21$.

21. $a^2 - 7a - 33$.

22. $n^2 + 15n - 16$.

23. $n^2 + 13n + 36$.

24. $n^2 - 6n - 60$.

25. $a^2 - 11a - 60$.

26. $a^2 + 10a - 24$.

27. $a^2 + a - 42$.

28. $a^2 b^2 - 16ab + 15$.

29. $n^4 - 4n^2 + 18$.

30. $x^2 - 5xy - 84y^2$.

31. $x^2 + 12xy + 27y^2$.

32. $1 + 5x - 14x^2$.

33. $a^2 - 14a + 40$.

34. $a^2 + 3ab - 54b^2$.

35. $1 - 13y - 68y^2$.

36. $x^2 - (a+b)x + ab$.

37. $x^2 - 7xy + 8y^2$.

38. $(m-n)^2 + 7(m-n) + 12$.

39. $(x+y)^2 - 5(x+y) - 14$.

Factor the following expressions by the methods given:

40. $x^2 y^4 - 16$.

41. $xy^2 - 4x$.

42. $xy^2 + 15xy - 34x$.

43. $a^2 y^6 - b^2 y^2$.

44. $bx^3 - a^2 bx$.

45. $3ax^2 - 18ax - 180a$.

46. $100x^4 - y^6$.

47. $a^8 b^4 - c^4 d^2$.

48. $9x^2 + 4y^2 + 12xy$.

49. $64x^9 - 16x^7$.

50. $16a^4 - 16x^4$.

51. $64x^8 + 16x^7 + x^6$.

52. $(x+y)^2 + 8(x+y) + 16$.

53. $(b-c)^2 + 16(b-c) + 64$.

54. $a^2 - 2a + 1 - x^2 y^2$.

55. $a^2 (b-c)^2 + 8a(b-c) + 16$.

56. $x^2 - 2y - y^2 - 1$.

57. $(x-y)^2 - 2ac(x-y) + a^2 c^2$.

The following are some of the answers of the above exercises. They should be consulted only after the factors are found.

4. $(x+4)(x-2)$.

12. No factors.

15. $(a+8)(a-9)$.

28. $(ab-15)(ab-1)$.

31. $(x+3y)(x+9y)$.

32. $(1+7x)(1-2x)$.

36. $(x-a)(x-b)$.

38. $(m-n+4)(m-n+3)$

44. $bx(x+a)(x-a)$.

45. $3a(x^2 - 6x - 60)$.

53. $(b-c+8)(b-c+8)$.

56. $(x+y+1)(x-y-1)$.

CHAPTER XXVI

EQUATIONS

236. If an equation has indicated multiplications and signs of grouping, it is usually best to perform the multiplications and remove the signs of grouping before proceeding with the solution of the equation.

Example 1. Find the value of c from

$$4c+3[2c-4(c-2)]=72-6c.$$

Solution.

(1) Given equation, $4c+3[2c-4(c-2)]=72-6c.$
(2) Simplifying, $4c+3[2c-4c+8]=72-6c.$
(3) Simplifying, $4c+6c-12c+24=72-6c.$
(4) Transposing, $4c+6c-12c+6c=72-24.$
(5) Collecting terms, $4c=48.$
(6) Dividing by the coefficient of c, $c=12.$

Test, $48+3[24-4(12-2)]=72-72,$ or $0=0.$

Example 2. Solve for x:

$$(1+3x)^2=(5-x)^2+4(1-x)(3-2x).$$

Solution.

(1) Given equation, $(1+3x)^2=(5-x)^2+4(1-x)(3-2x).$

(2) Removing parentheses, $1+6x+9x^2=25-10x+x^2+12-20x+8x^2.$

(3) Transposing, $9x^2-x^2-8x^2+6x+10x+20x=25+12-1.$

(4) Collecting terms, $36x=36.$

(5) Dividing by 36, $x=1.$

Test, $(1+3)^2=(5-1)^2+4(1-1)(3-2),$
         or $4^2=4^2+0,$ or $16=16.$

EXERCISES 78

1. $7x-5=x-23.$ *Ans.* $-3.$
2. $5x-12=6x-8.$ *Ans.* $-4.$
3. $7x+19=5x+7.$ *Ans.* $-6.$
4. $2x-(5x+5)=7.$ *Ans.* $-4.$
5. $3(x+1)=-5(x-1).$ *Ans.* $\frac{1}{4}.$

6. $7(x-18)=3(x-14)$.   *Ans.* 21.

7. $2(x-1)-3(x-2)+4(x-3)+2=0$.   *Ans.* 2.

8. $14x+20-12=-20x+35x$.   *Ans.* 8.

9. $2(x-1)+3(x-2)+4(x-3)=0$.   *Ans.* $2\frac{8}{9}$.

10. $5(2x+1)-7=3(2x-7)+51$.   *Ans.* 8.

11. $3(x+4)(x-2)-5=3(x+5)(x-3)+x$.   *Ans.* 16.

12. $(x+2)^2-x^2=x-5$.   *Ans.* -3.

13. $(x-4)(x+4)=(x-6)(x+5)+25$.   *Ans.* 11.

14. $3(x+1)-2(2x+5)=6(3-x)$.   *Ans.* 5.

15. $11a=3(x-2a)-5(2x-2a)$.   *Ans.* $-a$.

16. $3(2b-4x)-(x-b)=-6b$.   *Ans.* b.

17. $5(4x-3a)-6(3x-2a)=3a$.   *Ans.* $3a$.

Find values of a in exercises 18 to 24.

18. $3+(a+4)^2=(a+3)^2-4a+17$.   *Ans.* $\frac{7}{6}$.

19. $2.5a-6.75=1.25a-3$.   *Ans.* 3.

20. $8a-12=6a+4$.   *Ans.* 8.

21. $37a-(4+7)=41a+25$.   *Ans.* -9.

22. $12.75a+6.25=7.25a+17.25$.   *Ans.* 2.

23. $7(25-a)-2a=2(3a-25)$.   *Ans.* 15.

24. $5a-17+3a-5=6a-7-8a+115$.   *Ans.* 13.

Find values of y in exercises 25 to 31.

25. $2(y-1)-3(y-2)=4(3-y)-2$.   *Ans.* 2.

26. $5y-6(y+1)-7(y+2)-8(y+3)=0$.   *Ans.* $-2\frac{3}{4}$.

27. $(y+1)(2y+1)=(y+3)(2y+3)-14$.   *Ans.* 1.

28. $(y+1)^2-(y^2-1)=y(2y+1)-2(y+2)(y+1)+20$.   *Ans.* 2.

29. $6(y^2-3y+2)-2(y^2-1)=4(y+1)(y+2)-24$.   *Ans.* 1.

30. $2y-5[3y-7(4y-9)]=66$.   *Ans.* 3.

31. $3(5-6y)-5(y-5[1-3y+15])=23$.   *Ans.* 4.

Find values of x in exercises 32 and 33.

32. $84+(x+4)(x-3)(x+5)=(x+1)(x+2)(x+3)$.   *Ans.* 1.

33. $(x+1)(x+2)(x+6)=x^3+9x^2+4(7x-1)$.   *Ans.* 2.

34. Find two numbers whose difference is 25 and whose sum is $4\frac{1}{5}$ times their difference.   *Ans.* 40 and 65.

35. A rectangular field is 5 rods longer than it is wide. If it was 2 rods wider and 3 rods shorter it would contain 4 square rods less. Find dimensions of the rectangle.   *Ans.* 13 rd. long, 8 rd. wide.

Solution. Let $x=$ number of rods in width.

Then $x+5=$ number of rods in length,

and $x(x+5)=$ number of square rods in field.

Also $x+2=$ number of rods in width of second field,

and $x+2=$ number of rods in length of second field.

Then $(x+2)(x+2)=$ number of square rods in second field

$$\therefore x(x+5)-(x+2)(x+2)=4.$$
$$x^2+5x-x^2-4x-4=4.$$
$$x^2-x^2+5x-4x=4+4.$$
$$x=8.$$
$$x+5=13.$$

36. The difference between the squares of two consecutive numbers is 25. What are the numbers? *Ans.* 12 and 13.

37. The difference between the squares of two consecutive even numbers is 84. What are the numbers? *Ans.* 20 and 22.

38. The height of a flagstaff is unknown; but it is noticed that the flag rope, which is 4 ft. longer than the staff, when stretched out just reaches the ground at a point 25 ft. from the foot of the staff. If the ground is level, find the height of the staff. *Ans.* 76⅛ ft.

Suggestion. Fig. 198 shows the rope stretched to a point 25 ft. from the foot of the staff. This makes a right triangle which has the rope as hypotenuse. We then have the equation

$$(x+4)^2 = 25^2 + x^2.$$

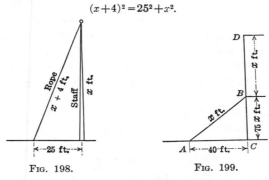

FIG. 198.   FIG. 199.

39. A flagstaff, *CD*, Fig. 199, 75 ft. high, breaks at point *B* and end *D* strikes at *A*, a distance of 40 ft. from *C*. Find the length *BD* that was broken off. *Ans.* 48⅛ ft.

Suggestion. Let $BD = x$, then $CB = 75 - x$.

40. A piece of sheet iron containing 625 sq. in. is bent into a cylinder 9 in. in diameter. How high is the cylinder? What is its volume? *Ans.* 22.1 in.; 1406+ in.³

41. At what rate simple interest will $75.00 amount to $106.50 in 6 years? *Ans.* 7%.

237. Equations solved by aid of factoring.—The equations considered so far have reduced to a form in which a certain number of times the unknown equaled some number. Thus, $6x = 12$ is such a form. They are called **simple equations.**

All equations do not reduce to such a form as this. For instance, when the equation has been reduced, we may have an equation in which the *square* of the unknown equals some number. Thus, $x^2 = 5$ is such a form. Such an equation is called a **pure quadratic equation.**

Again, when the equation is simplified and reduced, we may have a form containing the *square* and the *first power* of the unknown equaling some number.   Thus, $x^2 - 5x = 24$ is such a form.   Such an equation is called an **affected quadratic equation.**

Some of these forms of equations, together with certain other forms, can be solved by the *aid of factoring*.

Example 1.   Solve the equation $x^2 - 5x + 6 = 0$.

Discussion.   This equation puts the question: For what values of x does $x^2 - 5x + 6$ equal zero? If we factor the expression in the first member we get $(x-2)(x-3) = 0$. The question now is: For what values of x does the product $(x-2)(x-3)$ have the value zero? We know that the product of two factors is zero if either, or both, factors are zero and not otherwise.   Hence the product is zero, if $x - 2 = 0$, or if $x - 3 = 0$.   Thus, the solution of $x^2 - 5x + 6 = 0$ depends upon the solution of the two simple equations, $x - 2 = 0$ and $x - 3 = 0$. These give the values 2 and 3 for x.

That these are the values of x may be tested by substituting each one separately in the equation
$$x^2 - 5x + 6 = 0.$$
Substituting $x = 2$, gives $4 - 10 + 6 = 0$, or $0 = 0$.
Substituting $x = 3$, gives $9 - 15 + 6 = 0$, or $0 = 0$.

The values of the unknown number that satisfy the equation, that is, answer the question, are called **roots** of the equation.

A quadratic equation having one unknown letter always has two roots.

Example 1.   Solve the equation $x^2 - 25 = 0$.

First solution.

(1) Given equation, $x^2 - 25 = 0$.
(2) Factoring, $(x+5)(x-5) = 0$.
(3) Putting each factor equal to zero,
$$x + 5 = 0 \text{ and } x - 5 = 0.$$
(4) Transposing, $x = -5$ and $x = 5$.

Test for $x = -5$, $25 - 25 = 0$.
Test for $x = 5$, $25 - 25 = 0$.

Second solution.

(1) Given equation, $x^2 - 25 = 0$.
(2) Transposing, $x^2 = 25$.
(3) Taking the square root of each member of the equation,
$$x = \pm 5.$$

Here the sign $\pm$ is read "plus or minus." It means that 5 is a plus as well as a minus quantity. It should be noted here that we are saying that 25 has the two square roots, $+5$ and -5. Either of these is the square root of 25, for $(+5)^2 = 25$ and also $(-5)^2 = 25$. Hence both fulfill the definition of a square root, that is, one of the two equal factors into which a number may be divided.

Any positive number has two square roots, one positive and one negative, both equal in absolute value.

Example 3. Solve $(x+1)(x-3)(2x-16) = 0$.

Equating each factor to zero,
$$x+1 = 0, \ x-3 = 0, \text{ and } 2x-16 = 0.$$
Solving these, $\qquad x = -1, \ x = 3, \text{ and } x = 8.$

We have the following rule of procedure when solving an equation by the aid of factoring:

RULE. (1) *Simplify the equation as much as possible.*

(2) *Transpose all terms to the first member of the equation.*

(3) *Factor the expression in the first member.*

(4) *Equate each factor to zero.*

(5) *Solve each of these equations.*

EXERCISES 79

Solve the following by the aid of factoring:

1. $(x-4)(x-3) = 0$.
2. $(x-5)(x+6) = 0$.
3. $(x-2)(x+1)(x+3) = 0$.
4. $(x+1)(x-5)(x-3) = 0$.
5. $(2x-1)(x+4) = 0$.
6. $x(x-2)(3x+5) = 0$.
7. $x^2 - 16 = 0$.
8. $(x^2-9)(x^2-36) = 0$.
9. $x^2 - 16 = 48$.   *Ans.* 8 and -8.
10. $x^2 - x = 56$.   *Ans.* 8 and -7.
11. $(2x+1)(x+3) = x^2 - 9$.   *Ans.* -3 and -4.

Suggestion. It is necessary first to clear of parentheses, transpose, and unite before factoring.

Clearing of parentheses, $\quad 2x^2 + 7x + 3 = x^2 - 9$.
Transposing, $\qquad\qquad\quad 2x^2 - x^2 + 7x + 3 + 9 = 0$.
Collecting terms, $\qquad\quad\ x^2 + 7x + 12 = 0$.
Factoring, $\qquad\qquad\qquad (x+3)(x+4) = 0$.

12. If 24 is added to the square of a number, the sum equals 10 times the number. Find the number.   *Ans.* 4 or 6.

13. If 78 be subtracted from the square of a number, the difference equals 7 times the number. Find the number.   *Ans.* 13 or -6.

14. If 3 is added to a number, the square of the sum is 9 more than 13 times the number. What is the number?   *Ans.* 0 or 7.

19

15. A rectangle is 8 in. longer than it is wide. Find the dimensions, if the area is 240 sq. in.   *Ans.* **12** in. by **20** in.

16. Find the dimensions of a rectangle that is 4 rods longer than it is wide if, when the length is increased by 6 rods and the width by 4 rods, the area is doubled.   *Ans.* **10** rd. by **14** rd.

17. The base of a triangle is 3 in. longer than the altitude, and the area is 44 sq. in. Find the length of the base and the altitude.

Ans. **11** in. and **8** in.

18. The altitude of a triangle is 3 times the base, and the area is $37\frac{1}{2}$ sq. in. Find the length of the base and the altitude.

Ans. **5** in. and **15** in.

238. Formulas.—A formula as given usually stands solved for one letter in terms of several others. For instance, formula **[34]** is $T = ph + 2A$. Here T is stated in terms of p, h, and A.

It often happens that one wishes to express, say, h in terms of T, p, and A. To do this it is only necessary to solve the formula as an equation, and find the value of the particular letter desired in terms of the others.

Example. Solve the formula $T = ph + 2A$ for each of the other letters.

Solution. Here there are three other letters than T, and we will solve for p, h, and A in turn.

(1) Given equation, $T = ph + 2A$.

(2) Transposing, $-ph = -T + 2A$.

(3) Dividing by the coefficient of p which is $-h$, and indicating the division, since it cannot be performed,

$$p = \frac{T - 2A}{h}. \ Ans.$$

(4) Solving (2) for h, since it is properly transposed,

$$h = \frac{T - 2A}{p}. \ Ans.$$

(5) To solve for A transpose (1), $-2A = -T + ph$.

(6) Dividing by the coefficient of A, $A = \frac{T - ph}{2}. \ Ans.$

EXERCISES 80

In the following, the numbers in the brackets are the numbers of the formulas as given in previous chapters, where their meaning can be found. The ability to do such problems as these is very important.

1. **[32]** $A = \pi ab.$ Solve for a and b.   *Ans.* $\frac{A}{\pi b}$; $\frac{A}{\pi a}$.

2. **[33]** $S = ph.$ Solve for p and h.   *Ans.* $\frac{S}{h}$; $\frac{S}{p}$.

3. [42] $S = 2\pi rh$. Solve for r.   *Ans.* $\dfrac{S}{2\pi h}$.

4. [43] $V = \pi r^2 h$. Solve for h.   *Ans.* $\dfrac{V}{\pi r^2}$.

5. [46] $V = \pi R^2 h - \pi r^2 h$. Solve for h.   *Ans.* $\dfrac{V}{\pi(R^2 - r^2)}$.

6. [59] $A = 4\pi^2 Rr$. Solve for R.   *Ans.* $\dfrac{A}{4\pi^2 r}$.

7. [57] $Z = 2\pi rh$. Solve for r.   *Ans.* $\dfrac{Z}{2\pi h}$.

8. Using the answer of exercise 7, find the radius of a sphere on which a zone of altitude 3 ft. has an area of 32 sq. ft.   *Ans.* $1.698-$ ft.

9. [35] $T = 6a^2$. Solve for a^2 and then for a.   *Ans.* $\dfrac{T}{6}$; $\sqrt{\dfrac{T}{6}}$.

10. Using the second answer of exercise 9, find the edge of a cube whose total surface area is 3258 ft.^{2} *Ans.* $23.302+$ ft.

11. [60] $V = 2\pi^2 Rr^2$. Solve for r.   *Ans.* $\sqrt{\dfrac{V}{2\pi^2 R}}$.

12. [55] $S = 4\pi r^2$. Solve for r.   *Ans.* $\sqrt{\dfrac{S}{4\pi}}$.

13. Using the answer of exercise 12, find the radius of a sphere that has a surface area of 2756 ft.^{2} *Ans.* $14.82-$ ft.

14. [43] $V = \pi r^2 h$. Solve for r.   *Ans.* $\sqrt{\dfrac{V}{\pi h}}$.

15. Using the answer of exercise 14, find the radius of a right circular cylinder whose altitude is 16 in. and volume 2674 in.^{3} *Ans.* $7.294-$ in.

16. Disregarding the resistance of the air, $v = \sqrt{2gh}$ is a formula that gives the velocity in feet per second a body will have after falling from a height of h feet. Solve this for h and get a formula for the height to which a body will rise if thrown upward with a velocity of v feet per second.   *Ans.* $h = \dfrac{v^2}{2g}$.

Suggestion. First square both members of the equation, which gives $v^2 = 2gh$.

17. Use the formulas of exercise 16 and find (1) the velocity a stone will have after falling 125 ft., (2) the height to which a stone will go if thrown upward with a velocity of 200 ft. per second. ($g = 32.2$.)
     Ans. $v = 89.72+$ ft. per second; $h = 621.1$ ft.

18. The formula $v_t = v_0 + 32.2t$ gives the velocity that a falling body will have.

     $t =$ time in seconds the body has been falling,

     $v_0 =$ velocity in feet per second the body has at the start, that is, v_0 is the initial velocity,

     $v_t =$ velocity in feet per second after t seconds.

Solve for v_0 and for t.   *Ans.* $t = \dfrac{v_t - v_0}{32.2}$.

19. Using the formulas of exercise 18, find (1) the time for a falling body to have a velocity of 600 ft. per second if it started with a velocity of 40 ft. per second; (2) the initial velocity in order that a falling body may have a velocity of 340 ft. per second after falling 5 seconds.

Ans. 17.39+ seconds; 179 ft. per second.

20. Use the formula given in exercise 5 and find the height of a hollow cylinder having outer and inner radii of 14 in. and 10 in. respectively, that it may have a volume of 4.211 cu. ft. *Ans.* 24.13− in.

21. Given the formula $V = \frac{1}{3}\pi r^2 h = 1.0472\, r^2 h$, for finding the volume of a circular cone, solve for h and for r. *Ans.* $\dfrac{V}{1.0472 r^2}$; $\sqrt{\dfrac{V}{1.0472 h}}$.

22. Using the formulas of exercise 21, find (1) the altitude of a circular cone having a volume of 800 cu. in. and a radius of 8 in.; (2) the radius of the base of a circular cone having a volume of 456 cu. in. and an altitude of 10 in. *Ans.* 11.94− in.; 6.6− in.

23. In the formula given in the answer to exercise 35, page 240, $A = td + b(s+n)$. Solve this for t, d, b, s, and n successively.

Ans. $t = \dfrac{A - b(s+n)}{d}$; $s = \dfrac{A - td - bn}{b}$.

24. Using the formulas of exercise 23, find (1) t when $A = 3.35$ in.^{2}, $b = 2.04$ in., $s = 0.22$ in., $n = 0.56$ in., and $d = 8$ in.; (2) b when $d = 10$ in., $t = 0.24$ in., $n = 0.63$ in., $s = 0.24$ in., and $A = 4.45$ in.^{2}; (3) s when $d = 5$ in., $t = 0.19$ in., $b = 1.56$ in., $n = 0.45$ in., and $A = 1.95$ in.^{2}

Ans. 0.22 in.; 2.36 in.; 0.19 in.

25. In finding the area of a trapezoid, $2A = (b_1 + b_2)h$. Find b_1 if $A = 400$ in.^{2}, $b_2 = 15$ in., and $h = 20$ in. *Ans.* 25 in.

26. Find the volume of a sphere that has a surface of 201.0624 sq. in., the formula for the volume of a sphere being $V = \frac{4}{3}\pi r^3$. Use formula of exercise 12. *Ans.* 268.08 cu. in.

27. In reckoning simple interest, $A = prt + p$, where $A =$ amount, $p =$ principal, $t =$ time in years, and $r =$ rate per cent. Solve for each letter. *Ans.* $p = \dfrac{A}{1 + rt}$; $t = \dfrac{A - p}{pr}$; $r = \dfrac{A - p}{pt}$.

28. Using the formulas of exercise 27, find (1) t when $p = \$250$, $r = 6\%$, and $A = \$300$; (2) r when $t = 3$ years, $p = \$328$, and $A = \$377.20$; (3) p when $A = \$500$, $t = 5$ years, and $r = 4\%$.

Ans. $3\frac{1}{3}$ years; 5%; $\$416.67$.

CHAPTER XXVII

FRACTIONS

239. The same names and terms are used when referring to fractions in algebra as are used in fractions in arithmetic, and these terms have the same meanings. The same principles are applied and the same operations performed as in arithmetic.

Here only those processes will be considered that are necessary for the understanding of what follows.

When in doubt about an operation in algebra, carry out a similar operation using numerical numbers, and from this determine what the operation with the algebraic expressions should be.

REDUCTION OF A FRACTION TO ITS LOWEST TERMS

240. A fraction is in its lowest terms when there is no factor common to both numerator and denominator.

Example 1. Reduce $\frac{105}{120}$ to its lowest terms.

Process. $\quad \frac{105}{120} = \frac{3 \cdot 5 \cdot 7}{3 \cdot 5 \cdot 8} = \frac{7}{8}.$

Here each term of the fraction is factored and then the common factors are cancelled. We handle an algebraic fraction in the same way.

Example 2. Reduce $\dfrac{6x^2y^3}{12x^4y^4}$ to it lowest terms.

Process. $\quad \dfrac{6x^2y^3}{12x^4y^4} = \dfrac{2 \cdot 3 \cdot x \cdot x \cdot y \cdot y \cdot y}{2 \cdot 2 \cdot 3 \cdot x \cdot x \cdot x \cdot x \cdot y \cdot y \cdot y \cdot y} = \dfrac{1}{2x^2y}.$

Example 3. Reduce $\dfrac{x^2 - y^2}{x^2 + 2xy + y^2}$ to its lowest terms.

Process. $\quad \dfrac{x^2 - y^2}{x^2 + 2xy + y^2} = \dfrac{(x+y)(x-y)}{(x+y)(x+y)} = \dfrac{x-y}{x+y}.$

Example 4. $\quad \dfrac{x^2 + 16x + 63}{x^2 + 4x - 21} = \dfrac{(x+7)(x+9)}{(x+7)(x-3)} = \dfrac{x+9}{x-3}.$

EXERCISES 81

Reduce the following fractions to their lowest terms:

1. $\dfrac{125}{225}$.   *Ans.* $\dfrac{5}{9}$.   2. $\dfrac{144}{288}$.   *Ans.* $\dfrac{1}{2}$.

3. $\dfrac{135}{150}$.   *Ans.* $\dfrac{9}{10}$.   4. $\dfrac{21a^2x^3}{24a^3x^4}$.   *Ans.* $\dfrac{7}{8ax}$.

5. $\dfrac{28a^3x^4}{35a^3x^5}$.   *Ans.* $\dfrac{4}{5x}$.   6. $\dfrac{15b^4xy}{25cx^5y^2}$.   *Ans.* $\dfrac{3b^4}{5cx^4y}$.

7. $\dfrac{110mx^2y^3}{550m^2xy^5}$.   *Ans.* $\dfrac{x}{5my^2}$.   8. $\dfrac{12a^2x^3}{36a^3x^5}$.   *Ans.* $\dfrac{1}{3ax^2}$.

9. $\dfrac{45a^5c^3x^2}{15a^3c^3x}$.   *Ans.* $3a^2x$.

10. $\dfrac{216x^2y^2z^3}{1296x^2y^6z^3}$.   *Ans.* $\dfrac{1}{6y^4}$.

11. $\dfrac{792x^6y^7}{81x^6y^7}$.   *Ans.* $\dfrac{88}{9}$.

12. $\dfrac{(x+y)(x-y)^2}{x(x-y)^2}$.   *Ans.* $\dfrac{x+y}{x}$.

13. $\dfrac{a^2-5a+6}{a^2-7a+10}$.   *Ans.* $\dfrac{a-3}{a-5}$.

14. $\dfrac{n^2+7n-30}{n^2-7n+12}$.   *Ans.* $\dfrac{n+10}{n-4}$.

15. $\dfrac{a(x-y)^3}{(x^2-y^2)(x-y)}$.   *Ans.* $\dfrac{a(x-y)}{x+y}$.

16. $\dfrac{15a^4b+10a^3b^2}{6a^3b^4+4a^2b^5}$.   *Ans.* $\dfrac{5a}{2b^3}$.

17. $\dfrac{a^2-9a+18}{a^2+a-12}$.   *Ans.* $\dfrac{a-6}{a+4}$.

18. $\dfrac{25-a^2}{a^2-11a+30}$.   *Ans.* $\dfrac{5+a}{6-a}$.

19. $\dfrac{9x^2-49y^2}{28xy^2-12x^2y}$.   *Ans.* $\dfrac{3x+7y}{-4xy}$.

20. $\dfrac{a(x+y)+c(x+y)}{x(a+c)+y(a+c)}$.   *Ans.* 1.

21. $\dfrac{x^2-(y-z)^2}{z^2-(x+y)^2}$.   *Ans.* $\dfrac{y-x-z}{x+y+z}$.

22. $\dfrac{ax^2-2ax-8a}{ax^2-ax-6a}$.   *Ans.* $\dfrac{x-4}{x-3}$.

REDUCTION OF FRACTIONS TO COMMON DENOMINATORS

241. In arithmetic, fractions are reduced to a least common denominator before adding, so in literal fractions we change the fractions to fractions having the lowest common denominator before adding them.

The **lowest common denominator**, L. C. D., is the lowest common multiple, L. C. M., of the denominators of the fractions. We must then first consider the finding of the L. C. M. of algebraic expressions.

242. Lowest common multiple.—*Example* 1. Find the L. C. M. of 24, 32, and 40.

First separate into prime factors, and then find a number which contains all the factors of each.

Process. $24 = 2^3 \cdot 3.$

$\qquad 32 = 2^5.$

$\qquad 40 = 2^3 \cdot 5.$

$\qquad \therefore$ L. C. M. $= 2^5 \cdot 3 \cdot 5 = 480.$

Remark. The L. C. M. may also be found by the method of **Art. 19,** but that method is not as easily applied to algebraic expressions.

Example 2. Find the L. C. M. of $12x^2y$, $16xy^3$, and $24x^3y$.

Process. $12x^2y = 2^2 \cdot 3 \cdot x^2 \cdot y.$

$\qquad 16xy^3 = 2^4 \cdot x \cdot y^3.$

$\qquad 24x^3y = 2^3 \cdot 3 \cdot x^3 \cdot y.$

$\qquad \therefore$ L. C. M. $= 2^4 \cdot 3 \cdot x^3 \cdot y^3 = 48x^3y^3.$

The L. C. M. is found by taking each factor the greatest number of times it is found in any expression.

Example 3. Find the L. C. M. of $x^2 + 2xy + y^2$ and $x^2 - y^2$.

Process. $x^2 + 2xy + y^2 = (x+y)^2.$

$\qquad x^2 - y^2 \qquad = (x+y)(x-y).$

$\qquad \therefore$ L. C. M. $\qquad = (x+y)^2(x-y).$

EXERCISES 82

Find the L. C. M. of the following:

1. 72, 288, 64.   *Ans.* 576.

2. 576, 256, 128.   *Ans.* 2304.

3. $5a^3b^2$, $10a^2b^3$, $25a^2b$.   *Ans.* $50a^3b^3$.

4. $4c^2$, $2ab$, $9cd^2$.   *Ans.* $36abc^2d^2$.

5. $x^2 - y^2$, $x^2 - 2xy + y^2$.   *Ans.* $(x-y)^2(x+y)$.

6. $x^2 - 11x + 30$, $x^2 - 12x + 35$.   *Ans.* $(x-5)(x-6)(x-7)$.

7. $a^3 - ab^2$, $(a+b)^2$, $(a-b)^2$.   *Ans.* $a(a+b)^2(a-b)^2$.

8. $a^2b + ab^2$, $a^2 + 2ab + b^2$.   *Ans.* $ab(a+b)^2$.

9. $x^2 + 7x$, $x^2 + 8x + 7$.   *Ans.* $x(x+1)(x+7)$.

10. $a^2 + 3a + 2$, $a^2 - 4$, $a^2 - 1$.   *Ans.* $a^4 - 5a^2 + 4$.

243. Fractions having a L. C. D.—*Example* 1. Change $\frac{9}{16}$, $\frac{7}{24}$, and $\frac{7}{32}$ to equivalent fractions having a L. C. D.

The L. C. D. is found by the method of the preceding article to be 96. Now multiply both numerator and denominator of each fraction by such a number as will make the denominator in each case 96. How is the multiplier in each case found?

Process. $\dfrac{9}{16} = \dfrac{9 \times 6}{16 \times 6} = \dfrac{54}{96}$,

$\dfrac{7}{24} = \dfrac{7 \times 4}{24 \times 4} = \dfrac{28}{96}$,

$\dfrac{17}{32} = \dfrac{17 \times 3}{32 \times 3} = \dfrac{51}{96}$.

Example 2. Change $\dfrac{x}{y-2}$, $\dfrac{z}{y^2+4y-12}$, and $\dfrac{v}{y^2+6y}$ to fractions having a L. C. D.

Process. By the preceding article the L. C. D.
$$= y(y-2)(y+6).$$

$$\frac{x}{y-2} = \frac{x \cdot y(y+6)}{(y-2) \cdot y(y+6)} = \frac{xy^2+6xy}{y^3+4y^2-12y},$$

$$\frac{z}{y^2+4y-12} = \frac{z \cdot y}{(y^2+4y-12) \cdot y} = \frac{yz}{y^3+4y^2-12y},$$

$$\frac{v}{y^2+6y} = \frac{v \cdot (y-2)}{(y^2+6y) \cdot (y-2)} = \frac{vy-2v}{y^3+4y^2-12y}.$$

The multiplier in each case is found by dividing the L. C. D. by the denominator of the fraction. The division is most easily performed by striking out those factors in the L. C. D. which are found in the denominator of the fraction considered. For this reason it is best not to multiply together the factors of the L. C. D. Thus, in the above the L. C. D. is left in the form $y(y-2)(y+6)$ during the process, instead of in the form y^3+4y^2-12y.

EXERCISES 83

Reduce the following to equivalent fractions having a L. C. D.:

1. $\dfrac{7}{26}$, $\dfrac{9}{52}$, $\dfrac{41}{78}$.   *Ans.* $\dfrac{42}{156}$, $\dfrac{27}{156}$, $\dfrac{82}{156}$

2. $\dfrac{3}{4a}$, $\dfrac{4}{6a^2}$, $\dfrac{5}{12a^3}$.   *Ans.* $\dfrac{9a^2}{12a^3}$, $\dfrac{8a}{12a^3}$, $\dfrac{5}{12a^3}$.

3. $\dfrac{2}{a+b}$, $\dfrac{3}{a-b}$.   *Ans.* $\dfrac{2a-2b}{a^2-b^2}$, $\dfrac{3a+3b}{a^2-b^2}$.

4. $\dfrac{a}{x-a}$, $\dfrac{x}{x-a}$, $\dfrac{a^2}{x^2-a^2}$ *Ans.* $\dfrac{ax+a^2}{x^2-a^2}$, $\dfrac{x^2+ax}{x^2-a^2}$, $\dfrac{a^2}{x^2-a^2}$.

5. $\dfrac{3}{a^2+3a+2}$, $\dfrac{5}{a^2-2a-3}$.

Ans. $\dfrac{3a-9}{(a+1)(a+2)(a-3)}$, $\dfrac{5a+10}{(a+1)(a+2)(a-3)}$.

6. $\dfrac{2x}{x-b}, \dfrac{b}{2b-2x}, \dfrac{3x^2}{4(x^2-b^2)}, \dfrac{5b^2}{6(b^2-x^2)}.$

$Ans. \dfrac{24x(x+b)}{12(x^2-b^2)}, \dfrac{-6b(x+b)}{12(x^2-b^2)}, \dfrac{9x^2}{12(x^2-b^2)}, \dfrac{-10b^2}{12(x^2-b^2)}.$

7. $a+x, \dfrac{x^2}{a-x}.$ $\qquad\qquad Ans. \dfrac{a^2-x^2}{a-x}, \dfrac{x^2}{a-x}.$

8. $a-x, a+x, \dfrac{a^2+x^2}{a+x}.$ $\qquad Ans. \dfrac{a^2-x^2}{a+x}, \dfrac{a^2+2ax+x^2}{a+x}, \dfrac{a^2+x^2}{a+x}.$

ADDITION AND SUBTRACTION OF FRACTIONS

244. Fractions can be added or subtracted as in arithmetic, by first reducing them to fractions having a common denominator, and then adding or subtracting the numerators. The result should then be reduced to its lowest terms.

Example 1. Find the sum of $\dfrac{x}{a-x}, \dfrac{a}{a+x},$ and $\dfrac{a^2+x^2}{a^2-x^2}.$

Process. L. C. D. $= a^2-x^2.$

$$\dfrac{x}{a-x} = \dfrac{x(a+x)}{(a-x)(a+x)} = \dfrac{ax+x^2}{a^2-x^2},$$

$$\dfrac{a}{a+x} = \dfrac{a(a-x)}{(a+x)(a-x)} = \dfrac{a^2-ax}{a^2-x^2},$$

$$\dfrac{a^2+x^2}{a^2-x^2} = \dfrac{a^2+x^2}{a^2-x^2}.$$

Adding the numerators, the sum of the fractions is $\dfrac{2a^2+2x^2}{a^2-x^2}.$

Example 2. From $\dfrac{a+x}{a^2-ax}$ take $\dfrac{a+2x}{a^2-x^2}.$

Process. L. C. D. $= a(a+x)(a-x) = a^3-ax^2.$

$$\dfrac{a+x}{a^2-ax} = \dfrac{(a+x)(a+x)}{(a^2-ax)(a+x)} = \dfrac{a^2+2ax+x^2}{a^3-ax^2}.$$

$$\dfrac{a+2x}{a^2-x^2} = \dfrac{(a+2x)a}{(a^2-x^2)a} = \dfrac{a^2+2ax}{a^3-ax^2}.$$

Subtracting the numerator of the second fraction from the numerator of the first, the result is $\dfrac{x^2}{a^3-ax^2}.$

EXERCISES 84

1. to 8. Add the fractions in the preceding set of exercises.

9. Add $\frac{3}{4}, \frac{5}{6}, \frac{7}{8}, \frac{2}{3}.$ $\qquad\qquad Ans. 3\frac{1}{8}.$

10. Add $\dfrac{a}{3}, \dfrac{a}{4}, \dfrac{a}{12}, \dfrac{a}{18}, \dfrac{a}{6}, \dfrac{a}{9}$ $\qquad\qquad Ans. a.$

11. Add $\dfrac{a}{2y}, \dfrac{c-b}{3y}, \dfrac{c+b}{4y}$.   *Ans.* $\dfrac{6a+7c-b}{12y}$.

12. Add $\dfrac{a-3}{3}$ and $\dfrac{5+a}{6}$.   *Ans.* $\dfrac{3a-1}{6}$.

13. Add $\dfrac{m-n}{mn}$ and $\dfrac{n-r}{nr}$.   *Ans.* $\dfrac{m-r}{mr}$.

14. Add $7x+\dfrac{x-2}{3}$ and $8x+\dfrac{3x+4}{5x}$.   *Ans.* $\dfrac{230x^2-x+12}{15x}$.

15. From $\dfrac{4a+3x}{3a}$ take $\dfrac{5a+2}{3}$.   *Ans.* $\dfrac{3x+2a-5a^2}{3a}$.

16. From $3x$ take $\dfrac{3a+12x}{5}$.   *Ans.* $\dfrac{3x-3a}{5}$.

17. From $\dfrac{3a+2}{b}$ take $\dfrac{7ab-10b}{b^2}$.   *Ans.* $\dfrac{12-4a}{b}$.

18. Combine $\dfrac{3a-4b}{7}-\dfrac{2a-b-c}{3}+\dfrac{15a-4c}{12}-\dfrac{a-4b}{21}$.   *Ans.* $\dfrac{81a-4b}{84}$.

19. From $2x+\dfrac{5x-2}{7}$ take $3x-\dfrac{4x+5}{6}$.   *Ans.* $\dfrac{16x+23}{42}$.

20. Add $\dfrac{3}{x-2}, \dfrac{4}{x-3}$, and $\dfrac{7}{x^2-5x+6}$.   *Ans.* $\dfrac{7x-10}{x^2-5x+6}$.

21. Combine $\dfrac{1}{a}-\dfrac{1}{b}-\dfrac{1}{a-b}-\dfrac{1}{a+b}$.   *Ans.* $\dfrac{ab^2-a^3-a^2b-b^3}{ab(a^2-b^2)}$.

22. Combine $\dfrac{1}{x^2-9x+20}+\dfrac{1}{x^2-11x+30}$.   *Ans.* $\dfrac{2}{x^2-10x+24}$.

23. Combine $\dfrac{2}{x^2-3x+2}+\dfrac{2}{x^2-x-2}-\dfrac{1}{x^2-1}$.

                   Ans. $\dfrac{3x+2}{(x-2)(x-1)(x+1)}$.

24. Combine $\dfrac{1}{x^2+x-2}+\dfrac{1}{x^2-x-6}-\dfrac{1}{x^2-4x+3}$.

                   Ans. $\dfrac{x-6}{(x+2)(x-1)(x-3)}$.

25. Combine $\dfrac{a-b}{a^2-b^2}+\dfrac{b-a}{a^2+2ab+b^2}-\dfrac{21}{a-b}$.   *Ans.* $\dfrac{-2a^2-2ab-4b^2}{(a+b)^2(a-b)}$.

MULTIPLICATION AND DIVISION OF FRACTIONS

245. Multiplication of fractions.—As in arithmetic, the product of two or more fractions is the product of their numerators divided by the product of their denominators.

If we first cancel all factors common to both numerator and denominator, the result will be in its lowest terms when the multiplying is done.

Example 1. Multiply $\frac{35}{99}$ by $\frac{45}{91}$.

Process. $\frac{35}{99} \times \frac{45}{91} = \frac{5 \cdot \cancel{7}}{\cancel{9} \cdot 11} \times \frac{5 \cdot \cancel{9}}{\cancel{7} \cdot 13} = \frac{25}{143}$.

Here we cancel 7 and 9 in both numerator and denominator.

Example 2. Multiply 42 by $\frac{27}{28}$.

Process. $42 \times \frac{27}{28} = \frac{\cancel{2} \cdot 3 \cdot \cancel{7}}{1} \times \frac{3 \cdot 3 \cdot 3}{\cancel{2} \cdot 2 \cdot \cancel{7}} = \frac{81}{2} = 40\frac{1}{2}$.

Example 3. Multiply $\frac{x-y}{x^2+2xy+y^2}$ by $\frac{x+y}{x^2-2xy+y^2}$ by $\frac{x^2-y^2}{x^3}$.

Process. $\frac{x-y}{x^2+2xy+y^2} \times \frac{x+y}{x^2-2xy+y^2} \times \frac{x^2-y^2}{x^3} =$

$$\frac{x-y}{(x+y)(x+y)} \times \frac{x+y}{(x-y)(x-y)} \times \frac{(x+y)(x-y)}{x^3} = \frac{1}{x^3}.$$

246. Division of fractions.—One fraction is divided by another by multiplying the reciprocal of the divisor by the dividend.

The **reciprocal** of a number is 1 divided by that number. The reciprocal of a fraction is then the fraction inverted.

Thus, the reciprocal of 4 is $\frac{1}{4}$, of $\frac{2}{3}$ is $\frac{3}{2}$, and of $\frac{c}{b}$ is $\frac{b}{c}$.

Example. Divide $\frac{x^2-11x-26}{x^2-3x-18}$ by $\frac{x^2-18x+65}{x^2-9x+18}$.

Process. $\frac{x^2-11x-26}{x^2-3x-18} \div \frac{x^2-18x+65}{x^2-9x+18}$

$= \frac{x^2-11x-26}{x^2-3x-18} \times \frac{x^2-9x+18}{x^2-18x+65} = \frac{(x-13)(x+2)}{(x-6)(x+3)} \times \frac{(x-6)(x-3)}{(x-13)(x-5)}$

$= \frac{(x+2)(x-3)}{(x+3)(x-5)} = \frac{x^2-x-6}{x^2-2x-15}$.

EXERCISES 85

1. Multiply $\frac{25}{64}$ by $\frac{48}{125}$. *Ans.* $\frac{3}{20}$.

2. Find product of $17 \times \frac{2}{85} \times \frac{25}{26}$. *Ans.* $\frac{5}{13}$.

3. Divide $\frac{45}{91}$ by $\frac{9}{13}$. *Ans.* $\frac{5}{7}$.

4. Multiply $\frac{3m}{cx}$ by $\frac{c}{3}$. *Ans.* $\frac{m}{x}$.

5. Find product of $\dfrac{3ab}{4cd} \times \dfrac{16c^2x^2}{21b^2} \times \dfrac{7d^3}{4bx^2}$. $Ans.\ \dfrac{acd^2}{b^2}$.

6. Divide $\dfrac{14x^4m^3}{27y^4z^2}$ by $\dfrac{7x^3m}{9y^6z^4}$. $Ans.\ \dfrac{2m^2xy^2z^2}{3}$.

7. $\dfrac{2a^2}{41b^3x} \times \dfrac{11x^3b}{5a^2y}$. $Ans.\ \dfrac{22x^2}{205b^2y}$.

8. $-\dfrac{3cx}{5ay} \times \dfrac{2c}{3y^3}$. $Ans.\ -\dfrac{2c^2x}{5ay^4}$.

9. $\dfrac{2ax}{3by} \times \dfrac{5a^2}{7by^2}$. $Ans.\ \dfrac{10a^3x}{21b^2y^3}$.

10. $\dfrac{a^2-b^2}{bc} \times \dfrac{a^2+b^2}{b+c}$, $Ans.\ \dfrac{a^4-b^4}{b^2c+bc^2}$.

11. $\dfrac{x^2-1}{x^2-4} \times \dfrac{x+2}{x-1}$. $Ans.\ \dfrac{x+1}{x-2}$.

12. $\dfrac{x^n}{y^m} \times \dfrac{x^m}{y^n}$. $Ans.\ \dfrac{x^{m+n}}{y^{m+n}}$.

13. $\dfrac{3m^2x}{4a^2b} \div 3x$. $Ans.\ \dfrac{m^2}{4a^2b}$.

14. $\dfrac{3x+y}{9} \div \dfrac{4x}{3}$. $Ans.\ \dfrac{3x+y}{12x}$.

15. $\dfrac{4n}{2n-1} \div \dfrac{2}{n+1}$. $Ans.\ \dfrac{2n^2+2n}{2n-1}$.

16. $\dfrac{2a+b}{3a-2b} \div \dfrac{3a+2b}{4a+b}$. $Ans.\ \dfrac{8a^2+6ab+b^2}{9a^2-4b^2}$.

17. Simplify $\dfrac{5y^2}{7a^3} \times \dfrac{21c^3}{4ax} \div \dfrac{35c^2y}{7a^3x}$. $Ans.\ \dfrac{3cy}{4a}$.

18. Simplify $\dfrac{x-1}{x-2} \times \dfrac{x-2}{x-3} \div \dfrac{x-4}{x-3}$. $Ans.\ \dfrac{x-1}{x-4}$.

19. Multiply $\dfrac{x+y}{x^3-x^2y}$ by $\dfrac{xy-y^2}{x^2+xy}$. $Ans.\ \dfrac{y}{x^3}$.

20. Divide $\dfrac{x^2-14x-15}{x^2-4x-45}$ by $\dfrac{x^2-12x-45}{x^2-6x-27}$. $Ans.\ \dfrac{x+1}{x+5}$.

21. Simplify $\left(\dfrac{x^2-18x+80}{x^2-5x-50} \div \dfrac{x^2-15x+56}{x^2-6x-7} \right) \times \dfrac{x+5}{x-1}$. $Ans.\ \dfrac{x+1}{x-1}$.

22. Multiply $a^2+2ab+b^2$ by $\dfrac{a}{a^2-b^2}$. $Ans.\ \dfrac{a^2+ab}{a-b}$.

23. Multiply $\dfrac{1}{a}-\dfrac{1}{b}$ by $a-\dfrac{a^2}{b}$. $Ans.\ \dfrac{(b-a)^2}{b^2}$.

Suggestion. $\dfrac{1}{a}-\dfrac{1}{b}=\dfrac{b}{ab}-\dfrac{a}{ab}=\dfrac{b-a}{ab}$.

$$a-\dfrac{a^2}{b}=\dfrac{ab}{b}-\dfrac{a^2}{b}=\dfrac{ab-a^2}{b}.$$

Now multiply $\dfrac{b-a}{ab}$ by $\dfrac{ab-a^2}{b}$.

24. Multiply $\dfrac{a}{b}+\dfrac{b}{a}$ by $a-\dfrac{b^2}{a}$.   *Ans.* $\dfrac{a^4-b^4}{a^2b}$.

25. Multiply $1+\dfrac{3a}{1-a}$ by $1+\dfrac{a}{1+a}$.   *Ans.* $\dfrac{(1+2a)^2}{1-a^2}$.

26. Multiply $2+\dfrac{2y}{x-y}$ by $1-\dfrac{x-y}{x+y}$.   *Ans.* $\dfrac{4xy}{x^2-y^2}$.

27. Multiply $\dfrac{4xy}{2x^2+y^2}$ by $\dfrac{x}{y}+\dfrac{y}{2x}$.   *Ans.* 2.

28. Multiply $\dfrac{a^2bc}{ac+ab+bc}$ by $\dfrac{1}{a}+\dfrac{1}{b}+\dfrac{1}{c}$.   *Ans.* a.

Simplify the following:

29. $\dfrac{c-x}{a-x}\times\dfrac{3ax}{4by}\times\dfrac{a^2-x^2}{c^2-x^2}\div\dfrac{a^2+ax}{bc+bx}$.   *Ans.* $\dfrac{3x}{4y}$.

30. $\dfrac{xy-y^2}{xy+x^2}\times\dfrac{x-y}{(x+y)^2}\times\dfrac{3xz}{y}\times\dfrac{x+y}{(x-y)^2}$.   *Ans.* $\dfrac{3z}{(x+y)^2}$.

31. $\dfrac{x^2+xy}{(x-y)^2}\times\dfrac{xy-y^2}{(x+y)^2}\times\dfrac{4a+a^2}{x+a}\times\dfrac{x^2-y^2}{axy^2}$.   *Ans.* $\dfrac{4+a}{xy+ay}$.

32. $\dfrac{x^2-5x+6}{x^2-2x-8}\times\dfrac{x^2+2x}{x^2-4x+4}\times\dfrac{x^2-6x+8}{x^2-4x+3}$.   *Ans.* $\dfrac{x}{x-1}$.

33. $\dfrac{a^2-x^2}{x^2-3x-4}\div\dfrac{a-x}{x^2-x}\div\dfrac{a+x}{x-4}$.   *Ans.* $\dfrac{x^2-x}{x+1}$.

34. $\dfrac{x^2+2xy+y^2}{xy+y^2}\times\dfrac{y^2}{x^2-y^2}\div\dfrac{x^2-xy}{x^2-2xy+y^2}$.   *Ans.* $\dfrac{y}{x}$.

35. $\dfrac{a^2-a-6}{a^2-25}\times\dfrac{5a+a^2}{a^2+a-12}\div\dfrac{a^2+2a}{a^2-a-20}$.   *Ans.* 1.

36. $\dfrac{x^2-x-20}{x^2-25}\times\dfrac{x^2-x-2}{x^2+2x-8}\div\dfrac{x+1}{x^2+5x}$.   *Ans.* x.

37. $\dfrac{a^2+6a-7}{2a+b}\times\dfrac{ab^2+2a^2b}{a^2+a-42}\div\dfrac{a^3-10a^2+9a}{a^2-11a+30}$.   *Ans.* $\dfrac{ab-5b}{a-9}$.

38. $\left(\dfrac{a}{b}-\dfrac{b}{a}\right)\div\left(1-\dfrac{b}{a}\right)$.   *Ans.* $\dfrac{a+b}{b}$.

39. $\left(1-\dfrac{a^2}{b^2}\right)\div\left(\dfrac{b^4}{a^4}-1\right)$.   *Ans.* $\dfrac{a^4}{b^4+a^2b^2}$.

40. $\left(4-\dfrac{6}{x+1}\right)\div\left(8+\dfrac{8-2x}{x^2-1}\right)$.   *Ans.* $\dfrac{2x^2-3x+1}{4x^2-x}$.

41. $\left(x+\dfrac{8x}{x^2-9}\right)\div\left(x+\dfrac{2x}{x-3}\right)$.   *Ans.* $\dfrac{x+1}{x+3}$.

42. $\left(\dfrac{1}{1+x}+\dfrac{x}{1-x}\right)\div\left(\dfrac{1}{1-x}-\dfrac{x}{1+x}\right)$.   *Ans.* 1.

43. $\left(\dfrac{x+y}{x-y}+\dfrac{x-y}{x+y}\right)\div\left(\dfrac{x+y}{x-y}-\dfrac{x-y}{x+y}\right)$.   *Ans.* $\dfrac{x^2+y^2}{2xy}$.

44. $\left(-\dfrac{a}{x^2-y^2}\right)\left(-\dfrac{(x+y)^2}{a^5}\right)\left(-\dfrac{3m}{x+y}\right).$ *Ans.* $-\dfrac{3m}{a^4(x-y)}.$

45. $\left(-\dfrac{1-x^2}{1+y}\right)\left(\dfrac{1-y^2}{x^2+x}\right)\left(1+\dfrac{x}{1-x}\right).$ *Ans.* $\dfrac{y-1}{x}.$

46. $\left(1-\dfrac{x-y}{x+y}\right)\left(2+\dfrac{2y}{x-y}\right).$ *Ans.* $\dfrac{4xy}{x^2-y^2}.$

47. $(x^2-x+1)\left(\dfrac{1}{x^2}+\dfrac{1}{x}+1\right).$ *Ans.* $x^2+1+\dfrac{1}{x^2}.$

48. Simplify $\dfrac{ah^2x}{4}-\left(\dfrac{ax^2}{2}\right)\dfrac{2x}{3}-ax(h-x)\dfrac{x}{2}$ and get $\dfrac{a}{12}(3h^2x-6hx^2+2x^3).$

CHAPTER XXVIII

EQUATIONS AND FORMULAS

247. Subject matter.—In previous chapters a number of equations were presented for solution. These involved simplifications of various kinds, but were not what are called **fractional equations**; that is, equations in which fractions occur. In the present chapter, besides equations like those previously considered, will appear fractional equations.

248. Order of procedure.—The main steps in the solution of a simple equation have already been given, but for the sake of clearness they are repeated here.

(1) *Simplify the equation; that is, free of signs of grouping, perform indicated operations of multiplication and division if possible, clear of fractions, etc.*

(2) *Transpose all the terms containing the unknown to the first member and all other terms to the second member.*

(3) *Collect terms.*

(4) *Divide both members of the equation by the coefficient of the unknown.*

(5) *Test the results by substituting each in the original equation.*

249. Clearing of fractions.—A fraction is an indicated division, and usually a division that cannot be performed. Hence when an equation contains fractions, these must be removed by some other method than division.

An equation can be cleared of fractions by multiplying both members of the equation by the lowest common denominator of all the fractions in the equation.

Example 1.   Solve $\dfrac{x}{5} + \dfrac{x}{8} = 17 - \dfrac{x}{10}$.

Solution.   (1) Given equation, $\dfrac{x}{5} + \dfrac{x}{8} = 17 - \dfrac{x}{10}$.

(2) Clearing of fractions by multiplying each term by the L. C. D., 40, we have, $\qquad 8x + 5x = 680 - 4x.$

303

(3) Transposing, $8x + 5x + 4x = 680.$
(4) Collecting terms, $17x = 680$
(5) Dividing by coefficient of x, $x = 40.$

Test, $\dfrac{40}{5} + \dfrac{40}{8} = 17 - \dfrac{40}{10}$, or $13 = 13.$

Example 2.   In the equation $S = \dfrac{E - IR}{0.220}$ solve for I.

Solution.   (1) Given equation, $S = \dfrac{E - IR}{0.220}.$

(2) Clearing of fractions, $0.220S = E - IR.$
(3) Transposing, $IR = E - 0.220S$

(4) Dividing by coefficient of I, $I = \dfrac{E - 0.220S}{R}.$

EXERCISES 86

Solve the following equations for the unknown letters, and test the results.

1. $\dfrac{x}{2} + \dfrac{x}{6} = \dfrac{10}{3}.$ *Ans.* 5.

2. $\dfrac{2x}{3} - \dfrac{7x}{8} + \dfrac{5x}{18} + \dfrac{x}{24} = \dfrac{4}{9}.$ *Ans.* 4.

3. $\dfrac{3x}{4} - \dfrac{7x}{12} = \dfrac{11x}{36} - \dfrac{8x}{9} + \dfrac{3}{2}.$ *Ans.* 2.

4. $\dfrac{2x}{5} + \dfrac{x}{8} - \dfrac{x}{4} - \dfrac{11}{40} = 0.$ *Ans.* 1.

5. $\dfrac{x+1}{2} + \dfrac{x+3}{4} = 2.$ *Ans.* 1.

6. $\dfrac{2x+3}{11} + \dfrac{x-1}{3} = 2.$ *Ans.* 4.

7. $\dfrac{2(x+1)}{3} - \dfrac{3(x+2)}{4} = \dfrac{x+1}{6}.$ *Ans.* −4.

Solution. $\dfrac{2(x+1)}{3} - \dfrac{3(x+2)}{4} = \dfrac{x+1}{6}.$

Clearing of parentheses, $\dfrac{2x+2}{3} - \dfrac{3x+6}{4} = \dfrac{x+1}{6}.$

Clearing of fractions, $8x + 8 - 9x - 18 \quad = 2x + 2.$
Transposing, $8x - 9x - 2x = -8 + 18 + 2.$
Collecting terms, $-3x = 12.$
Dividing by coefficient of x, $x = -4.$

8. $\dfrac{x}{2}(2x+1) + 2 = \dfrac{x}{3}(3x - 2).$ *Ans.* −1⅝.

9. $\dfrac{x+1}{5} - \dfrac{x-1}{2} = \dfrac{3-x}{3}.$ *Ans.* 9.

10. $\frac{1}{2}(x+2) = \frac{1}{3}(x-3).$ *Ans.* −12.

11. $\dfrac{x+1}{4} - \dfrac{2(x-1)}{3} = 3.$ *Ans.* $-5.$

12. $\dfrac{2-x}{2} - \dfrac{5x+21}{5} = x+3.$ *Ans.* $-2\tfrac{12}{25}.$

13. $(x+1)^2 + 2(x+3)^2 = 3x(x+2) + 35.$ *Ans.* $2.$

14. $\dfrac{x+1}{2} + \dfrac{x+2}{3} + \dfrac{x+4}{4} + 8 = 0.$ *Ans.* $-9\tfrac{5}{13}.$

15. $\dfrac{3x+5}{8} - \dfrac{21+x}{2} = 5x - 15.$ *Ans.* $1.$

16. $x - \left(3x - \dfrac{2x-5}{10}\right) = \tfrac{1}{6}(2x-57) - \tfrac{5}{3}.$ *Ans.* $5.$

17. $\tfrac{5}{6}x + 0.25x - \tfrac{1}{3}x = x - 3.$ *Ans.* $12.$

18. $1.5 = \dfrac{0.36}{0.2} - \dfrac{0.09x - 0.18}{0.9}.$ *Ans.* $5.$

19. Given $3ac - 5c = 17$; solve for c.   *Ans.* $\dfrac{17}{3a-5}.$

20. Given $4abc - 5bc + 16 = 3bc$; solve (1) for a, (2) for b, (3) for c.

$$\text{\textit{Ans.}} \quad a = \frac{2bc-4}{bc}; \quad b = \frac{4}{2c-ac}; \quad c = \frac{4}{2b-ab}.$$

Solution for a. (1) Given equation, $4abc - 5bc + 16 = 3bc$.
(2) Transposing, $4abc = 5bc + 3bc - 16$.
(3) Collecting terms, $4abc = 8bc - 16$.

(4) Dividing by $4bc$, $a = \dfrac{8bc-16}{4bc} = \dfrac{2bc-4}{bc}.$

Solution for b. (5) Transposing, $4abc - 5bc - 3bc = -16$.
(6) Collecting terms, $(4ac - 8c)b = -16$.

(7) Dividing by $4ac - 8c$, $b = \dfrac{-16}{4ac-8c} = \dfrac{4}{2c-ac}.$

21. Given $(b-x)(b+2x) = b^2 - 2x^2 - 3b + 4$; solve (1) for b, (2) for x.

$$\text{\textit{Ans.}} \quad b = \frac{4}{x+3}; \quad x = \frac{4-3b}{b}.$$

22. $(a+b)x + (a-b)x = a^2.$ *Ans.* $\dfrac{a}{2}.$

23. $\tfrac{1}{2}(a+x) + \tfrac{1}{3}(2a+x) + \tfrac{1}{4}(3a+x) = 3a.$ *Ans.* $a.$

24. $4(t+b+y) + 3(t+b-y) = y$, solve for t.   *Ans.* $-b.$

The following are formulas that occur in physics, electricity, etc.

25. Given $PD = WD_1$, solve for P.   *Ans.* $\dfrac{WD_1}{D}.$

26. Given $F = \dfrac{WV^2}{gr}$, solve for W, g, r, and V.

$$\text{\textit{Ans.}} \quad \frac{Fgr}{V^2}; \quad \frac{WV^2}{Fr}; \quad \frac{WV^2}{Fg}; \quad \sqrt{\frac{Fgr}{W}}.$$

27. Given $I = \dfrac{En}{R+nr}$, solve for E, R, r, and n.

$$\text{\textit{Ans.}} \quad \frac{I(R+nr)}{n}; \quad \frac{n(E-Ir)}{I}; \quad \frac{nE-IR}{In}; \quad \frac{IR}{E-Ir}.$$

20

Solution for E.   (1) Given equation, $I = \dfrac{En}{R+nr}$.

(2) Clearing of fractions, $IR + Inr = En$.

(3) Dividing by coefficient of E, $E = \dfrac{IR+Inr}{n} = \dfrac{I(R+nr)}{n}$.

28. Given (1) $I = \dfrac{E}{R+r}$; (2) $I = \dfrac{nE}{R+nr}$; and (3) $I = \dfrac{E}{R+\dfrac{r}{n}}$; what value of

n will make (1), (2), and (3) identical?   Solve for n in (2) and (3).

$$Ans. \ 1; \ \frac{IR}{E-Ir}, \ \frac{Ir}{E-IR}.$$

29. Given $\dfrac{1}{f} = \dfrac{1}{p} + \dfrac{1}{q}$, solve for each letter in terms of the others.

$$Ans. \ f = \frac{pq}{p+q}; \ p = \frac{fq}{q-f}; \ q = \frac{fp}{p-f}.$$

Solution for p.   (1) Given equation, $\dfrac{1}{f} = \dfrac{1}{p} + \dfrac{1}{q}$.

(2) Multiplying by L. C. D., fpq, $pq = fq + fp$.

(3) Transposing, $pq - fp = fq$.

(4) Collecting terms, $(q-f)p = fq$.

(5) Dividing by $(q-f)$, $p = \dfrac{fq}{q-f}$.

30. If $\dfrac{1}{k} = \dfrac{1}{a} + \dfrac{1}{b} + \dfrac{1}{l}$, solve for k: and find the value of k if $a = 19,000$,

$b = 90,000$, and $l = 3180$. $Ans. \ \dfrac{abl}{ab+al+bl}; \ 2640.$

31. Given $\dfrac{E}{r} = \dfrac{E}{r_1} + \dfrac{E}{r_2}$, solve for r. $Ans. \ r = \dfrac{r_1 r_2}{r_1 + r_2}.$

32. Given $E = RI + \dfrac{rI}{n}$, find $I = \dfrac{E}{R + \dfrac{r}{n}}$.

33. Given $nE = RI + \dfrac{nrI}{m}$, find $I = \dfrac{E}{\dfrac{R}{n} + \dfrac{r}{m}}$.

34. Given $R_t = R_c(1+\alpha t)$, solve for R_0, α, and t in terms of the other quantities.

$$Ans. \ \frac{R_t}{1+\alpha t}; \ \frac{R_t - R_0}{R_0 t}; \ \frac{R_t - R_0}{R_0 \alpha}.$$

35. Given $R = $ radius of a circle, $h = $ height of a segment, and $W = $ length of the chord.   If W and h are known, find R.   (See **Art. 120.**)

Solution.   In the figure, AB is the chord, DC is the height, and AO is the radius. ADO is a right triangle.   Hence,

$$\overline{AO}^2 - \overline{DO}^2 = \overline{AD}^2$$

or

$$R^2 - (R-h)^2 = \left(\frac{W}{2}\right)^2.$$

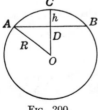

Fig. 200.

Simplifying, $\qquad R^2 - (R^2 - 2hR + h^2) = \left(\dfrac{W}{2}\right)^2.$

Simplifying, $\qquad R^2 - R^2 + 2hR - h^2 = \left(\dfrac{W}{2}\right)^2.$

Transposing and collecting, $\qquad 2hR = \left(\dfrac{W}{2}\right)^2 + h^2.$

$$R = \frac{\left(\dfrac{W}{2}\right)^2 + h^2}{2h}.$$

36. When a bar is balanced on a support F which is at a distance a from one end and b from the other, with weights m and n suspended from either end, we have found (see **Art. 68**) that $m:n = b:a$. This gives the equation, $am = bn$. A lever 10 ft. in length has a weight of 1000 lb. on one end. Where must the support be placed so that a weight of 250 lb. at the other end will make it balance? Disregard the weight of the lever.

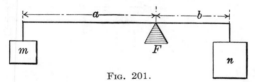

FIG. 201.

Solution. Let $d =$ the distance from support to heavier weight.
Then $10 - d =$ distance from support to lighter weight.
By proportion, $\qquad 250 : 1000 = d : 10 - d.$
$\qquad\qquad \therefore\ 2500 - 250d = 1000d.$
Transposing, $\qquad -250d - 1000d = -2500.$
Collecting terms, $\qquad -1250d = -2500.$
Dividing, $\qquad\qquad d = 2 =$ number of feet from the 1000-lb. weight to the support.

The weight at one end of the lever in Fig. 201 has a tendency to pull that end down, that is, it tends to make the lever turn about the fulcrum in that direction. The amount of this turning effect is known as a **moment,** and is the product of the weight by the length of its lever arm. Thus am is the moment of the weight m acting on the lever arm of length a.

Two moments that tend to turn in opposite directions balance each other when they are equal. *Two such moments put equal to each other give the equation used in solving a problem in levers.*

37. If a lever 16 ft. long is supported at a point 18 in. from one end, how heavy a weight can a man weighing 150 lb. on the long part of the lever balance? Disregard the weight of the lever. *Ans.* 1450 lb.

38. Two men are carrying a load, weighing 350 lb., on a pole 10 ft. long. Find the weight carried by each if the weight is 4 ft. from one end of the pole. Disregard the weight of pole. *Ans.* 210 lb. and 140 lb.

39. Place a fulcrum under a lever 12 ft. long so that a force of 150 lb.

at one end will balance a weight of 1750 lb. at the other end, if the lever
weighs 10 lb. per foot.   *Ans.* Nearly 1 ft. 3 in. from the weight.

When the weight of the lever is taken into consideration, the moment
of each arm of the lever is the weight of that arm multiplied by half the
length of the arm.   Thus, in exercise 39:

Let x = the length of the short arm in feet.

Then $12 - x$ = the length of the long arm in feet.

$$1750x = \text{moment due to weight.}$$

$$150(12 - x) = \text{moment due to force.}$$

$$\tfrac{1}{2}x \cdot 10x = \text{moment due to short arm.}$$

$$\tfrac{1}{2}(12 - x) \cdot 10(12 - x) = \text{moment due to long arm.}$$

The sum of the moments on one arm is equal to the sum on the other
arm if the lever is in balance.   Then the equation is

$$1750x + 5x^2 = 150(12 - x) + 5(12 - x)^2.$$

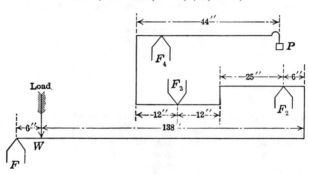

Fig. 202.

40. In the arrangement of levers for a platform scale shown in Fig.
202, find the lengths of the arms of the lever resting on F_4 so that a weight
of 1 lb. at P will balance a load of 1000 lb. at W.

Ans. 4 in. and 40 in.

In the following exercises, the numbers in the brackets are the numbers
of the formulas as given in previous chapters, where their meaning can
be found.

41. [30] $A = \tfrac{2}{3}hw$.   Solve for w.   *Ans.* $w = \dfrac{3A}{2h}$.

42. [60] $V = 2\pi^2 R r^2$.   Solve for R.   *Ans.* $\dfrac{V}{2\pi^2 r^2}$.

43. [46] $V = \pi R^2 h - \pi r^2 h$.   Solve for r^2 and then for r.

Ans. $\dfrac{\pi R^2 h - V}{\pi h}$; $\sqrt{\dfrac{\pi R^2 h - V}{\pi h}}$.

44. A hollow cylindrical cast-iron pillar 12 ft. high and 10 in. in outside
diameter is to weigh 1200 lb.   Find the diameter of the hollow.

Ans. 7.7 in.

Suggestion. Use the answer of exercise 43, and take cast iron at 450 lb. per cubic foot.

45. [47] $S = \frac{1}{2}ps$.   Solve for s.   *Ans.* $\dfrac{2S}{p}$.

46. [48] $T = \frac{1}{2}ps + A$.   Solve for p.   *Ans.* $\dfrac{2(T-A)}{s}$.

47. [49] $S = \frac{1}{2}(P+p)s$.   Solve for p.   *Ans.* $\dfrac{2S-Ps}{s}$.

48. [50] $T = \frac{1}{2}(P+p)s + B + b$.   Solve for s.   *Ans.* $\dfrac{2(T-B-b)}{P+p}$.

49. [56] $V = \frac{4}{3}\pi r^3$.   Solve for r.   *Ans.* $\sqrt[3]{\dfrac{3V}{4\pi}}$.

50. Given $F = -\dfrac{4\pi^2 mx}{T^2}$, solve for x.   *Ans.* $-\dfrac{FT^2}{4\pi^2 m}$.

51. Given $E = \dfrac{Ff}{(P-x)p}$, solve for x.   *Ans.* $\dfrac{EPp-Ff}{Ep}$.

52. Given $C = K\dfrac{rr'}{r+r''}$, solve for r'.   *Ans.* $\dfrac{Cr}{Kr-C}$.

53. Given $Q = K\dfrac{(t_2-t_1)aT}{d}$, solve for t_1 and a.

Ans. $\dfrac{aKt_2T-dQ}{aKT}$; $\dfrac{dQ}{KT(t_2-t_1)}$.

54. Given $p_t v_t = p_0 v_0\left(1+\dfrac{t}{273}\right)$, solve for t.

Ans. $\dfrac{273(p_t v_t - p_0 v_0)}{p_0 v_0}$.

55. Given $H = 1{,}600{,}000 \cdot \dfrac{b_1-b_2}{b_1+b_2}(1+0.004t)$, solve for t.

Ans. $\dfrac{H(b_1+b_2)-1{,}600{,}000(b_1-b_2)}{6400(b_1-b_2)}$.

56. Find the side of a square room such that if its length and width are increased by 3 ft., the area is increased by 81 sq. ft.   *Ans.* 12 ft.

57. Find the side of a square field such that if each dimension is decreased by 10 rods, the field will contain 400 sq. rd. less.   *Ans.* 25 rd.

58. A rectangle is 3 times as long as it is wide.   If the width is increased by 4 in. and the length decreased by 5 in., the area is increased by 15 in.^{2} Find the dimensions of the rectangle.   *Ans.* 5 in. by 15 in.

59. The difference between the base and the altitude of a triangle is 6 in. and their sum is 36 in.   Find the area of the triangle.

Ans. $157\frac{1}{2}$ in.^{2}

60. The altitude of a triangle is 7 in. longer than the base.   If the altitude is decreased by 4 in. and the base increased by 6 in., the area is increased by 25 in.^{2} Find the altitude and base.

Ans. 23 in. and 16 in.

61. Find the number such that we can take $\frac{1}{3}$ of it away and still have $\frac{6}{5}$ of 320.   *Ans.* 576.

62. From what price can I deduct $33\frac{1}{3}\%$ on goods which cost \$3.20 per yard, and still make 20%?   *Ans.* \$5.76.

63. Find the principal that invested for $4\frac{1}{2}$ years at $3\frac{1}{2}\%$ per annum will give an amount of \$694.50.   *Ans.* \$600.

Solution. Let p = number of dollars in principal.
Then $p \times 0.03\frac{1}{2} \times 4\frac{1}{2} = 0.1575p$ = number of dollars in interest,
and $p + 0.1575p$ = number of dollars in amount.

$\therefore p + 0.1575p = 694.50.$
$\quad 1.1575p = 694.50$
$\qquad p = 600.$

64. Find the rate in order that an investment of \$820 will amount to \$912.25 in 3 yr. 9 mo.   *Ans.* 3%.

65. The sum of \$1100 is invested, part at 5% and part at 6% per annum. If the total annual income is \$59, how much is invested at each rate?   *Ans.* \$700 and \$400.

Suggestion. Let x = the number of dollars invested at 5%,
then $1100 - x$ = number of dollars invested at 6%.

$\therefore 0.05x + 0.06(1100 - x) = 59.$

66. The interest on \$120 for a certain time at 6% is \$16.56. Find the time.   *Ans.* 2 yr. 3 mo. 18 da.

67. The interest on \$584 for 2 yr. 8 mo. 7 da. at a certain rate per cent is \$94.121$\frac{1}{2}$. Find the rate per cent.   *Ans.* 6%.

68. A man saves \$50 more than $\frac{1}{8}$ of his income, spends 3 times as much for living expenses as he saves, and spends the remainder which is \$600 for rent. Find his income.   *Ans.* \$2400.

69. If air is a mixture of 4 parts nitrogen to 1 part of oxygen, how many cubic feet of each are there in a room 40 ft. by 30 ft. and 12 ft. high?
               Ans. 11,520; 2880.

Suggestion. Let x = the number of cubic feet of oxygen in the room. Then $4x$ = the number of cubic feet of nitrogen in the room.

70. A room is $\frac{7}{10}$ as wide as it is long. If the length were decreased by 3 ft. and the width increased by 3 ft., the room would be square. Find the dimensions of the room.   *Ans.* 20 ft. by 14 ft.

71. A room is $\frac{4}{5}$ as long as it is wide, and its perimeter is 70 ft. Find the area of the room.   *Ans.* 300 ft.²

72. A man made a journey of 560 miles, part at the rate of 40 miles per hour and part at 50 miles per hour. If it took him 13 hours, how far did he go at each rate?   *Ans.* 360 mi.; 200 mi.

73. A tree 189 ft. tall was broken into two pieces by falling. If $\frac{2}{3}$ the length of the longer piece equals $\frac{3}{4}$ the length of the shorter piece, how long is each piece?   *Ans.* $100\frac{1}{17}$ ft.; $88\frac{16}{17}$ ft.

74. Sirloin steak costs $1\frac{1}{2}$ times as much as round steak. Find the cost of each per pound if 3 lb. of sirloin and 5 lb. of round cost \$2.28?
               Ans. 36 cents; 24 cents.

75. If 2 lb. of butter cost as much as 5 lb. of lard, and $4\frac{1}{2}$ lb. of lard and 6 lb. of butter cost \$5.46, find the cost of each per pound.
               Ans. 70 cents; 28 cents.

250. Thermometers.—Two kinds of thermometers are in common use. The Fahrenheit, which is used for common purposes, has the freezing point marked 32°, and the boiling point marked 212°. The centigrade, which is used for all scientific purposes, has the freezing point marked 0° and the boiling point marked 100°.

It is seen then that on the Fahrenheit scale there are $212° - 32° = 180°$ between the freezing point and the boiling point; while on the centigrade scale there are 100° in the same space. Hence 180° of the Fahrenheit scale = 100° of the centigrade scale. These relations are shown in Fig. 203.

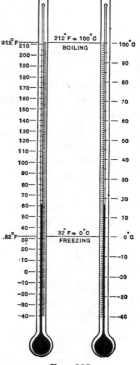

EXERCISES 87

1. If F stands for the number of degrees on the Fahrenheit scale and C for the number of degrees on the centigrade scale, find that

$$(1) \quad C = \tfrac{5}{9}(F - 32),$$
$$(2) \quad F = \tfrac{9}{5}C + 32.$$

2. A temperature of 176° Fahrenheit is what temperature centigrade? [Use (1) of exercise 1.]   *Ans.* 80°.

3. A reading of 24° centigrade is how many degrees Fahrenheit?

Ans. 75⅕°.

Fig. 203.

4. Given that the following metals melt at the given temperatures in Fahrenheit scale, find the melting point of each in the centigrade scale: Wrought iron, 2822°; steel, 2462°; cast iron, 2210°; silver, 1832°; lead, 620°; tin, 475°.

Ans. Wrought iron, 1550°; steel, 1350°; cast iron, 1210°; silver, 1000°; lead, 326⅔°; tin, 246⅑°.

5. 60° below 0° Fahrenheit is what on the centigrade scale?

Ans. 51⅓° below 0°.

6. At what temperature are the readings on the two thermometers the same?   *Ans.* 40° below 0°.

Solution. Let x = the reading on each thermometer scale. Then by the formulas of exercise 1,

$$\tfrac{5}{9}(x-32)=\tfrac{9}{5}x+32.$$
$$25x-800=81x+1440.$$
$$25x-81x=1440+800.$$
$$-56x=2240.$$
$$x=-40.$$

∴ the reading is the same when temperature is −40°.

7. With the oxyacetylene process of welding, the temperature of the flame is sometimes over 6000° Fahrenheit. What is this on the centigrade scale? *Ans.* Over 3315°.

251. Horse-power.—The term **horse-power** was first used by James Watt, the inventor of the steam engine. He ascertained that a London draught horse was capable of doing work, for a short time, equivalent to lifting 33,000 lb. 1 ft. high in 1 minute. This value was used by Watt in expressing the power of his engines, and has since been universally adopted in mechanics.

The expression **foot-pounds** is used to denote the unit of work. *It is equivalent to a force of* 1 *lb. acting through a distance of* 1 *ft.,* or a force of $\tfrac{1}{2}$ lb. acting through a distance of 2 ft., or $\tfrac{1}{10}$ lb. through a distance of 10 ft., etc. *Horse-power* is the measure of the rate at which work is performed. One horse-power is equivalent to 33,000 lb. lifted 1 ft. in 1 minute, or 1 lb. lifted 550 ft. in 1 second. We say then that *one horse-power equals* 33,000 *foot-pounds per minute, or* 550 *foot-pounds per second.*

Therefore, the horse-power of *any machine* can be found by dividing the number of foot-pounds of work done in 1 minute by 33,000, or

$$Horse\text{-}power = \frac{Number\ of\ foot\text{-}pounds\ of\ work\ per\ minute}{33,000}.$$

In *electric-power machines* where the *watt* is used, since 746 watts equal 1 horse-power, we have

$$Horse\text{-}power = \frac{volts \times amperes}{746}.$$

EXERCISES 88

1. What horse-power is necessary to raise a block of stone, weighing 3 tons, to the top of a wall 40 ft. high in 2 minutes?

Solution. The number of foot-pounds per minute is
$$\frac{6000 \times 40}{2} \text{ and hence the}$$

$$\text{h. p.} = \frac{6000 \times 40}{2 \times 33,000} = 3\tfrac{7}{11}. \quad Ans.$$

2. What horse-power is required to life an elevator, weighing 4 tons, to the top of a building 240 ft. high in $1\frac{1}{2}$ minutes?

Ans. 39 h. p. nearly.

3. What horse-power is required to pump 30,000 barrels of water per hour to a height of 45 ft.? (Use 1 bbl. = 4.211 cu. ft.)

Ans. 179.4+ h. p.

4. The following formula gives the horse-power of a steam engine:

$$H = \frac{PLAN}{33,000},$$

where H = indicated horse-power,

P = mean effective pressure of the steam in pounds per square inch,
L = length of stroke in feet,
A = area of piston in square inches, and
N = number of strokes of piston (twice the number of revolutions) per minute.

Solve the formula for each of the letters P, L, A, and N in terms of the others.

Ans. $P = \dfrac{33,000H}{LAN}$; $L = \dfrac{33,000H}{PAN}$; $A = \dfrac{33,000H}{PLN}$; $N = \dfrac{33,000H}{PLA}$.

Remark. It is to be noticed that the formula $H = \dfrac{PLAN}{33,000}$ has, in the numerator, an expression for the number of foot-pounds per minute. To see this, note that PA is the pressure on the piston in pounds. This times L, or PLA, is the foot-pounds for one stroke of the piston. Finally, multiplying this by the number of strokes per minute, N, gives $PLAN$, the number of foot-pounds per minute.

5. What horse-power will a steam engine with a cylinder 4 in. in diameter and a stroke of 6 in. develop at 300 R. P. M. of the crank, if the mean effective pressure is 95 lb.? *Ans.* 10.85+ h. p.

Suggestion. Express in form of cancellation,

$$H = \frac{4 \times 4 \times 0.7854 \times 95 \times 1 \times 600}{33,000 \times 2},$$

cancel what you can and compute by slide rule if you wish.

6. Find the horse-power of an engine with a cylinder 10 in. in diameter, a stroke of 30 in., the crank making 96 R. P. M., and the mean effective pressure 120 lb. *Ans.* 137+ h. p.

7. Find the diameter of a cylinder to develop 95 h. p. with a stroke of 34 in., the crank making 110 R. P. M., the boiler pressure being 80 lb., and the mean effective pressure 65% of the boiler pressure.

Ans. 11.1– in.

Suggestion. Find the area of the piston by the formula of exercise 4, and then the diameter by [27].

8. An engine is required to develop 50 h. p. with an average effective pressure of 46 lb. on a piston 13 in. in diameter, and a crank shaft speed of 100 R. P. M. Find the length of the stroke.

Ans. 1.351+ ft. or 1 ft. $4\frac{3}{16}$ in.

9. Find the mean effective pressure on the piston of a steam engine with a cylinder 12 in. in diameter and a piston stroke of 18 in., if the number of revolutions is 110 per minute and developed horse-power 40.

Ans. 35.37 —lb. per square inch.

10. In gas engines it is not easy to determine the mean effective pressure, so the formula $H = \dfrac{PLAN}{33,000}$ cannot well be used. As a result of experiments with engines used in automobiles, the formula $H = \dfrac{D^2 N}{2.5}$ is often used. Here D is the diameter of the cylinders in inches, and N is the number of cylinders. Find H, if $D = 4\frac{3}{4}$ in. and $N = 6$. *Ans.* 54.15.

11. In "Locomotive Data" of the Baldwin Locomotive Works, the following formula is given for the tractive power of a locomotive:

$$T = \frac{C^2 SP}{D},$$

where C = diameter of cylinders in inches,
$\quad\quad S$ = stroke of piston in inches ,
$\quad\quad P$ = mean effective pressure in pounds per square inch = 85% of boiler pressure,
$\quad\quad D$ = diameter of driving wheels in inches, and
$\quad\quad T$ = tractive power in pounds.

Solve for each of the letters C, S, P, and D in terms of the others.

Ans. $C = \sqrt{\dfrac{DT}{SP}}$; $S = \dfrac{DT}{C^2 P}$; $P = \dfrac{DT}{C^2 S}$; $D = \dfrac{C^2 SP}{T}$.

12. Use the formula of exercise 11 and find T when $C = 16$ in., $S = 22$ in., and $D = 64$ in., if the boiler pressure is 160 lb. per square inch.

Ans. 11,968 lb.

13. To find the pressure on a lathe tool in turning steel multiply the area in square inches of a section of the chip cut by 230,000. In cutting cast iron use 168,000.

What horse-power does it take to turn a 6-in. steel axle making 30 R. P. M., if the cut is $\frac{1}{32}$ in. deep with a feed of $\frac{1}{8}$ in.?

Ans. 1.3 nearly.

14. The power that is transmitted by a belt depends upon the pull of the belt and the rate at which it travels. The power may be given as a number of foot-pounds per minute or may be given as horse-power. Different makers of belts and writers on the subject give different values as the working strength for belts. The allowed pull for single belts is from 30 to 60 lb. per inch of width of belt. For double belts it is from 60 to 100 lb. per inch of width.

Show that the following formula gives the horse-power transmitted by a belt:

$$H = \frac{FWS}{33,000},$$

where H = horse-power,
$\quad\quad F$ = pull in pounds per inch of width,
$\quad\quad W$ = width in inches,
$\quad\quad S$ = speed of belt in feet per minute.

Solve for each letter involved in the formula.

15. Find the horse-power that can be transmitted by a belt 14 in. wide, if the pull allowed per inch of width is 90 lb. and the speed is 5000 ft. per minute. *Ans.* 190$\frac{10}{11}$.

16. Find the horse-power transmitted by a single belt 6 in. wide, running over a pulley 16 in. in diameter, and making 350 R. P. M., if the pull of the belt is 45 lb. per inch of width. Allow 2% for slipping.

Ans. 11.85.

17. If a single belt 6 in. wide transmits 7 horse-power, find its speed per minute, allowing 35 lb. pull per inch of width.

Ans. 1100 ft. per minute.

18. Find the horse-power transmitted by a 10-in. double belt, running over a 36-in. pulley, making 420 R. P. M. Use a pull of 75 lb. per inch of width. *Ans.* 89.96.

19. Assuming a tension of 50 lb. per inch of width for a single belt, and using D for diameter of pulley in inches, W for width of belt in inches, R for the number of revolutions per minute, and H for the horse-power transmitted, then

$$H = \frac{DRW}{2520}.$$

Use $\pi = \frac{22}{7}$ and derive this formula. Solve for W, D, and R in terms of the other letters.

Remark. In the above formula it is assumed that the pulleys are practically of the same size so that the arc of contact is 180°. If the pulleys differ in diameter the arc of contact of the belt on the smaller pulley should be found and the following table used in finding the horse-power that can be transmitted.

If angle of contact is.........	90°	100°	110°	120°	130°	140°	150°	160°	170°
Multiply by....	0.65	0.70	0.75	0.79	0.83	0.87	0.91	0.94	0.97

20. Using the notation of the preceding exercise and 80 lb. for the tension per inch of width for double belts,

$$H = \frac{DRW}{1575}.$$

Derive this formula if $\pi = \frac{22}{7}$. Solve for D, R, and W in terms of the other letters.

21. Find the width of a single belt to transmit 3 horse-power when running over a pulley 15 in. in diameter, making 220 R. P. M. Allow a pull of 50 lb. per inch of width. *Ans.* 2.3 in.

22. Find the number of R. P. M. a pulley 4 ft. in diameter must make that transmits 120 horse-power through a double belt 10 in. wide, having a pull of 80 lb. per inch of width. *Ans.* 393$\frac{3}{4}$.

23. How much work is done in lifting 150 lb. from a mine 1100 ft. deep? How many horse-power would it take to lift this weight from the mine in 1½ minutes? *Ans.* 3⅓ horse-power.

252. Relation of resistance, electro-motive force, and current.—Resistance, R, is measured in **ohms**; voltage or electro-motive force, E. M. F. or E, in **volts**; and current, I, in **amperes**. The law connecting these is stated as follows:

$$Amperes = \frac{volts}{ohms} \text{ or } I = \frac{E}{R}.$$

This law is **Ohm's Law,** and is the fundamental law for electrical work. It is an algebraic equation, and any one of the numbers can be found if the other two are given.

Exercises 27, 28, 32, and 33, pages 305 and 306, are forms of this equation.

EXERCISES 89

1. Solve the equation $I = \frac{E}{R}$ for E and R.   *Ans.* $E = IR$; $R = \frac{E}{I}$.

2. In a certain circuit the voltage is measured and found to be 1.5 volts. If the total resistance is 12 ohms, what is the current in amperes? *Ans.* 0.125 ampere.

3. Find the number of amperes of current sent through a circuit of 20 ohms resistance by one Daniell's cell which has an E. M. F. of 1.03 volts. *Ans.* 0.0515.

4. Find the strength of current from 50 Daniell's cells united in series, assuming the E. M. F. of each cell to be 1.03 volts, the resistance within each cell 0.3 ohm, and the external resistance 25 ohms.

Ans. 1.2875 amperes.

Remark. The student not familiar with the meaning of "cells united in series" can note the fact that 50 cells in series have 50 times the E. M. F. of a single cell, and the resistance within the cells is 50 times that of one cell. The formula of exercise 27, page 305, can be used.

5. An electric bell has a resistance of 450 ohms and will not ring with a current of less than 0.06 ampere. Neglecting battery and line resistance, what is the smallest E. M. F. that will ring the bell? *Ans.* 27 volts.

6. If an electric car heater is supplied with 500 volts from the trolley, how great must its resistance be so that the current may not exceed 2.5 amperes? *Ans.* 200 ohms.

7. A certain wire has a resistance of 1 ohm for every 30 ft. of its length. What must be the E. M. F. in order that a current of 0.4 ampere may flow through 1 mile of the wire? *Ans.* 70.4 volts.

253. Resistance of conductors.—Consider the formula,

$$R = \frac{l}{a}k,$$

where R is resistance in ohms, l the length of the conductor in *some unit*, a the area of the cross section of the conductor in *some unit*, and k a constant value depending upon the *material in the conductor and upon the units of length and cross section used*. This formula is the fundamental formula in wiring calculations.

In engineering practice, the length l is taken in *feet;* the area a is taken in *circular mils*, which equals the square of the diameter in thousandths of an inch when the conductor is circular (see **Art. 132**); and k is the resistance in *ohms* of 1 *ft. length of the conductor having a cross section of one circular mil*. That is, k is the *mil-foot* resistance of the conductor. The formula can then be written

$$R = \frac{l}{d^2}k.$$

If then it is required to find the resistance of any length of any size wire of any material, it is only necessary to know the mil-foot resistance for the material, and substitute the values in the formula.

The following table gives the mil-foot resistances for the materials named at zero degrees centigrade:

Aluminum	17.5 ohms.
Copper (commercial)	9.6 ohms.
German silver	125.7 ohms.
Iron (pure)	58.3 ohms.
Iron (telegraph wire)	90.0 ohms.
Platinum	54.3 ohms.
Silver	9.1 ohms.
Zinc	33.8 ohms.

Example 1. What is the resistance of 2 miles of No. 12, B. and S. gage commercial copper wire?

Solution. No. 12, B. and S. gage has an area of 6530 C. M.

$$2 \text{ miles} = 2 \times 5280 \text{ ft.}$$

$$\therefore R = \frac{2 \times 5280 \times 9.6}{6530} = 15.5 \text{ ohms. } Ans.$$

If it is required to determine the size of wire of a given length to have a given resistance, the formula is solved for d^2. This gives $d^2 = \dfrac{lk}{R}$.

Example 2.   Find the B. and S. gage of pure iron wire to have a resistance of 3 ohms per mile.

Solution.   Substituting in the formula,

$$d^2 = \frac{5280 \times 58.3}{3} = 102{,}608 \text{ C. M.}$$

$$d = \sqrt{102{,}608} = 320.3 \text{ mils} = 0.3203 \text{ in.}$$

The nearest to this size is No. 0, B. and S. which is 0.3249 in. in diameter.

If it is required to find the length of wire of a given size to have a given resistance, the formula is solved for l.   This gives $l = \dfrac{Ra}{k}$.

Example 3.   Find the length of a No. 20, B. and S. gage silver wire to have a resistance of 5 ohms.

Solution.   No. 20, B. and S. has an area of 1022 C. M.

$$\therefore l = \frac{5 \times 1022}{9.1} = 561.5 \text{ ft. nearly. } Ans.$$

EXERCISES 90

1. Find the resistance of 340 ft. of No. 25, B. and S. gage German silver wire.   *Ans.* 133.4 − ohms.

2. Find the resistance of 20 miles of trolley wire, made of commercial copper, and No. 00, B. and S.   *Ans.* 7.6 + ohms.

3. Find the resistance of 10 miles of the "third rail" conductor on an elevated railroad.   The "third rail" is iron and has a cross section of 5.88 in.²   *Ans.* 0.63 ohm nearly.

4. Find the resistance of 500 turns of No. 30, B. and S. gage silver wire, about a core ¾ in. in diameter.   *Ans.* 8.69 + ohms.

5. Find the B. and S. gage of commercial copper wire to give a resistance of 40 ohms per mile.   *Ans.* No. 19 nearly.

6. Find the length of No. 16, B. and S. gage commercial copper wire to have a resistance of 20 ohms.   *Ans.* 5381 ft.

7. The resistance of a certain commercial copper wire, 1 ft. long and 1 C. M. in cross section, is 10.79 ohms.   A wire, 525 ft. long, has a cross section of 4117 C. M.; what is its resistance?   *Ans.* 1.376 ohms.

CHAPTER XXIX

EQUATIONS WITH MORE THAN ONE UNKNOWN

254. In previous chapters the equations solved have involved only one unknown letter. In the present chapter will be considered equations involving more than one unknown letter. These letters will occur to the first power only, or if squared, will be such as are easily handled.

255. Indeterminate equations.—If we have the equation $x - y = 2$, and try to solve it for the unknown numbers x and y, it is evident that we can get numerous pairs of values for these numbers.

Thus, $x = 3$ and $y = 1$ is a pair of values that satisfy the equation; so are $x = 4$ and $y = 2$; $x = 5$ and $y = 3$; $x = 10$ and $y = 8$.

Such an equation is called an **indeterminate equation.**

Find pairs of values that satisfy the following:

1. $x + y = 10$.　　**2.** $x - y = 16$.　　**3.** $2x + y = 20$.
4. $3x + 2y = 40$.　　**5.** $7x - 8y = 27$.　　**6.** $3x - 8y = 16$.
7. $6x - 2y = -2$.　　**8.** $4x - 8y = -10$.

256. Simultaneous equations.—Take the two indeterminate equations

$$(1) \quad x - y = 2, \text{ and}$$
$$(2) \quad x + y = 12.$$

Pairs of values that satisfy (1) are $x = 3$, $y = 1$; $x = 4$, $y = 2$; $x = 5$, $y = 3$; $x = 6$, $y = 4$; $x = 7$, $y = 5$; etc. Pairs of values that satisfy (2) are $x = 2$, $y = 10$; $x = 3$, $y = 9$; $x = 6$, $y = 6$; $x = 7$, $y = 5$; $x = 8$, $y = 4$; etc.

It is noticed that the pair of values, $x = 7$ and $y = 5$, is found in both sets of values; that is, these values satisfy both equations. Such a set of two equations satisfied by a pair of values for the unknown is called a **system of simultaneous equations.**

319

If, as in the system just considered, there is only one pair of values that satisfy both equations, the equations are called **independent.**

If the equations are as in the set $x+2y=7$ and $3x+6y=15$, where there is no pair of values alike for both, the equations are called **inconsistent.**

If the equations are as in the set $2x+y=10$ and $6x=30-3y$, where every pair that satisfies one will satisfy the other, the equations are called **equivalent.**

257. Solution of independent equations.—It is evidently not convenient to find a pair of values that will satisfy two independent equations, by writing down pairs of values for each equation, and then selecting the pair which is the same in each. It remains then to devise a way that is shorter.

The different methods of solution that have been devised are alike in that an equation is obtained that has only one unknown. We say then that one unknown has been **eliminated.** There are three ways of eliminating an unknown. They are:

(1) *Elimination by adding or subtracting.*

(2) *Elimination by substitution.*

(3) *Elimination by comparison.*

258. Elimination by adding or subtracting.—

Example 1. Solve $x-y=2$ and $x+y=12$ for x and y.

Solution. (1) $x-y=2$.

(2) $x+y=12$.

Add equations (1) and (2), first member to first member and second member to second member, and we have

(3) $2x=14$.

∴ (4) $x=7$.

Substituting this value of x in (1) gives

(5) $7-y=2$.

∴ (6) $y=5$.

Hence the pair of values that will satisfy both equations is $x=7$ and $y=5$.

Example 2. Solve $3x+2y=21$ and $7x-5y=20$ for x and y.

Solution. (1) $3x+2y=21$.

(2) $7x-5y=20$.

Multiplying (1) by 7 gives   (3) $21x+14y=147$.

Multiplying (2) by 3 gives   (4) $21x-15y=60$.

Subtracting (4) from (3) = (5) $29y = 87$.

∴ (6) $y = 3$.

Substituting in (1) gives (7) $3x + 6 = 21$.

∴ (8) $3x = 21 - 6$.

(9) $3x = 15$.

(10) $x = 5$.

Hence $x = 5$ and $y = 3$ are the required values.

This way of eliminating one of the unknown numbers is called **elimination by adding or subtracting.** The following rule may be given for the process:

RULE. (1) *Multiply each equation, if necessary, by such a number as will make the absolute values of the coefficients of one of the unknown numbers the same in both of the resulting equations.*

(2) *Add or subtract the corresponding members of the resulting equations so as to eliminate the unknown number having coefficients equal in absolute value.*

It should be noticed that we add when the coefficients are of opposite signs, and subtract when they are of like signs.

259. Elimination by substitution.—The elimination can often be performed more easily by using a method called substitution. Consider the following system of equations:

$$y = 42 - 7x \text{ and } 3x - y = 8.$$

Solution. (1) $y = 42 - 7x$.

(2) $3x - y = 8$.

Substituting the value of y from (1) into (2) gives

(3) $3x - (42 - 7x) = 8$.

(4) $3x - 42 + 7x = 8$.

(5) $3x + 7x = 42 + 8$.

(6) $10x = 50$.

(7) $x = 5$.

Substituting in (1) gives (8) $y = 42 - 35$.

∴ (9) $y = 7$.

Hence $x = 5$ and $y = 7$ are the values.

This method of eliminating is called **elimination by substitution,** and can generally be used to good advantage when one equation is much simpler in form than the other. The following rule may be given for the process:

RULE. *Solve one of the equations for the value of one of the unknown numbers, and substitute this value in place of that*

21

number in the other equation. This will give an equation with but one unknown number.

260. Elimination by comparison.—

Example. Solve $x+4y=21$ and $3x-y=11$.

Solution. (1) $x+4y=21$.

(2) $3x-y=11$.

Solving (1) for x gives (3) $x=21-4y$.

Solving (2) for x gives (4) $x=\dfrac{11+y}{3}$.

By axiom (5), equations (3) and (4) give

(5) $\quad 21-4y=\dfrac{11+y}{3}$.

Clearing of fractions, (6) $63-12y=11+y$.

(7) $-12y-y=11-63$.

(8) $\quad -13y=-52$.

(9) $\quad y=4$.

Substituting in (3) gives (10) $\quad x=21-16$.

(11) $\quad x=5$.

Hence $x=5$ and $y=4$ are the values.

This method of elimination is called **elimination by comparison.** The following rule may be given for the process:

RULE. *Solve each of the equations for the value of one of the unknowns, and equate these values. This forms an equation having but one unknown.*

261. Suggestions.—Any method of elimination may be used. Usually one of the methods is shorter than the others. Elimination by adding or subtracting can usually be used to the best advantage.

Free the equations of signs of grouping before eliminating. Usually clear of fractions before eliminating.

Much practice and dealing with examples will help one to determine what method to use.

EXERCISES 91

In exercises 1 to 10 eliminate in each by all three methods.

1. $x+y=8$ and $x-y=2$.   *Ans.* $x=5$, $y=3$.
2. $2x+y=10$ and $x+2y=11$.   *Ans.* $x=3$, $y=4$.
3. $4x-3y=8$ and $2x+y=14$.   *Ans.* $x=5$, $y=4$.
4. $3x+2y=26$ and $5x-2y=38$.   *Ans.* $x=8$, $y=1$.
5. $7x+y=42$ and $3x-y=8$.   *Ans.* $x=5$, $y=7$.

6. $8x+6y=10$ and $5x+2y=1$.   *Ans.* $x=-1$, $y=3$.

7. $7x-9y=13$ and $5x+2y=10$.   *Ans.* $x=1\frac{57}{59}$, $y=\frac{5}{59}$.

8. $3x+5y=8$ and $2x-3y=12$.   *Ans.* $x=4\frac{8}{19}$, $y=-\frac{20}{19}$.

Solution.   (1) $3x+5y=8$.

          (2) $2x-3y=12$.

Multiplying (1) by 2 gives (3) $6x+10y=16$.

Multiplying (2) by 3 gives (4) $6x-9y=36$.

Subtracting (4) from (3) gives (5) $19y=-20$.

$$\therefore\ y=-\tfrac{20}{19}.$$

Substituting in (1), $x=4\frac{8}{19}$.

9. $5x+6y=17$ and $6x+5y=16$.   *Ans.* $x=1$, $y=2$.

10. $x-11y=1$ and $111y-9x=99$.   *Ans.* $x=100$, $y=9$.

In exercises 11 to 14 draw the graphs of the equations, determine values from these, and solve equations by some method of elimination. (See **Chapter XXXIII.**)

11. $x+y=17$ and $x-y=7$.   *Ans.* $x=12$, $y=5$.

12. $3x+4y=24$ and $5x-6y=2$.   *Ans.* $x=4$, $y=3$.

13. $5x+9y=28$ and $7x+3y=20$.   *Ans.* $x=2$, $y=2$.

14. $5x-2y=1$, and $4x+5y=47$.   *Ans.* $x=3$, $y=7$.

Solve the following by some method of elimination:

15. $\dfrac{x+1}{2}=\dfrac{y+2}{3}$ and $\dfrac{x+y}{4}=\dfrac{y+2}{3}$.   *Ans.* $x=5$, $y=7$.

16. $(y+1)(x+5)=(y+5)(x+1)$ and $xy+y+x=(y+2)(x+2)$

Ans. $x=-2$, $y=-2$.

17. $\dfrac{a}{3}-\dfrac{b}{6}=\dfrac{1}{2}$ and $\dfrac{a}{5}-\dfrac{3b}{10}=\dfrac{1}{2}$.   *Ans.* $a=1$, $b=-1$.

18. $\dfrac{a}{5}+\dfrac{b}{2}=5$ and $a-b=4$.   *Ans.* $a=10$, $b=6$.

19. $\dfrac{n+1}{10}=\dfrac{3m-5}{2}$ and $\dfrac{n+1}{10}=\dfrac{n-m}{8}$.   *Ans.* $m=3$, $n=19$.

20. $\dfrac{x-2}{3}-\dfrac{y+2}{4}=0$ and $\dfrac{2x-5}{5}-\dfrac{11-2y}{7}=0$.   *Ans.* $x=5$, $y=2$.

21. $\dfrac{x}{2}-\dfrac{y}{5}=4$ and $\dfrac{x}{7}+\dfrac{y}{15}=3$.   *Ans.* $x=14$, $y=15$.

22. $\dfrac{x}{a}+\dfrac{y}{b}=\dfrac{1}{ab}$ and $\dfrac{x}{c}-\dfrac{y}{d}=\dfrac{1}{cd}$.   *Ans.* $x=\dfrac{a+c}{ad+bc}$, $y=\dfrac{d-b}{ad+bc}$.

Solution.   (1) $\dfrac{x}{a}+\dfrac{y}{b}=\dfrac{1}{ab}$.

          (2) $\dfrac{x}{c}-\dfrac{y}{d}=\dfrac{1}{cd}$.

Clearing of fractions, (3) $bx+ay=1$.

          (4) $dx-cy=1$.

Multiplying (3) by c, (5) $bcx+acy=c$.

Multiplying (4) by a, (6) $adx-acy=a$.

Adding (5) and (6),   (7) $(ad+bc)x=a+c$.

$$(8)\ \therefore\ x=\dfrac{a+c}{ad+bc}.$$

Here it is best to solve for y by eliminating x rather than to substitute the value of y in (1) or (2).

23. The sum of two numbers is 15 and their difference is 1. What are the numbers?   *Ans.* 7 and 8.

24. Three times one number plus four times another number is ten, and four times the first plus the second is nine. What are the two numbers?   *Ans.* 2 and 1.

25. What is the fraction which equals $\frac{1}{3}$ when 1 is added to the numerator, but equals $\frac{1}{4}$ when 1 is added to the denominator?

Ans. $\frac{4}{15}$.

26. Given $S = \frac{\pi D N}{12}$ and $T = \frac{LF}{N}$, eliminate N and find the value of T in terms of the remaining letters.   *Ans.* $T = \frac{\pi DFL}{12S}$.

Suggestion. Solve each equation for N and eliminate by comparison.

27. The formulas of exercise 26 are used in lathe work. In these formulas, T is the time in minutes; S is the cutting speed in feet per minute; D is the diameter of the work in inches; N is the number of revolutions per minute; L is the length of the part to be turned in inches; F is the feed and is expressed as the numbers of turns to give a sidewise movement of 1 in. Thus, a feed of 16 means that each cut is $\frac{1}{16}$ in. wide. Find the time to turn a piece 3 in. in diameter and 2 ft. long, if the feed is 20 and the cutting speed 15 ft. per minute.   *Ans.* 25.13+ min.

28. In locating and boring holes in a drill jig, it is necessary to find the diameters of three circular disks tangent two and two, whose centers are at distances of 0.765 in., 0.710 in., and 0.850 in. Find the diameters of the three circles.

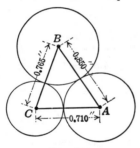

Fig. 204.

Solution. The disks are placed as shown in Fig. 204.

Let x, y, and z = the radii of the circles centered at A, B, and C respectively.

Then (1) $x + y = 0.850$.

(2) $x + z = 0.710$.

(3) $y + z = 0.765$.

Subtracting (2) from (1) = (4) $y - z = 0.140$.

Adding (3) and (4) = (5) $2y = 0.905$.

(6) $y = 0.4525$.

Substituting value of y in (1) gives $x + 0.4525 = 0.850$.

$\therefore x = 0.3975$.

Substituting value of y in (3) gives $0.4525 + z = 0.765$.

$\therefore z = 0.3125$.

The diameters of the circles are: at A, 0.795 in.; at B, 0.905 in.; at C, 0.625 in.

29. As in the last exercise, three holes are to be bored, the distance between whose centers shall be 0.650 in., 0.790 in., and 0.865 in. respectively. Find the diameters of the required disks.

Ans. 0.725 in.; 0.575 in.; 1.005 in.

30. Three points A, B, and C are located as shown in Fig. 205. Three disks are centered at these points and tangent two and two. Find the diameters of the disks.

Ans. At A, 0.8960 in.; at B, 0.9716 in.; at C, 0.9700 in.

Suggestion. Let x, y, and z = radii of circles centered at A, B, and C respectively.

Then $x+y = \sqrt{0.680^2 + 0.640^2}$.
$x+z = \sqrt{0.880^2 + 0.310^2}$.
$y+z = \sqrt{0.950^2 + 0.2^2}$.

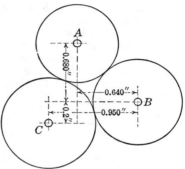

Fig. 205.

31. From geometry we know that the sum of the three angles of a triangle is 180°. Find the three angles of a triangle if the sum of twice the first and the second is 90° more than the third, and the sum of the first and twice the third is 70° more than twice the second. *Ans.* 50°; 60°; 70°.

32. A man has $98 in dollar bills, half-dollars, and quarters. Half of the dollars and $\frac{1}{3}$ the half-dollars are worth $31, and $\frac{1}{7}$ the half-dollars and $\frac{1}{3}$ the quarters are worth $10. How many pieces has he of each?

Ans. 48 dollars; 70 half-dollars; 60 quarters.

33. In a factory where 700 men and women are employed, the average daily pay for the men is $4.25, and for the women $2.25. If $2415 is paid daily for labor, find the number of men and the number of women employed. *Ans.* 420 men; 280 women.

34. A lever is balanced on a fulcrum with a weight of 40 lb. at one end and 50 lb. at the other. If 5 lb. is added to the 40-lb. weight, the 50-lb. weight will have to be placed 1 ft. farther from the fulcrum to balance the lever. Find the lengths of the two arms of the lever at first.

Ans. 10 ft.; and 8 ft.

Suggestion. Let x = the length in feet of the long arm,
and y = the length in feet of the short arm.
Then $40x = 50y$,
and $45x = 50(y+1)$.

35. A lever is balanced on a fulcrum with a weight w_1 on one arm and w_2 on the other. If p pounds are added to w_1, w_2 has to be moved over f feet to balance the lever. Find the lengths of the two arms of the lever.

Ans. $\dfrac{w_2 f}{p}$ and $\dfrac{w_1 f}{p}$.

36. A beam that is supported at its ends has a weight of 50 lb. placed upon it so that it causes an increase in pressure on the support at one end of 20 lb. It is also found that the same pressure is produced at this end by a weight of 60 lb. placed 3 ft. farther from this end. How long is the beam? *Ans.* 45 ft.

Suggestion. Consider the support where the increase is 20 lb. as the fulcrum. Then there is a pressure of 30 lb. at the other end.

Let $y =$ the length of the beam

and $x =$ the distance the 50-lb. weight is from the fulcrum.

Then $30y = 50x$.

Similarly, when the 60-lb. weight is applied,

$$40y = 60(x+3).$$

37. A glass full of water weighs 18 ounces. When the same glass is full of sulphuric acid of specific gravity 1.75 it weighs 27 ounces. Find the weight of the glass when empty. *Ans.* 6 ounces.

38. Given two grades of zinc ore, the first containing 45% of zinc, and the second 25% of zinc. Find how many pounds of each must be taken to make a mixture of 2000 lb. containing 40% of zinc.

Ans. 1500 lb. of 45% ore and 500 lb. of 25% ore.

Suggestion. Let $x =$ number of pounds of 45% ore,

and $y =$ number of pounds of 25% ore.

Then $x+y = 2000$,

and $0.45x + 0.25y = 0.40 \times 2000$.

39. The sum of the three sides of a triangle is 65 in. If the second side is 5 in. longer than the first and 7 in. shorter than the third, find the length of each side. *Ans.* 16 in.; 21 in.; 28 in.

CHAPTER XXX

EXPONENTS, POWERS, AND ROOTS

262. General statement.—In previous chapters, we have used **positive integral exponents.** In **Art. 185,** a positive integral exponent was defined as showing how many times the base is to be used as a factor.

The **negative exponent,** the **fractional exponent,** and the **zero exponent** are other kinds of exponents that occur in mathematics. They will be dealt with to some extent in the present chapter. **Logarithms** are exponents that will be considered in **Chapter XXXIV.**

The few facts and theorems concerning exponents, given in this chapter, are not intended to be a complete treatment of the subject, but they are sufficient for what follows, and will give the proper viewpoint for logarithms.

It should be carefully noted that the definition of a *positive integral exponent* cannot apply to an exponent that is *negative, zero,* or a *fraction.* For instance, in 8^2, the 2 shows that 8 is taken twice as a factor; but in $8^{\frac{1}{3}}$, the $\frac{1}{3}$ can in no sense show how many times 8 is taken as a factor. To say that 8 is taken $\frac{1}{3}$ times as a factor is to make a meaningless statement.

We shall therefore find it necessary to enlarge the definition of an exponent so as to make it include these new kinds of exponents.

263. Laws of exponents.—The **law of exponents in multiplication** (see **Art. 216**) has been stated and proved for *positive integral exponents.* It may be restated here in symbols as follows:

$$a^m \cdot a^n = a^{m+n}.$$

Likewise the **law of exponents in division** (see **Art. 223**) has been stated for *positive integral exponents.* A restatement in symbols is as follows:

$$a^m \div a^n = a^{m-n},$$

where m is greater than n. When $m = n$ it is

$$a^n \div a^n = 1.$$

In finding the **power of a power** *the exponents are multiplied.* That is, $(a^m)^n = a^{mn}$. This is found from the definition of a positive integral exponent.

Thus, $(a^m)^n = a^m a^m a^m \cdots$ to n factors $= a^{m+m+m} \cdots$ to n terms $= a^{mn}$. A numerical illustration is $(a^6)^3 = a^6 \cdot a^6 \cdot a^6 = a^{18}$.

The **power of a product** *is the same as the product of the powers of the factors.*

That is, $(abc \cdots)^n = a^n b^n c^n \cdots$

A numerical illustration is $(2 \cdot 3 \cdot 4)^3 = 2^3 \cdot 3^3 \cdot 4^3$.

The **power of a fraction** *equals the power of the numerator divided by the power of the denominator.*

That is, $\left(\dfrac{a}{b}\right)^m = \dfrac{a^m}{b^m}$.

A numerical illustration is $\left(\dfrac{2}{3}\right)^3 = \dfrac{2^3}{3^3} = \dfrac{8}{27}$.

If we take the **root of a power,** *we have the inverse of the operation by which we get* a^{mn}, *and have* $\sqrt[n]{a^m} = a^{m \div n}$.

A numerical illustration is $\sqrt[3]{3^4} = 3^{4 \div 2} = 3^2 = 9$.

The definition of a positive integral exponent gives us the right to state the above only when $m \div n$ is an integer.

A summary of the six laws of exponents mentioned is:

(1) $a^m a^n = a^{m+n}$.

(2) $a^m \div a^n = a^{m-n}$.

(3) $(a^m)^n = a^{mn}$.

(4) $(a \cdot b \cdot c \cdots)^m = a^m b^m c^m \cdots$

(5) $\left(\dfrac{a}{b}\right)^m = \dfrac{a^m}{b^m}$.

(6) $\sqrt[n]{a^m} = a^{m \div n} = a^{\frac{m}{n}}$.

Example 1.   Find the fourth power of $3a^2 x^3 y^4$.

$$(3a^2 x^3 y^4)^4 = 3^4 (a^2)^4 (x^3)^4 (y^4)^4 = 81 a^8 x^{12} y^{16}.$$

Example 2.   Find the cube of $\dfrac{3a^3 b^4 x}{2y^2}$.

$$\left(\frac{3a^3 b^4 x}{2y^2}\right)^3 = \frac{3^3 (a^3)^3 (b^4)^3 x^3}{2^3 (y^2)^3} = \frac{27 a^9 b^{12} x^3}{8y^6}.$$

Example 3.   Find the cube root of $3^6 b^9 x^{12}$.

$$\sqrt[3]{3^6 b^9 x^{12}} = 3^{6 \div 3} b^{9 \div 3} x^{12 \div 3} = 3^2 b^3 x^4.$$

EXERCISES 92

Raise to the indicated powers, or find the root indicated.

1. $(a^2y^3)^4$. $\qquad\qquad$ *Ans.* a^8y^{12}.
2. $(2y^3x^4)^6$. $\qquad\qquad$ *Ans.* $64y^{18}x^{24}$.
3. $(3a^2b)^3$. $\qquad\qquad$ *Ans.* $27a^6b^3$.
4. $(-4a^2x^6)^3$. $\qquad\qquad$ *Ans.* $-64a^6x^{18}$.
5. $(-3a^3b^2x)^4$. $\qquad\qquad$ *Ans.* $81a^{12}b^8x^4$.
6. $(-x^4y^6)^2$. $\qquad\qquad$ *Ans.* x^8y^{12}.
7. $(3^ab^c)^3$. $\qquad\qquad$ *Ans.* $3^{3a}b^{3c}$.
8. $(4a^cx^2)^b$. $\qquad\qquad$ *Ans.* $4^ba^{bc}x^{2b}$.
9. $\left(\dfrac{3x}{4b}\right)^3$. $\qquad\qquad$ *Ans.* $\dfrac{27x^3}{64b^3}$.
10. $\left(\dfrac{4x^2}{5b^3}\right)^3$. $\qquad\qquad$ *Ans.* $\dfrac{64x^6}{125b^9}$.
11. $\left(\dfrac{2a^3b}{4c^4x^2}\right)^4$. $\qquad\qquad$ *Ans.* $\dfrac{16a^{12}b^4}{256c^{16}x^8}$.
12. $\left[\left(\dfrac{a}{b}\right)^2\right]^n$. $\qquad\qquad$ *Ans.* $\dfrac{a^{2n}}{b^{2n}}$.
13. $\left(\dfrac{x^nb}{y^mc}\right)^d$. $\qquad\qquad$ *Ans.* $\dfrac{x^{dn}b^d}{y^{dm}c^d}$.
14. $(-x^2y^3z^4)^4$. $\qquad\qquad$ *Ans.* $x^8y^{12}z^{16}$.
15. $(7mn^3)^{xy}$. $\qquad\qquad$ *Ans.* $7^{xy}m^{xy}n^{3xy}$.
16. $(9x^2y^z)^{2z}$. $\qquad\qquad$ *Ans.* $9^{2z}x^{4z}y^{2z^2}$.
17. $\sqrt[4]{a^4b^8c^{12}}$. $\qquad\qquad$ *Ans.* ab^2c^3.
18. $\sqrt[3]{\dfrac{2^6b^9}{3^9x^{12}}}$. $\qquad\qquad$ *Ans.* $\dfrac{4b^3}{27x^4}$.

264. Zero exponent.—If we assume that $a^m \div a^n = a^{m-n}$ holds when $m = n$, we have $a^m \div a^n = a^{m-n} = a^0$, for $m - n = 0$
Also $a^m \div a^n = 1$ by **Art. 223,** if $m = n$.

$\qquad \therefore a^0 = 1$.

Making the above assumption is the same as stating by definition: *Any number other than zero affected by a zero exponent equals one.*

Examples. $\quad$ (1) $\quad 0.8^0 = 1$.
$\qquad\qquad\quad$ (2) $\quad 100^0 = 1$.
$\qquad\qquad\quad$ (3) $\quad 0.01^0 = 1$.

265. Negative exponent.—Assuming that the law $a^m \div a^n = a^{m-n}$ holds when n is greater than m, we have

$$a^2 \div a^6 = a^{-4}.$$

but $a^2 \div a^6 = \dfrac{a^2}{a^6} = \dfrac{1}{a^4}$.

$$\therefore \quad a^{-4} = \dfrac{1}{a^4}.$$

Similarly $a^{-n} = \dfrac{1}{a^n}$.

By definition then, *a number affected by a negative exponent equals 1 divided by the same number affected by a positive exponent, equal in absolute value to the negative exponent.*

Examples.   (1) $2^{-3} = \dfrac{1}{2^3} = \dfrac{1}{8}$.

             (2) $4^{-3} = \dfrac{1}{4^3} = \dfrac{1}{64}$.

266. Fractional exponent.—If we apply the law $\sqrt[n]{a^m} = a^{m \div n}$, when m and n have any values, we have

$$\sqrt[n]{a^m} = a^{\frac{m}{n}}. \quad \text{Also } \sqrt[n]{a} = a^{1 \div n} = a^{\frac{1}{n}}.$$

By definition then, *a fractional exponent indicates a root. The denominator is the index of the root, and the numerator is the exponent of a power.*

A form like $a^{\frac{m}{n}}$ means either $\sqrt[n]{a^m}$ or $(\sqrt[n]{a})^m$. That is, the number a may be raised to the mth power and then the nth root taken, or the nth root may be taken first and then the result raised to the mth power.

Thus, $8^{\frac{2}{3}} = \sqrt[3]{8^2} = \sqrt[3]{64} = 4$, or $8^{\frac{2}{3}} = (\sqrt[3]{8})^2 = 2^2 = 4$.

Examples.   (1) $4^{\frac{1}{2}} = \sqrt{4} = 2$.

             (2) $64^{\frac{1}{3}} = \sqrt[3]{64} = 4$.

             (3) $32^{\frac{3}{5}} = (\sqrt[5]{32})^3 = 2^3 = 8$.

             (4) $4^{-\frac{3}{2}} = \dfrac{1}{4^{\frac{3}{2}}} = \dfrac{1}{\sqrt{4^3}} = \dfrac{1}{8}$.

EXERCISES 93

Find the values of the following:

1. 10^0.	*Ans.* 1.	**6.** $16^{-\frac{1}{2}}$.		*Ans.* $\frac{1}{4}$.
2. 4^{-2}	*Ans.* $\frac{1}{16}$.	**7.** $27^{\frac{4}{3}}$.		*Ans.* 81.
3. 10^{-8}.	*Ans.* $\frac{1}{100000000}$.	**8.** $512^{-\frac{1}{3}}$.		*Ans.* $\frac{1}{64}$.
4. 8^{-3}.	*Ans.* $\frac{1}{512}$.	**9.** $(\frac{1}{125})^{-\frac{2}{3}}$.		*Ans.* 25.
5. $16^{\frac{1}{4}}$.	*Ans.* 2.	**10.** $100^{\frac{3}{2}}$.		*Ans.* 1000.

11. $1000^{-\frac{2}{3}}$. *Ans.* $\frac{1}{100}$. **14.** $(4^0)^6$. *Ans.* 1.
12. $10^{0.3^2}$. *Ans.* 9. **15.** $64^{-\frac{1}{3}}$ *Ans.* $\frac{1}{1024}$.
13. $(3^0)^{-3}$. *Ans.* 1. **16.** $9^{\frac{5}{2}}$. *Ans.* 243.
  17. Divide $a^{-2}x^{-\frac{1}{2}}$ by a^{-3}. *Ans.* $ax^{-\frac{1}{2}}$.
  18. Multiply $a^{-\frac{3}{4}}$ by $a^{\frac{5}{6}}$. *Ans.* $a^{\frac{1}{12}}$.
  19. Multiply $3a^{\frac{2}{3}}b^{\frac{1}{2}}$ by $4a^{\frac{1}{6}}b^{\frac{5}{6}}$. *Ans.* $12a^{\frac{5}{6}}b^{\frac{4}{3}}$.

267. Exponents used in writing numbers.—Often in engineering subjects we see such expressions as 4.25×10^9, or 726×10^{-8}. These forms are the result of an attempt to write certain expressions in a shortened form. Keeping in mind the meaning of an exponent,

$$4.25 \times 10^9 = 4.25 \times 1,000,000,000 = 4,250,000,000.$$

This last number means the same as the given expression, but in some ways is not so convenient a form to handle, neither is it so easily compared with others of its kind as is the first form. Neither does the eye catch its value as quickly as it does that of the shortened form.

The form $726 \times 10^{-8} = 726 \times \frac{1}{10^8} = 726 \times \frac{1}{100000000} =$

$$0.00000726.$$

EXERCISES 94

Express the following in the common notation.
  1. 3.5×10^7. *Ans.* 35,000,000.
  2. 8.67×10^{11}. *Ans.* 867,000,000,000.
  3. 523×10^{-8}. *Ans.* $\frac{523}{100000000} = 0.00000523$.
  4. 4.786×10^{-9}. *Ans.* $\frac{4.786}{1000000000} = 0.000000004786$.
  5. 9.376×10^{-6}. *Ans.* $\frac{9.376}{1000000} = 0.000009376$.
  6. 4.673×10^8. *Ans.* 467,300,000.
  7. 4.37×10^{12}. *Ans.* 4,370,000,000,000.
Express the following in the shortened notation:
  8. 4,768,000,000. *Ans.* 4.768×10^9.
  9. 23,600,000,000. *Ans.* 2.36×10^{10}.
  10. 37,600,000,000. *Ans.* 37.6×10^9.
  11. $\frac{367}{1000000}$. *Ans.* 3.67×10^{-4}.
  12. $\frac{4}{10000000}$. *Ans.* 4×10^{-7}.
  13. 0.000000367. *Ans.* 3.67×10^{-7}.
  14. 0.000000004676. *Ans.* 4.676×10^{-9}.
  15. $\frac{2.798}{1000000}$. *Ans.* 2.798×10^{-6}.

CHAPTER XXXI

QUADRATIC EQUATIONS

268. Definitions.—An equation that contains the square of the unknown number and no higher power of it is a **quadratic equation.**

A **pure quadratic equation** is one that has the square only of the unknown number, as $2x^2 = 4$.

An **affected quadratic equation** is one that has both the square and the first power of the unknown, as $x^2 + 3x = 10$.

THE PURE QUADRATIC EQUATION

269. Solution.—The solution of the pure quadratic equation is the same as that of the simple equation until the value of the square of the unknown is found. The next step is to take the square root of each member of the equation.

Example 1. Solve $3x^2 + 8 = 7x^2 - 8$ for x.

Solution.

(1) Given equation, $\quad 3x^2 + 8 = 7x^2 - 8.$

(2) Transposing, $\quad 3x^2 - 7x^2 = -8 - 8.$

(3) Collecting terms, $\quad -4x^2 = -16.$

(4) Dividing by -4, $\quad x^2 = 4.$

(5) Extracting the square root of both x^2 and 4, $\quad x = \pm 2.$

Here we use the sign $\pm$, and it indicates that the answer is either a $+2$ or a -2. (See **Art. 237.**)

Since the product of two minus numbers gives the same value as the product of the same plus numbers, we may always call a square root either plus or minus.

Thus, $\sqrt{4} = \pm 2$, $\sqrt{b^2} = \pm b$.

Example 2. Find the radius of a circle whose area is 4392 in.^{2}

Solution. (1) Let r stand for the radius,

(2) then $3.1416 r^2 = $ area of circle.

(3) But 4932 in.^{2} = area of circle.

(4) $\quad \therefore 3.1416 r^2 = 4932$, by axiom (5).

(5) $\quad r^2 = 1569.9007.$

(6) $\quad r = \pm 39.622.$

332

It should be noticed that the radius cannot be negative, hence the only value of r permissible is $+39.622$.

EXERCISES 95

Solve for x in exercises 1 to 10 and test.

1. $7x^2 + 25 = 2x^2 + 150.$ *Ans.* $\pm 5.$

2. $3x^2 - 10 - x^2 = 12 + 4x^2 - 54.$ *Ans.* $\pm 4.$

3. $53 - 7x^2 + 27 = -2x^2.$ *Ans.* $\pm 4.$

4. $x^2 + 1 = \dfrac{x^2}{4} + 4.$ *Ans.* $\pm 2.$

5. $\dfrac{x(9 + 2x)}{15} = \dfrac{3x + 6}{5}.$ *Ans.* $\pm 3.$

6. $\dfrac{2x}{3} - \dfrac{5}{4x} = \dfrac{7x}{9} - \dfrac{21}{4x}.$ *Ans.* $\pm 6.$

7. $2x(5 - x) + 8x^2 = 10(x + 2).$ *Ans.* $\pm 1.826 -.$

8. $\dfrac{13}{2x + 3} = \dfrac{3x + 2}{2 + x}.$ *Ans.* $\pm 1.826 -.$

9. $(3x + 6)(3x - 6) = (2x + 5)(2x - 5).$ *Ans.* $\pm 1.483 +.$

10. $\dfrac{x^2 + x + 1}{x - 1} - 6 = \dfrac{x^2 - x + 1}{x + 1}.$ *Ans.* $\pm 2.$

11. Given $\dfrac{5}{4 + y} + \dfrac{5}{4 - y} = \dfrac{8}{3},$ find the value of y.   *Ans.* $\pm 1.$

12. Given $F = \dfrac{Wv^2}{gr},$ find the values of v.   *Ans.* $\pm \sqrt{\dfrac{Fgr}{W}}.$

13. (a) Given $S = \frac{1}{2}gt^2,$ find values of t. (b) If $S = 5280$ and $g = 32.2,$ find values of t.   *Ans.* (a) $\pm \sqrt{\dfrac{2S}{g}};$ (b) $\pm 18.11.$

14. Given $l = \dfrac{gt^2}{\pi},$ solve for t.   *Ans.* $\pm \sqrt{\dfrac{\pi l}{g}}.$

15. Given $F = \dfrac{mna}{d^2},$ solve for d.   *Ans.* $\pm \sqrt{\dfrac{mna}{F}}.$

16. Given $n^2 = \dfrac{KS^2t}{l^2d},$ solve for S, l, and n.

$$\text{\textit{Ans.} } \pm \sqrt{\frac{n^2l^2d}{Kt}};\ \pm \sqrt{\frac{KS^2t}{dn^2}};\ \pm \sqrt{\frac{KS^2t}{l^2d}}.$$

17. Find the radius of a cylinder of altitude 12 ft. and volume 1400 cu. ft. (Use formula $V = h\pi r^2,$ substitute values and solve for r.)   *Ans.* $6.09 +$ ft.

18. Find the diameter of a right circular cone of altitude 20 in. and volume 145 in.^{3} *Ans.* $5.26 +$ in.

THE AFFECTED QUADRATIC EQUATION

270. Solution by factoring.—An affected quadratic equation in x, when simplified, can have a term in x^2, a term in x, a term not containing x, and no other term. Thus, $x^2 - 5x = -6$ is such an equation.

The solution of this equation has been discussed in **Art. 237**.

The steps in the solution of a quadratic equation that can be solved by factoring are restated here.

(1) *Simplify the equation.*

(2) *Transpose all terms to the first member of the equation.*

(3) *Factor the expression in the first member.*

(4) *Equate each factor to zero.*

(5) *Solve each of these equations.*

Example. Solve $x^2 + 23x = -102$.

Solution. (1) Given equation, $x^2 + 23x = -102$.

(2) Transposing, $x^2 + 23x + 102 = 0$.

(3) Factoring, $(x+6)(x+17) = 0$.

(4) $\therefore x+6 = 0$ or $x+17 = 0$.

(5) $\therefore x = -6$ or $x = -17$.

EXERCISES 96

Solve and test.

1. $x^2 + 15x + 56 = 0$.   *Ans.* -7 or -8.
2. $x^2 - 17x + 72 = 0$.   *Ans.* 8 or 9.
3. $x^2 - 16x = 36$.   *Ans.* -2 or 18.
4. $5x - 6 = x^2$.   *Ans.* 2 or 3.
5. $x^2 + 2x = 24$.   *Ans.* 4 or -6.
6. $x^2 + 26x + 160 = 0$.   *Ans.* -10 or -16.
7. $x^2 + 3x = 54$.   *Ans.* -9 or 6.

271. It was stated in **Art. 235** that there are many trinomials we had not learned to factor. It is necessary then to have some other method than factoring for solving affected quadratic equations.

272. Completing the square.—In **Arts. 229** and **230** we learned the form of a trinomial square. The first and last terms are perfect squares of monomials, and the middle term is twice the product of the square roots of the first and last terms. Keeping this in mind then, we can find the last term if we know the first two.

Thus, if we know that a^2+2ab are the first two terms, we can find the third term by taking the square of the quotient obtained by dividing the second term by twice the square root of the first. Twice the square root of the first term is $2a$. The second term divided by this gives b; which squared is b^2, the third term. We say then that we have **completed the square**, which is $a^2+2ab+b^2$.

Example. Complete the square of x^2+4x.

Twice the square root of x^2 is $2x$, $4x \div 2x = 2$, and the square of 2 is 4. Hence the completed square is x^2+4x+4.

When the coefficient of x^2 is 1, all that is necessary is to *add the square of one-half the coefficient of x.*

Complete the square of each of the following:

1. x^2+2x.   Result x^2+2x+1.
2. x^2-2x.   Result x^2-2x+1.
3. x^2-3x.   Result $x^2-3x+\frac{9}{4}$.
4. x^2-10x.   Result $x^2-10x+25$.
5. a^2-10ab.   Result $a^2-10ab+25b^2$.

273. Solution by completing the square.—We can best show how this is applied to the solution of an equation by an example.

Example 1. Given $x^2+4x=12$, find x.

(1) Completing the square of the first member we have x^2+4x+4. Since 4 is added to x^2+4x, we must also add 4 to 12 in order that the equality may be true.

$$\therefore x^2+4x+4=16.$$

(2) Extracting the square root of both members, we have

$$x+2=\pm 4.$$

(3) Transposing, $x=-2\pm 4$.

(4) $\therefore x=2 \text{ or } -6$.

Each of these results checks the original equation and is therefore a root of the equation.

Example 2. Given $x^2+12x=-35$, find x.

Solution.   (1) Given equation, $x^2+12x=-35$.

(2) Completing square, $x^2+12x+36=1$.

(3) Extracting roots, $x+6=\pm 1$.

(4) $\therefore x=-7 \text{ or } -5$.

Example 3.　Given $2r^2+4r=48$, find r.

Solution.　(1) Given equation,　$2r^2+4r=48$.

(2) Dividing by 2,　　　　　　　　$r^2+2r=24$.

(3) Completing square,　　　　$r^2+2r+1=25$.

(4) Extracting roots,　　　　　　$r+1=\pm5$.

(5)　　　　　　　　　　　　　$\therefore r=4$ or -6.

Example 4.　Given $3x^2-7x=6$, find x.

Solution.　(1) Given equation,　$3x^2-7x=6$.

(2) Dividing by 3,　　　　　　　　$x^2-\tfrac{7}{3}x=2$.

(3) Completing square,　　　$x^2-\tfrac{7}{3}x+\tfrac{49}{36}=\tfrac{121}{36}$.

(4) Extracting roots,　　　　　　$x-\tfrac{7}{6}=\pm\tfrac{11}{6}$.

(5)　　　　　　　　　　　　$\therefore x=3$ or $-\tfrac{2}{3}$.

It should be noticed that we always divide by the coefficient of x^2, unless it is 1, before completing the square.

Example 5.　Given $9x=4-3x^2$, find x.

Solution.　(1) Given equation,　　　$9x=4-3x^2$.

(2) Transposing,　　　　　　　　$3x^2+9x=4$.

(3) Dividing by 3,　　　　　　　　$x^2+3x=\tfrac{4}{3}$.

(4) Completing square,　　　$x^2+3x+\tfrac{9}{4}=\tfrac{4}{3}+\tfrac{9}{4}=\tfrac{43}{12}$.

(5) Extracting roots, $x+\tfrac{3}{2}=\pm\sqrt{\tfrac{43}{12}}=\pm1.893-$.

(6)　　　　　　　　　　$\therefore x=-\tfrac{3}{2}\pm1.893-$.

(7)　　　　　　　　　　$x=0.393$ or -3.393.

The method of solving an affected quadratic equation may be summarized in the following:

Rule.　(1) *Reduce the equation to the form* $x^2+bx=c$.

(2) *Complete the square by adding to both members the square of one-half the coefficient of* x.

(3) *Equate the square root of the first member to* $\pm$ *the square root of the second member, and solve the two equations thus formed.*

EXERCISES 97

Solve for x by completing the square.

1. $x^2-4x=60$.　　　　　　　　　　*Ans.* 10 or -6.

2. $x^2+11x=-24$.　　　　　　　　　*Ans.* -8 or -3.

3. $3x^2-10x+3=0$.　　　　　　　　*Ans.* 3 or $\tfrac{1}{3}$.

4. $36x^2-36x-7=0$.　　　　　　　　*Ans.* $\tfrac{7}{6}$ or $-\tfrac{1}{6}$.

5. $10x^2+7x=12$.　　　　　　　　　*Ans.* $\tfrac{4}{5}$ or $-\tfrac{3}{2}$.

6. $x^2+4x=2$.　　　　　　*Ans.* 0.4494 or -4.4494.

7. $x^2+2x=2$. *Ans.* 0.732 or -2.732.
8. $4x^2-4x=7$. *Ans.* 1.9142 or -0.9142.
9. $9x^2+6x-17=0$. *Ans.* 1.0809 or -1.7475.
10. $3x^2+121=44x$. *Ans.* 11 or $1\frac{1}{3}$.

274. Solution of the affected quadratic equation by the formula.—If we solve the general quadratic equation $ax^2+bx+c=0$, we shall have a formula which may be used to find the value of the unknown in any quadratic equation.

Example 1. Given $ax^2+bx+c=0$, find x.

Solution.

(1) Given equation, $ax^2+bx+c=0$.

(2) Transposing, $ax^2+bx=-c$.

(3) Dividing by a, $x^2+\dfrac{b}{a}x=-\dfrac{c}{a}$.

(4) Completing square, $x^2+\dfrac{b}{a}x+\dfrac{b^2}{4a^2}=\dfrac{b^2}{4a^2}-\dfrac{c}{a}$.

(5) Extracting roots, $x+\dfrac{b}{2a}=\pm\sqrt{\dfrac{b^2-4ac}{4a^2}}$.

(6) $\therefore x=-\dfrac{b}{2a}\pm\sqrt{\dfrac{b^2-4ac}{4a^2}}=\dfrac{-b\pm\sqrt{b^2-4ac}}{2a}$.

This last form is a formula that can be used in solving any quadratic equation.

In using the formula, care must be taken as regards the signs. They must be considered a part of the values of a, b, and c.

Thus, in $3x^2-2x-4=0$, $a=3$, $b=-2$, and $c=-4$.

Example 2. Substitute in the formula of example 1, and find the value of x in $6x^2+17x+7=0$.

Solution. Here $a=6$, $b=17$, and $c=7$.

Substituting these values in the formula,

$$x=\frac{-17\pm\sqrt{17^2-4\cdot6\cdot7}}{2\cdot6}=\frac{-17\pm11}{12}=-\tfrac{1}{2}\text{ or }-2\tfrac{1}{3}.$$

Example 3. By the formula, find the value of x in $6x^2+8x-30=0$.

Solution. Here $a=6$, $b=8$, and $c=-30$.

$$\therefore x=\frac{-8\pm\sqrt{8^2-4\cdot6(-30)}}{2\cdot6}=\frac{-8\pm28}{12}=1\tfrac{2}{3}\text{ or }-3.$$

22

EXERCISES 98

Solve the following equations by any method.

1. $x^2 - 3x = -2$.   *Ans.* 1 or 2.

2. $x^2 + 5x = -6$.   *Ans.* -2 or -3.

3. $x^2 - x = 6$.   *Ans.* 3 or -2.

4. $y^2 - 2y = 168$.   *Ans.* 14 or -12.

5. $y^2 + 2y = 120$.   *Ans.* 10 or -12.

6. $y^2 - 22y = 48$.   *Ans.* 24 or -2.

7. $5r^2 + 12r = 9$.   *Ans.* $\frac{3}{5}$ or -3.

8. $2r^2 + 5r = -2$.   *Ans.* $-\frac{1}{2}$ or -2.

9. $7a^2 + 9a = 10$.   *Ans.* $\frac{5}{7}$ or -2.

10. $7x^2 + 2x = 32$.   *Ans.* 2 or $-2\frac{2}{7}$.

11. $V + \dfrac{1}{V} - \dfrac{5}{2} = 0$.   *Ans.* 2 or $\frac{1}{2}$.

12. $\dfrac{S^2}{9} + \dfrac{S}{3} = \dfrac{35}{4}$.   *Ans.* $7\frac{1}{2}$ or $-10\frac{1}{2}$.

13. $x^2 + 4bx = \dfrac{9b^2}{4}$.   *Ans.* $\dfrac{b}{2}$ or $-\dfrac{9b}{2}$.

14. Given $S = Vt + \frac{1}{2}gt^2$, solve for V, g, and t.

$$\text{\emph{Ans.} } \frac{2S - gt^2}{2t}; \quad \frac{2S - 2Vt}{t^2}; \quad \frac{-V \pm \sqrt{V^2 + 2gs}}{g}.$$

15. Given $T = 2\pi rh + 2\pi r^2$, solve for r.   *Ans.* $\dfrac{-\pi h \pm \sqrt{\pi^2 h^2 + 2\pi T}}{2\pi}$.

16. Find three consecutive numbers, such that their sum is one-third of the product of the first two.   *Ans.* 9, 10, 11 or -1, 0, 1.

17. Find two numbers, one of which is 5 times the other, and whose product is 4500.   *Ans.* 150 and 30, or -150 and -30.

18. A walk containing 784 ft.^{2} is to be built around a garden 50 by 49 ft. How wide must the walk be?   *Ans.* 3 ft. $8\frac{1}{4}$ in. nearly.

19. There are as many square feet in the surface of a certain sphere as there are cubic feet in its volume. Find its radius.   *Ans.* 3 ft.

Solution. Let r = number of feet in radius.

Then $4\pi r^2$ = number of square feet in surface,

and $\frac{4}{3}\pi r^3$ = number of cubic feet in volume.

$$\therefore \tfrac{4}{3}\pi r^3 = 4\pi r^2.$$
$$4\pi r^3 - 12\pi r^2 = 0.$$

Factoring, $4\pi r^2(r - 3) = 0$.

$$\therefore 4\pi r^2 = 0 \text{ and } r - 3 = 0,$$

or $r = 0$ and $r = 3$.

20. Same as last exercise, but substitute cube for sphere and find the edge.   *Ans.* 6 ft.

21. Find two numbers whose sum is 25 and whose product is 144.

     Ans. 9 and 16.

22. Divide 71 into two parts, the sum of the squares of which is 2561.

     Ans. 40 and 31.

23. If a train traveled 5 miles an hour faster, it would take 2 hours less to go 420 miles. Find the rate of the train.

Ans. 30 miles an hour.

24. What is the radius of a circle whose area is doubled when the radius is increased by 2 ft.? *Ans.* 4.828 ft.

25. What is the diameter of a circle whose area is multiplied by 3 when the diameter is increased by 2 ft.? *Ans.* 2.732 ft.

26. The height of a right circular cylinder is 6 in., and the entire area is 100 in.² Find the radius of the base. *Ans.* 1.99+ in.

Suggestion. Let r stand for radius of base.

Then $2\pi r^2 + 12\pi r$ is the entire area.

$$\therefore\ 2\pi r^2 + 12\pi r = 100,$$

or $\qquad r^2 + 6r = \dfrac{100}{2\pi} = 15.915.$

27. The differences between the hypotenuse and the two sides of a right triangle are 3 and 6 ft. respectively. Find the sides and the area of the triangle. *Ans.* 15 ft., 12 ft., 9 ft., and 54 sq. ft.

28. The hypotenuse of a right triangle is 4 in. longer than one leg, and 8 in. longer than the other. Find the lengths of the three sides.

Ans. 20 in.; 16 in.; 12 in.

29. The circumference of the hind wheel of a wagon is 5 ft. more than that of the front wheel. If the hind wheel makes 150 fewer revolutions than the front wheel in going one mile, find the circumference of each wheel. *Ans.* 16 ft. and 11 ft.

30. An aeroplane which is at an altitude of 1200 ft. and moving at the rate of 100 miles per hour in a northerly direction drops a bomb. Disregarding the resistance of the air, where will the bomb strike the ground?

Ans. 1270 ft. north of starting point.

Suggestion. Find the number of seconds it will take the bomb to reach the ground from the formula $s = \frac{1}{2}gt^2$, where $s =$ height of aeroplane in feet, $g = 32$, and $t =$ time in seconds. This gives $t = 8.66$ seconds.

Then the bomb will strike as many feet north of the starting point as the aeroplane will travel in 8.66 seconds.

CHAPTER XXXII

VARIATION

275. General statement.—We depend upon the ideas dealt with in variation for most of our physical laws and formulas. The meaning of many of the formulas already used will be made much clearer by considering their meaning from the viewpoint of variation.

The relations considered in variation are those considered in ratio and proportion. In many ways, however, it will be found that the methods used in variation are more convenient than the methods of ratio and proportion. Familiarity with them gives the student another powerful mathematical instrument.

For the principles of ratio and proportion used in the present chapter the student is referred to **Chapter VII.**

276. Constants and variables.—A number whose value does not change is called a **constant.**

In mathematical problems, certain constants occur that are always the same.

The value of π, the ratio of the circumference to the diameter of a circle, is such a constant.

There also occur other constants that do not change in the same problem, but which may have another value in a different problem.

The radius of a circle and the side of a square are such constants.

A **variable** is a number that may take an unlimited number of values.

For example, the number expressing a person's age, the height of a growing corn stalk, or the distance a moving train is from a station it has just left.

277. Direct variation.—The idea of variation is a very common one. Nearly everything is affected by its surroundings; that is, things vary according as something else varies.

340

The growth of a tree depends upon the amount of light it receives; the more light it receives, the faster it grows, if other conditions are favorable. In such a case we say its growth varies **directly** as the amount of light.

The amount of pay a man gets varies directly as the time he works; that is, the longer he works the more pay he receives.

Definition. If two numbers are so related that their ratio is constant, that is, if either increases the other increases, or if either decreases the other decreases, the two numbers are said to **vary directly** as each other.

278. Mathematical statement.—Just as with many other ideas, there is a mathematical way of expressing the idea of variation. When the ideas are so expressed, they can be combined and handled according to the rules of mathematics. In this manner, new relations are seen and new results obtained.

The sign $\propto$ means "varies as."

If x and y are two variables that vary directly as each other, it may be written in the shorthand form $x \propto y$. It may also be written in the form $x = ky$. This last is an equation stating that the **ratio** of x to y is a constant k. The equation is the form most often used.

Example 1. If a train is moving away from a station at a uniform rate, express the relation between its distance d from the station and the time t since it left the station.

Here evidently the distance d varies directly as the time t.

$$\therefore \ d = kt.$$

The student should consider very carefully the meaning of the constant k in the different examples taken up. Here the k evidently represents the uniform rate per unit of time. If the time is in minutes, k stands for the rate per minute. This rate may be given in feet, rods, miles, or any other unit of length. The k then depends for its value upon the kind of units used, but this is not the only thing that may change the value of k.

Example 2. If two numbers x and y vary directly as each other, and when $x = 10$, $y = 4$, find x when $y = 25$.

Solution. Since the relation between x and y is direct,
$$x = ky.$$

Substitute the values of x and y given, and

   $10 = 4k$.

   $\therefore k = 2\frac{1}{2}$.

   $\therefore x = 2\frac{1}{2}y$ is the relation between the variables, and if $y = 25$ we have $x = 2\frac{1}{2} \cdot 25 = 62\frac{1}{2}$. *Ans.*

Such a relation as $x = 2\frac{1}{2}y$ is often spoken of as a **law.**

Example 3. The space passed through by a body falling freely from a distance above the ground varies as the square of the time. If $s =$ the space in feet and $t =$ time in seconds, write the law. Find the value of k, if the body will fall 402.5 feet in 5 seconds.

Solution. Since the variation is directly as the square of the time, $s = kt^2$. Substituting values of s and t,

$$402.5 = k \cdot 5^2.$$
$$\therefore k = 16.1.$$

Hence the law or formula to find the distance in feet a body will fall in t seconds is $s = 16.1t^2$. This is usually written $s = \frac{1}{2}gt^2$, where $g = 32.2$.

279. Inverse variation.—Consider a horizontal beam, resting at each end on a support, and having a weight at its midpoint. The size of the weight it will support depends upon its length; but here the *longer* the beam, the *less* it will support. In such a case the variation is said to be **indirect** or **inverse.**

The resistance to an electric current is less in a large wire than in a small one of the same material; the resistance varies inversely as the size of the wire in cross section.

The intensity of the light from a lamp decreases as we go away from it. Here the variation is an inverse one, but the intensity of illumination is not one-half as much when the distance is doubled. It decreases inversely as the square of the distance; that is, the intensity is one-fourth as much at twice the distance.

Definition. One number **varies inversely** as another when their product is constant. That is, if either increases, the other decreases, or if either decreases, the other increases.

280. Mathematical statement.—The shorthand way of writing the fact that x varies inversely as y is $x \propto \frac{1}{y}$.

The equation form is $x = \frac{k}{y}$, or $xy = k$.

Example 1.   If x varies inversely as y, state the law and find the value of the constant if $x = 10$ when $y = \frac{1}{2}$.

Solution. $xy = k$ is the mathematical statement of the variation.

Substituting, $10 \cdot \frac{1}{2} = k$. $\therefore\ k = 5$.

If this value of k is used, the law, or equation, becomes

$$xy = 5.$$

Example 2.   If $x = \frac{1}{100}$, find y from the law of example 1. Substituting in the law, $\frac{1}{100}y = 5$.

$$\therefore\ y = 500.\ Ans.$$

281. Joint variation.—*Definition.*   One number **varies jointly** as two or more other numbers when it varies directly as the product of the others.   Thus, x varies jointly as u and v when $x = kuv$.

A number may vary directly as one number and inversely as another.   It then varies as the quotient of the first divided by the second.

Thus, if x varies directly as y and inversely as z, it is written $x = k\dfrac{y}{z}$.

EXERCISES 99

1. If $x \propto y$ and when $x = 20$, $y = 60$, write the equation between x and y.   *Ans.* $3x = y$.

2. If $b \propto d$ and when $b = 10$, $d = 15$, find b when $d = 80$.   *Ans.* $53\frac{1}{3}$.

3. If x varies jointly as y and z, and when $y = 6$ and $z = 2$, $x = 120$, find the constant.   Find y when $x = 200$ and $z = 15$.

Ans. $k = 10;\ y = 1\frac{1}{3}$.

4. The area A of a triangle varies jointly as the base b and the altitude a.   Write the law if when $a = 6$ in. and $b = 4$ in., $A = 12$ in.^{2} What will be the area when the base is 25 in. and the altitude is 40 in.?

Ans. $A = \frac{1}{2}ab;\ 500$ in.^{2}

Remark.   The law here is the well-known formula for the area of a triangle, but we have not supposed that we knew anything about the formula in working the example.

5. Similar figures[1] vary in areas as the squares of their like dimensions. The diameter of one circle is four times that of another.   Using this principle, find the relation of their areas.   (Similar figures are those that are alike in shape.)

[1] The ideas used here are not new, but will help to show the intimate relation between variation and ratio and proportion.   (See **Art. 87.**)

Solution. Here the relation is best expressed as a proportion. Using A and a for the areas, and $4D$ and D for the diameters, we have

$$A:a = (4D)^2:D^2.$$
$$\therefore A:a = 16D^2:D^2.$$

Dividing both terms of the second ratio by D^2, we have

$$A:a = 16:1.$$
$$\therefore A = 16a.$$

6. A grindstone when new is 48 in. in diameter. How large is it in diameter when $\frac{1}{4}$ ground away? When $\frac{1}{2}$ ground away? When $\frac{3}{4}$ ground away? *Ans.* 41.57 $-$ in.; 33.94 $+$ in.; 24 in.

Suggestion. Let d_1 in. = diameter when $\frac{1}{4}$ ground away. Then since $\frac{3}{4}$ remains, $1:\frac{3}{4} = 48^2:d_1{}^2$. Solving for d_1, we have $d_1 = 41.57 -$.

7. To double the diameter of a circle has what effect on its area? To double the side of a regular hexagon has what effect on its area?

Ans. Multiplies area by 4.

8. Similar solids vary in volumes as the cubes of their like dimensions. A water pail that is 10 in. across the top holds 12 quarts. Find the volume of a similar pail that is 12 in. across the top. *Ans.* 20.736 quarts.

9. The number of vibrations made by a pendulum varies inversely as the square root of its length. A pendulum 39.1 in. long makes one vibration per second. How long must a pendulum be to make four vibrations per second? To make one vibration in 10 seconds?

Ans. 2.44 in. $+$; 325 ft. 10 in.

Solution. The law is $n = \dfrac{k}{\sqrt{l}}$, where n = number of vibrations per second, and l = length of pendulum in inches.

To find k, put $n = 1$ and $l = 39.1$.

$$\therefore 1 = \frac{k}{\sqrt{39.1}}, \text{ and } k = \sqrt{39.1}.$$

To find the length of a pendulum to vibrate four times per second, put $n = 4$.

$$\therefore 4 = \frac{\sqrt{39.1}}{\sqrt{l}}, \text{ and } l = \frac{39.1}{16} = 2.44 + \text{ in. } Ans.$$

To find the length of a pendulum to vibrate once in 10 seconds, put $n = \frac{1}{10}$.

$$\therefore \frac{1}{10} = \frac{\sqrt{39.1}}{\sqrt{l}}, \text{ and } l = 100 \times 39.1 = 3910 \text{ in.} = 325 \text{ ft. 10 in. } Ans.$$

10. If a lever with a weight at each end is balanced on a fulcrum, the distances of the two weights from the fulcrum vary inversely as the weights. If two men of weights 160 lb. and 190 lb. respectively are balanced on the ends of a 10-ft. stick, what is the length from the fulcrum to each end? *Ans.* $5\frac{3}{7}$ and $4\frac{4}{7}$ ft.

11. Could a 1-lb. weight balance a 100-lb. weight? How could they be placed on a 3-ft. bar?

Ans. Yes. Fulcrum $2\frac{98}{101}$ ft. from 1-lb. weight.

12. If $f \propto qq'$ and $f \propto \dfrac{1}{r^2}$, show that $f \propto \dfrac{qq'}{r^2}$.

13. If $R \propto E$, $R \propto l$, and $R \propto \dfrac{1}{d^2}$, find R in terms of E, l, and d.

Ans. $R = \dfrac{kEl}{d^2}$.

14. If the illumination of an object varies inversely as the square of the distance d from the source of light, and the illumination of an object at the distance 8 ft. from the source of light is 3, find the illumination of an object at 32 ft. from the source of light. At the distance of 20 ft. from the source of light. *Ans.* $\frac{3}{16}$; 0.48.

15. The number of units of heat H, generated by an electric current of I amperes in a circuit, varies as the square of the current I, as the resistance R, and as the time t in seconds during which the current passes. Write the law in the two forms. *Ans.* $H \propto I^2Rt$; $H = kI^2Rt$.

16. By trial in the above formula it is found that $H = 388,800$ if $I = 10$, $R = 9$, and $t = 30$ minutes. Find H when $I = 40$, $R = 50$, and $t = 45$ minutes. *Ans.* $H = 51,840,000$; $k = 0.24$.

17. Two parallelepipeds (rectangular solids) of the same shape have corresponding dimensions of $3\frac{1}{2}$ ft. and $7\frac{1}{2}$ ft. Find the relation of their volumes. *Ans.* 343:3375.

18. A circular sheet of steel 2 ft. in diameter increases in diameter by $\frac{1}{200}$, when the temperature is increased by a certain amount. Find the increase in area of the sheet. *Ans.* $\frac{401}{40000}$ or nearly $\frac{1}{100}$.

19. A wire rope 1 in. in diameter will lift 10,000 lb. What will one $\frac{3}{8}$ in. in diameter lift? *Ans.* $1406\frac{1}{4}$ lb.

20. A cone of cast iron 8 in. high weighs 50 lb. What will be the weight of a cone of the same shape and material and 5 in. high? *Ans.* $12.207 +$ lb.

21. Two persons of the same "build" are similar in shape. A man $5\frac{1}{2}$ ft. tall weighs 150 lb. Find weight of a man of same "build" and 6 ft. tall. *Ans.* $194.74 +$ lb.

22. A man 5 ft. 5 in. tall weighs 140 lb., and one 6 ft. 2 in. tall weighs 216 lb. Which is of the stouter "build"? *Ans.* The 216-lb. man.

23. The electrical resistance of a substance varies directly as the length L, and inversely as the area A of the cross section. If the resistance of a bar of annealed aluminum 1 in. long and 1 sq. in. in cross section is 0.000001144 ohm at 32° Fahrenheit, find the resistance of a wire of the same material 1 ft. long and 0.001 in. in diameter. *Ans.* $17.48 -$ ohms.

Note that you have in this exercise the law of **Art. 253.**

24. Find the resistance of 1 mile of wire $\frac{1}{32}$ in. in diameter of above material and at 32° F. *Ans.* $94.5 +$ ohms.

25. If the resistance of a coil of wire of the above material at 32° F. is 27.3 ohms, and the wire is 0.05 in. in diameter, find the length. *Ans.* 3904.7 ft.

26. If the resistance of a wire 9363 ft. long is 21.6 ohms, what would be the resistance if its length were reduced to 5732 ft. and its cross section made half again as large? *Ans.* $8.816 -$ ohms.

27. The resistance of 1 ft. of silver wire 0.001 in. in diameter at 32° F. is 9.023 ohms. Find the resistance of a silver wire 1 meter long and 1 mm. in diameter. *Ans.* 0.0191 ohm.

Suggestion. Use 0.001 in. = 0.0254 mm. and 1 ft. = 0.3048 m.

28. The resistance of 1 meter of German silver wire 1 mm. in diameter is 0.2659 ohm. Find the resistance of 1 ft. of wire of the same material and 0.001 in. in diameter. *Ans.* 125.6+ ohms.

29. Find the resistance of a coil of copper wire 0.03 in. in diameter, the coil being 18 in. in diameter and having 300 turns, if 1 ft. of copper wire 0.001 in. in diameter has a resistance of 9.803 ohms.

Ans. 15.4 − ohms.

30. There are three wires of diameters 2 mils, 3 mils, and 4 mils respectively. What length must the second and third have to have the same resistance as 20 ft. of the first? *Ans.* 45 ft. and 80 ft.

31. The size of a stone carried by a swiftly flowing stream varies as the sixth power of the velocity of the water. If the velocity of a stream is doubled, what effect does it have on its carrying power? What effect if changed from 5 miles per hour to 15 miles per hour?

Ans. Multiplies by 64. Multiplies by 729.

282. Transverse strength of wooden beams.—Other things being equal, the strength of a beam, rectangular in cross section, and supported at each end, varies (1) inversely as the length in feet, (2) directly as the breadth in inches, and (3) directly as the square of the depth in inches.

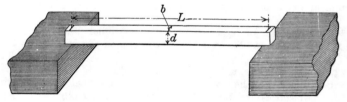

Fɪɢ. 206.

That the strength varies inversely as the length in feet means that if a beam, supported horizontally as in Fig. 206, has its length increased and everything else unchanged, the weight that it will support is decreased in the same ratio as the length was increased. That is, if the length is doubled it will support one-half as great a weight. If W is the weight and L the length, in the language of variation this fact is stated thus,

$$W \propto \frac{1}{L}, \text{ or } W = \frac{k_1}{L}.$$

The length L is the distance between the points of support.
That the strength varies directly as the breadth in inches
means that if the breadth b is **increased** in a certain ratio
and everything else is unchanged, the weight that it will
support is **increased** in the same ratio. That is, if the breadth
is doubled the weight that it will support will be doubled.
This law is expressed in symbols thus,

$$W \propto b, \text{ or } W = k_2 b.$$

That the strength varies directly as the square of the depth
in inches means that if the depth d is **increased** in a certain
ratio while other things remain the same, the weight that it
will support is **increased** by the square of the ratio of that
increase. That is, if the depth is doubled the weight that it
will support is four times as great. In symbols this is expressed thus,

$$W \propto d^2, \text{ or } W = k_3 d^2.$$

Finally, if the length, breadth, and depth are all changed we
have a combination of all these laws, and it may be expressed
thus (see **Art. 281**),

$$W \propto \frac{bd^2}{L}, \text{ or } W = \frac{Kbd^2}{L}.$$

By the expression "other things being equal" is meant
that the material must be the same, and the beams must be
similarly supported and similarly loaded. The nature of the
timber is an important factor, since timber, even of the same
kind, varies in strength to a considerable extent. Each
beam therefore has what is called a natural **constant,** the K
of the formula, which must be considered in the calculation
of its carrying capacity. This constant is the same for beams
when these "other things" are equal. That is, for beams
of exactly the same material, supported the same and weighted
the same.

283. The constant.—To find this constant, it is usual to
take a bar of similar material, 1 in. square in cross section, and
long enough to allow of its being placed on supports 1 ft. apart.
The constant to be used with beams weighted in the middle

is the weight of the central load which is just sufficient to break the bar. The constant may be expressed in pounds, hundred weight, tons, etc., and the carrying capacity of the beam it is applied to will always be in the same units.

284. Factor of safety.—For the man who wishes to apply these facts, another important consideration is the ratio which the *breaking load* bears to the *safe load*. This ratio is called the **factor of safety.** Its value depends upon whether the load is a **live load,** that is, a moving load; or a **dead load,** that is, a stationary load.

The factor of safety for a dead load is usually taken as 5, which means that the safe load upon a beam must not be more than one-fifth of the breaking load. The factor of safety for a live load is often taken as 10.

EXERCISES 100

1. Solve the formula $W = \dfrac{Kbd^2}{L}$ for each letter used.

$$Ans. \ L = \frac{Kbd^2}{W}; \quad b = \frac{WL}{Kd^2}; \quad d = \sqrt{\frac{WL}{Kb}}; \quad K = \frac{WL}{bd^2}.$$

2. The constant for white pine is 300 pounds. Find the weight a beam of this material, centrally loaded, and 10 ft. long, 3 in. broad, and 7 in. deep, will support. How much is the safe load if the factor of safety is 5?   *Ans.* 4410 lb.; 882 lb.

3. How long may a beam of white pine, centrally loaded, be between supports, if it is to have a safe load of 750 lb., and is 3 in. by 8 in. set on edge?   *Ans.* 15.36 ft.

4. By experiment we find that a beam of pine 40 ft. long, 1 ft. broad, and 1 ft. deep, will carry a load of 4500 lb. Find the depth of a beam of the same wood similarly loaded to carry a load of 1200 lb., when the length is 6 ft. and the breadth is 2 in.   *Ans.* 5.88 − in.

Solution. Use the formula $W = \dfrac{Kbd^2}{L}$, and substitute $W = 4500$, $L = 40$, $b = 12$, and $d = 12$. This gives $4500 = \dfrac{K \cdot 12 \cdot 12^2}{40}$. $\therefore K = \dfrac{625}{6}$.

Substituting $W = 1200$, $L = 6$, $b = 2$, and $K = \dfrac{625}{6}$ in the same formula,

$1200 = \dfrac{625 \cdot 2d^2}{6 \cdot 6}$.

Solving for d, $d = 5.88 −$.

5. In the above exercise find the depth if we allow a factor of safety of 10.   *Ans.* 18.6 − in.

6. In beams having the load uniformly distributed, the constant is twice as large as when the load is centrally located. Solve exercise 2 if the beam is uniformly loaded.   *Ans.* 8820 lb.; 1764 lb.

7. Find the breadth of a beam of oak, resting upon supports 18 ft. apart, the beam being 12 in. deep, to carry safely a uniformly distributed load of 5 tons. The constant is 500 lb. if loaded in center, and the factor of safety is 5.   *Ans.* $6\frac{1}{4}$ in.

8. A hall 16 ft. wide has the floor supported by joists of pine 3 in. by 12 in. set on edge; using the constant 300 lb. and a factor of safety of 5, find how far the joists must be placed from center to center to support a load of 140 lb. per square foot of floor surface. *Ans.* $17\frac{3}{8}$ in. nearly.

9. O'Connor gives the following formula to calculate the dead distributed safe load on timber, supported at both ends, and of rectangular cross section (this includes floor joists):

$$W = \frac{4bd^2K}{2L},$$

where W = load in pounds,
   b = breadth in inches,
   d = depth in inches,
   L = length of span in inches,
   K = 1900 for oak and 1100 for fir.

(Notice how this formula differs from the one previously given.) What safe weight distributed will an oak beam 6 in. by 10 in., set on edge, support if the span is 16 ft.?   *Ans.* 11,875 lb.

10. The joists in a room 14 ft. wide and 26 ft. long are fir 3 in. by 10 in. How far should their centers be placed apart if the floor is to support a crowd of men? (A crowd of men closely packed average 140 lb. per square foot.)   *Ans.* 2 ft. nearly.

11. From another source the following is taken: For white pine beams the formula $W = \frac{2000}{3} \times \frac{bd^2}{L}$ gives the safe load when the beam is supported at both ends and loaded in the middle.

   W = safe load in pounds, less weight of beam,
   L = length of beam in inches,
   d = depth of beam in inches,
   b = breadth of beam in inches.
   (1) Given $L = 12$ ft., $b = 3$ in., and $d = 8$ in., find W.
   (2) Given $L = 12$ ft., $b = 8$ in., and $d = 3$ in., find W.
   (3) Given $L = 16$ ft., $b = 4$ in., and $W = 1900$, find d.
   (4) Given $b = 6$ in., $d = 10$ in., and $W = 4100$, find L.
   Ans. (1) 889 lb.; (2) $333\frac{1}{3}$ lb.; (3) 11.7 – in.; (4) 8 ft. nearly.

12. The following are the results of some experiments on the strength of timbers when loaded in the middle. In each case find the strength of a stick of the same material 1 ft. long, 1 in. in breadth, and 1 in. in depth. This value is called K in the list.

Name of wood	Length in feet	Breadth in inches	Depth in inches	Breaking weight in pounds	K
White pine.................	2	2	2	1,430	357½
Yellow pine.................	10¾	14	15	68,000	232+
Pitch pine..................	10¾	14	15	118,500	404.4
Ash........................	2	2	2	2,052	513
Pitch pine.................	7	2	2	622	544¼
Ash........................	7	2	2	772	675½
Fir........................	7	2	2	420	367½

13. Suppose there are three pieces of timber of the following dimensions:

    (1) 12 ft. long, 6 in. deep, and 3 in. thick;
    (2) 8 ft. long, 5 in. deep, and 4 in. thick;
    (3) 15 ft. long, 9 in. deep, and 8 in. thick.

Compare their strengths.   *Ans.* In the ratio of 9:12.5:43.2.

14. Given a stick of timber 14 ft. long, 8 in. deep, and 3 in. thick; find the depth of another piece of the same material 18 ft. long and 4 in. thick that will support five times as much as the first. *Ans.* 17.6 − in.

Solution. Let W = weight first stick will support.

Then $W = \dfrac{Kbd^2}{L} = \dfrac{K \cdot 3 \cdot 8^2}{14} = \dfrac{96K}{7}.$

In the case of the second stick d is to be found when $5W = \dfrac{480K}{7}$ is the weight.

$$\therefore \frac{480K}{7} = \frac{K \cdot 4 \cdot d^2}{18}.$$

Solving, $d = 17.6 -$.

15. Given a piece of timber 12 ft. long, 6 in. deep, and 4 in. thick; find the thickness of another stick of the same material 16 ft. long and 8 in. deep that will support twice as much as the first.   *Ans.* 6 in.

16. Given a stick of timber 12 ft. long, 5 in. deep, and 3 in. thick; find the thickness of another stick of the same material 14 ft. long and 6 in. deep that will support four times as much as the first.
        Ans. 9.72+ in.

17. Given a stick of timber 12 ft. long, 6 in. deep, and 4 in. thick; find the depth of a stick of the same material 20 ft. long and 5 in. thick that will support twice the weight of the first.   *Ans.* 9.8 − in.

CHAPTER XXXIII

GRAPHICS

285. The graph.—The temperatures read each hour during March 21, 1917, were as given in the following table:

Hour, A. M........	12	1	2	3	4	5	6	7	8	9	10	11	12
Temperature........	45	45	45	45	43	42	41	40	42	51	57	59	62
Hour, P. M.........	1	2	3	4	5	6	7	8	9	10	11	12	
Temperature........	66	70	74	76	76	75	74	73	72	70	69	68	

The change in temperature is quite easily seen from a study of this table, but it may be seen at a glance if we put the facts into a diagram as shown in Fig. 207. Here the hours are located on a horizontal line and the degrees on a line perpendicular to it. The reading for any hour is located so as to be above the hour and to the right of the degree of temperature. In this manner we can locate 24 points.

Evidently if the temperature reading had been taken each minute instead of each hour, there would be determined 60 points in the same space in which we now have one. If we suppose no sudden change in temperature between the hourly readings, we may connect the points representing these by a line, and any point on this line will indicate the temperature for the corresponding time. Of course, if there had been a sudden rise and fall in temperature between the hours, it is not shown by this line. The oftener then we take the readings, the truer will the line indicate the changes.[1]

The representation, made as in Fig. 207, is called a **graph**;

[1] Cross-ruled paper, or paper ruled into squares of various sizes, can be obtained cheaply; and, by using this paper, the points can be located with greater accuracy than on plain paper.

and such a method of representing relations between numbers is called a **graphical method.**

The use of the graph is of very wide application. At the weather bureaus there are thermometers with an attachment which automatically traces the graph of the temperature and time. Engineers make constant use of the graph in their

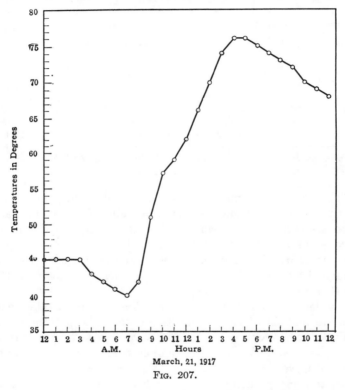

March, 21, 1917

Fig. 207.

work. Laboratory data are put in the form of a graph. Graphs can be made for algebraic equations, and relations are thus clearly shown that otherwise would be difficult to see.

Making the graph is often spoken of as **plotting.**

286. Definitions and terms used.—Since we often wish to plot negative as well as positive numbers, it is necessary to give certain definitions and make certain assumptions which will now be explained.

If in Fig. 208 *OX* and *OY* are drawn at right angles to each other, the position of any point, as *P*, may be located by measuring its distance from *OY* and from *OX*. These lengths, which in the figure are *OA* and *OB*, are called the **coördinates** of the point *P*. The length *OA* is called the **x-coördinate**; and *OB*, the **y-coördinate**.

The two lines *OX* and *OY* are called the **x-axis** and the **y-axis** respectively. Together they are spoken of as the **coördinate axes**. The point *O* where the two axes cross is called the **origin**.

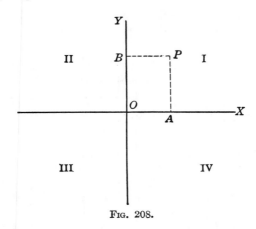

Fɪɢ. 208.

The *x*-axis is called the **axis of abscissas**, and the *y*-axis, the **axis of ordinates**. The *x*-coördinate and the *y*-coördinate are also called the **abscissa** and **ordinate** respectively of the point.

The coördinates are always measured from the origin. Any abscissa measured toward the right is **positive**, and measured toward the left is **negative**. Any ordinate measured upward is **positive** and downward is **negative**.

The four parts into which the axes divide the plane are called **quadrants**. These are called the **first, second, third, and fourth quadrants**, and are numbered in Fig. 208 by the numerals I, II, III, IV.

It is evident that, in the first quadrant, both coördinates are positive; in the second quadrant, the abscissa is negative and

23

the ordinate positive; in the third quadrant, both coördinates are negative; in the fourth quadrant, the abscissa is positive and the ordinate is negative. This is shown in the following table:

Quadrant......................	I	II	III	IV
Abscissa......................	+	−	−	+
Ordinate......................	+	+	−	−

287. Plotting points.—To plot a point is to locate it with reference to a set of coördinate axes. To plot a point whose

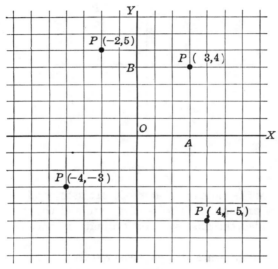

FIG. 209.

x-coördinate is 3 and y-coördinate 4, first draw the axes (see Fig. 209), then choose a unit of measure and lay off OA 3 units to the right of O. Through A draw a line parallel to the y-axis. Now lay off OB, 4 units above O, and through B draw a line parallel to the x-axis. The required point is located where these two lines meet. In the figure it is located as $P(3, 4)$, which is the usual manner of writing the coördinates of a point. The abscissa is placed first; they are separated by a comma and inclosed in parentheses. It is read: "The point P whose coördinates are 3 and 4."

In a similar manner the following points are located as given in the figure: $P(-2, 5), P(-4, -3), P(4, -5)$.

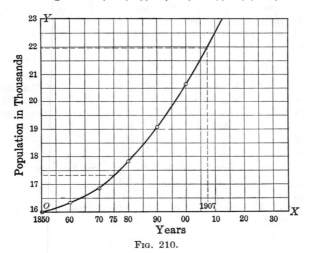

Fig. 210.

EXERCISES 101

1. Plot the following points: $(-1, 6), (7-2), (0, 4), (4, 0), (-6, 0), (-3, -8), (-6, 2), (0, 0)$.

2. The temperatures read each hour for the 24 hours ending Jan. 26, 1918, at 2 p. m. were as follows: Above zero 11, 11, 10, 6, 8, 5, 4, 3, 2, 2, 1, 0, 0; below zero 1, 1, 2, 3, 2; above zero 1, 3, 6, 8, 10, 12. Plot these using the hours as abscissas and the temperatures as ordinates, and connect by a smooth curve.

3. The population of a town in 1850 was 16,000; in 1860, 16,300; in 1870, 16,850; in 1880, 17,800; in 1890, 19,100; and in 1900, 20,700. Plot a curve showing the variation in population, and estimate the probable population in 1875 and in 1907.

Discussion. Draw the axes; lay off the years, beginning with 1850 at the origin, along the x-axis; and lay off the population in thousands along the y-axis, beginning with 16,000 at the origin. The curve will then be as in Fig. 210.

The population for any year is estimated by locating the year on the x-axis; drawing a perpendicular to the x-axis; and, from the intersection of this with the curve, drawing a parallel to the x-axis. The point where this parallel intersects the y-axis determines the population.

The process by which we determine the coördinates of any point on the curve is called **interpolating**.

4. A company began to sink a mining shaft on June 4; on June 11 it had reached a depth of 30 ft.; on June 18, 54 ft.; on June 25, 70 ft.; on July 2, 82 ft.; on July 9, 100 ft.; on July 16, 135 ft., and on July 23, 150 ft. Plot a curve showing the progress of the work.

5. The population of the United States by decades was as follows. Plot and estimate the population for 1913 and 1919.

Year	Population	Year	Population
1790	3,929,214	1860	31,443,321
1800	5,308,433	1870	38,558,371
1810	7,229,881	1880	50,155,783
1820	9,663,822	1890	62,669,756
1830	12,806,020	1900	76,295,200
1840	17,069,453	1910	91,972,266
1850	23,191,876		

6. Make a graph from which can be read the product of any number from −225 to 225 multiplied by 0.367.

Suggestion. Plot the numbers from −225 to 225 as abscissas and the products as ordinates.

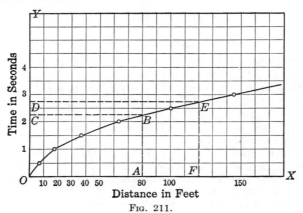

Fig. 211.

7. Make a graph from which can be read the quotient of any number less in absolute value than 500 divided by 12.7.

8. A stone, falling from rest, falls through 4 ft. in ½ second, 16 ft. in 1 second, 36 ft. in 1½ seconds, 64 ft. in 2 seconds, 100 ft. in 2½ seconds, and 144 ft. in 3 seconds. Find, by plotting a curve, how long a stone would be in falling 80 ft.; and also how far it falls in 2¾ seconds.

The graph for exercise 8 is as shown in Fig. 211. To find how long the stone would be in falling 80 ft., locate 80 ft. on the *x*-axis, draw a perpendicular line *AB*, and through the point *B* on the curve draw a line parallel to the *x*-axis to intersect the *y*-axis. This point of intersection *C* determines the number of seconds it will take the stone to fall 80 ft. To find how far the stone will fall in $2\frac{3}{4}$ seconds, proceed in a similar manner, starting on the *y*-axis.

9. The football accidents for the years given are as follows:

Year	Deaths	Injuries	Year	Deaths	Injuries
1901	7	74	1910	22	499
1902	15	106	1911	11	178
1903	14	63	1912	13	
1904	14	276	1913	14	
1905	24	200	1914	12	
1906	14	160	1915	16	
1907	15	166	1916	19	
1908	11	304	1917	12	
1909	30	216			

Plot two curves, using the years as abscissas and the deaths and injuries respectively as ordinates. State the conclusions that you can draw from the curves.

10. The monthly wages of a man for each of his first 13 years of work was as follows: $28, $30, $37.50, $45, $60, $65, $90, $95, $95, $137, $162, $190, and $210.

Plot the curve showing the change. Estimate his salary for the fourteenth and fifteenth years. Can you be certain of his salaries for these years? Why?

11. A cyclist starts from a town at 8 A. M. and rides 4 hours at the uniform rate of 9 miles per hour. He then rests 1 hour and returns at the rate of 8 miles per hour. At 11 A. M. a second cyclist starts from the same town and rides over the same route at the rate of 6 miles per hour. Plot curves showing where they will meet.

12. (a) Reckon the simple interest at 6% on $100 for the several years 1, 2, 3, · · · 10. Plot the years as abscissas and the interest as ordinates. Connect with a smooth curve from which may be read the interest on $100 at 6% for any time.

(b) Reckon the compound interest at 6% on $100 for the several years 1, 2, 3, · · · 10. Plot as in (a), using the same axes.

13. Plot the numbers 1, 4, 9, 16, 25, 36, etc., as abscissas and their square roots as corresponding ordinates. Make scale for ordinates 5 or 10 times that of abscissas. How can you determine roots of intervening numbers? (See discussion of exercise 3.) Find roots of 11, 14, 21,

29, 42 from curve. How do these agree with computed values of roots of these numbers?

14. If T is the tensile strength, in tons per square inch of cross section, of steel containing X per cent of carbon, and we are given the following values, plot a curve to show, as accurately as the data will allow, the tensile strength of steel containing any percentage of carbon from 0.1 to 1 per cent. What strength would you expect for 0.4 per cent of carbon?

X	0.14	0.46	0.57	0.66	0.78	0.80	0.87	0.96
T	28.1	33.8	35.6	40	41.1	45.9	46.7	52.7

15. Plot the Fahrenheit thermometer scale on the x-axis and the centigrade scale on the y-axis. Draw the line any point of which has as coördinates equivalent temperatures on the two scales. How can this graph be used to reduce from one scale to the other? Read from the graph the centigrade temperatures for the following Fahrenheit readings: 25°, 90°, 367°, −40°, 15°. Give in Fahrenheit the following centigrade readings: 33°, 76°, 15°, −46°, −9°.

16. In an experiment on the stretching of an iron rod the linear extension, L in inches, for a load, W in pounds, was found to be as follows:

W.......	600	1100	1600	2100	2600	3100	3600	4100	4600	5100
L........	0.005	0.009	0.013	0.018	0.022	0.027	0.032	0.037	0.043	0.050

Plot, choosing suitable distances on the x-axis for W, and on y-axis for L. Up to how great a load is the extension proportional to the load? That is, where does the curve change direction rapidly?

Remark. While the curve is a straight line, the relation between L and W can be expressed in the language of variation by the equation $W = kL$. Or we may say that the straight line is the graph of a direct variation where the ratio is constant.

17. A stick of white pine 1 in. broad and 0.5 in. thick is supported at points 24 in. apart and loaded in the middle. The deflection, d in inches, for a load, W in pounds, is as follows:

W......	0	5	8	18	28	38	48	58	63	68	69	70
d.......	0	0.088	0.14	0.35	0.56	0.77	0.99	1.22	1.35	1.685	1.765	1.85

Plot so as to show the deflection is proportional to the weight up to a certain point.

18. Plot the following data of the weight of railway locomotives. The weights are of the largest locomotives made each year. Plot time on the x-axis.

Year	Engine, pounds	Engine and tender, pounds
1898	230,000	334,000
1899	232,000	364,000
1900	250,300	391,400
1902	259,800	383,800
1904	287,240	453,000
1905	334,000	477,000
1909	425,900	596,000
1910	440,000	611,800
1911	616,000	850,000

19. A rifle sighted to 1000 yd. rests upon a support 5 ft. from the ground and is fired. The height of the bullet above the support at the various distances is given in the following table:

Distance in yards from firing point.	100	200	300	400	500	600	700	800	900	1000
Vertical height above support in feet.	7.3	11.2	15.0	18.5	21.0	23.3	25.0	22.5	16.5	0

Plot a representation of the path of the bullet. Show the ground level and the height of the support. Where does the bullet reach a height of 20 ft.?

20. Plot the relation between centimeters and inches.

Suggestion. Take the numbers of centimeters on the x-axis and the inches on the y-axis. Any point on the curve has as coördinates a number of centimeters and a number of inches that are equivalent in length.

21. Plot a curve showing the relation between yards and meters.

22. Plot a curve showing the relation between pounds and kilos.

23. Plot a curve showing the relation between dollars and francs. Use 1 franc = 19.3 cents.

288. Graph of an equation.—If we have an equation in two unknowns, as $3x+4y=12$, we can determine a number of pairs of values for x and y that will satisfy the equation. (See **Art 255.**) If we consider each of these pairs as the coördinates of a point, the value of x for the abscissa and y for the ordinate, then the graph determined by these points is called the **graph of the equation** or the **curve of the equation.**

To plot the curve of $3x+4y=12$, determine the pairs of values: $(0, 3)$, $(4, 0)$, $(2, 1\frac{1}{2})$, $(3, \frac{3}{4})$, $(5, -\frac{3}{4})$, $(8, -3)$, $(-8, 9)$,

(-4, 6), (12, -6). Plot these points and connect with a smooth line. The curve is shown in Fig. 212.

Whenever the equation is of the first degree the graph will be a straight line. Since a straight line is determined by knowing two points on it, the graph can be drawn when two points only have been plotted. Usually the most convenient points to take are those where the line crosses the two axes. These two points are found by putting $x = 0$ and finding y, and

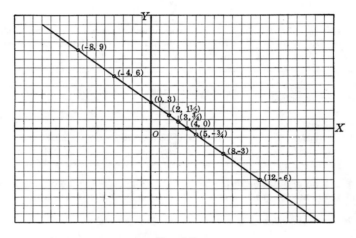

Fig. 212.

then putting $y = 0$ and finding x. The distances from the origin to these points are called the **intercepts** on the axes. If the line goes through the origin another point will be necessary. If the two points are near together the line will not be well determined unless the work is very accurate.

289. Simultaneous equations.—If we plot the graphs of two simultaneous equations they will intersect at some point if they are not parallel. The coördinates of the point of intersection evidently satisfy both equations and are the values obtained by solving the equations as simultaneous.

Example. Plot each of the following equations and solve them as simultaneous equations.

(1) $x + 4y = 3$ (2) $3x + 2y = 4$.

Pairs of values for first: $(0, \frac{3}{4})$, $(1, \frac{1}{2})$, $(3, 0)$, $(7, -1)$. Pairs of values for second: $(0, 2)$, $(2, -1)$, $(4, -4)$, $(-2, 5)$. These are plotted and the intersection is determined to be the point $(1, \frac{1}{2})$. Solving as simultaneous equations, we find $x = 1$ and $y = \frac{1}{2}$ as values of x and y. The plotting is shown in Fig. 213.

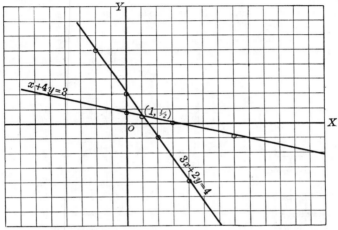

Fig. 213.

290. The graph of an equation of any degree.—The graph of an equation of any degree in two variables (unknowns) can be plotted by taking values for one variable and determining corresponding values for the other variable. Each pair of values determines a point, and a sufficient number of these points will determine the form of the curve.

A graph of an equation of higher degree than the first is not a straight line. The graph of an equation of the second degree in two variables is a conic section, that is, the section of a cone.

EXERCISES 102

Plot and solve the following systems of equations:
1. $x + y = 5$ and $3x + 2y = 12$.
2. $3x + 5y = 11$ and $4x + 7y = 15$.
3. $5x + 4y = 6$ and $7x + 6y = 10$.
4. $2x + 3y = 4$ and $4x - 6y = 8$.
5. $6x + y = 6$ and $4x + 3y = 11$.

6. Plot the curve of the equation $xy = 1$. This will give a curve from which can be read the reciprocals of any number. It is plotted by first finding a number of pairs of values for x and y which satisfy the equation, and then plotting the points that have these pairs as coördinates. It should be noticed that when x is negative, y is negative, and when x is positive, y is positive.

The pairs of values given in the table are found and plotted as shown in Fig. 214.

7. Plot the curve for $y = x^2$, and thus find the curve from which can be read squares and square roots of numbers.

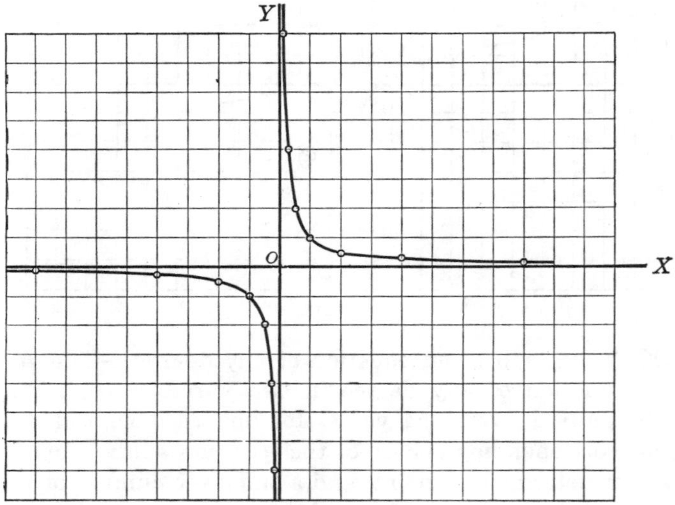

Pairs of values

x	y
$\pm\frac{1}{16}$	± 16
$\pm\frac{1}{8}$	± 8
$\pm\frac{1}{4}$	± 4
$\pm\frac{1}{2}$	± 2
± 1	± 1
± 2	$\pm\frac{1}{2}$
± 3	$\pm\frac{1}{3}$
± 6	$\pm\frac{1}{6}$
± 8	$\pm\frac{1}{8}$
± 16	$\pm\frac{1}{16}$

Fig. 214.

8. Plot the curve for $y = x^3$, and thus find the curve from which can be read cubes and cube roots of numbers.

9. In simple interest, if p stands for principal, t for time, r for rate, and a for amount, then $a = p(1 + rt)$. If now particular numerical values are given to p and r, and if the different values of a be taken as ordinates, and the corresponding values of t as abscissas, then the graph of this equation may be drawn. Draw the graph. What line in the figure represents the principal? What feature in the graph depends upon the rate per cent?

10. With the same axes as used in exercise 9, draw the graph for which interest and time are the coördinates of points on the curve.

11. Using the formula for the area of a circle $A = \pi r^2$, plot the curve, using radii as abscissas and areas as oridnates, from which can be read the areas of circles of radii from 0 to 6.

12. Follow directions similar to those in exercise 11 and plot the curve from which can be read the volumes of spheres.

13. If the temperature of a gas is constant, the pressure times the volume remains constant. Using p for pressure and v for volume, plot so as to show their relative change when $pv = 4$.

291. Simpson's Rule.—The area of the space included between a curve and a straight line can easily be found approximately by the use of *Simpson's Rule* which may be stated as follows: Let AB, in Fig. 215, be the curve and CD the straight line. Divide the length CD into an *even* num-

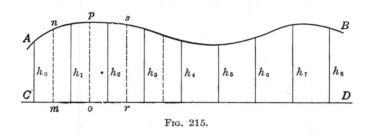

FIG. 215.

ber of equal parts, say 8, of length a, and erect the ordinates $h_0, h_1, h_2, \cdots, h_8$. Then the area of the figure $CDBA$ will be given by the formula:

$$\text{Area} = \tfrac{1}{3}a(h_0 + 4h_1 + 2h_2 + 4h_3 + 2h_4 + 4h_5 + 2h_6 + 4h_7 + h_8).$$

It is to be noticed that the coefficients of the ordinates are alternately 4 and 2, excepting the first and the last. The greater the number of divisions made the more accurate, in general, will be the result.

In words this may be stated in the following:

RULE. *Divide the base CD into an* **even** *number of equal parts, and measure the ordinate at each point of division. Add together the first and last ordinates, twice the sum of the other odd ordinates, and four times the sum of the even ordinates; multiply the sum by one-third the distance between consecutive ordinates. The result is the area inclosed (approximately).*

292. The average ordinate rule.—For approximate results the area between a curve and a straight line, base line, may be found as follows:

RULE. *Divide the base line into any number of equal parts; at the center of each of these parts draw ordinates. Take the average length of these ordinates and multiply by the length of the base line. The result is the area inclosed (approximately).*

In Fig. 215, *mn, op, rs,* etc., are the ordinates.

A convenient way for adding the ordinates is to draw a line of indefinite length; then with the dividers measure the ordinates successively on this line. The total length can then be measured at once. This will avoid errors to some extent.

293. Area in a closed curve.—Either of the methods given may be used in finding the area within a closed curve. Thus,

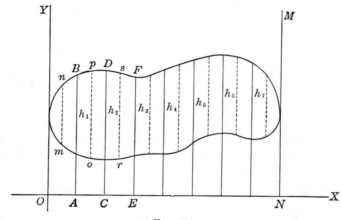

Fig. 216.

in Fig. 216, draw the two parallel tangents OY and MN, and draw OX perpendicular to these. Divide ON into any number of equal parts[1] (an even number for Simpson's Rule) and draw the ordinates AB, CD, etc. Call the several widths of the figure on these ordinates h_1, h_2, h_3, etc. These widths can be used in Simpson's Rule to find the area within the closed curve.

The widths *mn, op, rs,* etc., can be used in the average ordinate rule to find the area.

---

[1] To divide a line into any number of equal parts see **Art. 149.**

It should be noted that h_0 and h_8 for this figure are each 0.

294. The steam indicator diagram.—As a useful application of the discussion in the preceding articles, we will consider the steam indicator diagram.[1]

The steam indicator is a mechanical device to attach to a steam engine to make a graphical representation of the steam pressure acting on the piston throughout the stroke. Knowing

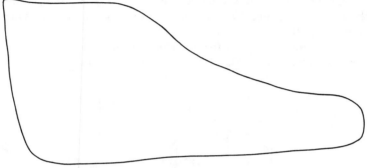

Fig. 217.

the pressure, the indicated horse-power of the engine can be calculated from the formula given in exercise 4, page 313,

$$H = \frac{PLAN}{33,000}, \text{ where}$$

H = indicated horse-power,

P = mean effective pressure in pounds per square inch,

L = length of stroke in feet,

A = area of piston in square inches,

N = the number of strokes per minute.

The **indicated horse-power** is the power developed by the steam on the piston of the engine, without any deduction for friction.

The **effective horse-power** is the actual available horse-power delivered to the belt or gearing, and is always less than the indicated horse-power, because the engine itself absorbs some power by the friction of its moving parts.

The indicator diagram may be as given, Fig. 217.

[1] For a full discussion of the steam indicator the student is referred to Peabody—*Manual of the Steam Engine Indicator.*

The width of a rectangle the same in length as this, and of the same area, would represent the **mean effective pressure** per square inch on the piston during the stroke.

The diagram is always to a certain scale, which is known from the indicator. For instance, the scale might be 60 lb. per inch in diagram. The mean effective pressure is then 60 lb. multiplied by the average width of the indicator diagram.

The average width of the diagram may be found by dividing the area by the length. The area can be found by Simpson's Rule or by the average ordinate rule.

A convenient method for locating the ordinates is to place a common ruler as in Fig. 218, and locate 10 ordinates, the two

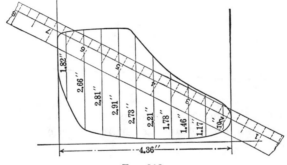

Fig. 218.

end ordinates being half as far from either end as the distance between the other ordinates.

The average length of these ordinates multiplied by the scale, taken from the indicator, gives the mean effective pressure.

Example. Taking the indicator diagram in Fig. 218, find the mean effective pressure of the steam if the scale is 30 lb. to the inch. Find the horse-power of the engine if the diameter of the piston is 18 in., length of stroke $2\frac{1}{2}$ ft., and number of revolutions 110 per minute. (The number of strokes of the piston is twice the number of revolutions.)

Solution. Adding together the ten ordinates, we have
1.82 + 2.66 + 2.81 + 2.91 + 2.73 + 2.21 + 1.78 + 1.46 + 1.17 + 0.70
= 20.25.

Since there are 10 ordinates, the mean is $20.25 \div 10 = 2.025$. Multiplying by the scale, we have $2.025 \times 30 = 60.75 =$ pounds pressure per square inch, the answer to the first part.

Area of piston $= 3.1416 \times 9^2 = 254.47$ in.^{2}

Formula for the horse-power is $H = \dfrac{PLAN}{33,000}$.

$$P = 60.75, \quad L = 2.5, \quad A = 254.47,$$
$$\therefore H = \frac{60.75 \times 2.5 \times 254.47 \times 220}{33,000} = 257.65.$$

EXERCISES 103

1. An indicator diagram has a length of 2 in. The ten ordinates, beginning at the left, are 0.70 in., 0.90 in., 0.97 in., 0.85 in., 0.67 in., 0.52 in., 0.42 in., 0.35 in., 0.23 in., 0.07 in. Draw a diagram that these ordinates will satisfy. If the indicator scale is 120 lb. to the inch, find the mean effective pressure. *Ans.* 68.16 lb. per in.^{2}

2. Find the indicated horse-power of an engine having the indicator diagram of exercise 1, if length of stroke is 3 ft., diameter of piston 23 in., and number of strokes 100 per minute. *Ans.* 257.4+ h. p.

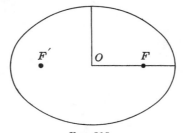

Fig. 219.

3. Draw a semicircle 2 in. in radius. Divide the diameter into four parts and find the area by Simpson's Rule. Divide the diameter into ten parts and find area by the same rule. Find the area by the formula. Compare the three results and state your conclusions.

4. Find the area of the ellipse in Fig. 219 by Simpson's Rule. Find the area by the formula $A = \pi ab$, and compare the two results.

5. Find the area of the indicator diagram of Fig. 217 both by Simpson's Rule and by the average ordinate rule, using ten divisions. Compare the results. *Ans.* 4.46 in.^{2} nearly.

6. If the indicator diagram of exercise 5 has a length of 3.73 in., and the scale is 50 lb., find the mean effective pressure. If the stroke is 2 ft. 6 in., the cylinder 18 in. in diameter, and the number of revolutions per minute 80. find the indicated horse-power of the engine.

Ans. 59.79 lb. per in.^{2}; 184.4+ h. p.

PART FOUR

LOGARITHMS AND TRIGONOMETRY

CHAPTER XXXIV

LOGARITHMS

295. Uses.—By the use of logarithms, the processes of multiplication, division, raising to powers, and extracting roots of arithmetical numbers are much simplified. The process of multiplication becomes one of addition, that of division becomes one of subtraction, that of raising to a power becomes one of simple multiplication, and that of extracting a root becomes one of simple division.

Many calculations that are difficult or impossible by ordinary arithmetical methods are readily carried out by means of logarithms. For instance, by the help of logarithms a square root is more readily found than by ordinary methods, and any other root is found as easily as a square root. The value of a number affected with any exponent, as $2.34^{1\frac{7}{16}}$, can be computed easily by logarithms.

296. Exponents.—For convenience the definitions and laws of exponents previously given are repeated here.

Definitions.

(1) $a^n = a \cdot a \cdot a \cdots$ to n factors. n an integer.

(2) $a^{-n} = \dfrac{1}{a^n}.$

(3) $a^0 = 1.$

(4) $a^{\frac{n}{m}} = \sqrt[m]{a^n}.$

Laws.

(1) $a^n \cdot a^m = a^{n+m}$.

(2) $a^n \div a^m = a^{n-m}$.

(3) $(a \cdot b \cdot c \cdot \cdot \cdot)^n = a^n b^n c^n \cdot \cdot \cdot \cdot$

(4) $\left(\dfrac{a}{b}\right)^n = \dfrac{a^n}{b^n}$.

(5) $(a^n)^m = a^{nm}$.

297. Definitions and history.—A **logarithm** of a number is the exponent by which the base must be affected to produce that number.

The logarithms of all the positive numbers to a given base are called a **system of logarithms,** and the base is called the base of the system.

Any base may be used in a system of logarithms; but the base 10 is commonly used because, as will be seen later, it makes a very convenient system of logarithms to work with.

Logarithms were invented by John Napier of Scotland, who lived from 1550 to 1617. They were described by him in 1614. Napier used the number 2.71828 · · · as a base. This base is still used in mathematics (see **Art. 315**).

Henry Briggs (1556 to 1631), professor at Gresham College, London, modified the new invention by using the base 10, and so made it more convenient for practical purposes.

Because of the time they save and the help they give in performing difficult computations, logarithms may be considered among the great inventions of the world.

298. Notation.—If we take 2 as a base, we may write in the language of exponents, $2^4 = 16$. In the language of logarithms, we may express the same idea by saying, the logarithm of 16 to the base 2 is 4. This is abbreviated and written thus, $\log_2 16 = 4$.

Similarly, we have the following expressed in the language of exponents and in the language of logarithms:

Language of exponents	*Language of logarithms*
$2^5 = 32$.	$\log_2 \quad 32 = 5$.
$3^4 = 81$.	$\log_3 \quad 81 = 4$.
$5^4 = 625$.	$\log_5 \quad 625 = 4$.

Language of   *Language of*
exponents   *logarithms*

$8^3 = 512.$	$\log_8 \ 512 = 3.$
$4^{0.5} = 2.$	$\log_4 \ 2 = 0.5.$
$8^{\frac{2}{3}} = 4.$	$\log_8 \ 4 = \frac{2}{3}.$
$64^{\frac{1}{3}} = 4.$	$\log_{64} \ 4 = \frac{1}{3}.$
$10^3 = 1000.$	$\log_{10} 1000 = 3.$

EXERCISES 104

Answer as many as you can orally. Cover the answers so that they will not be seen until the results are written.

1. Express the following in the language of logarithms:

(1) $2^6 = 64.$ (4) $16^{0.5} = 4.$ (7) $32^{0.4} = 4.$

(2) $5^3 = 125.$ (5) $10^4 = 10,000.$ (8) $10^{1.3979} = 25.$

(3) $7^3 = 343.$ (6) $125^{\frac{1}{3}} = 5.$ (9) $10^{2.5465} = 352.$

Ans. (1) $\log_2 64 = 6.$ (4) $\log_{16} 4 = 0.5.$ (7) $\log_{32} 4 = 0.4.$

      (2) $\log_5 125 = 3.$ (5) $\log_{10} 10,000 = 4.$ (8) $\log_{10} 25 = 1.3979.$

      (3) $\log_7 343 = 3.$ (6) $\log_{125} 5 = \frac{1}{3}.$ (9) $\log_{10} 352 = 2.5465.$

2. Express the following in the language of exponents:

(1) $\log_2 256 = 8.$ (4) $\log_{10} 643 = 2.8082.$

(2) $\log_6 216 = 3.$ (5) $\log_{10} 429 = 2.6325.$

(3) $\log_{16} \ 2 = 0.25.$ (6) $\log_{10} 999 = 2.9996.$

     Ans. (1) $2^8 = 256.$ (4) $10^{2.8082} = 643.$

          (2) $6^3 = 216.$ (5) $10^{2.6325} = 429.$

          (3) $16^{0.25} = 2.$ (6) $10^{2.9996} = 999.$

3. Find the logarithms of the following:

(1) $\log_7 49.$ (4) $\log_9 729.$ (7) $\log_8 2.$

(2) $\log_3 243.$ (5) $\log_4 256.$ (8) $\log_{16} 64.$

(3) $\log_5 3125.$ (6) $\log_{10} 100,000.$ (9) $\log_{10} 0.01.$

     Ans. (1) 2; (2) 5; (3) 5; (4) 3; (5) 4; (6) 5; (7) $\frac{1}{3}$; (8) $\frac{3}{2}$; (9) -2.

4. Find the value of x in the following:

(1) $\log_3 \ x = 4.$ (5) $\log_{10} x = -2.$ (9) $\log_{25} \ x = \frac{3}{2}.$

(2) $\log_{10} x = 6.$ (6) $\log_3 \ x = -3.$ (10) $\log_{16} \ x = \frac{3}{2}.$

(3) $\log_{16} x = \frac{3}{4}.$ (7) $\log_{10} x = -3.$ (11) $\log_{125} \ x = \frac{2}{3}.$

(4) $\log_{10} x = 0.$ (8) $\log_8 \ x = \frac{4}{3}.$ (12) $\log_{49} \ x = \frac{3}{2}.$

     Ans. (1) 81; (2) 1,000,000; (3) 8; (4) 1; (5) 0.01; (6) $\frac{1}{27}$; (7) 0.001;

(8) 16; (9) 125; (10) 64; (11) 25; (12) 343.

5. Find the value of x in the following:

(1) $\log_x 100 = 2$.	(5) $\log_x 4 = 0.5$.	(9) $\log_x 27 = 0.75$.
(2) $\log_x 81 = 4$.	(6) $\log_x 4 = 0.25$.	(10) $\log_x 2 = 0.125$.
(3) $\log_x 512 = 3$.	(7) $\log_x 16 = \frac{4}{7}$.	(11) $\log_x 49 = \frac{2}{3}$.
(4) $\log_x 1024 = 10$.	(8) $\log_x 17 = 0.5$.	(12) $\log_x 100 = \frac{2}{3}$.

Ans. (1) 10; (2) 3; (3) 8; (4) 2; (5) 16; (6) 256; (7) 32; (8) 289; (9) 81; (10) 256; (11) 343; (12) 1000.

299. Illustrative computations by means of exponents.— It is very important that the fundamental ideas of logarithms shall be well understood. In this article are given examples illustrative of the use of exponents, or logarithms, in making computations in multiplication, division, raising to powers, and extracting roots. These computations are made by the help of the following table in which 2 is the base. The work is kept in the language of exponents but can be easily translated into the language of logarithms.

$2^{-6} = \frac{1}{64}$	$2^1 = 2$	$2^8 = 256$
$2^{-5} = \frac{1}{32}$	$2^2 = 4$	$2^9 = 512$
$2^{-4} = \frac{1}{16}$	$2^3 = 8$	$2^{10} = 1024$
$2^{-3} = \frac{1}{8}$	$2^4 = 16$	$2^{11} = 2048$
$2^{-2} = \frac{1}{4}$	$2^5 = 32$	$2^{12} = 4096$
$2^{-1} = \frac{1}{2}$	$2^6 = 64$	$2^{13} = 8192$
$2^0 = 1$	$2^7 = 128$	$2^{14} = 16,384$

Multiplication. Multiply 512 by 32.

From the table, $512 = 2^9$,

and $32 = 2^5$.

$\therefore 512 \times 32 = 2^9 \times 2^5 = 2^{14}$.

From the table, $2^{14} = 16,384$.

$\therefore 512 \times 32 = 16,384$.

Division. Divide 512 by 4096.

From the table, $512 = 2^9$,

and $4096 = 2^{12}$.

$\therefore 512 \div 4096 = 2^9 \div 2^{12} = 2^{-3}$.

From the table, $2^{-3} = \frac{1}{8}$.

$\therefore 512 \div 4096 = \frac{1}{8}$.

Raising to a power. Find the value of 16^3.

From the table, $16 = 2^4$.

$\therefore 16^3 = (2^4)^3 = 2^{12}$.

From the table, $2^{12} = 4096$.

$\therefore 16^3 = 4096$.

Extraction of a root. Find the value of $\sqrt[4]{4096}$.

From the table, $4096 = 2^{12}$.

$$\therefore \sqrt[4]{4096} = \sqrt[4]{2^{12}} = 2^3.$$

From the table, $2^3 = 8$.

$$\therefore \sqrt[4]{4096} = 8.$$

EXERCISES 105

By the help of the table on page 372 find the value of the following. Do the work without using a pencil when possible.

1. 256×16.
2. 256×64.
3. 2048×8.
4. 128×128.
5. 32×256.
6. $\frac{1}{64} \times 16,384$.
7. $8192 \div 1024$.
8. $2048 \div 256$.
9. $16 \div 512$.
10. $8 \div 512$.
11. 16^3.
12. 64^2.
13. $\sqrt{16,384}$.
14. $\sqrt[6]{4096}$.
15. $\sqrt[7]{16,384}$.
16. $\dfrac{32 \times 2048}{512}$.
17. $\dfrac{16,384 \times 512}{2048}$.
18. $\dfrac{32 \times 64}{512 \times 8}$.
19. $(4096)^{\frac{2}{3}}$.
20. $(32 \times 128)^{\frac{3}{4}}$.
21. $(8192 \times 32)^{\frac{2}{3}}$.
22. $\dfrac{1024 \times 64}{512 \times 16,384}$.
23. $\left(\dfrac{512 \times 256}{1024 \times 8192}\right)^{\frac{1}{4}}$.
24. $\sqrt[3]{\dfrac{256 \times 1024}{4096^2}}$.

300. Logarithms of any number.—It is readily seen that, in the exercises of the last article, the numbers considered were all integral powers of 2. It is also readily seen that there are many numbers that cannot be expressed as integral powers of 2. The same thing is true for any base. Thus, for the base 3, we have as integral powers the numbers 3, 9, 27, 81, 243, etc., and no numbers except these between 3 and 243.

We can, therefore, with any given base write integral logarithms for only a small part of all possible numbers. That is, the logarithms of numbers to any given base are usually not integral. Thus, the logarithm of 95 to the base 3 is 4 and some fraction, because 95 is between 3^4 and 3^5. What this fraction is cannot easily be determined.

301. Logarithms to the base 10.—In what follows, if no base is stated, it is understood that the base 10 is used.

When the base is 10 we evidently have the following:

$$\log 100,000 = 5. \qquad \log 1 = 0.$$
$$\log 10,000 = 4. \qquad \log 0.1 = -1.$$
$$\log 1000 = 3. \qquad \log 0.01 = -2.$$
$$\log 100 = 2. \qquad \log 0.001 = -3.$$
$$\log 10 = 1. \qquad \log 0.0001 = -4.$$

The logarithm of any number between 1000 and 10,000 is between 3 and 4, or it is 3 and some fraction. Between 100 and 1000 the logarithm is 2 plus a fraction. Between 0.01 and 0.1 the logarithm is -2 plus a fraction or -1 minus a fraction. In order that the fractional part of the logarithm may always be positive, *we shall agree to take the logarithm so that the integral part only is negative.*

In general, the logarithm of a number consists of two parts, a whole number part and a fractional part.

The whole number part is called the **characteristic.**

The fractional part is called the **mantissa.**

The mantissas of the positive numbers arranged in order are called a **table of logarithms.**

The logarithm of 3467 consists of the characteristic 3 and some mantissa because 3467 lies between 1000 and 10,000. The logarithm of 59,436 is 4 plus a fraction because 59,436 lies between 10,000 and 100,000. The log 0.0236 is -2 plus a fraction because 0.0236 lies between 0.01 and 0.1.

It is readily seen that multiplying a number by 10 increases its characteristic by 1.

One of the great advantages in using the base 10 is that the characteristics can be determined by inspection. It is only necessary, then, to have the mantissas given in a table.

302. Rules for determining the characteristic.—From what has been said in the last article, and from a further consideration of the table given there, the following rules are evident:

(1) *For whole numbers, the characteristic is one less than the number of whole number figures and is positive.*

(2) *For decimals, the characteristic is one more than the number of zeros immediately at the right of the decimal point and is negative.*

(3) *In a number consisting of a whole number and a decimal, consider the whole number part and apply rule* (1).

Thus, the characteristics of the following are as given: of 326 is 2 by rule (1), of 37,265 is 4 by rule (1), of 0.046 is -2 by rule (2), of 0.000046 is -5 by rule (2), of 2.36 is 0 by rule (3), and of 276.36 is 2 by rule (3).

EXERCISES 106

State the characteristics to the base 10 of the following:

846	3956	2.325	87,654
44.36	43,968	0.0123	9.3264
173.94	39.267	0.00492	0.0003967
4.7654	3333.3	0.4689	0.039643

303. The mantissa.—The determination of the mantissa is more difficult than the determination of the characteristic. The mantissa is found from a table of logarithms.

Tables of logarithms are made only by a great deal of work. They are spoken of as three place tables, four place tables, ten place tables, etc., according to the number of decimal places given in the mantissas. The degree of accuracy in computations made by logarithms depends upon the number of places in the table used, the more places in the table the greater the degree of accuracy. The tables generally used are those having from four to six places.

The mantissa depends only upon the figures of the number, and not at all upon the decimal point. To illustrate this, consider the following: Suppose that we have given that log $867 = 2.9380$.

(1) This means that $10^{2.9380} = 867$.

(2) Now $10^2 = 100$.

(3) Dividing (1) by (2), $10^{0.9380} = 8.67$.

(4) ∴ log $8.67 = 0.9380$.

Hence the mantissa of 8.67 is the same as the mantissa of 867.

It is evident that if both members of (1) are multiplied or divided by any integral power of 10 the mantissa is unchanged. Hence the decimal point of a number can be moved as we please without the mantissa of the logarithm of the number being changed.

This also illustrates the fact that a change in the position of the decimal point of a number changes the value of the characteristic of the logarithm of the number.

304. Tables.—Upon examining a four place table of logarithms (see **Table X**), it is noticed that the first column has the letter N at the top. This is an abbreviation for number. The other columns have at their tops and bottoms the numbers

0, 1, 2, 3, · · · 9. Any number consisting of three figures has its first two figures in the column headed N and its third figure at the top of another column. For instance, take the number 456; 45 is found in the column headed N and 6 at the top of another column.

The columns, after the first, are made up of numbers consisting of four figures. These numbers are decimals, and are the mantissas of the logarithms of the numbers made up of the figures in the column headed N together with a figure from the head of another column.

The difference between two consecutive mantissas is called the **tabular difference**, that is, the table difference.

305. To find the mantissa of a number.—

(1) *When the number consists of three significant figures.*

Example. Find the mantissa of 347.

From the manner in which the table is formed, the first two figures of 347 are found in the column headed N, and the third figure at the top of the page. The mantissa of 347 is found to the right of 34 and in the column headed 7. It is 0.5403.

The mantissa of 3.47, 3470, or any number consisting of these figures in the same order is 0.5403.

(2) *When the number consists of one or two significant figures,* the number is found in the column headed N, and the mantissa to the right in the column headed 0.

Thus, the mantissa of 13 is 0.1139, and the mantissa of 4 is 0.6021; this is found to the right of 40.

(3) *When the number consists of four or more significant figures.*

Example 1. Find the mantissa of 7586.

Since 7586 lies between 7580 and 7590, its mantissa must lie between the mantissas of 7580 and 7590.

Mantissa of 7580 = 0.8797.

Mantissa of 7590 = 0.8802.

The difference between these mantissas is 0.0005, which is the tabular difference. Since an increase of 10 in the number increases the mantissa 0.0005, an increase of 6 in the number will increase the mantissa 0.6 as much, or the increase is 0.0005 ×0.6 = 0.0003. Hence the mantissa of 7586 = 0.8797+0.0003 = 0.8800.

The process of determining the mantissa as above is called **interpolation.** As carried out, the mantissa is supposed to increase in a constant ratio between the values taken; however, this supposition is only approximately true.

Example 2. Find the mantissa of 43,286.

Mantissa of 43,200 = 0.6355.

Mantissa of 43,300 = 0.6365,

and the tabular difference = 0.0010.

Since an increase of 100 in the number increases the mantissa 0.0010, an increase of 86 in the number increases the mantissa $0.0010 \times 0.86 = 0.0009$, to the nearest fourth decimal place. Hence the mantissa of $43,286 = 0.6355 + 0.0009 = 0.6364$.

The processes that have been given should seem reasonable; but, since the process of finding a mantissa has to be performed so often, it is best to do it by rule.

306. Rules for finding the mantissa.—

(1) *For a number consisting of three figures, find the first two figures of the number in the column headed N, and the third figure at the head of a column; then read the mantissa in the column under the last figure and at the right of the first two figures.*

(2) *For a number consisting of one or two figures, find the number in the column headed N, and the mantissa opposite in the column headed 0.*

(3) *For a number consisting of more than three figures, find the mantissa for the first three figures by rule (1), and add to this the product of the tabular difference by the remaining figures of the number considered as decimals.*

Illustrations. The mantissa of 243, 2.43, 0.0243, or any number consisting of these three figures in the same order, is found by rule (1) to be 0.3856.

The mantissa of 25, 0.025, or any number consisting of these two figures in this order, is found by rule (2) to be 0.3979.

The mantissa of 2364 is found by rule (3) to be 0.3736.

Process. Mantissa of 2360 = 0.3729. Tabular difference is 0.0018. $0.0018 \times 0.4 = 0.0007$. Adding this to the mantissa of 2360 gives the mantissa of $2364 = 0.3736$.

307. Finding the logarithm of a number.—In looking up the logarithm of a number, it is best to first determine the characteristic, and then the mantissa.

Example 1. Find the logarithm of 236.
By rule (1) for characteristic we find 2.
By rule (1) for mantissa we find 0.3729.
∴ log 236 = 2.3729.

Example 2. Find the logarithm of 7326.
Rule (1) for characteristic gives 3.
Rule (3) for mantissa gives 0.8649.
. ∴ log 7326 = 3.8649.

Example 3. Find the logarithm of 0.00037.
Rule (2) for characteristic gives −4.
Rule (2) for mantissa gives 0.5682.
∴ log 0.00037 = $\overline{4}$.5682.

It is not permissible to place the minus sign before the characteristic in writing a negative logarithm, for this would indicate that both characteristic and mantissa are negative, and we have agreed that the mantissa shall always be positive. To overcome the difficulty, the negative sign is placed above the characteristic. Another way of writing the negative logarithm is to increase the characteristic by 10 and subtract 10 at the right of the mantissa.

Thus, the logarithm of 0.00037 is written $\overline{4}$.5682 or 6.5682 − 10.

EXERCISES 107

1. Study the following to fix in mind the meaning of characteristic and mantissa:

log   4580 = 3.6609; that is, $4580 = 10^{3.6609}$.
log   458.0 = 2.6609; that is, $458.0 = 10^{2.6609}$.
log   45.80 = 1.6609; that is, $45.80 = 10^{1.6609}$.
log   4.580 = 0.6609; that is, $4.580 = 10^{0.6609}$.
log   0.4580 = $\overline{1}$.6609; that is, $0.4580 = 10^{\overline{1}.6609} = 10^{-1+0.6609}$.
log   0.0458 = $\overline{2}$.6609; that is, $0.0458 = 10^{\overline{2}.6609} = 10^{-2+0.6609}$.
log   0.00458 = $\overline{3}$.6609; that is, $0.00458 = 10^{\overline{3}.6609} = 10^{-3+0.6609}$.

2. Verify the following by the tables:

(1)   log 10 = 1.0000.   (2)   log 100 = 2.0000.
(3)   log 110 = 2.0414.   (4)   log 2 = 0.3010.
(5)   log 20 = 1.3010.   (6)   log 200 = 2.3010
(7)   log 0.2 = $\overline{1}$.3010.   (8)   log 542 = 2.7340.
(9)   log 345 = 2.5378.   (10) log 5.07 = 0.7050.
(11) log 78.5 = 1.8949.   (12) log 0.981 = $\overline{1}$.9917.

(13) log 1054 = 3.0228.

(14) log 1272 = 3.1045.

(15) log 0.0165 = $\bar{2}$.2175.

(16) log 0.1906 = $\bar{1}$.2801.

(17) log 21.09 = 1.3241.

(18) log 0.09095 = $\bar{2}$.9588.

(19) log 3.060 = 0.4857.

(20) log 4.411 = 0.6445.

(21) log 07854 = $\bar{1}$.8951.

(22) log 0.10125 = $\bar{1}$.0054.

(23) log 54.657 = 1.7377.

(24) log 0.09885 = $\bar{2}$.9950.

308. To find the number corresponding to a logarithm.— In nearly every problem involving logarithms it is not only necessary to find the logarithms of numbers, but the inverse process, that of finding a number corresponding to a logarithm, has to be performed.

Since the decimal point in no way affects the mantissa, we can determine only the *figures* of the number from the mantissa. The decimal point has to be placed by the rules for determining the characteristic.

(1) *When the mantissa of the given logarithm is exactly given in the table.* As an example, find the number having 2.8344 for a logarithm.

Find in the table the mantissa 0.8344. To the left of this mantissa, in the column headed N, find the first two figures, 68, of the number, and at the head of the column in which the mantissa is found, find the third figure, 3, of the number. The number then consists of the figures 683, but we do not know where the decimal point is till we consider the characteristic.

Since the characteristic is 2, there must be three figures at the left of the decimal point. Hence the number having 2.8344 for a logarithm is 683.

This means that $10^{2.8344} = 683$. Notice that a change in the characteristic would change the position of the decimal point. Thus, the number corresponding to 4.8344 is 68,300; while the number corresponding to $\bar{2}$.8344 is 0.0683.

(2) *When the mantissa of the given logarithm is not exactly given in the table.* As an example, find the number corresponding to the logarithm 3.4689.

Find the mantissas 0.4683 and 0.4698, between which the given mantissa lies. The number corresponding to 3.4698 = 2950. The number corresponding to 3.4683 = 2940. That is, an increase in the mantissa of 0.0015 makes an increase of 10 in the corresponding number. The given mantissa is 0.0006 larger than 0.4683. Then the required number is $\frac{0.0004}{0.0015}\times10$ =4 larger than 2940. Hence the number corresponding to the logarithm 3.4689 is 2944.

In dealing with the tabular difference, for convenience, it is best to drop the decimal point. Then we should have $\frac{6}{15}\times10=4$ instead of $\frac{0.0006}{0.0015}\times10=4$.

309. Rules for finding the number corresponding to a given logarithm.—(1) *When the mantissa of the given logarithm is exactly given in the table, the first two figures of the number are found to the left of the given mantissa in the column headed* N, *and the third figure is found at the head of the column in which the mantissa is given.*

(2) *When the mantissa of the given logarithm is not exactly given in the table, find the mantissa nearest the given mantissa but smaller. The first three figures of the number are those corresponding to this mantissa, and are found by rule* (1).

For another figure, divide the difference between the mantissa found and the given mantissa by the tabular difference. The quotient is the other figure. Always determine this figure to the nearest tenth.

In both (1) *and* (2) *place the decimal point so that the rules for determining the characteristic may be applied and give the given characteristic.*

Example 1. Find the number of which 2.8414 is the logarithm. The mantissa 0.8414 is found in the table to the right of 69 and in the column headed 4; hence the number consists of the figures 694. The decimal point must be placed so as to give a characteristic of 2 when the rule for characteristic is applied. Hence 694 is the number whose logarithm is 2.8414.

Example 2. Find the number whose logarithm is 1.7624. Mantissa nearest 0.7624 is 0.7619 which is the mantissa of 578. Tabular difference = 8. Difference between the mantissas is 5. 5 ÷ 8 = 0.6 nearly. Hence 1.7624 is the log 57.86.

EXERCISES 108

Find the value of x or verify the following:

1. $0.3010 = \log x$.	**2.** $1'.6021 = \log x$.
3. $2.9031 = \log x$.	**4.** $1.6669 = \log 46.44$.
5. $2.7971 = \log 626.7$.	**6.** $3.9545 = \log 9006$.
7. $0.8794 = \log 7.575$.	**8.** $3.9371 = \log x$.

9. 0.8294 = log 6.752.

11. 9.3685 − 10 = log x.

13. 8.9535 − 10 = log x.

15. 6.7016 − 10 = log 0.000503.

17. $\overline{3}$.4792 = log 0.003014.

19. $\overline{4}$.2975 = log 0.0001984.

10. 1.9039 = log 80.15.

12. 8.9932 − 10 = log 0.09845.

14. 7.7168 − 10 = log 0.00521.

16. 7.8654 = log x.

18. $\overline{4}$.9231 = log 0.0008378.

20. 4.2975 = log x.

310. To find the product of two or more factors by the use of logarithms.—RULE. *Find the sum of the logarithms of the factors. The product is the number corresponding to this sum.*

Example. Find the product of $3.76 \times 0.89 \times 7.628$.

Process.
$$\log 3.76 = 0.5752$$
$$\log 0.89 = \overline{1}.9494$$
$$\log 7.628 = \underline{0.8824}$$
$$\log \text{ of product} = 1.4070$$
$$\therefore \text{ product} = 25.53.$$

That this is an application of the law of exponents in multiplication will be seen from the following form:

$$3.76 = 10^{0.5752}$$
$$0.89 = 10^{\overline{1}.9494}$$
$$7.628 = 10^{0.8824}$$
$$\therefore 3.76 \times 0.89 \times 7.628 = 10^{0.5752} \times 10^{\overline{1}.9494} \times 10^{0.8824}$$
$$= 10^{0.5752 + \overline{1}.9494 + 0.8824}$$
$$= 10^{1.4070} = 25.53.$$

311. To find the quotient of two numbers by logarithms.— RULE. *Subtract the logarithm of the divisor from the logarithm of the dividend. The quotient is the number corresponding to this difference.*

Example 1. Find the quotient of $38.76 \div 7.923$.

Process.
$$\log 38.76 = 1.5884$$
$$\log 7.923 = \underline{0.8989}$$
$$\log \text{ of quotient} = 0.6895$$
$$\therefore \text{ quotient} = 4.892.$$

Example 2.   Evaluate $\dfrac{7.246 \times 0.8964 \times 5.463}{4.27 \times 0.3987 \times 27.89}$.

Process.

log 7.246	= 0.8601	log 4.27	= 0.6304
log 0.8964	= 9.9525 − 10	log 0.3987	= 9.6007 − 10
log 5.463	= 0.7374	log 27.89	= 1.4454
log of Num.	= 1.5500	log of Den.	= 1.6765
log of Den.	= 1.6765		
log of quotient	= 1.8735		
∴ quotient	= 0.7473.		

EXERCISES 109

1. Multiply the following by the use of logarithms:
(1) $226 \times 85 = 19{,}210.$ (2) $7.25 \times 240 = 1740.$
(3) $3272 \times 75 = 245{,}400.$ (4) $0.892 \times 805 = 718.1.$
(5) $1.414 \times 2.829 = 3.999.$ (6) $42.37 \times 0.235 = 9.958.$
(7) $2912 \times 0.7281 = 2120.$ (8) $289 \times 0.7854 = 227.$
(9) $7.62 \times 3.67 = 27.97.$ (10) $7.09 \times 3.99 = 28.29.$
(11) $10.00124 \times 89.5 = 0.1110.$ (12) $4.768 \times 9.872 = 47.07.$

2. Divide by the use of logarithms and check by actual division:
(1) $3025 \div 55.$ (2) $0.2601 \div 0.68.$
(3) $3950 \div 0.250.$ (4) $10 \div 3.14.$
(5) $0.6911 \div 0.7854.$ (6) $1 \div 762.$
(7) $6786 \div 4236.$ (8) $200 \div 0.5236.$
(9) $300 \div 17.32.$ (10) $0.220 \div 0.3183$

3. Find the product of $3.246 \times 98.768 \times 0.4376.$ *Ans.* 140.3.
4. Find the product of $0.00389 \times 9.876 \times 0.00468.$ *Ans.* 0.0001798.
5. Divide the product of 0.38765 and 7.498 by 4.3792.   *Ans.* 0.6637.

Evaluate the following by the use of logarithms:

6. $\dfrac{110 \times 3.1 \times 0.650}{33 \times 0.7854 \times 1.7}$.   *Ans.* 5.031.

7. $\dfrac{6000 \times 5 \times 29}{0.7854 \times 25{,}000 \times 81.7}$.   *Ans.* 0.5425.

8. $\dfrac{3.516 \times 485 \times 65}{3.33 \times 17 \times 18 \times 73}$.   *Ans.* 1.490.

9. $\dfrac{15 \times 0.37 \times 26.16}{11 \times 8 \times 18 \times 6.67}$.   *Ans.* 0.01374.

10. $\dfrac{78 \times 52 \times 1605}{338 \times 767 \times 431}$.   *Ans.* 0.05826.

11. $\dfrac{0.5 \times 3.15 \times 428}{0.317 \times 0.973 \times 43.7}$.   *Ans.* 50.

312. To find the power of a number by logarithms.—Rule.
Multiply the logarithm of the number by the exponent of the power. The number corresponding to this logarithm is the required power.

Example 1.   Find the value of $(2.378)^6$.
Process.   log $2.378 = 0.3762$
   $6 \times$ log $2.378 = 2.2572 =$ log of the power.
   $\therefore (2.378)^6 = 180.8$.

Example 2.   Find value of $(9.876)^{\frac{3}{4}}$.
Process.   log $9.876 = 0.9946$
   $\frac{3}{4}$ of log $9.876 = 0.7460 = \log(9.876)^{\frac{3}{4}}$.
   $\therefore (9.876)^{\frac{3}{4}} = 5.571$.

313. To find the root of a number by logarithms.—Rule.
Divide the logarithm of the number by the index of the root. The number corresponding to this logarithm is the required root.

Example 1.   Find $\sqrt[5]{27.658}$.
Process.   log $27.658 = 1.4418$
   $\frac{1}{5}$ log $27.658 = 0.2884 =$ log $\sqrt[5]{27.658}$.
   $\therefore \sqrt[5]{27.658} = 1.943$.

Example 2.   Find $\sqrt[6]{0.008673}$.
Process.   log $0.008673 = 7.9382 - 10$
   log $\sqrt[6]{0.008673} = \frac{1}{6}$ of $(7.9382 - 10)$
   $= \frac{1}{6}$ of $(57.9382 - 60)$
   $= 9.6564 - 10$.
   $\therefore \sqrt[6]{0.008673} = 0.4533$.

Note that, as in this example, when we are to divide a logarithm with a negative characteristic, not a multiple of the divisor, it is best to first add and subtract such a number of times 10, that after dividing there will be a -10 at the right. Thus, in the above, before dividing $(7.9382 - 10)$ by 6, we add and subtract 50.

314. Computations made by logarithms only approximate.—
By performing the above operations without the use of logarithms, it will be noticed that the results, in most cases, will vary slightly from those obtained by the use of logarithms. This emphasizes the fact that computations by the use of

logarithms are only approximately correct. However, *as great a degree of accuracy as desired can be obtained* by using tables of a large enough number of places. In general, we obtain an answer with about as many correct figures as the number of places in the logarithm tables.

315. Natural logarithms.—While in computations it is usually more convenient to employ logarithms to the base 10, often in theoretical work, and in some formulas, logarithms to another base are used. This base is a number that cannot be exactly expressed by figures. To seven decimal places it is 2.7182818. It is usually represented by the letter *e*, just as the ratio of the circumference of a circle to its diameter is represented by the Greek letter π. Logarithms to this base are called **natural logarithms, hyperbolic logarithms,** or **Napierian logarithms.**

Tables of natural logarithms are published; but, for purposes of computation, it is only necessary to remember that the natural logarithm of a number is approximately 2.3026 times the common logarithm of the same number. Or the common logarithm of a number is 0.4343 times the natural logarithm. Stated in symbols, this is, in the exponential form:

$$10^n = 2.71828^{2.3026n}, \text{ or } 2.71828^n = 10^{0.4343n};$$

and in logarithmic form it is

$$\log_e N = 2.3026 \log_{10} N, \text{ or } \log_{10} N = 0.4343 \log_e N,$$

where N is any number.

As an example of the occurrence of the Napierian logarithms in a problem of applied mathematics, consider the following: In finding the insulation resistance by the leakage method, the resistance R is found from the formula

$$R = 10^6 \cdot \frac{t}{C} \cdot \frac{1}{\log_e \left(\frac{V_0}{V}\right)},$$

where t is time in seconds, C capacity, and V voltage.

Compute the value of R if $t = 120$, $V_0 = 123$, $V = 115.8$, and $C = 0.082$.

Solution. In order that we may use the table of common logarithms, the formula may be written

$$R = 10^6 \cdot \frac{t}{C} \cdot \frac{1}{2.3026 \, \log_{10}\left(\dfrac{V_0}{V}\right)}.$$

Substituting values,

$$R = 10^6 \times \frac{120}{.082} \times \frac{1}{2.3026(\log 123 - \log 115.8)}.$$
$$\therefore \; R = 2.426 \times 10^{10}.$$

As other examples where the base of the natural system of logarithms occurs, consider the following: (1) In an alternating current circuit, the current i at any instant is given by the formula

$$i = I\left(1 - e^{-\frac{Rt}{L}}\right),$$

where I is the maximum current, R the resistance, L the coefficient of self-induction, t the time in seconds, and e the base of the natural system of logarithms.

(2) The work W done by a volume of gas, expanding at a constant temperature, from a volume V_0 to a volume V_1 is given by the following formula:

$$W = p_0 V_0 \, \log_e\left(\frac{V_1}{V_0}\right).$$

Formulas that involve logarithms to the base e occur frequently in applications of calculus.

EXERCISES 110

Use logarithms in evaluating the following:

1. $(0.543)^3$.	*Ans.* 0.1601.	**10.** $(1.4641)^{\frac{1}{4}}$.	*Ans.* 1.1.
2. $(4.07)^3$.	*Ans.* 67.42.	**11.** $(0.00032)^{\frac{1}{5}}$.	*Ans.* 0.2.
3. $(1.738)^3$.	*Ans.* 5.248.	**12.** $\sqrt[3]{2}$.	*Ans.* 1.260.
4. $(1.02)^5$.	*Ans.* 1.104.	**13.** $\sqrt[4]{4}$.	*Ans.* 1.414.
5. $(\frac{675}{1121})^3$.	*Ans.* 0.004394.	**14.** $\sqrt[3]{3}$.	*Ans.* 1.442.
6. $(z\frac{1}{13})^4$.	*Ans.* 2.868×10^{-10}.	**15.** $\sqrt[5]{2}$.	*Ans.* 1.149.
7. $(0.1181)^{\frac{1}{2}}$.	*Ans.* 0.3436.	**16.** $\sqrt[5]{0.032}$.	*Ans.* 0.5023.
8. $(1381)^{\frac{1}{4}}$.	*Ans.* 11.14.	**17.** $(4.56)^{4.56}$.	*Ans.* 1012.
9. $(1024)^{\frac{1}{5}}$.	*Ans.* 128.		

18. $(7.23)^{7.23}$.   *Ans.* 1,627,000.

19. $\dfrac{100^2}{48 \times 64 \times 11}$.   *Ans.* 0.2899.

20. $\dfrac{52^2 \times 300}{12 \times .31225 \times 400,000}$.   *Ans.* 0.5411.

25

21. $\sqrt{\dfrac{400}{55 \times 3.1416}}$.   *Ans.* 1.522.

22. $50 \times \dfrac{2^{1.5}}{81^{.63}}$.   *Ans.* 4.769.

23. $\sqrt{\dfrac{.434 \times 96^4}{64 \times 1500}}$.   *Ans.* 19.60.

24. $\sqrt{\dfrac{3500}{(1.06)^5}}$.   *Ans.* 51.14.

25. $\dfrac{3.8961 \times .6945 \times .01382}{4694 \times .00457}$.   *Ans.* 0.001743.

26. $\sqrt[4]{.0009657} \div \sqrt[3]{.0044784}$.   *Ans.* 1.070.

27. $\left(\dfrac{7.61 \times .0593}{1.307}\right)^{\frac{3}{4}}$.   *Ans.* 0.4505.

28. $\sqrt[8]{5106.5 \times .00003109}$.   *Ans.* 0.7945.

29. $\left(\dfrac{4400}{69.37}\right)^{\frac{2}{3}}$.   *Ans.* 5.259.

30. $(837.5 \times .0094325)^{\frac{2}{7}}$.   *Ans.* 1.805.

31. $(.01)^{\frac{3}{2}} \div \sqrt[3]{7}$.   *Ans.* 0.0005228.

32. $\dfrac{.0005616 \times \sqrt[7]{424.65}}{(6.73)^4 \times (.03194)^{\frac{5}{8}}}$.   *Ans.* 0.00001146.

33. $\dfrac{\sqrt{3929} \times \sqrt[4]{6548}}{\sqrt[6]{721.83}}$.   *Ans.* 188.2.

34. $\dfrac{\sqrt[5]{.05287}}{\sqrt[3]{.374} \times \sqrt[9]{.078359}}$.   *Ans.* 1.023.

35. In the formula $S = \dfrac{E - IR}{.220}$, find R if $S = 500$, $E = 220$, and $I = 12$.

Ans. 9.17.

Suggestion. Here, as in many exercises which follow, the computation can be more easily done without logarithms than with. Endeavor to use logarithms only when they are necessary or when they save time.

36. Using the formula for the horse-power of a steam engine, $H = \dfrac{PLAN}{33000}$, (see **Art. 251**):

(1) Find H when $P = 76.5$, $L = 2\frac{1}{4}$, $A = 231.8$, and $N = 116$.
(2) Find N when $H = 52$, $P = 49.12$, $L = 1.5$, and $A = 113.1$.

Ans. 140.3; 205.9.

37. Given $W = .0033 \times 10^{-7} n$, find W when $n = 75,000$.

Ans. 0.00002475.

38. If $E = $ E. M. F. in volts in moving conductor, $L = $ length of conductor in centimeters, $V = $ velocity in centimeters per second, $B = $ the number of lines of force per square centimeter, we have the formula $E = LVB10^{-8}$. Given $V = \dfrac{9 \times 100}{60}$, $B = 8000$, and $L = 0.6 \times 100$, find E.

Ans. 0.072.

39. Find the value of P from the following formula when $A = 11$, $B = 1.71$, and $C = 1.3$: $\qquad P = \sqrt[3]{\dfrac{A\,BC}{1.4\left(B + \dfrac{A^2}{C^2}\right)}}$ $\qquad$ *Ans.* 0.6199.

Suggestion. First find the logarithm of the expression under the radical, and then divide by 3. This will give the log P.

40. In measuring electrical resistance by a Wheatstone's bridge, the following data were taken:

(1) $R = 8$, $a_1 = 539.7$, $a_2 = 459$.
(2) $R = 9$, $a_1 = 510.1$, $a_2 = 488.4$.

Find the values of x from (1) and (2) by the formula

$$\frac{x}{R} = \frac{1000 + (a_1 - a_2)}{1000 - (a_1 - a_2)}.$$ $\qquad$ *Ans.* (1) 9.404; (2) 9.40.

41. In finding the diameter of a wrought-iron shaft that will transmit 90 horse-power when the number of revolutions is 100 per minute, using a factor of safety of 8, we have to find the diameter d from the formula

$$d = 68.5 \times \sqrt[3]{\frac{90}{100 \times \dfrac{50000}{8}}}.$$ Find the value of d. $\qquad$ *Ans.* 3.591.

42. Find the value of M from the formula $M = \dfrac{Wgl^3}{4bd^3B}$, when $g = 980$, $W = 75$, $l = 50$, $b = 0.98178$, $d = 0.5680$, and $B = 0.01093$.

$\qquad$ *Ans.* 11.69×10^{11}.

Solution.

log W	= 1.8751	log 4	= 0.6021
log g	= 2.9912	log b	= $\overline{1}$.9920
log l^3	= 5.0970	log d^3	= $\overline{1}$.2629
log Num.	= 9.9633	log B	= $\overline{2}$.0386
log Den.	= $\overline{3}$.8956	log Den.	= $\overline{3}$.8956
log M	= 12.0677		
$\therefore M$	= $1,169,000,000,000 = 11.69 \times 10^{11}$.		

43. Find the value of n from the formula $n = \dfrac{360Lmgl}{\pi^2 \theta r^4}$, when $g = 980$, $l = 28$, $\theta = 0.857$, $r = 0.477$, $L = 109.7$, and $m = 100$. $\qquad$ *Ans.* 2.476×10^{11}.

44. Use the same formula as in exercise 43, and find the value of n when $L = 69.6$, $m = 10$, $g = 980$, $l = 28$, $\theta = 1.1955$, and $r = 0.317$.

$\qquad$ *Ans.* 0.577×10^{11}.

45. If $m = ar^{-1.16}$, find r when $m = 2.263$ and $a = 0.4086$.

$\qquad$ *Ans.* 0.2287.

Solution. Solving for r, we have

$$r = \sqrt[1.16]{\frac{a}{m}} = \left(\frac{a}{m}\right)^{\frac{1}{1.16}} = \left(\frac{a}{m}\right)^{0.862}$$

log a = $\overline{1}$.6113
log m = 0.3547

log $\dfrac{a}{m}$ = $\overline{1}$.2566

It is now best to unite the characteristic and mantissa by algebraic addition.

Thus, $\overline{1}.2566 = -1 + .2566 = -.7434$.

Now multiply by the exponent .862, and get $-.7434 \times .862 = -.6408$.

This is next changed to the form of a logarithm as given in the table, that is, to a form where the mantissa is not negative.

$$-.6408 = \overline{1}.3592.$$
$$\therefore \log\left(\frac{a}{m}\right)^{.862} = \overline{1}.3592.$$
$$\therefore \left(\frac{a}{m}\right)^{.862} = 0.2287. \quad Ans.$$

46. Given $p = p_0\left(\dfrac{2}{\gamma+1}\right)^{\frac{\gamma}{\gamma-1}}$, find the value of p in terms of p_0 if $\gamma = 1.41$.

Ans. $p = 0.527p_0$.

Fig. 220.

(For the meaning of this formula see *Perry's Calculus*, page 55.)

47. If an open tank kept full of water has a rectangular notch cut on one side as shown in Fig. 220, the number of cubic feet of water that will flow through this notch per second is given by the formula:

$$Q = \tfrac{2}{3}cbh^{\frac{3}{2}}\sqrt{2g};$$

where $Q =$ the amount of flow in cubic feet,

         $c =$ a constant found by experiment,

         $b =$ the width of the notch in feet,

         $h =$ the depth of the notch in feet,

and $g = 32.2$.

Find Q when $h = 1\frac{1}{3}$, $b = 2$, and $c = 0.586$.   *Ans.* 9.654.

48. Using the formula of the last exercise, find Q when $h = \frac{5}{6}$, $b = 2.5$, and $c = 0.589$.   *Ans.* 5.991.

49. If Q is the number of cubic feet that will flow through a V-shaped notch per second and h the height in feet of the water above the bottom of the notch, then $Q \propto h^{\frac{5}{2}}$. If $Q = 7.26$ when $h = 1.5$, find h when $Q = 5.68$.

Ans. 1.360.

Suggestion. If $Q \propto h^{\frac{5}{2}}$ then $Q = Kh^{\frac{5}{2}}$.

Substituting values, $7.26 = K1.5^{\frac{5}{2}}$. $\therefore K = 7.26 \div 1.5^{\frac{5}{2}}$.

Using this value of K with $Q = 5.68$, gives

$$5.68 = (7.26 \div 1.5^{\frac{5}{2}})h^{\frac{5}{2}}.$$
$$\therefore h^{\frac{5}{2}} = \frac{5.68 \times 1.5^{\frac{5}{2}}}{7.26}.$$

50. The following is an approximate formula for determining the number of wires that can be enclosed in a pipe:

$$N = 0.907\left(\frac{D}{d} - 0.94\right)^2 + 3.7,$$

where N =the number of wires,

D =the diameter of the enclosing pipe,

d =the diameter of the wires.

Solve this formula for D and find $D = d \left(0.94 + \sqrt{\dfrac{N-3.7}{0.907}} \right).$

51. Use the formula of the preceding exercise and find the diameter of a casing to hold 100 wires each having a diameter of $\frac{1}{8}$ in.

Ans. 1.405 in.

52. The amount of a principal at compound interest for a certain time is given by the following formula:

$$A = P(1+r)^t,$$

where A =the amount, P =the principal, r =the rate per cent, and t =the time in years.

Find the amount of \$236 at compound interest for 14 years at 3 per cent. *Ans.* \$356.50.

53. Find the amount of \$3764 at compound interest for 21 years at $4\frac{1}{2}$ per cent. *Ans.* \$9478.

Remark. It should be noted that in such problems as those of exercises 52, 53, and the following, a four-place table of logarithms will not give results that can be relied upon when the exponent is large. For instance, if exercise 52 be computed by a six-place table of logarithms the amount is \$356.97, and that of exercise 53 is \$9486.07. Of course, all that is necessary to secure a desired degree of accuracy is to use a table of logarithms that has a sufficiently large number of decimal places. In life insurance computations a ten-place table is often used.

54. The government Farm Loan Banks loan money to farmers for a period of years at 5 or 6 per cent, and the money is paid back in equal annual installments. The following table, in use by the United States government, gives the annual installment necessary to discharge a loan of \$1000 with interest, the number of years and the rate of interest being indicated in the table.

Table for Loan of $1000

Number of years	Annual installment at 5%	at 6%
10	\$129.50	\$135.87
15	96.34	102.96
20	80.24	87.18
25	70.95	78.23
30	65.05	72.65
35	61.07	68.97
40	58.28	66.46

Compute the installments in this table by using the following formula:

$$p = \frac{Pr(1+r)^n}{(1+r)^n - 1}.$$

where $P=$ the amount of the loan,
$r=$ the rate per cent per annum,
$n=$ the number of annual payments,
$p=$ the amount of each installment.

Suggestion. If $P=\$1000$, $r=6\%$, and $n=10$, then

$$P=\frac{1000\times.06\times1.06^{10}}{1.06^{10}-1}=\$135.87.$$

55. The above formula will give the amount of each installment made at any equal intervals of time, in order to discharge a debt, if r divided by the number of intervals per year is used for the rate. Thus, if the installments are monthly, $\frac{r}{12}$ is the rate per month.

Find the amount of the equal monthly payments to discharge a debt of \$3000 in 5 years if the rate is 6%. *Ans.* \$58.34.

Suggestion. Here $P=3000$, $n=60$, and rate per month is $\frac{.06}{12}=0.005$.

56. Find the amount of the equal semi-annual installments to discharge a debt of \$4500 in 7 years at 6%. *Ans.* \$399.30.

57. If an indebtedness is paid in installments, the payments being equal and each including the interest to the date of the installment, then the number of installments necessary to pay the debt is given by solving the formula of exercise 54 for n and finding

$$n=\frac{\log p-\log (p-Pr)}{\log (1+r)},$$

where $P=$ the total indebtedness,
$p=$ the amount of one installment,
and $r=$ the rate per cent for the period between installments.

How many semi-annual installments of \$600 each will it take to discharge a debt of \$7000 bearing 5% interest. *Ans.* 14.

Suggestion. Here $P=7000$, $p=600$, and $r=0.025$. Substituting in formula,

$$n=\frac{\log 600-\log (600-175)}{\log 1.025}.$$

$$\therefore\ n=\frac{2.7782-2.6284}{0.0107}=\frac{0.1498}{0.0107}=14.\ Ans.$$

58. An indebtedness of \$1500 is to be paid in installments of \$15 per month, each installment to cover the interest to that date. Find the number of installments if the interest is at 8 per cent per annum.

Ans. 164.5.

59. An indebtedness of \$1800 is paid in installments of \$5.00 per week, each payment to cover the accrued interest to that date. How many payments will be required if the interest is at 5 per cent per annum, and 52 weeks are counted as one year? *Ans.* 461.5.

60. Find the radius of a sphere that contains 5263 cu. ft.

Ans. 10.79 ft.

Suggestion. Take the formula for the volume of a sphere, $V = \frac{4}{3}\pi r^3$, and solve it for r. This gives $r = \sqrt[3]{\dfrac{3V}{4\pi}}$.

61. In the equation $y = \log x$, find the values of y corresponding to the values 0.5, 1, 2, 5, 10, 25, 50, and 100 of x. Choose a pair of coördinate axes and plot these pairs of points. This will give a curve that shows the relation between a number and its logarithm. (It will be best to choose a unit on the y-axis 5 or 10 times the length of the unit on the x-axis.)

62. If the mixture in a gas engine expands without gain or loss of heat, it is found that the law of expansion is given by the equation $pv^{1.37} = C$. Given that $p = 188.2$ when $v = 11$, find the value of C, then plot the curve of the equation using this value of C. This curve shows the pressure at any volume as the gas expands. Consider values of v from 11 to 23.

Solution. Given $pv^{1.37} = C$.
Substituting $p = 188.2$ and $v = 11$, gives $C = 188.2 \times 11^{1.37}$.

Computing by logarithms,
$$\log\ 188.2 = 2.2747$$
$$1.37\ \log\ 11 = 1.4267$$
$$\log\ C = 3.7014$$
$$C = 5028.$$

The formula is then $pv^{1.37} = 5028$.
$$\therefore\ p = \frac{5028}{v^{1.37}}.$$

Now choose, say, six values of v, as given in the table, from 11 to 23 and compute the corresponding values of p.

v...........	11	13	15	17	20	23
p..........	188.2	149.7	123.1	103.7	82.98	68.53

These values are plotted in Fig. 221 and a smooth curve is drawn through the points. From this curve any value of p corresponding to values of v from 11 to 23 can be read. Such curves when accurately plotted are of great value in engineering.

63. D is the diameter of a wrought-iron shaft to transmit an indicated horse-power H at N revolutions per minute. Given $D = \sqrt[3]{\dfrac{65H}{N}}$; plot a curve showing the relation between D and H, from $H = 10$ to $H = 80$, when N is 100 revolutions per minute. From your curve find the diameters for horse-powers 35, 47, and 72.

Remark. Many of the following exercises can be worked without the use of logarithms. Some will review ideas previously discussed. Use logarithms only where they are more convenient.

64. The tractive power of a locomotive is found by the formula:

$$T = \frac{DP^2L}{W},$$

where D = the diameter of the cylinder in inches,

         P = the mean pressure of the steam in the cylinder in pounds per square inch,

         L = the length of the piston stroke in inches,

         W = the diameter of the driving-wheel in inches,

and T = the tractive force upon the rails in pounds.

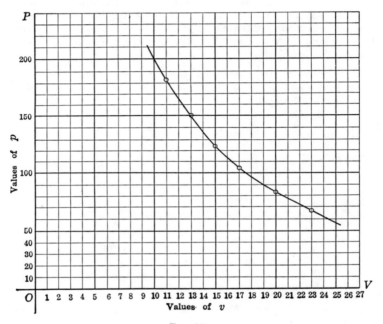

Fig. 221.

Find the tractive force for the following data:

(1) D = 16 in., P = 90 lb., L = 45 in., W = 78 in.;

(2) D = 20 in., P = 100 lb., L = 54 in., W = 84 in.

Ans. (1) 74,770; (2) 128,570.

65. To find the weight which a column of soft steel, with square bearings, will support per square inch of cross section we use the following formula:

$$P = \frac{45000}{1 + \frac{(12L)^2}{36000r^2}},$$

where P is the weight in pounds; L, the length in feet; and r, the radius of gyration in inches. Find P if $\dfrac{L}{r} = 5$. *Ans.* 40,910 lb.

Suggestion. $\quad P = \dfrac{45000}{1 + \dfrac{(12L)^2}{36000 r^2}} = \dfrac{45000}{1 + \dfrac{144}{36000}\left(\dfrac{L}{r}\right)^2} = \dfrac{45000}{1 + \dfrac{144 \times 5^2}{36000}}$.

66. In a column which is solid and circular in cross section, $r = \dfrac{d}{4}$, where d is the diameter of the cross section in inches. Find the weight such a column of soft steel will support per square inch of cross section, if $L = 16$ ft. and $d = 6$ in. Find the total weight this column will support.

Ans. 30,920 lb. per sq. in.; 874,400 lb.

67. In a hollow cylindrical column, $r = \dfrac{\sqrt{d^2 + d_1{}^2}}{4}$, where d and d_1 are the outer and inner diameters of the column respectively in inches. Find the weight the column in the preceding exercise will support per square inch of cross section and the total, if it is hollow and the shell is 1 in. thick. *Ans.* 34,220 lb. per sq. in.; 537,500 lb.

68. For a column whose cross section is a regular hexagon, $r = 0.264d$, where d is the diameter of the circle inscribed in the hexagon. Find the weight a solid hexagonal pillar of soft steel and square bearings will support, if the length is 12 ft. and the edge of the base is 2 in.

Ans. 276,900 lb.

Note. The safe load for the above columns is one-fourth or one-fifth of the value given. The formula used is Gordon's formula. For medium steel the 45,000 of the formula is changed to 50,000.

69. In any class of turbine, let P be the power of the waterfall; H, the height of the fall; and n, the rate of revolution. It is known that for a particular class of turbines of all sizes, $n \propto H^{1.25} P^{-0.5}$. In the list of a certain maker, when the fall equals 6 ft., and horse-power 100, the number of revolutions per minute is 50. Calculate n for a fall of 20 ft. and 75 horse-power. *Ans.* $n = 260$ nearly.

70. In transmitting power by means of a belt and pulley, if the belt embraces 180° of the pulley, the number of horse-power transmitted is given by the formula:

$$H = \frac{tws}{33000},$$

where $\quad H =$ horse-power,

$\qquad t =$ tension in pounds per inch width of belt,

$\qquad w =$ width of belt in inches,

and $\qquad s =$ speed of belt in feet per minute.

Solve for values of t, w, and s in terms of the remaining letters.

Ans. $t = \dfrac{33000H}{ws}$; $\; w = \dfrac{33000H}{ts}$; $\; s = \dfrac{33000H}{tw}$.

71. Using the formula of the preceding exercise, find t when $H = 50$, $w = 10$ in., and $s = 4000$ ft. per minute. *Ans.* 41.25 lb.

72. To determine the elevation of the outer rail in a curve in a railroad track, the following formula is used:

$$e = \frac{GV^2}{32.2R},$$

where e = the elevation in feet,
            G = gage of the track in feet,
            V = velocity of train in feet per second,
and R = radius of curvature of the curve in feet.

Find e for the following data, if G is 4 ft. 8½ in., the standard gage
(1) $R = 5730$ ft., (a) $V = 20$ mi. per hr., (b) $V = 50$ mi. per hr.
(2) $R = 2865$ ft., (a) $V = 15$ mi. per hr., (b) $V = 40$ mi. per hr.
(3) $R = 716.8$ ft., (a) $V = 25$ mi. per hr., (b) $V = 50$ mi. per hr.
Ans. (1) (a) 0.02 ft., (b) 0.14 ft.
           (2) (a) 0.02 ft., (b) 0.18 ft.
           (3) (a) 0.27 ft., (b) 1.10 ft.

73. In long water pipes, when the diameter and length of the pipes are constant, that is, do not change, the amount of discharge varies as the square root of the head. How many times must the head H be increased to double the amount of discharge G? To make the discharge five times as much? *Ans.* 4; 25.

Definition. The **head** is the distance the source of supply is above the point of discharge.

74. If the pipe is of such length and diameter that the discharge is 20 gallons per minute, what will it be if the head is doubled? *Ans.* 28.28+ gallons.

75. If when the head is 10 ft., the discharge through a certain pipe is 50 gallons per minute, what must be the head so that the same pipe may discharge 210 barrels per hour? *Ans.* 48.62 ft.

76. In long water pipes, when the lengths of the pipes are the same and when the head does not change, the amount of discharge varies directly as the square root of the fifth power of the diameter. Using D and d for the diameters, and G and g for the amounts of discharge, write this relation in the form of a proportion. *Ans.* $G : g = \sqrt{D^5} : \sqrt{d^5}$.

77. Write the above relation in the variation form both with and without the constant. What does the constant include in it? Would there be a different constant for each length of pipe? For each head? *Ans.* $G = K\sqrt{D^5}$; $G \propto \sqrt{D^5}$.

78. If the length and the head remain constant, what change in the discharge will be caused by a change in diameter from 3 in. to 4 in.? *Ans.* 2.05 times, nearly.

Suggestion. Increased in the ratio $\sqrt{3^5} : \sqrt{4^5}$.

79. A 3-in. pipe 100 ft. in length with a certain head discharges 110 gallons per minute; find the discharge from a 5-in. pipe of the same length and head. *Ans.* 394.5 gal. per minute.

Suggestion. $110 : x = \sqrt{3^5} : \sqrt{5^5}$.

80. How many 1-in. pipes will it take to discharge the same amount as one 6-in. pipe? Here we are considering long pipes so use $N = \dfrac{\sqrt{D^5}}{\sqrt{d^5}}$, where N = the number of small pipes, and D and d are the diameters of the large and the small pipes respectively. (See exercise 9, page 157.)

Ans. 88.2.

81. In long water pipes, when the discharge and the length are constant, the head will be inversely as the fifth power of the diameter. Using H and h for heads, and D and d for the diameters respectively, write this relation in the proportion form.   Ans. $H : h = d^5 : D^5$.

82. With a head of 4.1 ft. and a length of 100 ft. a 3-in. pipe will discharge 95.4 gallons per minute; find the head so that a 2-in. pipe of the same length will discharge an equal amount.   Ans. 31.13 ft.

83. Using H and D for head and diameter respectively, write the relation given in exercise 81 in the variation form. Using this formula solve exercise 82.   Ans. $H = \dfrac{K}{D^5}$.

84. In long water pipes when the head and the diameter are constant the discharge will be inversely as the square roots of the lengths. Using G for discharge and L for length, state this in the variation form. In the proportion form.   Ans. $G = \dfrac{K}{\sqrt{L}}$; $G : g = \sqrt{l} : \sqrt{L}$.

85. In a long water pipe of certain diameter and head, the discharge is 2000 gallons per minute. How many gallons will be discharged per minute under the same head and the same size of pipe if the length is doubled? If six times as long?   Ans. 1414 gal.; 816.5 gal.

86. In long water pipes, when the discharge and the diameter are constant, the head varies directly as the length. Using the letters given in the preceding exercises, state this in the form of a proportion, and in the variation form.   Ans. $H : h = L : l$; $H = KL$.

87. The square of the initial velocity of a projectile in feet per second varies as the number of pounds of powder in the charge and inversely as the weight of the projectile. If 5 lb. of a certain kind of powder will give a projectile weighing 10 lb. an initial velocity of 1850 ft. per second, how great a velocity will 50 lb. of powder give an 80-lb. projectile?

Ans. 2068 ft. per second.

Solution. Let p = number of pounds of powder in charge, w = weight of projectile, and v = velocity in feet per second.

Then $v^2 = k\dfrac{p}{w}.$

When $p = 5$ and $w = 10$, $v = 1850$.

$\therefore 1850^2 = k\dfrac{5}{10}$, and $k = 2 \times 1850^2$.

When $p = 50$ and $w = 80$,

$v = \sqrt{2 \times 1850^2 \times \dfrac{50}{80}} = 2068.$

88. Using the same quality of powder as in the last, find the charge necessary to give a 1200-lb. projectile an initial velocity of 2100 ft. per second.   Ans. 773 lb.

TRIGONOMETRY

CHAPTER XXXV

INTRODUCTION, ANGLES

316. Introductory.—Each advance step in mathematics is an attempt to do something more easily than it could have been done before, or to accomplish something that was before impossible. We have seen that many problems could be worked more easily by algebra than by arithmetic, and that many other problems could be solved by algebra that could not be solved by methods of arithmetic.

It was found that the area of a segment of a circle could not be obtained by geometry except in a few special cases; by methods of trigonometry, this area can be found in all cases where there are sufficient facts to do it by any means. By geometry, one side of a right triangle can be found if the other two sides are known; but there is no way by geometry of finding the acute angles when only the sides are known. By trigonometry, the angles as well as the sides can be found. Many such illustrations could be given in which trigonometry is a more powerful tool than either algebra or geometry. Trigonometry is based upon geometry, but makes use of the methods and machinery of algebra.

While trigonometry can be applied at once to the solution of various practical problems, it is also of great assistance in other branches of mathematics. In the following chapters will be given some of the direct applications of the subject.

317. Angles.—The definition of an angle as given in **Art. 90** admits of a clear conception of small positive angles only. In trigonometry we wish to deal with *negative* as well as *positive* angles, and these of any size whatever. We, therefore, need a more comprehensive definition of an angle.

If a line is turned about a fixed point in the line and kept in the same plane, it is said to **generate** or **sweep out an angle.**

The hand of a clock may be thought of as the line that is revolving and generating the angle.

The *size* of the angle is determined by the *amount of turning* made by the line.

If the line turns in a **counter-clockwise direction,** that is, opposite in direction to the hands of a clock, the angle described

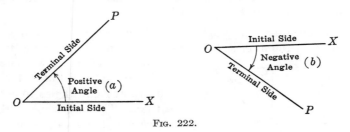

Fig. 222.

is called a **positive angle.** If the line turns in a **clockwise direction,** the angle described is called a **negative angle.**

The position of the line at the start is called the **initial line** or **side,** and the final position is called the **terminal line** or **side.**

A circular arrow drawn between the two lines and having its head in the terminal line shows the *direction of turning* and the *size of* the angle.

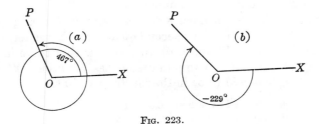

Fig. 223.

In Fig. 222(*a*), the line *OX* is imagined pinned at *O* and turning in a counter-clockwise direction to the position *OP.* The angle described is positive, and is read angle *XOP.* Notice that the initial line is read first.

In Fig. 222(*b*), the line *OX* is thought of as turning in a clockwise direction, and so describing the negative angle *XOP.*

It is evident that the idea of an angle given in this article allows it to be of any value whatever, positive or negative.

Thus, an angle of 467° is one complete turn and 107°. It is shown in Fig. 223(*a*).

An angle of —229° is a turn of 229° in the negative, clockwise, direction. It is shown in Fig. 223(*b*).

An angle of 720° is two complete turns of the initial line. An angle of 3760° is ten complete turns and 160° more.

318. Location of angles, quadrants.—For convenience in locating the angles, the agreement is made as for plotting

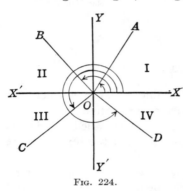

Fig. 224.

(see **Art. 286**). Two lines, $X'X$ and $Y'Y$ of Fig. 224, are drawn at right angles to each other. The directions of the lines and the location of the quadrants are as in the article referred to.

If the positive direction of the x-axis is taken as the initial side, the angle is said to be in the **first quadrant** if its terminal side lies between OX and OY. It does not matter how many turns are made. Thus the angles of 40°, 400°, 760° all lie in the first quadrant.

Similarly, if the terminal side lies between OY and OX', the angle is said to be in the **second quadrant**. If the terminal side lies between OX' and OY', the angle is said to be in the **third quadrant**. If the terminal side lies between OY' and OX, the angle is said to be in the **fourth quadrant**.

Thus, angle XOA is in the first quadrant.
Angle XOB is in the second quadrant.
Angle XOC is in the third quadrant.
Angle XOD is in the fourth quadrant.

If the terminal side falls on OX, OY, OX', or OY' the angle is said to lie **between** two quadrants.

319. Measurement of angles.—In **Chap. XIII,** the three units for measuring angles are discussed. These units are the *right angle*, the *degree*, and the *radian*.

By definition, the radian is an angle of such size that when placed at the center of a circle its sides intercept an arc equal to the radius. It is found in the chapter referred to that 2π radians are measured by a whole circumference. This is illustrated in Fig. 225. From the definition it is evident that the size of the radian does not depend on the size of the circle.

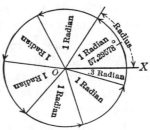

Fɪɢ. 225.

As before 1 radian $= 57.29578°-$ $= 57° 17' 44.8''$, and $1° = 0.017453$ $+$ radians.

The measurement of an angle by the radian unit is often called **circular measure** or **π-measure**.

Since 2π radians $= 360°$, π radians $= 180°$, $\dfrac{\pi}{2}$ radians $= 90°$, $\dfrac{\pi}{3}$ radians $= 60°$, etc., it is often convenient to represent some of the most frequently used angles by means of π.

In using circular measure, the word radian is usually omitted. Thus, we write π, $\dfrac{\pi}{2}$, $\dfrac{\pi}{4}$, 3, 0.5, meaning in each case so many radians.

To convert radians to degrees, multiply the number of radians by $\dfrac{180}{\pi}$ *or* $57.29578-$.

To convert degrees to radians, multiply the number of degrees by $\dfrac{\pi}{180}$ *or* $0.017453+$.

Example 1.   Reduce 2.5 radians to degrees, minutes, and seconds.

Solution.   1 radian $= 57.29578°$,

$$\therefore 2.5 \text{ radians} = 2.5 \times 57.29578° = 143.2394°.$$

To find the number of minutes, multiply the decimal part of the number of degrees by 60,

$$\therefore 0.2394° = 60 \times 0.2394 = 14.364'.$$

Likewise, $0.364' = 60 \times 0.364 = 21.8''$,

$$\therefore 2.5 \text{ radians} = 143° 14' 22''.$$

Example 2.   Reduce 22° 36′ 30″ to radians.

Solution.   First, change to degrees and decimals of degrees,

22° 36′ 30″ = 22.6083° +.

1° = 0.017453 + radians,

∴ 22.6083° + = 22.6083 × 0.017453 = 0.3946 − radians.

320. Relations between angle, arc, and radius.—From the definition of the radian, it is evident that the number of radians in an angle at the center of a circle can be found by dividing the length of the arc its sides intercept by the length of the radius.

That is, **number of radians in angle** $= \dfrac{\text{arc}}{\text{radius}}.$

In Fig. 226, angle *AOB* (in radians) $= \dfrac{\text{arc } AB}{\text{radius } OA}.$

If θ (the Greek letter theta) stands for the number of radians in an angle, *r* for the length of the radius of a circle, having its center at the vertex of the angle, and *s* for the length of the arc between the sides of the angle; then,

$$\theta = s \div r.$$

Solving, first for *s* and then for *r*,

$$s = r\theta,$$

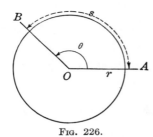

and

$$r = s \div \theta.$$

FIG. 226.

These relations are important as they may be used in solving many practical problems.

Example.   The diameter of a graduated circumference is 10 ft., and the graduations are 5 minutes of arc apart; find the distance, length of arc, between the graduations in fractions of an inch to three decimal places.

Solution.   By formula, $s = r\theta.$

From the example, $r = 12 \times 5 = 60$ in.,

and $\theta = 0.01745 \times \frac{5}{60} = 0.00145 +.$

Substituting in the formula, $s = 60 \times 0.00145 + = 0.087 +.$

∴ length of 5′ arc is 0.087 + in.

321. Railroad curves.—In the United States it is customary to express the curvature of railroad tracks in *degrees*.   The degree of a curve is determined by the central angle which is subtended by a chord of 100 ft. Thus, in a circle, a **5-degree curve** is one in which a 100-ft. chord subtends a central angle of 5 degrees.

In curves commonly used, the error is slight if the arc is taken in place of the chord. Then, assuming that 1 radian = 57.30°, the radius of a 1-degree curve is found by the formula for r of **Art. 320.** Thus,

$$r = s \div \theta = 100 \div \frac{1}{57.30} = 5730 \text{ ft.}$$

Hence 1 degree of curvature gives a radius of 5730 ft. It follows that 5730 divided by the number of degrees in the curve gives the radius of the curve; and 5730 divided by the number of feet in the radius gives the number of degrees in the curve.

EXERCISES 111

1. In what quadrant is each of the following angles: 27°, 436°, 236°, 4372°, −46°, −324°, −90°, −476°, −2342°, $\frac{1}{2}\pi$, 3π, $\frac{3}{2}\pi$, 4.3, 78.5, 82.3? Draw each angle.

2. Draw the terminal side of 237°, and give value of a negative angle having the same terminal side. How many such angles are there?

3. Draw the following angles: 76°, 25.6°, 425°, 5263°, −25°, −236°, −146°, −935°.

4. Can a positive and negative angle each have its terminal side in the same position? Illustrate.

5. Express the following angles as some number of times π radians: 30°, 45°, 54°, 60°, 81°, 90°, 120°, 135°, 150°, 180°, 210°, 225°, 240°, 270°, 300°, 315°, 330°, 360°, 540°, 720°.

Ans. $\frac{\pi}{6}$, $\frac{\pi}{4}$, $\frac{3\pi}{10}$, $\frac{\pi}{3}$, $\frac{9\pi}{20}$, $\frac{\pi}{2}$, $\frac{2\pi}{3}$, $\frac{3\pi}{4}$, $\frac{5\pi}{6}$, π, $\frac{7\pi}{6}$, $\frac{5\pi}{4}$, $\frac{4\pi}{3}$, $\frac{3\pi}{2}$, $\frac{5\pi}{3}$, $\frac{7\pi}{4}$, $\frac{11\pi}{6}$, 2π, 3π, 4π.

6. Reduce the following to radians:

(a) 47°,
(b) 75° 30′,
(c) 16° 43′ 10″,
(d) 125° 46′ 30″,
(e) 62° 40′,

(f) 135°,
(g) 120°,
(h) 175° 45′ 40″,
(i) 95° 10′ 10″,
(j) 127° 41′ 50″.

Ans. (a) .820+; (b) 1.318−; (c) .292−; (d) 2.195+; (e) 1.094−; (f) 2.356+; (g) 2.094+; (h) 3.068−; (i) 1.661+; (j) 2.229−.

26

7. Reduce the following (1) to degrees and decimals of degrees to four places, (2) to degrees, minutes, and seconds:

(a) $\frac{1}{4}\pi$,	(d) 4.23,	(g) 0.125,
(b) $\frac{3}{4}\pi$,	(e) 2.76,	(h) 2.236,
(c) $\frac{5}{6}\pi$,	(f) $\frac{17}{16}\pi$,	(i) 3.14159.

Ans. (a) 45°. (d) 242° 21′ 40″. (g) 7°9′ 43″.
  (b) 135°. (e) 158° 8′ 11″. (h) 128° 6′ 48″.
  (c) 150°. (f) 191° 15″ (i) 180°.

8. How many radians are in each of the angles of a right triangle, if one of the acute angles is 36° 47′?   *Ans.* $\frac{1}{2}\pi$; .642 −; .929 −.

9. How many degrees in each of the angles of an isosceles triangle, if the angle at the vertex is $\frac{1}{3}\pi$ radians?   *Ans.* 30°, 75°.

10. Two of the angles of a triangle are respectively $\frac{2}{3}$ and $\frac{2}{5}$ of a radian. Find the number of radians and degrees in the third angle.

Ans. 2.0749 radians = 118° 52′ 59″.

11. If an angle of 126° at the center has an arc of 226 ft., find the radius of the circle.

Solution.   Use the formula $r = s \div \theta$.

$\theta = 126 \times 0.017453 = 2.199.$

$r = 226 \times 2.199 = 102.77.$

∴ radius is 102.77 ft.

12. A flywheel 20 ft. in diameter has an angular velocity of 3π per second.   Find the rim velocity.   *Ans.* 94.25 ft. per sec.

13. The circumferential speed generally advised by makers of emery wheels is 5500 ft. per minute.   Find the angular velocity per second in radians for a 10-in. wheel.   *Ans.* 220 radians per sec.

Suggestion.   Use the formula $\theta = s \div r$.

14. Solve similar problems for the velocities of the following:

(a) Ohio grindstones, advised speed 2500 ft. per minute.

(b) Huron grindstones, advised speed 3500 ft. per minute.

(c) Wood, leather covered, polishing wheels, 7000 ft. per minute.

(d) Walrus hide polishing wheels, 8000 ft. per minute.

(e) Rag wheels, 7000 ft. per minute.

(f) Hair brush wheels, 12,000 ft. per minute.

15. A flywheel of 4-ft. radius is revolving counter-clockwise with a circumferential velocity of 75 ft. per second.   Find the angular velocity in radians per second.   *Ans.* $18\frac{3}{4}$ radians.

Solution. $\dfrac{75 \times 2\pi}{8\pi} = 18\frac{3}{4}.$

16. A train is traveling on a curve of half a mile radius at the rate of 30 miles per hour.   Through what angle does it go in 15 seconds?   Express the answer in both radians and degrees.

Ans. 0.25 radian = 14° 19′ 26″.

Suggestion.   Use the formula $\theta = s \div r$, where $s = \frac{1}{8}$ mile and $r = \frac{1}{2}$ mile.

17. Find the radius of a circle in which an arc of 20 ft. measures an angle of 2.3 radians at the center. In this circle, find the angle at the center measured by an arc of 3 ft. 8 in.

Ans. 8.70 − ft.; 0.421 + radians.

18. Find the angular velocity per minute of the minute hand of a watch. Express in degrees and radians. *Ans.* 6° = 0.1047 + radians.

19. A train of cars is going at the rate of 15 miles per hour on a curve of 600-ft. radius; find its angular velocity in radians per minute.

Ans. 2.2 radians.

20. A flywheel 22 ft. in diameter is revolving with an angular velocity of 9 radians per second. Find the rate per minute a point on the circumference is traveling. *Ans.* 5940 ft. per min.

21. Find the length of arc which, at the distance of 1 mile, will subtend an angle of 10′ at the eye. An angle of 1″. *Ans.* 15.36 ft.; 0.0256 ft.

22. The radius of the earth's orbit, which is about 92,700,000 miles, subtends at the star Sirius an angle of about 0.4″. Find the approximate distance of Sirius from the earth. *Ans.* 478 × 10¹¹ miles.

23. What radius has a 5-degree curve in a railroad track? A curve of 3° 15′? If the radius of curvature is 4550 ft., what is the degree of curve?

Ans. 1146 ft.; 1763 + ft.; 1¼° nearly.

CHAPTER XXXVI

TRIGONOMETRIC FUNCTIONS

322. Sine, cosine, and tangent of an acute angle.—In geometry we learn of certain relations between the sides of a triangle; here we find that the angles are related to the sides in a certain way. These relations are very useful in the con-

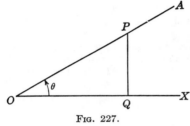

FIG. 227.

struction of angles and in solving various triangles and other figures.

Definitions. If an acute angle *XOA*, Fig. 227, is taken, and from *P*, any point in *OA*, a perpendicular *QP* is drawn to *OX*, a right triangle *QOP* is formed. It is evident because of similar triangles (see **Art. 104**) that the following ratios will not change no matter where the perpendicular *QP* may be drawn, so long as the angle *XOA*, or θ, does not change.

The ratio $\dfrac{QP}{OP}$ is called the **sine** of angle θ, written **sin θ**.

The ratio $\dfrac{OQ}{OP}$ is called the **cosine** of angle θ, written **cos θ**.

The ratio $\dfrac{QP}{OQ}$ is called the **tangent** of angle θ, written **tan θ**.

These lines can be measured, say, in inches, and numerical values of these ratios can then be found.

323. Ratios for any angles.—The same ratios may be written for an angle in any quadrant. Thus, in Fig. 228, angle *XOA* is in the second quadrant. *QP* is the perpendicular drawn from any point in the terminal side to the *x*-axis. The ratios are

$$\sin XOA = \frac{QP}{OP}, \ \cos XOA = \frac{OQ}{OP}, \ \tan XOA = \frac{QP}{OQ}.$$

404

As an exercise the student may write these ratios for the angles XOB and XOC.

As will be seen in the next article, some of the ratios are positive and some are negative numbers.

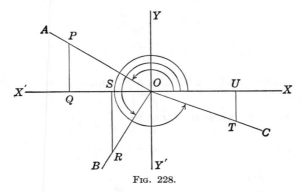

FIG. 228.

324. General form for ratios.—Let the distance from O along the terminal side to the point chosen be called the **distance**, represented by r, and *always* considered *positive*. The length of the perpendicular to the x-axis is the **ordinate**

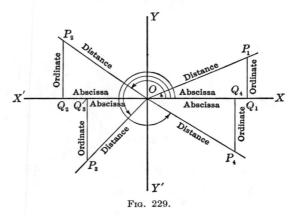

FIG. 229.

of the point, *positive* if extending above and *negative* if below the x-axis, and is represented by y. The distance from O to the foot of the perpendicular is the **abscissa** of the point, *positive* if extending to the right of the origin and *negative* if to the left, and is represented by x. The ratios for any angle θ (see Fig. 229) may then be written as follows:

$$\sin \theta = \frac{\text{ordinate}}{\text{distance}} = \frac{y}{r},$$

$$\cos \theta = \frac{\text{abscissa}}{\text{distance}} = \frac{x}{r},$$

$$\tan \theta = \frac{\text{ordinate}}{\text{abscissa}} = \frac{y}{x}.$$

The *reciprocals* of these ratios are often used and are named as follows:

cosecant θ, abbreviated **csc** $\theta = \dfrac{1}{\sin \theta} = \dfrac{r}{y}$,

secant θ, abbreviated **sec** $\theta = \dfrac{1}{\cos \theta} = \dfrac{r}{x}$,

cotangent θ, abbreviated **cot** $\theta = \dfrac{1}{\tan \theta} = \dfrac{x}{y}$.

These six ratios are called **trigonometric functions.** They are of the greatest importance in trigonometry and must be learned so that they can be given at any time without hesitation.

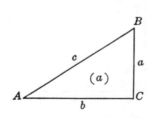 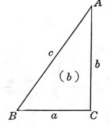

Fig. 230.

325. Acute angle in a right triangle.—In the right triangle ABC, Fig. 230, $\sin A = \dfrac{a}{c} = \cos B$, $\cos A = \dfrac{b}{c} = \sin B$, $\tan A = \dfrac{a}{b} = \cot B$, $\cot A = \dfrac{b}{a} = \tan B$, $\sec A = \dfrac{c}{b} = \csc B$, $\csc A = \dfrac{c}{a} = \sec B$.

These ratios for angle B will readily be seen if the triangle is placed in the position of Fig. 230(b).

In working with right triangles, the following forms of the

definitions of the trigonometric functions will be found convenient for either acute angle:

$$\sin A \text{ (or } \sin B) = \frac{\text{side opposite}}{\text{hypotenuse}},$$

$$\cos A \text{ (or } \cos B) = \frac{\text{side adjacent}}{\text{hypotenuse}},$$

$$\tan A \text{ (or } \tan B) = \frac{\text{side opposite}}{\text{side adjacent}},$$

$$\csc A \text{ (or } \csc B) = \frac{\text{hypotenuse}}{\text{side opposite}},$$

$$\sec A \text{ (or } \sec B) = \frac{\text{hypotenuse}}{\text{side adjacent}},$$

$$\cot A \text{ (or } \cot B) = \frac{\text{side adjacent}}{\text{side opposite}}.$$

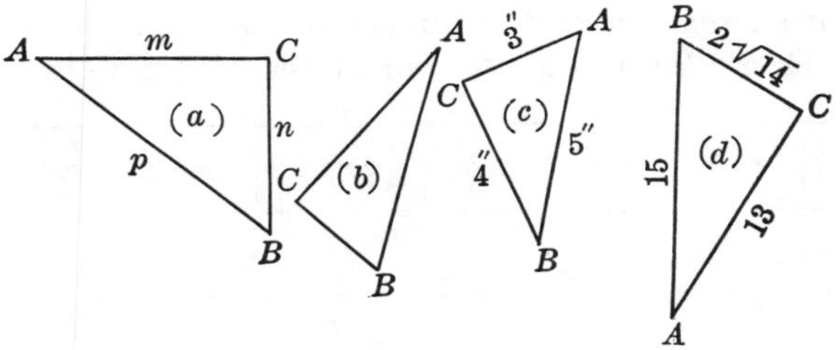

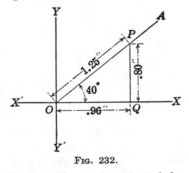

Fig. 231.

As an exercise give rapidly the functions of the acute angles of the right triangles shown in Fig. 231.

326. Relation between the functions of an angle and the functions of its complement. In the right triangle, angle $A +$ angle $B = 90°$. That is, angle A and angle B are complements of each other. (See **Art. 90.**) In the previous article it is seen that $\sin A = \cos B$; $\cos A = \sin B$; $\tan A = \cot B$; etc. From this, we see

Fig. 232.

that any function of an angle is equal to the **co-function** of the *complement* of the angle. For example, $\cos 30° = \sin 60°$, sec $22° = \csc 68°$.

327. Trigonometric functions by construction and measurement.—Let it be required to find the sine, cosine, and tangent of 40°.

Draw an angle $XOA = 40°$, Fig. 232.   Take a convenient distance OP on the terminal side and draw the perpendicular QP.   Then by measuring the lines we have the following:

$$\sin 40° = \frac{QP}{OP} = \frac{.80}{1.25} = .64,$$

$$\cos 40° = \frac{OQ}{OP} = \frac{.96}{1.25} = .77,$$

$$\tan 40° = \frac{QP}{OQ} = \frac{.80}{.96} = .84.$$

The measurements are made in inches.

As an exercise draw the angles and fill out the following table.   Carry the results to two places of decimals.

Angle	sin	cos	tan	Angle	sin	cos	tan
10°				50°			
15°				55°			
20°				60°			
25°				65°			
30°				70°			
35°				75°			
40°				80°			
45°				85°			

In the above table, compare the sine and cosine of 10° and 80°, 15° and 75°, 20° and 70°, etc.   As in **Art. 326,** it will be noticed that any function of any angle is the co-function of the complement of that angle.   It follows that any function of an angle larger than 45° is a function of some angle that is less than 45°.   If then a table is made for the functions of all the angles from 0° to 45°, it can be used for finding the functions of the angles from 45° to 90° as well. **Table XI** is arranged in exactly this way. It includes the angles for every 10′ from 0° to 90°.

328. Use of functions in constructing angles.—
Example 1. Construct an angle of 40°.

Construction. sin 40° = 0.64. By the help of this, the angle may be drawn as follows: Draw a straight line *AB*, Fig. 233. At some point *Q* erect a perpendicular *QP* 0.64 in. in length. With *P* as a center draw an arc with a radius of 1 in. cutting *AB* at *O*. Draw *OP*. Angle *QOP* is 40°, for sin *QOP* = 0.64 = sin 40°.

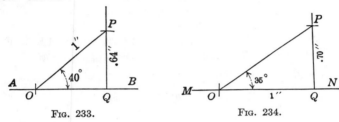

FIG. 233.   FIG. 234.

In constructing an angle of 40° all that is necessary is to make the sides *QP* and *OP* of such lengths that the ratio shall be 0.64. For this 1.28 in. and 2 in. could be used conveniently. Usually it is most convenient to make one of the sides unity. In making the construction, some other function of 40° could be used as well as the sine.

Example 2. Construct an angle of 35° by using tan 35°.
Construction. tan 35° = 0.70. Draw a straight line *MN*, Fig. 234. At some point *Q* erect a perpendicular *QP* to *MN* 0.70 in. in length. Locate *O*, making *OQ* = 1 in. Draw *OP*. Angle *QOP* is 35°, for tan *QOP* = 0.70 = tan 35°.

EXERCISES 112

1. Construct by the use of sines, angles of 25°, 65°, 47°, 53° 20′, and 25° 30′.
Suggestion. Use data from the table of **Art. 327** or from **Table XI**.
2. Construct by use of cosines, angles of 20°, 40°, 17° 20′, and 67° 40′.
3. Construct an angle θ whose tangent is 2. Find the other functions of this angle.
Ans. sin θ = .89; cos θ = .45; cot θ = .50; sec θ = 2.24; csc θ = 1.12.

4. Construct an angle θ whose cosine is .8.   Find the other functions of this angle.

   Ans. sin $\theta = .6$; tan $\theta = .75$; cot $\theta = 1.33$; sec $\theta = 1.25$; csc $\theta = 1.67$.

5. Construct θ when (a) sec $\theta = 3$;   (b) cot $\theta = 5$;   (c) csc $\theta = 2$;   (d) sin $\theta = .3$.

329. Values of functions by computation.—From our knowledge of geometry we know the relations between the sides and the angles of right triangles when the acute angles are 30°, 45°, or 60°.

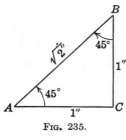

FIG. 235.

Thus, when the acute angles are 45° each, the two legs are equal; and if they are given the hypotenuse can be found.   If one acute angle is 30° and the other 60°, the shorter leg is one half the hypotenuse.

(1) *The 45° angle.* Draw a right triangle ABC, Fig. 235, with the angle $A = 45°$.   Then the angle $B = 45°$.   Let $AC = 1$ and $CB = 1$.   Then $AB = \sqrt{1^2 + 1^2} = \sqrt{2}$.

$$\therefore\ \sin 45° = \frac{1}{\sqrt{2}} = \tfrac{1}{2}\sqrt{2} = 0.707,$$

$$\cos 45° = \frac{1}{\sqrt{2}} = \tfrac{1}{2}\sqrt{2} = 0.707,$$

$$\tan 45° = 1.$$

(2) *The 60° and 30° angles.* Draw a right triangle with the acute angles 60° and 30° respectively, Fig. 236.   Let $AC = 1$, then $AB = 2$ and $CB = \sqrt{3}$.   The functions can now readily be written:

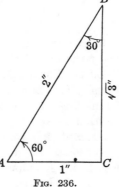

FIG. 236.

$$\sin 60° = \frac{\sqrt{3}}{2} = \tfrac{1}{2}\sqrt{3}, \qquad \sin 30° = \tfrac{1}{2},$$

$$\cos 60° = \tfrac{1}{2}, \qquad\qquad \cos 30° = \frac{\sqrt{3}}{2} = \tfrac{1}{2}\sqrt{3},$$

$$\tan 60° = \sqrt{3}, \qquad\qquad \tan 30° = \frac{1}{\sqrt{3}} = \tfrac{1}{3}\sqrt{3}.$$

330. Angles in other quadrants.—In the second quadrant, the angle $XOA = 120°$, Fig. 237, has the same numerical ratios between the abscissa, ordinate, and distance of the point P

in the terminal side as the ratios between the abscissa, ordinate, and distance of the point P' in the terminal side of the angle $XOB = 60°$ in the first quadrant.

Thus, using the values given in the figure,

$$\sin 120° = \frac{\sqrt{3}}{2} \text{ and } \sin 60° = \frac{\sqrt{3}}{2},$$

$$\cos 120° = -\tfrac{1}{2} \text{ and } \cos 60° = \tfrac{1}{2},$$

$$\tan 120° = -\sqrt{3} \text{ and } \tan 60° = \sqrt{3}.$$

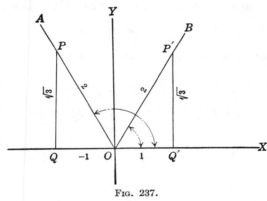

FIG. 237.

There are angles in the second, third, and fourth quadrants whose functions are connected in this way with the angles 30°, 45°, and 60° in the first quadrant. What are they?

The functions of these angles can easily be written by remembering (1) that the *distance* is always *positive;* (2) that the *ordinate* is *positive* in the first and second quadrants and *negative* in the third and fourth; (3) that the *abscissa* is *positive* in the first and fourth quadrants and *negative* in the second and third. (See **Art. 286.**)

331. Angles of 90°, 180°, 270°, and 0°.—For an angle of 90°, the ordinate equals the distance and the abscissa is zero. The functions are as follows:

$$\sin 90° = \frac{y}{r} = 1, \qquad \csc 90° = \frac{r}{y} = 1,$$

$$\cos 90° = \frac{x}{r} = 0, \qquad \sec 90° = \frac{r}{x} = \infty,$$

$$\tan 90° = \frac{y}{x} = \infty, \qquad \cot 90° = \frac{x}{y} = 0.$$

The symbol ∞ is read infinity, and here means that as the angle increases to 90°, the tangent and the secant increase without limit.

That the values of the functions are as given will readily be seen if one draws an angle XOP, Fig. 238, nearly equal to 90°, and considers the values of the ratios as the angle changes to 90°.

For an angle of 180°, the ordinate is zero and the abscissa and distance are equal. The functions are as follows:

$$\sin 180° = \frac{y}{r} = 0, \qquad \csc 180° = \frac{r}{y} = \infty,$$

$$\cos 180° = \frac{x}{r} = -1, \qquad \sec 180° = \frac{r}{x} = -1,$$

$$\tan 180° = \frac{y}{x} = 0, \qquad \cot 180° = \frac{x}{y} = \infty.$$

These values may be found by considering angle XOR, Fig. 238.

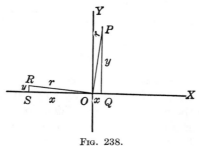

Fig. 238.

Similarly the functions for 270° and 0° are as follows:

$$\sin 270° = -1, \qquad \csc 270° = -1,$$
$$\cos 270° = 0, \qquad \sec 270° = \infty,$$
$$\tan 270° = \infty, \qquad \cot 270° = 0,$$
$$\sin 0° = 0, \qquad \csc 0° = \infty,$$
$$\cos 0° = 1, \qquad \sec 0° = 1,$$
$$\tan 0° = 0, \qquad \cot 0° = \infty.$$

332. The sine, cosine, and tangent of each of the angles mentioned in the previous articles are arranged in the following table. The student should carefully verify each result by drawing a figure and computing the ratios. Also express the results in decimals and compare with the values given in **Table XI.**

Deg.	Rad.	sin	cos	tan	Deg.	Rad.	sin	cos	tan
0°	0	0	1	0	210°	$\dfrac{7\pi}{6}$	$-\tfrac{1}{2}$	$-\dfrac{\sqrt{3}}{2}$	$\dfrac{1}{\sqrt{3}}$
30°	$\dfrac{\pi}{6}$	$\tfrac{1}{2}$	$\dfrac{\sqrt{3}}{2}$	$\dfrac{1}{\sqrt{3}}$	225°	$\dfrac{5\pi}{4}$	$-\dfrac{1}{\sqrt{2}}$	$-\dfrac{1}{\sqrt{2}}$	1
45°	$\dfrac{\pi}{4}$	$\dfrac{1}{\sqrt{2}}$	$\dfrac{1}{\sqrt{2}}$	1	240°	$\dfrac{4\pi}{3}$	$-\dfrac{\sqrt{3}}{2}$	$-\tfrac{1}{2}$	$\sqrt{3}$
60°	$\dfrac{\pi}{3}$	$\dfrac{\sqrt{3}}{2}$	$\tfrac{1}{2}$	$\sqrt{3}$	270°	$\dfrac{3\pi}{2}$	-1	0	∞
90°	$\dfrac{\pi}{2}$	1	0	∞	300°	$\dfrac{5\pi}{3}$	$-\dfrac{\sqrt{3}}{2}$	$\tfrac{1}{2}$	$-\sqrt{3}$
120°	$\dfrac{2\pi}{3}$	$\dfrac{\sqrt{3}}{2}$	$-\tfrac{1}{2}$	$-\sqrt{3}$	315°	$\dfrac{7\pi}{4}$	$-\dfrac{1}{\sqrt{2}}$	$\dfrac{1}{\sqrt{2}}$	-1
135°	$\dfrac{3\pi}{4}$	$\dfrac{1}{\sqrt{2}}$	$-\dfrac{1}{\sqrt{2}}$	-1	330°	$\dfrac{11\pi}{6}$	$-\tfrac{1}{2}$	$\dfrac{\sqrt{3}}{2}$	$-\dfrac{1}{\sqrt{3}}$
150°	$\dfrac{5\pi}{6}$	$\tfrac{1}{2}$	$-\dfrac{\sqrt{3}}{2}$	$-\dfrac{1}{\sqrt{3}}$	360°	2π	0	1	0
180°	π	0	-1	0					

CHAPTER XXXVII
TABLES AND THEIR USES

333. Nature of trigonometric functions.—From what has been done with the trigonometric ratios, it is seen that they are abstract numbers and, in general, cannot be expressed exactly as decimals. For convenience in computing, these ratios are arranged in tables somewhat similar to the tables of logarithms. The ratios in these tables may be carried to any number of decimal places. The larger the number of decimal places, the more nearly accurate the computations with the tables will be.

334. Table of functions.—In **Table XI** are arranged the natural and logarithmic functions of angles for every 10′ from 0° to 90°. The logarithms have 10 added when the characteristics are negative to avoid the writing of negative signs in the table. These logarithms are simply the logarithms of the natural functions that are in the adjoining columns, and are placed here for convenience.

Since, as stated in **Art. 327,** each acute angle above 45° has as a function the *co-function* of an angle less than 45°, each number in the table serves as the function of two different angles whose sum is 90°.

The angles less than 45° are found at the *left* of the page, and the names of the functions at the *top* of the page. The angles greater than 45° are found at the *right* of the page, and the names of the functions at the *bottom* of the page.

335. To find the function of an angle from the table.— To find the function of an angle from the table we proceed much the same as with the table of logarithms. It can best be illustrated by examples.

(A) *When the angle is given in the table.*

Example 1. Find the tangent of 23° 20′.

Find the angle of 23° 20′ at the left of the page and read 0.4314 in the column headed natural tangent,

$$\therefore \ \tan 23° \ 20' = 0.4314.$$

414

Example 2. Find the cosine of 86° 40'.

Find 86° 40' at the right of the page and read 0.0581 in the column with natural cosine at the bottom,

$$\therefore \cos 86° 40' = 0.0581.$$

(B) *When the angle is not given in the table.*
Example 3. Find sin 17° 27'.

Find sin 17° 20' = 0.2979. Find the tabular difference between 0.2979 and the next ratio below. This difference is 0.0028. Since this difference is for 10', the difference for 7' is 0.7 × 0.0028 = 0.0020,

$$\therefore \sin 17° 27' = 0.2979 + 0.0020 = 0.2999.$$

Note that the interpolation is very similar to that in logarithms, and gives approximate results only.
Example 4. Find tan 69° 43.6'.

Find tan 69° 40' = 2.6985.

Tabular difference for 10' = 0.0243.

Difference for 3.6' = 0.0243 × 0.36 = 0.0087.

$$\therefore \tan 69° 43.6' = 2.7072.$$

Example 5. Find cos 37° 57.3'.

Find cos 37° 50' = 0.7898.

Tabular difference for 10' = 0.0018.

Difference for 7.3' = 0.0018 × 0.73 = 0.0013.

$$\therefore \cos 37° 57.3' = 0.7898 - 0.0013 = 0.7885.$$

It is to be noted that a *subtraction* is to be made when interpolating in finding a cosine or a cotangent of an angle; while in finding a sine or a tangent, an *addition* is performed. This is because as the angle *increases* from 0° to 90° the sine and the tangent *increase*, but the cosine and the cotangent *decrease*.

336. To find the angle corresponding to a function.—
(A) *When the function is given in the table.*
Example 1. Find x if sin x = 0.2728.

Find 0.2728 in the column labeled natural sine and read 15° 50' in the column labeled angle.

$$\therefore x = 15° 50'.$$

(B) *When the function is not given in the table.*

Example 2. Find x if tan $x = 1.5725$.

In the column labeled natural tangent, find the ratio nearest 1.5725 and smaller. This is 1.5697 and is the tangent of 57° 30′. The tabular difference is 0.0101. The difference between 1.5697 and 1.5725 is 0.0028. Since a difference of 10′ gives a difference in the ratio of 0.0101, it will take a difference of as many minutes to give a difference in the ratio of 0.0028 as $\frac{28}{101} \times 10' = 2.8'$.

$$\therefore\ x = 57°\ 30' + 2.8' = 57°\ 32.8'.$$

Note again how similar the interpolating is to that in logarithms.

Example 3. Find x if cos $x = 0.7396$.

Since the cosine decreases as the angle increases, find the cosine nearest to .7396 but larger. This is cos 42° 10′ = 0.7412.

Tabular difference = 0.0020.

Difference of $0.7412 - 0.7396 = 0.0016$.

$$\tfrac{16}{20} \times 10' = 8'.$$

$$\therefore\ x = 42°\ 10' + 8' = 42°\ 18'.$$

Example 4. Find x if log sin $x = 9.3762 - 10$.

From table log sin 13° 40′ = 9.3734.

$$9.3762 - 9.3734 = 0.0028.$$

Tabular difference $\qquad = 0.0052.$

$$\tfrac{28}{52} \times 10' = 5.4'.$$

$$\therefore\ x = 13°\ 40' + 5.4' = 13°\ 45.4'.$$

EXERCISES 113

1. Find the sine, cosine, and tangent of 40° 10′, 59° 50′, 76° 30′, and 5° 40′.

2. Find the sine, cosine, and tangent of (a) 17° 36′, (b) 29° 29′, (c) 76° 14′, (d) 83° 33′, (e) 63° 47′.

Ans. (a) $\begin{cases} 0.3024 \\ 0.9532 \\ 0.3172 \end{cases}$ (b) $\begin{cases} 0.4922 \\ 0.8705 \\ 0.5654 \end{cases}$ (c) $\begin{cases} 0.9713 \\ 0.2380 \\ 4.0817 \end{cases}$ (d) $\begin{cases} 0.9937 \\ 0.1123 \\ 8.8468 \end{cases}$ (e) $\begin{cases} 0.8971 \\ 2.4418 \\ 2.0308 \end{cases}$

3. Find the angles having the following as sines: 0.5807, 0.2725, 0.4986, 0.9127, 0.0276.

Ans. 35° 30′, 15° 48.9′, 29° 54.4′, 65° 52.7′, 1° 34.8′.

4. Find the angles having cosines as follows: 0.3764, 0.8642, 0.9091, 0.4848, 0.0986. *Ans.* 67° 53.3′, 30° 12.7′, 24° 37.5′, 61°, 84° 20.3′.

5. Find the angles having tangents as follows: 0.2256, 1.7624, 2.8427, 0.1111, 3, 0.6666.
 Ans. 12° 42.9′, 60° 25.7′, 70° 37.1′, 6° 20.3′, 71° 33.9′, 33° 41.2′.
6. Find sin 34° 40′ and find the logarithm of this result from **Table X.**
Find log sin 34° 40′ from **Table XI** and compare results.
7. Verify the following by the tables:
  log sin 56° 35′ = 9.9215; log tan 34° 15.6′ = 9.8332;
  log cos 27° 55′ = 9.9462; log cos 19° 53.4′ = 9.9733;
  log sin 17° 9′ = 9.4696; log tan 75° 56.8′ = 0.6015.
8. Find x in each of the following:
  (a) log cos x = 9.8236;   (c) log tan x = 0.4293;
  (b) log sin x = 9.4737;   (d) log cot x = 9.4236.
    Ans. (a) 48° 13.6′; (b) 17° 19′; (c) 69° 35.3′; (d) 75° 8.8′.

337. Evaluation of formulas.—Formulas in various lines of work often contain trigonometric functions. As with other formulas, these can usually be evaluated with or without logarithms. Since logarithms are a very convenient and useful tool, they should be used whenever they can be used to advantage.

To indicate the power of a trigonometric function the exponent is placed before the symbol for the angle.

Thus, $\sin^2 30°$ means the square of sin 30°.

The logarithms of trigonometric functions are found in **Table XI** and those of numbers in **Table X.**

Example 1. Find $\sqrt[3]{\sin 47° + \tan^3 36°}$.

Solution.   sin 47° = 0.7314, from **Table XI.**

  log tan 36° = 9.8613 − 10.

∴ log tan³ 36° = 9.5839 − 10.

∴ tan³ 36° = 0.3836, from **Table X.**

∴ sin 47° + tan³ 36° = 0.7314 + 0.3836 = 1.1150.

  log 1.1150 = 0.0473.

  log $\sqrt[3]{1.1150}$ = 0.0158.

∴ $\sqrt[3]{1.1150}$ = 1.037.

∴ $\sqrt[3]{\sin 47° + \tan^3 36°}$ = 1.037. *Ans.*

Example 2. Given $x = \dfrac{\tan 72° 34'}{69° 40'}$, find the value of x to two decimal places.

In an example like this it is agreed that 69° 40′ shall be changed to radians to give the number to divide by.

  Solution.   tan 72° 34′ = 3.1846.
  27

69° 40' = 69⅔° = 69⅔ ×0.01745 radians = 1.216 radians.

3.1846 ÷ 1.216 = 2.62.

∴ $x = 2.62$. *Ans.*

Logarithms could be used in solving this example.

EXERCISES 114

1. Find the value of $\sqrt{\sin^3 49° 10'}$.   *Ans.* 0.6583.

2. Find the value of $\sqrt[5]{\tan 75° + 56}$.   *Ans.* 2.266.

3. Find the numerical value of $r^{\frac{2}{3}}(s^2 - t^2) \tan \theta$, where $r = 25.2$, $s = 90$, $t = 49.6$, and $\theta = 31° 52'$.   *Ans.* 30,140.

4. Find the value of $ae^{-bt} \sin (ct + \theta)$, if $a = 5$, $b = 200$, $c = 600$, $\theta = -0.1745$ radians, $e = 2.718$, and $t = 0.001$.   *Ans.* 1.69.

Suggestion. $(ct + \theta) = 0.6 + (-0.1745) = 0.4255$ radians.

0.4255 × 57.2957° = 24.379° = 24° 22.7'.

5. Given $x = \dfrac{\sin 45° 56' 20''}{36° 20'}$, find the value of x to three decimal places.

Suggestion. First change 36° 20' to radians.   *Ans.* 1.133.

6. Given $x = \dfrac{\tan 1.3788}{\sqrt{3 + \frac{1}{3}\pi}}$, find x to four decimal places.

          Ans. 0.8689.

7. Evaluate $\sqrt{a^2 + b^2 - 2ab \cos C}$, when $a = 231$, $b = 357$, and $C = 55°$.

          Ans. 293.6.

8. Evaluate $\dfrac{a \sin B \sin C}{\sin A}$, when $a = 126$, $A = 30°$, $B = 72°$, $C = 78°$.

          Ans. 234.4.

9. Find the value of $\sin x \cos y + \cos x \sin y$, when $x = 42° 10'$, and $y = 17° 50'$.   *Ans.* 0.866.

10. Find the value of each of the following:

(a) $\sin^2 20° + \cos^2 20°$.   (c) $\sin^2 40° + \cos^2 40°$.

(b) $\sin^2 30° + \cos^2 30°$.   (d) $\sin^2 62° 30' + \cos^2 62° 30'$.

Compare the results in the above and state conclusions.

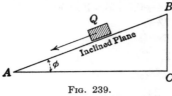

FIG. 239.

11. The velocity v of a body sliding a distance s down a smooth plane inclined at an angle φ with the horizontal is given by the formula $v = \sqrt{2gs \sin \varphi}$, where $g = 32$. Find v when $s = 50$ ft. and $\varphi = 27° 16'$.

          Ans. 38.3 ft. per second.

12. If the resistance of the air is disregarded, the distance along a horizontal plane that a projectile will go is given by the formula $d = \dfrac{v^2 \sin 2\alpha}{g}$, where v is the velocity at which the body is projected in feet per second, α the angle that the initial direction makes with the horizontal, and d the distance along the horizontal. The value of g may be taken as 32. Find d if v is 800 ft. per second and α is 5°. Using the same velocity, find d when α is 20°, 30°, 40°, and 45°.

Ans. 3472 ft.; 12,856 ft.; 17,320 ft.; 19,696 ft.; 20,000 ft.

13. Disregarding the resistance of the air, the highest point reached by a projectile is given by the formula $y = \dfrac{v^2 \sin^2 \alpha}{2g}$. Find the greatest height above the starting point reached by a projectile having an initial velocity of 2000 ft. per second, and having successive values for α of 5°, 10°, 20°, 30°, 45°, 60°, and 90°.

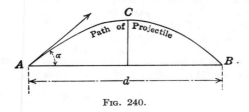

Fig. 240.

14. The height y that a projectile is after traversing a horizontal distance x, when projected with a velocity v in a direction making an angle α with the horizontal, is given by the following formula:

$$y = x \tan \alpha - \frac{gx^2}{2v^2 \cos^2 \alpha}.$$

Find y when $x = 1000$ yd., $v = 2000$ ft. per second, $\alpha = 5°$, and $g = 32$.

Ans. 226.2 ft.

15. If the resistance of the air is disregarded, the greatest horizontal distance a projectile will go is found by making the initial direction at an angle of 45° with the horizontal. Find the greatest horizontal distance that a shell having an initial velocity of 2200 ft. per second can reach.

Ans. 28.6+ miles.

16. If F is the force required to move a weight W up a plane inclined to the horizontal at an angle α, and μ (Greek letter mu) the coefficient of friction, then

$$F = W\,\frac{\sin \alpha + \mu \cos \alpha}{\cos \alpha - \mu \sin \alpha}.$$

Fig. 241.

Calculate F if $W = 800$ lb., $\alpha = 30°$, and $\mu = 0.2$. *Ans.* 703 lb.

17. In computing the illumination on a surface when the surface is not perpendicular to the rays of light from a source of light, the following formula is used:

$$E = \frac{I}{d^2} \times \cos \varphi,$$

where E = the illumination at the point on the surface in foot-candles
       I = the luminous intensity of the source in candles,
       d = the distance in feet from the source of light,
       φ = the angle between the incident ray and a line perpendicular
         to the surface.
Solve this formula for d and I, and obtain the following formulas:

$$d = \sqrt{\frac{I \cos \varphi}{E}}, \ I = \frac{Ed^2}{\cos \varphi}.$$

18. By means of the preceding formulas compute:
(1) E when $I = 50$, $d = $ 10, and $\varphi = 75°$.
(2) d when $I = 60$, $E = 0.25$, and $\varphi = 65°$.
(3) I when $E = $ 4, $d = $ 8, and $\varphi = 45°$.

               Ans. (1) 0.1294; (2) 10 ft.; (3) 362.

19. What do the formulas in exercise 17 become if $\varphi = 0°$? That is, if the rays are normal (perpendicular) to the surface.

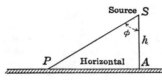

Fig. 242.

20. To compute the illumination on a horizontal surface from a source of light at a given vertical distance from the surface the following formula is used:

$$E_h = \frac{I}{h^2} \times \cos^3 \varphi,$$

where E_h = the illumination in foot-candles at a point on the horizontal
       surface,
       I = the luminous intensity of the source in candles,
       h = the vertical distance in feet from the horizontal surface to
       the source of light,
       φ = the angle between the incident ray and a vertical line.
Solve this formula for h and I, and obtain the following formulas:

$$h = \sqrt{\frac{I \cos^3 \varphi}{E_h}}, \ I = \frac{E_h h^2}{\cos^3 \varphi}.$$

21. By means of the preceding formulas compute:
(1) E_h when $I = 250$, $h = 12$, and $\varphi = 55°$.
(2) h when $I = 100$, $E_h = 65$, and $\varphi = 12°$.
(3) I when $E_h = 0.85$, $h = $ 8, and $\varphi = 37°$.

             Ans. (1) 0.3276; (2) 1.2 ft.; (3) 106.8.

CHAPTER XXXVIII

RIGHT TRIANGLES

338. Any triangle has three sides and three angles; these are called the six **elements** of the triangle.

The angles are usually represented by the capital letters A, B, and C; the sides by the small letters a, b, and c, the side a being opposite angle A, side b opposite angle B, and side c opposite angle C.

To **solve** a triangle is to find the values of the remaining elements when some of them are given.

339. Solving.—A triangle may be solved in two ways:

(1) By constructing the triangle from the known elements, and measuring the remaining elements with the ruler and the protractor.

(2) By computing the remaining elements from those that are known.

The first has already been done to some extent in **Chapter XIII.** The second has been done for some special triangles, as the right triangle, the isosceles triangle, and the equilateral triangle, in **Chapter XI,** but only for some of the elements, not including the angles.

By trigonometry a triangle can always be solved when the facts given are sufficient for its construction; and not only can the sides be found, but the angles also.

EXERCISES 115

If A, B, and C represent the angles of a triangle, and a, b, and c respectively the sides opposite these angles, construct carefully the following triangles, to scale if necessary, and measure the other elements. It is important that the student should carry out these carefully for it will help him to see when there are sufficient data for solution.

   1. $A = 40°$, $b = 2$ in., $c = 2.5$ in., find B, C, and a.
   2. $A = 50°$, $C = 70°$, $b = 2$ in., find B, a, and c.
   3. $A = 30°$, $a = 10$ ft., $c = 15$ ft., find B, C, and b.

Can more than one triangle be formed from the data in 3?

4. $a = 20$ ft., $b = 15$ ft., $c = 12$ ft., find A, B, and C.

5. $A = 40°$, $B = 80°$, $C = 60°$, find a, b, and c.

Can more than one triangle be formed from the data in 5?

The following are right triangles and C is the right angle:

6. $A = 29°$, $b = 2$ in., find B, a, and c.

7. $A = 42°$, $a = 4$ in., find B, b, and c.

8. $A = 47°$, $c = 3$ in., find B, a, and c.

9. $a = 4$ in., $b = 6$ in., find A, B, and c.

10. $a = 1.5$ ft., $c = 2.3$ ft., find A, B, and b.

340. The right triangle.—The right triangle has already been solved when any two sides are known, but the angles were not found. The previous exercises from 6 to 10 should lead us to expect that we could find the other elements when any two are given, other than the right angle, and including at least one side. Geometry will not do this but trigonometry will.

It is well to recall the following facts concerning the right triangle:

(1) *The hypotenuse is greater than either of the other two sides, and less than their sum.*

(2) *The square of the hypotenuse is equal to the sum of the squares of the other two sides.*

(3) *The sum of the two acute angles is 90°, that is, the acute angles are complements of each other.*

(4) *The greater side is opposite the greater angle, and the greater angle is opposite the greater side.*

An inspection of the problems of construction will show that all the possible sets of two given parts for the right triangle are included in the following cases:

CASE I. *Given an acute angle and a side not the hypotenuse.*

CASE II. *Given an acute angle and the hypotenuse.*

CASE III. *Given the hypotenuse and one other side.*

CASE IV. *Given the two sides not the hypotenuse.*

341. Directions for solving.—To solve a right triangle it is necessary that two elements be given, at least one of which is a side.

Each equation, as $\sin A = \dfrac{a}{c}$, contains three quantities. When two of these are given the third can be found. These equations together with the facts from geometry: (1) that the square of the hypotenuse equals the sum of the squares of the other two sides; and (2) that the sum of the two acute angles equals 90°, enable one to solve any right triangle.

These equations may be written thus:

(1) $\sin A = \dfrac{a}{c}$,

(2) $\cos A = \dfrac{b}{c}$,

(3) $\tan A = \dfrac{a}{b}$,

(4) $\cot A = \dfrac{b}{a}$,

(5) $c^2 = a^2 + b^2$,

(6) $\sin B = \dfrac{b}{c}$,

(7) $\cos B = \dfrac{a}{c}$,

(8) $\tan B = \dfrac{b}{a}$,

(9) $\cot B = \dfrac{a}{b}$,

(10) $A + B = 90°$.

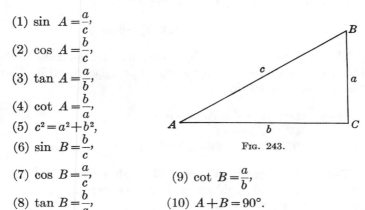

Fig. 243.

Notice that all of these except (5) and (10) are nothing but the definitions of the trigonometric ratios.

342. Case I.   Given A and b, A and a, B and a, or B and b.—
Example.   In a right triangle $A = 32°\ 20'$ and $b = 10$ ft., find B, a, and c.

Solution.   First, construct the triangle carefully; second, write equations using two of the known elements and one of the unknown in each.

Equations.   *Construction.*

(1) $A + B = 90°$, this gives B.

(2) $\cos A = \dfrac{b}{c}$, this gives c.

(3) $\tan A = \dfrac{a}{b}$, this gives a.

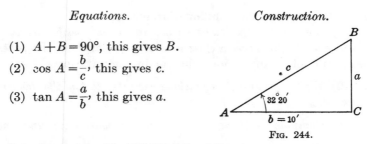

Fig. 244.

Substituting in (1), $32°\ 20' + B = 90°$.
∴ $B = 90° - 32°\ 20' = 57°\ 40'$.

Substituting in (2), $\cos 32° \ 20' = \dfrac{10}{c}$.

$\therefore \ c = 10 \div \cos 32° \ 20' = 10 \div .8450 = 11.83$ ft.

Substituting in (3), $\tan 32° \ 20' = \dfrac{a}{10}$.

$\therefore \ a = 10 \times \tan 32° \ 20' = 10 \times .6330 = 6.33$ ft.

This may be checked (a) by measuring the elements in the triangle constructed; (b) by using some other equation than the ones used in solving.

Thus, substitute values in $c^2 = a^2 + b^2$.
$\quad 11.83^2 = 6.33^2 + 10^2$.
$\quad 139.95 = 39.97 + 100 = 139.97$, which agrees closely.

This solution has been carried through with natural functions. Logarithms could be used to advantage in performing the multiplications and divisions.

Thus, in (2) $c = \dfrac{b}{\cos A}$

$\therefore \ \log c \ = \log b - \log \cos A.$
$\quad \log 10 = 1.0000$
$\log \cos 32° \ 20' = 9.9268 - 10$

$\rule{3cm}{0.4pt}$

$\quad \log c = 1.0732$
$\quad \therefore \ c = 11.83 +$ ft., which agrees with the result obtained before.

343. Directions for solution of triangles.—

(1) *Construct the triangle as accurately as possible with instruments.* This gives a clear idea of the relation of the parts, and will detect any serious blunder in computation.

(2) *Write down all the equations necessary to find the elements wanted.*

(3) *Compute the elements by natural or logarithmic functions.*

(4) *Check the work.*

(5) *Strive for neatness and clearness in the work.*

344. Case II.   Given A and c or B and c.—

Example.   Given $A = 67°$ $42.8'$ and $c = 23.47$ ft.

Formulas.   *Construction.*

(1) $A + B = 90°$, $\therefore B = 90° - A$.

(2) $\sin A = \dfrac{a}{c}$, $\therefore a = c \sin A$.

(3) $\cos A = \dfrac{b}{c}$, $\therefore b = c \cos A$.

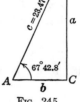

Fig. 245.

Computation by logarithms.

By (1), $B = 90° - 67°$ $42.8' = 22°$ $17.2'$.
By (2), $a = 23.47 \sin 67°$ $42.8'$.
By (3), $b = 23.47 \cos 67°$ $42.8'$.

$\log 23.47 = 1.3705$	$\log 23.47 = 1.3705$
$\log \sin 67°\ 42.8' = 9.9663$	$\log \cos 67°\ 42.8' = 9.5789$
$\log a = 1.3368$	$\log b = 0.9494$
$\therefore a = 21.72$	$\therefore b = 8.90$

Check.   Using $a^2 = c^2 - b^2 = (c+b)(c-b)$.

$\log (c+b) = 1.5101$
$\log (c-b) = 1.1635$

$\log (c^2 - b^2) = 2.6736 = \log a^2$.

345. Case III.   Given c and a or c and b.—

Example.   Given $c = 35.62$ ft. and $a = 23.85$ ft., find b, A, B.

Formulas.   *Construction.*

(1) $\sin A = \dfrac{a}{c}$

$\therefore A = \sin^{-1} \dfrac{a}{c}$.

(2) $\cos B = \dfrac{a}{c}$,

$\therefore B = \cos^{-1} \dfrac{a}{c}$.

(3) $\tan A = \dfrac{a}{b}$,

$\therefore b = a \div \tan A$.

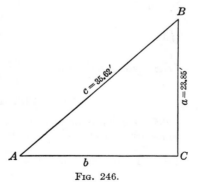

Fig. 246.

Computation.

log 23.85 = 1.3775

log 35.62 = 1.5517

log sin A = 9.8258 = log cos B

∴ $A = 42° 2.1'$ and $B = 47° 57.9.'$

log 23.85 = 1.3775

log tan A = 9.9549

log b = 1.4226

∴ $b = 26.46.$

Check.

log $(c+b)$ = 1.7930

log· $(c-b)$ = 0.9619

log $(c^2 - b^2)$ = 2.7549 = log a^2.

346. Remark on inverse functions.—The form $A = \sin^{-1} \dfrac{a}{c}$ is read "A = the angle whose sine is $\dfrac{a}{c}$." This is a convenient way of expressing the fact, and allows the angle symbol to stand alone. The -1 that is in the position of an exponent is not a negative exponent in meaning.

The form $\sin^{-1} \dfrac{a}{c}$ is called an inverse trigonometric function.

It is also written arcsin $\dfrac{a}{c}$ and invsin $\dfrac{a}{c}$. These forms are also read "antisine $\dfrac{a}{c}$," "arcsine $\dfrac{a}{c}$," and "inverse sine $\dfrac{a}{c}$."

347. Case IV. Given a and b.—

The equations are:

(1) $c^2 = a^2 + b^2$,   ∴ $c = \sqrt{a^2 + b^2}$.

(2) tan $A = \dfrac{a}{b}$,   ∴ $A = \tan^{-1} \dfrac{a}{b}$.

(3) tan $B = \dfrac{b}{a}$,   ∴ $B = \tan^{-1} \dfrac{b}{a}$.

Check. sin $A = \dfrac{a}{c}$, and cos $A = \dfrac{b}{c}$.

EXERCISES 116

Solve the following right triangles and check each by making an accurate construction and by substituting into a formula not used in solving.

1. $A = 27° 30'$, $a = 14$ in.; find B, b, and c.

Ans. $B = 62° 30'$; $b = 7.288$; $c = 15.78$.

2. $B = 46°\ 25'$, $a = 17$ ft.; find A, b, and c.

        Ans. $A = 43°\ 35'$; $b = 17.86$; $c = 24.66$.

3. $A = 75°\ 26'$, $b = 25$ ft.; find B, a, and c.

        Ans. $B = 14°\ 34'$; $a = 96.2$; $c = 99.38$.

4. $B = 62°\ 40'$, $b = 2$ ft.; find A, a, and c.

5. $A = 17°\ 50'$, $c = 47$ yd.; find B, a, and b.

6. $B = 53°\ 20'$, $c = 21$ ft.; find A, a, and b.

7. $a = 2$ ft., $c = 3$ ft.; find A, B, and b.

8. $b = 4$ ft., $c = 9$ ft.; find A, B, and a.

9. $a = 4.23$ in., $b = 7.23$ in.; find A, B, and c.

10. $a = 27$ in., $b = 20$ in.; find A, B, and c.

11. $B = 29°\ 45'$, $c = 2.36$ ft.; find A, a, and b.

12. $A = 32°\ 12'$, $c = 8.23$ in.; find B, a, and b.

348. Orthogonal projection.—If from a point P, Fig. 247(a), a perpendicular PQ be drawn to any straight line RS, then the foot of the perpendicular Q is said to be the **orthogonal projection** or simply the **projection** of P upon RS.

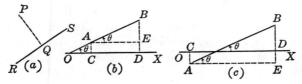

Fig. 247.

The **projection of a line segment** upon a given straight line is the portion of the given line lying between the projections of the ends of the segment.

In Fig. 247(b) and (c), CD is the projection of AB upon OX. In each case $AE = CD$ and $AE = AB \cos \theta$. Hence, if l is the length of the segment of the line projected, p the projection, and θ the angle between the lines, then

$$p = l \cos \theta.$$

Similarly, the projection of AB upon a line OY that is perpendicular to OX and in the same plane as OX and AB is

$$p' = l \sin \theta.$$

349. Vectors.—In physics and engineering, line segments are often used to represent quantities that have direction as well as magnitude. Velocities, accelerations, and forces are such quantities.

For instance, a force of 100 lb. acting in a northeasterly direction may be represented by a line, say, 10 in. long drawn in a northeasterly direction. The line is drawn so as to represent the force to some scale; here it is 10 lb. to the inch. An arrow head is put on one end of the line to show its direction.

In Fig. 248, *OP* is a line representing a directed quantity. Such a line is called a **vector**. *O* is the **beginning** of the vector and *P* is the **terminal**. *OQ* is the projection of the vector upon *OX*, and *OR* is the projection upon *OY*. *OQ* and *OR* are called **components** of the vector. As before, $OQ = OP \cos \theta$, and $OR = OP \sin \theta$.

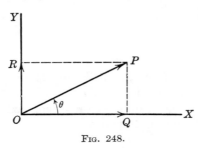

FIG. 248.

Example 1. Suppose that a weight *W* is resting on a rough horizontal table as shown in Fig. 249. Suppose that a force of 40 lb. is acting on the weight and in the direction *OP*, making an angle of 20° with the horizontal; then the horizontal pull on the weight is $OQ = 40 \cos 20° = 37.588$ lb., and the vertical lift on the weight is $OR = 40 \sin 20° = 13.68$ lb.

Example 2. A car is moving up an incline, making an angle of 35° with the horizontal, at the rate of 26 ft. per second. What is its horizontal velocity? Its vertical velocity?

Solution. Horizontal velocity $= 26 \cos 35° = 21.3$ ft. per second. Vertical velocity $= 26 \sin 35° = 14.9$ ft. per second.

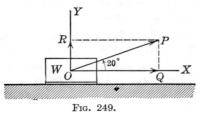

FIG. 249.

EXERCISES 117

1. The line segment *AB* 17 in. long makes an angle of 33° with the line *OX*. Find the projection upon *OX*. Find its projection upon the line *OY* perpendicular to *OX* and in the same plane as *OX* and *AB*.

Ans. 14.258 in.; 9.258 in.

2. A steamer is moving in a southeasterly direction at the rate of 24 miles per hour. How fast is it moving in an easterly direction? In a southerly direction?   *Ans.* 16.97 mi. per hr. in each.

3. The eastward and northward components of the velocity of a ship are respectively 5.5 miles and 10.6 miles. Find the direction and the rate at which the ship is sailing.

Ans. 11.94 mi. per hr., 27° 25.4′ east of north.

4. A roof is inclined at an angle of 33° 30′. The wind strikes this horizontally with a force of 1800 pounds. Find the pressure perpendicular to the roof. *Ans.* 993.4 lb.

5. A roof 20 ft. by 25 ft. and inclined at an angle of 27° 25′ with the horizontal will shelter how large an area? *Ans.* 443.85 ft.²

6. A hillside is on a slope of 16° and contains 5.2 acres. How much more is this than the projection of the hillside upon a horizontal plane? *Ans.* 0.2 acre.

7. Show in general that the projection of a plane area upon a fixed plane is equal to the given area times the cosine of the angle between the planes.

8. Show in general that the component of a force along any fixed line is equal to the magnitude of the force times the cosine of the angle between the direction of the force and the fixed line.

9. Two men are lifting a stone by means of ropes. The ropes are in the same vertical plane. One man pulls 85 lb. in a direction 23° from the vertical and the other 105 lb. in a direction 42° from the vertical. Determine the weight of the stone. *Ans.* 156.3 lb.

350. Definitions.—The **angle of elevation** is the angle between the line of sight and the horizontal plane through

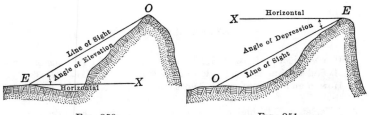

Fig. 250.   Fig. 251.

the eye when the object observed is above the horizontal plane. When the object observed is below the horizontal plane, the angle is called the **angle of depression.**

Thus, if *O* is the object observed by the eye at *E*, the angle *XEO* is the angle of elevation in Fig. 250, and the angle of depression in Fig. 251.

Directions on the surface of the earth are often given by directions as located on the mariner's compass. As seen from

Fig. 252, these directions are located with reference to the four cardinal points, north, south, east, and west.

Directions are often spoken of as **bearings**.

When greater exactness is required, the direction may be given as a certain number of degrees from a cardinal point. Thus, a direction given north 10° east means a direction 10° east of north; south 40° west means 40° west of south.

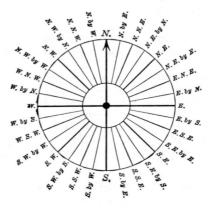

FIG. 252.—Mariner's compass.

EXERCISES 118

1. If a vertical staff 20 ft. high casts a shadow 26 ft. long on level ground, find the angle of elevation of the sun.   *Ans.* 37° 33.8′.

2. How many degrees east of north is N.E.? N.N.E.? N. by E.? N.E. by N.?   *Ans.* 45°; 22½°; 11¼°; 33¾°.

3. A flag staff 70 ft. high casts a shadow 40 ft. long. Find the angle of elevation of the sun above the horizon.   *Ans.* 60° 15.3′.

4. At 60 ft. from the base of a fir tree the angle of elevation of the top is 75°. Find the height of the tree.   *Ans.* 224 ft. nearly.

5. What is the inclination from the vertical of the face of a wall having a batter of ⅛?   *Ans.* 7° 7.6′.

A batter of ⅛ means that the wall slopes 1 ft. in a rise of 8 ft.

6. What is the angle of slope of a road bed that has a grade of 5 per cent? One with a grade of 0.25 per cent?   *Ans.* 2° 51.7′; 8.6′.

7. Find the angle between the rafter and the horizontal in the following pitch of roofs: two-thirds, half, third, fourth.

Ans. 53° 7.8′; 45°; 33° 41.3′; 26° 33.9′.

8. Certain lots in a city are laid out by lines perpendicular to B Street and running through to A Street as shown in Fig. 253. Find the widths of the lots on A Street if the angle between the streets is 28° 40'.

Ans. 114.0 ft.

9. A man whose eyes are 5 ft. 6 in. above the ground stands on a level with, and 150 ft. distant from, the foot of a flag staff 72 ft. high. What angle does his line of sight when looking at the top of the staff make with the horizontal line from his eyes to the pole? *Ans.* 23° 54.6'.

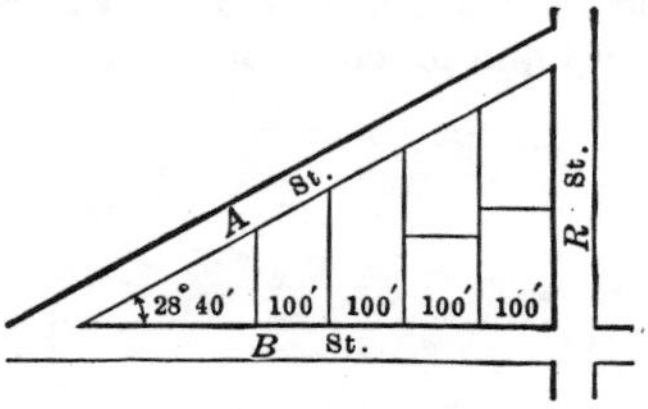

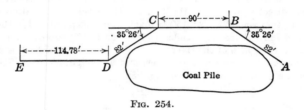

Fig. 253.

10. In surveying on the Lake Front in Chicago, measurements were taken as shown in Fig. 254. Find the distance on a straight line from A to E. *Ans.* 338.4 ft.

11. In an isosceles triangle one of the base angles is 48° 20', and the

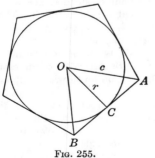

Fig. 254.

base is 18 in. Find the legs, vertical angle, and the altitude drawn to the base. *Ans.* Legs 13.54 in.; vert. ang. 83° 20'; alt. 10.11 in.

12. The side of a regular pentagon (five-sided figure) is 12 in. Find the radius of the inscribed circle, and the area of the pentagon.

Ans. Radius 8.258 in.; area 247.8 in.²

Suggestion. Draw the pentagon and inscribe a circle as in Fig. 255. Angle $AOB = 72°$. Triangle AOB is isosceles. We have $\tan 36° = \dfrac{6}{r}$, ∴ $r = 6 \div \tan 36°$.

Could this problem be solved as easily by geometry?

13. Find a side of the regular octagon circumscribed about a circle 20 ft. in diameter. *Ans.* 8.284 ft.

Fig. 255.

14. Given the right triangle ABC, with C the right angle, $CB = 20$ ft., and angle $CAB = 40°$. Produce CB to P making angle $CAP = 70°$, find the length of CP. *Ans.* 65.48 ft.

15. Find the shorter altitude and area of a parallelogram whose sides are 10 ft. and 25 ft., and the angle between the sides 75°.

Ans. Alt. 9.659 ft.; area 241.5 ft.[2]

16. Two points C and B are on opposite banks of a river. A line AC at right angles to CB is measured 40 rods long; the angle CAB is measured and found to be 41° 40′. Find the width of the stream.

Ans. 35.60 rd.

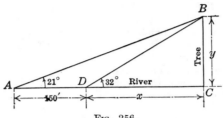

Fig. 256.

17. Wishing to determine the width of a river, I observed a tree standing directly across on the bank. The angle of elevation of the top of the tree was 32°. At 150 ft. back from this point and in the same direction from the tree the angle of elevation of the top of the tree was 21°. Find the width of the river.   *Ans.* 239 ft. nearly.

Suggestion. Let x = width of river, and y = height of tree. The relations of the parts are as given in Fig. 256.

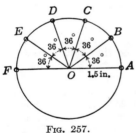

Fig. 257.

(1) $\tan 32° = \dfrac{y}{x}$.

(2) $\tan 21° = \dfrac{y}{150 + x}$.

Here are two equations and two unknown numbers. The solution of them will give the values of x and y.

18. Locate the centers of the holes B and C, Fig. 257, by finding the distance each is to the right and above the center O. The radius of the circle is 1.5 in. Compute correct to three decimal places.

Ans. B, 1.2135 in., 0.8817 in.; C, 0.4635 in., 1.4266 in.

19. A man surveying a mine measures a length $AB = 220$ ft. due east with a dip of 6° 15′; then a length $BC = 325$ ft. due south with a dip of 10° 45′. How much lower is C than A?   *Ans.* 84.57 ft.

20. A building 80 ft. long by 60 ft. wide has a roof inclined at 36° with the horizontal. Find the area of the roof, and show that the result is the same whether the roof has a ridge or not.   *Ans.* 5933 ft.[2]

21. In the side of a hill that slopes upward at an angle of 32°, a tunnel is bored sloping downward at an angle of 12° 15′ with the horizontal. How far is a point 115 ft. down the tunnel, below the surface of the hill?

Ans. 94.63 ft.

22. The angle of elevation of a balloon from a point due south of it is 60°, and from another point 1 mile due west of the former the angle of elevation is 45°. Find the height of the balloon. *Ans.* 1.225 miles.

23. From the top of a mountain 1050 ft. high two buildings are seen on a level plane and in a direct line from the foot of the mountain. The angle of depression of the first is 35° and of the second is 24°. Find the distance between the buildings. *Ans.* 858.8 ft.

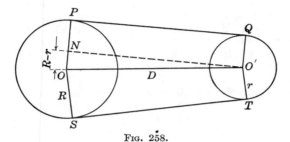

FIG. 258.

24. If R and r are the radii of two pulleys, D the distance between the centers, and L the length of the belt, show that when the belt is not crossed, Fig. 258, the length is given by the following formula where the angle is taken in radians:

$$L = 2\sqrt{D^2 - (R-r)^2} + \pi(R+r) + 2(R-r)\sin^{-1}\frac{R-r}{D}.$$

25. Show that when the belt is crossed, Fig. 259, the length is given by the following formula:

$$L = 2\sqrt{D^2 - (R+r)^2} + (R+r)\left(\pi + 2\sin^{-1}\frac{R+r}{D}\right).$$

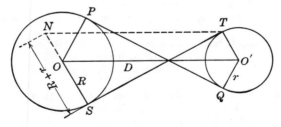

FIG. 259.

Note. These formulas would seldom be used in practice. An approximate formula would be more convenient, or the length would be measured with a tape line.

A rule often given for finding the length of uncrossed belts is: Add twice the distance between the centers of the shafts to half the sum of the circumferences of the two pulleys.

28

26. In exercise 24, given $R = 18$ in., $r = 8$ in., and $D = 12$ ft., find the length of the belt by the formula. Find the length by the approximate rule.   *Ans.* 30.87 − ft.; 30.81 − ft.

27. Use the same values as given in exercise 26, and find by the formula the length of the belt when crossed.   *Ans.* 31.20 − ft.

28. A belt connects two pulleys of diameters 6 ft. and 2 ft. respectively. If the distance between their centers is 15 ft., find the length of the belt, making no allowance for slack.   *Ans.* 42.83 ft.

29. Two pulleys, of diameters 7 ft. and 2 ft. respectively, are connected by a crossed belt. If the centers of the pulleys are 16 ft. apart, find the length of the belt.   *Ans.* 47.41 ft.

30. A chord of 2 ft. is in a circle of radius three feet. Find the length of the arc the chord subtends and the number of degrees in it.
Ans. 2.038 ft.; 38° 56.3′.

Suggestion. In Fig. 260, the chord $AB = 2$ ft. and the radius $OA = 3$ ft.

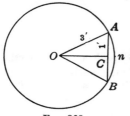

Triangle AOC is a right triangle. Angle $AOC = \frac{1}{2}$ angle AOB, and the central angle AOB has the same measure as the arc AnB.

31. Find the area of the sector $AnBO$ in exercise 30. Find the area of triangle AOB. Find the area of the segment ABn.
Ans. Sector 3.057 ft.²; triangle 2.828 ft.²; segment 0.229 ft.²

32. Find the area of the segment whose chord is 4 ft. in a circle of 5 ft. diameter.
Ans. 2.794 ft.²

Fig. 260.

33. Find the area of a segment whose chord is 6 ft. and height 2 ft.
Ans. 8.67 ft.²

34. In a circle of 60 in. radius, find the area of a segment having an angle of 63° 15′. Find the length of the chord and the height of the segment, take $\frac{2}{3}$ of their product, and compare with the area found.
Ans. 379 in.²

35. A cylindrical tank resting in a horizontal position is filled with water to within 10 in. of the top. Find the number of cubic feet of water in the tank. The tank is 10 ft. long and 4 ft. in diameter.
Ans. 106.7 ft.³

36. Compute the volume for each foot in the depth of a horizontal cylindrical oil tank of length 30 ft. and diameter 8 ft.
Ans. 108.8 ft.³; 294.8 ft.³; 516.4 ft.³; 754 ft.³; 991.6 ft.³; 1213.2 ft.³; 1399.2 ft.³

Note. In the same manner, the volume could be computed for, say, each ¼ in. In this way a gage could be made for determining the quantity of oil in a tank.

37. The slope of the roof in Fig. 261 is 30°. Find the angle θ which is the inclination to the horizontal of the line AB, drawn in the roof and making an angle of 35° with the line of greatest slope.
Ans. 24° 11.1′.

38. Find the angle between the diagonal of a cube and one of the diagonals of a face which meets it. *Ans.* 35° 15.9′.

39. A hill has a slope of 32°. A path leads up it making an angle of 45° with the line of greatest slope. Find the slope of the path.
Ans. 22° 0.3′.

40. Two set squares, whose sides are 3, 4, and 5 in., are placed as in Fig. 262 so that their 4-in. sides and right angles coincide, and the angle between the 3-in. sides is 50°. Find the angle θ between the longest sides. *Ans.* 29° 22.5′.

41. What size target at 30 ft. from the eye subtends the same angle as a target 4 ft. in diameter at 1000 yd.? Find the angle it subtends.
Ans. 0.48 in.; 4.6′.

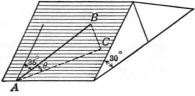

Fig. 261.

42. The description in a deed runs as follows: "Beginning at a stone, A, at the N.W. corner of lot 401; thence east 112 ft. to a stone, B; thence S. $36\frac{1}{2}$° W. 100 ft.; thence west parallel with AB to the west line of said lot 401; thence north on west line of said lot to the place of beginning." Find the area of the land described. *Ans.* 6612.88 ft.²

43. If the point of observation is at a distance of h feet above the surface of the earth, find the farthest distance that can be seen on the surface of the earth; that is, find the distance of the horizon.

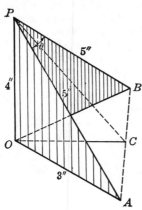

Fig. 262.

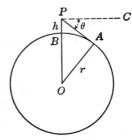

Fig. 263.

Discussion. In Fig. 263, let O be the center of the earth, r the radius of the earth, and h the height of the point P above the surface; it is required to find the distance from the point P to the horizon at A.

$$(PA)^2 = (PO)^2 - (OA)^2 = (r+h)^2 - r^2 = 2rh + h^2.$$
$$\therefore PA = \sqrt{2rh + h^2}.$$

For points above the surface that are reached by man, h^2 is very small as compared with $2rh$.

$$\therefore PA = \sqrt{2rh}, \text{ approximately.}$$

Here PA, r, and h are in the same units. Now let h be in feet, and r and PA be in miles. Also let $r = 3960$ miles. Then

$$PA = \sqrt{2 \times 3960 \times \frac{h}{5280}} = \sqrt{\frac{3}{2}h} \text{ miles.}$$

We may then state the following approximate rules:

The distance of the horizon in miles is approximately equal to the square root of $\frac{3}{2}$ times the height of the point of observation in feet.

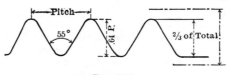

Fig. 264.

The height of the point of observation in feet is $\frac{3}{2}$ times the square of the distance of the horizon in miles.

Definition. The angle $APC = \theta$ is called the **dip of the horizon.**

44. Find the greatest distance at which the lamp of a lighthouse can be seen from the deck of a ship. The lamp is 85 ft. above the surface of the water and the deck of the ship 30 ft. above the surface.

Ans. 18 mi. approx.

45. A cliff 2000 ft. high is on the sea shore; how far away is the horizon? What is the dip of the horizon?   *Ans.* 54.8 mi. approx.; 47′.

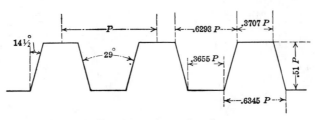

Fig. 265.—Acme thread.

46. Find the radius of a circle circumscribed about a polygon of 128 sides if one side is 2 in. What is the difference between the circumference of the circle and the perimeter of the polygon?

Ans. 40.81 in.; 0.417 in.

47. In Whitworth's English Standard screw threads, Fig. 264, the angle between the sides of the threads is 55°. If the top of a thread is rounded off ⅙ of the height and the bottom filled in the same amount, find the depth to four decimal places of the threads of the following pitches: 1, 8, 14, and 26.

Ans. 0.6403 in.; 0.0800 in.; 0.0457 in.; 0.0246 in.

48. In an acme thread, the angle between the sides of the threads is 29°. When the pitch is P, the depth and the other dimensions are as shown in Figs. 265, 267. (a) Suppose that the top dimensions and the depth are given, find the dimensions at the bottom. (b) Find the dimensions at the top and bottom and the depth for an 8-pitch acme thread.

Ans. (b) 0.0787 in.; 0.0463 in.; 0.0793 in.; 0.0457 in.; 0.0638 in.

49. In a worm thread, the angle between the sides is 29°. The dimensions are as shown in Figs. 266, 267. (a) Suppose the top dimensions

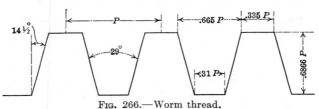

Fig. 266.—Worm thread.

and the depth are given, find the bottom dimensions. (b) Find the dimensions in a 7-pitch thread. (The above are the Brown and Sharp proportions.) What are the differences between a worm thread and an acme thread? *Ans.* (b) 0.0950 in.; 0.0479 in.; 0.0443 in.; 0.0981 in.

50. From a point A on a level with the base of a steeple the angle of elevation of the top of the steeple is 42° 30′; from a point B 22 ft. directly over A the angle of elevation of the top is 36° 45′. Find the height of the steeple and the distance of its base from A.

Ans. 118.9 ft.; 129.8 ft.

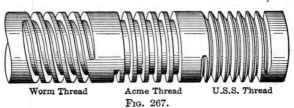

Worm Thread   Acme Thread   U.S.S. Thread

Fig. 267.

51. A ship sailing due north observes two lighthouses in a line due west; after an hour's sailing, the bearings of the lighthouses are observed to be southwest and south-southwest. If the distance between the lighthouses is 8 miles, at what rate is the ship sailing?

Ans. 13.66 mi. per hour.

52. Show that $R = \dfrac{50}{\sin \frac{1}{2} D}$, where $R =$ the radius of curvature and $D =$ the degree of the curve.

351. Widening of pavements on curves.—The tendency of a motorist to "cut the corners" is due to his unconscious desire to give the path of his car around a turn the longest possible radius. Many highway engineers recognize this tendency by widening the pavement on the inside of the curve as shown in Fig. 268. The practice adds much to the attractive appearance of the highway. If the pavement is the same width around the curve as on the tangents, the curved section appears narrower than the normal width; whereas if the curved section is widened gradually to the mid-point G of the turn, the pavement appears to have a uniform width all the way around.

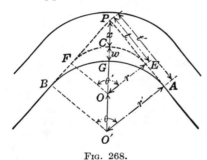

Fig. 268.

In order that the part added may fit the curve properly it is necessary to have the curve of the inner edge a true arc of a circle, tangent to the edge of the straightaway sections, and therefore it must start before the point E of the curve is reached. The part added may be easily staked out on the ground with transit and tape, by means of data derived from the radius r, the central angle θ of the curve, and the width w. In practice the width w is taken from 2 ft. to 8 ft. according to the value of r. The width added can be readily computed when values for r, w, and θ are given.

Referring to the figure, derive the following formulas:

$$x = r \sec \tfrac{1}{2}\theta - r = \frac{r}{\cos \frac{1}{2}\theta} - r.$$

$$x + w = r' \sec \tfrac{1}{2}\theta - r' = \frac{r'}{\cos \frac{1}{2}\theta} - r'.$$

$$\therefore \ r' = \frac{x+w}{\sec \frac{1}{2}\theta - 1} = \frac{(x+w)\cos \frac{1}{2}\theta}{1 - \cos \frac{1}{2}\theta}.$$

$$t = r \tan \tfrac{1}{2}\theta.$$

$$t' = r' \tan \tfrac{1}{2}\theta.$$

Area added $= BFCEAG = BPAO' - FPEC - BGAO'.$

$BPAO' = r't'.$

$$FPEC = FPEO - FCEO = rt - \frac{\theta}{360}\,\pi r^2.$$

$$BGAO' = \frac{\theta}{360}\,\pi r'^2.$$

$$\therefore \text{ area added } = r't' - \left(rt - \frac{\theta}{360}\,\pi r^2\right) - \frac{\theta}{360}\,\pi r'^2$$

$$= r't' - rt - \frac{\theta}{360}\,\pi(r' + r)(r' - r).$$

Exercise. Find the number of square feet in the area added if $r = 300$ ft., $w = 4$ ft., and $\theta = 100°$.   *Ans.* 1395 ft.[2]

352. Spirals.—If a line is drawn around a circular cylinder so that it advances a certain distance along the cylinder for each revolution, the curve thus formed is a **spiral** or a **helix.**

If a piece of paper is cut as shown in (*a*) Fig. 269, and lines *AB* and *CD* drawn, this piece of paper can be rolled into the

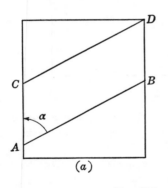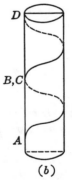

Fig. 269.

cylinder (*b*) Fig. 269, where the lines *AB* and *CD* of (*a*) form the spiral running from *A* to *D* of (*b*).

The advance along the cylinder for each turn of the spiral is the **lead of the spiral,** or the spiral lead. In Fig. 269, *AC* is the lead. It is customary to give the lead of the spiral as so many inches per one turn. For instance, a spiral that advances 8 in. in one turn is called an 8-in. spiral.

The angle α that the spiral makes with an element of the cylinder is the angle of the spiral. It is seen that

$$\tan \alpha = \frac{circumference\ of\ cylinder}{lead\ of\ the\ spiral},$$

or, in (a) Fig. 269, $\tan \alpha = \dfrac{CB}{AC}$.

In setting milling machines for cutting spirals such as worms, spiral gears, counter bores, and twist drills, it is often necessary to know the angle of the spiral.

To find the angle of a spiral or for the cutters in cutting a spiral, make a drawing as shown in Fig. 270; the angle C being a right angle, CB the circumference, and AC the lead. Angle A is the angle required, and may be measured with a protractor, or it may be found by finding $\tan A = \dfrac{CB}{AC}$ and using the table of tangents.

For ready reference the following rules are given:

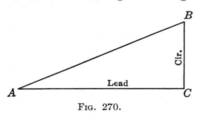

Fig. 270.

ANGLE. *Divide the circumference of the spiral by the lead (advance to one turn), and the quotient is the tangent of the angle of the spiral.*

LEAD. *Divide the circumference of the spiral by the tangent of the angle, and the quotient is the lead of the spiral.*

CIRCUMFERENCE. *Multiply the tangent of the angle by the lead of the spiral, and the product will be the circumference.*

When applying calculations to spiral gears, the angle is reckoned at the pitch circumference.

EXERCISES 119

1. Find the angle of the spirals in the following twist drills:

(1) Diameter of drill $\frac{9}{16}$ in., lead 2.92 in. *Ans.* 20° 35.2′.
(2) Diameter of drill $1\frac{1}{8}$ in., lead 9.33 in. *Ans.* 20° 44.8′.
(3) Diameter of drill $1\frac{3}{8}$ in., lead 7.29 in. *Ans.* 19° 13.3′.

2. Find the angle of the spiral thread on a double-threaded worm of pitch diameter $3\frac{1}{2}$ in. and having three threads in 2 in. *Ans.* 83° 5.1′.

3. In a tower the outer diameter of a winding stairway is 12 ft. Find the angle of the spiral formed by the outer end of the steps if the stairway makes one turn in ascending 18 ft. Find the angle of the spiral formed by the inner ends of the steps if the steps are 4 ft. long.

Ans. 64° 28.7′; 34° 55.1′.

4. The piece shown in Fig. 271 has a length of $3\frac{1}{2}$ in. and a diameter of $\frac{5}{8}$ in. If the spiral grooves make a half turn in the length of the piece, find the angle of the spiral. *Ans.* 15° 40′.

5. Find the angle for setting cutters in cutting the following spirals: (a) Diameter $\frac{1}{4}$ in. and lead 2.78 in.; (b) $\frac{3}{4}$ in. and 7.62 in.; (c) 2 in. and 10.37 in.; (d) $\frac{7}{8}$ in. and 22.5 in.

Ans. (a) 15° 46.7′; (b) 17° 10.9′; (c) 31° 13.1′; (d) 6° 59.2′.

FIG. 271.

6. A cylinder 2 in. in diameter is to have spiral grooves making angles of 20° with the center line of the cylinder. What will be the lead of the spiral? *Ans.* 17.26 in.

7. Find the length of one turn of a spiral around a cylinder 3 in. in diameter if the lead of the spiral is 9 in. *Ans.* 13.03 in.

8. Show that the length of any spiral is given by formula

$$L = n\sqrt{C^2 + l^2},$$

where L = length of spiral, n = the number of turns of the spiral, C = circumference of cylinder the spiral is on, and l = lead of the spiral.

9. Find the length of a spiral making 20 turns in 8 in. on a cylinder 3.5 in. in diameter. *Ans.* 220.0 in.

CHAPTER XXXIX

RELATIONS BETWEEN RATIOS, AND PLOTTING

353. Relations between the ratios of an angle and the ratios of its complement.—In **Art. 327** it was pointed out that the *function* of an acute angle is equal to the *co-function* of its *complement*. This gives the following relations. It can easily be shown that these relations hold for *any* value of the angle θ.

[62] $\sin\ (90° - \theta) = \cos\ \theta.$
[63] $\cos\ (90° - \theta) = \sin\ \theta.$
[64] $\tan\ (90° - \theta) = \cot\ \theta.$
[65] $\cot\ (90° - \theta) = \tan\ \theta.$
[66] $\sec\ (90° - \theta) = \csc\ \theta.$
[67] $\csc\ (90° - \theta) = \sec\ \theta.$

As previously explained, it is these relations that make a table of trigonometric functions do double duty.

Example. $\sin 60° = \sin (90° - 30°) = \cos 30°.$

354. Relations between the ratios of an angle and the ratios of its supplement.—The following relations between the ratios of an angle and its supplement are true for *any* value of θ. They are convenient when one wishes to find by means of the tables the functions of angles lying between 90° and 180°.

[68] $\sin\ (180° - \theta) = \sin\ \theta.$
[69] $\cos\ (180° - \theta) = -\cos\ \theta.$
[70] $\tan\ (180° - \theta) = -\tan\ \theta.$
[71] $\cot\ (180° - \theta) = -\cot\ \theta.$
[72] $\sec\ (180° - \theta) = -\sec\ \theta.$
[73] $\csc\ (180° - \theta) = \csc\ \theta.$

Proof.   In Fig. 272, angle $XOP = \theta$ is any angle, and angle $XOQ = 180° - \theta$.

From any point in the terminal side of XOP, as B, draw the perpendicular AB to the x-axis; and from D, any point in the

442

terminal side of XOQ, draw the perpendicular CD to the x-axis. The right triangles OAB and OCD are similar. Also OA, AB, OB, CD, and OD are positive, while OC is negative.

Then $\sin (180° - \theta) = \dfrac{CD}{OD} = \dfrac{AB}{OB} = \sin \theta.$

Also $\cos (180° - \theta) = \dfrac{OC}{OD} = -\dfrac{OA}{OB} = -\cos \theta.$

Example 1. $\sin 130° \ 15' = \sin (180° - 49° \ 45') = \sin 49° \ 45'$
$= 0.7633.$

Example   2. $\cos \ 160° = \cos \ (180° - 20°) = -\cos \ 20° = -0.9397.$

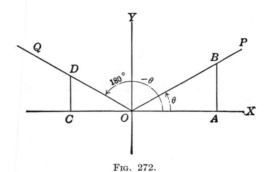

Fig. 272.

355. Relations between ratios of an angle θ and 90°+θ.— The following relations connect the ratios of any angle θ and $90° + \theta$. They are also convenient to use in finding, by means of the tables, the functions of angles lying between 90° and 180°.

[74] $\sin \ (90° + \theta) = \cos \ \theta.$
[75] $\cos \ (90° + \theta) = -\sin \ \theta.$
[76] $\tan \ (90° + \theta) = -\cot \ \theta.$
[77] $\cot \ (90° + \theta) = -\tan \ \theta.$
[78] $\sec \ (90° + \theta) = -\csc \ \theta.$
[79] $\csc \ (90° + \theta) = \sec \ \theta.$

Proof.   In Fig. 273, angle $XOP = \theta$ and angle $XOQ = 90° + \theta$.

From any point in the terminal side of each draw a perpendicular to the x-axis. The right triangles AOB and OCD thus formed are similar, and have all their sides positive except OC.

Then $\sin (90°+\theta) = \dfrac{CD}{OD} = \dfrac{OA}{OB} = \cos \theta$.

Also $\tan (90°+\theta) = \dfrac{CD}{OC} = -\dfrac{AB}{OA} = -\cot \theta$.

Example 1. $\sin 130° \ 15' = \sin (90°+40° \ 15') = \cos 40° \ 15'$
$= 0.7633$.

Example 2. $\tan 116° \ 20' = \tan (90°+26° \ 20') = -\cot 26° \ 20'$
$= -2.0204$.

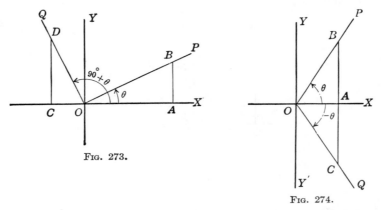

Fig. 273.

Fig. 274.

356. Relations between the ratios of an angle and the ratios of its negative.—The following relations connect the ratios of positive and negative angles, and are true for any value of θ.

[80] $\sin (-\theta) = -\sin \theta$.
[81] $\cos (-\theta) = \cos \theta$.
[82] $\tan (-\theta) = -\tan \theta$.
[83] $\cot (-\theta) = -\cot \theta$.
[84] $\sec (-\theta) = \sec \theta$.
[85] $\csc (-\theta) = -\csc \theta$.

Proof. In Fig. 274, angle $XOP = \theta$, and angle $XOQ = -\theta$.
From any point in the terminal side of each draw a perpendicular to the x-axis. The right triangles OAB and OAC

thus formed are similar, and have all their sides positive but AC, which is negative.

Then $\sin (-\theta) = \dfrac{AC}{OC} = -\dfrac{AB}{OB} = -\sin \theta$.

And $\cos (-\theta) = \dfrac{OA}{OC} = \dfrac{OA}{OB} = \cos \theta$.

Also $\cot (-\theta) = \dfrac{OA}{AC} = -\dfrac{OA}{AB} = -\cot \theta$.

Example 1. $\sin (-30°) = -\sin 30° = -0.5$.

Example 2. $\tan (-46° \ 10') = -\tan 46° \ 10' = -1.0416$.

EXERCISES 120

Draw a figure in each case and prove the following:

1. $\sin (90°-\theta) = \cos \theta$.	**7.** $\csc (180°-\theta) = \csc \theta$.
2. $\tan (90°-\theta) = \cot \theta$.	**8.** $\cos (90°+\theta) = -\sin \theta$.
3. $\sec (90°-\theta) = \csc \theta$.	**9.** $\cot (90°+\theta) = -\tan \theta$.
4. $\tan (180°-\theta) = -\tan \theta$.	**10.** $\sec (90°+\theta) = -\csc \theta$.
5. $\cot (180°-\theta) = -\cot \theta$.	**11.** $\tan(-\theta) = -\tan \theta$.
6. $\sec (180°-\theta) = -\sec \theta$.	**12.** $\sec (-\theta) = \sec \theta$.

By means of the tables find the following:

13. $\sin 140°$.	**16.** $\cos (-49°)$.	**19.** $\sin 159° \ 40'$.
14. $\cos 150°$.	**17.** $\tan (-17°)$.	**20.** $\cos (-117° \ 30')$.
15. $\tan 170°$.	**18.** $\cot (-125°)$.	**21.** $\tan (-156° \ 10')$.

Ans. Ex. 14. -0.8660.   Ex. 17. -0.3057.   Ex. 20. -0.4617.

357. Relations between the ratios of any angle.—As stated in **Art. 324,**

$$[86] \ \sin \theta = \frac{1}{\csc \theta} \ \text{or} \ \csc \theta = \frac{1}{\sin \theta}.$$

$$[87] \ \cos \theta = \frac{1}{\sec \theta} \ \text{or} \ \sec \theta = \frac{1}{\cos \theta}.$$

$$[88] \ \tan \theta = \frac{1}{\cot \theta} \ \text{or} \ \cot \theta = \frac{1}{\tan \theta}.$$

By definition,

[89] versedsine θ, abbreviated **vers** $\theta = 1 - \cos \theta$.

[90] coversedsine θ, abbreviated **covers** $\theta = 1 - \sin \theta$.

The truth of the following can easily be proved when θ is any angle.

[91] $\sin^2 \theta + \cos^2 \theta = 1.$

[92] $\sec^2 \theta = 1 + \tan^2 \theta.$

[93] $\csc^2 \theta = 1 + \cot^2 \theta.$

[94] $\tan \theta = \dfrac{\sin \theta}{\cos \theta}.$

[95] $\cot \theta = \dfrac{\cos \theta}{\sin \theta}.$

Proof of [91]. By definition (see Fig. 275),

$$\sin^2 \theta = \frac{y^2}{r^2} \text{ and } \cos^2 \theta = \frac{x^2}{r^2}.$$

Hence adding, $\sin^2 \theta + \cos^2 \theta = \dfrac{y^2}{r^2} + \dfrac{x^2}{r^2} = \dfrac{y^2 + x^2}{r^2}.$

But $y^2 + x^2 = r^2$ because the triangle OCB is a right triangle.

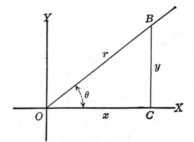

Fig. 275.

Hence $\sin^2 \theta + \cos^2 \theta = \dfrac{r^2}{r^2} = 1.$

Proof of [92]. By definition,

$$\sec^2 \theta = \frac{r^2}{x^2} \text{ and } \tan^2 \theta = \frac{y^2}{x^2}.$$

$\therefore \sec^2 \theta = 1 + \tan^2 \theta$ because $\dfrac{r^2}{x^2} = 1 + \dfrac{y^2}{x^2} = \dfrac{x^2 + y^2}{x^2} = \dfrac{r^2}{x^2}.$

EXERCISES 121

1. Prove [93], [94], and [95] by using the definitions.

2. From [91] derive (a) $\sin \theta = \pm \sqrt{1 - \cos^2 \theta}$, (b) $\cos \theta = \pm \sqrt{1 - \sin^2 \theta}$.

3. Solve [92] for sec θ and tan θ.

Ans. $\sec \theta = \pm \sqrt{1 + \tan^2 \theta}$; $\tan \theta = \pm \sqrt{\sec^2 \theta - 1}$.

4. Solve [93] for csc θ and cot θ.

Ans. $\csc \theta = \pm \sqrt{1 + \cot^2 \theta}$; $\cot \theta = \pm \sqrt{\csc^2 \theta - 1}$.

5. From the relations already given, write five other relations between the ratios.

6. Prove the following relations:

    (1) $\cos \theta \tan \theta = \sin \theta$.   (3) $\sec \theta \cot \theta = \csc \theta$.

    (2) $\sin \theta \cot \theta = \cos \theta$.   (4) $\tan \theta \csc \theta = \sec \theta$.

Use the formulas and find the other functions:

7. When $\sin \theta = \frac{1}{2}$.

8. When $\cos \theta = \frac{3}{4}$.

9. When $\tan \theta = 3$.

10. Find the following from **Table XI**: (1) sin 122° 20′, (2) cos 110° 44′, (3) tan 163° 15′, (4) cot 172° 50′, (5) cos (−42° 16′), (6) tan (−21° 49′).

    Ans. (1) 0.8450; (2) −0.3540; (3) −0.3010; (4) −7.9530; (5) 0.7400; (6) −0.4003.

358. Plotting the sine curve.—In **Chapter XXXIII** the plotting of the curve of an algebraic equation was considered. The trigonometric equations can be represented by curves plotted in a similar manner.

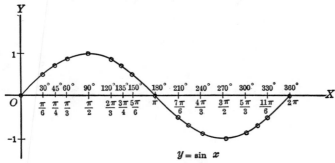

$y = \sin x$

Fig. 276.

Example. Plot the curve for $y = \sin x$.

Choose suitable angles for values of x and take the values for y from the table of **Art. 332** or from **Table XI.**

Values of x; 0° 30°   45°   60° 90° 120° 135° 150° 180°.

Values of y, 0 0.5   0.7   0.87   1 0.87 0.7   0.5   0.

Values of x,   210° 225° 240° 270° 300° 315°   330° 360°.

Values of y, −0.5 −0.7 −0.87 −1 −0.87 −0.7 −0.5 0.

Choose a convenient unit on the x-axis and y-axis and plot the points as shown in Fig. 276, using the angle as abscissa and the sine as ordinate.

The curve in Fig. 276 is called the sine curve. It extends

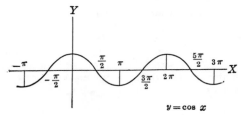

$y = \cos x$

Fig. 277.

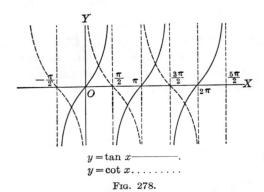

$y = \tan x$————.
$y = \cot x$........
Fig. 278.

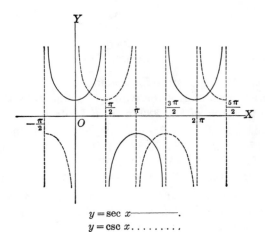

$y = \sec x$————.
$y = \csc x$........
Fig. 279.

both ways indefinitely, repeating the part given. That is, if values between 360° and 720° be taken the curve will be found to be of the same shape. The same will be true for values of the angle less than 0°.

A curve that repeats itself in this way is called a **periodic curve.** The equation giving rise to it is called a **periodic function.**

The relative lengths of the units representing x and y may be changed, and the curve thus drawn out or shortened. However, the curve will still be of the same general form.

359. Curves for cosine, tangent, cotangent, secant, and cosecant.—By choosing suitable angles for values of x and determining the corresponding values of y, the coördinates of points are obtained which, when plotted, give the curves of Figs. 277, 278, and 279.

EXERCISES 122

1. Plot $y = \sin x$, using various units for x and y.

2. Plot $y = \cos x$ from $x = 0°$ to $x = 360°$ and get form of Fig. 277.

3. Plot $y = \tan x$ and $y = \cot x$ from $x = 0°$ to $x = 360°$ and get forms of Fig. 278.

4. Plot $y = \sin x + \cos x$ from $x = 0°$ to $x = 180°$.

5. Plot $y = \cos^2 x - \sin^2 x$ from $x = 0$ to $x = \frac{1}{4}\pi$.

6. Plot $y = \cos^{-1}\frac{x}{4}$ from $x = 0$ to $x = 3$.

7. Plot $y = \sec x$ and $y = \csc x$ from $x = 0°$ to $x = 360°$ and get the forms of Fig. 279.

360. Projections of a point having circular motion.—

Example 1. A point P, Fig. 280, moves around a vertical circle of radius 3 in. in a counter-clockwise direction. It starts with the radius in a horizontal position and moves with an angular velocity of one revolution in 10 seconds. Plot a curve showing the distance from the center O of the projection of P on the vertical diameter at any time.

Discussion. Describe a circle with center O and radius 3 in., to scale if desired. In this circle the point P starts at A. After 1 second OP has turned to the position of OP_1 through an angle of 36° = 0.6283 radians, after 2 seconds to the position OP_2 through an angle of 72° = 1.2566 radians, and so on to the positions OP_3, OP_4, $\cdots OP_{10}$.

29

The points N_1, N_2, etc., are the projections of P_1, P_2, etc., on the vertical diameter.

Produce the horizontal diameter OA, and lay off the seconds on this to some scale.

For each second plot a point whose ordinate is the corresponding distance of N from O. Fractions of seconds may be taken and more points located if desired. Connect these points, and we have a curve for which any ordinate y is the distance from the center O of the projection of P on the vertical diameter at the time t, represented by the abscissa of the point.

It is to be noted that the ordinate of the curve increases from 0 to $+3$, decreases from $+3$ to 0 and from 0 to -3,

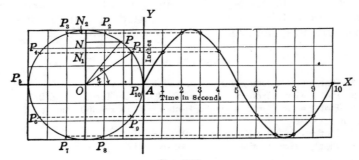

Fig. 280.

and increases from -3 to 0. The curve is made up of two like-shaped parts, one below and one above the horizontal line. Together they form a **cycle** of the curve.

It is evident that, for the second and each successive revolution, the curve repeats itself, that is, is a *periodic curve*.

Since OP turns through $36°$ per second, the angle $AOP = 36t° = 0.6283t$ radians. Because of the right triangle OPN,

$$y = ON = OP \sin 36t° = 3 \sin 36t°.$$

Or, in general, $y = r \sin \omega t$, where ω (Greek letter omega) is the angle turned through in one second, that is, the angular velocity. It is then the *equation of the curve*.

It is readily seen that if a straight line of length r, such as a crank, starts in a horizontal position when $t = 0$, and revolves in a vertical plane around one end at a uniform angular velocity

ω per second, the projection of the moving end on a vertical straight line has a motion which is represented by the equation

$$y = r \sin \omega t.$$

Similarly, the projection of the moving end on a horizontal straight line is given by the ordinates of the curve whose equation is

$$y = r \cos \omega t.$$

If OP represents the crank of an engine with a connecting rod which is very long compared with OP, the motion of the cross-head is represented approximately by that of the point N, and, hence, by the equation $y = r \sin \omega t$.

A simple periodic motion like the above is sometimes represented by the equation $y = r \sin \omega t$ and sometimes by $y = r$

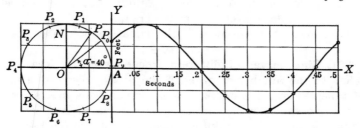

Fig. 281.

$\cos \omega t$.   The first, if the time is measured from the instant when OP is in the line of the simple periodic motion, and second, if measured from the instant when OP is perpendicular to the line of the simple periodic motion.

If the time is counted from some other instant than the above, we have $y = r \sin (\omega t + \alpha)$, where α is the angle that OP makes with the line OA at the instant t is counted from.

Example 2.   A crank OP, Fig. 281, of length 2 ft. starts from a position making an angle $\alpha = 40°$ with the horizontal line OA when $t = 0$.   It rotates in a vertical plane in the positive direction at the rate of 2 revolutions per second.   Plot a curve showing the projection of P on a vertical diameter.

Discussion.   As before, draw a circle of 2-ft. radius to some scale.   Extend the horizontal axis to the right, and represent the part of a second necessary for one revolution to some suitable scale.

When $t=0$, OP starts from the position OP_0 making an angle $AOP_0=\alpha=40°$. OP turns through $720°$ in 1 sec., or $36°=0.6283$ radians in 0.05 sec. Here we plot a point for every 0.05 sec. Any other convenient fraction of a second could be chosen. The position of the free end of the crank for each 0.05 sec. until a complete revolution is made is located by P_0, P_1, P_2, $P_3 \cdots$. These are at intervals of $36°$ starting with $40°$.

At any time t, the position of OP makes with OA an angle $AOP=\omega t+\alpha$. And the distance from O to the projection of P at N is

$$ON = OP \sin (\omega t+\alpha),$$
or
$$ON = 2 \sin (720t°+\alpha).$$

The curve of this example is periodic. It repeats itself for each complete revolution of the crank.

It follows that, in general, the equation of the curve is
$$y = r \sin (\omega t+\alpha).$$

361. Sine curves of different frequency.—The **frequency** refers to the number of *cycles* of the *periodic curve* in a unit of time. Thus, if a crank makes 4 revolutions in 1 second, the curve showing the motion makes 4 cycles in 1 second; while the curve for a crank that makes 2 revolutions in 1 second makes 2 cycles in 1 second. The frequency of the first is 4, of the second 2.

The angular velocity ω divided by $360°$ when measured in degrees, or by 2π when measured in radians, gives the frequency f,

$$\therefore f = \frac{\omega}{2\pi}.$$

The time necessary for one cycle is called the **period.** It is evident that the period T is given by the formula

$$T = \frac{2\pi}{\omega}.$$

Consider the following equations:

Equation	Angle ωt	Angular velocity ω	Frequency $f=\dfrac{\omega}{2\pi}$	Period $T=\dfrac{2\pi}{\omega}$
(1) $y=r \sin\frac{1}{2}t$	$\frac{1}{2}t$	$\frac{1}{2}$	0.0796	12.566
(2) $y=r \sin t$	t	1	0.1592	6.283
(3) $y=r \sin 2t$	$2t$	2	0.3183	3.1416

If r is taken as 1 and the three curves plotted, they are as in Fig. 282.

It is to be noted that the frequency of a sine curve varies directly

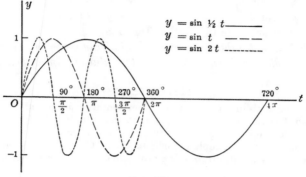

Fig. 282.

as the value of ω, that is, as the coefficient of t in the angle ωt. The number ω is sometimes called the **frequency factor**.

362. Variation in the amplitude of sine curves.—The am-

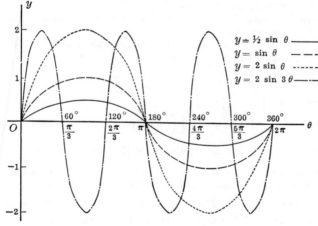

Fig. 283.

plitude of a sine curve is the difference between its greatest and least ordinate.

In the previous article all of the curves plotted have the

same amplitude, and it will be remembered that the radius in each case was taken equal to unity.

Consider the curves of the equations:

(1) $y = \frac{1}{2} \sin \theta$,   (3) $y = 2 \sin \theta$,

(2) $y = \sin \theta$,   (4) $y = 2 \sin 3\theta$.

These curves are plotted in Fig. 283.

It is to be noted that the amplitude of a sine curve varies directly as the coefficient of sin θ, that is, as the value of r in the generating circle.

EXERCISES 123

1. A crank 18 in. long starts in a horizontal position and turns in a positive direction in a vertical plane at the rate of 0.7854 radian per second. The projection of the moving end of the crank upon a vertical line oscillates with a simple periodic motion. Construct a curve whose ordinates show the distance of the projection from the center of its path at any time.

2. Write the equation of the curve in the previous exercise. Find the value of the ordinate when $t = 0.5$. When $t = 2.3$.

Ans. $y = 18 \sin(0.7854t)$; 6.89 in.; 17.50 in.

3. A crank 8 in. long starts in a position making an angle of 55° with the horizontal, and rotates in a positive direction at the rate of 20 revolutions per minute. Draw a curve to show the projection of the moving end of the crank on a vertical line.

4. Write the equation of the curve in the last exercise. Find the value of y when $t = 1.5$ seconds.

Ans. $y = 8 \sin(120t° + 55°)$; −6.55 in.

Plot the curves that represent the following motions:

5. $y = 3.5 \sin(35t° + 36°)$.

6. $y = 12 \sin(1.88t + 0.44)$.

7. $y = 2.5 \sin\left(\dfrac{\pi t}{8} + \dfrac{\pi}{12}\right)$.

8. Plot $y = r \sin \dfrac{\pi}{2} t$ and $y = r \sin\left(\dfrac{\pi}{2} t + \dfrac{\pi}{4}\right)$ on the same axes. Notice that the highest points are separated by the constant angle $\dfrac{\pi}{4}$. Such curves are said to be out of phase. The difference in phase is stated in time or as an angle; in the latter case it is called the phase angle.

9. Plot (1) $y = r \sin \dfrac{\pi}{4} t$, (2) $y = r \sin\left(\dfrac{\pi}{2} - \dfrac{\pi}{4} t\right)$, and (3) $y = r \cos \dfrac{\pi}{4} t$, all on the same axes. What is the difference in phase between (1) and (2)?

10. Plot on the same set of axes: (1) $y = r \sin \pi t$, (2) $y = r \sin \dfrac{\pi}{2} t$, (3) $y = r \sin \dfrac{\pi}{8} t$.

11. Plot on the same set of axes: (1) $y = 40 \sin \theta$, (2) $y = 30 \sin \theta$, (3) $y = 20 \sin 2\theta$.

CHAPTER XL

TRIGONOMETRIC RATIOS OF MORE THAN ONE ANGLE

363. In the present chapter will be given a number of formulas of very great use in more advanced subjects of mathematics and in their applications. These formulas are given for reference. But little attempt will be made here to prove them or illustrate their uses.

364. Functions of the sum or difference of two angles.—The following formulas express the functions of the sum or the difference of two angles in terms of the functions of the separate angles. These formulas are sometimes called the **addition** and **subtraction** formulas of trigonometry.

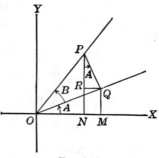

Fig. 284.

[96] sin (A+B) = sin A cos B+cos A sin B.
[97] sin (A−B) = sin A cos B−cos A sin B.
[98] cos (A+B) = cos A cos B−sin A sin B.
[99] cos (A−B) = cos A cos B+sin A sin B.

$$[100]\ \tan\ (A+B) = \frac{\tan A+\tan B}{1-\tan A \tan B}.$$

$$[101]\ \tan\ (A-B) = \frac{\tan A-\tan B}{1+\tan A \tan B}.$$

Proof of [96] *for* A<90°, B<90°, *and* (A+B)<90°. In Fig. 284, angle XOQ=A and angle QOP=B. Hence angle XOP=A+B.

Draw NP, QP, QR, and MQ perpendicular respectively to OX, OQ, NP, and OX. Then angle RPQ=A.

$$\sin\ (A+B) = \frac{NP}{OP} = \frac{MQ+RP}{OP} = \frac{MQ}{OP} + \frac{RP}{OP}.$$

455

But $MQ = OQ$ sin A, and $RP = QP$ cos A, from the right triangles. Putting these values in place of MQ and RP,

$$\sin (A+B) = \frac{OQ \sin A}{OP} + \frac{QP \cos A}{OP},$$

$$\therefore \sin (A+B) = \sin A \cos B + \cos A \sin B.$$

Formulas [97] to [101] may be proved in a similar manner.

Example 1. Given the functions of 45° and 30°, find the value of sin 15°.

Solution. sin $15° = \sin(45° - 30°)$
$$= \sin 45° \cos 30° - \cos 45° \sin 30°$$
$$= 0.7071 \times 0.8660 - 0.7071 \times 0.5 = 0.2588.$$

Example 2. Test formula [100] by using $A = 16°$ and B $= 27°$.

Substituting these values in the formula,

$$\tan (16° + 27°) = \frac{\tan 16° + \tan 27°}{1 - \tan 16° \tan 27°}.$$

Putting in the values of tan 16° and tan 27° from **Table XI,**

$$\tan 43° = \frac{0.2867 + 0.5095}{1 - 0.2867 \times 0.5095} = 0.9325.$$

365. Functions of twice an angle and half an angle.—By putting $B = A$ in the formulas for the sum in **Art. 364,** the following formulas are obtained:

[102] sin $2A = 2$ sin A cos $A.$

[103] cos $2A = \cos^2 A - \sin^2 A = 1 - 2 \sin^2 A = 2 \cos^2 A - 1.$

[104] tan $2A = \dfrac{2 \tan A}{1 - \tan^2 A}.$

These formulas are used to express the function of any angle in terms of the functions of one-half that angle.

From the above may be derived the following formulas, which are used to express the functions of any angle in terms of the functions of twice that angle.

[105] sin $A = \pm \sqrt{\dfrac{1 - \cos 2A}{2}}.$

[106] cos $A = \pm \sqrt{\dfrac{1 + \cos 2A}{2}}.$

[107] tan $A = \pm \sqrt{\dfrac{1 - \cos 2A}{1 + \cos 2A}} = \dfrac{\sin 2A}{1 + \cos 2A} = \dfrac{1 - \cos 2A}{\sin 2A}.$

Example 1. Test formula [**102**] by using $A = 20°$.
Substituting in the formula,
$\sin 40° = 2 \sin 20° \cos 20° = 2 \times 0.3420 \times 0.9397 = 0.6428$.
Example 2. Test formula [**106**] by using $A = 35°$.
Substituting in the formula,

$$\cos 35° = \sqrt{\frac{1 + \cos 70°}{2}} = \sqrt{\frac{1 + 0.3420}{2}} = 0.81915.$$

366. Formulas for changing products to sums or differences, and sums and differences to products.—The following four formulas are convenient for expressing a product of two functions as the sum or difference of two functions.

[**108**] $\sin A \cos B = \frac{1}{2} \sin (A+B) + \frac{1}{2} \sin (A-B)$.
[**109**] $\cos A \sin B = \frac{1}{2} \sin (A+B) - \frac{1}{2} \sin (A-B)$.
[**110**] $\cos A \cos B = \frac{1}{2} \cos (A+B) + \frac{1}{2} \cos (A-B)$.
[**111**] $\sin A \sin B = -\frac{1}{2} \cos (A+B) + \frac{1}{2} \cos (A-B)$.

The following four formulas express a sum or a difference as a product. They are often convenient when working with logarithms.

[**112**] $\sin A + \sin B = 2 \sin \frac{1}{2}(A+B) \cos \frac{1}{2}(A-B)$.
[**113**] $\sin A - \sin B = 2 \cos \frac{1}{2}(A+B) \sin \frac{1}{2}(A-B)$.
[**114**] $\cos A + \cos B = 2 \cos \frac{1}{2}(A+B) \cos \frac{1}{2}(A-B)$.
[**115**] $\cos A - \cos B = -2 \sin \frac{1}{2}(A+B) \sin \frac{1}{2}(A-B)$.

EXERCISES 124

1. Find $\sin 90°$, $\cos 90°$, and $\tan 90°$, using the addition formulas and $90° = 60° + 30°$.

2. Find $\sin (A+B)$ if $\sin A = \frac{3}{5}$ and $\sin B = \frac{4}{5}$, both being acute angles. Find $\cos (A+B)$. *Ans.* 1; 0.

3. Find $\cos (A-B)$ if $\cos A = \frac{5}{13}$ and $\cos B = \frac{12}{13}$, both being acute angles. Find $\sin (A-B)$. *Ans.* $\frac{120}{169}$; $\frac{119}{169}$.

4. Find $\tan (A+B)$ if $\tan A = 2$ and $\tan B = 3$, both being acute angles. What is the value of $(A+B)$? *Ans.* -1; 135°.

5. Given the functions of 30° and 45°, find $\sin 75°$, $\cos 75°$, and $\tan 75°$.

6. Take values from **Table XI** for the functions of 25° and 18°, and find $\sin 43°$, $\cos 43°$, $\sin 7°$, and $\tan 7°$.

7. Take values from **Table XI** for the functions of 15° and find $\sin 30°$, $\cos 30°$, and $\tan 30°$.

8. Using the functions of 45°, find $\sin 22\frac{1}{2}°$, $\cos 22\frac{1}{2}°$, and $\tan 22\frac{1}{2}°$.

9. Given $\sin 2\theta = \frac{3}{5}$, find $\tan \theta$ and $\cot \theta$. *Ans.* $\pm\frac{1}{3}$; ± 3.

10. Show that cos 5θ+cos 3θ=2 cos 4θ cos θ.

11. Show that sin 7θ−sin 3θ=2 cos 5θ sin 2θ.

12. Show that cos $125°$−cos $75°$ = −2 sin $100°$ sin $25°$.

13. Express sin 7α+sin 5α as a product.   *Ans.* 2 sin 6α cos α.

14. Express cos $46°$+cos $28°$ as a product.   *Ans.* 2 cos $37°$ cos $9°$.

15. Show that sin $575°$ cos $927°$+cos $575°$ sin $927°$=sin $1502°$.

16. Show that $\dfrac{\tan 327°+\tan 846°}{1-\tan 327° \tan 846°}$ = tan $1173°$.

17. Find the value of sin $\dfrac{11\pi}{6}$ cos $\dfrac{15\pi}{4}$+tan $\dfrac{9\pi}{4}$ cot $\dfrac{5\pi}{2}$.

Ans. −0.3536.

18. Find the value of

$$\cos\left(-\frac{11\pi}{6}\right)\sin\frac{19\pi}{6} + \cos\left(-\frac{4\pi}{3}\right)\sin\left(-\frac{7\pi}{3}\right).$$ *Ans.* 0.

19. If sin $\alpha = -\frac{1}{7}$ and α is in III quadrant, and cos $\beta = \frac{3}{4}$ and β is in I quadrant, find the value of sin $(\alpha+\beta)$, sin $(\alpha-\beta)$, and tan $(\alpha+\beta)$.

Ans. −0.7618; 0.5475; 1.1760.

20. Show that $\dfrac{\sin 47°+\sin 17°}{\cos 47°+\cos 17°}$=tan $32°$.

21. Show that $\dfrac{\sin 3\alpha+\sin 5\alpha}{\cos 3\alpha-\cos 5\alpha}$=cot α.

22. Show that $\dfrac{\sin 67°-\sin 23°}{\cos 67°+\cos 23°}$=tan $22°$.

23. In a right triangle cos $\alpha = \dfrac{b}{c}$ and cos $\beta = \dfrac{a}{c}$. Show that sin $\frac{1}{2}\alpha = \sqrt{\dfrac{c-b}{2c}}$ and sin $\frac{1}{2}\beta = \sqrt{\dfrac{c-a}{2c}}$.

24., If α is less than $360°$, in what quadrants may α be if sin $\frac{1}{2}\alpha$ is negative? Positive? If tan $\frac{1}{2}\alpha$ is negative? Positive? If cot $\frac{1}{2}\alpha$ is negative? Positive? If sec $\frac{1}{2}\alpha$ is negative? Positive?

CHAPTER XLI

SOLUTION OF OBLIQUE TRIANGLES

367. Cases.—A triangle that is not a right triangle is called an oblique triangle.

The student should now reread **Arts. 338** and **339** and the exercises following them. It is evident, then, that an oblique triangle can be solved when there are *three elements given at least one of which is a side.*

There arise the four following cases:

CASE I. *When any side and any two angles are given.*

CASE II. *When any two sides and the angle opposite one of them are given.*

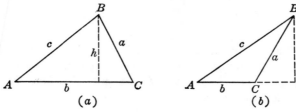

FIG. 285.

CASE III. *When any two sides and the angle included between them are given.*

CASE IV. *When the three sides are given.*

The oblique triangle can be divided into right triangles by drawing convenient altitudes, and so be solved by methods already given in the chapter on right triangles. It is, however, usually a saving of time to solve them by means of formulas derived especially for that purpose. The simpler of these formulas will now be derived.

368. The law of sines.—The law is: *In any triangle, the sides are proportional to the sines of the opposite angles.*

Proof. Let *ABC* in Fig. 285 be any triangle. Draw the altitude h from B to the side AC. Because of the right triangles, in either (*a*) or (*b*), $h = c \sin A$ and $h = a \sin C$,

$$\therefore a \sin C = c \sin A.$$

Dividing both members of this by $\sin C \sin A$,

$$\frac{a}{\sin A} = \frac{c}{\sin C}.$$

Similarly by drawing an altitude from C, $\dfrac{a}{\sin A} = \dfrac{b}{\sin B}.$

$$[116] \therefore \frac{a}{\sin A} = \frac{b}{\sin B} = \frac{c}{\sin C}.$$

From the law of sines there may be written the three equations: $\dfrac{a}{\sin A} = \dfrac{b}{\sin B}, \quad \dfrac{a}{\sin A} = \dfrac{c}{\sin C}, \quad \dfrac{b}{\sin B} = \dfrac{c}{\sin C},$ any one of which involves four elements of a triangle. It is evident that if any three of the elements involved in one of the equations are given, the remaining element can be found.

Thus, if in $\dfrac{a}{\sin A} = \dfrac{b}{\sin B},$ A, B, and b are given, then solving for a, $a = \dfrac{b \sin A}{\sin B}.$

369. The law of cosines.—The law is: *In any triangle, the square of any side equals the sum of the squares of the other two sides minus twice the product of these two sides times the cosine of the angle between them.*

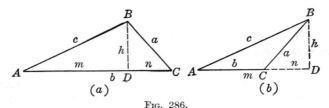

Fig. 286.

Proof. In Fig. 286, either (*a*) or (*b*), draw the altitude h from B to the side AC. Let $AD = m$ and $DC = n$.

Because of the right triangles, in either (*a*) or (*b*), $a^2 = h^2 + n^2$.

In (*a*), $n = b - m = b - c \cos A$.

In (*b*), $n = m - b = c \cos A - b$.

In either case, $n^2 = b^2 - 2bc \cos A + c^2 \cos^2 A$.

In either (*a*) or (*b*), $h^2 = c^2 \sin^2 A$.

Substituting these values for h^2 and n^2 in, $a^2 = h^2 + n^2$,

$$a^2 = c^2 \sin^2 A + b^2 - 2bc \cos A + c^2 \cos^2 A.$$

$$\therefore a^2 = b^2 + c^2 (\sin^2 A + \cos^2 A) - 2bc \cos A.$$

$$[117] \therefore \mathbf{a^2 = b^2 + c^2 - 2bc \cos A.}$$

Similarly there may be obtained:

$$[118] \quad \mathbf{b^2 = a^2 + c^2 - 2ac \cos B.}$$

$$[119] \quad \mathbf{c^2 = a^2 + b^2 - 2ab \cos C.}$$

Solving these for cos A, cos B, and cos C respectively:

$$[120] \ \cos A = \frac{b^2 + c^2 - a^2}{2bc}.$$

$$[121] \ \cos B = \frac{a^2 + c^2 - b^2}{2ac}.$$

$$[122] \ \cos C = \frac{a^2 + b^2 - c^2}{2ab}.$$

By these formulas the values of the angles of a triangle can be computed when the sides are known.

370. Directions for solving.—It will be noticed that each of the formulas from the law of sines and the law of cosines involves four elements of the triangle.

In solving a triangle, *select a formula that involves three known elements besides the element that is to be found, solve for the unknown element in terms of the known, substitute the numerical values, and evaluate.*

The work may be checked (a) by making a careful construction, and (b) by using some other formula than is used in solving.

371. Case I, a side and two angles given.—*Example.* Given $a = 45$, $B = 36°\ 17'$, and $C = 83°\ 32'$; to find b, c, and A.

Formulas.   *Construction.*

(1) $A = 180° - (B + C)$.

(2) $\dfrac{a}{\sin A} = \dfrac{b}{\sin B}$, $\therefore b = \dfrac{a \sin B}{\sin A}$.

(3) $\dfrac{a}{\sin A} = \dfrac{c}{\sin C}$, $\therefore c = \dfrac{a \sin C}{\sin A}$.

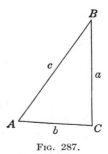

Fig. 287.

Computation by natural functions.

$A = 180° - (36°\ 17' + 83°\ 32') = 60°\ 11'$.

$$b = \frac{a \sin B}{\sin A} = \frac{45 \times .5918}{.8676} = 30.70.$$

$$c = \frac{a \sin C}{\sin A} = \frac{45 \times .9937}{.8676} = 51.54.$$

Computation by logarithms.

log 45 =	1.6532	log 45 =	1.6532
log sin 36° 17′ =	9.7722	log sin 83° 32′ =	9.9972
	11.4254		11.6504
log sin 60° 11′ =	9.9384	log sin 60° 11′ =	9.9384
log b =	1.4870	log c =	1.7120
∴ b =	30.69	∴ c =	51.53

Check by using the law of cosines.

372. Case II, two sides and an angle opposite one of them given.—With these parts given it is possible (a) that there is only one solution, that is, that only one triangle can be found; (b) that there are two solutions, that is, that there are two different triangles that fulfill the conditions; (c) that there is no solution, that is, that no triangle exists that will fulfill the conditions.

Whether there is one solution, two solutions, or no solution can readily be determined by making a careful construction of the triangle from the given parts.

Example 1. Given $a=15$, $c=10$, and $A=40°\ 30′$; to find b, B, and C.

The construction shows that there is only one solution.

Formulas.   *Construction.*

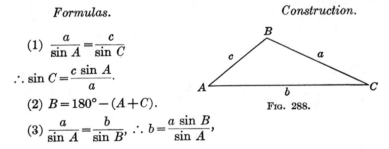

(1) $\dfrac{a}{\sin A} = \dfrac{c}{\sin C}$

∴ $\sin C = \dfrac{c \sin A}{a}$.

(2) $B = 180° - (A+C)$.

(3) $\dfrac{a}{\sin A} = \dfrac{b}{\sin B}$, ∴ $b = \dfrac{a \sin B}{\sin A}$,

Fig. 288.

Example 2. Given $a=20$, $c=25$, and $A=52°\ 40′$; to find b, B, and C.

From the construction it is seen that there are two triangles, ABC and ABC', that fulfill the conditions.

Formulas. *Construction.*

(1) $\dfrac{a}{\sin A} = \dfrac{c}{\sin C}$, $\therefore \sin C = \dfrac{c \sin A}{a}$.

(2) $C' = 180° - C$.

(3) $B = 180° - (A + C)$.

(4) $B' = ABC' = 180° - (A + C')$.

(5) $\dfrac{a}{\sin A} = \dfrac{b}{\sin B}$, $\therefore b = \dfrac{a \sin B}{\sin A}$.

(6) $\dfrac{a}{\sin A} = \dfrac{b'}{\sin B'}$, $\therefore b' = \dfrac{a \sin B'}{\sin A}$.

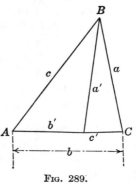

Fig. 289.

Example 3. Given $a = 12$, $c = 20$, and $A = 62° \ 20'$; to find b, B, and C.

From the construction, Fig. 290, it is evident that the side a is not long enough to form a triangle. Hence there is no solution.

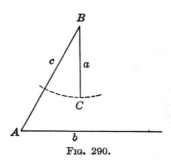

Fig. 290.

373. Case III, two sides and the angle between them given.—*Example.* Given $b = 45.2$, $a = 56.7$, and $C = 47° \ 45'$; to find c, A, and B.

Formulas. *Construction.*

(1) $c = \sqrt{a^2 + b^2 - 2ab \cos C}$.

(2) $\dfrac{a}{\sin A} = \dfrac{c}{\sin C}$,

$\therefore \sin A = \dfrac{a \sin C}{c}$.

(3) $\dfrac{b}{\sin B} = \dfrac{c}{\sin C}$,

$\therefore \sin B = \dfrac{b \sin C}{c}$.

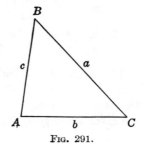

Fig. 291.

Computation.

$$c = \sqrt{56.7^2 + 45.2^2 - 2 \times 56.7 \times 45.2 \times 0.6723} = 42.56.$$

$$\sin A = \frac{56.7 \times 0.7402}{42.56} = 0.9861, \therefore A = 80^\circ\ 26'.$$

$$\sin B = \frac{45.2 \times 0.7402}{42.56} = 0.7861, \therefore B = 51^\circ\ 49'.$$

Check. $A + B + C = 180^\circ.$

$$80^\circ\ 26' + 51^\circ\ 49' + 47^\circ\ 45' = 180^\circ.$$

Logarithms cannot be used conveniently with formulas such as (1) above. Formulas in which logarithms can be used for the solution of examples under Case III can be derived from the law of sines. They are numbers 123, 124, and 125 on page 473.

374. Case IV, three sides given.—*Example.* Given $a = 10$, $b = 12$, and $c = 15$; to find A, B, and C.

Formulas.

(1) $\cos A = \dfrac{b^2 + c^2 - a^2}{2bc}.$

(2) $\cos B = \dfrac{a^2 + c^2 - b^2}{2ac}.$

(3) $\cos C = \dfrac{a^2 + b^2 - c^2}{2ab}.$

Construction.

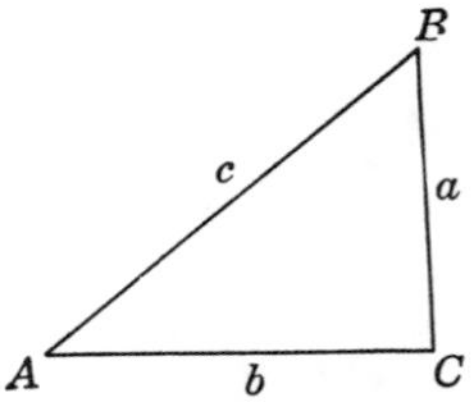

Fig. 292.

Computation.

$$\cos A = \frac{12^2 + 15^2 - 10^2}{2 \times 12 \times 15} = 0.7472, \therefore A = 41^\circ\ 39'.$$

$$\cos B = \frac{10^2 + 15^2 - 12^2}{2 \times 10 \times 15} = 0.6033, \therefore B = 52^\circ\ 53.5'.$$

$$\cos C = \frac{10^2 + 12^2 - 15^2}{2 \times 10 \times 12} = 0.0792, \therefore C = 85^\circ\ 27.6'.$$

Check. $A + B + C = 180^\circ.$

$$41^\circ\ 39' + 52^\circ\ 53.5' + 85^\circ\ 27.6' = 180^\circ\ 0.1'.$$

The above formulas are not suitable for work with logarithms; but formulas can be derived from them that lend themselves readily to logarithmic work. These formulas are given on page 473, numbers 126 to 134 inclusive.

EXERCISES 125

1. From the law of sines, find b in terms of a, A, and B. Find C in terms of b, c, and B. $Ans.$ $b = \dfrac{a \sin B}{\sin A}$; $C = \sin^{-1} \dfrac{c \sin B}{b}$.

With the following three elements given, find those remaining and check the results when the answers are not given.

2. $A = 44° 6.5'$; $B = 57° 42.5'$; $a = 4.23$ in.

3. $A = 48° 39.2'$; $C = 115° 23.8'$; $a = 14.83$ in.
   $Ans.$ $B = 15° 57'$; $b = 5.428$ in.; $c = 17.85$ in.

4. $B = 30° 36.8'$; $C = 107° 15.5'$; $b = 144$.

5. $C = 44° 17.3'$; $b = 14.33$; $c = 13.67$.
$Ans.$ $B = 47° 2.5'$; $A = 88° 40.2'$; $a = 19.57$; $B' = 132° 57.5'$; $A' = 2° 45.2'$; $a' = 0.940$.

6. $A = 53° 16.5'$; $c = 25.64$; $a = 31.4$.

7. $a = 79.8$; $b = 46.7$; $B = 23° 19.6'$.

8. $b = 17$; $c = 16$; $A = 47° 16.4'$.

9. $a = 99.4$; $c = 90.4$; $B = 11° 7.8'$.
   $Ans.$ $A = 110° 20.4'$; $C = 58° 31.8'$; $b = 20.5$.

10. $a = 21$; $b = 24$; $c = 31$.

11. $a = 61.52$; $b = 81.74$; $c = 75.34$.
    $Ans.$ $A = 45° 53.4'$; $B = 72° 33.2'$; $C = 61° 33.4'$.

12. $a = 2.46$; $b = 3.5$; $c = 4.2$.

13. To find the distance AB through the swamp, Fig. 293, the following data were measured: $a = 120$ rd., $b = 146$ rd., and $C = 41° 25'$. Compute the distance AB. $Ans.$ 97.14 rd.

14. Compute the inaccessible distance AB, Fig. 294, from the measured data $b = 450$ ft., $A = 82° 30'$, and $C = 67° 42'$. $Ans.$ 837.2 ft.

15. Two points, P and Q, Fig. 295, are on opposite sides of a stream and invisible from each other on account of an island in the stream. A straight line AB is run through Q, and the following measurements taken: $AQ = 756$ ft., $QB = 562$ ft., angle $QAP = 47° 28.6'$, and angle $QBP = 57° 45'$. Compute QP. $Ans.$ 852 ft.

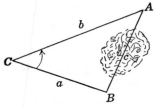

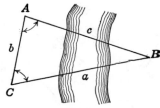

FIG. 293.   FIG. 294.

16. From a point on a horizontal plane the angle of elevation of the top of a hill is $23° 46'$; and a tower 45 ft. high standing on the top of the hill subtends an angle of $5° 16'$. Find the height of the hill. $Ans.$ 173 ft.

30

17. Two observers, A and B, 100 rd. apart on a horizontal plane observe at the same instant an aviator. His angle of elevation at A is 68° 25 and at B 55° 58.2'. The angles in the horizontal plane made by the projections of the lines of sight with the line AB are 43° 27' at A and 23° 45' at B. Find the height of the aviator.   *Ans.* 1820 ft.

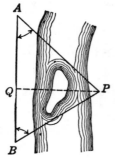

18. B is 42 miles from A in a direction W. 22° N., and C is 58 miles from A in a direction E. 73° N. What is the position of C relative to B?   *Ans.* 68.6 mi. E. 35° 21.1' N.

375. Resultant of forces.—If two forces, represented by the vectors PQ and PS, Fig. 296, act upon a body at point P, then the combined effect of these forces is the same as that of the force, represented by the vector PR, where PR is the diagonal of the parallelogram of which PQ and PS are two sides.

Fig. 295.

The force PR is called the **resultant** of the forces PQ and PS.

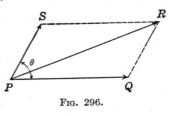

Fig. 296.

The resultant of any number of forces is a single force that will produce the same effect as the combined effect of all the given forces.

The resultant of any number of given forces can be found by finding the resultant of any two of the given forces, then the resultant of a third force and the first resultant, continuing till all the forces are used.

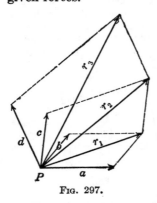

Fig. 297.

Thus, if a, b, c, and d, Fig. 297, are four forces acting at the point P, r_1 is the resultant of a and b, r_2 the resultant of r_1 and c, and r_3 the resultant of r_2 and d. Therefore r_3 is the resultant of a, b, c, and d.

376. Computation of a resultant.—If two forces act at *right angles* to each other, their resultant is evidently equal in magnitude to the *square root of the sum of the squares of their respective magnitudes.*

Thus, in Fig. 298, $r = \sqrt{a^2 + b^2}$. Also the direction of r can be found, for tan $QPR = \dfrac{b}{a}$.

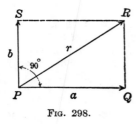

Fig. 298.

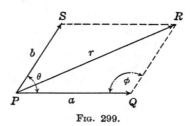

Fig. 299.

If two forces act at any angle θ to each other, their resultant can be found by using the law of cosines, **Art 369,** and is equal in magnitude to the *square root of the sum of the squares of their respective magnitudes increased by twice their product times the cosine of the angle between the two forces.*

Thus, in Fig. 299, $r = \sqrt{a^2 + b^2 - 2ab \cos \varphi}$ by the cosine law. But $\varphi = 180° - \theta$, and therefore $\cos \varphi = \cos(180° - \theta) = -\cos \theta$ by [69]. Substituting this value for $\cos \varphi$, $r = \sqrt{a^2 + b^2 + 2ab \cos \theta}$.

The angle between the resultant and either force can be found by the law of sines, **Art. 368.**

Velocities can be combined in exactly the same manner as forces.

EXERCIŞES 126

1. Given two forces of 40 lb. and 60 lb., acting at an angle of 30°. Find the magnitude of their resultant.   *Ans.* 67.66+ lb.

2. Given a force of 500 lb. acting toward the east and a force of 700 lb. acting northeast. Find the resultant in magnitude and direction.
                Anş. A force of 1111.3 lb. acting 26° 26.9′ N. of E.

3. An aeroplane, which is at an altitude of 1600 ft. and moving at the rate of 100 miles per hour in a direction due east, drops a bomb. Disregarding the resistance of the air, where will the bomb strike the ground if during its fall it is acted upon by a wind of 40 miles an hour from a direction 30° east of south?
                Ans. 1279 ft. 23° 24′ N. of E. of point where bomb was dropped.

Solution. To find the number of seconds it is in falling, use equation of exercise 30, page 339, $\frac{1}{2}gt^2 = 1600$, where $g = 32$. This gives $t = 10$, the time in seconds.

It would move east from the starting point as far as the aeroplane travels in 10 seconds if the wind is not considered.

This is $\dfrac{100\times5280\times10}{60\times60}=1467$ ft.

During 10 seconds the wind would carry the bomb

$$\dfrac{40\times5280\times10}{60\times60}=586.7 \text{ ft.}$$

The resultant of these displacements is

$$\sqrt{1467^2+586.7^2+2\times1467\times586.7\times\cos\ 120°}=1279 \text{ ft.}$$

By the sine law the direction is found to be 23° 24′ N. of E.

4. An automobile is traveling W. 36° N. at 27 miles per hour, and the wind is blowing from the N. E. at 30 miles per hour. What velocity and direction does the wind appear to have to the chauffeur?

Ans. 37.09 mi. per hr. from N. 59′ W.

5. A train is running at 30 miles per hour in a direction W. 35° S., and the engine leaves a steam track in the direction E. 10° N. The wind is known to be blowing from the N. E.; find its velocity.

Ans. 22 mi. per hr.

6. In a river flowing due south at the rate of 4 miles per hour, a boat is drifted by a wind blowing from the southwest at the rate of 15 miles per hour. Determine the position of the boat after 40 minutes if resistance reduces the effect of the wind 70 per cent.

Ans. 2.19 mi. E.14° 26′ S.

TABLES

TABLE I

Summary of Formulas

[1] $A = ab$, rectangle, parallelogram.

[2] $a = A \div b$, rectangle, parallelogram.

[3] $b = A \div a$, rectangle, parallelogram.

[4] $A = \frac{1}{2}ab$, triangle.

[5] $a = 2A \div b$, triangle.

[6] $b = 2A \div a$, triangle.

[7] $A = \sqrt{s(s-a)(s-b)(s-c)}$, where $s = \frac{1}{2}(a+b+c)$, triangle.

[8] $A = \frac{1}{2}(B+b) \times a$, trapezoid.

[9] $c = \sqrt{a^2+b^2}$, right triangle.

[10] $a = \sqrt{c^2-b^2}$, right triangle.

[11] $b = \sqrt{c^2-a^2}$, right triangle.

[12] $l:1 = t:T$, tapers.

[13] $x = \dfrac{D-d}{2} \times \dfrac{L}{l}$, tapers.

[14] $D_1 = D - \dfrac{1.732}{N}$, sharp V-threads.

[15] $D_1 = D - \dfrac{1.299}{N}$, U. S. S. threads.

[16] $r = \dfrac{(\frac{1}{2}w)^2 + h^2}{2h}$, segment of circle.

[17] $h = r - \sqrt{r^2 - (\frac{1}{2}w)^2}$, segment of circle.

[18] $w = 2\sqrt{h(2r-h)}$, segment of circle.

[19] $C = \pi d$, circle.

[20] $d = C \div \pi$, circle.

[21] $C = 2\pi r$, circle.

[22] $2r = C \div \pi$, circle.

[23] $A = \frac{1}{2}Cr$, circle.

[24] $A = \pi r^2$, circle.

[25] $A = \frac{1}{4}\pi d^2 = 0.7854 d^2$, circle.

[26] $r = \sqrt{A \div \pi}$, circle.

[27] $d = \sqrt{A \div \frac{1}{4}\pi}$, circle.

[28] $A_r = A - a = \pi R^2 - \pi r^2 = \pi(R^2 - r^2) = \pi(R+r)(R-r)$, ring.

[29] $A = \dfrac{\theta}{360} \times \pi r^2$, sector.

[30(a)] $A = \frac{2}{3}hw + \dfrac{h^3}{2w}$, segment.

[30(b)] $A = \frac{4}{3}h^2 \sqrt{\dfrac{2r}{h} - 0.608}$, segment.

[31] $A = \pi ab$, ellipse.

[32(a)] $P = \pi(a+b)$, ellipse.

[32(b)] $P = \pi[\frac{3}{2}(a+b) - \sqrt{ab}]$, ellipse.

[32(c)] $P = \pi\sqrt{2(a^2+b^2)}$, ellipse.

[33] $S = ph$, prism.

[34] $T = ph + 2A$, prism.

[35] $T = 6a^2$, cube.

[36] $p = S \div h$, prism.

[37] $h = S \div p$, prism.

[38] $V = Ah$, prism.

[39] $V = a^3$, cube.

[40] $h = V \div A$, prism.

[41] $A = V \div h$, prism.

[42] $S = Ch = \pi dh = 2\pi rh$, cylinder.

[43] $V = Ah = \pi r^2 h = \frac{1}{4}\pi d^2 h$, cylinder.

[44] $h = V \div A = V \div \pi r^2$, cylinder.

[45] $A = V \div h$, cylinder.

[46] $V = \pi R^2 h - \pi r^2 h = \pi h(R^2 - r^2) = \pi h(R+r)(R-r)$, cylinder.

[47] $S = \frac{1}{2}ps$, pyramid or cone.

[48] $T = \frac{1}{2}ps + A$, pyramid or cone.

[49] $S = \frac{1}{2}(P+p) \times s$, frustum.

[50] $T = \frac{1}{2}(P+p) \times s + B + b$, frustum.

[51] $V = \frac{1}{3}Ah$, pyramid or cone.

[52] $V = \frac{1}{3}h(B+b+\sqrt{Bb})$, frustum of pyramid or cone.

[53] $V = \frac{1}{3}\pi h(R^2 + r^2 + Rr)$, frustum of cone.

[54] $V = \frac{1}{12}\pi h(D^2 + d^2 + Dd)$, frustum of cone.

[55] $S = 4\pi r^2$, sphere.

[56] $V = \frac{1}{3}Sr = \frac{4}{3}\pi r^3 = \frac{1}{6}\pi d^3$, sphere.

[57] $Z = 2\pi rh$, area of zone.

[58] $V = \frac{1}{2}\pi h(r^2{}_1 + r^2{}_2) + \frac{1}{6}\pi h^3$, volume of segment.

[59] $A = 2\pi R \times 2\pi r = 4\pi^2 Rr$, solid ring.

[60] $V = 2\pi R \times \pi r^2 = 2\pi^2 Rr^2$, solid ring.

[61] $V = \frac{1}{6}h(B_1 + 4M + B_2)$, prismatoid.

[62] $\sin (90° - \theta) = \cos \theta.$

[63] $\cos (90° - \theta) = \sin \theta.$

[64] $\tan (90° - \theta) = \cot \theta.$

[65] $\cot (90° - \theta) = \tan \theta.$

[66] $\sec (90° - \theta) = \csc \theta.$

[67] $\csc (90° - \theta) = \sec \theta.$

[68] $\sin (180° - \theta) = \sin \theta.$

[69] $\cos (180° - \theta) = -\cos \theta.$

[70] $\tan (180° - \theta) = -\tan \theta.$

[71] $\cot (180° - \theta) = -\cot \theta.$

[72] $\sec (180° - \theta) = -\sec \theta.$

[73] $\csc (180° - \theta) = \csc \theta.$

[74] $\sin (90° + \theta) = \cos \theta.$

[75] $\cos (90° + \theta) = -\sin \theta.$

[76] $\tan (90° + \theta) = -\cot \theta.$

[77] $\cot (90° + \theta) = -\tan \theta.$

[78] $\sec (90°+\theta) = -\csc \theta$.

[79] $\csc (90°+\theta) = \sec \theta$.

[80] $\sin (-\theta) = -\sin \theta$.

[81] $\cos (-\theta) = \cos \theta$

[82] $\tan (-\theta) = -\tan \theta$.

[83] $\cot (-\theta) = -\cot \theta$.

[84] $\sec (-\theta) = \sec \theta$.

[85] $\csc (-\theta) = -\csc \theta$.

[86] $\sin \theta = \dfrac{1}{\csc \theta}$ or $\csc \theta = \dfrac{1}{\sin \theta}$.

[87] $\cos \theta = \dfrac{1}{\sec \theta}$ or $\sec \theta = \dfrac{1}{\cos \theta}$.

[88] $\tan \theta = \dfrac{1}{\cot \theta}$ or $\cot \theta = \dfrac{1}{\tan \theta}$.

[89] $\text{vers } \theta = 1 - \cos \theta$.

[90] $\text{covers } \theta = 1 - \sin \theta$.

[91] $\sin^2 \theta + \cos^2 \theta = 1$.

[92] $\sec^2 \theta = 1 + \tan^2 \theta$.

[93] $\csc^2 \theta = 1 + \cot^2 \theta$.

[94] $\tan \theta = \dfrac{\sin \theta}{\cos \theta}$.

[95] $\cot \theta = \dfrac{\cos \theta}{\sin \theta}$.

[96] $\sin (A+B) = \sin A \cos B + \cos A \sin B$.

[97] $\sin (A-B) = \sin A \cos B - \cos A \sin B$.

[98] $\cos (A+B) = \cos A \cos B - \sin A \sin B$.

[99] $\cos (A-B) = \cos A \cos B + \sin A \sin B$.

[100] $\tan (A+B) = \dfrac{\tan A + \tan B}{1 - \tan A \tan B}$.

[101] $\tan (A-B) = \dfrac{\tan A - \tan B}{1 + \tan A \tan B}$.

[102] $\sin 2A = 2 \sin A \cos A$.

[103] $\cos 2A = \cos^2 A - \sin^2 A = 1 - 2 \sin^2 A = 2 \cos^2 A - 1$.

[104] $\tan 2A = \dfrac{2 \tan A}{1 - \tan^2 A}$.

[105] $\sin A = \pm \sqrt{\dfrac{1 - \cos 2A}{2}}$.

[106] $\cos A = \pm \sqrt{\dfrac{1 + \cos 2A}{2}}$.

[107] $\tan A = \pm \sqrt{\dfrac{1 - \cos 2A}{1 + \cos 2A}} = \dfrac{\sin 2A}{1 + \cos 2A} = \dfrac{1 - \cos 2A}{\sin 2A}$.

[108] $\sin A \cos B = \frac{1}{2} \sin (A+B) + \frac{1}{2} \sin (A-B)$.

[109] $\cos A \sin B = \frac{1}{2} \sin (A+B) - \frac{1}{2} \sin (A-B)$.

[110] $\cos A \cos B = \frac{1}{2} \cos (A+B) + \frac{1}{2} \cos (A-B)$.

[111] $\sin A \sin B = -\frac{1}{2} \cos (A+B) + \frac{1}{2} \cos (A-B)$.

[112] $\sin A + \sin B = 2 \sin \frac{1}{2}(A+B) \cos \frac{1}{2}(A-B)$.

[113] $\sin A - \sin B = 2 \cos \frac{1}{2}(A+B) \sin \frac{1}{2}(A-B)$.

[114] $\cos A + \cos B = 2 \cos \frac{1}{2}(A+B) \cos \frac{1}{2}(A-B)$.

[115] $\cos A - \cos B = -2 \sin \frac{1}{2}(A+B) \sin \frac{1}{2}(A-B)$.

[116] $\dfrac{a}{\sin A} = \dfrac{b}{\sin B} = \dfrac{c}{\sin C}$.

[117] $a^2 = b^2 + c^2 - 2bc \cos A$.

[118] $b^2 = a^2 + c^2 - 2ac \cos B$.

[119] $c^2 = a^2 + b^2 - 2ab \cos C$.

[120] $\cos A = \dfrac{b^2 + c^2 - a^2}{2bc}$.

[121] $\cos B = \dfrac{a^2 + c^2 - b^2}{2ac}$.

[122] $\cos C = \dfrac{a^2 + b^2 - c^2}{2ab}$.

Formulas for solving Case III, oblique triangles, by logarithms:

[123] $\tan \frac{1}{2}(B-C) = \dfrac{b-c}{b+c} \tan \frac{1}{2}(B+C)$.

[124] $\tan \frac{1}{2}(A-C) = \dfrac{a-c}{a+c} \tan \frac{1}{2}(A+C)$.

[125] $\tan \frac{1}{2}(A-B) = \dfrac{a-b}{a+b} \tan \frac{1}{2}(A+B)$.

Formulas for solving Case IV, oblique triangles, by logarithms:

Let $s = \dfrac{a+b+c}{2}$.

[126] $\sin \frac{1}{2}A = \sqrt{\dfrac{(s-b)(s-c)}{bc}}$.

[127] $\sin \frac{1}{2}B = \sqrt{\dfrac{(s-a)(s-c)}{ac}}$.

[128] $\sin \frac{1}{2}C = \sqrt{\dfrac{(s-a)(s-b)}{ab}}$.

[129] $\cos \frac{1}{2}A = \sqrt{\dfrac{s(s-a)}{bc}}$.

[130] $\cos \frac{1}{2}B = \sqrt{\dfrac{s(s-b)}{ac}}$.

[131] $\cos \frac{1}{2}C = \sqrt{\dfrac{s(s-c)}{ab}}$.

Let $r = \sqrt{\dfrac{(s-a)(s-b)(s-c)}{s}}$.

[132] $\tan \frac{1}{2}A = \dfrac{r}{s-a}$.

[133] $\tan \frac{1}{2}B = \dfrac{r}{s-b}$.

[134] $\tan \frac{1}{2}C = \dfrac{r}{s-c}$.

[135] Area of a triangle $= \frac{1}{2} bc \sin A = \frac{1}{2}ac \sin B = \frac{1}{2}ab \sin C$
$= \sqrt{s(s-a)(s-b)(s-c)}$.

Other formulas for any angle.

[136] $\sin \theta = \sqrt{1-\cos^2 \theta} = \dfrac{\tan \theta}{\sqrt{1+\tan^2 \theta}} = \dfrac{1}{\sqrt{1+\cot^2 \theta}}$
$= \dfrac{\sqrt{\sec^2 \theta - 1}}{\sec \theta} = \dfrac{1}{\csc \theta}$.

[137] $\cos \theta = \sqrt{1-\sin^2 \theta} = \dfrac{1}{\sqrt{1+\tan^2 \theta}} = \dfrac{\cot \theta}{\sqrt{1+\cot^2 \theta}}$

$$= \dfrac{1}{\sec \theta} = \dfrac{\sqrt{\csc^2 \theta - 1}}{\csc \theta}.$$

[138] $\tan \theta = \dfrac{\sin \theta}{\sqrt{1-\sin^2 \theta}} = \dfrac{\sqrt{1-\cos^2 \theta}}{\cos \theta} = \dfrac{1}{\tan \theta}$

$$= \sqrt{\sec^2 \theta - 1} = \dfrac{1}{\sqrt{\csc^2 \theta - 1}}.$$

[139] $\cot \theta = \dfrac{\sqrt{1-\sin^2 \theta}}{\sin \theta} = \dfrac{\cos \theta}{\sqrt{1-\cos^2 \theta}} = \dfrac{1}{\tan \theta}$

$$= \dfrac{1}{\sqrt{\sec^2 \theta - 1}} = \sqrt{\csc^2 \theta - 1}.$$

[140] $\sec \theta = \dfrac{1}{\sqrt{1-\sin^2 \theta}} = \dfrac{1}{\cos \theta} = \sqrt{1+\tan^2 \theta}$

$$= \dfrac{\sqrt{1+\cot^2 \theta}}{\cot \theta} = \dfrac{\csc \theta}{\sqrt{\csc^2 \theta - 1}}.$$

[141] $\csc \theta = \dfrac{1}{\sin \theta} = \dfrac{1}{\sqrt{1-\cos^2 \theta}} = \dfrac{\sqrt{1+\tan^2 \theta}}{\tan \theta}$

$$= \sqrt{1+\cot^2 \theta} = \dfrac{\sec \theta}{\sqrt{\sec^2 \theta - 1}}.$$

[142] $\sin 3A = 3 \sin A - 4 \sin^3 A.$

[143] $\cos 3A = 4 \cos^3 A - 3 \cos A.$

[144] $\tan 3A = \dfrac{3 \tan A - \tan^3 A}{1 - 3 \tan^2 A}.$

TABLE II

Useful Numbers

1 cu. ft. of water weighs 62.5 lb. (approx.) = 1000 oz.

1 gal. of water weighs 8⅓ lb. (approx.).

1 atmosphere pressure = 14.7 lb. per sq. in. = 2116 lb. per sq. ft.

1 atmosphere pressure = 760 mm. of mercury.

A column of water 2.3 ft. high = a pressure of 1 lb. per sq. in.

1 gal. = 231 cu. in. (by law of Congress).

1 cu. ft. = 7½ gal. (approx.) or better 7.48 gal.

1 cu. ft. = ⅘ bu. (approx.).

1 bbl. = 4.211 − cu. ft. (approx.).

1 bu. = 2150.42 cu. in. (by law of Congress) = 1.24446 − cu. ft.

1 bu. = ⅘ cu. ft. (approx.).

1 perch = 24¾ cu. ft. but usually taken 25 cu. ft.

1 in. = 25.4001 mm. (approx.).

1 ft. = 30.4801 cm.

1 m. = 39.37 in. (by law of Congress).

1 lb. (avoirdupois) = 7000 grains (by law of Congress).

1 lb. (troy or apothecaries) = 5760 grains.
1 gram = 15.432 grains.
1 kg. = 2.20462 lb. (avoirdupois).
1 liter = 1.05668 qt. (liquid) = 0.90808 qt. (dry).
1 qt. (liquid) = 946.358 cc. = 0.946358 liter, or cu. dm.
1 qt. (dry) = 1101.228 cc. = 1.101228 liters, or cu. dm.
$\pi = 3.14159265358979+ = 3.1416 = \frac{355}{113} = 3\frac{1}{7}$ (all approx.).
1 radian = 57° 17′ 44.8″ = 57.2957795°+.
1° = 0.01745329+ radian.
Base of Napierian logarithms = e = 2.718281828· · · ·
$\log_{10} e$ = 0.43429448 · · · ·
$\log_e 10$ = 2.30258509 · · · ·
1 horse-power second = 550 foot-pounds.
1 horse-power minute = 33,000 foot-pounds.
$\sqrt{2}$ = 1.4142136. $\sqrt{3}$ = 1.7320508.
$\sqrt{5}$ = 2.2360680. $\sqrt{6}$ = 2.4494897.
$\sqrt[3]{2}$ = 1.2599210. $\sqrt[3]{3}$ = 1.4422496.

TABLE III

Decimal and Fractional Equivalents of Parts of an Inch

8ths	32nds	64ths	
1 = .125	1 = .03125	1 = .015625	33 = .515625
2 = .250	3 = .09375	3 = .046875	35 = .546875
3 = .375	5 = .15625	5 = .078125	37 = .578125
4 = .500	7 = .21875	7 = .109375	39 = .609375
5 = .625	9 = .28125	9 = .140625	41 = .640625
6 = .750	11 = .34375	11 = .171875	43 = .671875
7 = .875	13 = .40625	13 = .203125	45 = .703125
16ths	15 = .46875	15 = .234375	47 = .734375
1 = .0625	17 = .53125	17 = .265625	49 = .765625
3 = .1875	19 = .59375	19 = .296875	51 = .796875
5 = .3125	21 = .65625	21 = .328125	53 = .828125
7 = .4375	23 = .71875	23 = .359375	55 = .859375
9 = .5625	25 = .78125	25 = .390625	57 = .890625
11 = .6875	27 = .84375	27 = .421875	59 = .921875
13 = .8125	29 = .90625	29 = .453125	61 = .953125
15 = .9375	31 = .96875	31 = .484375	63 = .984375

TABLE IV

English Inches into Millimeters

In.	0	$\frac{1}{16}$	$\frac{1}{8}$	$\frac{3}{16}$	$\frac{1}{4}$	$\frac{5}{16}$	$\frac{3}{8}$	$\frac{7}{16}$	$\frac{1}{2}$	$\frac{9}{16}$	$\frac{5}{8}$	$\frac{11}{16}$	$\frac{3}{4}$	$\frac{13}{16}$	$\frac{7}{8}$	$\frac{15}{16}$
0	0.0	1.6	3.2	4.8	6.4	7.9	9.5	11.1	12.7	14.3	15.9	17.5	19.1	20.6	22.2	23.8
1	25.4	27.0	28.6	30.2	31.7	33.3	34.9	36.5	38.1	39.7	41.3	42.9	44.4	46.0	47	49.2
2	50.8	52.4	54.0	55.6	57.1	58.7	60.3	61.9	63.5	65.1	66.7	68.3	69.8	71.4	73.0	74.6
3	76.2	77.8	79.4	81.0	82.5	84.1	85.7	87.3	88.9	90.5	92.1	93.7	95.2	96.8	98.4	100.0
4	101.6	103.2	104.8	106.4	108.0	109.5	111.1	112.7	114.3	115.9	117.5	119.1	120.7	122.2	123.8	125.4
5	127.0	128.6	130.2	131.8	133.4	134.9	136.5	138.1	139.7	141.3	142.9	144.5	146.1	147.6	149.2	150.8
6	152.4	154.0	155.6	157.2	158.8	160.3	161.9	163.5	165.1	166.7	168.3	169.9	171.5	173.0	174.6	176.2
7	177.8	179.4	181.0	182.6	184.2	185.7	187.3	188.9	190.5	192.1	193.7	195.3	196.9	198.4	200.0	201.6
8	203.2	204.8	206.4	208.0	209.6	211.1	212.7	214.3	215.9	217.5	219.1	220.7	222.3	223.8	225.4	227.0
9	228.6	230.2	231.8	233.4	235.0	236.5	238.1	239.7	241.3	242.9	244.5	246.1	247.7	249.2	250.8	252.4
10	254.0	255.6	257.2	258.8	260.4	261.9	263.5	265.1	266.7	268.3	269.9	271.5	273.1	274.6	276.2	277.8
11	279.4	281.0	282.6	284.2	285.7	287.3	288.9	290.5	292.1	293.7	295.3	296.9	298.4	300.0	301.6	303.2
12	304.8	306.4	308.0	309.6	311.1	312.7	314.3	315.9	317.5	319.1	320.7	322.3	323.8	325.4	327.0	328.6
13	330.2	331.8	333.4	335.0	336.5	338.1	339.7	341.3	342.9	344.5	346.1	347.7	349.2	350.8	352.4	354.0
14	355.6	357.2	358.8	360.4	361.9	363.5	365.1	366.7	368.3	369.9	371.5	373.1	374.6	376.2	377.8	379.4
15	381.0	382.6	384.2	385.8	387.3	388.9	390.5	392.1	393.7	395.3	396.9	398.5	400.0	401.6	403.2	404.8
16	406.4	408.0	409.6	411.2	412.7	414.3	415.9	417.5	419.1	420.7	422.3	423.9	425.4	427.0	428.6	430.2
17	431.8	433.4	435.0	436.6	438.1	439.7	441.3	442.9	444.5	446.1	447.7	449.3	450.8	452.4	454.0	455.6
18	457.2	458.8	460.4	462.0	463.5	465.1	466.7	468.3	469.9	471.5	473.1	474.7	476.2	477.8	479.4	481.0
19	482.6	484.2	485.8	487.4	488.9	490.5	492.1	493.7	495.3	496.9	498.5	500.1	501.6	503.2	504.8	506.4
20	508.0	509.6	511.2	512.8	514.3	515.9	517.5	519.1	520.7	522.3	523.9	525.5	527.0	528.6	530.2	531.8
21	533.4	535.0	536.6	538.2	539.7	541.3	542.9	544.5	546.1	547.7	549.3	550.9	552.4	554.0	555.6	557.2
22	558.8	560.4	562.0	563.6	565.1	566.7	568.3	569.9	571.5	573.1	574.7	576.3	577.8	579.4	581.0	582.6
23	584.2	585.8	587.4	589.0	590.5	592.1	593.7	595.3	596.9	598.5	600.1	601.7	603.2	604.8	606.4	608.0

39.37 in. = 1 m. = 10 dm. = 100 cm. = 1000 mm.

TABLE V

U. S. Standard and Sharp V-threads

Diameter of screw	Threads per inch	Depth U. S. S.	Depth sharp V	Root dia. U. S. S.	Root dia. sharp V
1/4	20	.03247	.04330	.1850	.1634
5/16	18	.03608	.04811	.2403	.2163
3/8	16	.04059	.05412	.2936	.2668
7/16	14	.04639	.06178	.3447	.3139
1/2	13	.04996	.06661	.4001	.3668
9/16	12	.05412	.07216	.4542	.4182
5/8	11	.05905	.07873	.5069	.4675
3/4	10	.06495	.08660	.6201	.5768
7/8	9	.07216	.09622	.7307	.6826
1	8	.08119	.10825	.8376	.7835
1 1/8	7	.09277	.12371	.9394	.8776
1 1/4	7	.09277	.12371	1.0644	1.0026
1 3/8	6	.10825	.14433	1.1585	1.0863
1 1/2	6	.10825	.14433	1.2835	1.2113
1 5/8	5 1/2	.11809	.15745	1.3888	1.3101
1 3/4	5	.12990	.17325	1.4902	1.4035
1 7/8	5	.12990	.17325	1.6152	1.5285
2	4 1/2	.14433	.19244	1.7113	1.6151
2 1/4	4 1/2	.14433	.19244	1.9613	1.8651
2 1/2	4	.16238	.21650	2.1752	2.0670
2 3/4	4	.16238	.21650	2.4252	2.3170
3	3 1/2	.18557	.24742	2.6288	2.5052
3 1/4	3 1/2	.18557	.24742	2.8788	2.7552
3 1/2	3 1/4	.19985	.26647	3.1003	2.9671
3 3/4	3	.21666	.28866	3.3167	3.1727
4	3	.21666	.28866	3.5667	3.4227
4 1/4	2 7/8	.2259	.3012	3.7982	3.6476
4 1/2	2 3/4	.2362	.3149	4.0276	3.8712
4 3/4	2 5/8	.2474	.3299	4.2551	4.0901
5	2 1/2	.2598	.3465	4.4804	4.3070
5 1/4	2 1/2	.2598	.3465	4.7304	4.5500
5 1/2	2 3/8	.2735	.3647	4.9530	4.7707
5 3/4	2 3/8	.2735	.3647	5.2030	5.0207
6	2 1/4	.2887	.3849	5.4226	5.2302

TABLE VI

Chords of Angles in Circle of Radius Unity

Ang.	Lengths of chords for whole degrees										Differences to be added for tenths of a degree								
	0°	1°	2°	3°	4°	5°	6°	7°	8°	9°	.1°	.2°	.3°	.4°	.5°	.6°	.7°	.8°	.9°
0°	.000	.017	.035	.052	.070	.087	.105	.122	.140	.157	2	3	5	7	9	10	12	14	16
10°	.174	.191	.209	.226	.243	.261	.278	.296	.313	.330	2	3	5	7	9	10	12	14	16
20°	.347	.364	.382	.399	.416	.433	.450	.467	.484	.501	2	3	5	7	9	10	12	14	15
30°	.518	.534	.551	.568	.585	.601	.618	.635	.651	.667	2	3	5	7	8	10	12	13	15
40°	.684	.700	.717	.733	.749	.765	.781	.797	.813	.829	2	3	5	6	8	10	11	13	14
50°	.845	.861	.867	.892	.908	.923	.939	.954	.970	.985	2	3	5	6	8	9	11	12	14
60°	1.000	1.015	1.030	1.045	1.060	1.075	1.089	1.104	1.118	1.133	1	3	4	6	7	9	10	12	13
70°	1.147	1.161	1.175	1.190	1.203	1.218	1.231	1.245	1.259	1.272	1	3	4	6	7	8	10	11	12
80°	1.286	1.209	1.312	1.325	1.338	1.351	1.364	1.377	1.389	1.402	1	3	4	5	6	8	9	10	12

To find the length of a chord in a circle of any radius, multiply length of chord from table by radius of the circle.

For use of the table in laying out angles see **Art. 141.**

For use of the table in measuring an angle see **Art. 142.**

TABLE VII

Standard Gages for Wire and Sheet Metals

Diameter or thickness given in decimals of an inch

Number of gage	Birmingham wire gage	American, Brown and Sharp (B. and S.)	United States standard plate iron steel	British Imperial	American Steel and Wire Co.
0000000	. . . .	. . . .	.5	.5	. . . .
000000	. . . .	. . . .	.46875	.464	. . . .
00000	. . . .	. . . .	.4375	.432	. . . .
0000	.454	.46	.40625	.400	.3938
000	.425	.409642	.375	.372	.3625
00	.380	.364796	.34375	.348	.3310
0	.340	.324861	.3125	.324	.3065
1	.300	.289297	.28125	.300	.2830
2	.284	.257627	.265625	.276	.2625
3	.259	.229423	.25	.252	.2437
4	.238	.204307	.234375	.232	.2253
5	.220	.181940	.21875	.212	.2070
6	.203	.162023	.203125	.192	.1920
7	.180	.144285	.1875	.176	.1770
8	.165	.128490	.171875	.160	.1620
9	.148	.114423	.15625	.144	.1483
10	.134	.101897	.140625	.128	.1350
11	.120	.090742	.125	.116	.1205
12	.109	.080808	.109375	.104	.1055
13	.095	.071962	.09375	.092	.0915
14	.083	.064084	.078125	.080	.0800
15	.072	.057068	.0703125	.072	.0720
16	.065	.050821	.0625	.064	.0625
17	.058	.045257	.05625	.056	.0540
18	.049	.040303	.05	.048	.0475
19	.042	.035890	.04375	.040	.0410
20	.035	.031961	.0375	.036	.0348
21	.032	.028462	.034375	.032	.03175
22	.028	.025346	.03125	.028	.0286
23	.025	.022572	.028125	.024	.0258
24	.022	.020101	.025	.022	.0230
25	.020	.017900	.021875	.020	.0204
26	.018	.015941	.01875	.018	.0181
27	.016	.014195	.0171875	.0164	.0173
28	.014	.012641	.015625	.0148	.0162
29	.013	.011257	.0140625	.0136	.0150
30	.012	.010025	.0125	.0124	.0140
31	.010	.008928	.0109375	.0116	.0132
32	.009	.007950	.01015625	.0108	.0128
33	.008	.007080	.009375	.0100	.0118
34	.007	.006305	.00859375	.0092	.0104
35	.005	.005615	.0078125	.0084	.0095
36	.004	.005000	.00703125	.0076	.0090
37	. . . .	.004453	.006640625	.0068	. . . .
38	. . . .	.003965	.00625	.0060	. . . .
39	. . . .	.003531	. . . .	.0052	. . . .
40	. . . .	.003144	. . . .	.0048	. . . .

TABLE VIII

Specific Gravities and Weights of Substances

Name of substance	Pounds per cu. in.	Pounds per cu. ft.	Specific gravity
Air................................	.....	0.0795	
Aluminum......................	.....	162	2.6
Anthracite coal, broken.........	.....	52 to 60	
Antimony......................	.....	418	6.7
Asphaltum.....................	.....	87.3	1.4
Beech wood....................	.....	46	.73
Birch wood....................	.....	41	.65
Brass, cast (copper and zinc)....	.....	506	8.1
Brass, rolled..................	.....	525	8.4
Brick, common.................	.....	125	
Brick, pressed.................	.....	150	
Chalk.........................	.....	156	2.5
Coal, bituminous, broken.......	.....	47 to 56	
Coke, loose....................	.....	23 to 32	
Corundum......................	.....	....	3.9
Copper, cast..................	.....	542	8.6 to 8.8
Copper, rolled.................	.319.	555	8.8 to 9
Cork..........................	.....	15	.24
Ebony wood...................	.....	76	1.23
Elm wood......................	.....	35	.56
Flint..........................	.....	162	2.6
Glass.........................	.....	186	2.5 to 3.45
Gold..........................	.695	....	19.3
Granite.......................	.....	170	2.56 to 2.88
Hickory wood..................	.....	53	.85
Ice...........................	.....	57.5	.92
Iron, cast.....................	.26	450	6.7 to 7.4
Iron, wrought.................	.28	480	7.69
Lead..........................	.412	712	11.42
Marble........................	.....	168.7	2.7
Maple wood....................	.....	49	.79
Mercury.......................	.49	....	13.6
Nickel........................	.318	....	8.8
Oak wood, red.................	.....	46	.73 to .75
Pine wood, white..............	.....	28	.45
Pine wood, yellow..............	.....	38	.61
Platinum......................	.....	....	21.5
Quartz........................	.....	165	2.65
Silver.........................	.379	655	10.5

Specific Gravities and Weights of Substances—*Continued*

Name of substance	Pounds per cu. in.	Pounds per cu. ft.	Specific gravity
Steel............................	.29	490	7.85
Tin.............................	.....	459	7.2 to 7.5
Zinc.., ...	.....	438	6.8 to 7.2
Water, distilled at 32° F........	.....	62.417	
Water, distilled at 62° F........	.....	62.355	1
Water, distilled at 212° F	.....	59.7	

Specific gravities referred to air:

Air............................ 1
Oxygen....................... 1.11
Hydrogen..................... 0.07
Chlorine gas.................. 2.44

TABLE IX

Strength of Materials

Material	Ultimate tensile strength	Ultimate compressive strength	Coefficient of linear expansion
	Pounds per square inch	Pounds per square inch	For 1° Fahrenheit
Hard steel............	100,000	120,000	0.0000065
Structural steel........	60,000	60,000	0.0000065
Wrought iron..........	50,000	50,000	0.0000067
Cast iron.............	20,000	90,000	0.0000062
Copper...............	30,000	....	0.0000089
Timber, with grain.....	8,000 to 25,000	4,000 to 12,000	0.0000028
Concrete	300	3,000	0.0000055
Granite................	....	11,000	0.0000050
Brick.................	....	3,000	0.0000050

In the column of ultimate tensile strengths are given the pulls necessary to break a rod of one square inch cross section of the given material.

In the column of ultimate compressive strengths are given the weights necessary to cause a support of one square inch cross section to give way under the pressure.

In the column of coefficient of linear expansion are given the fractional parts of their length, bars of the different materials will increase when the temperature rises one degree Fahrenheit.

31

TABLE X.—COMMON LOGARITHMS

N.	0	1	2	3	4	5	6	7	8	9
10	0000	0043	0086	0128	0170	0212	0253	0294	0334	0374
11	0414	0453	0492	0531	0569	0607	0645	0682	0719	0755
12	0792	0828	0864	0899	0934	0969	1004	1038	1072	1106
13	1139	1173	1206	1239	1271	1303	1335	1367	1399	1430
14	1461	1492	1523	1553	1584	1614	1644	1673	1703	1732
15	1761	1790	1818	1847	1875	1903	1931	1959	1987	2014
16	2041	2068	2095	2122	2148	2175	2201	2227	2253	2279
17	2304	2330	2355	2380	2405	2430	2455	2480	2504	2529
18	2553	2577	2601	2625	2648	2672	2695	2718	2742	2765
19	2788	2810	2833	2856	2878	2900	2923	2945	2967	2989
20	3010	3032	3054	3075	3096	3118	3139	3160	3181	3201
21	3222	3243	3263	3284	3304	3324	3345	3365	3385	3404
22	3424	3444	3464	3483	3502	3522	3541	3560	3579	3598
23	3617	3636	3655	3674	3692	3711	3729	3747	3766	3784
24	3802	3820	3838	3856	3874	3892	3909	3927	3945	3962
25	3979	3997	4014	4031	4048	4065	4082	4099	4116	4133
26	4150	4166	4183	4200	4216	4232	4249	4265	4281	4298
27	4314	4330	4346	4362	4378	4393	4409	4425	4440	4456
28	4472	4487	4502	4518	4533	4548	4564	4579	4594	4609
29	4624	4639	4654	4669	4683	4698	4713	4728	4742	4757
30	4771	4786	4800	4814	4829	4843	4857	4871	4886	4900
31	4914	4928	4942	4955	4969	4983	4997	5011	5024	5038
32	5051	5065	5079	5092	5105	5119	5132	5145	5159	5172
33	5185	5198	5211	5224	5237	5250	5263	5276	5289	5302
34	5315	5328	5340	5353	5366	5378	5391	5403	5416	5428
35	5441	5453	5465	5478	5490	5502	5514	5527	5539	5551
36	5563	5575	5587	5599	5611	5623	5635	5647	5658	5670
37	5682	5694	5705	5717	5729	5740	5752	5763	5775	5786
38	5798	5809	5821	5832	5843	5855	5866	5877	5888	5899
39	5911	5922	5933	5944	5955	5966	5977	5988	5999	6010
40	6021	6031	6042	6053	6064	6075	6085	6096	6107	6117
41	6128	6138	6149	6160	6170	6180	6191	6201	6212	6222
42	6232	6243	6253	6263	6274	6284	6294	6304	6314	6325
43	6335	6345	6355	6365	6375	6385	6395	6405	6415	6425
44	6435	6444	6454	6464	6474	6484	6493	6503	6513	6522
45	6532	6542	6551	6561	6571	6580	6590	6599	6609	6618
46	6628	6637	6646	6656	6665	6675	6684	6693	6702	6712
47	6721	6730	6739	6749	6758	6767	6776	6785	6794	6803
48	6812	6821	6830	6839	6848	6857	6866	6875	6884	6893
49	6902	6911	6920	6928	6937	6946	6955	6964	6972	6981
50	6990	6998	7007	7016	7024	7033	7042	7050	7059	7067
51	7076	7084	7093	7101	7110	7118	7126	7135	7143	7152
52	7160	7168	7177	7185	7193	7202	7210	7218	7226	7235
53	7243	7251	7259	7267	7275	7284	7292	7300	7308	7316
54	7324	7332	7340	7348	7356	7364	7372	7380	7388	7396

| N. | 0 | 1 | 2 | 3 | 4 | 5 | 6 | 7 | 8 | 9 |

TABLE X.—COMMON LOGARITHMS—*Continued*

N.	0	1	2	3	4	5	6	7	8	9
55	7404	7412	7419	7427	7435	7443	7451	7459	7466	7474
56	7482	7490	7497	7505	7513	7520	7528	7536	7543	7551
57	7559	7566	7574	7582	7589	7597	7604	7612	7619	7627
58	7634	7642	7649	7657	7664	7672	7679	7686	7694	7701
59	7709	7716	7723	7731	7738	7745	7752	7760	7767	7774
60	7782	7789	7796	7803	7810	7818	7825	7832	7839	7846
61	7853	7860	7868	7875	7882	7889	7896	7903	7910	7917
62	7924	7931	7938	7945	7952	7959	7966	7973	7980	7987
63	7993	8000	8007	8014	8021	8028	8035	8041	8048	8055
64	8062	8069	8075	8082	8089	8096	8102	8109	8116	8122
65	8129	8136	8142	8149	8156	8162	8169	8176	8182	8189
66	8195	8202	8209	8215	8222	8228	8235	8241	8248	8254
67	8261	8267	8274	8280	8287	8293	8299	8306	8312	8319
68	8325	8331	8338	8344	8351	8357	8363	8370	8376	8382
69	8388	8395	8401	8407	8414	8420	8426	8432	8439	8445
70	8451	8457	8463	8470	8476	8482	8488	8494	8500	8506
71	8513	8519	8525	8531	8537	8543	8549	8555	8561	8567
72	8573	8579	8585	8591	8597	8603	8609	8615	8621	8627
73	8633	8639	8645	8651	8657	8663	8669	8675	8681	8686
74	8692	8698	8704	8710	8716	8722	8727	8733	8739	8745
75	8751	8756	8762	8768	8774	8779	8785	8791	8797	8802
76	8808	8814	8820	8825	8831	8837	8842	8848	8854	8859
77	8865	8871	8876	8882	8887	8893	8899	8904	8910	8915
78	8921	8927	8932	8938	8943	8949	8954	8960	8965	8971
79	8976	8982	8987	8993	8998	9004	9009	9015	9020	9025
80	9031	9036	9042	9047	9053	9058	9063	9069	9074	9079
81	9085	9090	9096	9101	9106	9112	9117	9122	9128	9133
82	9138	9143	9149	9154	9159	9165	9170	9175	9180	9186
83	9191	9196	9201	9206	9212	9217	9222	9227	9232	9238
84	9243	9248	9253	9258	9263	9269	9274	9279	9284	9289
85	9294	9299	9304	9309	9315	9320	9325	9330	9335	9340
86	9345	9350	9355	9360	9365	9370	9375	9380	9385	9390
87	9395	9400	9405	9410	9415	9420	9425	9430	9435	9440
88	9445	9450	9455	9460	9465	9469	9474	9479	9484	9489
89	9494	9499	9504	9509	9513	9518	9523	9528	9533	9538
90	9542	9547	9552	9557	9562	9566	9571	9576	9581	9586
91	9590	9595	9600	9605	9609	9614	9619	9624	9628	9633
92	9638	9643	9647	9652	9657	9661	9666	9671	9675	9680
93	9685	9689	9694	9699	9703	9708	9713	9717	9722	9727
94	9731	9736	9741	9745	9750	9754	9759	9763	9768	9773
95	9777	9782	9786	9791	9795	9800	9805	9809	9814	9818
96	9823	9827	9832	9836	9841	9845	9850	9854	9859	9863
97	9868	9872	9877	9881	9886	9890	9894	9899	9903	9908
98	9912	9917	9921	9926	9930	9934	9939	9943	9948	9952
99	9956	9961	9965	9969	9974	9978	9983	9987	9991	9996
N.	0	1	2	3	4	5	6	7	8	9

TABLE XI.—TRIGONOMETRIC FUNCTIONS

Angles	Sines		Cosines		Tangents		Cotangents		Angles
	Nat.	Log.	Nat.	Log.	Nat.	Log.	Nat.	Log.	
0° 00'	.0000	∞	1.0000	0.0000	.0000	∞	∞	∞	90° 00'
10	.0029	7.4637	1.0000	0000	.0029	7.4637	343.77	2.5363	50
20	.0058	7648	1.0000	0000	.0058	7648	171.89	2352	40
30	.0087	9408	1.0000	0000	.0087	9409	114.59	0591	30
40	.0116	8.0658	.9999	0000	.0116	8.0658	85.940	1.9342	20
50	.0145	1627	.9999	0000	.0145	1627	68.750	8373	10
1° 00'	.0175	8.2419	.9998	9.9999	.0175	8.2419	57.290	1.7581	89° 00'
10	.0204	3088	.9998	9999	.0204	3089	49.104	6911	50
20	.0233	3668	.9997	9999	.0233	3669	42.964	6331	40
30	.0262	4179	.9997	9999	.0262	4181	38.188	5819	30
40	.0291	4637	.9996	9998	.0291	4638	34.368	5362	20
50	.0320	5050	.9995	9998	.0320	5053	31.242	4947	10
2° 00'	.0349	8.5428	.9994	9.9997	.0349	8.5431	28.636	1.4569	88° 00'
10	.0378	5776	.9993	9997	.0378	5779	26.432	4221	50
20	.0407	6097	.9992	9996	.0407	6101	24.542	3899	40
30	.0436	6397	.9990	9996	.0437	6401	22.904	3599	30
40	.0465	6677	.9989	9995	.0466	6682	21.470	3318	20
50	.0494	6940	.9988	9995	.0495	6945	20.206	3055	10
3° 00'	.0523	8.7188	.9986	9.9994	.0524	8.7194	19.081	1.2806	87° 00'
10	.0552	7423	.9985	9993	.0553	7429	18.075	2571	50
20	.0581	7645	.9983	9993	.0582	7652	17.169	2348	40
30	.0610	7857	.9981	9992	.0612	7865	16.350	2135	30
40	.0640	8059	.9980	9991	.0641	8067	15.605	1933	20
50	.0669	8251	.9978	9990	.0670	8261	14.924	1739	10
4° 00'	.0698	8.8436	.9976	9.9989	.0699	8.8446	14.301	1.1554	86° 00'
10	.0727	8613	.9974	9989	.0729	8624	13.727	1376	50
20	.0756	8783	.9971	9988	.0758	8795	13.197	1205	40
30	.0785	8946	.9969	9987	.0787	8960	12.706	1040	30
40	.0814	9104	.9967	9986	.0816	9118	12.251	0882	20
50	.0843	9256	.9964	9985	.0846	9272	11.826	0728	10
5° 00'	.0872	8.9403	.9962	9.9983	.0875	8.9420	11.430	1.0580	85° 00'
10	.0901	9545	.9959	9982	.0904	9563	11.059	0437	50
20	.0929	9682	.9957	9981	.0934	9701	10.712	0299	40
30	.0958	9816	.9954	9980	.0963	9836	10.385	0164	30
40	.0987	9945	.9951	9979	.0992	9966	10.078	0034	20
50	.1016	9.0070	.9948	9977	.1022	9.0093	9.7882	0.9907	10
6° 00'	.1045	9.0192	.9945	9.9976	.1051	9.0216	9.5144	0.9784	84° 00'
10	.1074	0311	.9942	9975	.1080	0336	9.2553	9664	50
20	.1103	0426	.9939	9973	.1110	0453	9.0098	9547	40
30	.1132	0539	.9936	9972	.1139	0567	8.7769	9433	30
40	.1161	0648	.9932	9971	.1169	0678	8.5555	9322	20
50	.1190	0755	.9929	9969	.1198	0786	8.3450	9214	10
7° 00'	.1219	9.0859	.9925	9.9968	.1228	9.0891	8.1443	0.9109	83° 00'
10	.1248	0961	.9922	9966	.1257	0995	7.9530	9005	50
20	.1276	1060	.9918	9964	.1287	1096	7.7704	8904	40
30	.1305	1157	.9914	9963	.1317	1194	7.5958	8806	30
40	.1334	1252	.9911	9961	.1346	1291	7.4287	8709	20
50	.1363	1345	.9907	9959	.1376	1385	7.2687	8615	10
8° 00'	.1392	9.1436	.9903	9.9958	.1405	9.1478	7.1154	0.8522	82° 00'
10	.1421	1525	.9899	9956	.1435	1569	6.9682	8431	50
20	.1449	1612	.9894	9954	.1465	1658	6.8269	8342	40
30	.1478	1697	.9890	9952	.1495	1745	6.6912	8255	30
40	.1507	1781	.9886	9950	.1524	1831	6.5606	8169	20
50	.1536	1863	.9881	9948	.1554	1915	6.4348	8085	10
9° 00'	.1564	9.1943	.9877	9.9946	.1584	9.1997	6.3138	0.8003	81° 00'
	Nat.	Log.	Nat.	Log.	Nat.	Log.	Nat.	Log.	
Angles	Cosines		Sines		Cotangents		Tangents		Angles

TABLE XI.—TRIGONOMETRIC FUNCTIONS—*Continued*

Angles	Sines		Cosines		Tangents		Cotangents		Angles
	Nat.	Log.	Nat.	Log.	Nat.	Log.	Nat.	Log.	
9° 00′	.1564	9.1943	.9877	9.9946	.1584	9.1997	6.3138	0.8003	81° 00′
10	.1593	2022	.9872	9944	.1614	2078	6.1970	7922	50
20	.1622	2100	.9868	9942	.1644	2158	6.0844	7842	40
30	.1650	2176	.9863	9940	.1673	2236	5.9758	7764	30
40	.1679	2251	.9858	9938	.1703	2313	5.8708	7687	20
50	.1708	2324	.9853	9936	.1733	2389	5.7694	7611	10
10° 00′	.1736	9.2397	.9848	9.9934	.1763	9.2463	5.6713	0.7537	80° 00′
10	.1765	2468	.9843	9931	.1793	2536	5.5764	7464	50
20	.1794	2538	.9838	9929	.1823	2609	5.4845	7391	40
30	.1822	2606	.9833	9927	.1853	2680	5.3955	7320	30
40	.1851	2674	.9827	9924	.1883	2750	5.3093	7250	20
50	.1880	2740	.9822	9922	.1914	2819	5.2257	7181	10
11° 00′	.1908	9.2806	.9816	9.9919	.1944	9.2887	5.1446	0.7113	79° 00′
10	.1937	2870	.9811	9917	.1974	2953	5.0658	7047	50
20	.1965	2934	.9805	9914	.2004	3020	4.9894	6980	40
30	.1994	2997	.9799	9912	.2035	3085	4.9152	6915	30
40	.2022	3058	.9793	9909	.2065	3149	4.8430	6851	20
50	.2051	3119	.9787	9907	.2095	3212	4.7729	6788	10
12° 00′	.2079	9.3179	.9781	9.9904	.2126	9.3275	4.7046	0.6725	78° 00′
10	.2108	3238	.9775	9901	.2156	3336	4.6382	6664	50
20	.2136	3296	.9769	9899	.2186	3397	4.5736	6603	40
30	.2164	3353	.9763	9896	.2217	3458	4.5107	6542	30
40	.2193	3410	.9757	9893	.2247	3517	4.4494	6483	20
50	.2221	3466	.9750	9890	.2278	3576	4.3897	6424	10
13° 00′	.2250	9.3521	.9744	9.9887	.2309	9.3634	4.3315	0.6366	77° 00′
10	.2278	3575	.9737	9884	.2339	3691	4.2747	6309	50
20	.2306	3629	.9730	9881	.2370	3748	4.2193	6252	40
30	.2334	3682	.9724	9878	.2401	3804	4.1653	6196	30
40	.2363	3734	.9717	9875	.2432	3859	4.1126	6141	20
50	.2391	3786	.9710	9872	.2462	3914	4.0611	6086	10
14° 00′	.2419	9.3837	.9703	9.9869	.2493	9.3968	4.0108	0.6032	76° 00′
10	.2447	3887	.9696	9866	.2524	4021	3.9617	5979	50
20	.2476	3937	.9689	9863	.2555	4074	3.9136	5926	40
30	.2504	3986	.9681	9859	.2586	4127	3.8667	5873	30
40	.2532	4035	.9674	9856	.2617	4178	3.8208	5822	20
50	.2560	4083	.9667	9853	.2648	4230	3.7760	5770	10
15° 00′	.2588	9.4130	.9659	9.9849	.2679	9.4281	3.7321	0.5719	75° 00′
10	.2616	4177	.9652	9846	.2711	4331	3.6891	5669	50
20	.2644	4223	.9644	9843	.2742	4381	3.6470	5619	40
30	.2672	4269	.9636	9839	.2773	4430	3.6059	5570	30
40	.2700	4314	.9628	9836	.2805	4479	3.5656	5521	20
50	.2728	4359	.9621	9832	.2836	4527	3.5261	5473	10
16° 00′	.2756	9.4403	.9613	9.9828	.2867	9.4575	3.4874	0.5425	74° 00′
10	.2784	4447	.9605	9825	.2899	4622	3.4495	5378	50
20	.2812	4491	.9596	9821	.2931	4669	3.4124	5331	40
30	.2840	4533	.9588	9817	.2962	4716	3.3759	5284	30
40	.2868	4576	.9580	9814	.2994	4762	3.3402	5238	20
50	.2896	4618	.9572	9810	.3026	4808	3.3052	5192	10
17° 00′	.2924	9.4659	.9563	9.9806	.3057	9.4853	3.2709	0.5147	73° 00′
10	.2952	4700	.9555	9802	.3089	4898	3.2371	5102	50
20	.2979	4741	.9546	9798	.3121	4943	3.2041	5057	40
30	.3007	4781	.9537	9794	.3153	4987	3.1716	5013	30
40	.3035	4821	.9528	9790	.3185	5031	3.1397	4969	20
50	.3062	4861	.9520	9786	.3217	5075	3.1084	4925	10
18° 00′	.3090	9.4900	.9511	9.9782	.3249	9.5118	3.0777	0.4882	72° 00′
	Nat.	Log.	Nat.	Log.	Nat.	Log.	Nat.	Log.	
Angles	Cosines		Sines		Cotangents		Tangehts		Angles

TABLE XI.—TRIGONOMETRIC FUNCTIONS—Continued

Angles	Sines		Cosines		Tangents		Cotangents		Angles
	Nat.	Log.	Nat.	Log.	Nat.	Log.	Nat.	Log.	
18° 00′	.3090	9.4900	.9511	9.9782	.3249	9.5118	3.0777	0.4882	72° 00′
10	.3118	4939	.9502	9778	.3281	5161	3.0475	4839	50
20	.3145	4977	.9492	9774	.3314	5203	3.0178	4797	40
30	.3173	5015	.9483	9770	.3346	5245	2.9887	4755	30
40	.3201	5052	.9474	9765	.3378	5287	2.9600	4713	20
50	.3228	5090	.9465	9761	.3411	5329	2.9319	4671	10
19° 00′	.3256	9.5126	.9455	9.9757	.3443	9.5370	2.9042	0.4630	71° 00′
10	.3283	5163	.9446	9752	.3476	5411	2.8770	4589	50
20	.3311	5199	.9436	9748	.3508	5451	2.8502	4549	40
30	.3338	5235	.9426	9743	.3541	5491	2.8239	4509	30
40	.3365	5270	.9417	9739	.3574	5531	2.7980	4469	20
50	.3393	5306	.9407	9734	.3607	5571	2.7725	4429	10
20° 00′	.3420	9.5341	.9397	9.9730	.3640	9.5611	2.7475	0.4389	70° 00′
10	.3448	5375	.9387	9725	.3673	5650	2.7228	4350	50
20	.3475	5409	.9377	9721	.3706	5689	2.6985	4311	40
30	.3502	5443	.9367	9716	.3739	5727	2.6746	4273	30
40	.3529	5477	.9356	9711	.3772	5766	2.6511	4234	20
50	.3557	5510	.9346	9706	.3805	5804	2.6279	4196	10
21° 00′	.3584	9.5543	.9336	9.9702	.3839	9.5842	2.6051	0.4158	69° 00′
10	.3611	5576	.9325	9697	.3872	5879	2.5826	4121	50
20	.3638	5609	.9315	9692	.3906	5917	2.5605	4083	40
30	.3665	5641	.9304	9687	.3939	5954	2.5386	4046	30
40	.3692	5673	.9293	9682	.3973	5991	2.5172	4009	20
50	.3719	5704	.9283	9677	.4006	6028	2.4960	3972	10
22° 00′	.3746	9.5736	.9272	9.9672	.4040	9.6064	2.4751	0.3936	68° 00′
10	.3773	5767	.9261	9667	.4074	6100	2.4545	3900	50
20	.3800	5798	.9250	9661	.4108	6136	2.4342	3864	40
30	.3827	5828	.9239	9656	.4142	6172	2.4142	3828	30
40	.3854	5859	.9228	9651	.4176	6208	2.3945	3792	20
50	.3881	5889	.9216	9646	.4210	6243	2.3750	3757	10
23° 00′	.3907	9.5919	.9205	9.9640	.4245	9.6279	2.3559	0.3721	67° 00′
10	.3934	5948	.9194	9635	.4279	6314	2.3369	3686	50
20	.3961	5978	.9182	9629	.4314	6348	2.3183	3652	40
30	.3987	6007	.9171	9624	.4348	6383	2.2998	3617	30
40	.4014	6036	.9159	9618	.4383	6417	2.2817	3583	20
50	.4041	6065	.9147	9613	.4417	6452	2.2637	3548	10
24° 00′	.4067	9.6093	.9135	9.9607	.4452	9.6486	2.2460	0.3514	66° 00′
10	.4094	6121	.9124	9602	.4487	6520	2.2286	3480	50
20	.4120	6149	.9112	9596	.4522	6553	2.2113	3447	40
30	.4147	6177	.9100	9590	.4557	6587	2.1943	3413	30
40	.4173	6205	.9088	9584	.4592	6620	2.1775	3380	20
50	.4200	6232	.9075	9579	.4628	6654	2.1609	3346	10
25° 00′	.4226	9.6259	.9063	9.9573	.4663	9.6687	2.1445	0.3313	65° 00′
10	.4253	6286	.9051	9567	.4699	6720	2.1283	3280	50
20	.4279	6313	.9038	9561	.4734	6752	2.1123	3248	40
30	.4305	6340	.9026	9555	.4770	6785	2.0965	3215	30
40	.4331	6366	.9013	9549	.4806	6817	2.0809	3183	20
50	.4358	6392	.9001	9543	.4841	6850	2.0655	3150	10
26° 00′	.4384	9.6418	.8988	9.9537	.4877	9.6882	2.0503	0.3118	64° 00′
10	.4410	6444	.8975	9530	.4913	6914	2.0353	3086	50
20	.4436	6470	.8962	9524	.4950	6946	2.0204	3054	40
30	.4462	6495	.8949	9518	.4986	6977	2.0057	3023	30′
40	.4488	6521	.8936	9512	.5022	7009	1.9912	2991	20
50	.4514	6546	.8923	9505	.5059	7040	1.9768	2960	10
27° 00′	.4540	9.6570	.8910	9.9499	.5095	9.7072	1.9626	0.2928	63° 00′
	Nat.	Log.	Nat.	Log.	Nat.	Log.	Nat.	Log.	
Angles	Cosines		Sines		Cotangents		Tangents		Angles

TABLE XI.—TRIGONOMETRIC FUNCTIONS—*Continued*

Angles	Sines		Cosines		Tangents		Cotangents		Angles
	Nat.	Log.	Nat.	Log.	Nat.	Log.	Nat.	Log.	
27° 00′	.4540	9.6570	.8910	9.9499	.5095	9.7072	1.9626	0.2928	63° 00′
10	.4566	6595	.8897	9492	.5132	7103	1.9486	2897	50
20	.4592	6620	.8884	9486	.5169	7134	1.9347	2866	40
30	.4617	6644	.8870	9479	.5206	7165	1.9210	2835	30
40	.4643	6668	.8857	9473	.5243	7196	1.9074	2804	20
50	.4669	6692	.8843	9466	.5280	7226	1.8940	2774	10
28° 00′	.4695	9.6716	.8829	9.9459	.5317	9.7257	1.8807	0.2743	62° 00′
10	.4720	6740	.8816	9453	.5354	7287	1.8676	2713	50
20	.4746	6763	.8802	9446	.5392	7317	1.8546	2683	40
30	.4772	6787	.8788	9439	.5430	7348	1.8418	2652	30
40	.4797	6810	.8774	9432	.5467	7378	1.8291	2622	20
50	.4823	6833	.8760	9425	.5505	7408	1.8165	2592	10
29° 00′	.4848	9.6856	.8746	9.9418	.5543	9.7438	1.8040	0.2562	61° 00′
10	.4874	6878	.8732	9411	.5581	7467	1.7917	2533	50
20	.4899	6901	.8718	9404	.5619	7497	1.7796	2503	40
30	.4924	6923	.8704	9397	.5658	7526	1.7675	2474	30
40	.4950	6946	.8689	9390	.5696	7556	1.7556	2444	20
50	.4975	6968	.8675	9383	.5735	7585	1.7437	2415	10
30° 00′	.5000	9.6990	.8660	9.9375	.5774	9.7614	1.7321	0.2386	60° 00′
10	.5025	7012	.8646	9368	.5812	7644	1.7205	2356	50
20	.5050	7033	.8631	9361	.5851	7673	1.7090	2327	40
30	.5075	7055	.8616	9353	.5890	7701	1.6977	2299	30
40	.5100	7076	.8601	9346	.5930	7730	1.6864	2270	20
50	.5125	7097	.8587	9338	.5969	7759	1.6753	2241	10
31° 00′	.5150	9.7118	.8572	9.9331	.6009	9.7788	1.6643	0.2212	59° 00′
10	.5175	7139	.8557	9323	.6048	7816	1.6534	2184	50
20	.5200	7160	.8542	9315	.6088	7845	1.6426	2155	40
30	.5225	7181	.8526	9308	.6128	7873	1.6319	2127	30
40	.5250	7201	.8511	9300	.6168	7902	1.6212	2098	20
50	.5275	7222	.8496	9292	.6208	7930	1.6107	2070	10
32° 00′	.5299	9.7242	.8480	9.9284	.6249	9.7958	1.6003	0.2042	58° 00′
10	.5324	7262	.8465	9276	.6289	7986	1.5900	2014	50
20	.5348	7282	.8450	9268	.6330	8014	1.5798	1986	40
30	.5373	7302	.8434	9260	.6371	8042	1.5697	1958	30
40	.5398	7322	.8418	9252	.6412	8070	1.5597	1930	20
50	.5422	7342	.8403	9244	.6453	8097	1.5497	1903	10
33° 00′	.5446	9.7361	.8387	9.9236	.6494	9.8125	1.5399	0.1875	57° 00′
10	.5471	7380	.8371	9228	.6536	8153	1.5301	1847	50
20	.5495	7400	.8355	9219	.6577	8180	1.5204	1820	40
30	.5519	7419	.8339	9211	.6619	8208	1.5108	1792	30
40	.5544	7438	.8323	9203	.6661	8235	1.5013	1765	20
50	.5568	7457	.8307	9194	.6703	8263	1.4919	1737	10
34° 00′	.5592	9.7476	.8290	9.9186	.6745	9.8290	1.4826	0.1710	56° 00′
10	.5616	7494	.8274	9177	.6787	8317	1.4733	1683	50
20	.5640	7513	.8258	9169	.6830	8344	1.4641	1656	40
30	.5664	7531	.8241	9160	.6873	8371	1.4550	1629	30
40	.5688	7550	.8225	9151	.6916	8398	1.4460	1602	20
50	.5712	7568	.8208	9142	.6959	8425	1.4370	1575	10
35° 00′	.5736	9.7586	.8192	9.9134	.7002	9.8452	1.4281	0.1548	55° 00′
10	.5760	7604	.8175	9125	.7046	8479	1.4193	1521	50
20	.5783	7622	.8158	9116	.7089	8506	1.4106	1494	40
30	.5807	7640	.8141	9107	.7133	8533	1.4019	1467	30
40	.5831	7657	.8124	9098	.7177	8559	1.3934	1441	20
50	.5854	7675	.8107	9089	.7221	8586	1.3848	1414	10
36° 00′	.5878	9.7692	.8090	9.9080	.7265	9.8613	1.3764	0.1387	54° 00′
	Nat.	Log.	Nat.	Log.	Nat.	Log.	Nat.	Log.	
Angles	Cosines		Sines		Cotangents		Tangents		Angles

TABLE XI.—TRIGONOMETRIC FUNCTIONS—*Continued*

Angles	Sines Nat.	Log.	Cosines Nat.	Log.	Tangents Nat.	Log.	Cotangents Nat.	Log.	Angles
36° 00′	.5878	9.7692	.8090	9.9080	.7265	9.8613	1.3764	0.1387	54° 00′
10	.5901	7710	.8073	9070	.7310	8639	1.3680	1361	50
20	.5925	7727	.8056	9061	.7355	8666	1.3597	1334	40
30	.5948	7744	.8039	9052	.7400	8692	1.3514	1308	30
40	.5972	7761	.8021	9042	.7445	8718	1.3432	1282	20
50	.5995	7778	.8004	9033	.7490	8745	1.3351	1255	10
37° 00′	.6018	9.7795	.7986	9.9023	.7536	9.8771	1.3270	0.1229	53° 00′
10	.6041	7811	.7969	9014	.7581	8797	1.3190	1203	50
20	.6065	7828	.7951	9004	.7627	8824	1.3111	1176	40
30	.6088	7844	.7934	8995	.7673	8850	1.3032	1150	30
40	.6111	7861	.7916	8985	.7720	8876	1.2954	1124	20
50	.6134	7877	.7898	8975	.7766	8902	1.2876	1098	10
38° 00′	.6157	9.7893	.7880	9.8965	.7813	9.8928	1.2799	0.1072	52° 00′
10	.6180	7910	.7862	8955	.7860	8954	1.2723	1046	50
20	.6202	7926	.7844	8945	.7907	8980	1.2647	1020	40
30	.6225	7941	.7826	8935	.7954	9006	1.2572	0994	30
40	.6248	7957	.7808	8925	.8002	9032	1.2497	0968	20
50	.6271	7973	.7790	8915	.8050	9058	1.2423	0942	10
39° 00′	.6293	9.7989	.7771	9.8905	.8098	9.9084	1.2349	0.0916	51° 00′
10	.6316	8004	.7753	8895	.8146	9110	1.2276	0890	50
20	.6338	8020	.7735	8884	.8195	9135	1.2203	0865	40
30	.6361	8035	.7716	8874	.8243	9161	1.2131	0839	30
40	.6383	8050	.7698	8864	.8292	9187	1.2059	0813	20
50	.6406	8066	.7679	8853	.8342	9212	1.1988	0788	10
40° 00′	.6428	9.8081	.7660	9.8843	.8391	9.9238	1.1918	0.0762	50° 00′
10	.6450	8096	.7642	8832	.8441	9264	1.1847	0736	50
20	.6472	8111	.7623	8821	.8491	9289	1.1778	0711	40
30	.6494	8125	.7604	8810	.8541	9315	1.1708	0685	30
40	.6517	8140	.7585	8800	.8591	9341	1.1640	0659	20
50	.6539	8155	.7566	8789	.8642	9366	1..1571	0634	10
41° 00′	.6561	9.8169	.7547	9.8778	.8693	9.9392	1.1504	0.0608	49° 00′
10	.6583	8184	.7528	8767	.8744	9417	1.1436	0583	50
20	.6604	8198	.7509	8756	.8796	9443	1.1369	0557	40
30	.6626	8213	.7490	8745	.8847	9468	1.1303	0532	30
40	.6648	8227	.7470	8733	.8899	9494	1.1237	0506	20
50	.6670	8241	.7451	8722	.8952	9519	1.1171	0481	10
42° 00′	.6691	9.8255	.7431	9.8711	.9004	9.9544	1.1106	0.0456	48° 00′
10	.6713	8269	.7412	8699	.9057	9570	1.1041	0430	50
20	.6734	8283	.7392	8688	.9110	9595	1.0977	0405	40
30	.6756	8297	.7373	8676	.9163	9621	1.0913	0379	30
40	.6777	8311	.7353	8665	.9217	9646	1.0850	0354	20
50	.6799	8324	.7333	8653	.9271	9671	1.0786	0329	10
43° 00′	.6820	9.8338	.7314	9.8641	.9325	9.9697	1.0724	0.0303	47° 00′
10	.6841	8351	.7294	8629	.9380	9722	1.0661	0278	50
20	.6862	8365	.7274	8618	.9435	9747	1.0599	0253	40
30	.6884	8378	.7254	8606	.9490	9772	1.0538	0228	30
40	.6905	8391	.7234	8594	.9545	9798	1.0477	0202	20
50	.6926	8405	.7214	8582	.9601	9823	1.0416	0177	10
44° 00′	.6947	9.8418	.7193	9.8569	.9657	9.9848	1.0355	0.0152	46° 00′
10	.6967	8431	.7173	8557	.9713	9874	1.0295	0126	50
20	.6988	8444	.7153	8545	.9770	9899	1.0235	0101	40
30	.7009	8457	.7133	8532	.9827	9924	1.0176	0076	30
40	.7030	8469	.7112	8520	.9884	9949	1.0117	0051	20
50	.7050	8482	.7092	8507	.9942	9975	1.0058	0025	10
45° 00′	.7071	9.8495	.7071	9.8495	1.0000	0.0000	1.0000	0.0000	45° 00′
	Nat.	Log.	Nat.	Log.	Nat.	Log.	Nat.	Log.	
Angles	Cosines		Sines		Cotangents		Tangents		Angles

INDEX